How We Were
– in the parish of Kilbarron-Terryglass Co. Tipperary

How We Were
– in the parish of Kilbarron-Terryglass Co. Tipperary

Bridie O'Brien

Published by

in association with
Kilbarron-Terryglass Publication Committee

Published in 1999 by
RELAY Books
Tyone, Nenagh, Co. Tipperary, Ireland
Phone/Fax (067) 31734 e-mail relaybooks@ti.ie
in association with Kilbarron-Terryglass Publication Committee

© Copyright, Bridie O'Brien, 1998

No part of this publication may be reproduced, copied or transmitted in any form or by any means without written permission of the publishers, or else under the terms of any licence permitting limited copying issued by the Irish Copyright Licensing Agency, The Writer's Centre, 19 Parnell Square, Dublin 1.

ISBN 0 946327 25 4

British Library Cataloguing-in-Publication Data
A catalogue record for this book
is available from the British Library.

Cover design: RELAY Books – incorporating photographs of Drominagh tower house; O'Meara family of Kilbiller; Ashgrove House.
Typesetting: RELAY Books
Typeface: Times 11pt on 12pt leading
Page size: 235 x 160 mm

Printed by Nenagh Guardian Ltd

Dedication

*To the memory
of my parents, Patrick and Agnes Carroll,
and of my sister, Gretta Corbett*

Heritage

My parents' people
charted their inward sea of peatland,
pegs hammered down, lines taut between them;

they bent, and dug, and saved, while I
holding the reins, stood on the cart-shafts
legs apart and balancing –

Aeneas setting out, with
yup there yup! to the old ass;
now I explain the process

to my children on the road before me,
drain, bank, scraw, bog-banquet tea;
leave this waste, I tell them,

to lie in peace a thousand years
it will put down roots and, unlike man,
recreate its rich, soft flesh.

A heron stands, still as a shape of bog-oak;
eels have squirmed, like memories, back into the pools.
I turn towards the white-washed villages

and would escape, half-willingly, this wilderness,
shake from my shoulders
my parents' people's weight of faith.

– John F. Deane

Contents

Heritage, John F. Deane		vi
Acknowledgements		viii
Foreword		x
Preface		xi

1 An Overview of the Parish — *1*

2 Castles and Tower Houses — *16*
  A Lament for the O'Kennedys, May O'Meara *33*

3 Religion — *34*

4 Education — *73*
  Parish Schools *73*, Curriculum *91*, Personal Memoir *93*,
  Kyle Park Agricultural School *100*

5 How We Were — *108*

6 Families and Their Houses — *119*
  Cambies: Castle Cambie, Brookfield & Kilgarvan *119*
  Biggs: Castle Biggs, Bellevue, Cornalack *134*
  Minchins: Annagh, Col. F. F (Jack), aviator *145*
  Parkers: Brookfield *163*
  Bruces: Lesserragh *167*
  Breretons: Oldcourt *174*
  Hickies: Slevoir, Major-General Sir William B. Hickie *177*

7 Eugene Esmonde, VC, DSO — *184*

8 Other Houses and Gate Lodges — *201*

9 Islandmore — *230*
  Shannon's Lough Derg Shore, Michael Moran *239*

10 Villages — *240*
  Coolbawn *240*
  Kilbarron *250*, Carney Commons *257*
  Ballinderry *258*, Kilgarvan Anglers *272*
  Terryglass *275*, Carrigahorig *283*

11 Parish Personalities — *287*
  Paddy Tierney *287*
  Harold C. Kent *295*
  Michael Conway *299*
  John Francis Waller *303*
  Henry G. Burgess *309*

12	***Across the Seas***	**310**
	John Carroll, Lisquillibeen & USA *310*	
	Mary Carroll, Brookfield & USA *315*	
	Leaving Bellevue for USA *321*	
	Kennedy Letters, Lisquillibeen to Australia *322*	
	Patrick Moran, Bellevue & Australia *325*	
	A Journey 1943, Bridie O'Brien *332*	
13	***Trades and Occupations***	**333**
	Forges *333*	
	Limekilns *337*, Sawmills *340*, Orchards *341*	
	Charcoal *341*, Artichokes *342*, Tobacco *343*,	
	Dressmaking *343*, Ploughing *344*, Carpentry *346*	
	Tree Nursery *346*	
	My Three Oak Trees, May O'Meara *349*	
	Lakeshore Foods *350*	
14	***Some Parish Folklore***	**352**
15	***Hurling***	**356**
	Salute to the Shannon Rovers, May O'Meara (song) *367*	
16	***Wars at Home and Abroad***	**375**
	VE Day 1945, Bridie O'Brien *380*	

Appendix: Census, 1659-1996	381
Publication Committee & Sponsors	384
Index	387

ACKNOWLEDGEMENTS

It is very difficult to apportion gratitude and appreciation fairly, but there are a few names that I must mention particularly as having helped me beyond the call of duty and friendship. Many, many others helped as well with old traditions, stories and photographs and they are all, I hope, acknowledged in the text and/or in the sources at the end of each chapter.

I must first and foremost thank Wilsie Nolan, Terryglass, whose help and encouragement knew no bounds. He was constantly at my beck and call and spared neither enthusiasm, time nor petrol in his constant efforts to help. Amongst many others were Michael Parkinson who actually wrote pieces for me; Bill Donoghue, Michael Conway, Christy Gleeson and his wife Biddy (née Kennedy); James Hickie (son of Manuel) for much information on the Hickie family; Elsie Hogan, Marty O'Meara, Donie O'Meara, Marie Cormican, Rev. Michael O'Donoghue, Mrs Patricia Lyons (Trush Darcy), The Deasy family; Michael McMahon, Corofin (formerly of Portumna) who allowed me to use extensive extracts from his article on Terryglass in *Cois Deirge*; Rev. Johnny Hogan, our priest for twenty-three years, who encouraged me to write this book. Three or four weeks before he died he penned the Foreword in Irish. I treasure that Foreword. Eamonn Dillon, NT, Nenagh, kindly translated it.

I am very grateful to Brian Minchin, Commander Harry Minchin's son, for the extensive help he gave me from the Minchin papers in his possession, and to Mrs Alice Minchin Gloster for putting me in touch with him.

I feel sad for those who had looked forward to the book and who had given me much help but who passed to their eternal rewards before it was finished. Amongst those I would particularly like to mention Mrs Julia Slevin, Pat Carroll, Brookfield, Frank Flannery, Glenbower, Michael Tiernan of the Island. Frank and Michael gave me most of the information which I have on Islandmore.

I also acknowledge help from Mary Guinan-Darmody of the Local Studies Section in the County Library, the National Archives, Dublin, the Irish Folklore Commission. I also express thanks to Nenagh District Heritage Society for allowing me use of their 'Historical Dwellings' Survey, and Tipperary North Family History Research Centre, in particular Nora O'Meara, for genealogical data; Edward Lalor Cambie, Wexford (formerly of Killoran, Moyne) and Mrs Rosamund Sterling for Cambie and Towers papers; Mrs Heather Bell (née Parker-Reeves) for information on the Parker and Reeves families, and photographs; the Australian descendants of the Kennedy family of Lisquillibeen for the Kennedy letters; Justin Moran, Australia, for allowing me to include his Moran story. I also thank my USA-based cousins, Betty Osborne and her brother Joe Schlosser, and Sr Ruth Cecilia Dowd who did so much research on the two Carroll emigrants.

I also acknowledge permission from Dúchas to quote from their archaeological report; from Chaz Bowyer to quote and use photographs from his biography of Eugene Esmonde, VC, DSO; from John F. Deane for his poem, 'Heritage', and from my sister May O'Meara for her two poems and one song, and Michael Moran for his poem. Professor Patrick O'Farrell, Australia, kindly allowed me to reproduce what is a unique picture of an early Kilbarron or Borrisokane hurling scene which found its way to Australia.

I thank especially my brother Paddy for taking most of the photographs in the book, and Alan Kelly for researching and writing parts of the profile of the late Paddy Tierney, TD. I also thank Liam Hogan, Shannon Rovers GAA club, for allowing me to use material from their 1992 and 1994 programmes.

I am grateful to the publication committee and to the sponsors who have helped to make publication possible with financial assistance. I thank especially Deirdre Cox and her colleagues of LEADER for their patience and understanding of delays in bringing to completion this project, which they have grant-aided, and Deirdre especially for her unfailing helpfulness.

I thank particularly Donal and Nancy Murphy and Elaine Burke Houlihan of RELAY Books, Nenagh, for their help beyond the call of duty. Nancy, figuratively speaking, held my hand and at times had to grasp it very hard in my moments of despondency. Donal read the first and final drafts and made useful suggestions. I thank Danny Grace for his help and encouragement, for reading all of the typescript, and all of them for correcting errors.

Finally, I thank my husband Jimmy, without whose help and support this book would never have been finished including acting as courier between Nancy and myself, and my son Anthony for his encouragement and support.

Foreword

Fearaim fíor-chaoin fáilte roimh an leabhar staire seo, *How We Were,* le Brigid Ó Brien. Is maith is fiú an pobal seo go neosfaí a scéal, pobal go bhfuil spioraid an mheithil beo bríomhar gníomhach in a measc, fíor-spioraid na Críostaíochta, agus dul ar aghaidh iontach déanta acu le blianta anuas. Agus is maith an cás Bridie chun a insithe, and deis a labhartha aici, an tsuim is dual don sean-ionsdóir in a muintir féin, agus taighde thar na bearta déanta aici le fada an lá i gcúrsaí na paróiste.

I extend a heartfelt welcome to this history book, *How We Were*, by Brigid O'Brien. It is very worthwhile that this community's story be told, a community in which the spirit of co-operation is alive, vigorous and active, the true spirit of Christianity – and where great progress has been made over the years. It's well able Bridie is to tell it, with her facility with words, with the interest that is natural to someone long absorbed in her own community, and with the huge amount of research which she has done for a long while past into parish events.

John Hogan, PP
August 1995

Preface

I am, perhaps, the least qualified person to write the story of 'How We Were' in the combined parishes of Finnoe, Kilbarron and Terryglass, having spent by far the greater part of my life, and all my working days, away from these shores. I never lost touch with home because my late sister Gretta kept me informed of local events in her long, newsy and almost weekly letters tucked into the *Nenagh Guardian* in defiance of all Post Office regulations.

The arrival of the *Guardian* and her letter was the highlight of my week and every inch of that newspaper – even the advertisements – was avidly read. It is a mystery to me how she 'minded' the paper long enough to have it wrapped up on the Monday and dispatched to whatever part of the U.K. I happened to be living in at the time.

My main anxiety when embarking on the task of writing this book was how I was going to cope with Terryglass. As I grew up in Kilbarron I felt I could manage that area but I hardly knew Terryglass at all, apart from visiting the bog there in my childhood, and to be examined by the bishop for Confirmation. I ended up knowing as much, if not more, than I knew about Kilbarron. I have come to the conclusion that people live longer in Terryglass – it must be the bog air! I found more people willing and anxious and old enough to impart information to me about 'how we were' in Terryglass than I could have imagined possible.

Michael Joseph O'Rahilly (1875-1916) of Ballylongford, Co. Kerry, the only one of the leaders of the 1916 Easter Rising to be killed in action, is reputed to have said, or written, that 'Love of one's country begins with love of one's own place'. He had an intense interest in, and love of, local history. The homesick exile does not dream of Ireland or Munster or Tipperary but of the little townland, the parish or town where he or she was born and grew up.

I first became interested in local history while still living in England and wrote a few articles for *Cois Deirge*, that excellent magazine edited by Martin Power. They were reminiscences rather than local history but they did include some traditions and stories I had heard from old people. I stumbled along and eventually began to do a little research. I had no background in history and made many mistakes. I slowly got the idea that I might gather enough material to write a short parish history.

Strictly speaking, the book, which grew to be longer than I intended, is a collection of 'fragments' of history and tradition. I decided that the title 'How We Were' would best describe what I had in mind to achieve. I know that I have exceeded my brief in many ways but felt it was worth putting on record certain things, for example the story of the death of Eugene Esmonde, VC, DSO. I make no apology for including Islandmore which was in Kilbarron until 1898 and for all practical purposes still is. Kyle Park Agricultural School is in Borrisokane parish but very close to the border with Kilbarron-Terryglass. Over many years people from our parish, including my own father, attended it.

I suppose the people of Finnoe, Kilbarron and Terryglass are as typical as those of any rural parish in Ireland. This was certainly true until almost twenty years ago when the proximity of Lough Derg brought an influx of newcomers anxious to enjoy the beauty and amenities of the lake. These strangers are welcome and are, on the whole, an asset to the community. But there is still in the parish a hard core of old inhabitants with their own culture, their own folk memories, their own way of looking at life. I trust my collection of 'fragments' will give some pleasure to those who are of the old stock and to our new neighbours from faraway lands.

1
An Overview of the Parish

The parish of Kilbarron-Terryglass, which incorporates the medieval parish of Finnoe, is situated in the barony of Lower Ormond. It is traversed by the main Nenagh to Portumna road. It is bounded on the west by the River Shannon's largest lake, Lough Derg, having an estimated shoreline of 15.5 miles/ 25km. Borrisokane parish lies to its east, Monsea & Killodiernan parish to its south-east, and the parish of Lorrha to its north.

Finnoe, Kilbarron and Terryglass combined have a total of eighty-eight townlands of which the largest is Ballinderry with 838 acres and the smallest Stonepark with 25 acres. There are also three small islands, the largest of which is Bounla with a little over ten acres, Brieny's has two, and Goat a little over one acre. The census record for 1841 and 1851 also lists '33 other islands' with a total of 13 acres, 3 roods and 7 perches. Most were in Kilbarron parish and all were uninhabited.

In 1984-6 the Tipperary branch of the Irish Wildbird Conservancy (IWC) carried out restoration work to the perimeter of Goat Island to increase the overall area for the Common Terns which had begun to nest and breed there. Terns winter off the west African coast and fly north every year to breed. Their food is mostly fish which they catch by diving into the water from the air. Terns still frequent Luska Bay area.

Kilbarron's topography is hilly with many small freshwater lakes. Finnoe is very flat with lakes also, while Terryglass has some low hills but no lakes. Standing at the Long Lane Cross on the road between Coolbawn Cross and Kilbarron village, now that the hedges have been trimmed, you see before you a great plain which takes in Finnoe and places further afield. If, however, you pause for a moment at the Round Hill in Borrisokane you can see Kilbarron Hill in the distance, and as you get to the Pound of Finnoe you can positively identify landmarks in Kilbarron, such as Thade's Castle and the Forty Acre Field in Annagh.

Our parish has some of the finest land in Ireland and there are no finer scenic views anywhere in the country than that from the top of Glenbower Hill (below),

where Tipperary (NR) Co. Council's regional water scheme reservoir is situated. There are other points on the Kilbarron hills from which splendid views can be seen, but none finer than this.

Land Use
The dominant soil type in the parish is limestone, with some sandstone and shale. There are intermittent pockets of peat soils.

Drystock farming (cattle/sheep) is practised on about 45 per cent of the land area. This is followed by dairying on approximately 30 per cent of the area. The main crops are sugar beet and spring barley. A small amount of winter cereals are grown. Total crops account for about 20 per cent of the area.

Upwards of 200 acres/80 hectares of forestry has been planted in the parish in recent years. A high percentage of this consists of broadleaf trees. About 5 per cent of the parish area is now devoted to forestry.

This contrasts with the figures given in Lewis's *Topograpical Dictionary* of 1837, which stated that the 7,575 statute acres in the parish of Kilbarron is chiefly under tillage and that in Terryglass, where the land is light, there were 4,066 statute acres partly under tillage, with 2,000 acres of bog out of a total of 9,762 acres. In Finnoe parish, of its total of 4,003 statute acres, 800 were bog and the remainder mostly pasture land.

In his poem, 'The Planter's Daughter', Austin Clark wrote: 'The house of the planter is known by its trees'. In this parish when you see in the distance a thickly wooded area you can tell you are nearing what was a landlord's demesne. Curiously enough, it is the incoming settlers of the seventeenth century, and their descendants, that we can thank for any old timber which exists in the parish today.

At the end of the eighteenth century wood was becoming scarce in Great Britain and the Napoleonic wars were raging, much of the fighting being at sea. Landowners were encouraged to plant oak, elm, ash, birch, sycamore etc. By the time the trees had matured steel-clad ships had come into use so we still have many of those great trees in little pockets all over the countryside, some of which were planted about 200 years ago.

There are many woods in this parish. The Cambies planted trees in great numbers, as did the Minchins. Bassett Holmes planted the trees on Islandmore in the middle of the nineteenth century. Kylenoe Wood is quite famous, and there are splendid woods around Gortalougha House. Much of the old timber in the parish is past its best and some is even a danger in storms.

It is indeed a great boon that the agricultural advisory service, Teagasc, with the voluntary organisation Crann and the Department of Forestry's commercial arm, Coillte, are encouraging the planting of trees again, particularly broadleaf ones like beech, oak, lime and elm. Ireland was at one time a thickly wooded land but with the coming of the invader, the constant wars and the complete disregard for the environment the country had become denuded of trees. We are all familiar with the 'Lament for Kilcash', reputed to have been written in Irish by Rev. Francis Lane, when the magnificent woods around Kilcash, near Carrick-on-Suir, were cut down at the end of the 1700s. The poem was translated by Frank O'Connor.

Cad a dhéanfaimíd feasta gan adhmad/Tá deire na gcoillte ar lár.
What shall we do without timber/The last of the trees are down.

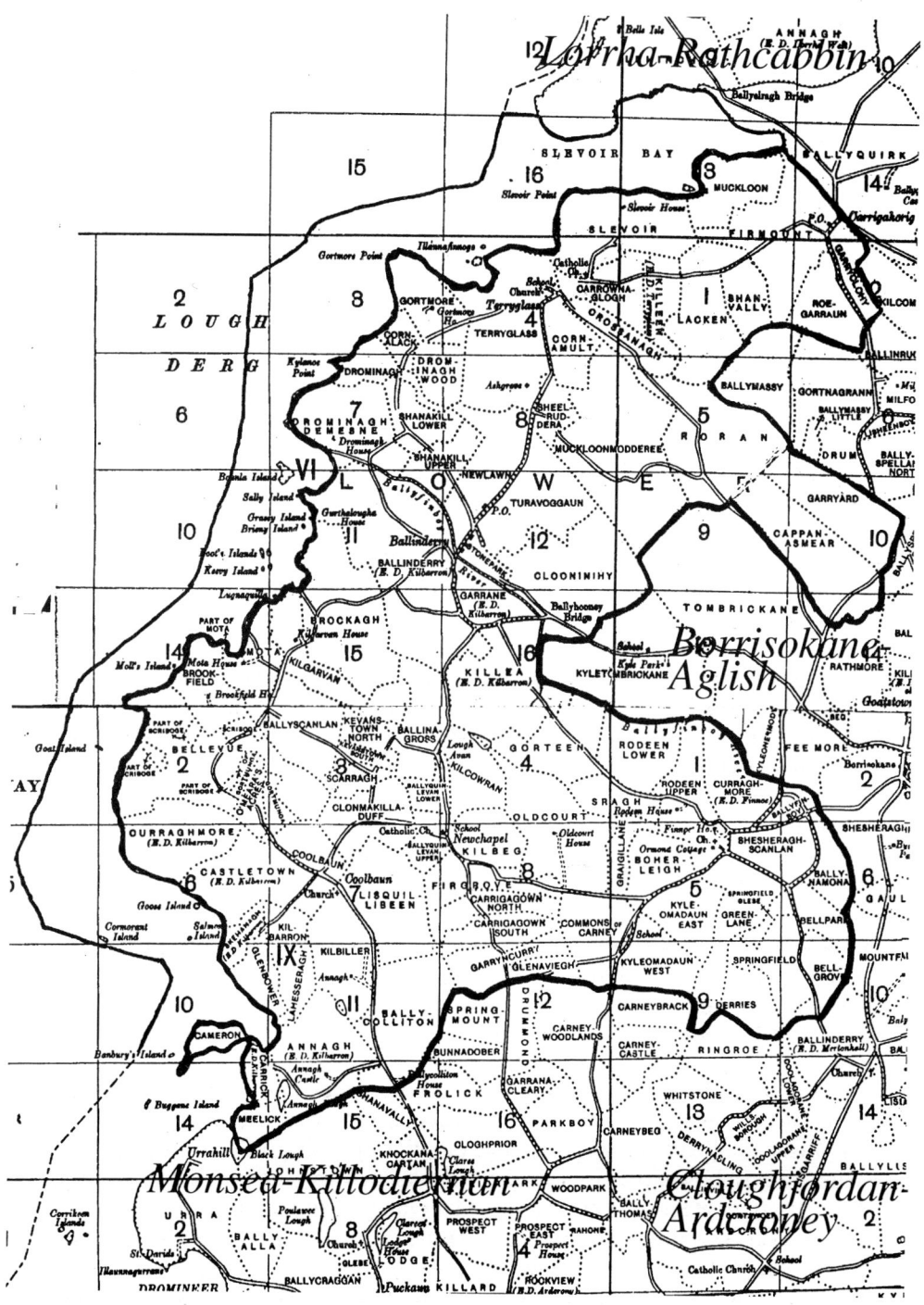

Parish of Kilbarron-Terryglass (reproduced by kind permission of the Government, permit No. 6793)

LANDSCAPE

17th Century
The *Civil Survey* of 1654, which purports to be a record of who owned the land in 1641, i.e. before the rebellion by the Irish against the Crown, also recorded other information. One of the striking bits is that relating to boundaries between properties. The countryside was not divided into fields as it is now. A recurring entry in the Survey goes: 'the sd. lands are not clearly divided betweene the sd. proprietors whereby each pprietor's portion may be particularly meared and bounded'. There were no hedgerows. The land was worked in common and divided into strips which were tilled in rotation for the cereal crops. Until about fifty years ago there was a plot of land in Bellevue referred to as the 'continent'. A strip of this piece of land was owned in this way by five or six small holders. The word 'continent' springs from the Latin word *continere:* to contain.

The pasture land, also held in common, would be outside the tillage so that animals could roam free. The inhabitants lived in clusters of houses called 'clacháns' adjacent to their common land. These clacháns were much more common in the west and south-west of Ireland and in the islands off these shores. The Blasket Islands are an excellent example. There were some such settlements in this parish. Until recently there existed the remains of a little street of houses in Gurteen townland. They were on land at the back of Donie O'Meara's old home.

The old people in Coolbawn used speak of 'a street of houses' at the boundary of Sterling's Fort field and Michael Carroll's Whittaker's field. Also, according to Bill Donoghue, Ballinderry, there was a settlement of about twenty houses near the shoreline at Gortalougha at the end of the eighteenth century.

In the *Civil Survey* also there is mention in many of the townlands of the existence of cottages – there were eight cottages in Coolbawn. There is no indication as to whether these cottages were in a cluster or not, or where they were, but I assume that for safety sake they probably huddled together. Drominagh tower house had twelve cottages near it and they were most likely just outside the bawn walls, while at Castletown there were eight, also very likely in close proximity to the bawn walls. As well as cottages the *Civil Survey* mentions a few, but not many, 'thatched' houses. One wonders what sort of roof the cottages had – obviously something inferior to thatch!

Rivers and Streams
There are two main rivers in the parish: the Ballyfinboy, which separates Kilbarron parish from Borrisokane parish and empties into Lough Derg in the vicinity of Drominagh House, and the Ballycolliton, which separates Kilbarron from Monsea & Killodiernan parish and empties into Lough Derg at Luska Bay.

The Ballyfinboy river rises in the Knockshegowna area and is called the Ballinderry river where it flows through that village. The short Ballycolliton river rises at Hough's well in Lisquillibeen near the old Hough family home in which Michael Donoghue now lives, flows along by Lisquillibeen tower house, and is fed by a big spring at Springmount and other streams. In the *Civil Survey* the Ballyfinboy river is called the river Inihy, hence the name Clooninihy, *cluan* meaning fertile land bounded by a marsh or between a river and a bog. Two little rivers flow through Terryglass – one of the translations of Terryglass is the land of the two streams. The Carrigahorig river forms part of the bounds between

Terryglass and Lorrha parishes. A network of streams feeds into all four rivers.

Lakes
There are freshwater lakes in Kilbarron and Finnoe parishes but none in Terryglass. Cornaling Lake in Oldcourt (Breretons) has a swallow hole which is thought to send water underground to link up with the various other loughs in the area. Someone once tested it by putting dye in the hole but I don't know the result.

Other freshwater lakes are: Ballyquinlivan Lough; Ballinagrass Lough; Maggie Smith's Lake (now called Dunne's) which may be a turlough. The Loughawn, between Coolbawn and Lisquillibeen, is in front of Tony Halifax's house. It may be a turlough as I have known it to go completely dry in very hot summers. It was there we watered our cattle in the long ago, driving them down Ryan's lane.

Lough Avon, which straddles the townlands of Oldcourt and Killea, at 11 acres 16 perches, is one of the biggest lakes. The name means the lake of the swans.

Swans nest every year in The Loughawn also, the pen and cob flying out over Coolbawn, and when the cygnets are able to get along under their own steam they are brought on foot up through O'Halloran's land, they then come out at O'Halloran's house, walk up the road about 200 yards to Ryan's old house, go inland through Sterling's fields, come out somewhere below Kilbarron well, cross the road and go inland again behind the former Bruce house (now Mary Ryan's) and thus arrive at Lough Derg shore.

Driving home one day we came on them, father and mother swan and three cygnets doing their bit of road journey from Kilbarron well to Mary Ryan's. Two must have got lost in Sterling's cornfield that day as my brother Michael had seen them earlier in the day promenading from O'Halloran's to Ryan's old farm and there were five cygnets then. Hopefully, the two missing ones turned up.

Annagh Lough is beside the road on the left as you go towards Luska bay from the main road. What people call the Black Lough is not really a lough but an inlet of the lake. You can row a boat from the main lake into it through a wide passage hedged at each side by reeds. It is supposed to be bottomless, or so we were told as children, and is an excellent breeding ground for pike. In June the yellow water irises make the journey into the Black Lough a delight.

The Priest's Lough of 1.8 acres lies in Scarragh townland opposite John and Kathleen Dwyer's house – Lakeview House as it is now called and which may be built on the site of the house recorded by ordnance surveyors in 1840 as 'the Cottage'. He said it was used as a hunting lodge by the Tabideau family who lived in Annagh Castle at the time.

In Bellevue townland there are two little lakes in the two fields just past Lesserragh House entrance. We used call the one nearest the house 'Bruce's Loughawn', and that in the next field near Treacy's house, 'Trassey's Loughawn'. I think they may be turloughs.

Samuel Lewis, who compiled his *Topographical Dictionary* in 1837, writes that ten years earlier, i.e. 1827, a lake covering about 60 acres was drained in Finnoe parish The land was reclaimed and became very productive. The stone-lined culvert or canal that was built to drain the water away is still working efficiently. When the weather is wet small pools of water collect in the field but the culvert keeps it under control. It is about 300 yards long and carries the water towards the Ballyfinboy river.

The earliest census which survives for the parishes of Finnoe, Kilbarron and Terryglass is 1659, though it is not necessarily a complete head count.

Parish	1659	1841	1851	1861	1871	1881	1891	1901	1911	1986	1991	1996
Finnoe	70	1,576	1,045	786	630	618	587	490	389	157	150	155
Kilbarron	324	2,853	1,878	1,273	1,064	909	707	721	600	541	530	553
Terryglass	61	2,953	1,986	1,408	1,060	1,032	955	867	738	485	464	450

Antiquities

Unlike neighbouring Monsea & Killodiernan parish, where quite a few prehistoric monuments have been identified and, indeed, two excavated, nothing of that vintage has been discovered in our parish.

There is a prehistoric cooking place, known as a 'fulacht fiadh' in the Cow's Field on the Castletown estate just inside the avenue gates. It was discovered a few years ago by John Feehan and his field survey team. A fulacht fiadh is a horseshoe-shaped mound of burnt stones with its opening towards a stream. Usually within the hollow of the mound is a hearth of flat stones and nearby is a trough for water. The method of cooking was to heat the stones in a fire, fill the trough and drop the hot stones in until the water came to the boil, followed by the meat to be cooked. The stones became black and brittle from repeated heating and plunging into water.

However, having heard the story of the Céide Fields in North Mayo where some people discovered walls when cutting turf which turned out to be the remains of a New Stone Age settlement (circa 3,000-2,500 BC), I was interested in the following snippet of information given me by Michael Parkinson of Slevoir.

When the Parkinsons' house was being built in 1918 there was a stonemason named Paddy Hackett, a local man who lived in Turavoggaun, working on the house. He told the following story to Michael Parkinson's father and grandparents and I quote Michael exactly.

> When cutting turf in Turavoggaun Bog in the early part of the twentieth century people used to talk about the ridges of stones they used to uncover in the bottom of the bog. The looked like remains of walls. They could not understand how they came to be there.

Turavoggaun [there are several spellings] is situated quite near Ballinderry village on the right-hand side of the main road to Terryglass.

In Nolan's bog on the border between Lacken and Shanbally people used find stakes under the bog. They assumed them to have been used for snares to catch elk.

Ring Forts

A survey and valuation of Ireland was ordered by the House of Commons in 1824. The first set of ordnance maps is the result. The survey was carried out by the army's Royal Engineers (sappers). The director of the survey was Civil Engineer Captain Thomas A. Larcom. He decided to extend the scope of the work to include topography, history, antiquities, economic state, and social conditions. Accordingly, an antiquarian department was set up within the overall survey. George Petrie was entrusted with the antiquities and topography section of this. He then made up a team of workers to be lead by John O'Donovan and Eugene O'Curry.

Petrie stayed in Dublin while O'Donovan, sometimes accompanied by O'Curry, covered the country, systematically examining antiquities and making investigations on the spot into placenames and traditions associated with them.

Both O'Donovan, and O'Curry particularly, were authorities on the Irish language and Irish manuscripts. The team worked from 1835 to 1842. The findings of the field workers were sent to Dublin in letter form – hence the OS Letters of which one hundred and three volumes were compiled. Fortunately for us, the Co. Tipperary letters were typed up by Rev. Michael Flanagan in 1930.

The Sites and Monuments record for Tipperary North Riding, compiled by the Office of Public Works in 1992, lists as many as thirty-six enclosures, a crannóg in Carrick near Luska bay, and a cairn in the Commons of Carney. They do not define what an enclosure is and it is not necessarily what we call a ring fort – also known as a rath, lios, or dún, words which often form part of a placename, such as Lisquillibeen in our parish and Rathmore in Borrisokane.

1840 Surveyor, John O'Donovan, as was the fashion of the time, called them 'Danish forts' as they were supposed to have been built by the Danes or Norsemen. Archaeologists now tell us that these forts were in fact the farmsteads of farmers of the first 500-800 years of the Christian era. They varied in size, depending on the prosperity of the farmer, and had defensive features. A fort excavated in Thurles in the 1970s uncovered evidence of a free-standing wooden structure, a probable hearth site and some shallow pits and trenches.

Ring forts were generally called 'fairy forts', as the fairies were supposed to live in them and hold high-jinks therein. Scary stories, and tales of mysterious scenes and sounds seen and heard in their vicinity, is an integral part of Irish folklore. There are well-known poems, like 'The Stolen Child', which illustrate this. Tales of the bad luck and misfortune which befell families and individuals who interfered with them are legion and, it must be said, helped in no small way to insure their preservation. However, the decline in that belief, coupled with the arrival of powerful machinery, made removal easy so that in some cases all that is left is a circular outline in the field or on the hillside.

Lisquillibeen: According to the Ordnance Survey, this townland abounded with 'Danish forts'. There were two forts there that we knew of – one at the back of Casey's, down Lisquillibeen lane, the other on Costelloe's land. Both have since been removed, probably in the last few years.

Clonmackilladuff: 'In Clonmackilladuff there are two 'Danish forts' in the south end', wrote O'Donovan. Two forts still exist in James Bourke's field in that townland not far from his new house.

Coolbawn: O'Donovan stated that there were two 'Danish forts' near the centre of the townland. One I do not know about but there was a splendid example of a three-ringed fort in the field belonging to the Sterling family opposite Brendan Carroll's and Tony Halifax's houses. It is still known as the Fort Field. Another fort in Sterling's ruined the field as modern machinery, such as a reaper and binder not to mention the later combine harvesters, could not function within them, so it was removed

It was Easter and the weather was beautiful. I happened to be at home for the holidays. For days and days on end the constant drone of the bulldozer went on. At the time I had very little knowledge of or interest in local history or antiquities and was not thinking of the bulldozing of the fort as a calamity.

Ballinderry: O'Donovan wrote: 'In the east side of the townland of Ballinderry, about five and a half mile west of Borrisokane, is a Danish fort or rath in which unbaptised infants are buried. It is thickly overgrown with whitethorns'.

It is still there. This fort or 'lios' is in Ryehill on the farm of Mrs Julia McDonnell (née Hogan). The field in which it is situated has always been called the 'lios field'. At present corn is grown there and the lios is very overgrown. When the field was in pasture cattle kept down the overgrowth. and the outline could be seen. Julia's father-in-law, the late Tom McDonnell, told her that unbaptised infants were buried there in the past. Everyone gave it a wide berth.

Kilbiller: O'Donovan says: 'Kilbiller contains several Danish forts'. One of these was in a 'divide' which my brother Michael Carroll acquired. It was spoiling the field but he felt bad about getting rid of it. He went to Fr Comerford for advice. Fr Comerford told him to work away but at the same time indicated that 'there are more things in heaven and earth than are dreamed of in our philosophy'. The fort was removed.

Holy Wells

Other antiquities which have survived in the parish are holy wells. The cult of springs and votive offerings in water was known among the Celtic peoples in Europe since pagan times. In Ireland, after the coming of St. Patrick, the cult became absorbed by the Christian religion, even to the extent that holy wells became the focus of many of the early monastic sites. But whatever its origins, the custom of reciting prayers at holy wells became sanctified by usage, particularly during the Penal times when the holy well was one of the few externals of Catholic devotion to escape proscription.

The 'pattern' or practice of going to a holy well in great numbers on a particular Sunday was quite common until forbidden by the bishops at the beginning of the nineteenth century as people tended to turn the pattern into a jollification with a certain amount of 'drink taken'.

Holy wells became associated with cures for such as eye disease. As many people became blind on becoming older, not having the modern remedies against such common conditions as cataracts, they felt their only hope was the holy well. The water from other wells was said to have healed headaches.

As already stated, John O'Donovan, Eugene Curry and other scholars were the members of the Ordnance Survey team whose task was to collect information on topographical features. Information on Terryglass was given to O'Donovan by Edward Biggs, Benjamin Talbot, Rev. Fr Bugler, CC, and Mr O'Callaghan. One feels that he would have got much more accurate information from the local peasantry. I cannot imagine Mr Biggs or Mr Talbot knowing much about holy wells, and Fr Bugler was not a native of the parish. I do not know who Mr O'Callaghan was.

Information about points of archaeological and other interest in Kilbarron were given to the surveyors by John Parker, Ballycolliton; Solomon B. Cambie, Kilgarvan; David Hogan, Hugh Costelloe, Garrancurra; Edward Talbot, and Robert Holland – probably from Whitegate on the Clare side of the lake and who gave information about the islands.

St. Augh's Well is located in Shannon Lane, Terryglass, fairly close to the lakeshore, and is still venerated as an 'eye well'. The rounds are begun at the four sides of the well, saying at each the Creed, five Our Fathers and five Hail Marys. When the prayers are completed the eyes are washed in the water and some little token or offering is left on the nearby bush.

St. Colum's Well is in Shannon Lane, on the same side, in a marshy hollow. It is near a steep mound covered with trees and shrubs, marked on maps as the 'Greenan', and dates back to Terryglass's monastic days. The well provides a cure for headaches.

Tobar Atáin /Aughan or the well of the little ford, a so-called holy well in Slevoir townland about one-quarter mile north-east of Terryglass, was also identified. It was somewhere behind the parish priest's house and the late Canon Darcy set great store by its water and would allow no other water to be used in the church or his house. It was in a marshy place and there is no longer any trace of it. Near that field was a fulacht fiadh or cooking place. There are still fire-blackened stones scattered around.

Kilbarron Well was, according to the surveyors, 'an excellent well at the end of the townland convenient to the ruined Old Abbey. Catholics frequented it some time ago to do penance for their sin.' I lived near Kilbarron well and we drew our water from it. I never heard the story of the penance. The greatest penance the unfortunate people of Coolbawn suffered was drawing two barrels of water, lashed precariously on a horse and cart, up that hilly road to Coolbawn Cross, the barrels constantly in danger of falling off. Anyone fortunate enough to possess two barrels and a horse and cart would be met at the Cross by those not fortunate enough to possess such amenities and was asked for a bucket or two of spring water. The pump at the Cross, the only other source of spring water, was dry as often as not. In fact, Kilbarron well was an excellent well and used until quite lately when it became silted up. It was a wonderful source of watercress.

Tobar Naomh Eoin /St. John's Well, or *Tobar na Shane*, is at the south-west end of Garryncurry townland and is enclosed on three sides by limestone blocks. A small stream flows out of it.

Spellman's Well was near the Belvedere quay. It got its name from a family of the same name. Their house burned down as a result of a child losing his pet bird and searching for it under the bed with a candle. Tradition does not say whether there was any loss of life.

The family did not rebuild but moved away. Some of them went to America. There is a tradition in the neighbourhood that Cardinal Spellman, New York, was descended from one of them.

Flora

Rev. John Hogan developed a keen interest in the wild flora in the parish after he was appointed parish priest here. He soon became very knowledgeable on the subject and took many photographs of the very rare species. His bible was *The Concise British Flora in Colour*. Twenty years ago he listed the species he had identified in *Cois Deirge*. They are still there today. Golden Cellandines on the road between Coolbawn Cross and the old graveyard, wild roses in Glenbower, orchids at Luska, Terryglass, and in the new cemetery at Kilbarron. He was particularly pleased with his discovery of tufts of white campion growing in a hostile, stony environment near his house in Kilbarron village. At Luska, Glenbower and Slevoir he noted the extremely rare *Inula Salicina*, which resembles a golden daisy or small sunflower. The Lough Derg shoreline is the only place it now survives in the British Isles. Another favourite spot of his was the bank opposite the children's play area in Glenbower – a herbaceous border of wild flowers and plants of up to twelve different species.

Amenities

The parish has a share of amenities, both natural and acquired. Development of the natural ones has concentrated mainly on the extensive shoreline of Lough Derg. The main developments have been at Terryglass and Kilgarvan quays which have been well exploited for boating, fishing, walks and scenic views. There is a children's play area in Glenbower near Kilbarron quay and at Terryglass. More recently there has been a successful development away from the water – at Comenthus, an uphill 2m/3km circular forest walk in the townland of Bellevue. Additional attractions include panels with poems, seats and picnic tables.

There is a sportsfield with amenities, a pitch and putt course, and two community centres. There is a very active branch of the Irish Countrywomen's Association in Terryglass, a Ladies Club and a club for over-60s in Kilbarron. Fishing enthusiasts are catered for by Kilgarvan Angling club who hold regular competitions. An annual festival is held in Kilbarron village in June or August. Each village has its own Improvements Committee.

Regional Water Scheme

Since 1997 water has been taken from the lake at Skehanagh, treated, stored in a reservoir above Glenbower and sent by gravity feed to Nenagh and surrounding areas. The total cost of this development was £12m. The treatment plant, using computer-controlled technology, is designed to produce a maximum throughput of 3.5m gallons of water per day. The present daily output is about half that.

SOCIETY

Notwithstanding the outstanding scenery, antiquities and other topographical features which the parish can boast of, in the end its most important asset is its people. The characteristics of successive generations were governed by circumstances of birth, religion, social status, customs and practices within their social environment. Some crossed the religious and social divides during the course of their lives.

Arising from the allocation of extensive tracts of land in the parish to an officer of the Parliamentary/Cromwellian forces in the mid-1600s, and the later purchase of lands by persons of like faith and background, three equally distinct classes – as distinct from one another as were the British and Indians under the Raj – evolved in the parish. This occurred more so in the stretch of territory which had Lough Derg as its immediate boundary. The outcome of this was the emergence of a three-tiered society comprised of (a) land-owning descendants of the planters, whose religion in most cases was Protestant; (b) prosperous Protestant tenant farmers, and (c) those of the Gaelic race whose religion was Roman Catholic and who were, in most instances, tenants of smallholdings or employees of the other two groups.

The settlers never lost this complete difference in class, religion and culture. And while relations were friendly and mutually respectful, there were very few, if any, instances of intermarriage or socialising between the two. However, not a single Big House was burnt in the parish of Kilbarron-Terryglass during the War of Independence or the Civil War.

We were a different race. In the course of this book I have written much about the Anglo-Irish. The reason is simple. People like us, the peasantry, the remnants of the old septs who ruled the country before the 1650s, have no history. We have kept no records. We had no education, and even if we had books and could read them where would they go in our smoky cabins. The gentry on the other hand kept some records, although in this parish such are hard to find. Those that are there enable one to piece the story together from, for example, the family papers of the Cambies and the Minchins who came in the 1650s and 1660s respectively. The Catholic Esmondes and Hickies are well documented also but they were later arrivals in this area. Property seems to have changed hands very rapidly in Terryglass and it is difficult to trace the land-owning families, apart from the Biggs family, in the eighteenth century.

At first there was little distinction between one downtrodden eighteenth century Catholic and another. Gradually, as the nineteenth century grew older a pyramid of class distinction made itself visible. Nobody owned land but some could lease it and one must be honest and say that some leased more, had more ambition and worked harder than others. So you got strong farmers at the top of the pyramid, smaller ones beneath them with, perhaps, between ten and twenty acres, then those who held a house and perhaps an acre or two or even four, finally the cottier with a garden to grow enough potatoes for his family. This was the class and to a lesser extent the class above it which was wiped out in the Great Famine.

After that, the holding of land changed. Farms became bigger as tenants accumulated the tiny holdings of those who had emigrated or died. There was a movement of farmers also as some moved to larger holdings, perhaps a couple of parishes away. Their origins could still be traced until a few years ago because even when families moved they always brought back their dead to be buried with their own people. It still happens in rare cases. Thus one can always tell which families always lived in the parish as their burial grounds are usually in the local old pre-Reformation churchyards. Now that new local authority-controlled cemeteries have been introduced that distinction is dying away.

Marriage

So, apart from the gentry class which do not concern us in this context, there were social strata and I am speaking now of the late nineteenth century; strong farmers; small farmers; small holders and cottiers. The distinction from the point of view of marriage, for example between a strong farmer's son and a cottiers's daughter, was nearly as great as that between a strong Catholic farmer's son or daughter marrying into the gentry.

There were practical reasons for this. One of the reasons was the dowry. The custom of 'made' matches between members of the farming classes was very strong in the nineteenth century and at least into the first two or three decades of the twentieth century. Families were large and the average farm could only sustain one family. If a girl had a dowry she could marry the eldest son of a neighbouring farmer. Her 'match could be made'. I heard my mother speak of several friends who had their 'matches made' for them. Sometimes the couple would not see each other until the families met to do the deal. The deal accomplished, that 'dowry' which a girl brought in would be used to 'fortune' her husband's sister into another farm and so on. But there was a limit to dowry money and, as I said, families were large. One great outlet was emigration. A girl would go out to America and save the fare for her next sister. If you can possibly get a copy of the late John Healy's book, *Nineteen Acres*, do so. It describes this process vividly, if crudely, but lovingly. This sister in turn would send for her sister. I believe more women emigrated than men. I do not have the statistics, just an impression. Emigration crossed all social frontiers and it is not often realised that the gentry emigrated in great numbers after their estates had to be sold in the Encumbered Estates courts after the Famine. In this parish the Cambies emigrated following such an event. Children of all classes emigrated, mostly to the USA but sometimes to Australia or New Zealand.

Careers
To return to our strong farmer and what is left of his large family after he has fortuned off two daughters, acquired a daughter-in-law and, perhaps, helped one or two to emigrate. If he were a very strong farmer he might send a son to be a priest. Missionary Orders did not require money for education but to become a member of the diocesan clergy did. There was status attached to being a member of the diocesan clergy – the possibility of becoming a bishop existed! Nevertheless it was not unusual in the early nineteenth century for members of Orders to become bishops.

Our strong farmer has now disposed of four out of a possible eight children. What to do with the other four. One great outlet for girls was to become nuns and a great many did. The convents of England, America and Australia were at one time overflowing with Irish nuns. Many of them had novitiates in Ireland.

The earlier generations of nuns became teachers or nurses if they had the ability to profit from the training – or were already trained before entering. Without a dowry or a profession, or the intellect to train for a profession, a nun became a 'lay' sister. Almost all orders had this grade. Certainly the Sisters of Mercy, where I was educated, had. They performed the same menial tasks as servants in a Big House. They were visibly distinguished by the wearing of aprons at all times. For everyday wear it was a check gingham type, blue and white, and for chapel an elegant little pleated affair. Even in God's house they were different.

I have a memory from my youth of a young woman from this parish entering a convent as a lay sister and Canon Darcy's reaction to the event. He was furious and delivered a sermon – he had a fine voice – on the subject. He forbade any of his congregation to allow his or her daughter to become a lay sister in a convent. He left the parents of the parish in no doubt that they might as well send a daughter to work as a servant in a big house where at least she would get wages. In hindsight, Canon Darcy is to be admired for that brave statement so much before its time.

Very often two or even three girls from a large family would 'join the nuns'. The probability of actually having a call to the religious life was seldom dwelt on, which is not to say that many of these girls did not have a vocation. Nor was it often a probability in the case of the son who became a priest. Mothers were not unknown to have had the 'vocation' in the first place.

The Christian Brothers were another great outlet for boys from most classes. Many young men got their education in this way. They were recruited very young – about thirteen or fourteen years – and given full secondary educaton free and, in some instances, third level as well.

The Royal Irish Constabulary (RIC), the predecessors of the Garda Síochána, gave employment to bright boys, irrespective of class, provided they were respectable and intelligent and at least 5 feet 9 inches tall. They had to have a certain level of education but sufficient could be gained in a good national school. The career prospects were not good as, until the late 1880s, it was not possible to reach even the rank of sergeant unless one was a Protestant. It was quite unheard of for a Catholic to become a District Inspector (DI) which was officer class, until well into the War of Independence, 1918-21. At that period men were resigning in great numbers and some DIs were getting shot before the first Catholic DIs were appointed and then only a few. Head Constables did not have to be Protestants, probably as of 1895 when the embargo was removed from the post of sergeant. A young man over 6 feet might get into the Dublin Metropolitan Police.

Another outlet for farmers' children was a career in business. Shops were the only sources of such employment; in our case Nenagh, Borrisokane or. possibly, Roscrea; they might go further afield to a distant town or even Dublin. It was quite respectable to work in a draper's shop. One had to 'serve one's time' and it is likely that a fee would have to be paid. Later on the trained draper might open his own shop. There were no boutiques then and it was quite a skilled occupation. The girls often 'lived in'. Those who enjoy reading William Trevor will have gleaned the atmosphere of such drapers' shops vividly portrayed in particular in his novella *Reading Tunganev*. He makes those country town drapers' shops of the 1920s and 1930s come to life. The last one in Nenagh to have the overhead cash railway for carrying the bill and money and bringing back the change was Hodgins in Pearse Street.

Working in a grocery or bar was not quite as respectable as a draper or indeed as a hardware store. Still it must have been pleasant with all the lovely smells of still unpackaged groceries and the fun of the rough and tumble in the public bar.

Other boys 'served their time' to carpenters and blacksmiths and some managed to acquire their own forge and joinery business. Girls became dressmakers. These boys and girls would usually be the children of small farmers.

The children of small farmers emigrated, naturally, but the girls also went into 'good' service, while the younger sons went to work on the farm of the local landowner. The daughters of cottiers, if they were unlucky, went into service with a farmer. As a rule that was in many cases the nearest thing to slavery that society had to offer. After World War II 'good' service was hard to find as the class which was employing it was no longer able to afford the wages. The great houses with their armies of servants – not that such ever existed in this parish – were a thing of the past. Labour had become expensive and the employers poorer. It was usual in the Big Houses to employ girls from the next parish or county or even farther away. In Kickham St in Nenagh, where Harry Martin's shop now is, was a shop kept by a Miss Day. She sold odds and ends, stationery and such like, but not, I think, sweets. She had an agency through which prospective employers found maids and maids found employers. These 'foreign' girls very often married into the community and brought much needed new blood.

During the nineteenth century and early part of the twentieth century marriages, both those arranged and otherwise, took place between members of the same community or a neighbouring one. People did not travel far because of lack of transport, so there was a great deal of intermarriage. As any student of bloodstock knows this is not 'a good thing'. It did not only happen in rural Ireland but amongst the aristocracy and royalty of Europe where it also proved to be 'not a good thing'. These servant girls who came from some distance remedied this in a small way. Unfortunately, the sons of strong farmers rarely married servant girls and it was mainly that class which suffered from inbreeding. In towns there would be an influx of new blood from girls coming to work in shops. Another source of new blood was the police force. There were RIC barracks all over the place because of the constant agrarian and other troubles and police, particularly sergeants, were never left long in one place – the obvious reason being that they might get too friendly with the inhabitants. Nevertheless many, indeed most, RIC men met and married their wives while stationed a long way from home; it was the policy of the Government to station them as far away from home as possible.

Role of Clergy

Father Ignatius Murphy in his *History of the Diocese of Killaloe in the Eighteenth Century* gives us a vivid picture of the life of the Catholic clergy during the eighteenth century. When not positively persecuted, a rare occurrence anyway, they were allowed to carry out their duties as best they could. Their lot was often no better than that of their parishioners. But they felt at one with their people and helped them as best they could. This was true up to the latter part of the nineteenth century. After 1850-60, when a certain prosperity followed the famine years, the relationship between priest and people seemed to change. It had probably begun with the first priests who came out of Maynooth, whose setting up was supported financially by the British government to supply priests who had hitherto been educated on the Continent. This new breed of priests, sons of strong farmers, quickly became part of the Establishment and, with many honourable exceptions, became somewhat superior. They also adopted the Victorian morals then fashionable, frowning on young people enjoying themselves and forbidding as far as possible the gatherings where they met, calling them 'occasions of sin'. They were particularly hard on any sexual frailty and woe betide the unfortunate girl who found herself pregnant outside marriage. Such a girl would be 'read off the altar' unless her father had at least 50 acres of land! With the collusion of the parents she would be spirited away to some convent from which the child would be adopted. Then the young mother might, or might not, be allowed back into society. Very often the poorer girls had such children in the county home.

Employment
A later chapter, 'Trades and Occupations', shows that in the past employment was also found in areas unconnected with argriculture. People were employed in the various trades; small industries like lime burning, saw mills and corn mills; on the large estates and in the Big Houses – the latter being a particularly important source for young girls and women. Of these only the trades have survived. Today, pockets of employment within the parish centre on mustard making in Ballinderry, crafts, furniture making, building construction, and the various tourist-oriented businesses at or near the lake.

Sources:
Teagasc, Nenagh. Coillte, Nenagh.
Civil Survey, Co. Tipperary, Vol 2, 1654-6. Census of Ireland, Pender (ed), 1659, Census 1841-1996. Ordnance Survey Letters 1840, Rev. Michael Flanagan (ed) 1930. Ordnance Survey sheet No.s 6, 7, 9, 10.
Sites and Monuments Record, Co. Tipperary (NR), Office of Public Works, 1992.
Archaeological Survey – Holy Wells, Elizabeth Fitzpatrick, for Nenagh District Heritage Society, 1985. *Cois Deirge*, 1978.
Author's personal memories.
Photographs on pp. 1, 15 supplied by Paddy Carroll, Coolbawn.

An aspect of parish culture: Paddy Ryan, Ballyscanlon (left), All-Ireland traditional accordion champion, 1965 – his son George won the u/14 in 1967; Pat Joe Maloney, Ballinagrass (right), traditional flute champion, 1957.

2
Castles and Tower Houses

LANDOWNERSHIP

Before 1600 land was owned by the Gaelic septs and the 'Old English' descendants of the Norman invaders. This lasted in a rather shattered form until after the confiscations in the mid-1650s and the arrival of new owners, largely English. This was brought about by a parliamentary act of 1653 which designated the baronies of Upper and Lower Ormond, Owney and Arra, Kilnamanagh and Slieveardagh in Co. Tipperary to be divided by lot amongst the soldiers of the parliamentary forces in lieu of army service. The rest of county Tipperary was set aside for 'adventurers' – people who had adventured money to finance the keeping of an army in Ireland.

This did not happen, in fact, as approximately only one-third of confiscated land in Lower Ormond (16,225 acres) went to soldiers. According to the Book of Survey and Distribution of 1662 there is only one person clearly identified as a soldier who received land in the parishes of Finnoe, Kilbarron and Terryglass – Captain Solomon Cambie who got approximately 958 acres in the parish of Kilbarron.

We must bear in mind that it was the Irish owners of land who were displaced at this time – not tenants or labourers. Accordingly, the others, and indeed the owners themselves, most likely remained on in their own areas as tillers of the soil. This is reflected in the census of 1659 which shows that in the parish of Finnoe there were 31 English and 39 Irish; in Kilbarron 41 English and 280 Irish; and in Terryglass 2 English and 76 Irish.

The Great Upheaval

Two documents from the seventeenth century set out the owners of the land in the three civil parishes which make up our Catholic parish – Finnoe, Kilbarron and Terryglass. The first is the *Civil Survey* which is a record made in the year 1654 of who owned the land in 1641, i.e. before the rebellion by the Irish against the Crown. Fortunately, the Co. Tipperary survey was printed by the Irish Manuscripts Commission in 1934. However, the survey does not record tenants, only owners.

The second record, called the Book of Survey & Distribution and referred to above, is a handwritten document listing the owners as recorded in the *Civil Survey* in one column and opposite that are the names of persons granted land either for service in the Parliamentary/Cromwellian army or for 'adventuring' money. The document shows those of both groups confirmed as the owners by the Act of Settlement & Explanation of 1662, after Charles II had been restored to the English throne.

As the Book of Survey and Distribution was transcribed at different times there are slight differences in the various surviving copies.

Finnoe

The *Civil Survey* recorded that in this parish there were 2,463 Irish acres of which 2,223 were 'profitable' and 240 'unprofitable' An Irish acre was three-eighths bigger than a statute acre. 2,103 acres were owned by members of the O'Kennedy sept holding 'in fee by descent from their ancestors' and bearing names such as Keadagh, Brien, Rory, Philip, Donogh, Dermot and William. The exceptions were in the townland of Ballintrially where James Butler, 12th earl of Ormond, held one plowland and John Hogan, one-half plowland, 'in fee by descent' from their ancestors, and in Kyleomadaun, where Daniell Hally (probably Healy) and Morrogh Morisy held one-quarter and one-eight of a plowland, respectively, by descent from their ancestors. All were returned as 'Irish Papists', but this is not quite correct as James Butler had been brought up in the Anglican religion. Ballintrially is not a townland name now but it adjoined Graigellane and Carrigagowan.

In 1662 the confirmed owners were Sir Nicholas White, William Fitzgerald, Lord Dungan, David (or it might be Daniel) Kennedy, and the countess of Ormond and the earl of Anglesea.

Kilbarron

This parish's total acreage was 3,842, of which 3,768 were profitable and 74 unprofitable. Again, the Kennedys were the biggest landowners with 1,934. The *Civil Survey* shows a little movement in change of ownership. Sir Nicholas White of Leixlip, Co. Kildare, had bought in to Ballycolliton 'long before the rebellion' from Edmond Kennedy, and John Hurly, Annagh, likewise from Mortagh O'Bryen. In all Hurly had 948 acres. James Butler also had a holding 'by inheritance', as had a James Geoghgan, Sir John Dungan, Co. Kildare, Marcus Magrath, Blean Toomevara, and Donogh Hogan. Another outside proprietor was John Carroll of Behagh (probably modern Behamore) in the parish of Modreeny. The Kilbarron Kennedy names included Rickard, Morrogh, Hugh and Therlagh.

Castletown and Glenboure (Glenbower) contained 664 acres. Of that 500 were arable, 20 meadow, 60 pasture and 80 shrubby and rocky lands. There were 4 acres of bog and the value of the 'whole and each of the said lands', which presumably included the tower house and 8 cottages, was £50. The tower house was described as 'one old ruined castle with bawne, the walls onely standing'. The whole was owned by Philip Kennedy of Castletowne, Bryan McMorrogh (Kennedy) of the same, William Kennedy, Richard McMorrough (Kennedy), Jeffrey McMorrough and Teige McMorrough (Kennedy) of the same. Another part owner was above-mentioned John Carroll of Modreeney. All were described as 'Irish Papists'.

All these people, except John Carroll, appeared to be living at Castletown with their families and each owned a certain portion of the land, but 'said lands were not clearly divided'. Philip Kennedy owned more than half the land.

However, in the copy of the Book of Survey and Distribution found in Castletown some years ago by Mrs Stirling, Philip Kennedy is also shown as the sole owner of Raheen's 213 acres. This is not shown in the Minnitt, Annaghbeg, copy of the Book. These are the 200 acres Philip Kennedy tried and failed to get back after the Restoration. John Briggs definitely got Raheen according to the Castletown copy. There are still fields in Castletown called 'The Raheens'.

The confirmed owners in 1662 were Captain Solomon Cambie, John Briggs, the earl of Ormond, Lord Dungan, Nicholas White, William Fitzgerald, the earl of Anglesea and Walter Lawless. Cambie got in the region of 915 acres and Briggs 2,022. We have no way of knowing if they, or any of the others, purchased debentures from other soldiers or adventurers. The debenture was a legal document which set out a person's land entitlement and was a very saleable commodity.

Terryglass

The Kennedys also held a substantial portion of the land in this parish with 1,456 acres out of the total 2,350, of which 2,120 was profitable. A Philip Hogan held one-quarter of a plowland 'by inheritance'. John Grace of Ballinvoyne, had acquired 270 acres in Cappansmeare by his marriage to Joan (then deceased) daughter of John Kennedy, Ballingarry. The only woman proprietor in the three parishes was the Countess of Ormond, née Elizabeth Preston, and wife of James Butler the 12th earl, who had a nice holding of 330 acres 'by descent'. She was heiress in her own right through her mother, the only daughter of the 10th earl. Richard Butler of Ballyquirke had bought in to Terryglass townland, while James Butler, Tullow, Co. Carlow had 70 acres in Roran 'by inheritance'.

The confirmed new owners in this parish were the the earl of Cork & Orrery, the earl of Anglesea and Sir Nicholas White. White recovered his lands as 'an innocent Catholic'.

So what of the 1654 owners? Dermot F. Gleeson, in his *Last Lords of Ormond*, concluded from his analysis of the Hearth Money Rolls that in the barony of Lower Ormond only 120 out of the total 1,028 families were 'new planters'. He saw this as an indication that the old Gaelic families remained on as tenants of the new owners. This would have been greatly facilitated in Finnoe and Terryglass, and to a lesser extent in Kilbarron, by the fact that White, Dungan and the earls of Anglesea and Cork lived outside of the area.

The following are the only persons appearing in Robert C. Simington's *The Transplantation to Connacht, 1654-58*, who can be identified as belonging to our three parishes

Name	Origin	Barony Destination	Acres (Irish) Allotted
Brian McBrian, Mary Oge [Kennedy]	Annagh	Tulla, Co. Clare	55
Morris Hurly, minor, son and heir of John	Annagh	Bunratty, Co. Clare	195
Tirlag Kennedy	Scriboge	Ballymoe, Co. Galway	40
William Kennedy	Tombricane	Dunmore, Co. Galway	156
William Kennedy	Lismagrid	ditto	62
William Kennedy	Ballynagrist	ditto	40
John Kennedy	Gurteen	Longford, Co. Galway	435
Teige Kennedy	Coolbane	Loughrea, Co. Galway	183
Daniel Kennedy	not given	Bunratty, Co. Clare	33
Philip Kennedy jointly held with two Kennedys of	Ballyfinboy Tombricane	Longford, Co. Galway ditto	108

Transactions relating to land are complex documents, as evidenced in the summary of the Cambie court case and the Minchin and Ballycolliton leases quoted in later chapters.

CASTLES AND TOWER HOUSES

According to the *Civil Survey* the tower houses in the three parishes were in ruins. As it was locals who gave the information to the juries compiling the survey it is quite possible that they said they were ruined for the same reason that they gave undermeasures of the land – reckoned to be about 7 per cent more than declared.

However, the *Civil Survey* is a return of landowners only; we know nothing of their tenants and/or workers. The same applies when it comes to dwellings. The centuries have swept away all signs of the homes of these lesser folk, leaving only the remains of substantial landowners' castles and tower houses.

The Normans brought the building of stone castles to Ireland in the twelfth century. Nenagh castle dates back to within a couple of decades of the arrival of the first Normans in Co. Tipperary. Its building was initiated by Theobald fitzWalter whose task was to colonise the lands granted to him by Prince John in 1185. These lands lay in what is now Co. Tipperary. Theobald was appointed Pincerna Hiberniae or Chief Butler of Ireland. By about 1250 title and surname had become Le Botiller which evolved to become the surname Butler. This first Theobald's descendants became earls of Ormond and, later still, dukes of Ormonde.

In the fourteenth century the Gaelic chieftains of O'Brien and O'Kennedy purged this area of Co. Tipperary of the descendants of Theobald and other Norman settlers and reasserted their rights as landowners. In the fifteenth century their descendants turned their attention to building substantial stone dwellings or tower houses. These were not as extensive or elaborate as the Norman castles, but were smaller, still well-fortified, edifices. The buildings were usually surrounded by a high bawn walls inside which the livestock could be kept.

Harold G. Leask, Inspector of National Monuments, summarises this progression very well in his *Irish Castles and Castellated Houses* (1973).

> From about 1440 onwards there was a great building revival, signalised especially by the addition of belfry towers and cloister arcades to the monasteries and to the erection of completely new houses for the Friars – both Fransciscan and Dominican – particularly in the western part of the country.
>
> About the middle of the century laymen seem to have begun to build for themselves and for another hundred and fifty years or more they kept the masons at work.
>
> It is to this period that by far the greater number of the single towers – fortified residences – belong. ... Rich lands have, as might be expected, the greater numbers ...

Leask gives the figure of 253 castles and tower houses for County Tipperary. Studies made since Leask's time would make that number higher and put an earlier date of construction on some.

The Buildings

The combined parishes of Finnoe, Kilbarron and Terryglass have one Norman castle and seven tower houses. With one splendid exception, all are in a ruinous state. While one ruin is a national monument, the others are in a somewhat neglected condition. Collectively they present fine examples of key architectural tower house design and features – some of which are in an excellent state of preservation.

The pre-Reformation parish was the territorial unit on which surveys, reports, valuations and so on were based. Accordingly, it is easier and, hopefully, more comprehensible for the reader if we examine the castle and tower house legacy of each of our three parishes separately. However, these ruins are all on private lands and cannot be visited without the owner's permission.

Terryglass

Terryglass is the only one of the three parishes with a castle dating from the Norman period. It is known as 'Old Court castle' and stands on an elevated site in close proximity to Lough Derg in the townland of Terryglass and a short distance from the village.

The castle (below) is a national monument in private ownership as it is part of the nearby Old Court House property.

The Norman practice was to first throw up an earthen mound or motte and surmount this with a timber fortification. Later on a stone castle might be built on or near the motte. As Terryglass was part of the territory granted to Theobald fitzWalter it followed that this important crossing point to Connacht, where the River Shannon narrowed above Lough Derg, merited a fortification.

Some archaeologists are of the opinion that Terryglass castle is an unfinished building and was never any higher than it is today. This view is credible when one takes this fourteenth century description of it into account – 'a solid base of one castle with four towers of the height of 12 feet' [3.6m]. The elevated site which it surmounts may well be an earlier motte. This 'base' may have been built by John Marshal, a Norman who settled in the area, as he figures in a document of 1219 when the Justiciar, Geoffrey de Marisco, tried to confiscate Terryglass from him because he had 'not fortified it as others had fortified neighbouring lands.' However, by 1289 it seems to have been in the hands of the powerful de Burgos or Burkes, who by then were majority landowners across the bay in Co. Galway.

Old Court appears to have been the caput or head of a Norman manor, i.e. the property controlled by a lord. In the escheator's return for 1291 there is a receipt for £19 11*s* 4*d* being 'rent of the manor and ferry of Tyreaglas from Michaelmas 1289 to 7 June following when it was delivered to Richard De Burgo'. 'The Ferry' as a placename still survives; and is applied nowadays to the area adjoining Portumna bridge on the Tipperary side of the river.

In 1290 Old Court was in the possession of a Robert fitzDavid (probably a Burke) for a period. This can be inferred from an account which John De Saunford, archbishop of Dublin (1286-94) and also Justiciar of Ireland, gives of his journey through Ormond in the summer of that year. The archbishop was at Loughrea on Saturday and Sunday, 8-9 July 1290. He dined there with the earl of Ulster (Richard De Burgo) on both days. On Monday he was at 'Tyreglas' where he dined with Robert fitzDavid, having spent the previous night with him – presumably in Old Court castle.

The Ruin
The building at Terryglass is a roughly rectangular keep, 15m/49ft x 10.80m/35ft in dimension internally, with an average wall thickness of 3m/10ft, with strong circular towers on its north-east, south-east, north-west and south-west corners. The towers are not all of the same dimension.

It is built of roughly-cut limestone laid down in irregular courses. The keep is divided unternally into two distinct compartments. Each compartment has access to two of the towers via round-headed doorways. The area directly overhead each doorway is vaulted. A spiral limestone stairway is located in the north-west tower.

Externally, the round-headed windows are narrow slits but widely splayed on the inside for use by bowmen. Some conservation work was carried out on this castle by the Office of Public Works in 1940.

The Bawn
In the heart of Terryglass village, behind the two public houses, is the remains of a bawn or fortified enclosure. No evidence has surfaced to show that it ever had a tower house attached like, say, at Carney in Cloghprior parish. The *Civil Survey* of 1654 is unambiguous in its description of the state of this one and of Old Court – 'upon sd lands [Terryglass townland] stands two ruined old castles and Bawnes totally demolished …'. There was also 'fower cottages'.

The ordnance surveyors of 1840 recorded a tradition that this bawn stood on the site of the Early Christian monastic college. The surveyors' estimated date of its erection was 'during the reign of Queen Elizabeth 1 to secure the pass of the Shannon'. Elizabeth was on the throne from 1558 to 1603. They also recorded the local tradition of the 'Cobbler's Box' – a deep recess high up in the north-west corner of the west wall. The story was that when the castle was been stormed the cobbler took refuge in this recess in the curtain wall. It is still to be seen high up on the wall over The Derg Inn petrol pump.

The bawn was examined for an 'Urban Archaeological Survey: Co. Tipperary North Riding,' carried out by the Office of Public works in 1994. The archaeologists' report was as follows:

The south, east and west walls of this limestone bawn survive. The main entrance is in the east wall and consists of a beautifully carved doorway with elaborate punch tooling and knot, perhaps some form of mason's mark, on the lower arch stone on the south side. There are two eye-stones, that on the north side being particularly finely dressed. The jambs on the south side are rebated and there are two draw-bar holes. While the fine decoration on the doorway is a credit to the aesthetic sensibilities of the builders, the main function of the building was military. Thus the bawn was equipped with a wall-walk, gun-loops and at least one bartizan.

The west wall is 1.39m/4.5ft wide with an internal alure [a passage] which terminates short of the north end of this wall. In the remaining wall, near the north-west corner, there is a deep recess 80cm high. It would appear that if the alure was continued it would cut across this feature ... The terminus of this wall has been levelled off with re-used blocks of stone.

There are no remains of the north wall.

At the north end of the west wall there is a doorway slightly splayed internally, which is 1.5m/5ft above the internal ground level and accessed by five steps. There are a number of putlogs [holes] in this wall c.1.6m above ground and another row c.1.5m/5ft above this. It is 1.55m/5ft above ground level internally but at ground level externally.

A concrete shed has been built onto the internal face of this wall.

Surmounting the north end of the external face there is a semi-circular base and supporting corbels [stone projections for supporting the roof timbers] of a bartizan.[a small overhanging turret]. These roughly-dressed limestone corbels, two large and one small, are pyramidal in shape.

A recent concrete block storage shed and toilets have been built up against the internal east face of the bawn. A large recess in this wall, which contains traces of wicker-centring, houses two gun-loops, the holes of which have been blocked up. The decorated entrance, described above, is also in this wall.

The external face of the wall, which has a base batter 1.23m/4ft high and 10cm-15cm/4.5 inches wide, has been modified.

A plaque to Flann, poet of Connacht, has been inserted and also a niche with a plaque. A rockery has been built up against it and a wooden lean-to erected between the rockery and the entrance to the bawn. The doorway itself is recessed in the batter. Above the doorway the bawn wall is slightly higher and inserted in it are two loops with corbels in their base. Immediately north of this doorway is a modern single-storey extension to the premises, above which the bawn wall is visible.

The south wall survives to a lower level than the west wall and what remains of the wall-walk has been rendered with concrete. A portion of this wall has a slight internal base batter. Externally the wall bulges slightly in the centre and has no visible features.

Drominagh tower house stands quite near the edge of Lough Derg in the grounds of Drominagh House in the townland of Drominagh Demesne, on the old road between Ballinderry and Terryglass.

Its erection is attributed to the O'Maddens of Co. Galway. However, it passed into O'Kennedy ownership and Owney O'Kennedy would appear to be the freeholder in 1580. Donagh Kennedy of Lackeen in Lorrha parish is returned as

Drominagh tower house, before the wall collapsed, with the outline of the 'lean-to' house visible.

owner in the *Civil Survey* of 1654 when it was in a ruinous state and had a bawn.

Historically, Drominagh (above) is a very important building as it was Redmond Burke's headquarters while he was fighting a private war against the earl of Ormond during the two-year rebellion against the Crown commenced by Hugh O'Neill, earl of Tyrone, in 1598. While Munster was laid waste in a most terrible way during the rebellion, O'Kennedy territory in north-west Tipperary more or less escaped because of the Butler lordship. O'Neill's efforts came to a sad end at the battle of Kinsale in 1601.

For some unknown reason John O'Donovan did not make a detailed examination of the ruin in 1840, confining his description of it to 'the ruins of a square castle'. It was, however, examined by the archaeologist who conducted a 'Historic Dwellings' survey for Nenagh District Heritage Society in 1985. The south wall and part of the east wall had collapsed following the severe frost of 1979.

The 1985 survey recorded:

> a strong four-storey structure with projecting tower at its north-east corner and possibly a similar tower at the south-east corner since collapsed? The external dimensions (including the north-east tower) are 11.85m/39ft x 10.59m/35ft. The walls average 1.08m/3ft in thickness. ... The masonry is composed of uneven courses of rough limestone bonded together with a gritty lime mortar. The corners are neatly finished with a series of cut and dressed quoin stones. ... the original entrance was possibly situated in the recessed face of the east wall, first floor (indicating an early date of building).

The 1985 survey also records the remains of five large corbels on the north wall which formerly supported a bartizan. ... There are seven windows in all on this side. These include five cut and dressed loops, one roughly cut loop set into the batter and a fine cut and dressed two-light, cusped-ogee window with its mullion intact.

... Traces of the gable lines of two buildings, which projected out from the north wall, are still visible'. The uppermost gable line has a steep pitch, the lower one is more flattened.

There are four surving windows in the west wall – one two-light, cusped-ogee window with tracery and mullion intact, one loop and two later inserted windows which include a rough rectangular single-light and a large rectangular window with a flat arch ... On the top floor, running in line with the bartizan corbels, there are four square apertures containing dripstones, which formerly drained rainwater from the wall-walk.

In the recessed face of the part of the east wall which was still standing, the remains of a 'two-light window with hood moulding, sidestones, sill and spandrels' was noted as being still intact.

The spandrels (the space between the curve of the arch and the moulding) were decorated with interlaced trefoils or three-leaved motifs. A gable line of an additional building was noted in what remained of the collapsed south wall. Inside this bit of wall was the remains of the stairs – about twelve stone steps.

Inside, the barrel-vaulted roof and remains of a fireplace and an inaccessible mural passage could be seen at first-floor level. In the north wall a rectangular doorway gave access to a staircase 'which occupies the north-east tower ...'. Also noted was a building located south of the tower house.

> This is divided internally by a partition wall running north-south. It appears to have been a two-storey structure, now unfortunately obscured by the collapsed masonry of the south wall of the tower house. The gable line on the latter suggests that this structure projected out from the south wall. ...

Noted too were remains of another rectangular structure which projected out from the north wall of the tower house. The maximum height of these remains were 4.20m/14ft. They contained remains of a window and door.

Remains of the bawn were also found to have survived, the best portion of which was 'at the west where the wall survives to a height of 4.10m/13.5ft', and

> within the bawn wall, just east of the present entrance to the site, there is a small, single-storey vaulted structure – a guardhouse. It survives to a maximum of 3m/10ft. The vault, which is mortared and bears impressions of wickerwork centering, is of barrel type, semi-circular in section. The entrance to the guardhouse ... occurs in the south wall ... Within the bawn wall and to the north-west of the tower house there are two, long, low adjoining tunnels above ground, roofed with flat lintels. Both tunnels are open-ended, 9.65m in length, 1.05m in height and 90cm wide internally. ... They may have been used as storage space or, perhaps, they had a defensive purpose.

The traces of two gables described above supports the tradition that the incoming Cromwellian grantee, John Briggs, or his descendants, built a 'lean-to' dwelling on to the former O'Kennedy tower house.

KILBARRON

Kilbarron pre-Reformation parish has five tower houses. All were built by the O'Kennedys. Four are in a ruinous state while one is still lived in.

Annagh (below), is located in the townland of that name and prominently sited on a hillock overlooking Lough Derg almost beside the bye-road which runs from the main Puckane-Coolbawn road to Luska quay. It is a well-known landmark to both road and lake users.

Donogh Duff McBrian O'Kennedy was returned as occupier of the townland in a list of 1580 freeholders. According to the Patent Rolls of 1604 it was given in a Crown grant to a Sir Oliver Lambert as '1/8 part of the castle of Annagh in Ormond, thatched and with a bawne … the lands of Morrogh McTeige McBrien O'Kennedy, late of Anngh, Gent, slain in rebellion'. Historian Dermot F. Gleeson identifies him as 'O'Kennedy Fionn, killed at Ballyhough 2nd December 1599' during the Hugh O'Neill, earl of Tyrone, rebellion.

A half century later the *Civil Survey* described it as having 'the walles only standing'. Presumably this meant the roof was off. John Hurly was the occupier of the townland.

When Eugene O'Curry and John O'Donovan examined it in 1840 they found:

> The ruin of a square castle four stories high and measuring forty-two feet ten inches on the outside from east to west and thirty-two feet from north to south. The third

floor rested on a stone arch, part of which still remains, the others were of wood. The staircase led to the top at the south-east corner and still remains. The east and north side of this building are destroyed except for small fragments at the corners. The walls are seven feet six inches in thickness at the base and very well built of hammered limestone. The corners and all the windows are cut limestone. This was a strong and beautiful tower.

This century-and-a-half-old description still applies today. As seen from the road to Luska it looks like an intact building but, as the OS surveyors recorded, the walls on the lake side are destroyed. The advantage of this is that one can see the internal architectural features close-up from ground level.

Annagh tower house was also examined as part of the 'Historical Dwellings' survey team. It was noted that there still existed a garderobe (lavatory) outlet at the southern end of the west wall, a spiral staircase leading to the first and second floors, corbels, joist holes, a slop stone, and on the first floor 'a long rectangular chamber'. The entrance to this chamber from the staircase has a semi-pointed doorway, equipped with an intact 'dressed hanging-eye'. The roof over the second floor is vaulted. Remains of an L-shaped garderobe passage was detected in the thickness of the walls between the second and third floors. The garderobe chute was also there, though blocked up with rubble.

Ballycolliton (right), located in the townland of that name, is clearly visible to the right at the turn-off for Luska quay. The date of building has been put at 1434.

William McDiarmada O'Kennedy was the freehold occupier per a 1580 list. Ballycolliton was the location of a battle in 1598 in which the O'Kennedys, O'Briens and others joined with Redmond Burke in his rebellion against the Crown.

Owney McEdward O'Kennedy of Ballycolliton was one of the several O'Kennedys who lost their lives. Like Annagh, this tower house and some lands were granted to Sir Oliver Lambert by the Crown after the rebellion. In the grant it is described as 'a small thatched castle'.

Three different people, Sir Nicholas White, John Hurly, Annagh, and Rory

Kennedy, Criagh (in Killodiernan parish), were the occupiers of the townland according to the *Civil Survey*. White was a property speculator. The Kennedys probably sold some of their lands to him when plantation of the area was under consideration during the reign of King Charles I (1625-48).

The *Civil Survey* also recorded that 'uppon the sd lands stands the ruines of an old little castle ye walls onely standing'. A new life began for this 'old little castle' in the post-Cromwellian era and this is told in later chapters.

Ordnance Surveyors John O'Donovan and Eugene O'Curry examined it in October 1840 and described it as a square castle surrounded by out-offices which, O'Donovan noted, concealed all but one of the windows. They estimated its height to be about 23 feet. It measured 21 feet 3 inches from east to west and 17 feet from north to south with walls about 4 feet 7 inches thick (this approximates to about half the size of Annagh).

The only window visible was on the south side and was quadrangular in shape and constructed of cut lime stone. They also noted that the quoin stones were 'chiselled and a little rounded at the corners'.

The 1985 Heritage Society survey found little changes from the above, other than noting it was four-storey with no floors or staircase, that the roof over the second floor was vaulted, and that a water tank had been constructed on its top.

Castletown, located in the townland of the same name, a short distance down, and in to the right, on the road which leads from Coolbawn Cross to Kilbarron quay. While 'Ye walls only standing', is the recurring description in the *Civil Survey* of the other tower houses in Kilbarron parish, Castletown, though 'ruined', has its bawn, a very important feature, a garden, and eight cottages – quite a little colony.

'Gilladuff O'Kennedy, gent', is returned as a freeholder in the 1580 list. In 1654 Philip Kennedy of Castletown was owner of the townland together with five O'Kennedys and a John Carroll from Modreeny parish.

It is the only tower house in Kilbarron parish not described by John O'Donovan in his 1840 letters. The explanation for this would appear to be that it was not then a historic ruin but the lived-in home of the Cambies.

Castletown (right) is the only tower house which has been, as far as we can deduce, used almost continuously as a family home since it was built by the O'Kennedys in the fifteenth or sixteenth century. It is also one of the few to enjoy this state in the county today. It may have been uninhabited for a period after the sons of Cromwellian grantee, John Briggs, disposed of it. It is described as 'Castle

Camby' on the Taylor and Skinner road maps published in 1778.

The Cambie story is recounted in some detail in chapter 6. It is possible that some of the bawn wall still existed into the nineteenth century as Henry J. Cambie in his reminiscence says: 'a courtyard in front of the house was enclosed with high walls' – as it still is today.

Obviously due to its being inhabited, it was not surveyed either in 1985, so there is no 'professional' description of it to hand. It is three storeys high with castellations. It has a straight stone stairs to the first floor. The stonework has been plastered over.

The original roof-draining system, via projecting stones as visible in the photograph, is still in operation.

Lisquillibeen, the jewel among the ruins (below), is also called the Black Castle and marked on earlier maps as Tullaghan or Tullawn castle – that being the earlier name of Lisquillibeen townland. It too is adjacent to the main Puckane-Coolbawn road and can be seen across the fields to the right after Annagh Lodge gates.

In the 1580 list of Ormond freeholders it is spelled *Tulaghan* and is the residence of Diarmod na Brosny O'Kennedy. According to the *Civil Survey* Rory and William Kennedy, Brockagh, Arthur McJames Geoghegan, Tulloghane, and John Kennedy of Knigh parish, were the owners of the townland. Like the other tower houses in the parish this one was also 'ruined'. Its story ends here for, unlike Annagh, Ballycolliton, Castletown and Drominagh, no incoming Cromwellian settler set up home in its vicinity. This is understandable, given its inhospitable location.

O'Donovan and O'Curry visited the ruin in 1840. It is in fact a four-storey rectangular, rather than a square, building. Their report went as follows:

> In the townland of Lisquillibeen in this parish on a rocky hill in the middle of a bog stands a square castle of great strength measuring on the outside 38 feet 3 inches from east to west and 31 feet from north to south and its walls grouted 7 feet in thickness and now about 50 feet in height, but they were originally much higher.
>
> The third floor over the ground one rested on a stone arch still remaining, all the others were of wood and have long since disappeared.
>
> There is a pointed doorway on the east side and a staircase leads to the top through the thickness of the south wall.
>
> The part of this building remaining is lighted by 20 windows which are some pointed, some rectangular and some round topped, and all constructed of cut lime stone.
>
> This castle was built by O'Kennedy to whom it proved a great fortress in its day.

The 1840 surveyors made no mention of the very well-preserved internal features of this tower house – loops, corbels, slop stones, wall cupboards, murder hole, mural passages, the garderobe chute (lavatory), and an open fireplace on the second floor – which are all described in the 1985 survey, which concluded with the observation:

> Great attention was paid to stone dressing by the masons who constructed Tullaun tower house. The type of dressing generally used is neat pocking and linear pecking. They also engaged in some ornamentation as is indicated by the tulip and torch-like carvings on some of the pointed tops of the window embrasures, third floor hall.

This tower house has always been known locally as the 'Black Castle' because it was clothed in ivy which in the distance made it look black. The ivy was cleared away and some repairs made to the structure by the Office of Public Works in the 1950s. It is the only one of the ruins which has a complete upper floor. Standing on this floor in the evening light one get the impression of being in a room. The sconces in which the torches or rushlights were stuck are still there.

Thade's Castle, Knockballyea, or Caisleán Tadgh Bhoict/poor Taidhg's [Timothy's] castle is now the most ruined and diminished of the tower houses. Tradition says stones from it were used to build the Protestant church near Coolbawn Cross in 1822.

Four Kennedys and Arthur McJames Geoghegan were the landowners in 1654. Of this tower house (left) the survey records noted that 'the walles only were standing'.

As well as recording the features and measurements in 1840 O'Donovan and O'Curry recorded the local tradition that it once belonged to a Teige O'Kennedy who was surnamed bocht or poor because he squandered all his property.

> In the townland of Knockballylea and about 3/4 mile to the north of the castle just described [Lisquillibeen], there is another called Caislean Taidhg Bhoicht, i.e.

poor Teige's castle (below).

It is situated on the summit of a conspicuous rocky hill and is seen from a considerable distance on every side. The greater part of its south-west side is destroyed down to the ground as is also about one half of the southeast side, but the other sides remain to the height of about 25 feet. It was 33 feet from north-west to south-east and 28 feet in the opposite direction, and the walls are 7 feet in thickness, and built of hammered lime stone, grouted.

All the windows are destroyed except one round topped one constructed of cut lime stone. The first floor over the ground one rested on a stone arch which is now nearly destroyed.

The Heritage Society's 1985 survey team found little change in the wall heights from 1840 and observed that the building was composed of 'very rough, undressed limestone'. They also noted the probable garderobe passage inside, and its outlet in the western end of the north wall outside, evidence of wall cupboards, and two vaulted chambers with traces of 'mortar and impressions of wickerwork centering'. They found no traces of the stairs or upper floors.

FINNOE

This parish has one tower house in the small townland of Ballyfinboy on the bank of the river of the same name. It stands close to a byroad off the Borrisokane-Ballinderry road.

In the 1580 list of freeholders James Óg O'Kennedy and Donald McEdmond O'Kennedy are returned for the townland. Ballyfinboy was also granted to Sir Oliver Lambert. In the grant it is described as 'thatched and walled around' and was on the lands of 'Dermot McDonnell O'Kennedy, Gent, slain in rebellion'.

Philip and Keadagh Kennedy were the townland's owners in 1654 and, in keeping with the other tower houses in the area, this one was returned as in a ruined state.

John O'Donovan recorded that it was built 'about the beginning of the reign of Queen Elizabeth', which puts the date at 1560 or thereabouts. O'Donovan has left us a very good description of it at it was in 1840.

> I find no remains of antiquity in this parish (Finnoe) but the old castle of Ballyfinboy [above] which was a large strong square tower measuring on the outside 38 feet 6 inches from E. to W. and 31 feet 4 inches from N. to S. and having walls 6 feet 4 inches in thickness and built of hammered stones not grouted, as usual with castles of its age but cemented with lime and sand mortar.
>
> The doorway which is in good preservation is on the east side; it is constructed of cut limestone in the pointed style and measures 6 feet 8 inches in height and 3 feet 9 inches in width.
>
> When you enter this doorway you observe three other pointed doorways, one to the left communicating with a spiral staircase leading to the top in the s.e. corner, another to the right leading into a square tower at the n.e. corner, and the third directly opposite you communicating with the lowest chamber of the castle.
>
> The two first floors over the ground one were of wood, and have disappeared, but the third floor rested on a stone arch which still remains. The remainder of its height is gone. It was probably five stories high originally.
>
> All its windows are narrow; some are pointed and some rectangular and constructed of chiselled lime stone.
>
> On a quoin stone in the southeast corner, about eleven feet from the ground, is

to be seen sculptured in a rude style, a representation of a woman in naked majesty.

The latter refers to what is termed a 'Sheela-na-Gig'. Much interest has been shown in these figures in recent years and those researching them have concluded that most likely they are fertility symbols.

An attempt was made to remove the Ballyfinboy sheela at one time but her lofty position from the ground probably protected her. These sculptures are also to be seen on the south-facing walls of some pre-Reformation churches. That several have been removed from their original location can be deduced by the fine collection housed in the basement of the National Museum in Dublin.

Like Lisquillibeen, the tower house in Ballyfinboy, though more conveniently sited, missed out on any significant development in the post-Cromwellian era.

All the features identified in 1840 were still intact in 1985. However, that recent survey also recorded that the tower house was constructed on a low earthen mound, which had 'slipped outwards to the north and south'.

Summary
We can see from the foregoing the stature the Gaelic O'Kennedys held in the parish up to the confiscation of their lands in the mid-seventeenth century. We get brief glimpses of their participation in rebellion.

Sources:
Civil Survey, County of Tipperary, Vol 2, 1654-6.
Dermot F. Gleeson, *Last Lords of Ormond* (London, 1938).
Robert C. Simington, *The Transplantation to Connacht 1654-58.*
'The Book Of Survey and Distribution', 1662
Harold G. Leask, *Irish Castles.*
Conrad Cairns, 'Tower Houses of County Tipperary', Ph.D. thesis, Vols 1 & 2, 1984.
'Historical Dwellings', survey conducted for Nenagh District Heritage Society, 1985.
The 1604 Calender of Patent Rolls, p. 40, quoted in NDHS 1985 survey, names Sir Oliver Lambert as a grantee of Annagh and Ballycolliton.
Ordnance Survey Letters, 1840, Rev. Michael Flanagan, ed., 1930.
George Cunningham, *The Anglo-Norman Advance in the south-west midlands of Ireland, 1185-1221* (his source for 14th century description of Terryglass is *Ormond Deeds*, 1172-1350, no. 36, p. 9).
Michael McMahon, 'Terryglass', *Cois Deirge*, 1981.
H G. Leask on Terryglass in JRSAI 1943, vol. 73.
The Urban Archaeological Survey: Co Tipperary (NR), 1994 (Office of Public Works now Dúchas).

Photographs taken by Paddy Carroll, Coolbawn.

Lament For The O'Kennedys

Written by May O'Meara on the death of Robert Kennedy in America in 1968 and printed in the Nenagh Guardian at the time.

They come no more as once, fleet-footed, young
They came in days when life was free and fair,
Our blue-eyed chieftains of the gold-brown hair.
These Ormond hills they loved and fought among
Are silent now, the wild deeds all unsung;
The dreams and hopes, the hatred and despair
Like tapestries have crumbled;
Unaware
The ivy triumphs where the trophies hung.

Yet, strangely, sometimes on a Western wind
I seem to hear their names, their voices call
In greeting and farewell beyond the sea.
Strong hand, brave heart and undefeated mind
Their bright heads in that alien dust will fall –
A ransom paid? The price of liberty?

3
Religion

The Roman Catholic parish of Kilbarron-Terryglass can lay claim to having had within its bounds an important Early Christian monastic settlement – that of St Colum at Terryglass.

Though no discernible physical remains of that foundation now survive, apart from a few parts of the monastic enclosure and a possible section of a high cross, adequate proof of its existence and importance is to be found in annals relating to the Early Christian and medieval periods.

Despite the fame of that monastic settlement, the site was not selected for a Norman-sponsored religious foundation like, say, at nearby Lorrha which acquired both Dominican and Augustinian Canons foundations on the site of St. Ruadhan's monastery. They maintained a presence there throughout the medieval period, combining their monastic life with the exercise of a pastoral curacy in the surrounding districts.

The early Irish church was centred on monastic settlements under the jurisdiction of abbots. The introduction of dioceses and parishes brought the Irish church into the system which had already prevailed for up to three centuries on the continent of Europe. Dioceses were carved out after the Synod of Kells in 1152; sub-divisions of these territories into parishes followed. While it is probable that the creation of parishes had already begun before the coming of the Normans, some historians hold the view that parishes are largely a Norman creation.

The parish therefore is an ecclesiastical and administrative unit of considerable antiquity. Each parish had distinct boundaries, its own resident priest and its own church. The priest was supported by a levy or tithe, which was originally a tenth of the produce of land or stock but later on was converted to a monetary charge.

This secure pattern of parish and universal faith was thrown into disarray by the great religious revolution of the sixteenth century known as the Reformation; it spread to England circa 1534. This brought about the division of the Christian church and the emergence of reformed religions. Conflict between those who upheld the centuries-old Catholic precepts and those who advocated the reformed religion was inevitable.

After the Reformation the parishes of Finnoe, Kilbarron and Terryglass remained unchanged territorially. But, as elsewhere, major changes within the parish extended to church property and the freedom to practice Catholicism. Thereafter, church buildings and land became the property of the new Anglican or Protestant religion, and Catholic clergy were prohibited from pursuing their religious calling.

It is not intended to go into any great detail on the trials and tribulations encountered by adherents of the old religion in the early post-Reformation years. There are numerous history books available on the period. Suffice it to say that the upheaval of the Reformation is reflected in many aspects of Finnoe's, Kilbarron's and Terryglass's ecclesiastical history. In time each parish acquired congregations, clergymen and churches subscribing to the Anglican religion.

The pre-Reformation parish, also called a civil parish because of its administrative role, was the territorial unit on which was based surveys, reports, valuations, ordnance letters, directories and numerous other documents of historical interest.

After the Reformation the Catholic church continued to service the parishes as individual units. Amalgamation into one administrative unit, such as Kilbarron-Terryglass is of comparatively recent origin – sometime in the early 1800s and, apart from the parish registers, is not of significance in nineteenth century historical sources. For years Kilbarron and Terryglass kept separate registers which suggests a reluctance on Kilbarron's part to concede that the other was the caput or principal one.

At the time of the Reformation Finnoe, Kilbarron and Terryglass each had a stone church which became the property of the Anglican religion – in time the Church of Ireland. A rector was duly appointed to each parish. His dilemma was that the number who had conformed to the Anglican religion was extremely low. This presented the immediate problem of church maintenance.

We get some idea of the state of affairs in the three parishes from a report known as the 'Royal Visitation of Killaloe diocese 1615' – just over eighty years on from the Reformation.

Rectory de Fennoh: Petrus [Piers or Pierce] Butler, a clerical reading minister. A church (i.e.) nave only in repayr. No chauncell [chancel].

Rect de Kilbarrain: Impropriat [i.e. pays dues] to the Monastery of Owney [in Co, Limerick]. Sir Edm Walsh impropriator. Nave and chancel in ruins.

Rectory de Tirreglas: is a membrum [member attached to] of the rectory of Finnoe. Petrus Butler reading minister. Chancel covered.

In 1622, in reply to an inquiry during the reign of King James I as to the state of the church in Ireland, John Rider, Bishop of Killaloe, gives the following account of churches in the three parishes. It is known as the 'Loyall Answer'.

ffinnoh Rectory of value £20.0.0. Incumbent Piers Butler. Vicarage value £10.0.0. Incumbent the same; Cure not served. Patron, the Bishop.

Kilbarraine Rectory: Value £20.0.0. Impropriat to ye Aby of Ony [Owney] Vicarage, value £10.0.0. Incumbent Richard Burk, native, and preacher graduat of ye Colledge of Dublin, a man of good life. Inducted 1st June 1617. Cure served by ye Deane. Patron Earl of Cork & the Bishop.

Tirraglasse Rectory: value £16.0.0. appropriat to ye Rectory of ffinnoh. Vicarage appropriate to ye Deanery. Cure served by ye Deane. Patron the Bishop.

There we see that Kilbarron had its own Rector, while Terryglass and Finnoe shared the services of Piers Butler. From the same source we find that 'ye Deane of the diocese' who served Terryglass was a Hugh Hogan.

We get a little insight into Rev. Butler from the Bishop's response to the Sixth **Article** which asked: 'What graunts have bene made from ye crowne of **approp**riations or church-living to any person for maintenance or provision of able **ministe**rs?'

In ye yeare 1606 His Majesty by his letters Patents gave unto Piers Butler, a native **and** a minister, ye Rectory of Modrenith, Rectory of ffinnoh (under wch he carries **away** ye Rectory of Tirraglasse) and Vicarage of ffinnoh wth other livings, ye **bette**r to incourage him in his ministery to take paines to instruct ye people in theyr **langu**age, he being theyr countrey man: but he taketh no paines or care atall, neythr **doth** live wthin ye Diocesse.

Canon Philip Dwyer's interpretation of this in his history of Killaloe Diocese was:

The Bishop is very sore about Piers Butler, who contrived with aid of the Crown **to sec**ure £70 per annum as a Pluralist, and gave no value for it in clerical services, **altho**ugh possessing high powers of usefullness from his familiarity with the Irish **tong**ue.

The massive confiscation of Irish lands after Ireland was conquered by the **Parliam**entary/Cromwellian forces in 1652 changed the fortunes of the Anglican **Church** in the above three parishes in the long term. This was brought about by the **fact that** confiscated property was used to pay off the arrears of pay due to officers **and so**ldiers in the Parliamentary forces, and to reimburse persons who had **'adven**tured' money to keep an army in Ireland. The outcome of this was the **injecti**on of Protestant settler families who, within a few generations, had **multip**lied. Within a few decades the small band of first settlers was supplemented by persons of like faith buying into an area with immense potential for financial gain.

As we have seen, after the Restoration of the monarchy and the accession of King Charles II in 1660 there was no major change insofar as the land allocated by the Cromwellian regime was concerned.

In 1693 Henry Ryder (Rider) was Bishop of Killaloe. He gave a report of the state of parishes etc. in the diocese to Richard Aldworth, Dublin Castle. He complained of the state of the livings and the fact that the earl of Thomond acted as if he were bishop and he hoped that matters be put in order. The report stated that Joseph Amirath, archdeacon (1693-1713) had eight livings: two were served by himself – Ffiniagh (Finnoe) and Larha (Lorrha). Both churches were stated to be 'in repair'. The other livings included Terryglass, Kilbarron and Cloghprior.

FINNOE PARISH

The following is quoted by Canon Dwyer in his history and gives some fascinating information on some of the problems encountered by the Protestant community and how they resolved them. From it we see that though the three parishes had been united a certain degree of disunity prevailed. We also learn that in 1684 it was the pre-Reformation church in Finnoe, rather than Kilbarron's or Terryglass's, which was selected to be the 'mother' church and accordingly kept in repair.

In presence of
Benjamin Lloyd,
Jno McNamara
To the Right Rev. Lord Bishop of Killaloe

The Representation of the Church wardens of the United Parishes of Finnoe, Cloghprior, Kilbarron and Terryglass.

Showing that ever since the Restoration these foresaid parishes have been united and consequently by the Act of Settlement, s. 137, are to be understood as one parish, and in pursuance of which the several churches in ye above union, being out of repair, a vestry was called by Rev. John Hall L.L.D., then incumbent, to be held in Ballinderry, near ye centre of these United Parishes, in ye year 1683 or 1684 unto which all the freeholders and farmers of said Union came to consider which of the churches would be most convenient to be pitched up for the Mother Church. And after a full hearing of all parties it was at length unanimously agreed that the church of Finnoe should be the Mother Church, and to be repaired by the aforesaid United Parishes for Divine services, and it was accordingly unanimously agreed upon that the sum of £50 should be laid upon the foresaid parishes to repair the Church of Finnoe and to fit it for Divine service, and that John Hunt Esquire and Mr Edward Legge should be Church wardens of the said Union to raise the said sum for the use of the said Church, and Mr McMerritt should be overseer of the said reparation.

This Act was confirmed by the Right Rev Dr John Roan, the Bishop of Killaloe, and the said money was raised and employed to the repair of the said Church of Finnoe, and that ever since, under the several Rectors, the aforesaid Union has unanimously joyned in the keeping of the said Mother Church of Finoh in constant and decent repair without any opposition.

Notwithstanding of which some ill disposed persons upon frivolous pretences, in the parish of Terryglass, refuse to pay their proportion of the money laid upon the Union in this year, of 1728, for the repair of their Mother Church, the names of whom are here unto adjoined and presented to your Lordship's Court.

Humbly entreating that your Lordship will order a vigorous prosecution to oblige them to repair their Mother Church, as they have always done, according to the Ecclesiastical Laws in that case made and provided.

Rev James Greenshields was the rector and Edward Legge, Kilburne [Kilbarron], was the church warden. The defaulters' names appended to the report are familiar ones. Indeed, some figure in some detail in other chapters.

	£	s	d
John Barry	0	5	10
Mr Chas. Minchin	0	9	9
Mr Sam Robbins	0	7	8
Mr Richard Biggs	0	18	6
Mr Thomas Talbot	0	5	0
Hugh Hogan	0	2	6
M. Luscurry	0	2	6
E. Kingsboro	0	8	0

New Church

In 1776 a new church (above) was built on the site of the pre-Reformation church, dedicated to St. Ruadhan, presumably using the old church's stones. It is a long, narrow cut-stone building with a high tower and was one of the earliest rural Protestant churches to be erected. In 1837 it was described in Lewis's *Topographical Dictionary* as follows:

> a neat edifice, repaired and improved by aid of a loan of £323.00 in 1822 from the late Board of First Fruits; there is also a glebe of 28 acres for which the incumbent pays £17.0.0. per annum.

The ordnance surveyors found no trace of the old pre-Reformation church when they examined the site in 1840.

Vestry Records

Distribution of Church Sittings – Finnoe – as settled by lot at a vestry meeting in 1824.

Name	No of seats
Thomas Waller, Finnoe House [came from Limerick in 1821]	2
Joseph Falkiner, Rodeen	1
Samuel Barry, Bellpark	2
Counsellor Saunders, Ballinderry Park	1

Benjamin Falkiner, Springfield	1
John Falkiner, Springfield	1
Samuel Waller, [Ormond Lodge]	1
George Waller, Prior Park	2
William Woodward, Cloghprior	1
Samuel Cleburne, Springmount	2
John Falkiner, Prospect	2

William Woodward got the 4th seat on reading desk side.
Samuel Cleburne got the 1st and 2nd seats on reading desk side.
John Falkiner, Prospect, got the 6th and 7th seats on reading desk side.

From Lewis's *Topographical Dictionary* we can also glean that the parish had a glebe house lived in by Rev. Pierce Gould. The living was a rectory and vicarage in the diocese of Killaloe. We also learn from the same source that Finnoe was episcopally united to the rectory and vicarage of Cloghprior in 1790 and that the tithes amounted to £217.

Fortunately, a list of the rectors going back to 1612 has survived. The list was originally on a board in the 1776 church. The board has now disappeared but it was transcribed by Mrs Roland Kent (née Powell) who lived in the rectory before the present owner bought it.

Finnoe's first Protestant rector, Rev. Piers/Petrus Butler, if he were so inclined, would have taken services in the pre-Reformation church, which he was quite legally entitled to do since, as already stated, all church property had been taken over by the Anglican Church. Everyone was expected to attend these services.

There is a gap in the list between 1633 and 1667. This would take in the rebellion of the 1640s, the Cromwellian campaign, and the arrival of the new settlers.

Name	*Duration of Ministry*	*Status*
Piers (Petrus) Butler	1612-1633	
John Thompson	1667-1672	
Jasper Pheasant	1672-1673	Afterwards Dean of Killaloe
John Hall L.L.D.	1673-1691	Archdeadon
Joseph Amirath	1693-1713	Archdeacon
Walter Thomas B.A.	1714-1715	
Rev James Greenshields	1715-1744	
Rev. Wm. Greenshields	1744-1772	
William Trench M.A.	1772-1789	Archdeacon
James Martin M.A.	1789-1825	
Pierce Gould M.A.	1825-1851	
Rev James Martin	1852-1888	
Canon Massey	1890-1895	
Canon Gillespie	1895-1911	
Rev. John Westropp	1912-1915	Curate

Finnoe Church of Ireland parish was amalgamated with the parish of Borrisokane in 1915. The church was deconsecrated in 1988 but is still owned by the Church

Representative Body. Sadly, it is now in quite a bad state of repair. Plaques in the church, which commemorated Edward Waller Stoney (1844-1931), the engineer son of Thomas George Stoney, Kyle Park, and Jane Woodward, and Francis Sadleir Woodward, are now in Borrisokane Church of Ireland church.

Church Silver

The Church silver used at Finnoe was dated to the late eighteenth century. It was made of Dublin silver with beaded decorations. Both chalice and paten were made by Joseph Jackson and inscribed 'Union of Finnough 1792'. The paten has been dated to 1785 while the chalice bears the date 1791.

The Graveyard

The graves of the two Greenshields rectors and of Archdeacon William Trench are near one another by the side door of the church.

Canon Philip Dwyer in his diocesan history, published in 1878, quotes the following which was communicated to him by the then Rector of Finnoe, Rev. R. J. Martin, M.A.:

> Overhead is a coat of arms, or, more properly speaking, a shirt of arms, with a two-handed sword erect in the centre and a motto underneath, 'The Lord is my Shield'.

The Greenshields memorial is inscribed as follows:

> Underneath this tomb do lie ye remains of Elizabeth Greenshields ye elder, who died in ye year of our Lord 1739, aged 74. Also of ye Revd James Greenshields, Rector of Finnoe 26 years, and died in ye year [17]44 aged 76. Also of Elizabeth Greenshields ye younger, who died in ye year [17]48 aged 24. Also of ye Revd William Greenshields, Rector of Finoe for 30 years who died in ye year 1772 aged 68. His son Wm. Greenshields caused this monument to be erected in token of his prefound respects to ye deseasd.

Canon Dwyer continues:

> The Very Rev. Wm Reeves D.D. Dean of Armagh promises a life of Mr Greenshields, which like every other production of his learned pen, must prove full of interest and of great value to the Church.

One assumes Canon Dwyer is referring to Rev. Wm. Greenshields as the possible subject of Dr Reeves's eventual biography. He must have been a person of some special importance or achievement.

This tomb takes one back in time to when the pre-Reformation church was being used for Church of Ireland services. The coat of arms is now slightly defaced, probably by the weather. All that remains of the motto is 'my Shield'.

The graveyard is still used occasionally for burials by both Catholics and Protestants. Apart from that of the Greenshields rectors and that of Archdeacon Trench, there are two or three other interesting headstones. Anna Waller of Finnoe House, who married Thomas George Stoney of Kyle Park is buried here by her own request, with her murdered father Thomas Waller and her aunt Miss Vereker.

The gruesome story of how Thomas Waller and his sister-in-law met their deaths is recounted in chapter 9.

Rev. Charles Minchin, son of Falkiner Minchin of Annagh in Kilbarron parish, is also buried here, having died a violent death. That parish's Church of Ireland church, although built in 1823 on Minchin land, was probably not yet consecrated and so without a burial ground. The inscription reads:

> Here lie the remains of the Rev. Charles Minchin who departed this life on the 17th day of June 1826, aged 28 years. He possessed all the qualities which constitute an honourable and affectionate son and brother and a kind-hearted and sincere friend.

Charles Minchin was probably destined to be the first rector of Kilbarron. His murder is part of the parish folklore. He lived at Skehana beside Kilbarron (Clery's) quay on the shores of Lough Derg and not far from the parish's pre-Reformation church, known locally as the Old Abbey. His house is now occupied by Tim and Marina Cleary.

The story goes that as he was returning late at night from visiting at Curraghmore House, home of the Alt family, he came upon some men near the big rock which stands near Cleary's quay. They were apparently stealing either wool packs or turf from a boat. Having recognised them, he appealed to them to desist, they refused and, fearing he would denounce them, they killed him with stones.

It is said that one, at least, was transported but there was not enough evidence to have any of them condemned to death. The old people used to say that one of those who was transported returned to tell the tale.

Finnoe Glebe, now called Curraghmore House

Another feature of the Church of Ireland parish was its glebe house where the rector resided. Finnoe's, (below) situated on four acres, three roods, twenty-six perches, lies about half a mile from the church. Its building was financed by a gift of £400 and a loan of £400 from the late Board of First Fruits in 1819 during the rectorship of James Martin. After Rev. John Westropp left in 1915 it ceased to be

used as a glebe house.

In 1919 the house and 65 acres was sold by the Church Representative Body to Abraham Powell, a Methodist, for £3,110. He died in 1934 and is buried in Finnoe graveyard. His daughter, Mrs Roland Kent, inherited it and sold the house and some land to Des Conroy, a teacher at Borrisokane Community College, after she went to live in a nursing home. Des has done a really superb job of restoring it to its original elegance. A typical glebe house of the period, it is two-storey over a basement – the basement being as large as a modern bungalow – and shows the comfort and affluence in which these rectors, usually members of the gentry class, lived.

The last clergyman in Finnoe, Rev. John Westropp, described as a curate, was a wealthy man in his own right and built the lawn tennis court which is still there. Pat Dunne, who lived nearby, was his coachman. Rev. Westropp succeeded Canon Gillespie who had served the parish for sixteen years.

Prior to his appointment to Finnoe Rev. Westropp ministered in Castletownarra, during which time a young local boy, Michael Joy (1875-1946), went to work with him. Michael moved to Finnoe with him and lived in a house in the rectory yard. He emigrated to the United States in 1911 with two young Rogers men who worked with Samsons of Rodeen, and stayed there for thirteen years. He subsequently returned to his native parish, married and settled down in Curragh, Portroe. Local historian and Ormond Historical Society member, Michael Joy, is his son.

Catholicism in Finnoe
In the aftermath of the Reformation adherents of the Catholic faith in Ireland were faced with two major obstacles. Firstly, they were deprived of the use of the parish churches and, secondly, they were faced with legal restrictions on religious practice and the imposition of severe penalties for breaches. However, it would appear that the Catholic church found ways to maintain a form of organisation despite the restrictions and penalties.

The 'Loyall Answer' of 1622, already quoted, contained the following:

> Eleventhly I complaine of ye multitude of Popish Priests within my Dioces [Killaloe] who drawe ye people from theyr obedience to His Majesty [King James I] and then especially when pclamation or direction comes from his Highnes hindering also ye minister in ye work of his calling and drawing back those whom ye minister had formerly gained.

The document lists thirty-seven 'Popish priests' by name and parish. There is no one named for Finnoe, or indeed for Kilbarron or Terryglass, but it is not a complete list being only 'for so many as yet are remembered ...'. There are names for some nearby parishes, notably Killodiernan, Monsea and Uskane.

In 1704 all secular Catholic clergy who wished to continue in the priesthood had to register. All members of religious orders were banished from the country under pain of death as were senior secular clergy, i.e. bishops, archdeacons, deans. Nenagh and Ennis were the two centres where registration took place in the diocese of Killaloe.

At Nenagh fifty-four priests registered. There were to be no more registrations.

So when the 1704 generation had died out the theory was that there would be no more Catholic priests. At Nenagh in 1704 we find the name of Dennis Kennedy, resident of Gurteene, aged 27, parish priest of Finnoe. He was ordained in 1701 by John Slyne, Bishop of Cork. The ordination took place in Cork jail where the Bishop was incarcerated. Rev. Dennis Kennedy is buried within the ruins of Kilbarron pre-Reformation church. The graveslab (above) is inscribed:

DONATUS KENDY
SACERDOS 27 ANNOS NATUS: 11: 8 BRIS 1706 OBVT — MEMENTO MORI

This translates roughly as: Dennis Kennedy priest, born 27 years, died 11 Oct 1706. Remember you must die.

The fact that Protestant services were being held in Finnoe's pre-Reformation church was obviously an inhibition on burying Fr Kennedy there, hence his interment in Kilbarron.

After the registration of priests in Nenagh in 1704 the next overview we get of the church in the diocese is 'The Report on Popery' in 1731. This arose when the House of Lords requested an account of the state of Catholicism in Ireland to be sent in by the Protestant clergyman of each parish to his Bishop. It tells the number of priests, Mass houses and other religious houses – convents, monasteries – in each parish. The report relates to the union of four Protestant parishes – Finnoe, Kilbarron, Terryglass and Cloughprior – not to the Catholic union.

> There have been two mass houses in this union which consists of four small parishes of 22,000 acres ever since I came to the parish which was the year 1715. They are served by one Connolly Egan, Parish Priest and one Anthony Kennedy, his assistant, and there are three popish schoolmasters – two of which are in private Protestant homes.

This is attested by me this 29th day of November 1731.
J. A. Greenshields , Rector of Finoh.

This shows the presence of an organised and accepted Catholic church with two Mass houses in existence for at least fifteen years. The Mass houses would have been in Terryglass and Carney Commons. It also shows a degree of tolerance and the ignoring of the Penal Laws regarding the teaching of school by Catholics by the fact that such schools were held in private Protestant houses. Secular Catholic clergy, provided they had registered, were allowed to function undisturbed. However, we cannot say from the report if either Fr Egan or Fr Kennedy was in fact appointed specifically to Finnoe.

Old Mass House in Carney Commons

Finnoe parish seems to have had its own place of Catholic worship up to the time the present church was built in 1814 in what is popularly known as Kilbarron village in the townland of Ballyquinlivan Upper in Finnoe parish. This was a Mass house in Carney Commons townland – also, of course, in Finnoe parish.

It was situated on the road from Kilbarron to Borrisokane on the right side of the road, a little way past Oldcourt House gate on the left, and the old Sullivan home on the right. There is a little lane leading into a clearing about 100 yards after the Sullivan home. The clearing is very pleasant. I have heard that stone artefacts, e.g. a holy water font, were found within living memory. The fact that the Mass house was in the Commons might bear out the fact that landowners would not, or were reluctant to, have a Mass house on their land. Such a building probably existed there from the time the parish church ceased to be used for Catholic services once the Anglican religion got established in the parish. A new improved structure may have been built in Carney Commons in 1782 because I have heard it said that the building dated from that period.

It is thought that the building material from this old Mass house was used in the building of the 1814 chapel.

Though located in the parish of Finnoe, the new chapel seems to have been identified with Kilbarron parish from the beginning. A full account of it is given in the next section of this chapter. Finnoe does not figure as part of the Catholic parish name in a list of priests compiled by Bishop McMahon in 1835 and quoted by the late Monsignor Ignatius Murphy in volume 2 of *The Diocese of Killaloe 1800-1850*.

Sources:
Canon Philip Dwyer, *The Diocese of Killaloe from the Reformation to the close of the Eighteenth Century*, pp. 94-5.
Samuel A. Lewis, *Topograpical Dictionary of Ireland* (1837).
Ormond Historical Society, Gravestone Inscriptions, Finnoe graveyard.
'Report on the State of Popery' *Archiv. Hib.* vol ii (1913).
Rev. R. Wyse Jackson, 'Old Church Silver of East Killaloe', *NMAJ*, 1940.

Photographs: pp. 32, 41, taken by Paddy Carroll; p. 39 loaned by Des Conroy.

Kilbarron Parish

As recorded in the report on the state of the churches in 1615 the nave and chancel of Kilbarron parish church were 'in ruins'. Notwithstanding this, the parish had its own rector, one Rev. Richard Burk 'graduat of ye Colledge of Dublin'. There is mention of an 'Edmundus Hurley, Vicarius eide eccie' in a roll of clergy of the Anglican Church in the diocese in 1633. Hurley was ordained in 1621.

The decision taken in 1684 to repair Finnoe's old church as the Anglican religion's 'mother' church for the united parishes of Finnoe, Kilbarron and Terryglass destroyed any possibility of the restoration of Kilbarron's old church thenceforth.

Burials were already taking place within the ruins. Though legally the pre-Reformation churches could not be used by the Catholic population, they were allowed to make burials in the adjoining graveyard. Because the Catholic priest was not permitted to officiate there a custom evolved in which a portion of earth was blessed by the priest and a relative would throw this consecrated earth on the grave. In fact, according to Monsignor Ignatius Murphy's diocesan history, burials were forbidden anywhere except in a graveyard attached to a Protestant church.

In the list of priests who registered at Nenagh in 1704 we find the name of Donnogh Kennedy, aged 60, who gave his place of abode as Glenbouin (Glenbower). He was identified as parish priest of Kilbarron, Cloghprior and Terryglass. Fr Kennedy was ordained in 1668 at Dublin by Patrick Plunkett, Bishop of Meath, a brother of Oliver, now Blessed Oliver Plunkett. He is buried in the Franciscan friary graveyard, Nenagh.

A gravestone in Killoscully graveyard, near Newport and in the diocese of Cashel & Emly, has an inscription in Latin, translated thus: Here lies the body of Laurence Ryan, parish priest of Terryglass & Kilbarron who died in Feb. 1760 aged 30 [it could be 50].

At this time, provided he registered and kept a low profile, a priest could say Mass. Individual or combined parishes had a 'Mass house' and a priest. Priests wore the same dress as the laity. It was not until the beginning of the nineteenth century that they began to wear black; the roman collar came much later. The Mass houses were barn-like structures with thatched roofs, at worst wretched cabins, and were never big enough to hold the congregation, hence the custom until quite recently of some men staying outside during Mass. These buildings were used for other purposes, e.g. school, public meetings – and even threshings – but such activities were frowned upon. The sacraments of baptism, marriage and confession, and funeral Masses took place in the houses of the people or in the priest's house. It was not until towards the middle of the nineteenth century that the chapels began to be used for administering the sacraments.

As seen in relation to Finnoe in 1731, Rev. Connolly Egan, PP, and his assistant Rev. Anthony Kennedy, were also servicing the three parishes for which Rev. Donough Kennedy registered in 1704 – Kilbarron, Terryglass and Cloghprior.

It would seem, therefore, that apart from two or three short periods, from 1715 onwards Catholics could practise their religion, priests could live publicly, if unobtrusively, provided Mass houses were kept well out of sight of public highways and had no belfry. Such practices were still forbidden by law but the law was ignored. Those short periods of persecution which coincided with the attempt by James III, son of James II and known as the 'old Pretender', and his Stuart followers to regain the English throne gave rise to the legends of Mass rocks and hedge schools. The Mass rock stories mainly go back to the post-Cromwellian period when some priests and bishops were thrown into prison and Mass houses boarded and nailed up.

After the death in 1766 of James III, Rome allowed priests to give their allegiance to the new Hanoverian monarch on the English throne – George I.

The 'Old Abbey'

Judging by the Irish name of the parish, Cill Barrfhionn, a church was founded here in the early years of the Christian period – probably in the sixth century – by St. Barron, of whom we know very little. Such an early church would have been a timber structure, probably replaced a few times.

Kilbarron parish, unlike Finnoe, has extensive remains of its pre-Reformation church. It stands on an elevated site overlooking Lough Derg and the Clare hills beyond, and is about a half-mile from the shore. It is in the townland of Kilbarron and is always referred to as the 'old abbey'. It has a nave and chancel separated by an ivy-covered arch. It originally had a square tower at the west end of which only a fragment remains. There is a narrow room at the back of the nave which may have been the priest's abode.

This church was examined in detail by the ordnance surveyors in 1840. Their findings are reproduced below:

> It has a nave, choir and a square tower at the west end, but this tower is now destroyed except for a fragment of the height of the side walls.
>
> *The nave* measures on the inside 34 feet 6 inches in length and 24 feet in breadth and the choir 29 feet in length and 21 feet 8 inches in breadth.
>
> *The east window* is disfigured on the inside but in tolerable preservation on the outside, where it is pointed and constructed of cut limestone and measures five feet one inch in height and seven inches in width.
>
> At a distance of five feet seven inches from the east gable the south wall contained *a small window* which is now totally disfigured on the inside and nearly so on the outside. Its east side and the stone in which its pointed top was (is) formed only remaining; it was constructed of cut limestone and it can be ascertained from

what remains that it was three feet ten inches in height and ten inches in width.

The choir arch was pointed and constructed of cut limestone, but its southern half is now totally disfigured. It was 11 feet in height, but its width cannot now be easily determined.

At a distance of five feet from the middle gable, the south wall of the nave contains *a rectangular window* measuring on the inside 5 feet in height and 2 feet 5 inches in width, but it is entirely disfigured on the outside. It is constructed of hammered limestone on the inside.

At the distance of seven feet eight inches from this there is, on the same wall, *another window of similar form* and dimensions on the inside, but its form cannot be seen on the outside as it is filled and entirely covered with the roots and leaves of strong luxuriant ivy. It is constructed of brown sandstone chiselled, but the stones are displaced by the roots of the ivy.

The north wall has another window placed at the distance of five feet from the middle gable; it is rectangular on the inside where it measures 6 feet 2 inches in height and 2 feet 4 inches in width and round topped on the outside, where it is three feet five and a half inches in height and 6 and a half inches in width.

The tower at the west end is 9 feet 4 inches by 24 feet. Its first floor rested on a stone arch which is now nearly destroyed but no idea can be formed of its original height from what remains. This tower communicated with the nave of the church by a pointed **doorway**, measuring 5 feet 7 inches in height and 3 feet 5 inches in width.

The doorway of the nave must have been on the north wall near the west end where there is now a breach.

The side walls of this church are 3 feet thick and about 12 feet high and built of limestone of a good size (now quarried) cemented with lime and sand mortar.

In 1991 a scheme to do some further tidying up was planned. The Office of Public Works required an archaeologist's report before any work could be undertaken. In her report she drew attention to a division between the nave and

(left): window in the nave
(right): window behind the high altar

chancel which was discernible inside and outside.

This division is visible on the two outside (north and south) walls where the east end walls project slightly and are clearly corners of what was originally a separate building ... On the north external side there are three square putlog holes (at 1.5m from ground level) ... possible indication of a building on this side. At the northeast corner is a buttress (extension of east wall).

The Graveyard

A large graveyard surrounds the church ruin and is still in use. Until the new graveyard was opened in the village in the 1960s this one was the only Catholic burial place in Kilbarron parish and was used by all the old inhabitants. There were also graveyards attached to the Protestant churches in Terryglass and Finnoe and used by both Christian traditions. With the exception of the Clebourne father and daughter of Ballycolliton, in 1684 and 1682 respectively, Kilbarron graveyard seems to have been used exclusively by Catholics.

The graveyard, in common with most others of its kind, was in a state of extreme neglect and heavily overgrown by nettles and other weeds. In the early 1950s a clean-up was done under the auspices of the parish branch of Muintir na Tíre. This organisation is described in more detail in relation to Kilbarron village. A three-person sub-committee including Joe Slattery, Kilbiller, and Paddy Treacy, Bellevue, oversaw the project. Muintir paid Jack Barry £50 to do a general clean-up. It was a contract job and I am told he did far more work than the payment warranted. Tipperary (North Riding) County Council then intervened, possibly at the behest of the Office of Public Works/OPW (now Dúchas). Martin Moran was paid by them to do a certain amount of repairs to the masonry work – he also did some work on the Black Castle at the same time.

Other Council workers who worked in the graveyard at various times were Jer Boucher, Paddy Lynch, Billy Ducie, Willie Quirke and Rody Burns.

In the course of the clean-up some gravestones were covered by displaced material. Amongst those was the Rev. Donatus Kennedy stone within the church ruins referred to on page 43. When I returned from holidays in England I noticed that this historic stone was missing but Jack Barry was able to show me exactly where it was – in the chancel on the right of the altar facing you. It had been covered by about two feet of soil which was then removed. It is probably in its original position.

At the left-hand side of the high altar is a large vault. On a horizontal tombstone on the roof of the vault is the following inscription.

> Guliellmus Cleburne de Ballycolletan, Armiger obit vigessimo Secundo Die Mensis Octobris Anno Dom 1684.

This translates as: William Cleburne, Ballycolletan, Gentleman, died twenty-second day of month of October year of Our Lord 1684.

On a plaque on front of the vault beside the entrance is an inscription as follows:

> Here lyeth the body of Elizabeth Cleburne Aged Thirteene Dayes Who Departed this life 4th Day of June 1682.

The 1682 plaque (right) is the earliest inscription that can be deciphered in the graveyard. The graveyard itself contains mainly eighteenth and nineteenth century stones. Erection of gravestones only became common in the seventeenth century.

Another Ancient Stone
Near the Donatus Kennedy stone is an upright one against the wall which divides the chancel from the nave (at the head of the Moran burial plot).which may well be as early as the tenth century and would confirm an Early Christian association with the site.

In 1992 a FÁS Social Employment Scheme, sponsored by Tipperary (NR) County Council, got underway. The perimeter wall of the graveyard was repaired, a fine stone entrance built, some gravestones cleaned and many old horizontal ones uncovered, and a general cleaning up done. A local committee now look after the site, the grass is cut regularly and all is presented very well.

The Church of Ireland in Kilbarron
The parish acquired its own Protestant church in 1822-3 (right) when one was erected in the townland of Kilbiller on land donated by the Minchin family. Stones from Thade's Castle (see previous chapter) were reputedly used in its construction. Lewis's *Topographical Dictionary* of 1837 notes that the Board of First Fruits gave £1,000 for its erection in 1822.

The first rector was Rev. Edward Sinclair but there is a gap of two or three years between the building of the church and his appointment. Rev. Thomas Lyon was vicar from 1844 until his death in 1877. He and his wife are buried in the adjoining graveyard. Inside the church the stained glass window overlooking the altar has the following inscription:

> To the glory of God and in loving memory of Rev'd Thomas Lyon and Anne his wife.

Given by their affectionate children'.

Rev. Lyon was succeeded by Rev. F. S. Samuels, D.D., who is described on his gravestone as 'rector of this parish'. Rev. Samuels was rector for forty-four years and died in June 1921, aged 78 years After his death the parish was served from Killodiernan, so he was the parish's last resident rector. The list of rectors is:

Rev. Edward Sinclair	1825-40
Rev. Thomas George	1841-43
Rev. A. M. Evanson	1843-47
Rev. Thomas Lyon	1844-77
Rev. F. F. Samuels, D.D.	1877-1921

The church was deconsecrated in 1975. It is now in private ownership, having been bought in 1993 by the internationally-known film actor, Patrick Bergin of 'Sleeping With The Enemy' fame. The graveyard is still in use.

Memorial Inscriptions Within the Church
There were two Minchin memorials and a Parker one within the church. One commemorated Col. Jack Minchin (see chapter 6) and the other John Minchin. The latter is now on the new Minchin burial plot. Col. Jack's plaque is now in Nenagh District Heritage Centre. The plaque to John (Jack) Parker, Brookfield, is on the Parker-Reeves burial plot.

The Glebe House
There existed until about twenty-five years ago a handsome glebe house built on the ancient glebe lands in Kilbarron townland about a quarter of a mile from the pre-Reformation church ruin on the Coolbawn cross side.

It was a two-storey house over a half basement and was typical of glebe houses which were built in the first two decades of the nineteenth century. It was probably built at the same time as the church, *c.*1822. After the death of Rev. Samuels in 1921 the Dagg family from Kevinstown took it over. On the death of the last member of that family it remained uninhabited until bought by James O'Meara of Illaunmore who demolished it and built a bungalow on the site.

Kilbarron RC Church
As already stated, a new Catholic church was erected in 1814 which, though located in Finnoe parish, about a quarter-mile from the Kilbarron parish border, seems to have been known, firstly, as the New Chapel and later on as Kilbarron church.

A stone plaque over the original main entrance (now enclosed by a porch) has the inscription:

This chapel was built by the Rev. Ja. MacCormac A.D.1814
Erected by Patrick Clear

Patrick Clear is dealt with in the chapter which covers the villages in the parish.

Of the sixteen churches built in the diocese of Killaloe between 1811 and 1815, Kilbarron's is one of the four which still remain in use.

Below is the account of the church as written into the parish register by an earlier priest and kindly given to me by the late Rev. John Hogan, who was parish priest from 1972 until his retirement in 1993.

> Kilbarron is the ecclesiastical name of the parish which is made up of the medieval parishes of Kilbarron and Finnoe. It is called after St. Barrfhionn who flourished about the beginning of the sixth century. He was abbot of Drumcullen, Co. Meath, and died about 550 A.D. The old church of Kilbarron was founded in the townland of the same name, overlooking the lordly Shannon and quite near to Islandmore. There is a tradition that a body of monks founded a church on Islandmore which the people of Kilbarron attended for worship. On one occasion when returning from worship in a great storm the tochar (ford) was swept away and some of the congregation were drowned, whereupon the monks built on the mainland the old church of Kilbarron which continued to be used until the seventeenth century when it fell into disrepair.
>
> The present church was built in the townland of Ballyquinlivan (on the border between the parishes of Finnoe and Kilbarron) by the then Parish Priest, Father McCormack, in the year 1814. It had the distinction of being the first slated church in the surrounding country after Penal Times and was called the New Chapel, which name it bears to this day. In February 1903, during a great storm, the roof was destroyed and a new roof was put on by the Rev. J. Darcy, PP, and the front aisle was seated.

It would appear that the pews were constructed in situ and amongst the carpenters who made them was Tommy O'Brien of the Convent lodge, Nenagh, who with his cousin John O'Brien was shot by Crown Forces at Knigh in 1920. A monument to their memory stands at Knigh Cross. The cost of the pews was £331, all of which was generously subscribed by the people of Kilbarron and

Finnoe. Only the pews in the side aisle were privately owned.

In 1888 the present Stations of the Cross were installed by Rev. John Darcy, then a curate.

Since its modest beginnings, all of one hundred and eighty-four years ago, the church has undergone much renovation, refurbishment and enhancement.

In 1920 a beautiful baptismal font was presented by Ellie Brereton of Oldcourt in memory of her brother John. She also presented a ciborium, value £50. The first child to be christened at the font was the late Breda Brereton and, as far as I know, my sister Nora Carroll was the second – in April 1920.

In 1934-5 Canon John Darcy renovated the whole church both inside and out, putting down drainpipes, roughcasting and attaching the plinth course all around, putting in a new wooden floor set in cement (the original floor was earthen), repairing doors and windows with new door sills, breaking out two new windows, one on each side of the altar (the existing windows were smaller and the one nearer the altar had been blocked out when a sacristy was built, date unknown).

He also had new altar rails and two beautiful new altars with mosaic backgrounds inserted. Mike Whelan, Borrisokane, grandfather of Mrs Teresa Burke, did the stone and plaster work, while the carpentry was carried out in the coach house by Danny Tierney of Terryglass. Bob Markison, a craftsman from Dublin who worked for the Dublin firm which supplied the altars, did all necessary work in assembling them and also probably applied the mosaic. He lodged at Donoghues (now Hanigans) while the work was in progress. Apart from John Meagher of Coolbawn, who was a paid employee, all the labouring work was done by volunteers from the parish. All this work was carried out according to plans supplied free by M. J. Kennedy, County Surveyor, Galway, who was Canon Darcy's nephew. The people of the whole parish of Kilbarron and Finnoe contributed generously to this work.

Ellie Esmonde, Killeen, presented £100 for the erection of a sanctuary lamp in memory of her parents and brothers. Dr Esmonde, Nenagh, contributed £25. Mrs Mary Clancy, Newlawn, donated the altar rails in memory of her husband, Joe Clancy, and her uncle, Rev. John Kennedy (Fr Darcy's predecessor), at a cost of £150. Mrs O'Connell, Ballycolliton, presented the side altar and statue in honour of the Immaculate Conception, in memory of her husband John and family, at a cost of £126. The handsome vestment bench in the sacristy was donated by Mrs Daniel Hough, Borrisokane (née Ryan, Coolbawn), in memory of her husband Daniel and their daughter Madge Seymour. The high altar and mosaic work cost £420. The approximate cost of all the work was £1,400.

In 1968 a sum of £5,380 was spent on repairs by the then parish priest, Canon Daniel O'Donohoe, and Rev. Thomas Comerford, CC. Michael Egan, builder, received £3,875 for the main work – new floor (cement, the previous wooden one having rotted), plastering of walls inside and out, repairs to bell, new stairs to gallery (the old outside stone stairs having been removed by voluntary labour). The altar was changed by Murray of Nenagh at cost of £265. Our Lady's altar was brought outside the rails. New gas heaters were installed at a cost of £188. John Bray, Nenagh, tiled the floor at a cost of £383. O'Brien Brothers (painters) cleaned and varnished seats, painted doors etc. at a cost of £378. Gunnings received £135 for brass work. Eamonn Slevin, Borrisokane received £70 for wiring and new lights. Finally, amplification was installed in 1975, also by Eamonn Slevin, at a cost of £125.

In May 1981 a chalice was presented to the church in memory of Mr John Tuohy of Pelham Manor, New York, by Mrs Bridie (née Tuohy) McCarthy, and a set of vestments by Mr and Mrs Walter Doherty and Mr and Mrs Peter J. Smith and family of New York. Other donations: figures for crib by Mrs Thomas Cormican, Kilbarron; a ciborium by Mr and Mrs James Burke; Paschal candlestick by Michael and Mary Parkinson; altar and lectern hanging by Elsie Hogan who embroidered them herself. Mick Maloney donated the carriage for wheeling out coffins.

In 1981 more renovations took place under the direction of Rev. John Hogan, PP, and Rev. P. J. O'Connor, CSSP, curate. The sanctuary was extended and a celebrant's chair provided. A new porch was added and the entrance gate and walls lowered and side entrance ramped and railed. Total cost, £13,000. Later on, the walls of the church grounds were faced with stone and painted, and the church floor carpeted. Christy Cormican did all the work. A new organ was installed and new gas heaters were put in - cost, £4,500.

The church holds the Kearney chalice – silver with gilt bowl inscribed 'Orate pro D. Daniel Kearney 1621'. Which translates: 'pray for Daniel Kearney 1621. The chalice has a panel with cross, lance, reed, sponge and ladder.

An interesting entry in the baptismal register gives an account of how the parishioners expressed their disapproval of a clerical appointment in the 1830s. A similar incident, which escalated and became prolonged, occurred in Newport in the 1820s and in Nenagh in the 1840s. The entry reads as follows:

> On the death of Rev. Francis Neylan, P.P., the people of the parish of Kilbarron and Terryglass petitioned the Bishop to appoint Rev. E. Malone, the then C.C., as P.P. The Bishop could not see his way to accede to the request and appointed Rev. Ambrose Bowles as P.P. When Father Bowles arrived at Terryglass he found the door of the church nailed up against him. Father Bowles quieted the Schism and those who nailed the door against faded off the face of the earth. Their families had no one to represent them in 1900.
>
> Registry of baptisms lost from 12 April 1832 to 4th Dec 1832.

Another entry from the baptismal register of 1888-98 also makes for interesting reading a century on. The practice of private pew ownership is well within living memory, having been phased out only in the 1950s.

Rules governing the ownership of seats in Kilbarron church

All seats in long house are common, one side for men and the other for women, except as reserved by the Parish Priest.

In side wings seats have been purchased by individual families and such families have right to their exclusive use as long as they live or remain as residents of the parish. When individual families die out or remove to other parishes the seats used by them become vested in the Parish Priest. No seat can be disposed of by Will or Sale or in any other way without the sanction of the Parish Priest.

Sources:
Canon Philip Dwyer, *History of Diocese of Killaloe.*
Monsignor Ignatius Murphy, *History of the Diocese of Killaloe*, vols. I & II.

Ormond Historical Society, Gravestone Inscriptions, Killoscully, Kilbarron.
Daniel Grace, *Portrait of a Parish: Monsea & Killodiernan*.
Tipperary North Family History Research Centre – notes from RC registers of Kilbarron-Terryglass and Newport-Birdhill.
Daniel Grace, 'The Barricading of Nenagh Chapel in 1849', *Tipperary Historical Journal*, 1990.
Ordnance Survey Letters, 1840.
The late Rev. John Hogan, PP.

Photographs: pp. 44-5, 47, 49, taken by Paddy Carroll.

Drawing of Kilbarron church and sculpted angel made by Hilary Gilmore for the *History of the Diocese of Killaloe*, vol II, by Monsignor Ignatius Murphy, and reproduced here with her kind permission.

Terryglass Parish

While Kilbarron parish's connection with the Early Christian church is tenuous, Terryglass's has a history stretching back almost to the dawn of Irish Christianity. Adamnan, the seventh-century monk, in his life of St. Colmcille, refers to this place: *ager duorum rivorum* : land of the two streams. Thereafter in the frequent references in the annals it is always *Tír-Dá–Glas*.

The earliest historical figure associated with the district was St. Colum (Mac Cremthainn) who founded a monastery here around the year 548 AD. Its fame endured for six hundred years and the name of the founder was included amongst the '12 apostles of Ireland'. It became especially famous for its association with the great monastic reform movement of the Célí Dé (servants of God) in the eight century.

Who Was St. Colum?

There is a life of the saint extant but the story is so laced with mythological allusions, after the fashion of early Irish literature, that the bounds between history and fancy are obscure in some places. We are told that Colum was of Leinster royal stock and got his early training in the celebrated school of St. Finian at Clonard. Several writers attest to his reputation for sanctity. After spending some time at Clonenagh in Co. Laois, Colum finally settled at Terryglass, probably about the year 548 AD.

The only visible signs today of this great foundation are traces of the monastic enclosure revealed in cropmarks by aerial photography immediately to the east of the village, and two holy wells – St. Colum's and St. Augh's. The archaeological survey of 1994, already referred to in relation to Terryglass bawn, identified a 79m/260ft long 'linear earthwork', referred to as the 'Grianán', in the vicinity of St. Colum's well. The reports states that the 'east side is particularly steep. There is a further bank on the flat areas between the mound and the stream. This bank is intermittent and irregular. At the south end, the bank is 14.2m/46.6ft wide and at the north side it is 10.3m/33.8ft.

There is also a possible part of a high cross which once stood in the vicinity of the old chapel in the village. The story of its relocation to the parish's new cemetery beside the new church in 1937 is told later in this chapter.

Flann the Poet

Medieval and later buildings intruded on Terryglass's monastic site. These too have disappeared in turn or degenerated into ivy-clad ruins. The derelict remains of a sixteenth-century courtyard now occupy the spot where tradition had placed the monastic church. On the eastern curtain wall of this ruin a latter-day sculptor has carved the legend: Flann Poet of Connacht, rests within: slain 893 AD. The notice is a reminder of the turbulent history of this monastic foundation.

The slain poet was son of Lonan, Ollamh (master of arts and poetry) of Ireland, and one of the three principal poets of Connacht. He is said to have been buried with his kinsfolk and three kings of the ancient Múscraighe Tíre in the middle of the monastery. He is the earliest professional poet of whom any definite tradition survives.

Mention of the poet recalls a verse found in the margin of a ninth-century manuscript. Its begins as follows:

Fierce and wild is the howling wind to-night/It tosses the tresses of the sea to white;
On such a night as this I take my ease:/Fierce Northmen only course the quiet sea.

This verse, which gives an insight into the plight of the defenceless Irish monks in the face of the Viking raids, could well have been written at Terryglass. Indeed, the concern expressed in the poem must have been more keenly felt in that monastery than in many of its contemporaries, for the annals mention the burning or plundering of Tír-Dá-Glas on six occasions between 805 and 1164 AD.

This troublesome history was due to some extent to the location of the monastery on the great waterway of the Shannon where the Viking King, Turgesius, maintained a 'great royal fleet'. Other monasteries along the river suffered in the spoliation, Clonmacnoise enduring the greatest humiliation of all when Ota, wife of Turgesius, gave heathen oracles from its high altar.

Pinpointing the Vikings as plunderers should not ignore the far greater intensity of raids on the wealthy monasteries by the native Irish in all periods, including 'long before the first Viking set foot in Ireland', to quote Donncha Ó Corráin in *Ireland Before the Normans* who gives the detailed evidence. The attackers in 1140 were, according to the Annals of Connaught, 'the people of O'Many [the small territory in the Co. of Galway in which the town of Clonfert is situated] who, with their accustomed barbarity, destroyed the Shrine of the Saint'.

Aside from the association with Flann, chief ollamh of Connacht, the monastery at Terryglass had other literary associations. Sometime between 1151 and 1225 AD. Aedh, abbot of Terryglass, 'prime historian in wisdom and knowledge', compiled the Book of Leinster at the behest of bishop Finn of Kildare. This book has been described as a summary of all the learning of the monastic period of Irish writing. It is now one of the treasures of the Royal Irish Academy in Dawson Street, Dublin.

A fairly complete list of the abbots of Terryglass appears in the Ordnance Survey Letters, pp. 28-38, compiled from the *Annals of the Four Masters* and other sources. They extend from St Colum in 548 to Annudh Ó Lonnargan, who died in 1099. No abbot is named after this.

Perhaps it was its very vulnerable riverside location which inhibited any take-over by one of the European religious orders that followed the Norman colonisation. An example of this is to be found at nearby Lorrha where Dominican and Augustinian monasteries were established on the old foundation of St. Ruadhan. These orders maintained a presence there throughout the medieval period and, indeed up to the end of the nineteenth century, combining their monastic life with the exercise of a pastoral curacy. Terryglass, after the middle of the twelfth century, appears as an ordinary diocesan parish.

The pre-Reformation Church
Whatever remained of the old monastic buildings at Terryglass would appear to have become absorbed in later developments on the site. The first of these was a fourteenth-century parish church. The second and most imposing ruin on the site is a large oblong courtyard with three of its curtain walls remaining. As this building has no religious significance it has been dealt with in the previous chapter, 'Castles and Tower Houses'.

Like the churches in Finnoe and Kilbarron parishes, the one in Terryglass gradually fell into decay after the Reformation. In 1615 its chancel (sanctuary area) was 'covered' and, presumably, being used for service by Rev. Piers Butler, Finnoe. There is no rector named for Terryglass parish in 1622.

The first comprehensive description of this church is in the Ordnance Survey Letters of 1840 where the surveyor recorded:

> Of this church only *the nave* remains in bad preservation; it is forty-two feet in length and twenty-seven feet eight inches in breadth and its walls are three feet four inches thick and built of hammered stones cemented with lime and sand mortar.
> *The choir arch* is pointed and constructed to a very rude style of hammered limestones and measures nine feet ten inches in width and thirteen feet in height.
> The south wall is destroyed down to the very foundations. The west gable is surmounted by a small belfry, which serves for the modern [Protestant] church.

According to local people, who remember the old ruin as children, there were two gable ends and a belfry with a bell which was still used by the Church of Ireland church. Michael Parkinson and Wilsie Nolan remember as boys (circa 1930) throwing stones at the bell to make it ring. At some later stage the bell was sold or given to a Mr Clarke of Roscrea who collected bells. No trace of the belfry now remains.

The ruin has deteriorated considerably since O'Donovan described it. The 1994 archaeological survey, referred to above, has some interesting additional material – not least being the finding of a *piscina*. The normal location of this would be on the right side of the altar, as that was where the sacred vessels were washed after use. It had a hole in the base for the water to flow away. The archaeologists noted:

> Only *the north and west walls, and a possible east wall*, of this church survive, though in a much modified condition. They are constructed of very poor quality limestone which has recently been repointed in a crude fashion. Externally, these walls are composed of 'cyclopean' blocks of masonry arranged in courses. There is also an external plinth.
> *The west gable* collapsed in the 1960s. As it now stands it is 9.4m/30.8ft long, an average of 1.3m/4.26ft high and 78cm/2.5ft thick. ... the north-west corner of this west wall steps up to meet the north wall .... In the north wall, centrally placed between the west wall and an internal butress there is a large blocked doorway, 2.45m/8ft high and 1.5m/4.9ft wide, with a curving arch of shattered voussoirs. The north wall is 12.76m/41.3ft long internally to the buttress and a further 8.54m/28ft beyond this. Seemingly, there was an east wall where the buttress is now. This may have been the wall containing the chancel arch [of the 1840 Ordnance Survey]. If this is so, then the stretch of north wall east of the buttress and the east wall may be part of the chancel. In this length of north wall there is the west side of a possible embrasure, with an internal splay. The wall beyond, which contains an entrance to the graveyard, survives at a lower height of c.1.1m/1.2ft. ...
> Inserted on top of an undulating wall between the ruinous church and the bawn, is *a piscina*, currently forming part of the crenellation which surmounts the wall. The limestone block measures 52cm/20ins x 31cm/12ins and is 12cm/4.7ins thick.

The bowl carved into this block is 24cm/9.5ins x 23cm x 10cm/4ins deep. The stone, including the bowl, is decorated with stab-line tooling which radiates around the circumference of the bowl.

Another interesting architectural fragment was discovered when part of the graveyard wall was being demolished. It is a block of stone, 28cm/11ins high, 20cm/7.8ins wide and 25cm/9.8ins thick, carved on one face is a cross-motif. Harbison dates this piece to the eleventh-twelfth century and suggests that it formed part of the arch or lintel of a church doorway.

There is no local knowledge as regards this cross-inscribed block of stone, which is mentioned in Peter Harbison's *Guide to National Monuments*. However, one wonders did he actually see it or was he bringing forward what appeared in the *Guide to the Shannon*, compiled by Lord Killanin and Michael Duignan in 1962: 'in the graveyard are early gravestones and cross slabs. There are also some fragments in the Catholic churchyard'.

The piscina mentioned above has since been relocated from its vulnerable position and is now directly above the Peace Tree on the roadside end of the courtyard wall which bounds the graveyard.

The Graveyard

There are over 200 inscribed gravestones in the graveyard (below) now occupying the site of the pre-Reformation church and grounds. Persons of both religious persuasions are interred there. The oldest commemorates a Thomas Cleary who died in 1741. There are quite a few pre-1800 stones. The dominant surnames are Hogan and Meara/O'Meara.

There are no stones commemorating any of the parish's Catholic clergy. There are memorials to two Church of Ireland rectors: Rev. Benjamin B. Talbot who died in 1878, and Rev. Canon Henry Massey, A.M., who died in 1895 after serving the parish for twenty-three years.

Michael Parkinson recalls that the ruins of the old church at Terryglass were, according to the old people, those of the monastery church. They had great reverence for it. When a funeral arrived at the cemetery the coffin was carried around by the wall and laid down where the high altar was supposed to have stood and certain prayers were said. At that moment, it was said, the soul entered heaven. The coffin was carried

in a complete circuit of the cemetery before being laid in the grave. During the 1800s, when many people were dying of consumption and the fever, a watch had to be kept on new burials in case body snatching would occur. Some doctors paid well for a fresh corpse for anatomical study. Two men from Portumna came across the lake on at least one occasion and took a young girl's body across to a doctor there.

Terryglass Old Catholic Church
Very little material now survives from which to reconstruct the history of Catholicism in the parish after the Reformation. There was a Mass rock in Slevoir townland where the parish's new church was built in 1886. We know, however, that an Act of 1709 compelled all priests to take the Oath of Abjuration under the penalty of transportation. As only some thirty-three conformed, the general body of clergy became outlaws and were forced to put themselves upon the people or hide in the woods and mountains. On 1 July 1714, five Justices of the Peace met at Nenagh and examined on oath the Petty Constables of the North Tipperary parishes as 'to what priests officiated without being registered'. From their report we learn that they did 'not hear of any person going abroad for foreign education nor of any person exercising ecclesiastical jurisdiction except one Denis Kennedy, priest of Kilbarron, against whom we have issued our warrants ....'

According to tradition, there was always a Mass house on the site where a new stone chapel was erected in Terryglass village sometime in the late 1700s or early 1800s. Monsignor Ignatius Murphy says this new church was built at the same time as Kilbarron's, i.e. 1814. There is no primary record of its date of building or of the parish priest responsible, or of the builder who did the construction. It is simpler in building style than Kilbarron church. It is situated in the village nearly opposite the former Protestant church and became Terryglass's first national school in 1887 after the new church was brought into use. It is now on its third life as a vibrant parish hall.

When the hall was being reconstructed and renovated a few years ago Frank Moran, of Morecome builders, found a hardwood plank on which was a date which included the Roman numeral seven, VII. The piece of wood was inadvertently made into egg cups by Jed Molloy before it could be inspected. The fact that there is no plaque indicating the name of the parish priest or the builder – unlike at Kilbarron – might point to an earlier date than that church.

New Church
The extraordinary story of how the new church in Terryglass came to be built in 1880-6, together with construction and other details is best recounted by Brigadier Séamus Hickie, Slevoir, grandson of the generous benefactors.

> In 1873 my grandfather and grandmother – Lieutenant Colonel James Francis Hickie from Kilelton, Co. Kerry, and Mrs. Hickie, née Lucila Larios y Tashara from Andalucia, Spain – having bought the Slevoir estate and rebuilt the house, came to live there. A few years later my grandmother accidentally injured herself; the injury became malignant and surgery failed to stem its spread. She decided to make the pilgrimage to Lourdes, where only nineteen years previously Our Blessed Lady had appeared. Travelling at that period was indeed exacting, but,

accompanied by her eldest daughter, Mary Pauline, she bore the journey with supreme fortitude. Whilst at Lourdes she made a promise to Our Lady that she would build a church at Terryglass in her honour.

She returned home, not having been the beneficiary of a cure and set about making plans to build the church. Daniel O'Connell, a grandson of the Liberator and a great friend of the family, had recently qualified as an architect, having had to leave the Royal Navy. While serving in this he had contracted yellow fever and had gone deaf, and on learning of my grandmother's project offered her the plans as a gift.

Meanwhile, the surgeons had given up all hope of my grandmother's recovery and she accepted that it was the Holy Will of God that she should not receive the cure she had hoped for. She pressed on with the work of building her church, of which the foundations were started on 25 November 1879 on the site of the Mass Stone of former days, so she died a happy woman when God called her to Himself on 6 March 1880. The foundation stone was laid on 19 August 1880, her husband's birthday anniversary.

The first ceremony to be celebrated in the new Church of the Immaculate Conception – the first church in Ireland to be so dedicated – was the wedding of the founder's eldest daughter, Mary Pauline, to Morgan Ross O'Connell of Lakeview, Killarney, on 15 September 1884. The church (below) was opened to the public on 15 August 1886, the anniversary of my grandfather's birthday. It was transferred to the care of the bishop of Killaloe by deed dated 14 August 1886.

The next event in the history of the church was its consecration which was performed on 25 June 1910 by His Lordship, Dr Michael Fogarty, Bishop of

Killaloe. It was of particular interest as at that time, and for forty years after, there were only three other churches in the diocese which were consecrated. [A church could not be consecrated while there was still a debt on it.]

When, on 5 February 1913, my grandfather died he was interred in the vault under the high altar alongside my grandmother and their second daughter, Amelia Victoria, who had died young. A detachment of his regiment – the 7th Royal Fusiliers – fired three volleys over his coffin and a bugler sounded the Last Post and Reveille. At that time the tower on the church had not been built, although provision was made for such in Daniel O'Connell's plans, and it had always been my grandfather's intention that it should be built, so much so that his eldest son, later Major-General and Senator, Sir William Bernard Hickie, KCB, put a note in his father's hand before his coffin was closed stating that his children would see his wishes carried out and the tower built. Under the stained glass windows is recorded in Latin the names of the donors, mostly members of the Larios family, with some words of commendation. One window was donated by Rev. George Corbett, PP, 'to his well-deserving mother'. Under the Stations of the Cross hang brass memorial tablets given in memory of deceased members of many families in the parish.

The First World War intervened and it was not until 15 August 1923 that the bell due to be hung in the tower, when built, was erected in the church grounds and blessed by Bishop Fogarty. The bell, named 'Columbia', was the gift of the children of the founders; it called the faithful of the parish to Mass and rang the Angelus for the first time on 15 August 1923. The bell was cast by Matthew of Dublin.

A few years were to elapse before work on the actual building of the tower was to commence, although the decision to do so had been taken by the family in 1923. Building of the tower, designed by Fuller & Jermyn, architects, Dublin, commenced on 1 August 1927 under the supervision of the founder's youngest son, Manuel Domingo Hickie. It was completed in 1929 when, on 8 December, the Feast of the Immaculate Conception, it was dedicated by Bishop Fogarty. Dan Mohilly of Nenagh was the stone cutter and John Glynn of Portumna the mason.

Several years before this ceremony, Major-General Sir William Hickie made a beautiful gift to the parish priest, Very Reverend John Darcy, on 15 August 1920.

Dick Stanley, Ballinderry, attending to the clock in the tower of Terryglass church.

It bears the inscription in Gaelic: *Do Chum Glóire Dé agus Onóra na hÉireann* (For the Glory of God and the Honour of Ireland). The bronze figure of Christ came from Paris; the wood of the cross was originally oak from the woods of Slevoir; this split and was replaced in 1933 with teak, the work being done by Manuel Hickie, assisted by his eldest son James Francis.

There are a number of items of special interest within the church:

The high altar was the gift of my grandfather's sister and brother-in-law, Mr and Mrs Jerome Murphy of Cork. The Lady altar that of the parish priest, at the time the church was built, Very Reverend George Corbett, and the Sacred Heart altar that of Mrs Dolores Deasy, the founder's youngest daughter, and Miss Ellie Esmonde E de M of Drominagh. The memorial tablets to my grandmother and grandfather on either side of the chancel arch were the gift of their children. Major-General Sir William Hickie made the arrangements with the Metropolitan School of Art in Dublin where the work was carried out; they were put in place and blessed by Father Darcy in 1925. The work was a great achievement at the time, entailing as it did the figures, etc. being worked in a fusion of gold, silver and enamel on a base of bronze.

The stained glass windows and stations of the cross came from the firm of Meyer of Munich in Germany, who presented the statue of Our Lady on the Lady altar to my grandfather. The picture of the Virgin and Child which hangs above this altar was the gift of the founder's third son, Brigadier-General Carlos Joseph Hickie, CMG. The church furniture and in fact most of the interior woodwork of the building was the work of James Griffin and his team of carpenters; he had been employed by the contractors who rebuilt Slevoir House for my grandfather circa 1872 and had been retained as the estate carpenter. Much of the ironwork was cast in the forge of the Kennedy family which stood by the roadside in the townland of Lacken. Martin Costelloe of Ballinderry was the foreman of works.

The bishop's throne in the sanctuary is of carved ebony; it was a wedding present to Manuel Hickie and Mary MacDermott on their marriage in 1914, from Count Gerald O'Kelly de Gallagh, uncle of Mrs Deasy of Firmount.

Until 1972 a very fine old brass sanctuary lamp hung in front of the high altar, another gift from my grandfather. It was removed in 1972, cut down and re-erected in its present form.

There are many memorials to dead members of the parish around the walls, of which probably the most remarkable is that to Lieut. Commander Eugene Esmonde, Royal Naval Fleet Air Arm, of Drominagh, who was killed during the World War of 1939-45, winning both the Victoria Cross and Distinguished Service Order for great gallantry.

In the private chapel of the Hickie family, the Chapel of the Holy Cross, there hangs a silver crucifix containing a relic of the True Cross formerly in the possession of the founders; below it stands the prie-dieu at which the foundress used to kneel whilst living in Slevoir. The altar and prie-dieu were formerly in the oratory at Ramore, Co. Galway, the home of Mary MacDermott, wife of Manuel Hickie; she carved part of the altar embellishment. The crested chairs came from the founder's childhood home, Kilelton, Co. Kerry.

The illuminated framed altar cards beneath the altar were the work of the founder's second daughter Amelia Victoria, who had studied in Paris. They were used on the high altar for 75 years; now that Mass is said in the vernacular the cards have been placed in the private chapel.

Outside the church and alongside the high altar, an engraved stone erected by the Hickie family in 1937 is let into the wall; it came from Lourdes and was emplaced by Manuel Hickie. Close by is the burial ground of the Hickie family. Here lie the remains of the founder and foundress with all their children except Arthur Francis who died during World War II and whose remains could not be brought home. The last of their children to die was buried on the Feast Day of the Immaculate Conception to whom the church is dedicated; he was Brigadier-General Carlos Joseph Hickie, CMG, my father.

Next to that burial ground lies the present parish cemetery which opened in 1940. It is dedicated to the Holy Cross of Our Lord Jesus Christ, the gift to the parish of Manuel Hickie in memory of his first wife, Mary. The area was part of the Slevoir estate; it was developed by the donor along very special lines so that it is now a most dignified and pleasing burial ground.

The stone in the middle of the area was originally outside the former Catholic church in Terryglass village; it is of great age but its origin is unknown – the cross is not old. The celtic cross in the cemetery is a replica of the cross in the cemetery at Guinchy, France, where the members of the 16th Irish Division, killed at the battle of the Somme are buried. Most of the division, commanded by Sir William Hickie, was wiped out in the battle. The design of the standard headstones is taken from the shape of the west door of the church. The cemetery was consecrated on 26 September 1940 by Bishop Fogarty. Manuel Hickie, the donor, was buried on the feast day of the Holy Cross to which he had arranged for the cemetery to be dedicated. In his wife Mary's coffin is a relic of the true cross which influenced my uncle Manuel in naming the cemetery.

High Cross?

Manuel Hickie attached conditions to his donation of land for the cemetery: the chief one was that there should be only one design of headstone. He had a long struggle with the parish priest, Canon Darcy, and Dr Michael Fogarty, the then bishop of Killaloe, over this, but they gave way in the end. The burial of the relic of the True Cross occurred after it was placed with Manuel Hickie's wife Mary when she was laid out. Its presence was forgotten and it was buried with her.

As Séamus Hickie states the stone (right) in which the central Guinchy cross is set is of great antiquity and was for many years in front of the old school, formerly the parish chapel. No one knows its origin but it had a square hole in it – obviously to take the shaft of a cross. Jack Egan, and Manuel Hickie's son James, brought it up from the village using a Fordson tractor and an old trailer in 1937 and put it in its present position. The Guinchy cross, which was placed in the ancient stone, was designed by James's uncle, General Sir William Hickie. It is not a true celtic cross design as the arms are slightly curved.

Michael Parkinson has collected an interesting story about the base of this Guinchy cross from Willie Kennedy of Lacken who gave him this account in the summer of 1997.

> The stone in the centre of the new cemetery is thought to date back to the monastery in Terryglass. It was beside the old chapel in the village. When the chapel was in use there was a wooden cross on the stone. When the stone was being removed to its present site Manuel Hickie organised all the school children to pull it out to load it onto a low trailer. Two ropes were attached to the stone with the girls on one and the boys on the other. Before we started Mr Hickie told us to always remember that day as it was of great importance in our lives. He treated all the pupils to a feast of sweets purchased at Glynn's shop for £2. The two boxes of sweets were taken up to the school by two senior pupils.

The Calvary

The figure on the Calvary in the cemetery is the work of a young sculptor who worked in Paris. James Hickie comments on the beauty of the figure and is very attached to it. When it arrived there was no way of fixing it to the cross so Manuel Hickie sank two nuts in the back to take bolts through the cross. When he had finished the figure was lying on the grass by the front door of Old Court, their home. The young James, about seven years old at the time, ran out for some reason and when he saw the figure lying there got the fright of his life.

The New Church

Michael Parkinson has added the following detail to Séamus Hickie's memoir relating to the building of Terryglass new church.

> The limestone for Terryglass church was quarried in Lacken townland on Hickies' own land. All the work was done by hand. The holes for blasting were bored with a drill called a jumper. One man held it while another man struck it with a sledgehammer. The stone was carted to the church site with horses. There were teams of stone cutters and masons working. The tradesmen were known as 'tramp cutters' or masons. They were perfect workers but they never stayed very long on the job, particularly the stone cutters. Sometimes they were sacked for something small. All they had were the clothes they wore and the tools of their trade – a few chisels, mallet and trowel. They drew whatever few shillings were due to them and went out on the road and threw up the mallet. Whatever way the handle pointed was the direction they went looking for another job. Work was plentiful at that time. Work on the building stopped for the winter. A few tradesmen stayed around during the winter doing building for local farmers. The stone cutters were always on the lookout for a suitable stone to make a land roller to sell to local farmers. Everything they earned was spent in the parish on lodgings and in the pubs. In order to set themselves above the ordinary workers they always wore a collar and tie.

On the inside of the church a special stone was used. It was a soft white stone imported from Scotland. It was used for all the window arches and trim for the corners of the walls and sanctuary arch. On Sundays, during the building, the local women used collect the chips of stone, crush them to powder and use it for scouring tables and pots and pans. The chapel was heated in the early years by a solid fuel stove in the front of the sanctuary. The chimney entered the wall behind where the fourteenth station of the cross is at present.

The tower was built at a much later date. Manuel Hickie was engineer and organiser of the job (below, in the white hat, with James Griffin in the workshop). The stone was brought up from Galway and cut at Fogarty's quarry at Shannonview. A concrete base was laid there and the tower was built on this with sheets of asbestos between the stones instead of mortar. The stones were all numbered and then brought to the site at the church. The mason who started it was John Glynn of Portumna. He was in failing health at the time and he went astray with measurements and had to be let go. After him Mr Hickie got Mike Whelan of Borrisokane to complete the job. Some stone was left after completion and remained beside the church. It was used around the doorway of the new school in Terryglass.

Mike Whelan was not a mason – he was a plasterer and slater by trade – but he did a perfect job. Dan Mohilly from Nenagh was the stone cutter and is buried in the new cemetery in Terryglass. Lime for the tower was burned at Fogarty's quarry in a kiln built at that time. The remains of it are still there. The clock was given by Dan Hogan of Lacken who left money in his will. He was dead before the tower was started.

Parochial Residences

The first parochial residence for a Catholic priest in the parish was built in 1905 during the ministry of Rev. John Darcy. It is a handsome dwelling named 'St. Columba's' on a scenic site overlooking Lough Derg. The foundation stone was laid on 23 June 1904 and the building was ready for occupation by 10 May the following year. Up to this priests lived in rented houses, e.g. Rodeen House, Finnoe, or in lodgings, e.g. in Newlawn, Ballinderry, the rooms being known afterwards as 'the priests' rooms'.

The Silver Trowel

After laying the foundation stone of the residence (above) Fr Darcy was presented with the silver trowel he had used. It was inscribed: 'A souvenir of the laying of the Foundation Stone of Terryglass Presbytery by Rev. John Darcy, PP, 23rd June 1904'. After Canon Darcy's death in 1940 his effects were being auctioned and amongst them was the silver trowel. Fr Tuohy, who had been the curate in 1904, was present at the auction and felt that such a memento should not go under the hammer. Accordingly, he presented it to Rev. Tim Gleeson, Canon Darcy's nephew, who was ordained that year. When Rev. Tom Seymour, a close friend of Fr Gleeson's, became PP of Kilbarron-Terryglass, this year (1998) Fr Gleeson presented him with the trowel. So it is now back in Terryglass parochial house. The trowel is solid silver with a white ivory handle. The back, on which the inscription is written, is highly decorated.

Around this time Mill House in Ballinderry was taken as a curate's residence and continued as such for about sixty years. Rev. John Moloney, CC, left in 1959 and was succeeded by Rev. John Cooney who remained until 1961. Rev. William Harty came as curate in 1961 but, sadly, died suddenly in 1964. He was followed by Rev. Thomas Comerford who stayed until 1972 when he left to become parish priest of Cournaganeen (Bourney).

During Fr Comerford's curacy, in April 1965, a new curate's house was erected on the Coolbawn road on the outskirts of Kilbarron village. Paddy Ryan, Ballyscanlon, was the builder (his sons were still schoolboys so the firm was not then Paddy Ryan & Sons as it is now). The agreed cost was £4,805. This was kept to within app. £100. The men who worked on the house were Jack Gaynor Nenagh, plumber; John (Golly) Carroll, Borrisokane, blocklayer; Oliver Kennedy, Brocka,

William O'Mahoney, Cloughjordan, Martin Guest, Ballinderry (now Borrisokane), carpenters; Denis Ryan, Borrisokane, painter & decorator. Others who also worked on the building were Michael Donnelly and Mick Gleeson, Borrisokane; Jack Dwyer, Ballinderry, and Mick Foote, Brocka.

Mill House, Ballinderry was then sold to Dr Vincent Ryan and his family. Canon Daniel O'Donoghue retired the same year as Fr Comerford's departure, 1972, and was replaced as parish priest by Rev. John Hogan, with Rev. Michael O'Donoghue becoming curate.

Fr Hogan elected to make his home in the new house in Kilbarron which facilitated Fr O'Donoghue going to live in Terryglass with his uncle, the retired parish priest. After the death of Canon O'Donoghue in 1979 his nephew went to Coolderry parish near Birr as parish priest.

However, Fr Hogan chose to live on in Kilbarron. Rev. P. J. O'Connor, a Holy Ghost father who had been on the missions, came as curate in 1979 and lived in Terryglass. When Fr Hogan retired as parish priest in 1993 he continued living in Kilbarron as assistant pastor until his death in August 1995. His successor as parish priest, Rev. John O'Driscoll, on transfer from Templederry parish took up residence in Terryglass which was now vacant as Fr O'Connor had already retired.

After an interval of nearly two years, during which time the parish was served by the parish priest only, a retired priest from Australia, Rev. Michael Downes, a native of Co. Clare, was appointed as assistant priest in 1996. On his arrival Fr O'Driscoll moved to Kilbarron while Fr Downes made his home in the parochial residence in Terryglass. He has since become a convent chaplain in Clare. In August 1998 Fr O'Driscoll transferred as PP to Lissycasey, Co. Clare. He was replaced by Rev. Tom Seymour who took up residence in the parochial house, Terryglass.

PRIESTS APPEARING IN THE BAPTISMAL REGISTERS
1827-1911

	1st appearance	last appearance
Francis Neylan,	01.07.1827	18.12.1831
Wm. D. O'Brien, PP	04.09.1827	03.01.1829
Thomas Downey, CC	08.01.1829	19.03.1829
Eugene Malone, CC	22.03.1829	12.04.1832
Ambrose Bowles, PP	09.12.1832	09.08.1846
M. Corbett, CC	04.12.1832	08.07.1833
John P. Conway, CC	21.07.1833	21.01.1835
Josh Kerin, CC	26.03.1835	21.06.1836
James Bowles, CC	25.02.1841	09.10.1841
Patrick Mailley	21.10.1843	13.10.1844
J. Stack	18.11.1844	31.08.1845
J. McMahon	07.09.1845	28.06.1846
Michael Scanlan, CC	30.07.1846	23.07.1848
J. Moloney, PP	13.09.1846	23.07.1848
M. Burke	29.07.1848	07.08.1848
P. Kennedy, PP	17.03.1849	05.01.1856
D. O'Meara	14.10.1849	27.04.1851

	1st appearance	last appearance
Michael Donoghue	21.03.1852	20.05.1855
Cornelius Gleeson	10.06.1855	03.02.1856
Timothy Gleeson	03.02.1856	04.03.1862
P. Horan	24.02.1856	13.07.1856
P. Hurley	30.11.1856	08.04.1857
Michael Gleeson	25.04.1857	15.04.1860
Francis O'Keane	02.05.1860	05.03.1862
John Gleeson, CC	08.03.1862	30.03.1867
Timothy Gleeson, PP	11.05.1862	25.04.1869
Peter McDonnell, CC	19.05.1867	21.04.1872
George Corbett, PP	03.10.1869	20.11.1881
Daniel Flannery, CC	05.05.1872	22.01.1873
James Menton, CC	05.04.1873	09.06.1873
John McNamara, CC	23.07.1873	22.07.1876
M. J. Lynch, CC	08.08.1876	29.09.1878
Wm. Marrinan	08.10.1878	27.10.1883
John Kennedy, PP	28.12.1881	08.04.1899
W. Bourke	14.11.1883	06.07.1886
Daniel O'Meara	05.08.1886	10.07.1887
John Darcy, CC	02.08.1887	10.08.1890
Patrick Gunning, CC	30.09.1890	04.07.1895
Michael Hayes, CC	22.08.1895	05.01.1897
Patrick M. Kinnerk, CC	13.01.1897	15.04.1899
Dan Day	30.05.1899	03.12.1899
John H. Molony, CC	23.12.1899	05.01.1900
John Darcy, Adm later PP	28.01.1900	04.01.1940
Thomas Meehan, CC	06.01.1901	04.07.1907
Michael Murray, CC	02.08.1907	05.02.1911
Michael Foley, CC	1904. continuing	

Curates after 1911

Joseph Houlihan
Michael Flannery
Daniel Clohedy
James Moloney
William Harty, 1961-4 (died)

T.D. Tuohy
Michael McNamara
John Cleary
John Cooney 1959-61

Rev. Canon John Darcy, PP, 1887-1940

Canon Darcy (right) was a native of Barbaha in the parish of Youghalarra-Burgess. His ministry in the parish was in two spells, serving firstly as a curate from 1887 to 1890. After curacies in Monsea & Killodiernan, Kilmihill, Kilfarboy, and Birr, he returned as curate in 1899. He was Adm until Fr Kennedy died and then became PP and remained here until his death in the parochial house, Terryglass, on 4 January 1940. His first appointment after

ordination in 1885 had been as chaplain to Birr workhouse, followed by a year as curate in Kilcolman, Co. Offaly.

In the mid-1930s Canon Darcy initiated the first major refurbishment of Kilbarron church.

Rev. Daniel O'Donoghue, PP, 1940-72

Daniel O'Donoghue was born on 2 July 1887 at Lacken in the parish of Templederry. His parents, Michael and Ellen (née Fogarty, Kilcoleman in Youghalarra parish), were farmers and Daniel was one of a family of ten children. Two of his brothers, Matthew and Patrick, also joined the priesthood, and two sisters, Madelene and Teresa, joined the religious life – Madeleine being a Sister of Mercy and matron of Nenagh hospital until she retired in the early 1950s.

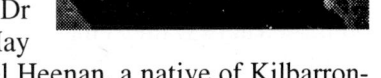

The young Dan O'Donoghue received his primary education in Latteragh national school and Templederry national school prior to going to St. Flannan's College, Ennis, in 1901.

He studied for the priesthood at the Irish College in Paris and was ordained in Ennis by his uncle, Dr Michael Fogarty, Bishop of Killaloe, on 1 May 1912. Also ordained that day was Rev. Michael Heenan, a native of Kilbarron-Terryglass parish.

Daniel O'Donoghue was appointed curate of O'Callaghan's Mills in Co. Clare after ordination. He subsequently served at Doonbeg, Co. Clare, Toomevara, and Kilrush. In 1940 he was appointed parish priest of Kilbarron-Terryglass on the death of Canon John Darcy.

During Fr O'Donoghue's time as parish priest primary schools were built in Kilbarron (1941), and Terryglass (1954). A new house for the curate was built in Kilbarron village in the 1960s.

Fr O'Donoghue was appointed a Canon of the Cathedral Chapter in 1956. He celebrated the Golden Jubilee of his ordination to the priesthood in 1962, and the Diamond Jubilee in 1972. He retired that year.

Canon O'Donoghue was held in great affection by the people of Kilbarron-Terryglass and he had a good relationship with them. He enjoyed a long and fruitful ministry and died on 19 April 1980 at the fine age of 92 years.

Rev. John Hogan, PP, 1972-93, AP 1993-5

Rev. John Hogan (right) was born in 1917 in the townland of Creggane in the parish of Youghalarra-Burgess, His parents were John and Elizabeth (née McGrath) Hogan.

He received his primary education in Youghalarra national school, where his teacher was Mick Nealon, before going on to St. Flannan's College, Ennis. He went from there to St Patrick's College, Maynooth, to study for the priesthood and was ordained there in 1942, having also obtained a degree in Classics, Greek and Latin. He then returned to St. Flannan's where he was to remain on the staff for twenty-seven years teaching Latin and Irish, becoming vice-President in 1958.

His first appointment to a parish was in 1969 when he went to Dunkerrin as a curate. Three years later he became parish priest of Kilbarron-Terryglass. He retired from this position in 1993, but spent the last two years of his life as assistant pastor to the new PP, Rev. John O'Driscoll. Fr Hogan (right) had a great affinity with the parish, its people and, particularly, the children with whom he had a great rapport. He loved hurling all his life and was there for Shannon Rovers at all times, sharing in their wins and defeats.

He was an avid reader and a keen photographer, with a special interest in the environment. He liked nothing better than identifying and photographing the wild flowers and plants – some very rare – to be found in the lakeside areas. He shared his knowledge on the subject freely, writing about them in *Cois Deirge* and, on one occasion, was persuaded to talk about them to members of the Ormond Historical Society.

He was a noted poet in the Irish language. A collection of his work was published in 1987 under the title *Dióscain*. The themes reflect his deep spirituality. He died in Nenagh hospital on 25 August 1995 and was buried in the grounds of Kilbarron church.

Rev. John O'Driscoll, PP, 1993-8

Fr O'Driscoll is a native of Killimer, Co. Clare. He was educated in the local national school and in St Flannan's College, Ennis. Since his ordination in Maynooth in 1953 he has served in Brentwood, London, as chaplain to Sean Ross Abbey, Roscrea, and as Director of Religious Education, 1955-68. This was followed by a curacy in Nenagh, during which he studied at the Irish Institute for Pastoral Liturgy, 1974-5. He was appointed parish priest of Templederry in 1987, transferring to Kilbarron-Terryglass in 1993, and to Lissycasey, Co Clare, in August 1998.

Rev. Tom Seymour, PP, 1998 - ongoing

Fr Seymour (right) was born in Lansdowne, Portroe, in 1935 to James Seymour and Johanna Ryan. He is a past pupil of Portroe national school, Nenagh CBS, and St Flannan's College, Ennis. He studied for the priesthood at St Patrick's College, Carlow, where he was ordained in 1961. He has served as curate in Annaclone and Banbridge, two separate parishes in Co. Down. He returned to his

native diocese in 1969 to the parish of Lorrha-Rathcabbin. He was in Borrisokane parish, 1969-81, where he combined parochial duties with teaching religion in Borrisokane Community College. He returned to Lorrha-Rathcabbin parish in 1981 and remained there for six years. There followed a seven-year term in Roscrea, followed by four years in Broadford, Co. Clare, as PP. He was appointed PP of Kilbarron-Terryglass in August 1998.

The Church of Ireland in Terryglass

We have seen in an earlier section that in 1684 Finnoe was selected to be the 'mother' church and was put into repair to serve the united parishes of Finnoe, Kilbarron, Cloghprior and Terryglass. It will also be remembered that in 1728 church warden Edward Legge made a complaint that some 'ill-disposed persons, upon frivolous pretences, in the parish of Terryglass, refuse to pay the proportion of the money laid upon the Union this year'.

There is, however, some evidence that there was some type of church in Terryglass parish in 1692. This is gleaned from an entry under 'Crimes and Penances' quoted in Canon Dwyer's *The Diocese of Killaloe*. In this a Roger Cleary and a Daniel Hogan, having been found guilty of fornication, 'and being contumacious were adjudged by public sentence delivered in the parish churches of Larha and Tirraglas, *excommunicated;* and the congregation was also exhorted to have no commerce, consort, or dealings whatsoever with the above-mentioned under penalty'.

The parish got a new church in 1809, erected with the aid of a grant of £600 from the Board of First Fruits. As in Finnoe, it was built in the grounds of the pre-Reformation church – again probably using some of the old stones. However, it was built to one side and to the front of the ruins rather than directly on the site.

The new church had fallen into some disrepair by 1837 when Rev. Ralph Stoney had it refurbished and a tower, with neatly-crenellated battlements, added to the western end. This undertaking was part-financed by a grant of £138 by the Ecclesiastical Commissioners. Rev. Stoney, a brother of Thomas George of Kyle Park, was pepetual curate here until his death in 1856.

An attempt is now made here to chart the succession of clergy by noting the date of each one's first and last appearance in the baptismal registers. As there are overlaps obviously some are curates.

Name	*Years*
Ralph Stoney	1809-56 (curate)
William ?Jones	1828-41
Henry A. Sadleir	1831-32
Benjamin Talbot	1836-56
John C. Head	1849-70
Henry Massey	1872-94.
G. W. Sall	1886-89
Henry Gillespie	1895-1911
R. N. Perdue	1913-19
Wesley Daly	1921-22
W. E. Hipwell	1928-34

D. Clarke	1956-57
D. G. Caddoo	1957-59
James Camier	1962-82

Terryglass church was deconsecrated and sold into private ownership in the early 1980s. The purchaser, Tom Saunders, had it tastefully adapted as a residence, craft shop and art gallery. It is now owned by the well-known artist Jenny Boelens and her husband Jeremy Castles. She carries on the same type of business there.

Terryglass Glebe House
This elegant Georgian house lies in an avenue to the right after the new Catholic church and in the townland of Killeen. It was erected in 1816 at a cost of £500. It was owned successively by the Kents of Terryglass, Ellie Esmonde in the 1930s, followed by Maurice and Lucila O'Connell. After the O'Connells died it was sold to the late Klaus Mahnke, a German national, whose son Michael still lives there. It is dealt with in more detail in Chapter 8.

Sources:
OPW, Urban Archaeological Survey, 1994.
Peter Harbison, *Guide to National Monuments*.
Canon Philip Dwyer, *History of the Diocese of Killaloe*.
TNFH Research Centre.
OHS Gravestone Inscriptions, Terryglass graveyard.
Ordnance Survey Letters, 1840.
Monsignor I. Murphy, *History of the Diocese of Killaloe*, vols I & II.
James Hickie, Wilsie Nolan, Michael Parkinson.
Rev. Michael O'Donoghue (for the biographical note on Canon Daniel O'Donoghue), Liam Hogan, Newtown, Rev. John O'Driscoll, Rev. Tom Seymour.

Photographs: pp, 59, 65, taken by Paddy Carroll; pp. 62, 64, loaned by James Hickie; p.67, loaned by Rev. Tim Gleeson; p. 68, loaned Rev. M. O'Donoghue; p. 69 (2), courtesy of Liam Hogan, loaned by Rev J. O'Driscoll; p. 70, loaned by Rev. T. Seymour.

4
Education

Early in the 1700s, after the Williamite wars had ended and contrary to promises made at the Treaty of Limerick in 1691, Penal Laws against the Catholic population were passed. As well as placing restrictions on Catholic clergy, as outlined in the previous chapter, education was affected. This included a prohibition on sending students abroad. The wealthy Catholics could overcome this by employing private tutors, but for the great majority of our eighteenth-century ancestors there was no real provision for education.

This deprivation gave rise to the so-called hedge schools, or schools kept mainly by local men who had picked up some education and who, for a few pence a week per pupil, taught the rudiments to the children of their neighbours. In the early part of the century some of those teachers may have received some formal education; perhaps they were ex-students of the teachers of disbanded bardic schools which flourished until the late seventeenth century when they were finally dispersed under post-Cromwellian rule, or they may have been educated abroad. Towards the last quarter of the century they would, in the main, have themselves been products of the hedge schools. If caught teaching they were liable to be imprisoned or, at best, fined, so there grew up the practice of teaching in the open, in the shelter of a hedge, where teacher and pupils could quickly disperse at the first sign of danger.

The practice of sometimes holding classes in the open died out in the middle of the 1700s but the schoolhouses were mainly miserable cabins with mud floors. School was sometimes held in the chapels. These chapels were really only Mass houses in which Mass was celebrated on Sunday; other religious observances, such as baptisms, marriages, confessions and funeral Masses, were held in people's homes until the middle of the nineteenth century. In one instance in Kilbarron parish, as Table 1 shows, school was held in the home of a local landowner.

In 1782 acts of parliament were repealed which had been passed in the reigns of William & Mary and later of Anne and which forbade 'persons of the popish religion' to teach. However, the teacher could teach only under licence and to obtain this licence had to take the Oath of Allegiance to the Crown, could not have Protestant children in his school or teach in a Protestant school. None of the teachers with whom we are concerned, i.e. teachers in remote rural areas, bothered to apply for a licence, and Catholic and Protestant children were taught together, sometimes by Catholic and sometimes by Protestant teachers. The scriptures were read if the teacher so wished. Again, it was sometimes the Authorised (Protestant) version and sometimes the Douai (Catholic) version which was used, as can be seen in Table 1. Miss Cambie, a Protestant, kept a school in a room in her brother's house at Brookfield. She read the Douai version to her 2 Protestant and 28 Catholic pupils, see Table 1. These would probably have been the children of workers from the Cambie and neighbouring estates.

Early Schools in the Parish
In the British Library there are many eighteenth and nineteenth century records of the dioceses of Killaloe and Cashel. Historian Dermot F. Gleeson, writing in the *Nenagh Guardian* in 1936, gave an account of the schools in the Ormond parishes as prepared by the vicars of the various parishes and forwarded by them to the Protestant bishop of the time. These are dated December 1807 and January 1808 and thus pre-date those in the First Report of the Commissioners of Irish Education Inquiry, 1826-7, Table 1.

In the reports, as quoted by Gleeson, Terryglass parish and most of Kilbarron parish are omitted, but there is a Protestant teacher, Leonard Piggott, in Springfield townland, near Carney, with 6 Protestant and 14 Catholics pupils. In the Commons of Carney Will Eldaer, a Protestant, had 12 Protestant and 15 Catholic pupils. In Ballyscanlon Patrick Dwyer, a Catholic, taught 2 Protestant and 18 Catholic pupils.

In Dorrha parish (now united with Lorrha as Lorrha-Rathcabbin RC parish) Patrick Moran, a Catholic, was teaching 35 Catholics. The vicar of Lorrha comments on this school: 'In cold weather the children bring a sod or two of turf. Fees per quarter are Reading one shilling and one penny, Writing and Reading two shillings and two pence, Reading, Writing & Arithmetic three shillings and three pence'.

As Table 1 shows, Patrick Moran later returned to his native Coolbawn where he taught in a cabin, the ruins of which can still be found hidden in fuschia opposite Noel and Sally Anne Teefy's house near Coolbawn Post Office.

The 1826-7 Report of the Commissioners of Education also gives details of the names and religion of the teachers, how much they were paid, the kind of buildings in which they operated, numbers and religion of the pupils, whether or not the scriptures were read, and, sometimes, which version. In the 1835 report we are told how much the pupils paid, the average daily attendance, and whether it was increasing, decreasing or stationary. In 1835 the population of Ireland was in the region of 8 million, with 5,000 in the parish of Kilbarron.

Establishment of the National Schools
In 1831 E. G. Stanley, the chief secretary for Ireland, established the national system of education for Ireland when parliament provided for it in the British educational budget. The Irish national schools followed and spread very gradually through the rural parishes. In some places the same buildings and teachers were brought into the system.

The new national schools were strictly non-denominational. Every care seems to have been taken to omit anything from the Board's textbooks that might tend to arouse a spirit of nationalism. In the whole music manual in use in 1864 there was not a single Irish air. The textbooks, which for the period were well printed, well illustrated and well bound, were sold to the pupils for a few pence, and in certain necessitous cases given free. As they were continually in use in the schools for about seventy years, they were usually passed on from the older members of a family to the younger and even from parent to child – a practice which continued well into this century.

In some areas a continuing hedge school was preferred to the new national schools. The Church of Ireland, and to an even greater extent the Presbyterian

Townland	Teacher's Name	Religion	Pay	Schoolhouse	Pupil, Religion, Sex and numbers		Whether Scriptures read
Coolbawn	Pat Moran	RC	£25 p.a	A thatched cabin cost about £60.	40 m, 20f, 10 EC, 50 RC	No connection with Societies. Not parish school.	Scriptures not read.
Ballinderry	Michael Moran	RC	£8 p.a.	ditto	40 m, 20f, 60 RC	ditto	Douai.
Brookfield	Miss Cambey	EC	None	A room in her brother's house in Brookfield.	2 EC, 28 RC, sex not given	Miss Cambey and ladies of the neighbourhood superintend this school and teach the children.	Douai version read.
Curraghmore	Miss Mary Alt	RC	None	not stated.	1m, 8f, 9RC	Miss Alt instructs the poor children herself through charity.	not stated.

TABLE 1 (The 1824 position, from the second report of the Commissioners of Irish Education Inquiry, HC Papers, 1826-7, vol. xii)

church, disapproved of the new national schools because the religious teaching was not based on the scriptures. In the Archdiocese of Tuam Dr John McHale, the Catholic archbishop, refused to have anything to do with them. He demanded Catholic schools for Catholic children and so strong were his representations in Rome that 'in July 1839 the Irish National Schools System stood condemned by the Congregation of Propaganda'. The other bishops disagreed with him and in 1841 Rome allowed every bishop discretionary powers in his own diocese. Another of Dr McHale's objections was that the new schools would kill the Irish language which was then spoken almost universally in his archdiocese. This was a valid point. It had little relevance in north Tipperary where the language had been almost dead for nearly 150 years.

The formal training of teachers began in 1838 when Marlborough Street Training College, Dublin, was set up. Women were admitted to it in 1845. It was non-denominational. There had been Model Schools set up in 1814, one of which was situated in Birr, then called Parsonstown, and in which pupil-teachers got a certain amount of training in the art of teaching.

Kilbarron's First National School

Lorrha was the first parish in the barony of Lower Ormond to have a national school but Kilbarron was not far behind, building one in 1841 which was taken into connection by the National Board of Education in 1842.

It served the Kilbarron end of the parish for a full century. It was known to older parishioners as the 'old Boys School' and stood in Kilbarron village where Our Lady's grotto now is – having being demolished when the present school was built in 1941.

The application for the school was received by the National Education Board on 10 December 1841 from the Rev. Mr Kerins, RCC, Newlawn, Borrisokane. The correspondent was Rev. Ambrose Bowles, PP. Their application extended to seeking grants for the school and towards the teacher's wages. The Education Board responded to the application by arranging for the school to be inspected. This duly took place on 18 November 1842. The following report, filed by Patrick Quinlan, Superintendent of Schools, gives us an amount of information.

> The school was established 1st June 1842 in Ballyquinlivan, 3 miles easterly from Borrisokane. There are no other national schools in the vicinity, only one or two hedge schools. It is built on the chapel grounds but the Inspector's suggestion will be acted upon by having the door removed to the end of the house with an entrance from the road. It has no connection with any religious establishment. The building is stone and lime mortar, slated and all new. The outside dimensions 321/2 feet long, 171/2 feet broad. 9 feet high. It consists of one room and the internal measurements are 281/2 feet long, 131/2 feet broad, 9 feet high.
>
> The funds are supplied locally, no rent, and is held by prescription. It is sufficiently ventilated and warmed. There are 4 double desks, 28 forms [a long narrow stool without a back] each 12 feet, a desk and seat for teacher but no press.
>
> The teacher is Dennis Maguire aged 35 years. He has no instruction in the art of teaching but has testimonials from Rev. Mr Curran, PP, Moyross, and manager of Carna (Co. Galway) N.S. which Maguire controlled for 2 years. The documents

have been seen by the Inspector. Maguire had £8 p.a. salary in Carna until it was suspended in consequence of Dr McHale's opposition in 1839. Maguire's literary acquirements are 'middling', his character 'excellent', and his method of conducting the school 'middling'. Local funds towards paying the teacher are £12 p.a. The scholars pay this in sums of 1s 6d., 2s, 3s 6d, 4s 0d. No children are admitted free yet.

The words NATIONAL SCHOOL are to be put up conspicuously on the school door. The General Lesson is to be hung up in the school. It is open to children of all religions. Bona fide access is to be given to the public at all times to visit the school, examine the register, witness the mode of teaching etc., though not to interfere with the business of the school. The Board's books are to be used and all those published are available in the school. There are books for 75 pupils. One hour each day is to be set aside for religious instruction. This must not impede the business of the school and parents must be satisfied. The population of the parish is 5,000. Children of cottiers and small farmers will mainly attend.

Present at the time of inspection: 33 males, 27 females. On books last 6 months: 40 males, 30 females, average daily attendance last 6 months: 25 males, 20 females. Increase expected: 20 males, 15 females.

There is no committee. The school is under the management of Rev. Mr Kerins, Roman Catholic Curate. There is 6-day schooling 9 a.m.-3 p.m. Sat. 9 a.m.-12. There is no resident Protestant clergyman in the parish but Rev. Mr Stoney, Terryglass, has no objection. The school will be locally supported if taken into connection.

The 1840s-1870s

The average attendance in the school to 31 March 1843 was 43. In 1845 the manager of Kilbarron Loan fund informed the committee that he had received an impertinent letter from Dennis Maguire, teacher of Kilbarron, which he transmitted to the committee. They ordered that the teacher be reprimanded, the committee being of the opinion that the note sent by him to the trustees of the Loan Fund was couched in objectionable and disrespectful language.

In 1846 Kilbarron-Terryglass's parish priest, Rev. Ambrose Bowles, was drowned while bathing in Lahinch where he was on holiday. His successor, Rev. John Moloney, was appointed correspondent. He died of fever in 1849.

Dennis Maguire resigned as teacher in 1849. James Moran was then appointed and resigned in 1853. He may have been a brother of Patrick Moran or even a son – more likely a son. William McGoldrick was then appointed. He resigned in 1855 and went to teach in Borrisokane. In 1855 Patrick Meagher, of a Coolbawn family, was appointed.

My information about Patrick Meagher does not come solely from the public records but from my aunt who knew him. I did not get my information directly from my aunt who died in 1935 but from her daughter Mary Moran. Patrick became a teacher in the first place because, as a child, he had a badly burned arm and, not being able to do the normal farm work, was kept 'at his books'. At that time a teacher probably earned less that a farm labourer but had more status in the community.

In 1858 a girls' school – now the 'Small Hall' and of which more anon – had been built and taken into connection by the Board so there were now two national schools in the village – an amenity which was to obtain for sixteen years.

Patrick Meagher taught the boys until 1874 during which time he was often, according to the records, in trouble and admonished. What the records do not tell is that he was in poor health and was suffering from tuberculosis from which he subsequently died. In 1869 he was threatened with severe censure but was too young to warrant the award of a retiring allowance.

In 1874 Rev. George Corbett, PP, who had been the school manager since 1869, was informed by the National Education Board 'that it is quite clear that these scholars, male and female, cannot separately command a sufficient average and steps must be taken before the end of the quarter to amalgamate the two schools under one teacher'.

This came about on 22 December 1874 when, the average attendance (26) being too low, the boys' school was struck off the roll and grants cancelled from the end of that month. Pat Hough, who had replaced Pat Meagher as teacher for a short while, left on 31 December.

The intention was that all the boys would transfer to the newer girls' school. However, this did not actually happen in some cases. For instance, my father, Patrick Carroll, who would have been ten years old at that time, was sent instead to Kyle Park N.S. in Borrisokane parish, which was almost as near to his home as the Kilbarron one. Kyle Park's unusual story is recounted at the end of this chapter.

Many children from other parishes walked long distances to go to Kyle Park where the teacher, John Gallagher, had a very good reputation. Among those who went was Jack Collins of Claree in Monsea & Killodiernan parish, father of the late Martin, onetime member of Tipperary (NR) County Council, and grandfather of Michael, solicitor in Borrisokane. Jack afterwards joined the Royal Irish Constabulary. In 1878, when the boys' school got back its grants, my father returned there and remained for quite a long time, becoming a paid monitor under Richard Meredith.

The re-opening of the boys' school was due to the unstinting efforts of Rev. George Corbett who made a new application for a grant for the closed school. The Board at first ordered that the application be not granted for the following reasons:
(a) no privies [toilets];
(b) no local aid secured;
(c) floor of schoolroom not boarded;
(d) no evidence that a sufficient average for two separate schools would be maintained.

However, Fr Corbett persisted and renewal of the grant was re-considered on 19 July when the Board recorded that 'the applicant, Rev. George Corbett, having called at this office and stated that he will guarantee local aid to the amount of at least £10 p.a. and will have [the] floor boarded as soon as possible'.

The application was granted and a salary of £32 per year, with results fees, was awarded to Richard Meredith, Class 3, from 1 January 1879. Free stock £4. Sale stock £1 5s 0d. Meredith had been the Literary Master at Kyle Park Agricultural School until 16 May 1873. He had probably been a pupil-teacher at Birr Model School.

The 1880s
We get an insight into the school from the Inspectors' reports of the 1880s.

1880 Rules observed. Supply of books, repairs, efficiency of teacher, school accounts, proficiency of pupils, all satisfactory (report of 26 May).
1881 Rev. John Kennedy appointed manager when Rev. George Corbett resigned.
1884 Ups and downs with teacher Richard Meredith, as he was often absent – ostensibly through illness.
1886 Application for a retiring grant for Richard Meredith refused as medical certificate did not state that he was permanently incapacitated.
1887 Medical certificate now says Richard Meredith permanently incapacitated and the Board will consider application for retirement gratuity. Salary withdrawn from Richard Meredith as he is permanently incapacitated and his claim referred to the teachers' pension office. He received a retiring gratuity of £111 (report of 15 February).

Meredith died in Borrisokane in November 1911 aged 70 years. Going on that record he was 38 years on appointment and 46 on retirement.

Patrick Curtin from Miltown Malbay, Co. Clare, was appointed teacher. He was a native Irish speaker and had come into the area as a substitute at Ardcroney. He was trained at the Royal Botanical Gardens School, Glasnevin, Dublin, and had skills which would have given him a more remunerative post than that of teacher. However, when the Kilbarron post became vacant he applied for it and was successful. My father, who had been acting as paid monitor, also applied for the post. As he was unsuccessful, not having sufficient qualifications, he joined the RIC.

The 1890s-1900s
1893 Inspector forwards letter from management stating a site cannot be obtained for out-offices.
1895 Grants continued only on condition an average of 30 be maintained with 64 on rolls.
1898 Management requested to have out-offices roofed and school roof replastered.
1899 Manager requested to state what action he proposed to take to provide suitable accommodation for pupils of school.

There was a difficult situation here as the manager, Rev. John Kennedy, PP, had been ill for some time and his curate, Rev. John Darcy, acted as administrator up to Fr Kennedy's death in 1901. Fr Darcy then became parish priest and manager of the schools.
1902 The need for a new school indicated by the Board of Education. Many defects identified – bad roof, floor broken, roof of porch stripped of slate. 'Manager says he will see to roof and floor and other defects will be looked into as soon as possible'.

The Board wished to amalgamate the boys' and girls' schools and have a new school built. Fr Darcy, as manager, was totally opposed to the amalgamation and the schools were not amalgamated until after his death in 1940 when he was replaced by Rev. Daniel O'Donoghue. The original, voluminous and illuminating correspondence on the subject of amalgamation, is extant in the National Archives, Dublin.

There was no improvement to either school from 1902, when the need was first highlighted, until 1941 when the new school was built. This took in the period of my own primary education, 1923-9. The schools were exactly as they had been when built in 1841 and 1858 respectively, except that they had deteriorated. The same was true of the Terryglass school, which had been the old parish chapel and built towards the end of the 1700s or early 1800s.

When the Kilbarron schools were amalgamated in 1941 the two buildings continued in use until the new school could be built, but now in a co-educational manner. The Seniors (third, fourth, fifth and sixth classes) of both sexes were housed in the former 'all boys' building under Mr Buckley, and the Juniors (infant, first & second classes) were put in the former 'all girls' school under Mrs Margaret Concannon.

The new school was built in 1942. It had three classrooms, a children's cloak room, staff room and flush toilets.

Latter-Day Teachers
Patrick Curtin retired in 1924 and died in 1929. Timothy Concannon from Co. Galway, whose wife Margaret was already principal of the girls' school, took his

Kilbarron Boys N.S., *c.* 1908
Michael Kennedy, Brocka, father of Biddy Gleeson and Mick (Mouse) Kennedy, is fifth from left in the second row. Apart from teacher Patrick Curtin we can find no other names. This photo was in the possession of Michael Kennedy.

Kilbarron Boys N.S. (? senior or Confirmation class), c.1918
Back (l to r): Pat Carroll, Comenthus, Mick Quirke, –, Paddy Hough, Mikey Hogan (? Clonmakillduff), Harry Donoghue, Ballyscanlon; Willie Donoghue, Ballyscanlon, Danny Brereton, –. **Front**: Jack Gorman, Willie Donoghue, Lodge, Tommy Treacy, Jack Costelloe, Mick Ryan, Ballyscanlon, Jack Fleming, Pat (?) Donoghue, Lodge.

Kilbarron Boys Confirmation class of 1923

place. An assistant, Miss Neville, from Co. Mayo, had been appointed to the boys' school in 1923. She was succeeded by May Graham from Dingle c.1927. Miss Graham taught there until her retirement in 1964 when she returned to her native Dingle. Then came Mrs May Sullivan who retired in February 1993.

Timothy Concannon resigned c.1937 and went to teach in a Christian Brothers' school in Dublin. He was succeeded by Martin Walsh from Nenagh who in turn was replaced by Mr Buckley from Cork.

Mr Buckley was followed in 1942 by Séamus Collins (right) from Ballinaclough, Nenagh. Séamus Collins became like a native of the parish and was very involved in the Local Defence Force during the 'Emergency'. Had Kilkeary school, near his home parish, not become vacant he would probably have spent all his teaching life in Kilbarron of which he had become very fond and where he was greatly liked. His place was taken for a short period by a substitute, Mr Hilliard. Paddy Fogarty, Drominagh (right), a native of the parish, was then appointed and served until his retirement in 1996. He was the first native-born teacher and took a full part in the life of the community. He was replaced by Michael O'Dwyer, Moneygall. The other teachers in the school at present are Mrs Bernadette Grace (née Looby), Ballywilliam, and Mrs Emer Browne (née Bergin), Nenagh.

Kilbarron's Second School – Bellevue, 1852-1857

There is a record of a school built in Bellevue by George W. Biggs. It measured 17 feet by 13 feet and was to cater for 30-40 scholars. This information comes from the records of the Society for Promoting the Education of the Poor of Ireland, popularly known as the Kildare Place Society, so called after the Dublin street where its headquarters was located. The Society was non-denominational in character and its rules forbade it to interfere with other religions. However, the Bible had to be read without comment in all its schools. In 1830 Biggs applied to the Society for a grant of £15 but the school does not seem to have been admitted to membership.

The Second Report of the Commissioners of Public Instruction in Ireland, 1835, shows that a John O'Brien kept a 'hedge school' in Kilbarron (see Table 2 overleaf). It does not specify where in the parish but it was undoubtedly in Bellevue – perhaps in the Biggs building.

In 1851 Rev. Philip Kennedy, PP, applied to the National Board of Education for a newly-established national school in Bellevue to be taken into connection. The request was sanctioned on 2 July 1852. The school had two rooms 14 feet x 13 feet and 9 feet x 13 feet. It stood on the Ballinderry road at the junction facing the avenue to Bellvue House. The ruins are still there. As the measurements furnished here differ only slightly from George Biggs's 1830 school it is reasonable to presume it was brought back into use in 1851.

Description of School	Sources of Support	No. of Children	Avg. daily attendance	Increasing Diminishing Stationary	Kind of Instruction
1. Hedge school kept by John O'Brien in Bellview.	Payment of children from 1s6d to 2s6d per quarter.	Males 36	32	Increasing	Reading Writing Arithmetic
2. Hedge School kept by Patrick Moran (in Coolbawn).	Payment of children from 1s6d to 4s per quarter.	Males 36 Females 16	35	Stationary	ditto
3. Hedge School kept by John Sullivan.	Payments of children from 1s6d to 3s per quarter.	Males 35 Females 25	40	Increasing	ditto
4. Hedge School kept by Michael Lynch.	Derived from the Baptist Irish Society.	Males 29 Females 25	20	Stationary	ditto
Number of Children on Books of Daily Schools Males 136; Females 58; TOTAL 194					
Finnoe Hedge School kept by Michael Fahy.	Payments of children 1s6d to 2s6d per quarter.	Males 41 females 32	40	Increasing	Reading Writing Arithmetic
Cloghprior Hedge School kept by John Revoker.	Payments of children 1s6d to 2s6d per quarter.	Males 81 Females 38	?	Stationary	ditto

TABLE 2 (from the Second Report of the Commissioners of Public Instruction in Ireland, HC Papers, 1835, vol. xxxiv)

John O'Brien was appointed as teacher in this new national school on 1 February 1852 with a salary of £11 p.a. and books for 100 children. However, the attendance declined, the building deteriorated, and the Board threatened to withdraw O'Brien's salary unless things improved. There is no indication in the records that it was a new building and the fact that it fell into disrepair so quickly makes one think that it was the one built by George W. Biggs circa 1830 and in which O'Brien had been keeping his hedge school in 1835.

In 1856 Rev. Philip Kennedy was replaced as manager by Rev. John Gleeson, PP. Fr Gleeson wrote to the Board requesting that the grants not be withdrawn, but in spite of this they were cancelled on 22 April 1857, the average daily attendance having dropped further and no improvement having been made to the building.

Despite the withdrawal of the grants John O'Brien continued to teach, presumably in the same school building. Many, if not all, of the pupils remained with him notwithstanding the existence of the grant-aided national school in Kilbarron village.

My aunt, Anne Carroll of Brookfield, later Mrs Moran of Coolbawn, and Anne Costello of Kilbarron, later Mrs Flannery and, on her second marriage, Mrs Gleeson of Lahesseragh, were two of those who attended John O'Brien's school after it ceased to be a registered national school. Anne Carroll was born in 1858 and in 1868 she and Anne Costello, who had both reached the age of ten years, were still pupils at the school. They were told by the parish priest that unless they transferred to the girls' school in the village they could not be prepared for or receive First Holy Communion – then received at age ten. They both then transferred and became very fond of their female teacher, Mary Kennedy.

My father and his brothers and sisters were fortunate in that John O'Brien, a near neighbour, 'rambled' at their house in Brookfield and he would gather them around the table in the evening and go over their lessons with them. They profited from the extra help and were good scholars and beautiful writers.

John O'Brien's only child, Sarah, married Michael Molamphy of Bellevue, grandfather of Michael who now keeps Coolbawn Post Office.

KILBARRON'S THIRD SCHOOL – THE GIRLS', 1858-1941

Known to all now as the 'Small Hall', this girls' school was applied for by Rev. John Gleeson and established on 10 May 1858. It was taken into connection by the Board in October of the following year. It was a purpose-built, one-roomed building, measuring 25 feet x 14 feet x 10 feet high, erected, the official report states, 'on chapel ground but with the door facing outward' – it would seem that it was important that the door did not open into the chapel yard, thus linking it with a particular religion. Anne Connors was appointed as teacher with her salary unspecified but was to get school fees of £2 4s. 3d per quarter. She left on 27 March 1863 and Mary Kennedy was appointed. She lived in Ryehill, Ballinderry, and came to school by ass and trap. She retired on 3 August 1894.

Margaret Gleeson, who came from Bodyke, Co. Clare, was appointed on 12 November 1894. She married Mark Bourke and remained at the school until 1914. She was replaced by Hannah Nealon from Newtown. Miss Nealon left about 1920 to enter a convent and her sister Josephine, not yet trained, took over from her until another sister, Margaret Concannon, who had been teaching in Roscrea, was free to come. Miss Josephine, as we called her, and Mrs Concannon were the teachers when I first went to school in 1923. Josephine was my first teacher and I liked her very much. She soon left to go to Training College and there were several assistant teachers after her. Miss O'Reilly from Newtownmountbutler in Co. Fermanagh is the assistant teacher most of us remember best as she remained for a long time and was very well liked. Mrs Concannon remained principal teacher at the girls' school until the amalgamation of both schools in 1941. She left and took a position elsewhere in 1943. She loved Kilbarron and chose to be buried in its new graveyard. She gave a great deal to the parish and is remembered with affection by the generations whom she taught. She was replaced by Miss Hastings from Newmarket-on-Fergus.

Margaret (née Nealon) Concannon and her husband Timothy

SCHOOLS OF THE CHURCH OF IRELAND

In the grounds of the now disused Protestant church near Coolbawn Cross are the ruins of a schoolhouse. It was a fine two-roomed slated building, much superior in structure to the 1841 and 1858 national schools in the village. It was there in 1850 according to the Griffith/Primary Valuation list and was probably the Protestant parish school. The immediate lessor is given as Rev. Thomas Lyon, Rector.

Stanley's old house facing Castletown avenue gates was also, according to the old people in Coolbawn, a Protestant school. It is likely that it was the school kept by Michael Lynch (see Table 2) whose sources of support derived from the Baptist Irish Society. Note that it is described as a 'school', unlike the others which are described as 'hedge schools'.

Finnoe Parish

An application was made in January 1880 for a school in the townland of Carney Commons. The applicant was John Frances Waller, Finnoe House, who is dealt with in some detail in a later chapter. The former school had closed in 1879 because of low average attendance and no teacher. Its manager was William Waller.

Robert Dennison, Belfast, aged 18½ years, Protestant, was appointed teacher to the 1880 school. He had been a pupil teacher in Belfast for one and a half years up to 31 December 1879. His salary was £32 per annum, plus results fees, provided the average did not fall. However, the report stated that no salary would be granted until the schoolroom floor was boarded and privies provided.

SCHOOLS IN TERRYGLASS

In the 1820s there was a school in the vicinity of the Glebe house in Killeen townland on the Terryglass-Carrigahorig road. This belonged to the Society for Promoting the Education of the Poor of Ireland/Kildare Place Society.

Kilbarron Girls' School, c.1924-5

Back (1 to r): Bridget Cleary, Nancy Quinlan, Molly Foley, Kitty Sammon, Mary Donoghue, Ballyscanlon, Margaret Quinlan, Nora Carty. **4th Row:** May Grady, –, Bridget Cunningham, Kitty Mary Burke, Mary Burke, Carrigagown, Chrissie Sullivan, Nellie Tuohy, Nellie Starr. **3rd Row:** Kitty Sullivan, Christina Curtin, Una Costelloe, Mary (Molly) Carroll, Lisquilibeen, Bab Lalor, Mary (Ciss) Hogan, Bridget Quirke, Pauline Harkins, Eileen (Nell) Curtin, –, Bridie Ryan. **2nd Row:** Mary Cormack, Margaret Burke, Carrigagown, Nora Cleary, Pauline Quinlan, Kitty Cahalan, Nellie Donoghue, Moira Carroll, Nora Barry, Sarah (Sal) Cormack, Madge Carroll. **Front:** Bridie Carroll, Bridget Cormack, Nancy Ryan, May Carroll, Sarah Madden, Annie Kitson, May Loughnane, Bessie Kitson, Mary Jo Sheedy, Jo(anna) Carroll.

From its surviving records we can glean that Rev. Ralph Stoney, Rector of Terryglass, was involved in securing it in April 1823. A slated limestone building, measuring 40 feet x 17 feet, was erected by him at a cost of just over £64. A trained teacher named John Horan was employed at £7 10s per annum.

The original application was for a grant of £30 for a projected attendance of 100 children. £20 was granted. A report for 1823 shows that the school was progressing well and that 'the parish priest approves of the establishment and at his wishes Mr Stoney supplies copies of the Romish testament to be read in the school'.

The inspector's reports for the years 1823-5 chart the attendance for that period.

	Roll	Present	Average
1823	M67	33	68
	F50	24	34
1824	M17	50	80
	F34	60	20
1825	M80	46	59
	F40	25	28

Two female teachers are also named in the record – Anne Holland and Jane Boland. The latter was the school's second teacher in 1825 on a salary of £7.10s per annum. In 1827 Rev. Stoney indicated that he intended rebuilding the schoolhouse at an estimated cost of £90 but that no local aid could be obtained. James Kennedy and George Hodgins are mentioned as teachers at that time.

Towards the end of 1828 the school was withdrawn from the Kildare Place Society. It seems to have fallen into disfavour because of its connection with the Hibernian Society who were suspected of engaging in proselytising (attempting to convert persons to another religion – a very sensitive subject where Catholic children were attending interdenominational, or wholly Protestant, schools). It was re-admitted again in 1829 with 100 pupils but disagreement over the reading of Scripture caused a falling off in attendance. 78 males and 36 females were returned as on the roll in 1830. However, it closed the following year, due to the ill-health of the patron, and did not re-open.

Dame School

The Terryglass end of the parish did not get its own national school until 1887. Up to then the children went to either the national school in Lorrha parish or Kyle Park national school in Borrisokane parish, The names of a great many Terryglass children are to be found in a Kyle Park register which still exists.

Lorrha or Kyle Park was a long way for small girls to walk, and as a result Catherine Griffin (born 1832) opened what in England would be called a 'Dame School'. She had a sister called Jane (born 1834) and they lived on the narrow road called Shannon Lane which linked the village with the quay. They were sisters of James the carpenter who did much work on the new RC church. Their father plied a barge on the Shannon.

Catherine had been a governess with 'good' families and taught the local girls needlework, deportment and good manners generally, as well as the 'three Rs'. When they were considered 'hardy' enough they went to a national school.

Michael Parkinson's aunts attended Catherine Griffin's school and then went to Lorrha.

Before 1887, but later than any available records, i.e. the Inquiry of 1835, there was a private (hedge) school in Lacken townland kept by Michael Hogan (Shelter), grandfather to the present occupier, John Hogan, whose great-grandfather came from Puckane. O'Donovan, in 1840, mentions a schoolhouse but does not say where – it may have been on the Ballinderry road as there is a strong local tradition that there was a school there at one time.

In the 1852 Primary Valuation List a national school is recorded in Roran but there is no mention of this in the education records or in local tradition.

Terryglass's Old and New National Schools

The first move to acquire a school under the national school system for Terryglass was taken by the parish priest, Rev. John Kennedy, towards the end of January 1887 when he informed the Commissioners of Education:

> I beg you to bring under your notice that I have opened at Terryglass, in the old RC Chapel on Monday Jan. 17th a mixed school and I now ask you kindly let me have the grants usually given by the Commissioners in such cases.
>
> There was a most urgent necessity for a school at Terryglass. The room I have had fitted up is capable of accommodating about eighty children. The teacher in charge of it has a Certificate of Competency from Mr Purser, District Inspector, and the daily average attendance for the first week was 47.2 and is likely to increase to at least 60.

It will be recalled that the Hickie-sponsored new church had been brought into use in Terryglass the previous August.

The church-cum-school was inspected on 22 February and Inspector A. Purser's report submitted a week later to the Commissioners. His report was in the form of answers to a questionnaire. The following were some of the main points.

• The school is conducted in strict accordance with the principles of National Education. There are no denominational emblems of any sort.

• The schoolroom is part of the former, now disused, RC Chapel of Terryglass. It has no connection with any religious establishment.

• It is built of stone and mortar, slated, one storey and in good repair. There are no privies. The dimensions are 27 1/2 feet long 22 1/2 feet broad, 13 1/2 feet high. Suitable provision is made for light, warmth and ventilation. It is not ceiled, but the floor is boarded and the walls plastered.

• Sufficient school furniture has been provided for pupils and teacher, there is a properly shelved book-press with door, lock and key, and racks are provided whereon to suspend the Time Table, General Lesson, Board's Rules etc.

• The teacher is John Scales, 19-years-old RC, who was last employed as Pupil Teacher in the Parsonstown (Birr) Model School which he left on 31 March 1886.

• The local funds towards teacher's support will be annually provided by school fees of £15. No local aid is secured. Fees are from 1s to 3s per quarter and all labourers' children – about half the pupils – are free. The school is bona fide open to children of all religious denominations.

• Religious instruction is given in the schoolroom from 3.30 to 4 o'clock daily.

Schooling is 5 days each week from 10 to 3.30 o'clock.
- Present on the day of inspection were: 39 males and 24 females, Total 63. On the rolls at the time were 54 males and 41 females, a total of 95.
- The clergy of other denominations have no objection to the school – quite the contrary. The inspector had an interview with the manager and confirms that he is resident in the locality and is quite fit to be manager. About one-third of the pupils have been withdrawn from Lorrha and Kyle Park national schools. These schools were at an inconvenient distance.
- The establishment of this school will not have a serious effect on these two national schools as regards their average attendance.
- If the Commissioners insist upon out-offices being built the manager will at once convert another part of the old chapel into offices but it will be almost impossible to find a suitable outlet.

However, the Commissioners decided they would not come to a final decision until out-offices have been provided.

There then followed a lively correspondence between Fr Kennedy and the Commissioners on the subject of the need for out-offices. In March he told them that 'relative to the above school. I beg to state that out-offices for the children of the peasantry in an open country, are by no means as necessary as you may consider'. He continued:

However, in order to qualify for the grants without which I cannot expect the services of an efficient teacher I hereby promise to have offices erected within three weeks from this date, but I do not undertake to say they will be of much utility to children who have never been accustomed to such.

By April he was able to tell the Commissioners:

I beg to inform you that the out-offices for the above school have been erected as required. I trust you will most kindly give the usual grants.

The 'unwanted' out-offices were passed by Inspector Allman in mid-May 1887.

Teacher John Scales was granted a salary of £35 p.a. with Results fees backdated to 1 February 1887. A grant of free stock of £4 10s 0d was made on condition that a Sale Stock of the value of 17s 6d be purchased.

There is a tradition locally that Scales was given leave of absence to train and that a John White took his place. This is not in the official reports.

In 1892 an application was made for an assistant teacher. The response from the Commissioners was that the school could not have one unless evidence of increased attendance was maintained. If not less than an average of 70 pupils could be maintained for two quarters a renewed application would be considered. They obviously managed to achieve this and an Elizabeth Kelly was appointed in October 1892.

John Scales was awarded £5 Carlyle & Blake Premium for 1894. The out-offices question surfaced again towards the end of the 1890s and it was recommended that new ones be built. At this time Fr Kennedy became ill. On his

Terryglass N.S., 1911

Back (l to r): Bill Guest, –, –, Tom Donoghue, Mick Leenane, Mick Tierney, Michael Cahalan, Matt Farrell, Jim Tierney. **3rd row:** Timmy Tierney, Willie Donoghue, Tone Fox, Jack Fox, Tom Meagher, – Hough, Mick Meagher, Willie Tierney, Jack Hogan, Willie Starr. **2nd row:** Lizzie Cooney, Nan Cooney, Maggie Cooney, Nan Meagher, –, –, Geraldine Buckley, Nora Hogan. **Front:** Murt Conway, Mick Neill, Jim Neill, Dennis Starr, Neil Conway, Mary Ann Donoghue, Kathleen Hough, Nan Keeshan, Nora Starr, –, –, Bess Hough, Nora Carroll, Ballinderry.

death in 1901 his curate, Fr John Darcy, who became the new parish priest, also bcame manager of the school.

John Scales died in 1913, aged 46 years, and John Gleeson from Bodyke, Co. Clare, was appointed. He died in 1938 and was succeeded by Desmond Gordon who served until he died in 1970.

Terryglass got a fine new school in 1954 following ongoing representations by the local branch of Muintir na Tíre to the parish priest, Rev. Daniel O'Donoghue, and the Department of Education. By then, the Terryglass end of the parish had been making do with the redundant Catholic church for educational purposes for over thirty-three years. The builders of the new school were Paddy Fox and Brian Williamson.

John Leenane, Newlawn, a native of the parish, succeeded Mr Gordon. He retired in 1997 and was succeeded by Noreen Sheridan, Portroe. The second teacher, as of early 1998, is Bernadette (née Ryan) Molamphy, Coolbawn, replacing Evelyn (née Kennedy) Smith of Templemore.

CURRICULUM AND EXTRA-CURRICULAR

Gradually in all schools the three Rs – r(eading), (w)r(iting) (a)r(ithmetic) – were augmented by the teaching of singing, a certain amount of history and geography, book-keeping and a bit of Euclid. I have access to many of the Kilbarron principal Patrick Curtin's books and they include texts on mechanics, physics, then called natural philosophy, quite advanced arithmetic, the poetry of Sir Walter Scott and other poets of that period, and an excellent 'Fifth Reader'. Many of those texts bore the imprimatur, 'Sanctioned by the Commissioners of National Education, Ireland'. The history book, *Historical Course for Schools,* published in 1872 and edited by a graduate of Trinity College Dublin, gives a general sketch of European and British history from the Greek civilisation until 1872. It gives a good and objective account of the Reformation in England and on the Continent of Europe. There is one paragraph only on the history of Ireland and that on the penultimate page. I feel it is worth quoting.

> The whole island of Great Britain has long been firmly joined together, notwithstanding the differences of race and speech in different parts which have still not wholly died out. But the remembrance of ancient misgovernment has constantly kept up the spirit of disaffection in Ireland, which has broken out into more than one conspiracy and rising, though none of any great scale. Every care has been taken by a succession of measures to do justice to Ireland, by the admission of the Roman Catholics to equal rights with Protestants, by the disestablishment of the dominant Protestant Church, and by laws for the benefit of the occupiers of land. But it would seem that the memory of old wrongs is even now [1872] stronger than the feeling of recent benefits.

In the national schools girls were taught needlework and there was simple drill. After Independence was achieved in 1922 teaching of Irish became compulsory. Many of the teachers had little Irish and in my first year at school in Kilbarron, 1923, we had three months summer holidays, to allow teachers to go to Irish Colleges or the Gaeltacht to improve their knowledge of the language. However, Patrick Curtin, the principal in Kilbarron, was a native Irish speaker and had

Terryglass N.S., undated
Back (l to r): O. Allen, T. Ryan, Paddy Hogan (Bawn), Tommy Hogan, Gerard Flynn, Tim Darcy. **Middle:** ?T Burns, Mary Nolan, Cornamult, Bridget Nolan, Bridge Donoghue, Bridie Starr, Bridie Kennedy, Mick Kirwan, John Gleeson, NT. **Front:** Janey Donoghue, Madeline Flynn, Gretta Kennedy, Gretta Ryan, Lizzie Hogan, Margaret Cahalan.

Terryglass N.S., undated
Back (l to r): Marty Ryan, P Heenan, Roran, Dan Hough, Billy Burns, Johnnie Hogan (Duck), Pake Starr, Tim Hogan, Aidan Fox, Dan Loughnane. **Middle:** Paddy Hogan (Bawn), Bridie Conway, Gretta Ryan, K. Kennedy, Lacken, Mary Anne Donoghue, Nell Darcy, Nora Kennedy, Willie Ryan, Drominagh. **Front:** Din Ryan, Gretta Darcy, Nan Burchell, Bab Starr, Maisie Burchell, Mary Ryan, Mary Joe Costelloe, Mary O'Neill, Mary Jo Heenan, Bridie Starr, Paddy Hough.

Terryglass N.S., 1926/7
Back (l to r): Johnnie Hogan (Duck), Edward Maher, –, Jack Kirwan. **Middle:** Billy Lucas, Joe Mackey, ? Jim Kirwan, T. Hogan, Bawn. **Front:** Bobby Lucas, Tom Hogan (Duck), Michael Hogan (Mountain), Tom Ryan, Tim Darcy, Bill ?Leenane, Joe Nevin.
They are all so well-dressed. Tim Darcy has the knee britches and the lovely stockings.

already been teaching some Irish in the school before 1922. He also cycled to Borrisokane to give Irish classes to members of the Gaelic League. He came from a very musical West Clare family. His brother Hugh, a noted musician on the flute, tin whistle, bagpipes and fiddle, is featured in the Heritage Centre at Corofin near Ennis with fellow-musician Peadar Clancy. He had influenced Clancy to take an interest in the bagpipes. The set of pipes, or one of the sets he used, is on display in Corofin with photos of the two men. Patrick Curtin's daughter, Eileen Carroll, Clonmackilladuff, has told me that every St. Patrick's Day the first thing her father did when he got up was to take down his fiddle and play a jig called 'St. Patrick's Day'. They still have his fiddle in the house.

John Gleeson, the teacher in Terryglass, also gave Irish classes to members of the Gaelic League.

KILBARRON GIRLS' SCHOOL – A PERSONAL MEMOIR

As outlined already, an 'all girls' school was built in Kilbarron village in 1858 and the first national school became an 'all boys' one. From 1874 to 1878 education was co-educational in the new school. Then came a return to two schools, catering for boys and girls separately. This is what obtained when I first attended this school in 1923 and was to continue for another twenty years or so. The boys kept to their end of the playground and hurled mostly. I do not know what the boys' toilet facilities were like. Ours was a tin-roofed shed with a wooden seat in which there were two round holes, underneath which was a zinc tub which was emptied periodically.

In 1923 there were between 50 and 60 girls on the roll with two teachers. It was a one-roomed building with no frills; you lifted the latch and walked straight in. There was one fireplace, which had a high grate and two hobs. When the weather was very cold, the little ones, whose desks were inside the door, were allowed up to warm themselves. We brought a penny a week for turf. The boys each brought two or three sods of turf on Monday for their school. The kettle for the mistress's tea was boiled on this fire in winter.

In summer a fire was lit in the playground to boil the kettle. Lighting this outdoor fire was a delightful and much-coveted task. It meant missing that last half-hour, usually catechism, and gaining the freedom of the blazing, crackling, twig fire and the spluttering, steaming kettle. We ate our bread-and-butter lunch and drank our milk as we tended the fire. I can still recall sharply the acrid-sweet savour of those far-off half-hours – the taste of bread and butter and cold milk, combined with wood smoke.

In summer we took a bottle of milk to wash down the two slices of bread. In winter there was no bottle of milk. I never remember feeling thirsty, just as I never remember feeling hot or cold. We must have been hot and thirsty after the wild games of 'Spy' all over Mark Bourke's farmyard, and I know we went to drink at Armitage's well. However, this amenity was closed after an adult death from typhoid in the area.

The Playground

In retrospect the playground games seem magical. The girls kept to their side and the boys to theirs. 'Spy' and 'Tig' were perennial but there were other more ritualistic games. One was called 'Janey Joe'. A ring of girls formed around Janey Joe and her mother. The ring would go backwards and forwards chanting:

We've come to see Janey Joe, Janey Joe, Janey Joe,
We've come to see Janey Joe, how is she now?

The answer would come each time from the mother:

Janey Joe's washing, she's washing, she's washing,
Janey Joe's washing all the day long.

And so right through the household tasks and finally the sickness and death of Janey Joe, with the girls who played Janey Joe and her mother miming all the actions.

Janey Joe's dead, she's dead, she's dead,
Janey Joe's dead all the day long.

'Jackstones' was a summer game in which some big girls were very skilled. It involved five smooth, rounded pebbles and miming household actions.

'Skipping' came with springtime. Winter brought marathon slides on the

Kilbarron Girls' N.S., 1926/28

Back (l to r): Pauline Harkins, Bridget Quirke, Nellie Donohoe, Christina Curtin, Kathleen Cahalan, Bridie Carroll, Madge Carroll, Mary Cormack. **4th Row:** Margaret Burke, Frances Cahalan, Eileen Curtin, Margaret Quinlan, Christina Sullivan, Sarah Cormack, Kathleen Sullivan, Christina Costelloe. **3rd Row:** Nancy Quinlan, Pauline Quinlan, Moira Carroll, Babs Lalor, Annie Kitson, Nora Barry, May Carroll, Bridget Cormack, Maura Byrnes, Breda Brereton (partially hidden). **2nd Row:** Agnes Cormack, Nancy Burns, Mary (?) Madden, Bessie Kitson, Mary Sheedy, Agnes Hogan, Mary Jo Sheedy, Bridget Burns, Bridget Sheedy, –. **Front:** Nonie Carroll, Johanna (Jo) Carroll, Bridie (?) Madden, Una Costelloe, Bridie Ryan, Nancy Ryan.

frozen pond. Our nailed or studded boots were like skates. One hard winter Maggie Smith's lake froze over and we adjourned daily to skate there while the teachers, all unknowing, warmed their shins at the fire. One day one of our number fell through the ice and narrowly escaped drowning. Someone told the teachers and that ended the skating.

In summer we all went barefoot. I read some years ago in a review of a new book by Mary Kenny that she removed her shoes as she first walked off the boat at Liverpool and subsequently dined out on the barefoot Irish emigrant story. We loved going barefoot. Once the month of May arrived we nagged our parents to let us 'leave off the boots'. 'So-and-so had the boots left off today'. The feel of the cool, soft grass under bare feet, after the long winter in heavy boots and thick socks, comes back to me still with intense pleasure. Sometimes a toe was stubbed. Blackthorns were a constant hazard. When it rained the limestone dust of the roads turned into soft, white mud and squelched deliciously through the toes.

Visitors
There were high days and holidays. The visits of the Inspector and the Diocesan Inspector ('the Dioss') were very exciting. We always knew when they were coming and wore our Sunday clothes and new hair ribbons and had our boots polished. We also liked funerals. The school windows looked out on the chapel yard so all the comings and goings were visible. We had to keep very quiet. Once there was a particularly grand funeral. It was the bishop's brother, Patrick Fogarty, Drominagh Lodge. The Fogarty family lived at Terryglass but the church there was undergoing repairs so the funeral was held in Kilbarron. There were crowds of clergy and the bishop was expected to visit the school. We had been instructed to kneel down when he came in and to say, 'Welcome my Lord'. He finally arrived after we had knelt at least twice to welcome perfectly ordinary priests. I remember that particular day because it was the day I got my first slap. As we awaited the episcopal visit with ever-growing tension, a girl who was sitting beside me urged me to sing. She probably gave me a pinch to encourage me because I obligingly piped up. The mistress was, understandably, furious and ordered Miss Josephine to slap me.

I do not recall exactly what we learned at school or how. It seems to have been mostly Irish and catechism. We must have picked up other skills such as the ability to work buttonholes, to write reasonable English, and do tables.

The introduction of mandatory teaching of Irish in 1923 was undoubtedly a great upheaval for teachers and children alike – and indeed also for parents. I disliked doing Irish so much, and was so bad at it, that when I arrived at the Convent of Mercy secondary school in Nenagh and was told I had to do French I began to cry. I went on to do a degree in French and spent half my life teaching it!

An inordinate amount of time was given to the teaching of Catechism, most of it now irrelevant. Coming on towards Confirmation and to the annual visit of the Diocesan Inspector we seemed to do nothing at all except Catechism. We were all budding theologians! We might not have known the number of angels who could dance on the head of a pin, but we knew to a crumb the amount we could eat at the two collations allowed as well as the main meal on fast days. Our kindly teacher did not readily resort to corporal punishment but in the weeks prior to these episcopal and diocesan visitations she certainly wielded the switch! Catechism was combined with bible stories from Schuster's Bible History. We never had the bible straight and it seems to have been always Old Testament.

Schoolbooks
Our schoolbooks consisted of an English reader, an Irish book, an arithmetic and table book, the bible history, modern geography, which was anything but modern, and a history book, *A Child's Story of Ireland*, which was a joy. It had pictures of Brian Boru about to be struck down by Brodar as he prayed, crucifix aloft, outside his tent after Clontarf, and of Patrick Sarsfield and Wolfe Tone.

Having just recently got our own government, history could at last be taught as it appeared to Irish eyes. Up to this time not only had history to be seen from the English point of view, but in the schools no poetry or stories with an Irish flavour were taught. All the poems and stories learned by our parents were English, Scottish or American – the works of such writers as Tennyson, Scott and Longfellow. The old Irish stories were handed down, but around the firesides – never in the schools, and certainly never officially. There were no other books in the school apart from schoolbooks. I once found a ragged copy of *Lamb's Tales from Shakespeare* on a window sill and managed to sit by that window as often as possible until I had finished reading it. I had never heard of Shakespeare but I relished *Lamb's Tales*.

The school walls were covered with maps. There were the British Isles – all pink – the World and Europe. The map of Europe was pre-1914 with an enormous Austria, little Serbia, and no sign of Czechoslovakia or Yugoslavia.

Singing was an important lesson. Our teacher was very musical. The songs we learned were often of the rather sentimental Edwardian variety: 'Sweet Belle Mahone', 'Say Au Revoir but not Good-bye'. We learned the usual hymns and the 'Veni Creator', 'Adeste Fidelis', 'Tantum Ergo' and 'O Salutaris' for Benediction.

Going and Coming
We liked school. If a morning came very wet there was the danger that we might be kept at home and this would cause great dismay, even tears. If we were lucky my uncle, wearing his wet-weather garb of old sack and battered bowler, would look up at the sky and say, 'I can see enough blue in the sky to make a jacket and trousers for a gooseberry', the horse would be harnessed and yoked to the trap, and we would be taken to school.

In summer we dawdled home along the dusty roads. The hedges were thick with woodbine, robin-run-the-hedge and dog roses – the eglantine, convolvulus and sweetbriar of the poets we were yet to meet. A shower would come and wash away the white dust, releasing the heady summer scents.

We would get down on all fours and drink the cool, clear water from Meredith's well. Sometimes the boys threw stones at us and we shouted rudely back at them. Sometimes we went into the fields and picked cowslips and made didgy-dodgies and played, chanting

Didgy-dodgy, four and fodgy,
How many years have I to live?
One, two, three, four . . .

keeping the soft yellow ball in the air as long as we could until it fell at the fatal figure. Sometimes, particularly if two of us had stayed behind 'to sweep', we sat at the roadside and did home exercises, swapping skills.

Neighbours working in the fields watched the 'scholars' go by and judged the time of day by their passing. Time seemed to be without end.

As a postcript I give the names of the scholars of 1930, in the sequence in which they appeared from back to front in a photograph which, unfortunately, was of too poor a quality to reproduce.

Sarah Madden, Nancy Ryan, May Carroll, Nora Cleary, Nora Corbett, Julia Garry, Mota, Eileen Chapman, Mota, Mary Madden, Breda Brereton, Bridget McCormack, Kitty Sullivan. Oldcourt, Gretta Ryan, Bridget Quirke, Moira Carroll, Una Costelloe, Bridie Ryan, Carney, Josie Carroll, Pauline Quinlan, Nora Barry, Bellevue, Annie Kitson, Oldcourt, Pauline Harkins, Mary McCormack, Charlotte Chapman, Eithna Concannon, Bridget Garry, Mota, Ann Sheedy, Peg Starr, Margaret McCormack, Monica Lynch, Hazel Stanley, Kitty Stanley, Eileen Stanley, Rene Grey, Gretta Carroll, Margaret Burns, Nellie Corbett, Margaret Sheedy, Nonie Carroll, Coolbawn, Kathleen Burns, Carney, Eileen Flannery, Glenbower, Mary Sheedy, Mary Jo Sheedy, Bessie Kitson, Bridie Madden, Oldcourt, Katie Foote, Mota, Eileen Cahalan.

Sources:
Second Report of the Commissioners of Irish Education Inquiry, 1826-7, Parliamentary Papers, vol. 12.
Second Report of the Commissioners of National Education in Ireland, 1835, PP, vol. 35.
The National School records in the National Archives, Bishop St, Dublin.
P. J. Dowling, *The Hedge Schools of Ireland.*
Dermot F. Gleeson, *Nenagh Guardian,* 19 December 1936.
Church of Ireland College of Education, Kildare Place, Records.

Photographs: loaned by Biddy Gleeson, p. 80; Michael Conway, p. 81; Sheila Collins and Paddy Fogarty, p. 82; Eithne (née Concannon) Maguire, p. 85, Mary Joe (née Starr) Sheedy, p. 86; Wilsie Nolan, p. 90; Patricia (née Darcy) Lyons, p. 93, John Leenane, p. 99.

Terryglass N.S., early 1970s

Back (l to r): John Dwyer, Pádraig Walsh, Michael Keane, Michael King, Dolores Quirke, N.T., John Leenane, N.T., Brendan Tierney, Niall Heenan, Johnny Dwyer, Seán Fox, John Egan. **Middle:** Joseph Starr, Geoffrey Kent, James Mulvihill, Donal Hogan, Helen Donoghue, William Gleeson, Noreen Starr, Mary Keane, Helena Kexane, Teresa Donoghue, Paula King, Kevin Hogan, Martin Nolan, Martin Mulvihill, Tommy Dwyer, Michael Egan, Johnny Nevin. **Front:** Brian Leenane, Jer Leenane, Joseph Hogan, Caroline Corboy, Anne Marie Egan, Carmel Dwyer, Alice Egan, Anne King, Bridget Nevin, Bernadette Leenane, Linda Kent, John Mulvihill, John Molloy, Bernard Molloy, Anne Fox.

Kyle Park Agricultural School

As outlined in the previous chapter, a school, grant-aided and sanctioned by the Commissioners for Education, opened in Kilbarron village in 1841-2. In May of that year the parish priest of Borrisokane parish, Rev. George Bermingham applied to the Commissioners for grants for a national school in the town of Borrisokane. The accommodation he offered was a room in a three-roomed house, the other two rooms being occupied. This room may have been an existing hedge school, with the master and his family in the other two rooms.

This schoolroom had one double desk and five forms, all old. There was no other furniture. The room could accommodate 35 children. The Commissioners agreed to give the grants provided the patron looked for a better place. James Egan, aged 22, the clerk at the RC chapel, was appointed teacher at a salary of £4 per annum . He had no training.

At the same time Thomas George Stoney (1808-1886) (right), a landowner and justice of the peace, who lived at Kyle Park, in the townland of Kyletombricane, a few miles from Borrisokane on the road to Ballinderry, got the idea that he would, in conjunction with the Commissioners, set up a national school at Kyle Park to which he would attach a farm and in which a skilled agricultural teacher would be employed to teach the boys the latest agricultural methods.

Thomas George Stoney, then thirty-four years old, was son of George and Marianne (née Smith) Stoney. As George was dead, Thomas G. had inherited Kyle Park and Kyletombricane on the death of his grandfather, Thomas Stoney, Arran Hill, in 1826. The latter had been Deputy Lieutenant of Co. Tipperary in 1793. He was twice married and decreed in his will that on the death of his second wife Arran Hill was to revert to Thomas G. Thomas G. Stoney was of a philanthropic turn of mind, very well educated and a skilled draughtsman. He married Anna Waller, daughter of Thomas Waller, Finnoe House. They had at least four sons, one of whom was Edward Waller Stoney (1844-1931), a railway engineer in India.

Thomas George was five generations on from George Stoney who had come to North Tipperary in the late 1600s from Rilston, Yorkshire. George's son Thomas had married Sarah Robinson, Knockshegowna, and lived in Greyfort, Borrisokane. Their son George (1713-87) married Elizabeth Johnstone, of Rath and Emmel Castle, near Cloughjordan but just across the county border in Co. Offaly. In time this Johnstone property was inherited by Elizabeth Stoney's grandson.

Thomas George Stoney was most generous in the offer he made to the Commissioners for National Education when he wrote to them from Kyle Park on 13 February 1843.

> I therefore, apply to the Commissioners of Education for a grant of two hundred pounds in aid of the expenses of the erection of suitable buildings, the cost of which

I estimate at £300, to accommodate what may be expected as the average attendance of children, namely 80 boys and 50 girls for whom two rooms would be required.

I beg respectfully to add that in the event of this application being complied with it is my intention as Patron of said school to attach thereto a farm of six acres (Irish) to be cultivated under my management and under the Superintendence of a skilful Agriculturist to be employed and paid by the Committee of the Borrisokane Loan Fund Society, the rent of £1 per acre to be paid me out of the proceeds thereof. The surplus of said proceeds to be applied to the uses of the said school generally, the work of the farm to be carried out by a senior class of boys who shall have instruction in the improved system of agriculture imparted to them by the Agriculturist. At the same time not holding the Commissioners of Education in any wise accountable for the rent of the said farm or for the expenses thereof – only asking that the Agriculturist may be accommodated with apartments in said building.

The next step was for the Commissioners to obtain an official report on the application for aid towards the proposed school. This was duly furnished in March 1843. It named Thomas George Stoney as 'patron and correspondent' and the title of the school as 'Kyle Park Agricultural School'. The report went as follows.

The quantity of ground required will be given. It is a healthy situation for a schoolhouse. The plot will be enclosed with a wall. Plot is 6 acres. It is not portion of a Church, Chapel or Meeting House. It is not in connection with any religious establishment. Nearest Post Town is Borrisokane 2 1/4 miles.

Thomas George Stoney, Proprietor in fee of the ground. Lease 3 lives or 31 years. Ground liable to rent of 1*s*. p.a.

Trustees not yet chosen. Their names will be forwarded to office in a few days.

Pupils

80 males and 70 females, but 156 may be expected to attend the school. The population of the parish is large – exact amount not known. By far the greater portion has need of such a school. There is no committee.

The value of £100 sterling at the least will be contributed by the applicant in cash and building materials towards the erection of the schoolhouse which will be kept in repair by the patron of the school. A great and obvious necessity exists for the building of a schoolhouse.

The names of other such National Schools and correspondents for the poor within a radius of 3 mile are

Borrisokane National School – not vested.

Borrisokane Church – not vested.

The Parish Priest has been consulted and has no objection. Did not communicate with Rector as the Protestant clergy will not participate in the establishment of a National School. (Scriptures not taught).

A copy of the Trust Deeds have been presented to the applicant (in the absence of Trustees) which he is willing to execute and will observe the rules thereon set forth.

The portion of Lower Ormond in which Kyle Park is situated is almost entirely destitute of a well regulated school – and in a sadly backward state with regard to literary and moral education. We have interviewed the Patron of the school and we recommend that this application be favourably entertained.

No other individual has been communicated with personally on the subject.

Special Report for Board

B.O. 20/4/43. Grant £200 on expenditure of cash £300 on lease of 3 lives or 31 years including privies and furniture. The whole of the School Premises, the Farm Buildings and Teacher's Residence (but not the Farm itself) to be vested in trustees.

Mr. Stoney's detailed plan of building is approved. The School Room to be 30 feet x 18 feet x 10 feet high to accommodate 90 children and usual conditions – 8 desks. 2 rooms 30 feet x 18 feet each. To call for plan when payment claimed.

Stoney's elegant design won a Silver Medal at the Exhibition of the Royal Agricultural Society in Dublin in 1844.

Underway

Kyle Park school opened on 14 Oct 1844, with teachers John Nevin and Frances Nevin, aged 26 years and 24 years respectively. Their salaries were to be £15 and £12 per annum. John had been properly trained in Marlborough St Training College, Dublin. It was unusual to have such a qualified person in a rural school. Frances may have been untrained. Both were Roman Catholics. Previously they taught at Eglish female national school in King's County (Offaly). It is not known if they were brother and sister or husband and wife – more likely the latter.

Thomas G. Stoney's official report of 23 October to the Commissioners noted that as no local funds were yet available for salaries the scholars paid one penny a week on average. There were two schoolrooms and a female workroom. The report confirmed the size of the schoolrooms – 30 feet x 18 feet, with a workroom measuring 22 feet x 14 feet 6 inches.

His report also stated than an average of 138 males and 210 females had been present each week since opening of school. It concluded optimistically that 'it is expected that numbers will increase to 100 males and 100 females'.

One year later Thomas G. informed the Board that he intended dismissing John Nevin for having made a false statement 'and for general inattention to his duty as a teacher'. He said he also intended dismissing the mistress. He was told by the Board that he had the right of dismissal if he disapproved of a teacher.

At this point Thomas G. proposed to the Board the appointment of an agriculturist at a salary of £30 per annum and retaining John Nevin as his assistant. The Board more or less agreed to this but stipulated that they would only grant the salary after a due trial of the appointee. They stalled on approving the salary for John Nevin unless the daily average of attendance was in excess of 100 pupils.

There is correspondence in the *Nenagh Guardian* of 28 June 1845 regarding Mr Stoney's move to appoint an agricultural teacher. It appears that Stoney put an advertisement in a newspaper called the *Monitor* for a 'headmaster ... whose especial office will be the agricultural department. Salary – £30 per annum from the National Board and £20 from the patron, with apartments and fuel. ... None but Protestants need apply etc.' I note that the Borrisokane Loan Fund is no longer mentioned.

The leading article entitled 'Romish Assurance' in the *Nenagh Guardian* of that date begins:

> That portion of the Press of Ireland which advocates the political treason of Repeal and the sectarian supremecy of Romanism assumes to itself a right of dictation ... respecting the conduct of a private man.

It goes on to attack those who have accused Stoney of bigotry in his advertisement. Mr Stoney's letter to the *Monitor* in which he justifies his advertisement is an excellent letter and, to my mind, does justify his wish for a Protestant teacher. He already had two RC teachers, the Nevins, and, as he hoped to have Protestant children attending the school, he felt it only right that there should be a Protestant teacher to teach them their religion. He writes:

> furthermore, having on former occasions published advertisements which did not contain the limitations as to religious profession, I felt most painfully circumstanced in being afterwards obliged to decline the services of Roman Catholics who offered, placing me in a position which I, on this present occasion, determined to avoid.

In July 1845 Robert Smyth, a highly qualified agriculturist, a native of Scotland and recently employed on the Tyrone estate of the earl of Aberdeen, was appointed to Kyle Park school. But soon Stoney was complaining to the Board again – this time about the conduct of Frances Nevin, who, he said, 'employed one Bess Peters, a reputed dealer in witchcraft, to restore them their butter which had been spirited away by some persons'. The Board again assured him that he had the right to dismiss an unsatisfactory teacher, so Frances was duly removed.

Closed

The autumn of 1845 brought the first season of the dreaded potato blight. In July of 1846, when failure of the potato crop was again being forecast, Thomas G. felt compelled to abandon his ambition of an agricultural school. However, the Commissioners of Education informed him that they had no powers to 'release the Trustees from the Covenant in the lease by which they were bound to keep open the school as a Model Agricultural School'. Nevertheless, Stoney went ahead and terminated Robert Smyth's employment in September 1846. The school seems to have been closed altogether between May and October 1847.

Three more teachers now make an appearance – Patrick Darragh, who was kept for only a short period, James Neville, a trainee agriculturalist, and Thomas Madden who, though a qualified agricultural teacher, was appointed as literary teacher.

1850 saw the introduction of an innovative 'industrial class' on the recommendation of the Agricultural Inspector. The class was to consist of six pupils who would receive six shillings a week for their labour. A grant of £30 was also made available so that boarding pupils could be taken. A John McCabe and Anthony Barnes were the first two pupils to come on to this scheme as boarders on the recommendation of the Inspector.

The Dowlings

January 1851 saw the appointment of two new literary teachers, John and Elizabeth Dowling – presumably to replace Thomas Madden. John's recommended pay was £10 per annum in addition to his classed salary and boys' school fees. Elizabeth was to receive £7 per annum, plus her classed salary and school fees from the girls. The Dowlings were given living accommodation in the school which extended to 'a parlour, bedroom, kitchen, with a bedroom overhead for a servant'. The agriculturist was provided with a similar suite of rooms.

front elevation

Plan of Kyle Park Agricultural School, 1844
Designed by Thomas G. Stoney
Copy made by Desmond Fogarty, Annagh, 1997

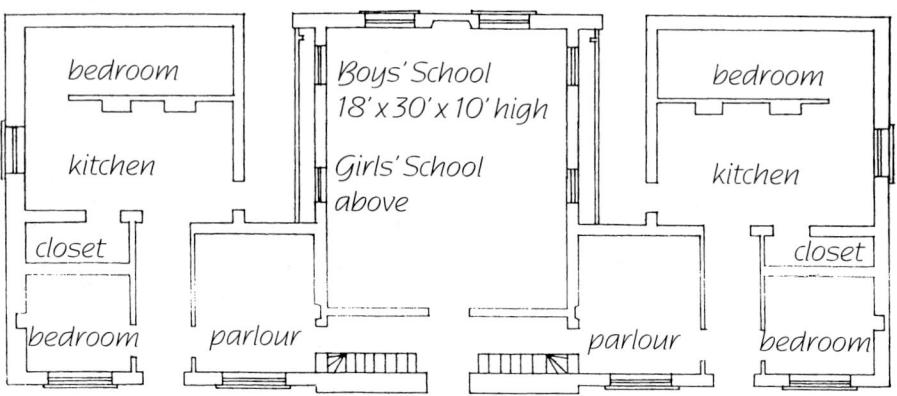

From a report made by James Neville to the Agricultural Inspector we can see that Stoney's ambition was being realised. The farm of sixteen acres, it was stated, was divided into four more or less equal parts. Crops sown were potatoes, turnips and mangolds, as well as wheat, oats and barley. A crop of flax is also mentioned. The school had four cows, two calves, a pig and a pony. There was also a good collection of farm implements, tools and other items. Extra labour to work the farm was employed, as the pupils, who were receiving instruction in agricultural methods, did not do the regular farm work. There were about eight 'agricultural students' at this time.

Sometime in 1850 Thomas George Stoney transferred the function of patron to his brother Rev. Ralph Stoney, rector of Terryglass. The school must have been a great drain on Thomas G.'s resources. He lost the rent of his poor tenants who could not pay and became involved in a major famine relief scheme trying to drain the Ballyfinboy river. It was said that at one time he had hundreds men employed on it. He became bankrupt. In the *Nenagh Guardian* of 1851 we find an advertisement headed

In Chancery

In the matter of R. Hewitt, Solicitor, Petitioner
Thomas George Stoney Respondent ... on Friday 11th April 1851 ... in my Chambers Inns Quay County of Dublin ... to let to the highest bidder for 7 years three lots (1) Kyle Park with house and lands 356 acres, corn mill worked by stream; (2) Ballycasey 52 acres etc; (3) Bonaguga 34 acres.

As there was no further mention of T. G. in relation to the school I thought he might have died. I wrote to his great-great-grandson, also Thomas George Stoney, who lives in Cork and with whom I was put in touch by Mrs Alice Gloster, formerly Minchin and whose mother was a Stoney. Mr Stoney of Cork never knew his ancestor had built the school at Kyle Park in spite of the fact that his own father had attended the school before going to Tipperary Grammer School.

But he supplied the reason for his ancestor's disappearance. It appears he left his wife and family and went away with another woman. However, his great-great-grandson, who had only discovered this through a letter from a descendant of his second family, requested me not to publish the facts – and I promised not to.

In the meantime I discovered that the facts were actually in the public domain in the Kyle Park area and elsewhere. It appears that the house in Kyle Park, in which a near neighbour of mine in Coolbawn, Marina Cleary (née Tierney), was born and reared, was built by Thomas George Stoney for his mistress.

It was also well-known that he and his wife, Anna Waller, had not get on and that he had formed a liaison with the beautiful daughter of a blacksmith who lived in the forge at Kyle Park. Her family may have been from Scotland.

Thomas G. built the house for her opposite the forge. John Tierney, Macloon, bought it in 1932 and all the Tierneys – four girls and Rev. Tadhg – were born there. The house had one room which had no door. It is now owned by the Hough family who have renovated it completely.

It is not known for certain, but it is likely that this was the lady with whom he settled in Co. Roscommon. Local tradition is that they already had children before leaving Kyle Park.

When I found out all this I told it to Mr Stoney in Cork and he released me from my promise, since it was known locally and of some historical interest.

Having gone bankrupt, T. G. Stoney was fortunate, unlike some of his neighbours, in not having to sell off his estates in the Encumbered Estates Courts. Instead, he merely leased his three properties for seven years. At the end of that period, 1878, Anna and whatever children were left, returned to Kyle Park where she lived until her death in May 1880, aged 75 years. At her own request she was buried in Finnoe alongside her father, Thomas Waller.

The Stoney direct connection with the school was finally severed in 1855 when, on the death of Rev. Ralph Stoney, management was passed on to Rev. James Phelan, parish priest of Borrisokane, later followed by Rev. John Meagher. However, the Stoney family were still the landlords.

Under Rev. Ralph in the 1850s

The literary Dowlings and agriculturist James Neville became embroiled in petty disputes over pupil access to study rooms, parties thrown by Neville, and borrowed pieces of furniture. The inspector had to come down and examine these complaints. The outcome was that Neville was dismissed and a Matthew Ryan appointed at a salary of £36 per annum with an extra £11 for board. He and the Dowlings seem to have had a good working relationship.

However, by 1853 trouble loomed again. This time Ryan's 'neglect of the accounts' brought a fine and admonishment from the Commissioners and ultimately dismissal. A Patrick Stephens took up duty in February 1854 on the same terms as Ryan had.

The Dowlings resigned in August 1855 and their going closed the literary section of the school until the following February when John and Kate Gallagher were appointed.

Patrick Stephens fell foul of the Commissioners of Education in 1860 arising from the fact that he also had a farm near the school. His position in the school was terminated by them.

Michael Costelloe, an agriculturist based in Co. Donegal, now comes on the scene. In December 1860 it was decided to let the school to him at a rent of £16 per year. The conditions stated he was to receive a salary for giving instruction in agriculture and have use of the house and furniture. Costelloe ran the agricultural side of the school until that aspect finished in 1875 and his position terminated. It had not grown during his tenure. The Commissioners decided to sell off the farm vested in them. Costelloe was the only bidder and got it for the sum of £30.

In 1909 Martin Costelloe became the accepted tenant after Michael's death. The fee simple of the farm was purchased outright by John Costelloe in 1917.

The Commissioners of Education records of 1858 show that salary was granted to John Connors and John Carroll as Senior Monitors from 1 November 1856. As already stated in the previous section, when Kilbarron Boys' School closed in 1874 my father, Patrick Carroll, and other boys from the school transferred to Kyle Park school and remained there until Kilbarron re-opened in 1878.

Richard Meredith, who taught in Kilbarron Boys' School until he retired, also taught in Kyle Park for some time, leaving in 1873.

After the farm was sold Kyle Park seems to have become an ordinary national school, but it did continue to have a garden. John Doorley, Nenagh, uncle to Bess Moran, Borrisokane, taught the boys gardening.

Other teachers after the Gallaghers included a Miss McArt who resigned in 1937. Before she did she commissioned James ('Guardian') Cahalan to replace the old rotting windows of the school at her own expense. She was succeeded by Anne Harrihill, Borrisoleigh. The following year she married Jimmy Kelly, Borrisokane, and remained as principal until retirement in 1977. Thomas G. Stoney's award-winning design had ceased as a school in 1953 when a new one was erected on a nearby site.

Mrs Anne Kelly was succeeded by Gwen Darcy (now Mrs Cooney), Borrisokane, who continues to teach in what is now a one-teacher school.

Sources:
Reports of the Commissioners of National Education, National Archives, Dublin.
Diary of George Stoney, Arran Hill, privately held.
Correspondence with Thomas G. Stoney, Cork.
Memorial Inscriptions, Borrisokane C. of I. church, and gravestone, inscriptions Finnoe graveyard.
Bess Moran, Borrisokane, Marina Tierney Cleary, James Cahalan.
Nenagh Guardian files.
TNFH Research Centre.

Photographs: p. 100 loaned by Thomas G. F. Stoney, Cork; p. 107 taken by Paddy Carroll.

The former Kyle Park Agricultural School and later National School

5
How We Were

The Kilbarron end of the modern parish is big and stretches from Finnoe Cross to Luska bay. Since the present church was built at New Chapel in 1814, and before roads improved and means of transport became more available, people who lived a long distance from the church, and children who lived a long way from the national school, would take any available short-cut through the fields.

Most areas had recognised Mass paths – which served also as school paths but for convenience we shall call them all Mass paths. Many of these took the travellers across farmers' fields. This was not strictly legal but was such an accepted tradition that no farmer would dare plough a field which contained a Mass path. After World War II, when bicycles and other forms of conveyances, such as traps and motor cars. became commonplace, and the government was keen to have land reclaimed, tilled and sown with crops, this tradition died out and fields, which had been fallow for generations, if not centuries, were ploughed up.

School Path to Puckane
This path was an exception to the rule. People who lived on the Annagh road, Carrick, Luska and Ballycolliton, were in the parish of Kilbarron and so were obliged to go to Mass in that parish or the parish priest would want to know why! However, the children went to school in Puckane which was closer, in fact quite near across the fields.

The following is the account written for me by Mrs Annie Burke (née Whelan) of Carrigagown, formerly of Annagh, of their journey to school. This particular path can still be walked.

> People would sometimes go to Mass in Puckane using the path. You started on the Kilbarron side of the Ballycolliton river on the road between Whelan's house and Ellen Lynch's, now demolished, but the site is on Pat Cleary's land. The bridge across the river was a small, wooden one just for foot traffic and known as the 'Craobh'. Originally, I suppose, they would simply throw a large branch of a tree across the river and pick their way over it, *craobh* being the Irish word for branch.
>
> Once across the river you were in Puckane parish and went through land belonging to Gleesons of Peterfield, then through the lands of Johnstown owned by the Headech family. The Ballycolliton river flows into the Shannon at Luska Bay.
>
> The fields they passed through each had its own name – the Rabbit Park, which Annie assumes got its name from the plenitude of rabbits it accommodated; next the Wilderness, renowned for its fine timber of oak and walnut. The Church Meadow was named after Killodiernan pre-Reformation church; the graveyard and Headech's house came next. Then came Keane's Field, where someone

named Keane had once lived, then by Coen's farm down the lane and out at Johnstown lodge – now Teach an Gheata, the well-known craft shop run by the Walsh family whose mother was Julia Coen.

At the time of which Annie is speaking – the late 1920s and early 1930s – it was the residence of George Hodgins and Fanny Thomas. I always heard it referred to as 'Fanny Thomas's'. Later it was the residence of Mrs Fox, a member of the Keane family of the Frolic, and her son Michael. Other houses passed on the way were Jim Egan's, now the home of the McGrath family, and Paddy Coen's. Paddy Coen's grandmother was Vina Costelloe of Lisquillibeen, the eldest of the Costelloe family.

Mass Path from Lisquillibeen to Kilbarron village.

The path started from the entrance gate to Carroll's yard. You then went over the stile into Starr's field and along the path that led to the Black Castle field on Costelloe's land, keeping the castle on your right, and then on to Casey's callow. You then crossed the stream by stepping stones on to Waller's Hill (now Burke's). You continued to the Sand Pit field, then on to the White Stick Gate, and over a double stile into the Pump field. You then skirted the field, which is now the new cemetery, the path going down by Hannigan's (then Donoghue's) side of the field.

People from Annagh, Carrick, Luska and Ballycolliton, had quite a long way to come before arriving at Carroll's yard and would drive in their horse carts or donkey carts as far as there, then leave them and take the path to Mass.

I have heard many stories of mitching from school, or 'schaming' (scheming) as it used to be called in this area, which took place on that heavenly walk from home to school.

Mass Path from Gurteen and Rodeen to Kilbarron Village

Leaving O'Meara's of Gurteen you went first through Big Field and Connor's Field, then into Gurteen Lane and into Brereton's field known as the Hilly Field. You then passed Ring Grove, went across a tributary of the Ballyfinboy river at a spot known as the Hunting Bridge or the Ford. This tributary leads from Loch Avon to the Swallow Hole in Coreling. You then went into one field in the townland of Kilcowran and then through four fields in Kylebeg. You came out at the left of where the parish hall stands now, then down a path through a field of Mark Bourke's and across the road to the 'old' Girls' School of 1858-1941, now the small hall.

Mass Path from Curraghmore to Kilbarron

This came through Castletown. May Tierney (née Grady) told me that Gradys and Clearys used it. They came into Castletown avenue at the sheds and walked on to Coolbawn Cross where we would often meet them and go on together.

Mass Path from Bellevue to Kilbarron

There was a stile opposite Bruce's little wicket gate and we went up through two of Bruce's fields, now owned by Tommy Slattery, then on through two of Sterling's (then Towers') fields and through Michael Carroll's Whittaker's field and out over a stile and on to the road at the ruins of a house known as Dick Meredith's.

In the summer when the grass was long we would tie the blades of grass across the path to trip the ones coming after us!

The long-gone ruins were of the house belonging to schoolmaster Richard Meredith. He taught my father who was a monitor under him in the 1880s. It was said he was the illegitimate son of a scion of one of the gentry families who provided him with enough education to become a schoolmaster. I do not know if he had the formal Marlborough St training, but I think not. On the roadside outside his house was a well, known as Meredith's well, where we used refresh ourselves after the dusty walk from school. A stream from it ran across the road into the field opposite. Well and stream have disappeared, probably having gone underground where they appear every winter in the form of a lake in the field opposite. This lake soon disappears.

Modes of Transport
Until nearing the end of the nineteenth century the peasantry walked everywhere. Bicycles appeared and some people were fortunate enough to possess one. My father cycled home from Wicklow to Brookfield in 1889 when his mother died. He often did this journey by bicycle, later with his dog either trotting beside him or sitting on the handlebars.

The gentry had carriages and other vehicles such as phaetons, dog carts (for carrying the dogs) and back-to-back traps. A strong farmer would have a horse or two to ride and pull the plough and draw what was known as a 'common cart'. Up to about 1900 farmers attended funerals on horseback. People walked great distances. There were vehicles called brakes which served the purpose of today's coaches. They resembled very large pick-up trucks with seats and were pulled by a pair of horses, or maybe three, and were used to take people to hurling matches, political meetings and other such outings.

Gradually the rural population acquired various means of transport depending on their stations in life. My aunt Eliza in Brookfield kept a donkey and car to drive her father to Mass and any necessary outing to town, or to visit a relative. The better-off farmer would take his family to Mass in the common car. Sometime in the latter half of the nineteenth century what became known as the 'side' or 'outside' car was introduced. This was soon in universal use and most strong farmers would have one. When speaking or writing of a 'car', in the context of the late nineteenth century and early twentieth century Ireland, a side car is meant, just as when one speaks of a car now one means a motor car.

By the time we came, as very small children, to live in Coolbawn the side car was giving way to the round or 'tub' trap. One did not buy a trap as one buys a car today. It was built by a coachbuilder. My father ordered a trap from Culberts of Nenagh who were the local coachbuilders. I remember we were very excited when our new trap was driven into the yard for the first time. While waiting for the trap to be built we were taken to Mass and to Borrisokane in our aunt's sidecar. Our aunt lived next door. They had a mare called Dolly who pulled it. I loved riding on the sidecar behind Dolly who stepped out smartly. It was much more exciting than the staid trap. It was so high up and you could see everything going by.

I made my first trip to Borrisokane on Aunt Anne's (Moran's) sidecar when I was four; it was by far the most exciting expedition of my life. No trip to the moon could equal that journey as I sat perched on the coachman's seat, my cousin Martin driving, as we swayed through the Commons of Carney. In Borrisokane we had lemonade and biscuits in Houghs (now Seymours). Mrs Hough (née Ryan) had been born in the house we lived in, in Coolbawn.

Some traps were bigger than others and meant to be pulled by a big horse, others were for ponies and there were smaller ones to be drawn by donkeys. Some were more elegant than others. A rubber-tyred trap was a status symbol – like having an élite brand of motor car today. Ours did not have rubber tyres.

The first two motor cars in the district were at Castletown and Lesserragh. The Castletown car was a large yellowish tourer with the soft roof always open. The Lesserragh car was black of the same make. Neither owner ever passed a child on the way to or from school without giving him or her a lift. My uncle, Peter Carroll, Brookfield, had the next car – a very temperamental Model T-Ford. He used it to go to Nenagh to County Council meetings of which he was a Labour member and also to transport hampers of rabbits to the railway station for export to England.

From a seat on or in all these vehicles one had a grand view of houses, bridges, mills, hills, crossroads and every other possible landmark. Thus one was familiar with every inch of the road travelled. One even got to know the road better than when walking.

Hills on the road were important as the animal had to put more effort into his task, as would the cyclist and walker. So every hill on the road had a name. These usually came from the name of a family which at one time, often a couple of centuries ago, had lived there.

I had always assumed that everyone knew these familiar names of hills and other landmarks. I had forgotten the change in people's lifestyles and happened to mention in the presence of my youngest niece that a house was being built on Onny Dunne's hill. She looked at me in wonder, 'Onny Dunne's hill? Where's that?'; she had never heard of it. I then realised that the children and not just the children but the virtually middle-aged people of today had never walked the roads of the parish or even cycled them and had no knowledge of the names of these landmarks. Children have been going to school by bus and driving elsewhere in motor cars with their parents for at least two generations.

A few of the hill names which come to mind in Kilbarron are:

Onny Dunne's hill just before you come to Kilbarron village coming from the Long Lane Cross.

Crone's hill on the Bellevue road just after Eoin Slattery's new house and before you come to Tommy Slattery's. This hill was alive with ghost stories – so much so that we were afraid to pass there after dark. It had the proverbial great black dog with wild red eyes, a headless pedestrian or two and a 'walking dresser'. We imagined the dresser waddling up and down the hill complete with dishes and other accoutrements. When we came to have some sense we realised that our neighbour, Tim Ryan, had invented the stories.

Mick Donoghue's hill, sometimes called Hogan's Hill, went from Jerry Carroll's house to the entrance to Lisquillibeen lane. Hogans did have a public house where Jerry Carroll's house stands and I suppose at some stage a Mick Donoghue lived alongside the hill. There were many houses along that road early in the nineteenth century.

Kane's hill or Poulavickdeeragh hill is on the road to Ballinderry. Matt Costello's house, formerly Whelan's, is beside it.

Long Lane hill stretches from the Long Lane Cross – half way between Coolbawn and Kilbarron village – on to Burke's house, which used to be Paddy Smith's and before that Robert Waller's farm yard. Ordnance Surveyor John O'Donovan, writing in 1840, makes quite a feature of the Long Lane. I had always understood that it was a road constructed as part of Famine relief and we were told that men got 6 pence a day for the work. O'Donovan described it thus: 'In the centre of the townland of Clonmackilladuff, about 5 miles w.s.w. of Borrisokane, a straight part of a road finely shaded with large trees'.

So far I have written the names of hills on roads only. Kilbarron is hilly – unlike Terryglass – and I understand the highest point in the parish is the King's hill, lying beyond the Comenthus. Those whose parents lived through the Boer War (1899-1902) called it Spion Kop for the same reason that the Lahorna hurling team called themselves the Lahorna De Wets. De Wet was a famous Boer general and Spion Kop was an equally famous South African hill which the British took weeks to capture. Anti-British feeling was quite strong in Ireland in relation to the Boer War, as the bitter fight for Irish land was not yet over. Pamela Hinkson .gives a vivid description of the view from the King's hill, as seen from horseback, in her book written in Drominagh, *Irish Gold*.

Needham's hill is the old Knockballyea straddling Lisquillibeen and Clonmackilladuff, with the Loughawn in the valley between, and looking down over Coolbawn. It must have been Cnocbaileaodh/the hill of the townland of Hugh away back in the time of the O'Kennedys. The hill is crowned by 'Thade's Castle'.

Costelloe's hill, now topped by the great reservoir of the regional water scheme which sends water to Nenagh and other areas from Lough Derg, looks out over the lake to Islandmore with Tountinna and the Arra hills and the shores of Galway and its hills beyond – surely one of the most splendid views in the whole, wide world. The Costelloes lived there until recently.

Barry's hill, between Carrick townland and Luska bay. There is a quarry and a lime kiln on this hill. As the Costelloes had not been there for more than a century and a half, and the Barrys for far less, the hills must have had some older names.

Field Names

Fields get their names in different ways. The most common is the name of a person who owned it or lived there at one time. These names change as the ownership of the fields change but many go back to the Famine when people either gave up their holdings and emigrated or just died. The field or garden would then be taken over by a neighbour and the name of the old owner of the field would be kept. Some of the names are those of quite recent owners.

For example *Whittaker's Field*, opposite Tony Halifax's house (formerly Needham's), was a Waller divide given to John and Mary Hogan (a bonesetter), who lived in a cottage now known as Coonan's garden opposite Whittaker's. The Hogans had no family so a Whittaker nephew – a sister's child – in England inherited it and sold it to the present owner. Other fields in the Coolbawn and Lisquillibeen areas get their names from long-dead owners – *Ned Healy's* (pronounced Haley), *Kelly's Gardens*, *Feeney's*.

Other fields got their names from their shapes, e.g. the *Fiddle* in Terryglass; the *Sleeve* on Needham's hill, which is the only cleared place on the hillside and, looking at it from Coolbawn, does look like a sleeve; the *Bell* and the *Handkerchief* in Slevoir, Terryglass. The *Sleeve* is now overgrown.

In the Terryglass area, especially around Slevoir, there are fields which indicate the uses to which they had once been put, or where they were near. There is the *Stockyard* near the haggard, the *Cot* joining the lake where the little boat or 'cot' was kept; the *Chapel Garden* near the church; *Orchard Park* adjoining the orchard; *Paddy's Field* named after a Spanish ass belonging to the Hickies who ended his days there; *Shannon Grove* field near a wood between it and the lake; the *Lodge Field* at the back of Slevoir gate lodge; the *Cottage Field*, which is the next field to Slevoir steward's cottage. There are field names which cannot be explained, or are self-explanatory, e.g. *America*, the *Piper's Rock, Dick's Fort, Gough's* in Michael Fogarty's farm, the *West Hill, Kilkee,* the *Sugar Gardens, Dancers*, the *Burrow*, the *Terrace. O'Briens Field* was the local hurling field.

Other names go back to the time when Irish was spoken, e.g. the *Kosheer*; the *Slig Field*, meaning a slatey, stony place. It contained a lot of sligs or flagstones. *Snáile*; the *Inches*; the *Reiske* meaning marshy pasture; *Poor Field*; *Cooleen* meaning little corners or haggard end. The name *Carrigeen* occurs regularly, meaning a little rocky field. The *Dispensary Field* is near Drominagh and goes back to the time when Dr William Ledger Biggs and his son, Dr Edward, had a dispensary there.

Hill Names in Terryglass
As Terryglass is much less hilly than Kilbarron there are not as many hill names. Some examples are Burke's hill at Knockanleen. Knockanleen itself must have been the original name as Knock/cnoc means a hill. It must have been the hill of the *faileen*: cliff. Sydney's hill at Gortmore after the family who lived there; Glennon's hill at Clooniniha; Flannery's hill at Roran; Heenan's hill at Crossanagh; Hough's hill at Newlawn; Bollard's hill at Firmount; Firmount hill at Firmount; Barry's hill at Ashgrove.

Rambling
There was little else to do in the long winter evenings except go 'rambling' – or 'cuardaidheacht' as it is called in some areas. Groups of neighbours would gather in a particular house round the burning turf and log fire, the hearth swept and the lamp lit. Every kitchen had the same open hearth with a timber form in each corner. These were favourite spots, often occupied by the owner and his wife. Most houses had regular ramblers. The men smoked their pipes, spat and reminisced. Live coals would be picked up and pressed into the bowl of the pipe with a roughened forefinger. Ghost stories were told. I have heard of people who were almost afraid to go home after listening to these tales. But it was not only ghost or fairy stories. It was by telling and retelling that stories of past wars, tragic incidents, local incidents, ballads and poetry were passed on from generation to generation, not always accurately and often embellished, but nevertheless preserved in the folk memory. Card playing was a popular pastime in many houses.

People who had read the local newspaper would recount what was in it. Some houses had music and dancing. Fiddles and melodeons would be played and sets and quadrilles danced on the flag or earthen floor.

Girls and women did not 'ramble' as a rule, but would go to a neighbour's when there was dancing and music. For the generation before mine a great rambling

Paddy Ryan, nephew of Mick's, a master accordion player and builder.

house was Slattery's beside Kilbarron old graveyard.

In summer much of the dancing was at the crossroads on the 'boards' or platforms. These were usually made from lengths of timber, but one or two were concrete. Different locations enjoyed favour at different times – sometimes it might be Coolbawn, other times Lahorna or Carney. I remember the summer of 1939, just before World War II broke out – Lahorna was in full swing. However, it was the Coolbawn boards that were most familiar to us. The late Mick Ryan of Ballyscanlan was one of the chief musicians. He would sit, with head back and eyes closed, on the wall behind the pump, playing for the sets and quadrilles and the popular music of the day for the waltzes and foxtrots.

The Gentry

Adding extra colour to our lives in Coolbawn were the comings and the goings of the residents of the Big Houses – Minchins, Bruces, Towers, Biggs and Parker-Reeves. Each house still kept a gardener and two or three indoor servants. Every Saturday evening the gardener from each Big House went up to the Protestant church to mow the grass on 'their' family's grave and generally make the place smart for Sunday. The result was a beautifully kept graveyard – just like a park, and in sad contrast to our own overgrown burial ground beside the 'old abbey'.

On Sundays the gentry usually walked to church. We enjoyed these parades. Funerals were the real highlights in our lives, as were Harvest Thanksgiving when people from the neighbouring parishes of Finnoe and Killodiernan came in various conveyances, some of which were put up in our yard. Funerals were still quite grand with plumed horse-drawn hearses. An additional treat when a funeral was over was going to the graveyard to admire the exotic wreaths and crosses spread out over the new grave.

At this time the church was cleaned by Onnie Kennedy. Onnie was a Protestant and lived in a little house on the Castletown estate quite near the lakeshore at Skehanagh. All traces of her house are now gone. Onnie came once a week to do her job. She called at Moran's on her way up to get the key, to us on the way back, and always had a cup of tea and then to Molamphy's shop to get her messages and, of course, to visit and probably drink tea again. She was quite old then, perhaps seventy years, but was trim and upright. She dyed her hair and wore a navy-blue serge costume with a long, fitted jacket and full skirt down to her toes. With this went a high-necked lace blouse, a cameo brooch and the rather low-crowned, wide-brimmed hat of the pre-1914 period fastened with hatpins. She had twinkling dark eyes and pouchy cheeks. Her brother Jim lived in the little house near the pump at Coolbawn Cross.

Onnie's grandniece, Kitty, sometimes 'minded' us and if Onnie were ill Kitty did the church cleaning, taking us with her. Kitty was a Catholic and Onnie, a

Protestant, was meticulous about seeing that she learned her catechism and prayers.

The church was different from ours – a different smell, beeswax I suppose, and an odour of leather book bindings and, perhaps, a faint lingering fragrance of the scent worn by the ladies on Sunday. It was darker than our chapel and so bare! No candles or smell of them, no statues or stations of the cross, but soft cushions on which to kneel. We would go up into the pulpit and pretend to preach. There was always a delicious feeling of doing something that was not quite right. Onnie was a true Christian, if you take the word to mean one who loves and gives. I always stand by her unmarked grave when I go up to the graveyard and think of her lying there amongst all the grand folk awaiting resurrection. That she lies there at all is a small footnote to our history. Her parents 'turned' during the 'bad' times.

The Pensioners

Living in the post office, as we did, gave us an opportunity of coming into contact with people of an earlier generation. Some of the very old coming for the pension must have been the very first to benefit from the Old Age Pensions Act introduced in 1908. This non-contributory pension for persons over 70 years was means tested so some got only got 2s 6d (12.5p) and others the maximum of 10s (50p). Friday night was pension night and was quite a sociable occasion for us. We had to hurry and get the supper over, tidy up as the pensioners would sit around the fire, drink tea, chat and tell stories. However, women rarely came, their pensions being fetched by sons or other relatives.

I can still remember quite few of the pensioners. Rode Cleary, Curraghmore, was a very tall man and wore a sort of a round-crowned hat. He rarely sat down but lit his pipe and paced the floor holding forth on most subjects. Jim Kennedy, Onnie's brother, came during the day and did not visit. He shuffled along very fast with the aid of a stick. He had a full beard and I think we were slightly afraid of him. Tom Hough, Lisquillibeen, another big man with a beard, also came during the day, but we liked him. He called us 'the babbies' and gave us 6d (2.5p). He never walked around by the road but came over the hill. As he got older he came by road with the ass and cart but walked beside it and only brought it in case he needed to be carried!

Another pension-collecting character was Tom Maher, Kevanstown, who came in the daytime for his mother's. He 'skipped' around the kitchen in the exuberance of describing the performance of his Raleigh racing bicycle. He could do 'Borris and Nenagh in one day'. His mother was one of the few old ladies still wearing Victorian dress – a bonnet beaded with jet, and a black cape, which was the fashion in the time of Queen Victoria who had died in 1901. Most elderly women wore the Edwardian type of dress – big hats, fitted jackets and full skirts. The hats had to be constantly retrimmed and freshened up as they could no longer be bought.

Travellers

Tramps and travellers loomed large in our lives. We had tramps who came on a regular basis. Jimmy Casey was our most constant and familiar one. He carried a sack in which he collected potatoes which he would sell when he got to a town. We understood that he had a house somewhere where he spent the winter. Then there was the lady tramp called 'Trouble you too much', because she began her request for help that way. She was always laden with bags and parcels.

The travellers were different – they travelled in convoys of cars, carts, loose ponies and asses. As they travelled so widely they would sometimes bring news of friends or relatives in distant parts. One particular man, who frequented north Co. Galway for the horse fairs, would bring my mother quite authentic news of her family, who lived near Tuam.

My favourite traveller was Jim Hutchinson who had served in the British Army in the Connaught Rangers regiment. He like to give his opinion on topical events. 'Sad about the poor ould Pope, mam', he remarked to my mother on the death of Pius XI. Jim always swept our chimney.

Another class of traveller was the pedlar. They had houses but went around the countryside in donkeys or ponies and cart – buying rabbit skins and selling delph and tin kettles. Skins, when removed from the rabbits, were hung on the fire crane to dry until the pedlar called. One regular pedlar took all our skins and kept us supplied with delph in return, after a bit of bargaining. Joe Carroll and his wife were also regular callers. They travelled in a donkey and cart and sold trinkets, hair slides and combs, as well as delph. They were always warmly welcomed and got tea. We had a fantasy that Joe was the last descendant of the head of our clan, the O'Carrolls of Ely.

Life in remote parishes like Kilbarron-Terryglass had hardly changed for centuries until the coming of the motor car and the outbreak of the first world war. My generation was just in time to get a whiff of the old pagan times as we listened to the stories of the old people and watched old customs. My mother never omitted to shake the Easter (deenach) water on newly-sown crops. This was an old pagan fertility rite given a veneer of Christianity. People still feared that their neighbours would take their crops.

You would not dare enter a kitchen where the churning was in progress without taking you turn at the churn, lest you be accused of 'taking the butter'. There are still many pagan customs about. My aunt used tell how one parish priest, Rev. John Kennedy, I think it was, threatened 'to quench the candles on the altar (i.e. stop saying Mass) unless the "pishoguery" ceased'.

Electricity and Steam
Electricity did not come to our parish until 1953. From crane and pot hooks over the open fire to the electric cooker was considerable progress. Up to then the baker or oven was used for all baking and roasting. It was placed on a nest of nice hot coals on the hearth. The bread or cake or meat was put in it. and some more hot coals placed on the lid. That was the easy part. The hard part came when you had to lift the lid to inspect the contents. You had to get the knack of balancing the lid in the tongs so that ash did not drop into the baker. It sometimes did.

We made our own butter, first with a dash churn until we graduated to an end-over-end one. Milk was set in large basins for about twenty-four hours. Then the cream was skimmed off and held in a large crock container until churning day.

Children were kept busy on Saturdays and during the school holidays. They had jobs like bringing in the cows, thinning turnips, sowing and picking potatoes, and helping at harvest time. Before the advent of the reaper and binder the corn was cut with an ordinary mowing machine and bound into sheaves by hand. I could never master the knotting of the straw rope one made to bind them.

The first steam threshing machine which I remember belonged to Lynchs of Carney Commons. Another important farming job was the spraying of potatoes with 'bluestone' to ward off the blight. This was usually done with a horse-drawn sprayer, whose owner moved from farm to farm. In our area Jimmy Brannigan, Rodeen did this. Patrick Kavanagh comes to mind:

> The flocks of green potato stalks/Were blossom spread for sudden flight,
> The Kerr's Pinks in a frivelled blue,/The Arran Banners wearing white.

Sources:
Mrs Annie Burke (née Whelan) of Carrigagown (school path to Puckane).
Donie and May O'Meara, Gurteen (Gurteen & Rodeen to Kilbarron path).
Jerry and Josephine Carroll and Mrs Jo Carroll Comerford, Borrisokane (Lisquillibeen to Kilbarron path).
Mick Molamphy, Snr (for Bellevue to Kilbarron path, plus author's personal memoir).
Author's personal memoirs.

Photographs: pp. 114. 117, 118, taken by Paddy Carroll.

Three harvesting scenes in Kilbarron, courtesy of Paddy Carroll

6
Families and Their Houses

Chapter 3, Castles and Tower Houses, showed that in the mid-seventeenth century the landowners in the three parishes were mostly of Gaelic origin, with the Kennedys owning the most. We have seen how Ireland was conquered by the Parliamentary/Cromwellian forces by the summer of 1652, and how this was followed by confiscation of the land of Catholic owners unable to provide proof of loyalty to the Cromwellian cause. We also saw the names of the persons confirmed in their ownership of these lands in our parish by the Act of Settlement of 1662.

In that list there is only one soldier confirmed as a settler – Captain Solomon Cambie who received approximately 915 acres in the parish of Kilbarron.

Sir Nicholas White, who was a substantial landowner in the area before the 1640 rebellion, recovered his property as an 'innocent Catholic'. A descendant of his figures in an interesting Cambie-Kennedy story.

The other recipient of interest to us for this chapter was John Briggs, who got land in Kilbarron parish in the region of 2,022 acres.

William Nolan, writing on 'Patterns of Living' in *Tipperary History and Society*, states that:

> ... between 1670 and 1850 a well defined suite of settlement features developed through Tipperary countryside. The Big House was sometimes found contiguous to the older skeletal remains of the castle. ... The term Big House denotes the fact that it was the house of a substantial and usually resident landlord, rather than its mere size.

The houses erected by the gentry in Kilbarron-Terryglass fit into the category of 'classical houses of the middle size', with the possible exception of Drominagh and Slevoir.

The identification of Big Houses with family names still persists in this area long after they have left. Older people still talk of Biggs of Bellevue, Towers of Castletown, Minchin of Annagh.

THE CAMBIES OF CASTLETOWN, BROOKFIELD, KILGARVAN

In 1920 a member of the Cambie family, Vancouver, wrote an account of the family's origins. He claimed that the family was descended from a 'David Cambie who was a Colonel in Queen Elizabeth's army and in charge of one of the ships which went against the Spanish Armada in 1588'. Colonel David, he stated,

> followed some of the Spanish vessels round the North of Scotland and along the West coast of Ireland and in Galway Bay took one of them. And from it he took

for himself the Spanish Captain's Sea Chest of red cedar, handsomely carved, which is still in the possession of the family of my brother A. J. Cambie in Vancouver B.C. and has always passed to the eldest son in each generation. They also have David Cambie's French Bible printed in Geneva in 1588.

The writer identifies Solomon of the Parliamentary/Cromwellian forces as David's son. He concludes the account with the statement that his brother's family had Solomon's sword.

Lalor Cambie Papers

However authentic the story of the Armada, we do have fully documented in the Lalor Cambie papers the background of the Kilbarron Cambies from the time they left France and came to England.

They were Huguenots (French Protestants) fleeing from persecution in France. The father of the Captain Solomon Cambie who received the grants of land in Ireland was also named Solomon and came from around Lille and Tournai in the northern region of France where he had been engaged in the cloth trade.

He arrived at Sandwich, England, in 1580 and later moved to Canterbury (there are references to them in relation to the cathedral there) and thence to Norwich in Norfolk where many of these 'Strangers', as they were called, had settled. They had their own church. This Solomon – the name, both as first name and surname, is spelt in various different ways – joined the church and in it married Esther Desbonnet, also a Huguenot. Their children, all born in Norwich, were: Solomon, 1613, John, 1615, Suzanne, 1617, and Elizabeth, 1618. The eldest son, Solomon, married Alice Craine of Norwich in the same church.

In Norwich the Cambies were merchants, specializing in the weaving and dyeing of cloth, even pioneering new dyeing methods. In 1593 a Gyles Cambie, a brother of Solomon the emigrant from France, got a testimonial from the Mayor of Norwich for 'dyeing, dressing and currying Norwich stuffs'. They made a great deal of money. In 1621 the name Solomon Cambre (sic) appears in the Militia Company of Officers in Norwich. After 1646 they all seem to have left Norwich as there is no more mention of them there. The last Cambie entry in Norwich is dated 1658.

When the Civil War broke out in England the Cambies were strongly on the side of parliament and the puritans. Markham, in his life of Fairfax, a famous Cromwellian general, mentions a Captain Cambie who served under the earl of Manchester at the battle of Marston Moor (1641). A David Cambie was a lieutenant in Cromwell's army under Major Nathaniel Barton in 1659.

The First Cambie in Ireland

Solomon Cambie (born 1613) and his wife Alice Craine brought his brother John with him to Ireland, also his sisters Suzanne and Elizabeth (who later married a Hatton from Gorey, Co. Wexford). As already told, according to the *Book of Survey and Distribution*, Captain Solomon Cambie drew land in Lisquillibeen (Tullaghan), Annagh, Ballycolliton, Kilbiller and Bundadubber in lieu of arrears for 'army service in Ireland'.

In the Census of 1659 Solomon Cambier (sic) Esq., is living in Annagh while a John Briggs Esq and a Marish Thomas, gent, are living in Castletown, which in time was to become synonmous with the name Cambie. Solomon Cambie was later to sell off his Annagh lands to Captain Charles Minchin. This transaction is recounted in the section below relating to Minchin of Annagh.

In the Hearth Money Rolls for 1665 Solomon Cambie has the only house with four hearths in the parish. In the 1666 roll he has five hearths and his brother John has two. These rolls were compiled under a 1662 act of parliament which lasted until 1793.

Solomon Cambie, stated to be of Ballycolliton and Annagh Castle, Co. Tipperary, his wife Alice, and his son, Samuel Cambie of Galway, were parties with William Cleburne of the city of Kilkenny, gent, to an indenture dated 20 July 1677, for the sale of 'Castletown, Ballyculleton, Killenboy, Kilbulloir [Kilbiller], Burnadubber and part of Annagh, with all the castles, towns, villages, lands, premises, their rights, marches & appurtenances situate in the Co. Tipperary' to the said William Cleburne, gent, his heirs & assigns forever. In another version of this indenture Castletown is not included.

The Cleburne Branch

The Cleburne family tree in John O'Hart's *The Irish and Anglo-Irish Landed Gentry*, shows this William (d.1682) was of St John's Manor, Wexford. He had two sons, William and Richard, and a daughter Mary. From the same source we learn that his son William of Ballycolliton Castle, married Solomon Cambie's daughter, Elizabeth, by whom he had one child, a daughter named Elizabeth, who was born on 22 May 1682 and died on 4 June 1682. The inscription on the stone which marks her grave in Kilbarron's pre-Reformation church is still legible and is reproduced in Chapter 2.

In view of the early demise of William Cleburne, aged 42 years, it is unlikely that there were any more children. However, the Cleburne name did survive in the area through his brother Richard, Bunadubber, whose grandson, John of Ballycolliton, Castletown and Springmount, married a Grace Palmer in the mid-1700s. Also, there is an Eleanor Cleburne, died 1787, interred in Knigh graveyard. The name hereabouts died out with Samuel Cleburne (1826-1907), who was married to Anna Minnitt, Annaghbeg,. and lived in Springmount, Cloghprior parish.

William Cleburne, Ballycolliton, had made a will, but its contents are not known apart from the request that he be buried in Kilbarron old cemetery – where his child was already buried.

After the return to the throne of King Charles II in 1660, Philip Kennedy, in common with several others, tried to get back Castletown and 200 acres but failed. Solomon Cambie's grants were confirmed, as were practically all others, by the Act of Settlement in 1662.

In contrast, those who had supported the Royalists in the Civil War in England mostly recovered their land on the restoration of the monarch. However, this did not happen widely in Ireland, although some persons did get all or portions back.

First Irish Cambie Offspring

No further information has come to light in the Kilbarron area about John Cambie, Captain Solomon's brother, other than his appearance in the Hearth Money Rolls. Solomon's eldest son, Samuel, also a captain and said to have fought in the siege of Limerick, went to Galway and became an alderman of that city.

The fact that Captain Cambie's wife was called Alice creates a puzzle as to the identity of the ladies whose names are on the gravestone in Cloghprior graveyard, which reads: 'Here lieth Mary the wife of Soloman Cambie deceased the 11 day of Feb 1684 and Rachel Harding his 2 Feb 1687'.

Captain Solomon's second son, **Solomon of Ballycolliton** (d. 1713), married Anne Minchin and had

1 **Thomas** (d. 1743), of Ballycolliton who seems not to have married.

2 **David of Kilbiller,** who married Anne, daughter of Edward and Elizabeth Ledger, Ballinderry. Their known issue were:

   1   Elizabeth, and

   2   George, both of whom are named in a deed of 1747.

3   **Solomon Ledger** Cambie of Brookfield and Castletown who, in 1762, married Elizabeth, daughter of William Ryan of Ballymackeogh, Newport. This Solomon L. died in 1792 and the children named below were mentioned in his 'last will and testament' in which he divided up the lands between his sons and left the sum of £1,000 to his daughter Catherine. His debts were to be paid by his executors, one of whom was his eldest son David, out of Solomon L.'s 'personal property'.

     i. David of Brookfield and Castletown, born in 1764, married Mary Walsh in 1799, and died in 1813.

     ii. Edward of Mota & Kilgarvan, born in 1768, married Eliza Watkins and died in 1836.

     iii. Richard [of Kilgarvan] born 1770, married Charlotte Ledger of Ballyrickard. In his will Solomon L. left Richard his interest in the Hill of Annagh, Carrick, Cameron, Meelick, Kilbarron and Glenbower. We have no definite follow-up on him but it seems likely he was the father of Catherine Cambie, described as a daughter of the late Richard, Sedgemore, Ardcroney, who died in 1838 aged 25 years. There is a child commemorated on a gravestone in Cloghprior – 'Richard William Camac Cambie died 1853 aged 17 years'. He could have been the above Richard's son, but agewise it is unlikely he was.

     iv. Thomas (who was blind) married Mary Lalor of Killoran, Moyne, near Thurles. He became a Catholic to marry her in 1798 and founded the Lalor Cambie branch of Killoran House, Moyne near Thurles. Mary was a daughter of Thomas Lalor who died in 1814. His Cambie grand-children of four boys and three girls were the main beneficiaries of his will made in 1812. In the will he made it a condition of the inheritance that the name Lalor be appended to their Cambie surname, which they did.

     v. Elizabeth married G. Lewis, Dysart, Queen's Co.

     vi. Catherine married John Sabatier, Summergrove, Queen's County.

     vii. Charlotte married David Baldwin.

David Cambie (1764-1813), Solomon L.'s eldest son, who married Mary Walsh in 1796, appears to have been living in Brookfield while his father was still living in Castletown.

David had four children, Charles, Sarah, Mary and Elizabeth. David inherited huge debts from his father and mismanaged his affairs badly, even to the extent of getting his brother Edward to act as his guarantor for further borrowings which arose from his father's will of 1792 in which Solomon L. divided up the lands between his sons and left substantial legacies to two of his daughters. The legal document of 1817 quoted on page 127, in which David's widow and issue were summoned by Edward, shows David's various transactions which led to the court case.

David's debts had become so great that he transferred his interests in his lands, except Brookfield House, to his brother-in-law David Baldwin, in exchange for Baldwin handling his debts. In a marriage settlement when David Cambie married Mary Walsh in 1796 he had transferred the lands of Castletown and Brookfield (subject to the debts) to a James R. Gray and Henry Palmer, to hold them in trust.

David died in 1813, leaving his wife Mary with four children under eighteen years, and only Brookfield House. She took guardianship proceedings on behalf of her children and, apparently, succeeded in regaining possession of the lands, i.e. Brookfield and Castletown, from David Baldwin.

She returned with her children to live at Castletown, probably having transferred the ownership of Brookfield to a John Parker. She and her four children, Charles, Sarah, Mary and Elizabeth, lived for some time in Castletown. They must have been already grown up when they left Brookfield as we know that one of Charles's sisters kept a private school for the estate children in her brother's house at Brookfield in 1824. Mary died in Castletown in 1845, aged 78 years. Charles Cambie married Jane Disney. They had at least four children – one boy and three girls.

The Castletown estate, of which this Charles Cambie was the occupier, was sold in the Encumbered Estates Court in June 1856. The petitioner was his brother-in-law, Thomas Towers, Bushy Park, Borrisokane, married to his sister Elizabeth.

This was probably the extent of Castletown when it was sold in 1856. The sale prospectus said that the owner had spent 'a large sum of money on its restoration'.

In the prospectus prepared for the sale Sarah Cambie was named as a tenant in Castletown of 196 Irish acres, lease dated 22.11.1850 between Thomas Sadleir and Charles Cambie. The lease was for the lives of above Sarah [his sister] now aged 50, Alex, aged 21, and Henry John, aged 19. Castletown was held under a lease dated 1.2.1747 from Charles Sadleir [son of Thomas who bought it from John and George Briggs in 1706] to Anne (Ledger) Cambie for lives renewable for ever at £50 renewal fine. The next renewal was from Thomas Sadleir to Charles Cambie 25.10.1826 for lives of Edward (since dead), Charles Cambie and Richard Baldwin. The Edward here is Charles's brother who lived in Kilgarvan and is dealt with below.

Charles emigrated to Canada around the time of the sale, taking with him his wife, daughter Jean and son Henry John, who became an eminent engineer and whose memoir is on page 130-1.

Sarah Cambie went to live in South Terrace, Borrisokane, and died unmarried there on 10 Feb 1872, leaving property to the value of £1,000 according to her will. As far as is known the third sister, Mary Anne, also died unmarried.

The Towers Branch

Thomas and Elizabeth Cambie Towers had three sons. Thomas died unmarried. Charles (Anthony Charles) married Honora Moran (probably of Courthill) and emigrated to Canada, settled in Ontario about 1854, and had seven children.

Benjamin, the third son, born 1833, married Lucy Ellen Wolf (Woulf) and bought back Castletown from the Encumbered Estates Commissioners in 1856. They had seven children; Frances, Elizabeth, Caroline (Carrie), Lucy Ellen, Margaret (Marjorie), Johanna (Anne) and Thomas.

Only Frances married. She had become Matron of the Dental Hospital in Dublin and married a Mr Manning. They had no children.

Benjamin Towers died in a tragic accident in 1881, aged 48 years. His widow Lucy Ellen died in 1893. As their son Thomas did not marry there was nobody in Ireland to inherit Castletown so when Marjorie, the last of his unmarried sisters, died in 1956 a godson of Frances Manning, George Myles (Jimmy) Sterling, inherited the castle and estate. He had been coming on visits to Castletown since his boyhood. He died in 1988 and the property now belongs to his widow Rosamund.

From time to time Cambie and Towers descendants come back from Canada and Australia to visit Castletown. They came while the Misses Towers were alive and still come to visit Mrs Rosamund Sterling.

During the Great Famine there was a soup kitchen near Castletown avenue gate in an old building which is still there and which had been a school supported by the Baptist Society circa 1830. It is now in a ruined condition. At some time between 1840 and 1850 the constabulary barracks, which is still there near the entrance to Castletown, was built.

Charles Cambie of Castletown does not seem to have taken any active part in parish affairs unlike his relative Solomon of Kilgarvan. It was always a tradition in the locality that the Cambies did not evict for non-payment of rent and this is supported by the fact that they went bankrupt. The poor law rates were very high during and after the Famine and landlords were obliged to pay the rates of tenants under £4.00 valuation. Many of Cambies' tenants would have come into this category.

Kilgarvan Cambies

Edward of Mota (1768-1836), the second son of Solomon Ledger Cambie and Elizabeth Ryan and who later lived in Kilgarvan, married an Elizabeth Watkins and had five children that we know of: Solomon Baldwin born 1801, Lucy, 1806, David, 1807, John, 1808, Fanny, 1809.

Edward was left Kilgarvan by his father, not outright, but to be held 'in trust for him throughout his natural life' and from his death 'to the use ... of his eldest son'.

In 1835 Mrs Elizabeth Cambie, then aged 68, and three of the children, John, aged 27, Lucy, aged 29, and Fanny, aged 30, were drowned in the Shannon on 10 October 1835 when returning from a 'party of pleasure', as their gravestone inscription in Cloghprior graveyard reads. At this time their eldest brother, Solomon B., was thirty-four. In 1836 Edward Cambie Sen., died suddenly, aged 66. All five are buried beneath a tomb erected by the second eldest son, David.

This David married a Catherine Carlton. Their son, David Solomon, was born in Kilgarvan in 1841. The family emigrated soon afterwards to Melbourne, Australia. Catherine was delicate and died the day they arrived there. David Solomon went to New Zealand and took part in the Maori wars, for which service he was paid in Crown lands just as his ancestor was with Irish lands. David married and had ten children. He died in 1923, aged 82 years. His family is well documented and descendants visit Ireland and were here in 1997.

Solomon Baldwin Cambie (1801-71), the eldest surviving son of Edward and Elizabeth Watkins, married a Miss St, Ledger. He played an active part in parish affairs during the Famine and was elected a Guardian of Nenagh Poor Law Union and member of the Famine Relief Committee in 1846-7. On 8 May 1849 we learn from the Board of Guardian minutes that he resigned his office of Guardian.

He had at least two sons, Edward, who married Mary Walsh and went to Canada where he drowned in the Ottawa River in 1880, and David. This is according to the family tree which is unclear in several places and lacks dates mostly. Compiling a full Cambie family tree is impossible without Kilbarron church registers. Those prior to 1878, unfortunately, do not survive.

Some light is thrown on Edward's emigration by an advertisement in the *Nenagh Guardian* in 1863, to the effect than 'E. J. Cambie, changing his residence, has directed to sell unreservedly at Kilgarvan, sheep, cattle etc. ...' This is explained in a memorial of March 1863 made between Edward and a Richard Thomas Sweny, Kingstown, Dublin, a captain in the Royal Navy, to the effect that Edward had been adjudged a bankrupt and that Captain Sweny had lodged the amount owing, £908. Cambie promised to repay this and undertook that when his bankruptcy was annulled he would convey the lands of Kilgarvan to Sweny.

Solomon B. died in 1871 and sometime in that decade Kilgarvan was purchased by Edward Reeves who gave it to his son Willie on his marriage to Anne Parker of Brookfield.

Kennedys and Cambies

There are two original documents in the Lalor Cambie papers which relate to

Kilgarvan. They are undated but probably stem from the end of the 1700s. The queries are made to Richard Ryan, barrister, Dublin, and concern the legality of Solomon Cambie's title to the town (sic) and lands of Kilgarvan containing 200 acres. They are of interest in that they feature an O'Kennedy as a land purchaser.

1st Query: [paraphrasing] Mr Cambie states that in 1666 Charles White of Leixlip sold the town and lands of Kilgarvin (sic) in the Co. of Tipperary to Andrew Kennedy for £300 to hold and hand on to his heirs for ever. Andrew Kennedy died leaving sons John, Philip, another unnamed son, besides daughters, which said John Kennedy was his eldest son and entered into possession of said lands and continued in the peaceful possession thereof.

In the year 1737 the said John Kennedy intermarried with Honora Wall and in order to secure a provision for said Hanora in case she should survive him he forfeited his bond to Patrick Wall in trust for the principal sum of £300 on the day of his [the said John Kennedy's] death.

The said John Kennedy, dreading that his two brothers and sisters might claim a right in Gavel of his father's during the said Andrew Kennedy's lifetime, conformed to the Established Religion soon after his intermarriage, whereby it is apprehended that he [John] as the first protestant vested the estate wholly in himself and made his father [Andrew] his tenant for life.

[paraphrasing] The said John Kennedy got heavily in debt. In the year 1769 the said John Kennedy was prevailed on to perfect his Bond for £240 principal money unto his daughter Mary Kennedy and another for £200 principal money unto his other daugher Margaret Kennedy.

In 1776 John Kennedy, finding he could not pay off his debts and mortgage, allowed his lands to be sold to the highest bidder, whereupon Solomon Cambie [Solomon L who died in 1792] of Castletown in said County, Esq. agreed to purchase the same and a deed was executed in pursuance of the agreement which deed is herewith sent (No. 4). In some short time afterwards Mr Cambie paid off the principal and interest due on the mortgage.

There is a great deal of, sometimes indecipherable, legal jargon regarding what Cambie's duties or rights are regarding 'the old couple' and the son who is in 'foreign parts'

Mr Cambie's query to his barrister is as to the safety of his title to the lands of Kilgarvan and the answer from the barrister is that the title is 'good'.

2nd Query: John Kennedy having been in possession for 33 years [1742-75] undisturbed, having educated Andrew, his only son, a protestant. Andrew having joined in the original deed to Mr Cambie. John having, after the death of his son, levied a fine on Mr Cambie in consideration of money bona fide paid – the purchaser being a protestant & in the actual possession; have we at this day any right to apprehend a claim to a right of Gavel or any other claim of that nature that may be set up by either the Brother [Philip] of John or by his daughters [Mary, Margaret] who are all and ever have been Papists.

3rd Query: Additional case of Solomon Cambie Esq.
For Richard Ryan, Esq., with reference to the first. Mr Cambie (paraphrased) began to have doubts as to the Conformity of John Kennedy in the lifetime of his

father, Andrew. He searched the Books (Convert Rolls) minutely as to the time of filing the Bishop's certificate and ascertained that the said John Kennedy had filed the Certificate in 1740 but it did not appear that he had taken the oath until 1762, nor is the identity of the man ascertained by any proper addition being only 'stiled John Kennedy, Gent'.

Your opinion is required – whether, if the Conformity of John be Irregular (having been from 1742 to 1775 in the uninterrupted possession of the lands), has sufficiently vested the fee (freehold) in him no person whatsover having claimed a right of Gavel or any other right or title during that time.

Counsel's Opinion.
I am of opinion that Mr Cambie has purchased a good title in Lands of Kilgarvan from John Kennedy, the said John Kennedy having had the fee & inheritance of said lands vested in him and capable of disposing of same.
Rich. Ryan

One aspect of interest in the case stated is that the Brehon Law type of tenure called gavelkind was still adverted to in 1740 when John Kennedy became a Protestant to ensure that such ancient custom of tenure would not apply. Gavelkind provided for land tenure to descend equally to all sons, which would have allowed Philip joint ownership with John. John apparently did not have a surviving son who would have given entitlements after his death to his daughters, that is if gavel(kind) still applied some time after 1775 – Solomon Cambie's worry.

Cambies in Conflict
We get a further insight into the complexities of Cambie property from a Court of Chancery hearing in November 1817 involving Edward of Kilgarvan, married to Elizabeth Watkins and father of five young children, and the widow of his brother David, née Mary Walsh. The problem had its origins in the generous nature of the will made by their father, S. L. Cambie. The following is a summary of the contents.

'BRIEF ON BEHALF OF PLAINTIFF'
Court of Chancery Nov 26 1817

This is a brief of a summons/court action dated 26 Nov 1817 by Edward Cambie (Plaintiff) against various others. It is an action to settle a dispute arising from the administration of the will of his father, Solomon Cambie.

By the will of the said Solomon Cambie (S.L.C.) dated 1 June 1792 he first of all left a £999 charge on the lands to his daughter Charlotte. [She married David Baldwin, Queen's Co.] He also left his eldest son David [b. 1765] (Plaintiff's brother) the lands of Brookfield, Islandmore and part of Carney all in Co. Tipperary and also the lands of ?Conmilaine in Co. Galway.

He gave the lands of Kilroan and Kilburrer [Kilbiller] Co. Tipperary to his son Thomas (he had a lease-hold interest in these). He also gave Thomas a charge/ annuity of £500 on the lands of Castletown, Clonmackilladuff and Kylebeg in Co. Tipperary. [S.L.C. must have been entitled to do this under some settlement involving the latter lands]. He gave Richard Cambie his interest in the lands of the Hill of Annah, Carrick, Cameron, Meelick, Kilbarron and Glenbower, Co. Tipperary, and his leasehold interest in the lands of Ardcroney.

He gave his post chaise and horses and 20 guineas to his wife Elizabeth and furniture etc. to children. The residue after payment of debts to go to his children.

On 20 July 1792 S.L.C. added a codicil to his will specifically instructing that David should be the one to deal with S.L.C.'s debts after his death.

S.L.C. died on 20 July 1792 leaving sizeable debts (e.g. £1,000 owed to a Richard Biggs, the engineer who built Drominagh toll bridge). David didn't deal with the debts for the time being and instead put a charge on his Brookfield lands as security for them.

In 1796 David married Mary Walsh and in a money settlement transferred the lands of Castletown and Brookfield (subject to the debts) to a James R. Gray and Henry Palmer to hold them in a trust. Richard Biggs assigned the benefit of his debt to his niece Mary Ledger, Ballinderry, who then sought repayment from David. Edward alleges that David 'pushed' him into signing a type of letter of Guarantee for David's debts, i.e. Edward used his lands to further secure David's debts.

In the meantime David obtained a better legal interest in his Brookfield and Islandmore lands (which were held on a medium term lease) from the holding landlord, Mr Sadleir, i.e. David obtained a lease with a covenant that it would be renewed perpetually [i.e. as good as freehold, except the rent of £2 per acre would attach].

Sadleir was also entitled to take all the timber on these lands, but David wished to save the trees and paid Sadleir £300 to leave them there. David had to borrow this from a Mike Hogan, again getting Edward to act as Guarantor.

David found himself in serious financial difficulty with the debts of S.L.C, the amounts due to the rest of the family under S.L.C.'s will, and the debts he had incurred himself.

Consequently he transferred his interest in his lands (except Brookfield House) to his brother-in-law David Baldwin [who had married his sister Charlotte] in exchange for Baldwin handling his debts.

David died in 1813 leaving his wife Mary (née Walsh), only son Charles and three daughters Elizabeth, Mary and Sarah (all four children were under 18) [and living in Brookfield].

Mary took guardianship proceedings on behalf of her children and apparently succeeded in regaining possession of the lands from David Baldwin [including Castletown].

Mary Ledger (see above) again applied to have her debt repaid by Mary [Walsh] Cambie. Mary Cambie made various attempts to hold her off and claimed that SL.C's [her father-in-law] debts weren't her responsibility. Mary Ledger then pursued Mary's brother-in-law, Edward Cambie (Plaintiff), who had given letters of Guarantee for his late brother David's debts.

Eventually Mary Ledger got an order for possession of Edward Cambie's lands of Kilgarvan and Ballyscanlon and as a result, Edward and his family, who lived near Mary Cambie's Brookfield House, suffered great hardship.

Edward made several unsuccessful attempts to obtain help from Mary and he alleged that she made empty promises and used her cunning to avoid helping him, except for occasional small offerings.

Consequently, this proposed court action by Edward requests that Mary Cambie give full account of her earnings from her lands, give full account of S.L.C.'s debts and the debts of her husband and that she be liable for same and that Edward be given such other remedy as the court decides.

Unfortunately, there is no outcome of the court case amongst the papers. A search in Dublin proved negative as most of the Chancery documents were destroyed in the burning of the Four Courts in 1922. But we have seen that the Cambies continued in Kilgarvan for two more generations.

KILGARVAN HOUSE

We know that the above Edward Cambie was occupier of Mota in 1805 and 1812, as amongst the Cambie papers are two original leases which he granted to local tenant farmers on these dates. The first one was made on the 'first day of May in the year of Our Lord 1805 between Edward Cambie, Esq, of Mota and William Corboy of Bellvie'. William Corboy signed the document with his mark.

The term of the lease was thirty-one years from the above date 'provided the said Edward Cambie's interest may so long continue in said farm'.

Leaving out all the legal language, the farm consisted of that part of the land of Ballyscanlon containing 45 acres 2 roods plantation measure (and some perches not to be charged) to be the same more or less and subject to a survey, bounded on the north by Kilgarvan, on the east by Kevanstown, on the south by the road leading through Ballyscanlon, and on the west by that part of Ballyscanlon held by Cornelius Dwyer situate lying and being in the parish of Kilbarron Barony of Lr Ormond & Co. of Tipperary aforesaid. To have and to hold the said demised premises yielding & paying therefrom a thousand fifty six pounds seventeen shillings & sixpence sterling being at the rate of one pound five shillings per acre to be paid in 2 equal instalments. 1st day Nov., 1st day of May.

Then the standard conditions: And it is agreed by both parties that the sd Wm Corboy his heirs etc shall have liberty to plant, till or turn up the soil or surface as he thinks proper with liberty to burn the same the better to enable him to pay his rent.

There is a PS:
Corboy shall not have liberty to draw off any straw, dung or manure of said land.

In presence of	Edward Cambie
James Donohue	His
Patrick Dwyer	William X Corboy
	Mark

I do not know if this was a fair rent but I am struck by the leniency of the terms when compared with the lease given to John O'Connell in 1878 as outlined in relation to Ballycolliton in Chapter 8, 'Other Houses and Gate Lodges'.

The second lease of 1812 is between Edward Cambie and Dennis Phelan of Kilgarvan for 'that part of the land of Kilgarvan down from the road to the Shannon containing 41 acres 3 roods and 1 perch plantation measure exclusive to the copse and road to the Shannon and Islands as a commonage'.

The term of the lease is 17 years at the yearly rent of £69 3s 5d. There are no extra conditions apart from standard printed ones on all such leases. The lease is signed thus:

In the presence of	Edward Cambie
Michael ?Phelan [not clear]	His
	Dennis X Phelan
	Mark

We know from this latter lease that Edward Cambie was in possession of Kilgarvan as early as 1812. Mota House is dealt with in more detail in 'Other Houses and Lodges'.

Kilgarvan House is situated on the main Nenagh-Ballinderry road about a mile and a half beyond Coolbawn Cross, close to the shore of Lough Derg and close to Kilgarvan quay. Heather Bell (née Parker Reeves) is of the opinion that Kilgarvan was bought by her great-grandfather, Edward Reeves, from the Cambies. This is unlikely because as we have seen the last Cambie to reside there, Edward J. was declared bankrupt in 1863 and undertook to convey the lands to a Richard Thomas Sweeny who had paid off his bankruptcy debt.

Edward Reeves passed Kilgarvan to his son William when William married Annie Parker, Brookfield House, whose story is told in a later chapter. It remained in the Reeves family until December 1976 when it was sold to a syndicate and subsequently resold.

Brookfield Cambies

Two sources provides the information that a family of Cambies lived in Brookfield House – the 'First Report of Enquiry into Irish Education 1824-1826' in Chapter 2, and in the Tithe Applotment list of 1827. The report noted that 'Miss Cambie has a private school in a room in her brother's house in Brookfield'. The Tithe Applotment list recorded a Charles Cambie as a resident in Brookfield.

Interestingly, Lewis's *Topographical Dictionary* of 1837 makes no mention of Brookfield. It may well have been empty. The full story of Brookfield and its later Parker owners is recounted later on in this chapter.

Henry J. Cambie of Castletown & Vancouver

Henry J. Cambie was the son of Charles Cambie and Jane Disney of Castletown. Arising from the sale of Castletown the parents had emigrated to Canada, taking Henry J. and their daughter Jean with them. Two other daughters had already married and remained in Ireland. A fragment of Henry J.'s reminiscences is reproduced below.

Most of the information we get of his career as engineer comes from a rather turgidly written article in a Canadian magazine, *MacLean's Magazine*, dated 15 Dec.1923, in which the writer, Noel Robinson, interviews Mr Cambie, then aged 87.

He begins by stating that at first Mr Cambie, whom he describes as having the ruddy complexion of a young man, held out for a long time against any sort of publicity. Finally, he was persuaded that it was the duty of every pioneer of achievement to leave behind him some written record of his life's work.

Robinson recounts how the Cambies came to Canada in the 1850s, sailing from Liverpool to Philadelphia in the *City of Manchester*, the first ship of the Inman Line –later known as the American Line, and took eighteen days on the passage, landing on 23 May and eventually arriving in Toronto.

Henry J. spent the first seven years of his career with Gzowski & Co who were engaged in building the G.T.R. from Toronto to Detroit. He then entered the service of Punchard, Clarke & Co. and located and constructed the Windson, Annapolis Railway (which was acquired by the Canadian Pacific Railway before the commencement of the Great War, 1914-18). After completing that railway in 1869 he took charge of some of the most extensive works on the Inter-colonial Railway of Canada, in the provinces of New Brunswick and Quebec. Prior to this he had been exploring for that railway in various parts, and particularly in the country between the St. Lawrence and Bay Chaleur. In 1874, with an established reputation as a railway builder, he was sent out to British Colombia and conducted many important explorations and surveys through some of the wildest portions of that province. These explorations took him to many and hitherto almost inaccessible parts of the province and finally away up into the Peace River country – then largely unknown territory – and he explored, among other parts, the western heads of the Nechaco River. During this expedition he discovered and mapped the Ootsa Lakes.

His Crowning Achievement

Following this he was ordered by Mr (afterwards Sir) Sandford Fleming, the distinguished chief engineer of the Government railways, to survey the canyons of the Fraser. Eventually he was placed in charge of the tremendous task of building a railway through these canyons, a feat which he successfully accomplished after surmounting many stupendous difficulties. This was the crowning achievement of his career, although he accomplished afterwards much important railway construction work in British Columbia.

Mr Cambie retired only in 1920 and was still at the disposal of the Canadian Pacific Railway at the time of the interview in 1923. According to the interviewer, Cambie had been one of that historic little group gathered about the late Lord Strathcona when that G.O.M. of the Canadian Pacific Railway drove the last spike at Craiglahachie in British Columbia. The biographical note continues:

The old pioneer spoke nostalgically to the interviewer of his boyhood on the banks of the Shannon in the old grey Castle, a portrait of which had pride of place in the room. He also spoke with great feeling and affection of his first railway work in Nova Scotia on LA East Coast. He recalled with pride and pleasure that first little railway he built and which runs through the scene in which the poet Longfellow laid the action of his famous poem, 'Evangeline'. Here, too, Henry met and fell in love with the girl who was to be his wife.

There are some who will argue that there is little romance in railway building. Yet the building of railways in a new, wild, unopened country is one of the most romantic callings a man can pursue. This is borne out by following the career of Henry J. Cambie of Castletown and Vancouver, who surveyed and planned the whole course of the Canadian Pacific Railway and personally supervised its construction through the rugged canyons of the Fraser.

Reminiscences of Henry J. Cambie, 1923

In connection with my Professional Record, it might be of interest to some Members of the E.I.C. to give a few reminiscences of events which have occurred during a long, busy life.

I was born in the County Tipperary, Ireland, in 1836 and brought up on the banks of the River Shannon (Lough Dearg) [sic] and terrible as is the unsettled state of that Country at present with the almost daily murders which are taking place, the same sort of things were common during my childhood, and were just as brutal, differing only in frequency.

My father's house consisted of an old Castle which had been repaired and extended to make a comfortable residence. A courtyard in front of the house was enclosed with high walls, and during part of my boyhood, if any visitor came after dark, he had to ring a bell outside the courtyard gate and give an account of himself to someone at an inaccessible window, and if satisfactory he was admitted to the courtyard and to the hall door. But I do not remember a case when the visitor was not admitted. ...

The next day [after the ship docked] we travelled by rail to Perth-Amboy, and thence to New York by boat. On that evening, and the next, the lower end of Broadway and the Battery was lit by arc lights on high poles. The carbons were just such as are in use today, but the electricity for each was furnished by a large number of cell batteries. They were found to be unreliable and very expensive and were abandoned in two or three days. I saw the lights myself, but only knew of the batteries by hearsay. Of course they did not come into actual use for nearly thirty years later, when the dynamo had been invented.

The Hudson River Railway had not been built, so we came by steamer to Albany and thence by rail to Buffalo, which was a hard night's journey as Pullman sleepers did not come into use for fifteen years or more afterwards. Next day we took a small ferry boat from Buffalo to Chippewa, about two miles above Niagara Falls, and from there to Queenstown we travelled by a railway which was, I believe, the only one then operating in the Province of Upper Canada (Ontario) and is worth describing.

The Line was on very much the same location as that occupied by the Electric Railway of late years. We were carried in an old-fashioned English type of coach, with two or three compartments, which each had seats for six or eight persons. It ran on wooden rails, reinforced with iron straps, and was drawn by one horse. The luggage was carried on top, covered by tarpaulins. Eventually, by boat, we arrived at what is now Toronto.

Henry J. Cambie has the distinction of having a street named after him in Vancouver.

Sources
John P. Prendergast, *The Cromwellian Settlement of Ireland*.
Indenture enrolled in Record Office Dublin, 20 July 1677.
Civil Survey, 1654.
Book of Survey & Distribution, 1662.
Lalor Cambie Papers, Co. Library, Thurles (by kind permission of Lalor Cambie family).
Registry of Deeds, Deed No.s 35-445-23264, 37-412-23623, 1863-18-227.
Ormond Historical Society, Cloghprior and Knigh Gravestone Inscriptions.
Samuel A. Lewis, *A Topographical Dictionary of Ireland*, 1837.
Tithe Applotment, Kilbarron parish.
TNFH research centre for genealogical data.

Photographs taken by Paddy Carroll.

THE BIGGS FAMILY AND THEIR HOUSES

We have seen that in the plantations after the Cromwellian wars John Briggs drew as his share of the spoils a considerable amount of land in Kilbarron parish. Unlike the Cambies, whose previous history in France and England is documented, little is known of John Briggs. We know from the 1659 census that he was living in Castletown, which tower house, according to the *Civil Survey*, was a ruin with only the walls and curtain (bawn) walls standing.

However, in the Hearth Money Rolls of 1665-6-7 there is no mention of a Briggs in the parishes of Finnoe, Kilbarron, or Terryglass. These rolls were compiled on a civil parish basis. Though the original rolls were destroyed when the Four Courts was burnt in 1922, Co. Tipperary is lucky, inasmuch as Dr Thomas Laffan transcribed the entries for 1665-6-7 and had them printed in 1911. But he had difficulty reading the handwriting so there are omissions and errors, and some townlands are placed in the wrong parishes.

We know from later land transactions that John Briggs of Castletown, Co. Tipperary, and Dunstable, Bedfordshire, married Elizabeth, daughter of Thomas Sadleir, a Cromwellian officer who had settled on the former MacEgan lands at Kilnalahagh (in Uskane parish) which was later renamed Sopwell. Captain John Briggs died in 1694.

In 1706 John Briggs, his wife Judith, and his brother George, sold to their uncle, Thomas Sadleir, for the sum of £2,930, the lands named in their father's grant in the townlands of Kevanstown, Brockagh, Mota (part of Scribogue), Ballinderry, Ballyscanlon, Castletown, Glenbower, Clonmackillduff, Coolbawn and Raheen.

I had always assumed that the name Biggs and Briggs were one and, accordingly, that the successive generations of Biggs, who lived in the parish up to the 1970s, were descendants of John Briggs, the grantee of Castletown.

However, this appears not to be so. In 1711 Godfrey Boate of Dublin and Benjamin Frend of King's County, leased William Biggs, Cloughjordan, a total of 618 acres in Drominagh, Gortmore and that part of Shanakill then in Biggs's possession – all in Terryglass parish. The lands included 29 acres of bog. The lease was for three lives – John and Richard Biggs, sons, and William Biggs, Jun., grandson, 'with covenants for renewal for ever at the yearly rent of £80 sterling'. Boate and his heirs retained the rights to some oak trees in Shanakill townland.

The Biggs name next surfaces on an inscribed vault in Terryglass old churchyard. Going on the birth year, 1704, of the man commemorated one could conjecture that he is the grandson named in the document referred to above. Shanakill adjoins Newlawn townland.

> Here is what is mortal of William Biggs Esq. late of New Lawn in the county of Tipperary and Mary Mason, otherwise Biggs, his wife. Mary departed this life Feb 25th 1779, aged 70, and William departed Feb 21st 1782, aged 78 yrs.

There is no record of any children, but there must have been at least one, otherwise the inscription would hardly have been put on the vault. We know Newlawn passed out of the Biggs family before 1840. Some of the Biggs family were medical doctors and are very often referred to just as Dr Biggs in the various written records – Tithe Applotment list and so on – which makes it difficult to differentiate between them.

The Biggs left a fine legacy of dwellings in the parish, all of which are dealt with below.

Biggs in the West Indies

There is a story about the early Biggs family told by the last surviving male Biggs, Samuel (Uel) of Bellevue (d. 1974), to Mrs Betty Williams when she was living in Bellevue House, having leased it from Uel who was living in nearby Rowdly House at the time. It appears that at least one Biggs member went out to the West Indies to seek a fortune in the sugar trade. According to Uel's story it was a very early Biggs who went.

Dr William L. Biggs

The first Biggs dwelling erected in the parish was, in all likelihood, Castle Biggs or, as it later became known, Drominagh House.

Dr William Ledger Biggs, and his wife Phidelia Matilda, lived in Castle Biggs. He died there in 1837, aged 74, and is buried in the grounds of the house. William L.'s father and mother may well have been buried there also, since there is no inscribed gravestone to them locally.

William's mother may have been one of the Ballinderry Ledgers. It is a name which crops up also in the Cambie family. It was common practice for sons to bear their mother's surname as their second Christian one.

Dr William L. and Phidelia Matilda had seven or eight children. Dr Edward, who inherited sometime between 1837 and 1840, was the eldest but his birth is not recorded in the parish register. He was one of those who gave much information about the neighbourhood to John O'Donovan at the time of the Ordnance Survey in 1840. There is no record of his marriage or of any children born to him.

He may well be the Edward Biggs, Kilgarvan, who committed suicide in March 1876 aged 69. He was a widower and a 'gentleman farmer'.

William L.'s other children were: Robert, no birth date; Triphenia Anne, 1810; William, 1811; Samuel Dickson, 1813; Frederick, 1815; Richard, 1820; Charlotte, 1824.

Frederick became a doctor and married Elizabeth Anderson of Borrisokane in 1851. They had a son Edward born in 1853. Frederick died in 1858, aged 42.

Triphenia Anne married a Major Brooke Firman of Firmount on 29 November 1831. One wonders if the name Triphenia had anything to with the sojourn in the West Indies. There is no record of the marriages of the other children. A Robert and Richard Biggs died in 1876 and 1877, aged 59 and 57 years, respectively.

However, details of Samuel Dickson are known and will be recounted later on.

When Phidelia Matilda Biggs died in 1864, aged 78, she was buried in the Biggs vault in Kilbarron Protestant graveyard. This had been built to house the mortal remains of George Washington Biggs and a Thomas Biggs, both of whom died in 1844 aged 61 years and 27 years respectively – possibly a brother and nephew or son of Dr William Ledger Biggs.

The Toll Bridge

The Ballyfinboy river separates Drominagh from Ballinderry townland wherein Gorthalougha House is located. There is a bridge near the entrance to the two demesnes. It has two covered recesses for the collection of tolls. The datestone over the recess on the upriver side proclaims Richard Biggs, Esqr, to have been the overseer for its construction in 1776.

Flax Industry

There is lore in the locality (but we have no idea of the date) that a flax industry flourished at Drominagh and that the owner, probably William Ledger Biggs, brought a flax comber from Northern Ireland to teach the trade to the local people. A Biggs girl fell in love with this comber and they got married (no record) and became known as Comber-Biggs. She has not been positively identified.

The Biggs Priest

There is a tradition that a member of the Biggs family converted to Catholicism and became a priest and is buried in Rathcabbin. In his *History of Ely O'Carroll* Rev. John Gleeson states that going back to the year 1269 Lorrha parish had been served by Dominican priests. During the Penal Days they lived in a house in Rathcabbin. He continues:

> The succession of Dominicans was broken by Father Biggs, who was a convert and who left after him a reputation for sanctity. He died in 1796 and is buried in Rathcabbin church.

Monsignor Ignatius Murphy, in his *History of the Diocese of Killaloe*, gives 'John Biggs, a Dominican, 1780-?1796', as parish priest of Lorrha. He also writes that Bishop MacMahon (himself a Dominican) in 1765 appointed Denis McGrath, OP, parish priest of Lorrha. Denis McGrath was followed by three more Dominican priests – John Dominic McGrath (1775-80); John Biggs (1780-96) and Alexander Fitzgerald (1796-1817). The latter built the old church at Rathcabbin.

I had thought Fr Biggs might have been a son of William L., but by the date of his death he could be his brother – and also a brother of the Richard of the toll bridge. This ties in with the local folklore that Richard was so incensed at his brother/relative having turned Catholic and becoming a priest, that he built the toll bridge in place of the little wooden bridge over the Ballyfinboy river used by the locals on the way to Mass in Terryglass so that they would have to pay to cross it. They never used the new bridge and found another way to Mass.

All sorts of folklore has survived about the Biggs priest, some of it patently untrue. One story is that he arrived home from Rome, or wherever he had been ordained, on a Friday and meat was served for dinner. He commented that even the dogs would not eat meat on a Friday. He put down his plate to the dog who refused to eat the meat. The Richard of the next generation – Dr William Ledger's son, born in 1820 – was living in the Talbot-built Shannon View House in 1857. He was a member of the petty jury which convicted William and Daniel Cormack for the alleged murder of land agent John Ellis, Kilrush, Thurles. They were hanged in Nenagh in May 1858.

Samuel Biggs of Cornalack

The Tithe Applotment list of 1825 shows that the small Cornalack townland, adjoining Drominagh, was owned by a Dr Biggs, presumably Dr William L., and occupied by a John Hough. There is a Samuel in Gortmore, presumably the father of the Samuel in the Primary Valuation list of 1852. This 1852 Samuel Biggs is occupier of 48 acres in Cornalack with Edward Biggs as landlord, but the valuation of the buildings suggests that there was no large dwelling there. He is also returned as the occupier of 205 acres in Gortmore, with buildings valued at £11.10s.

John Hough was a tenant on 10 acres in Cornalack, but had a house and some land in the not-too-far-away townland of Cornamult.

Biggs-Haugh
Sometime in the late 1850s Samuel Biggs married a Sarah Hough (probably the daughter of that John). We do not know the exact date of their marriage as it is not recorded in either the Catholic or Protestant registers for Terryglass or Kilbarron. He most likely built a house on his Cornlack holding. He and Sarah had three daughters and a son. In those days couples in a mixed marriage made their own arrangements. That was before 'Ne Temere', the papal decree of 1907 that all children of mixed Catholic and Protestant marriages should be brought up as Catholics. The most common solution was for the boys to be brought up in the father's faith and the girls in that of the mother.

Samuel and Sarah's first child, Adelaide, was baptised on 7 February 1857 in the Catholic chapel in Terryglass. She was followed by Samuel, 1860, also baptised in the Catholic faith. He was only twenty-two years and unmarried when he died of septicaemia in 1884. Mary was also baptised in the Catholic chapel, Terryglass, on 21 April 1865. Lastly, Harriet (Babe) was christened in Terryglass C. of I. church on 26 February 1868.

Eccentric Harriet
There is a sequel to this break in practice, recounted by Rev. William Leenane, PP, Monsea & Killodiernan, a native of Newlawn, Terryglass. The story is that Harriet was secretly taken by her mother to a house down in the bog belonging to a relative of Fr Leenane. Stations were being held in one of the houses, possibly Leenanes, and it was the custom to bring children for baptism to the station. So the local Catholic priest came and baptised the Biggs child. Fr Leenane's relative, Mike Leenane, was a sponsor. The fact that Harriet practised the Catholic religion, and in the 1901 census gave her religion as RC, gives credence to the story.

Samuel Biggs died in 1888. In 1901 Sarah, aged 65, his widow, and Harriet, aged 39, his daughter, were living at Cornalack. When Sarah died Harriet continued to live there and farmed the land with the help of a workman named John Meagher. She had always been slightly eccentric. Wilsie Nolan remembers his mother giving her a lift from Mass once when he was a small boy and she was smoking Woodbines (the cheapest cigarettes on the market). She wore trousers which women then rarely did, wore a man's cap, and always kept a gun. Bill Donoghue also remembers her.

When Harriet Biggs sold Cornalack she built a pretty, wooden house on a piece of ground which she was given. She kept a donkey, a cow and a sheepdog. For a time all went very well but then some difference arose with the man from whom she had got the land – a Coolbawn man – and he treated her rather badly, preventing her from getting fodder for her animals. The aggravation upset her mental equilibrium to the extent that she planned to shoot him and lay in wait for him with her gun. Fortunately, he did not come by. Her poor mind must have been gone completely because she then set about burning down her own house. She had some good silver which she arranged in the middle of the floor. She surrounded it with the donkey's tackling, poured paraffin oil over the lot, and set it alight. The house, being timber, burnt like tinder down to the concrete foundations.

Gardaí Michael McGowan and Joe Cusack, who had just come from the Garda Depot, were sent for and they got an ambulance to take her away to care. The neighbours looked after the dog and other animals.

Bill Donoghue remembers as a small lad poking with his pals amongst the charred remains to try to find a bit of silver.

This story of Samuel Biggs and Sarah Hough is an interesting, if sad one. I feel sure there is much more that could be read between the lines of the bare facts.

Without church records it is not possible to establish the relationship of the Cornalack and Drominagh Biggs families, but one can reasonably assume they are both descended from the William who obtained the lease in 1711.

Cornalack House

This house (left) is situated near the lake shore not far from Gortmore point. There is a little quay nearby. Edward Biggs told O'Donovan in 1840 that he had some old deeds of Cornalack going back to 1711 – which corresponds to the date William Biggs, Cloughjordan, secured the lease from Godfrey Boate.

In the late 1930s Harriet (Babe) Biggs sold her Cornalack property to Dr Anthony Esmonde, a medical practitioner in Summerhill, Nenagh, and later Sir A. Esmonde, TD for Co. Wexford. His youngest son, Tony Esmonde, who now lives in a chalet beside Lesserragh House, was born in Cornalack. When Dr Esmonde moved to Wexford Willie Hogan of Ryehill bought Cornalack and lived there for many years. Several of his family were born there. After his death his son Willie Joe sold the house to a Dutchman, and the land to Christy Gleeson of Gortmore.

The Dutch family later sold the house to Tony Brock and his wife Madeline, who is a sister of Frank Moran, Coolbawn. It is now the Brock home (left).

Biggs of Bellevue

There is a vault in Kilbarron Protestant church graveyard inscribed: 'The family vault of George Washington Biggs' – presumably the man named in

the Tithe list as occupier of 274 acres in Bellvue which was owned by Thomas Sadleir.

Interred in the vault are Dr William L. and Phidelia Biggs's son, Samuel Dickson Biggs (1818-1904), his wife Elizabeth Goodwin (1843-1921). Their eldest son, Major George W. Biggs (1872-1957) (left)°, late 4th Royal Irish Regiment, was a contemporary of my father's and I remember him very well. It appears he married a very pretty, rather sophisticated young lady from Dublin, named Grace Robinson. Some people said she was an actress but I do not think that is true – and they had three children, a girl and two boys: Zelie, Samuel (Uel) and Cecil. The young Dublin girl could not stand the rather lonely country life in Bellevue and returned to live in Dublin with her youngest son Cecil. My aunt remembered her and took pleasure in describing her.

Cecil Biggs was very skilful in the making and repairing of watches. He died in 1959, aged 53, and is commemorated on the family vault as is his father. Samuel (Uel) died tragically in 1974 when gored by a bull. He was not buried in the vault at his own request and has no headstone. Zelie (right), whom most people remember, died in 1983, aged 81. She lived in Ashley Park which she had inherited from her uncle Thomas, who had assumed the name Biggs-Atkinson after his marriage to Alice Margery Atkinson, Ashley Park, in 1903. They had no children. Zelie has an inscribed headstone in Kilbarron Church of Ireland graveyard: born Jan 26th 1902, died 31 Jan 1983. She was the last of the Biggs family of Bellevue.

In 1932, when the Eucharistic Congress took place in Dublin, most people in this parish were unable to attend, or indeed listen to a broadcast of, the ceremonies as there were very few wirelesses in the parish in those days. Uel Biggs (right) built wireless sets as a hobby and was able to fit up loudspeakers to one set. His father, Major George Biggs, decided to invite all the neighbours who did not have a wireless to come to Bellevue to listen to the ceremonies and all the singing. The workmen spent the day before cleaning up the old courtyard

at the back and on the great day the yard was thronged. Uel had his loudspeaker rigged up but at the last minute there was a hitch. Bertie Bruce and her sisters were present and Bertie somehow managed to get rid of the gremlin. All were able to hear the words and music of the historic ceremony, including John McCormack's incomparable rendering of 'Panis Angelicus', as if they had been in the Phoenix Park. I remember George Biggs giving threshing dances in the big barn on a few occasions in the 1930s.

There is no record, either in folklore or documentation, that the Biggs family evicted during the 'bad times' as the Talbots and Synges did. In 1905 the Bellevue tenants were endeavouring to buy out their tenancies under the 1903 Land Act, known as Wyndham's, which paved the way finally for all tenants to purchase their holdings and for division of estates.

I have in my possession a letter written to my uncle William (Bill) Carroll who was a tenant on a farm in Bellevue – the Comenthus – at the time and who appears to have been the spokesman of the group of neighbours. The letter is from Rev. Thomas Meehan, CC, and is headed Ballinderry, Borrisokane, 15/3/1905.

> In reply to yours of today I wish to say that I had nothing whatever to do with the Bellevue people and Captain Biggs. If I had I would not advise them to buy at that many years and again I think when they buy out they should be sole masters of everything connected with their holdings.
>
> I would not give any landlord the right of the game and if they do I think they are more than foolish. Father Darcy took it up for them at first and when he saw the number of years Capt. Biggs wanted he would not have anything to do with it. But I believe that some of the tenants lately made an offer of 23 years to him and also gave him the game rights.
>
> I suppose they think themselves the best judges in the matter. Father Darcy P.P. has lately interested himself on behalf of other tenants in the parish and the highest bought at was 21 and a half years. I think they should take their time in Bellevue.
> T. Meehan CC

I believe that when the tenant farmers bought out their holdings under the 1903 Land Act some of the landlords were allowed to keep the game rights if they so wished, and that many did – as far as I can glean Biggs did so for above Bill Carroll's holding.

Under this Act a landlord was offered a bonus of 12 per cent, as well as the agreed price, as an incentive to sell. The whole purchase price was advanced to the tenant at 3.25 per cent to be repaid over 68.5 years. By 1908 the Exchequer had advanced £28m, the average cost per acre being £12. Successive Land Acts took care of extra financing and the reinstatement of evicted tenants. The Act allowed the landlord to sell untenanted land. He could also sell his demesne land and buy it back on the same annuity as the tenants.

The Cambies and the Biggs were the two chief post-Cromwellian landlords in the parish. However, they never amassed large estates like, say, Thomas Sadleir. Descendants of these two settler families built almost all of the mid-eighteenth century houses which still exist. As recounted in the previous chapter section the Cambies died out in the parish when Marjorie Towers, Castletown, whose

grandmother was a Cambie, died in 1956.

Drominagh House

This house (above) was built sometime between 1720 and 1740. It is a handsome early- to mid-eighteenth century mansion, the finest house in the parish. Material from the tower house bawn wall, or even from the house, could have been used for its building. Indeed what I believe to be a fragment of the bawn wall is still attached to the side of the house facing the lake.

We know from the *Civil Survey* that Drominagh townland in 1654 had a settlement of 'twenty cottages', and 'a decayed orchard', as well the 'old ruined castle and bawne, the walls only standing'. As it is accepted generally that the land acreage recorded in the Survey was understated, one can reasonably presume that the recurring description of the tower houses as 'ruined' was, in many instances, an overstatement.

It appears that the first building put up by a Biggs was a small Tudor-style house built up against the tower house wall on the lake side. The outline of its roof was visible until that wall of the castle collapsed in 1989 due to frost erosion. The Biggs family continued to live in this Tudor house until the mid-1700s or thereabouts when the present fine house was built. As was the practice at the time it was given the grand name of 'Castle Biggs'.

In August 1857 Dr Edward Biggs sold Drominagh to a Frederick Smythe, a captain in the 14th regiment of infantry. Smythe probably paid around £17,000 for the house and what remained of the original Biggs estate. He owned the house for seventeen years and was in partnership with a lawyer in Nenagh. They bought land along the River Shannon as far as Co. Longford. Eventually Smythe had to sell Castle Biggs to settle a debt with his partner. His son, Edward Cecil, was born in Castle Biggs in 1869.

The Smythes sold the house and in the region of 600 acres of lush farmland to James Esmonde who came from the ancient Esmonde family of County Wexford. The tragic story of his grandson, Eugene, is told in a later chapter. In 1946 Owen, another grandson, sold it to Geoffrey MacNeill Moss (Geoffrey Moss the writer). Geoffrey's son Gilbert, and Gilbert's wife Fiona, now own Drominagh and use it as a holiday home. They have the deeds, going back to the early 1700s.

There is a field at Drominagh called the Dispensary Field. The Castle Biggs dispensary was there in the 1840s.

Newlawn
It would appear that the next Biggs house to be built was Newlawn (above). The builder here was probably the William Biggs (1704-82) interred in the vault in Terryglass. There is a tradition in the Leenane family, who live there now, that it was the second house to be built on the estate. It had passed out of Biggs hands before 1840. We can only assume that the third Biggs residence, Bellevue House, was built by the grandfather, or even father, of George Washington Biggs (1783-1844). The Leenanes acquired Newlawn sometime between 1865 and 1901 – possibly in the 1880s.

Bellevue House
This house is situated on the Lough Derg shore between Mota Quay and Kilgarvan quay. It is approached by a long avenue off the Nenagh-Portumna road, about half way between Coolbawn Cross and Ballinderry. It may have been built around the same time as the original Brookfield House which dates from *c.*1766.

Bellevue was the only house which a Biggs built in Kilbarron parish. It survived longest in their ownership, Zelie Biggs having lived there until she inherited Ashley Park house and estate near Ardcroney.

The George Washington Biggs, who was born in 1783, was living here in 1837

– at the same time as Dr Wm L. Biggs was living at Castle Biggs. It is not correct to say, as some people do, that the Biggs family left Drominagh and went to live at Bellevue (above).

Samuel (Uel) Biggs was the last of the family to own Bellevue House (above). He married Ruby Jupe and they lived at Rowdly House near Mota Quay.

In the 1970s Uel Biggs made over Bellevue to the Williams family who sold it to a Limerick businessman in July 1997.

Gortmore House
This is situated on the road from Terryglass going towards Drominagh and near Gortmore point on the lake. The Tithe Applotment lists show that this house was there in 1825. It was owned by 'Dr Biggs', obviously William L. It is not mentioned in the *Topographical Dictionary* of 1837 or in the *Parliamentary Gazeteer* of 1846.

The house and 212 acres was still in Biggs ownership when the Primary Valuation list was compiled in 1852. Samuel Biggs is returned therein as a tenant of Edward Biggs, the son of Dr William L. The tenant and landlord were almost certainly brothers. Sometime between 1850 and towards the end of the century it became the property of the Sydney family who are mentioned in Chapter 8 in relation to Garrane House.

Gortmore was taken over by the Land Commission in the 1930s and divided, first preference being given to the descendants of those who had been evicted by Talbots of Ashgrove. Four of the evicted families took up the offer – including three Donoghue families, i.e. Bill's family, the family of 'Big' Mick Donoghue and the 'Gunner' Donoghue.

A few families who had not been evicted got land also, for example the Mackeys and Paddy Ryan of Coolbawn. The house and lawns were purchased by John Gleeson, the principal teacher in Terryglass school. It is now the home of his son Christy, married to Bridget (Biddy) Kennedy, Brocka.

From Biggs to Fogarty

According to an archaeologist friend of the present occupier, Matt Fogarty, whose tree nursery story is told in chapter 13, Drominagh Lodge was built by the Biggs family sometime between 1790 and 1820. Dr William L. Biggs was living in Castle Biggs/Drominagh in 1837 and his oldest son, Edward, was living in Drominagh Lodge. William died that year and Edward moved to the parental home and was there in 1840, according to the Ordnance Survey Letters. Later occupants of the Lodge were a Fortune family.

In the early 1880s Matt's grandfather, Patrick Fogarty, Kilcolman in the parish of Youghalarra, bought it. His brother Michael became Bishop of Killaloe in 1904.

There is a story that the gate piers of the house were won by a Biggs at a card game in Galway.

Sources:
Appendix to 5th Report of Deputy Keeper of Public Records, PROI (Briggs sale to Sadleir).
OHS, Gravestone Inscriptions of Kilbarron and Terryglass cemeteries.
TNFH research centre for genealogical data.
Tithe Applotment Lists, Hearth Money Rolls, Primary Valuation Lists, 1901 census.
Rev. John Gleeson, *History of Ely O'Carroll Territory*,
Monsignor I. Murphy, *History of the Diocese of Killaloe*, vol. I.
Registry of Deeds, Deed no. 284 (Captain Smythe' purchase of Drominagh on 8 August 1857). The daughter of his son Edward Cecil Smythe (b. 17 Jan 1869), and her husband Edward Morris visited Drominagh in 1996 from Zimbabwe; they sent back the information to Helen Fox who looks after Drominagh for the present owners Gilbert and Fiona MacNeill Moss.
Mrs Betty Williams, Matt Fogarty.
Carroll family.

Photogaphs: p. 138, loaned by Tony Brock; p. 139, loaned by Laura (née Grady) Dwyer; pp. 141-2, taken by Paddy Carroll; p. 143, loaned by Heather (née Reeves) Bell; p, 144 loaned by Matt Fogarty.

The Minchins of Annagh

In the *Civil Survey* – which describes the ownership of land in 1640 – Annagh is given as the property of John Hurly, 'Irish Papist'. The Hurlys had acquired those lands through marriage with a member of the O'Kennedy family. An earlier reference to Annagh in the year 1580 described it as the property of Dónal Duff MacBrien O'Kennedy. The survey recorded that Annagh was divided into two 'ploughlands' and was estimated to contain a total of 400 plantation or Irish acres. 250 acres were described as 'arable', 66 as 'pasture', 20 as 'meadow' and the remaining 60 acres as 'unprofitable bog'. The entire lands of Annagh were valued at £30.

The boundaries of the lands were given as follows:

The said two ploughlands of Annagh are bounded on the east with the two ploughlands of Cloghprior in the parish of Cloghprior, on the west with the River Shannon, on the north with the ploughland of Kilbiller in the said parish of Kilbarron, on the south with the lands of Killodiernan in the parish of Killodiernan.

The survey also remarked that 'the said John Hurly is proprietor in fee by descent from his ancestors' and that 'upon the said lands stands an old castle, the walls only standing'.

Annagh was one of the many properties in the parish of Kilbarron granted to Captain Solomon Cambie in 1652. In 1669 he sold Annagh to Captain Charles Minchin, who had already acquired the O'Carroll property at Busherstown near Moneygall by royal grant from Charles II under the Act of Settlement of 1662, and this despite the fact that Colonel Anthony O'Carroll had held Nenagh castle for the Crown against General Ireton of the Parliamentary forces. Charles Minchin also acquired a partial interest in Ballinakill castle on the Roscrea side of Dunkerrin.

The details of the sale of Annagh and neighbouring properties are recorded in two agreements found among the Minchin Papers, kindly shown to me by Mr Brian Minchin, son of Commander Harry Minchin, RN.

(1) Articles of Agreement dated 18 February 1668 between Solomon Cambie of Ballinullitant (?Ballycolliton) and Charles Minchin of Ballinakill for sale of all Cambie's rights and interests in Annagh, Kilbarron, Kilbullior [Kilbiller], Tollohan [Tullawn, part of present Lisquillibeen], Knockballion [Knockballyea, i.e. Needham's Hill, etc., part of present Lisquillibeen], a total of 185 plantation acres in consideration of £640.

(2) Indenture dated 19 April 1669 between Solomon Cambie and Charles Minchin, whereby Cambie assigns by bargain and sale and enfeoffs the latter of the lands of Annagh (243 acres), Kilbarron (195 acres) and Knockballion (Knockballyea) (183 acres). Witnesses: Giles Martin, Adam Warren, Will Woodward, Humphrey Minchin, John Daniell, Henry Legg.

Minchin Background

The Minchins of Annagh almost certainly came from a family of Minchins who were farming land at the village of Wyck Rissington in Gloucestershire in Tudor and Jacobean times. They probably acquired land at the time of the plantation of Munster under Elizabeth I in the sixteenth century. There were three brothers; one brother John had a son Charles already referred to. The names of Lieutenants Humphrey and Charles Minchin appear among those who served as soldiers in the Parliamentary forces in Ireland in the 1650s. However, there is no reference to them among the lists of troops dispatched to Ireland during that period. The name Minchin appeared earlier among the list of the English forces sent to relieve Kinsale at the time of the siege in 1601, but there does not seem to be any other reference to them in Ireland before the Cromwellian period.

Captain Charles Minchin's eldest son, Thomas, as heir-at-law, inherited Busherstown and acquired Annagh and the lease in Ballinakill and other property under his father's will. Thomas completed the purchase of Ballinakill and made his home there; Busherstown was occupied by his brothers and their families. He also entered into an agreement with his father's executors whereby the lands of Annagh and other property were to be held by them as security for the payment of various bequests to the younger sons. When Thomas died in 1686, leaving daughters but no sons, Ballinakill and Busherstown passed to his eldest brother, Humphrey whose eldest son Paul inherited Ballinakill in 1733; Busherstown passed to the second son, also named Humphrey.

Annagh Castle

John Minchin, fourth son of Captain Charles Minchin, occupied Annagh which he appears to have redeemed from the executor-trustees. He seems to have lived partly at Busherstown and partly at Annagh. At that time the only habitation at Annagh was a small building constructed against the walls of the old O'Kennedy tower house.

After the death of his first wife, Frances Ryan of Inch House near Thurles, John Minchin married Penelope, daughter of Joseph Cuffe of Castle Inch, Co. Kilkenny. This was a marriage of considerable advantage as in 1689, one year before the marriage, the battle of the Boyne had confirmed the ascendancy of William of Orange in Ireland and the Cuffes had been his bankers. Penelope brought with her the lands of Castle Inch, which lay to the north of the principal Cuffe estate. Castle Inch became John Minchin's home for the rest of his life.

The lands of Annagh were conveyed to trustees as part of the Minchin-Cuffe marriage settlement. It was probably about this time that the new residence was built at Annagh – lower down the hill from the tower house, and so less exposed. It was known as 'Annagh Castle' and was obviously built in the late 1600s or early 1700s. It was a plain, solid, two-storey, L-shaped house with slated gables and marvellous chimney stacks.

When John Love, Kilkenny, was selling off the remaining years of his lease in 1898 the house was described as 'having ten apartments, pantry and dairy, good out-offices; houses all slated, walled-in garden (remunerative) fully-stocked with best fruit trees'. This was the house and farm which the Cleary family, parents of P. J. Cleary, purchased from John Love in 1900. The house was demolished in 1993.

In 1725 John Minchin's son, Charles, married Catherine Green, daughter of John Green of Old Abbey, Co. Limerick, and Annagh was transferred to them as part of the marriage settlement. Charles was killed in a duel in 1736. This may have

been the duel which, according to tradition, took place between a Minchin and a Cambie in a field on the Castletown estate called the Buckle Park, beside Coolbawn Cross. That tradition did not specify when the duel took place, or if it ended in a fatality. Charles Minchin left a son, John, aged about ten years, who was brought up at Annagh by his mother. He became a merchant in Limerick, and Annagh was leased to tenants called Lane from Dublin.

Followng the death of John Minchin, the merchant, in 1802, aged about 76, Annagh Castle (above) seems to have been left unoccupied some of the time while Falkiner, John's second but eldest surviving son, born in 1757, was living with his family in Dublin. In 1815 a new settlement of the Annagh estate was executed to secure the interest of this Falkiner's son John, born 1791, who seems to have taken over the administration of the Annagh estate and was living in Kilbiller on 140 acres according to the Tithe Applotment list of 1824.

This John's father, Falkiner, died in 1825 and from then onwards John seems to have continued to live in the new house in Kilbiller and farmed the land at Annagh. In Lewis's *Topographical Dictionary* of 1837 there is a Joseph M. Tabideau living at Annagh Castle. In the Primary Valuation list of 1852 Arbuthnot Goold was the occupier of Annagh and 87 acres, while John Minchin still occupied the land in Kilbiller. The Kilbiller buildings were valued at £18 10s.

This John of Kilbiller is the person commemorated on the plaque in Kilbarron Church of Ireland church: 'Sacred to the memory of John Minchin of Annagh, who departed this life, April 17th 1855, aged 64'. He never married. It was in the time of this unmarried John, that the new Annagh Lodge (above) on the main Coolbawn-Ballinderry road was built, circa 1815-22.

On John's death Annagh passed to his nephew, Falkiner John, aged twelve years. As a minor, Falkiner John must have had a good land agent and probably a strong and intelligent mother.

Looking at the dates of the leases in the section, 'Some Minchin Leases', below, it is interesting to note that the first two were given in 1829 and the third

in 1840. These leases, then, were granted during the life of the unmarried John Minchin. His policy of granting favourable leases to tenants was carried on by his nephew and heir, Falkiner John, who granted the fourth lease, dated 1858. He continued to grant leases during the nineteenth century. Most of the families still occupy the holdings in question and the bloodlines of others survive where the name has gone. Falkiner John Minchin and his uncle both appear to have been enlightened and humane landlords.

The Old General
When Falkiner John Minchin died in 1916 the estate passed to his eldest son, Frederick, an officer serving in the Royal Artillery. Owing to ill-health he left the army, with the rank of Major-General, towards the end of World War I and came home to Annagh. He had twice married. His first wife, Marjorie Abbott, died suddenly in her forties. She was mother of Commander H. F. (Harry) Minchin, Col. F. F. (Jack) Minchin the aviator, and Violet (Mrs Austin).

His second wife, Lena, who came home with him to Annagh, had three children, Peggy, Dick and Dennis. Dennis was our contemporary and, during walks through Coolbawn with his nurse, would play with us in our garden while my mother chatted to Nurse Clarke. I well remember his grey flannel suits and hat. We were saddened when we heard that he had been killed in a road accident somewhere in England while on military service during World War II.

The 'Old General', as he was called, kept up quite an establishment at Annagh Lodge. There were two gate lodges. The one nearest to Coolbawn, where the gardener lived, is still lived in. The other lodge stood on the site of John Slattery's farm yard and was the home of Robert Brien, the coachman, during my childhood in the early 1920s. Robert Brien drove his elegant, black-clad wife and the two house servants to Mass every Sunday in a beautiful, pale yellow, rubber-tyred trap drawn by a smart, high-stepping pony.

In conversation about the old days some months ago with the late Sarah Waller, formerly of Prior Park and then of Rockvalley, we exchanged memories of Robert

Brien and his trap. She shared a governess with Peggy Minchin, and every Monday morning Sarah would be driven from Prior Park to Annagh and on the following Friday would be delivered back to Prior Park in Robert Brien's trap. I believe the General and his wife still had a horse-drawn carriage; I do not remember a motor car. I remember his funeral in 1922 very well. Huddled behind the hedge of Moran's (now O'Halloran's) 'Corrigeen', which faces the church gate, we watched the coming and going of the grand folk. Ireland had just got Independence, so there were no army uniforms, only tall silk hats and, I suppose, frock coats and pin-striped trousers. I do not recall seeing any ladies present.

Commander F.H. (Harry) Minchin R.N.

After the General's death Mrs Minchin and her children moved to Garrykennedy and we lost touch with them. Annagh Lodge was inherited by the elder son of the first marriage, Harry (below), who had a distinguished career in the Royal Navy in both World Wars. In World War 1 he served throughout the Gallipoli campaign as a lieutenant on HMS *Cornwallis* and, as ordnance officer, directed the shelling of the forts during the Navy's attempts to force the Dardenelles, otherwise known as The Narrows. He took part in the landing on 'S' beach and was active in the fighting. This was one of the fiercest and bloodiest battles of the war.

He was on the *Cornwallis* in January 1917 when she was torpedoed and sunk. In 1918-19 he was serving on HMS *Centaur* for the evacuation of Allied wounded and prisoners of war in North Germany.

During 1919-20 he was attached as liaison officer to the Royal Hellenic Navy in Thrace during the war between Greece and Turkey. He was on the Greek naval vessel *Kilkis* during landing operations as gunning instructor and liaison officer, when he supervised the unloading of supplies during shell fire. He was made an honorary vice-Admiral of the Greek navy and was awarded the War Cross, B. Class.

Harry Minchin retired from the navy in 1926 and came home to run the farm at Annagh. He had married for a second time – this time to a distant cousin, Alice Minchin of Busherstown, who happily is still alive and well in Ashlawn Nursing Home outside Nenagh. He had two sons by his first wife, Brian and Myles; and another, William A. R. (Billy), by his second marriage who, sadly, was killed in a motor bicycle accident coming home from Dublin in 1956, aged 21 years.

Some Minchin Leases

The first mention of the name 'Liskillebeene' (Lisquillibeen) for the two ancient townlands of Tullawn and Knockballyea occurs in a lease dated 1 May 1762. This lease of the lands of 'Liskillebeene' was made between John Minchin and Solomon Cambie at a rent of

£100 per annum. This Solomon Cambie was the great-grandson of the original Cromwellian grantee.

Another lease between John Minchin of Annagh and Solomon Cambie, Castletown, of Knockballyea and Tullawn (Lisquillibeen), 250 acres at 9s per acre is dated 12 May 1762. Here only Tullawn is equated with the present Lisquillibeen. The spelling of placenames is very erratic, 'Liscullen' also being given for Lisquillibeen.

The following leases were all granted to tenant farmers on the Minchin estate during the course of the nineteenth century, although many of the lessees held very small holdings.

(1) Lease dated 9 April 1829 of 'part of Annaghshan', 30a 10r 1p, made between John Minchin and Patrick Boucher for the lives of Patrick Boucher and his heirs at rent of £6 3s 8d per annum.

It would appear that the Bouchers had a perpetual lease, and the last heir was Terry Hogan whose mother was a Boucher. He sold the property to Frank Donoghue of Ballinderry about four years ago and the house is now a holiday home.

(2) Lease by John Minchin 'of Annaghshan' of 4 acres plantation to John Smith for lives, at £12 per annum. Dated 9 April 1829.

(3) Lease of 'part of lands of Kilbeller' (Kilbiller) by John Minchin to Joseph Slattery of Coolbawn, Shopkeeper, for lives of his sons, Patrick, John and William, 35a 2r 22p at £1 10s 0d per acre, dated 20 August 1840. The same with notes on the will of Joseph Slattery etc, dated 21 August 1840.

(4) Lease of 'part of the lands of Lahesseragh', 26a 0r 2p, by F. J. Minchin to Henry Lynch for 21 years at annual rent of £22 15s. Counterpart lease dated 9 April 1858. Witness: John Exshaw.

(5) Draft copy of lease dated 1858 of 'part of lands of Annagh', 38 acres, by F. J. Minchin to Michael Toohey for 21 years at annual rent of £48. Bounded on east by Ballycolliton, and on west and south by Arbuthnot Gould's farm and on north by Kilbiller.

I believe this is the farm now owned by Ger and Breda Fogarty.

(6) Lease dated 1858 of 'part of lands of Lisquiallabeen', 15a 1r 31p, by F. J. Minchin to William Hogan for 21 years. Bounded on east by John D'Arcy's farm, on west by the road leading from the Cross at Coolbawn to the Cross at Ballycolliton, and on the north by Mary Slattery's farm.

(7) Draft copy of lease of 1858 of 'part of the lands of Lisquillibeen', 23 acres, by F. J. Minchin to Matthew Costelloe, farmer, for 21 years at a rent of £25 17s 6d per annum.

(8) Draft copy of lease of 'part of lands of Annagh', being 35a 1r 20p by F. J. Minchin to James Gaynon (Gaynor) for 21 years at rent of £39 16s 0d.

(9) Draft copy of lease of 1858 of 'part of lands of Lisquillibeen' by F. J. Minchin to Martin Moran, being 7a 2r 5p for 21 years at rent of £10 2s 0d per annum.
'Assignment of the lands of Kilbelleer' (Kilbiller). John Minchin dec. demised these lands to Joseph Slattery. Mrs Mary Slattery, widow, assigns the lease to John Exshaw junior for £26. Dated 28 November 1859. John Exshaw was Minchin's agent.

(10) Lease of 26a 2r 3p of lands of Annagh by F. J. Minchin to Patrick Hobbins for 21 years at a rent of £25 per annum. Dated 27 April 1869.
In 1824 Hobbins held land in Glenbower in common with Matthew Slattery. The Whelan's grandmother was Hobbins. John Whelan of Ballinderry married in.

(11) Lease of 33a 0r 6p part of lands at Skehanagh by F. J. Minchin to John Cleary, farmer, for 21 years at a rent of £34 9s 1d per annum. Dated 27 April 1869.

(12) Lease of 26a 2r 38p of lands of Lisquillibeen by F. J. Minchin to John Casey. The land is bordered on north by John Gough's farm, on south by Mrs. Slattery's farm, on the east by Rod. Kennedy's farm and on west by Mrs. Slattery's and Loughnane's farms. Dated 28 April 1869.

(13) Lease of 13 acres of lands of Kilbarron by F. J. Minchin to John Slattery for 21 years at a rent of £18 5s 0d per annum. Dated 28 April 1869.
This is the John Slattery of Glenbower who married into the Kennedys of Kilbarron and is ancestor of Mrs Kitty Cormican (née Sammon) whose mother was Penelope Slattery.

(14) Lease of 7a 2r 5p of lands at Lisquillibeen by F. J. Minchin to Martin Moran for 21 years at annual rent of £10 3s 0d. Dated 28 April 1869.

(15) Lease dated 4 February 1870 of 121 acres of 'lands of Castle Division' by F. J. Minchin to John Love of Annagh Castle at a rent of £194 15s 8d per annum. A bill for carpentry, etc dated 1869 is attached to lease.

(16) Draft lease dated 1871 of 16a 1r 24p of lands at Lisquillibeen, lately in tenure of John Sheehan, by F. J. Minchin to Alice Starr, widow, for 21 years at a rent £20 9s 4d per annum.
This Alice Starr was grandmother of the late Mrs Peg Donohue, Kilbiller, and Mrs Liz Moore, Borrisokane.

(17) Lease dated 21 February 1874 of road and passage etc., by F. J. Minchin to Robert Cleburne of Kilbiller for 31 years at a rent of 4s per annum.
The demise of the passage leading from the main road to the houses of the workmen of Robert Cleburne of Kilbiller for 31 years.

Cleburne lived in the old Georgian house at the back of Rody O'Meara's new house in Kilbiller.

The Toohey Eviction

There is only one recorded ejectment or eviction on the Annagh estate – that of Laurence Toohey from Glenbower in 1860. A document among the Minchin Papers, dated 22 May 1860, records that F. J. Minchin sought to recover 6a 30r 0p of the land of Glenbower with dwelling thereon, held at a rent of £6 3s 9d per year, from Laurence Toohey and Michael, John, Joseph, Daniel, Judith and Matthew Toohey. The Toohey eviction was also mentioned in the Kennedy of Lisquillibeen letters which came back from Australia and which appear in Chapter 12. There is also a folk memory of a Toohey eviction, the name quoted being Michael Toohey, Annagh, the same name as in lease (5) above.

A Laurence Toohey is recorded as living at Lisquillibeen in 1824 according to the Tithe Applotment lists. There were also Tooheys living in Cameron, at Meelick and on Annagh Hill.

Early in the nineteenth century several families were moved from their original holdings to other locations nearby. This was in order to have big fields to grow corn which became very profitable at the time of the Napoleonic wars and the Industrial Revolution in England. For example, there were several smallholders on the stretch of road on the right going towards Nenagh from Kilbarron Church of Ireland church stretching to the turn-off for Luska. Some of these families were moved into Lisquillibeen Lane. I know of two for certain from reliable tradition in the families of their descendants.

Hogans kept a public house where Jerry and Josephine Carroll's house now stands. Mrs Eileen Carroll (Paddy Carroll's wife), whose mother was a Hogan of Lisquillibeen, recounts that her ancestor, possibly her great-grandfather – her grandfather was William Hogan who got the lease in 1858 – kept this public house which was licensed and not a shebeen. He travelled to Birr at regular intervals with a jennet and cart to bring back the supplies of porter etc. He had come originally from Bellevue townland. The family was moved down Lisquillibeen Lane and was the first house in the lane. The house fell into disrepair when Tom Hogan – the above Mrs Carroll's uncle and last of the family, died but the ruins are still there. The land is still in the family – the property of Pat Carroll who lives in Jersey.

The other family whom we know was moved from the high road down the lane was the O'Meara (Eel) family. One of the family, Martin (Sandy) Meara, died at Ballyhogan near Puckaun in 1996. His grandfather Jack lived down Lisquillibeen Lane, as did Jack's son Martin whose family, including Martin (Sandy), were all born there.

When the original Minchin land on the high road was being divided by the Land Commission sometime in the 1950s, Jack and his second wife camped out on the site of what had been their ancestral home, down the road from Jerry Carroll's, in the hope of getting it back from the Land Commission. They used light a fire there and make tea. However, they did not succeed in getting a 'divide', as they did not have the land necessary to qualify.

Other families may have been moved down to Lisquillibeen Lane also, but I have no information on them. The Houghs of Lisquillibeen originally lived down the lane beyond Caseys but moved, at some stage, to what was their last home – the foot of Thade's Castle where Michael Donoghue now lives. The old Hough home stood in the townland of Knockballyea.

Most of those families who were moved may only have had a garden and since that was less than an acre they would not appear in the 1824 Tithe Applotment list. That the area was quite thickly populated we know from tradition and indeed from the early census returns.

Division of the Minchin Estate
When Commander Harry Minchin came back from service in the first World War he continued to farm as his grandfather and great-grandfather had done. His father, the General, had concentrated on rearing cattle and had no tillage. He employed a fair number of men. Joe Slattery was his steward. All went well until the mid-Thirties when what became known as the 'Economic War' between Ireland and Great Britain broke out.

When the first Fianna Fáil government, under de Valera, came into power in March 1932 they decided to fulfil their pre-election pledge that the 'land annuities' would no longer be returned to the British Exchequer, as had been done since the setting up of the Free State. He argued that we should not still be paying for the land that had been taken from our ancestors by force. Great Britain retaliated by imposing a heavy tariff on our agriculture produce and cattle. At that time, unlike now, Britain was our only customer. The bottom fell out of the cattle trade and farmers who depended solely on cattle were in a very bad way and many went broke. It put Commander Minchin out of business and he decided to sell his land voluntarily to the Land Commission. I understand he got a very poor price – something like £8 per acre. He kept about 50 acres around the house.

The Land Commission considered 30 acres a viable farm. Joe Slattery, the steward, got a full 40-acre farm. Mike Ryan of Coolbawn got a couple of fields behind the church and wood, Jerry Moran got the Church Field. Joe Coonan, whose cottage had been built on Minchin land, got a few acres. Mrs Heffernan, also a cottier whose husband had worked in Annagh, got some land. Bill Carroll got the Quarry Field. Jack Barry got a full farm. Jer Bouchier and the Ducies each got a divide of eight or nine acres.

After this distribution there was still some land left which had not been allocated. A meeting was held in the Fort Field near the Protestant church, now known as Smith's field and owned by Michael Carroll. This field was still not apportioned at the end of the meeting. The Land Commission official offered it to Jack Meagher who replied that he already had enough 'forts'. There were two forts on the land he had got in the Waller divide at Onny Dunne's hill! Land was a glut on the market, farmers couldn't pay their rates, nobody wanted land.

The Land Commission official next offered it to Jack Needham who refused. He was hoping Castletown would be divided and it would suit him better to get some land there. Tommy Smith, the part-time postman, was passing by and went into the field to see what was going on. Tommy had got a small divide in Wallers. The official asked 'well, what about the postman, perhaps he would take it?' Taken unawares Tommy, who needed more land like he needed a hole in his head, accepted. Tommy and his brother Dan both died unmarried and their brother Paddy's son, Danny, inherited their land, including the Fort Field.

At this time there was talk of the Biggs estate in Bellevue being divided and Pat Tiernan, who had lived at Lesserragh gate lodge before he built his own house, wanted a divide of it. It was becoming less easy to get land in the late 1930s and the Land Commission was only giving it to people who already had a small holding. The Tiernans were advised to buy a bit of land, so they bought the Fort Field from Danny Smith. Thus they qualified for, and got, a farm on the Biggs estate. The Land Commission then offered Smith's field to Michael Carroll at £8 half-yearly rent and he accepted it. You could buy out entirely at half what was owed or continue paying until the expiry date of the annuity.

The Last Minchin in Annagh

When Britain declared war on Germany in 1939 Harry Minchin rejoined the Royal Navy and was posted to Glasgow as adviser on ordnance with the substantive rank of captain. Alice and their young son went to join him and were there throughout the heavy bombing of the dockyards.

Harry Minchin sold Annagh Lodge and what was left of the estate after the earlier sale to the Land Commission. He and his wife took up residence in a house on the estate, formerly a hunting lodge called 'Murroughboro'. They changed the name to 'Lochiel'. The present owners, Aggie and Duncan Bane, have changed the name back to 'Murroughboro'.

The first owners of Annagh Lodge after Minchins were a Burke family who ran it as a guest house. They sold it to Robin Cubitt, a member of a wealthy English family. He farmed it for many years until his untimely death in the 1980s. His sons sold it to Mrs Rosamund Sterling, Castletown. It is now the home of her younger son, Andrew, and his wife Rachel (née Henry, Waterloo Lodge and Dublin). They run it as Country House accommodation.

Commander Minchin died in January 1973, aged 83 years; his widow later married Vivian St. Claire (Edward) Gloster, who died in 1988. She has two sets of stepsons, Harry's sons, Brian and Myles, and Vivian's sons – all of whom come to visit her regularly from distant parts.

Sources:
Brian Minchin, Cheltenham, England (son of late Commander H. F. Minchin), who holds the original Minchin documents.
Civil Survey, Vol 2, 1654.
Tithe Applotment List, 1824.
Primary Valuation List, 1852.
1901 census.
OHS, Kilbarron civil parish Gravestone Inscriptions.
Samuel A. Lewis, *Topographical Dictionary of Ireland*, 1837.
My own and Carroll family personal memories.

Photographs: p. 147, taken by Nancy Murphy; p. 148 loaned by Rachel Sterling; p. 149 loaned by Brian Minchin.

Colonel Jack Minchin's Last Flight

It was the last day of August 1927 and unseasonably misty. Thick fog clung over Annagh woods. It was school holidays and my sisters and brother and I were playing outside. At mid-morning a throbbing noise could be heard coming from behind the church tower. Looking over the woods we saw the dark shape of an aeroplane flying low. We watched in wonder. In 1927 an aeroplane was a rare sight in Coolbawn and it was flying so very low and so slowly. As we watched, it turned and flew back over the lake, over Islandmore, and vanished beyond the Galway shore. 37-year-old Colonel 'Jack' Minchin was saying 'Hail and Farewell' to Annagh and Murroughboro before voyaging out into the bleak Atlantic in an attempt, with his two companions, to be the first fliers to cross the great ocean from east to west.

There had been several crossings from west to east, the last only a month earlier when Charles Lindbergh had flown from New York to Paris; the first in 1919 when Alcock and Brown had flown from Newfoundland and landed in a bog near Clifden in Co. Galway. In 1919 a British airship, R.34, had made the east to west crossing. The flight from east to west was much more difficult and dangerous than that in the opposite direction. On this route the aviators had to risk encountering the full fury of a south-westerly gale, as the prevailing winds across the Atlantic are westerly at all seasons of the year.

Fogs off the coast of Newfoundland had to be contended with and the westward-sloping contour of the North American coastline did not help. Several fliers had met their deaths latterly, i.e. summer 1927, in east-west attempts – the very latest, two Frenchmen, Nungessor and Coli, only a few days before.

Col. Frederick Frank Reilly Minchin, or 'Jack' as he was known to family and friends, had long had an ambition to fly the Atlantic. He had spoken of it to friends in Canada fifteen years before when Lindbergh (born 1902) and his generation were small boys.

Born in Madras

The Minchin background in military service was outlined in the previous section. Captain Frederick F. Minchin was in the army and stationed at Madras when a second son was born to him and his wife Marjorie Abbott in 1890. Frederick Frank Reilly/Jack was a delicate child and had to wear irons on his legs to correct a curvature. When Captain (later Major-General) Minchin was transferred to Ceylon, his wife brought the children back to England. She comes across as a devoted mother who did not send her little sons to school in England at age five or six, as was the custom then, but kept them with her until she could accompany them. Captain Minchin soon joined them to take up an appointment as Inspector in the Ordnance Department at Woolwich. He remained there and was in charge of munitions during the the First World War until his health broke down and he came home to Annagh where he died in 1923.

When Jack was fourteen years old his mother died suddenly, and after a year his father remarried. From Eastbourne College he went to Sandhurst in 1909. In 1910 he was gazetted to the 2nd Batt. Connaught Rangers, stationed at the Curragh. While there he first learned to fly. Keeping polo ponies and generally leading an expensive lifestyle he got into debt and had to resign his commission. In those days, and indeed until World War II, officers had to have private means;

they were not meant to live on their pay, and there would have been no private income for young Jack. His father had a new, young family and Annagh was not a big estate. It was, indeed, simply a large farm. Jack went to Winnipeg in Manitoba, Canada, in 1912. While there he did a series of boring jobs which he hated.

Rare Foresight
But he had rare foresight in aviation matters and advocated the formation of a Canadian Air Force. He set about forming in Winnipeg the first company ever incorporated in Canada to carry on civil aviation in a practical way. He wrote endless articles for Canadian papers on the subject and brought a rattle-trap machine which would form, he hoped, the nucleus of a great air fleet. In 1914 the Great War was declared before anything could be done about it. He joined Princess Patricia's Canadian Light Infantry as a private and came back to Europe. He soon gained a commission and in March 1915 was seconded to the Royal Flying Corps as a Lieutenant. He rose to the rank of Lieut.-Col. and fought in Europe on the Western Front, in Macedonia and in the Middle East, with conspicuous bravery and skill, being awarded almost all the war decorations possible, including the M(ilitary) C(ross) with bar, the D(istinguished) S(ervice) O(rder) and several mentions in dispatches.

In March 1919 he went to India to command No. 52 Wing, returned to England in January 1920, and left the service in March 1920 with the rank of Colonel. The Royal Air Force was still not a separate service. In July he was made a Commander of the Military Division of the Order of the British Empire (OBE). In October 1920 he was married in Dublin to Betty Selby-Lowndes, but the marriage failed and they were divorced in May 1925. In 1924 he joined Imperial Airways as a pilot. Early in 1925 he was selected as one of the two to try out a new airmail service between Cairo and Calcutta. In 1926 he and Frank Barnard, set up speed and distance records while testing the new Bristol Scout Amphibian Airliner.

About this time Jack Minchin became acquainted with the Princess von Lowestein-Wertheim, formerly Lady Anne Savile, daughter of the fourth earl of Wexborough near Leeds in Yorkshire. She had a home, Ditton Lodge, at Thames Ditton near Kingston-upon-Thames, Surrey. It was she who was to finance the Atlantic flight. Having learned to fly herself, she was very interested in aviation generally and had, since 1922, been laying plans for an attempt to make the first transatlantic flight from east to west and also to be the first woman to fly the Atlantic.

Though 61, she was petite and elegant and did not look her age. She asked Minchin if he would be her pilot and he agreed. She then asked Capt. Leslie Hamilton, who had piloted her around a great deal, if he would act as co-pilot. He agreed, but regretted it afterwards as he was not a long-haul pilot as Minchin was. However, he was too much of a gentleman to go back on his word so he went ahead with the project. He was younger than Minchin and was known as the 'Aerial Gipsy'. He operated a flying taxi service between the European capitals.

Preparations for the Flight
Once the pilots agreed to take on the task it was decided to get going as soon as possible as several other outfits were also preparing to attempt the flight, notably

the American millionaire Levine with Capt. Hinchcliffe of Imperial Airways. The Princess wanted the expedition to be all-British – the flight was originally to be from London to Ottawa. No suitable British plane was available so a Dutch Fokker monoplane VIIA was ordered from Amsterdam but to have a British engine of the latest type – a radial air-cooled Bristol Jupiter, 450 horse power.

They had hoped to take off from Clifden in Co. Galway to save fuel and the two pilots flew to Baldonnel en route to Clifden where they failed to find a suitable runway. Baldonnel was then thought of, but Upavon on Salisbury Plain in Wiltshire, England, was finally decided on. This had the advantage of being near the engineers at Filton, Bristol. On 18 August Minchin and Hamilton flew the Fokker VIIA from Amsterdam to Croydon, then on to Filton where technical experts of the Bristol Co. gave the engine a thorough overhaul and re-tuning. Meanwhile, the cabin seating was removed and eight additional petrol tanks fitted, giving a total capacity of 795 gallons and an endurance of over 40/41 hours.

From Upavon to Ottawa was approximately 3,600 miles. If they could average 100 miles an hour, they could get there in 36 hours but even at 80/85 m.p.h. it could be done inside the 40/41 hours. Everything would depend on the winds. The monoplane had a white body and great golden wings. It was named the St. Raphael for two reasons: St. Raphael is the patron of fliers, and the church where the princess's Catholic family worshipped was St. Raphael's in Kingston-upon-Thames near her home. Her great-uncle, Alexander Raphael, a rich recluse, had built it in 1848 as Kingston's first RC church.

Waiting

On 26 August Minchin and Hamilton flew the plane from Filton to Upavon and waited for favourable weather conditions. The princess remained in London. On 30 August she telephoned Hamilton to say that Levine and Hinchcliffe were ready to start. 'We've got to get away tomorrow. I've been on to the Air Ministry and the weather reports are favourable. I'll be at Upavon at 6.30 in the morning', she said. Until now the pilots did not know if the princess really meant to accompany them. It is probable they would have been much happier to have gone without her, but she was paying and there was nothing they could do. That night there was a party in the Officers' Mess. The pianist played over and over again a popular hit of the day which was Leslie Hamilton's favourite tune: 'I took one look at you, That's all I had to do ... my heart stood still'.

Next morning he had a bad hangover. Minchin on the other hand looked fresh and confident. The princess arrived in her Rolls at 6.30 a.m. Soon afterwards the Archbishop of Cardiff, accompanied by Monsignor Mostyn and two priests, arrived. They got into the princess's car and drove to the plane. There was a short service when the Archbishop blessed the plane, wished the two pilots luck and shook their hands warmly. The princess knelt for a blessing. One of the priests, Father O'Reilly, gave the princess a four-leaf shamrock, carved out of Irish bog oak, for luck. The pilots climbed into the cockpit, Minchin into the pilot's seat, and the princess, helped by the Archbishop, crawled into her niche amongst the petrol tanks, where she sat on a wicker armchair surrounded by a hamper and two red hatboxes. The hamper contained eggs, cheese and ham sandwiches, and two thermos flasks of coffee. She was wearing purple riding breeches, fur-lined yellow top boots, a belted purple jacket and a black toque hat of a kind then fashionable.

The Take-Off

There were anxious moments at the start because of the very heavy load of fuel being carried. Wing Commander Vernon Browne, the station commander, and his Adjutant, Flight Lieut. Freddie West, VC, doubted if they would be able to take off, and had ambulances stationed at strategic points on the runway. The Fokker took a run of 1,020 yards before it rose into the air. The successful take-off (below), was due to the skill and courage of the pilot and to the pulling power of the Bristol Jupiter engine. The total load was 11,000 lbs. The plane had no floats or seaplane hull; it carried a small raft which would not stay long afloat in Atlantic seas. The intention of the pilots was not only to get safely to Ottawa but to land there, refuel and return at once to Vienna, thus breaking the world distance record set up by Chamberlain and Levine a few weeks earlier.

Before they set off Hamilton had told Flight Lieut West that he did not think they would make it. He had given his word to go and would not go back on it. He kept repeating, 'This is a grim ordeal', as the mechanics swung the propeller. On the surface, at least, Minchin exuded quiet confidence. He was a pilot who had never had a serious accident. Somehow or other, in popular mythology, at least in Co. Tipperary, he had the reputation of being a dare-devil flier, but this was not at all the case. He was a serious professional aviator who would not take unnecessary risks. 'Minchin is one of the finest civil pilots the world has ever seen', an official of Imperial Airways is quoted as saying at the time, 'He would never lose his head. In a difficult situation Minchin is your man'.

On Course

After take-off the plane moved very slowly westward. The weight of fuel ruled out any speed or height. At 10.15 a.m. Captain Harvey of Bargy Castle, Co. Wexford, reported seeing the plane at a height of approximately 500 ft. going in a north west-by-west direction, travelling slowly, but engine running well. Captain Harvey believed that the machine must have crossed the Irish coast between Rosslare and Carnsore Point. It was next reported at 10.40 a.m. over Thurles, flying low and slowly. The exact time they flew over Coolbawn was not noted by us. At 12.10 p.m. the Gardai at Inverin, Co. Galway, reported seeing it fly out over the coast at approximately 900-1,000 ft. It was beginning to gain height. The throbbing of the engine could be plainly heard and the flight of the machine was watched by hundreds of farmers and fishermen as it sped out over the Atlantic between Garumna Island and Inis Mór.

The next and last authentic sighting of the St. Raphael came from a ship in mid-Atlantic, the *Josiah Macey*, a tanker owned by the Standard Oil Co., and making for Germany. It was 9.44 p.m. on that Wednesday 31 August, and she was flying at latitude 53.50 and longitude 20.45.5 in a direct line with the north of Scotland. This position would have fitted in with the known speed of the plane. The ship's crew signalled with a Aldis Lamp and the St. Raphael replied with a succession of flashes from its own signalling lamp in recognition and reassurance. The radio operator of the tanker sent out a message to say that the St. Raphael was in mid-Atlantic holding her course for the direct flight to Ottawa, her engine running smoothly and strongly.

Since leaving the Irish coast the plane had covered nearly 900 miles against headwinds which had reduced her average speed to 85 m.p.h. This speed could be expected to improve as more fuel was burned and providing the headwinds did not get much stronger. The margin for Ottawa was still just adequate. The message from the *Josiah Macey* had been picked up by an Irish wireless station on the west coast and had been relayed to the Air Ministry in London. Minchin had a contingency plan to land at Harbour Grace in southern Newfoundland if he felt he could not reach Ottawa non-stop.

Hope Fades
With the hopeful message from the *Josiah Macey* it was felt that the aviators were going to make it to Ottawa and great preparations were made to welcome them. The Prince of Wales and his brother Prince George (later King Edward VIII and the Duke of Kent), who were in Ottawa and due to leave for Montreal, postponed their departure. Hamilton's wife came up from New York. An all-night vigil was kept all along the coast and flares were sent up to guide them in. Suddenly, banks of fog drifted in off the ocean. The St. Raphael would have had to fly through this treacherous mist which probably stretched for nearly a third of the way across the Atlantic.

Towards mid-day 1 September the fog cleared but there was no sign of the plane. Possibly it had slipped over the coast unseen in the fog and would still arrive in Ottawa. Crowds gathered from far and near. Journalists and photographers abounded. They waited in hope. Darkness fell. The night wore on. Slowly the crowds dispersed.

By the morning of 2 September it became clear that there was going to be no triumphant arrival at Ottawa. Hope was not completely lost however. The crew might have been picked up by a ship which carried no radio. This had happened to a flier a little while before and he had turned up safe and sound after six days. They might have been blown off their course and force-landed somewhere in the wastes of Labrador.

That possibility was borne out the following year when the first successful east-west flight was carried out by an Irishman, Captain (later Colonel) Fitzmaurice and two Germans, Captain Kohl and Baron Von Huenefeld flying a German plane, The Bremen, and taking off from Baldonnel, Co. Dublin. It landed at Greenly Island off Labrador.

World Opinion
The world's press was full of the lost fliers. News items and leading articles proliferated in the *Irish Independent, Irish Times, The Times, The Sunday Times, The Observer, The Daily Telegraph, Daily Mail, Daily Express, Daily Mirror*, not

to mention the *Nenagh Guardian* and the *Offaly Chronicle*, as well as newspapers outside Ireland and Britain. *The Daily Mail*'s leading article of 7 September reads:

> Probably never before has the whole civilised world been so touched by sympathy and anxiety as it has been over the fate of the Princess von Lowenstein-Wertheim and her gallant pilots ... Sometimes unreflecting people ask 'what is the use of these daring exploits?' The answer is that 'the safety of this country may depend, within the next generation, on supremacy in the air. The flight of the St. Raphael is as great and splendid an adventure as the voyage of the *Mayflower* long ago.

The Irish Times, in a leading article on 6 September entitled 'Pioneers', posed the question: 'Does the world gain anything from these so perilous flirtations with death?' and quotes, in answer to the question, Air Vice-Marshal Sir. W. Sefton Brancker, Head of Civil Aviation.

> We cannot stop people from attempting to fly the Atlantic and we do not want to stop them. All our great achievements have involved danger and death in the early stages. Let these pioneers go on.

In the *Daily Mirror* of 7 September, Sir Sefton is quoted as having said to a reporter at Liverpool:

> You can no more prevent a man from attempting to fly the Atlantic than you can prevent him from attacking Mount Everest. I could have put money on Minchin getting across safely.

The Sunday Times of 4 September wrote:

> It seems that the airmen were either forced down on to the sea before they reached America or else drifted off their course and ran out of petrol in the wide area of sea south of Newfoundland.

Hope Dies at Home

And what of hopes and fears at home in Annagh and Coolbawn during those days after 31 August where Jack's brother, Commander Harry Minchin, and other relatives waited anxiously for news? There was no television or wireless. The only news came from the daily paper.

My parents kept the post office at Coolbawn. The only telephone for miles around was in that post office. Any news, good or bad, would come over the telephone. Anxiously we waited. On 3 September a telegram arrived: 'Delighted to hear Master Jack safe'. Sender: Nora, and handed in at Nenagh. Nobody was thinking logically. Here was news, good news, nobody doubted it, nobody wanted to doubt it.

My father took the telegram to Annagh himself, so happy to be the bearer of good news. Normally, we children would take the telegram, walking through the woods. But this was special. My father rode up the avenue on his bicycle and gave the telegram to the Commander. He too suspended disbelief. He looked at my father, shook his head and said, 'He was a devil'.

The Three Fliers

Colonel Jack Minchin

I have read all the material I could find on Jack Minchin (below) but have not succeeded in meeting anyone who knew him. I knew people who knew him well, such as his cousins, Dot and Gwen Bruce and, of course his brother Harry, but they were all dead when my interest in him first arose.

Physically, he was over 6'3', tall, dark and handsome. He appears to have been a man everyone liked. He had personal charm and a kindly nature. He was admired for his skill and courage as a pilot and was a very good commanding officer. One person who knew him well in Canada, writing in a Canadian paper, comments that 'somehow in civil life he failed to find a job worthy of his war record'. He goes on to say that Jack Minchin struck him as a man 'possessed by some constant sadness and that perhaps his end was welcome'.

In many ways his life had been sad: his mother's sudden death when he was fourteen, the failure of his marriage, the experience of having to resign through lack of funds. He was always short of money while having expensive tastes, making the Cavendish Hotel his headquarters while in London. I believe that his feelings when setting out on his last expedition probably were: 'well and good if I make it and perhaps make some money as well – if I don't, what the hell!'

> He balanced all, brought all to mind.
> The years to come seemed waste of breath.
> A waste of breath the years behind
> In balance with this life, this death.

Commander Harry Minchin had a wall plaque erected in Kilbarron Church of Ireland church commemorating the memory of Jack and his two companions. When the church was deconsecretated and sold into private ownership the plaques within the church were relocated to the grounds. However, the people involved in this process felt that because of this one's historical significance the most appropriate place for it would be the Heritage Centre in Nenagh. This was done in 1990, in agreement with his sister-in-law, Mrs Alice Minchin Gloster. It is on display there since with an abridged version of this story.

Captain Leslie Hamilton

Leslie Hamilton (below with the Princess) had a splendid war record and was a brilliant aviator. He was pale-faced, handsome, and not as tall as Minchin. He was said to be irresistible to women. He had married but the marriage was in difficulties. Until 1924 he was an instructor and test pilot with the RAF, but left for a commercial career, flying his own Vickers Napier Amphibian throughout Europe. His was probably the greatest courage of all as he felt the expedition was going to fail but went because he had given his word.

Princess Anne von Lowenstein-Wertheim
The former Lady Anne Savile had married a German prince named Ludwig von Lowenstein-Wertheim in 1887. He had been killed two years after their marriage, fighting in the Phillipines with the Spaniards against the Americans. After World War I she had regained her British nationality. She was a very wealthy woman. By all accounts, she was well liked and charming. The Princess had faith in her pilots and believed they would get there – otherwise why the hatboxes? There are some who say that, had she not opted to go, there would have been room for that much more fuel, which might have made the difference between success and failure.

There is a marble plaque in her memory and in memory of 'her two brave pilots' in the church her great-uncle built – St. Raphael's in Kingston-upon-Thames.

MEMORY OF AVIATORS.

VICTIMS OF DISASTERS.

LAKES NAMED IN CANADA.

(Received January 15, 5.5 p.m.)
A. and N.Z.   OTTAWA, Jan. 14.

The Canadian Government has named some newly discovered lakes in North-western Ontario after the men and women who lost their lives in transoceanic and other flights last summer. The first has been named Lake Doran, after Miss Mildred Doran, who perished in the Dole prize flight to Honolulu. Others have been named after Princess Lowenstein and Messrs. Tully, Medcalf, Minchin, Bertaud and Payne.

Sources:
Author's personal knowledge.
Sunday Graphic, 28 August 1927, *The Illustrated London News*, 1927, for text and photographs (courtesy of the Imperial War Museum, London)

Photograph p. 161, loaned by Brian Minchin.

The Parkers of Brookfield

Brookfield House stands about a quarter of a mile from the shores of Lough Derg, about half-way between Skehanagh quay and Kilgarvan quay. By road it is approached via a long avenue which leads off the main Nenagh-Portumna road about half-way between Coolbawn Cross and Ballinderry. It is only a short distance along the shore from Bellevue House. Brookfield and Bellevue are two new townland names – the territory seems to be all part of Scriboge in the *Civil Survey*.

It is said to be called Brookfield because of a brook separating the two properties. The present house is a reconstruction of an earlier house, which was probably built by the Cambies about the middle of the 1700s. An indication of the date of the building of the house can be found in the diary of George Stoney, Greyfort, Borrisokane, which contains an entry for 3 May 1766 thus: 'Tom went to Brookfield to housewarming'. Tom was his second son and lived at home in Greyfort.

Description
Brookfield is a rather plain, but nevertheless very handsome, two-storey L-shaped building (below). The front part is said to have been built by John Parker, the then owner, prior to his marriage to Helena Biggs circa 1860. It would have an older look about it were it not for the added bay window and veranda on the south side. This was put on at his wife's request and is a copy of that at Bellevue, her old home.

The hall door is approached by fine wide steps. The entrance hall is large and there is a splendid staircase leading to the upper storey. Opening off the hall are two finely-proportioned reception rooms – dining-room to the right and drawingroom to the left.

The Parkers
Cambie ownership of Brookfield in the eighteenth century continued until sold or tenanted in the mid-1800s. Henry D. Grady is returned as the immediate lessor, with

John Parker the occupier, in the Primary Valuation list of 1852. This John Parker was son of John Parker of Ballycolliton who was of the Lansdowne (near Portroe) branch.

It was John Parker, Jun., who married Helena Biggs. They had two children, Jack and Annie. The following tablet was erected to Jack's memory in Kilbarron Church of Ireland church.

In loving memory of John George (Jack) Parker, Brookfield, Co. Tipperary, Captain, Princess Victoria's Royal Irish Fusiliers.
Born April 6th 1865. Died at Bhamo, Upper Burmah, Feb 3rd 1896 of enteric fever.
This tablet was erected by his sorrowing mother and sister whom he dearly loved.

That sister was Annie Parker who later married William Reeves – hence the name Parker-

Three generations: Mrs Helena (née Biggs) Parker, her daughter Mrs Annie Parker-Reeves and Annie's daughter Eileen, beside Brookfield's bay window with veranda, circa 1910.

Reeves. After the church was deconsecrated and sold, this tablet was placed on the Parker-Reeves burial plot, which also contains a vault.

Parker-Reeves

William Reeves of Kilgarvan and Annie Parker had three children: John (Jack) who married Elizabeth (Babs) Griffiths and was the father of Heather who married Alec Bell and lives in Dublin; Eileen who married a Kennedy from Dublin and had two children; and Robert William George (Laddie) who married a Miss Waterstone and lived at Kilgarvan and had no children. The young Parker-Reeves' nurse was Bridgie Smith of Bellevue whose home was quite near Brookfield and whom I remember very well. The nursery regime was strict and only very plain food was allowed. Heather Bell and her two Kennedy cousins are the only known descendants of the Biggs, Parker and Reeves families.

Heather Bell understands that the lands of Brookfield (212 acres at that time) were acquired by the Cambies from the Biggs. As already stated the owner was Thomas Sadleir. The Biggs may have had it on lease from him and sold that on to Cambies.

William Reeves died in 1904 at the early age of 37. The family continued to live at Kilgarvan and when his mother-in-law, Mrs Helena Parker, became too old to live alone at Brookfield she took up residence with her daughter, the widowed Annie, at Kilgarvan. Helena died there in 1924, aged 97. After this her daughter,

Mrs Annie Parker-Reeves, left Kilgarvan and made her home in Monkstown, Dublin. She died there on 14 May 1954, aged 91 years.

Brookfield House remained empty for many years. Then in 1926 an army of workmen came and the old house was renovated and came to life again. The eldest son, Jack, was coming to live there with his wife Elizabeth (Babs). Heather is their only child. Elizabeth Parker-Reeves died in 1995, aged 87, and is buried with Jack who died in 1974, aged 80 years. Her mother, Mrs Griffiths, and other members of the Parker family are also buried in the Parker plot in the cemetery attached to the now deconsecrated Kilbarron Church of Ireland church.

Brookfield was sold out of Parker-Reeves family ownership in 1967. It has had several owners since then, as well as a period when it was unoccupied. Among the owners were a Belgian, Paul Roels, and his wife, a Welsh couple, and the present owners Philip and Beulah Garcin as of 1988.

There was no division of the Brookfield (Parker-Reeves) and Kilgarvan (Reeves) estates. They were sold privately in 1967 and 1976 respectively.

THE BELVEDERE – THE VELVET AIR, BROOKFIELD

During the eighteenth and early nineteenth centuries many of the gentry sought to have places within easy reach of their houses and usually elevated, where they could go for a picnic or after-dinner stroll and admire the view. Sometimes they would build little Greek temples on the spot. They were called 'Belvederes' from the Italian words *bel* meaning 'beautiful' and *vedere* meaning 'to view'. Sometimes they were referred to as 'follies'. The belvedere at Brookfield was probably constructed sometime in the eighteenth century by the Cambie family. It is very close to the boundary between Brookfield and Mota which was also Cambie property at one time. The Cambies must have decided they would take advantage of the lake for their 'pleasuance'. It was very well sited and gave a view of the surrounding countryside, as well as a base for looking out over Lough Derg to the Clare Hills beyond, and for watching the beauty of the sunsets.

It consisted of about half a statute acre of water between two walls about 12 feet wide to meet in a V and facing out to the lake. Inside the walls was a lily pond which, it is said, contained exotic water lilies brought back by members of the Cambie family from different parts of the world. The family and guests could stroll along the walls, enjoy the view and take the air. Years later, when the Parkers lived at Brookfield and after John Parker died, his widow Helena would proceed in a little pony chaise, probably led by a groom, up and down the walls around the lily pond and enjoy the view and balmy air. The local people corrupted the word Belvedere to Belvedare, then Velvedare and, finally, to 'the Velvet Air' which it is known as locally.

After Helena Parker died and her daughter Mrs Annie Parker-Reeves went to live in Dublin in the 1920s, and probably much before that, the Belvedere became neglected and finally was used as a port for turf boats. The boat would anchor at the V, the empty horse and cart with its creel would drive along the right-hand wall, be filled with turf, proceed back on the left-hand side, and so several horses and carts could work away at the same time.

The little water enclosure still remains and is about to be returned to its former glory. A holiday village based on the concept of the old Irish 'clachán', or a rather irregular collection of houses of different shapes and sizes, has been built beside the Belvedere. The little harbour has been dredged and may be turned into a marina, a swimming pool or, perhaps, even a lily pond! The village is nearing completion and should be good for tourism in the area.

Brookfield Gate Lodge

In 1850 my grandparents, Patrick Carroll of Lisquillibeen and Mary Fennell from the Cloughjordan area, got married and came to live in the gate lodge to Brookfield House. Mary Fennell's family had been evicted sometime during the Great Famine and she never saw any of her six brothers again. My grandfather was the herd at Parkers. I do not know how they met; Mary may have been in service in the Big House or he may have worked in the Cloughjordan area. The record of their marriage is in that parish register.

The lodge was situated a short distance down the avenue from the road. It was a two-roomed building, with a remarkably stout oak front door which may have been there for security reasons. It was already an old house when Brookfield House was extended and, when digging around the back of the lodge, my grandparents found quantities of mutton bones and other household detritus. It is likely that the lodge was built at the same time as the original Big House circa 1766. Like Brookfield, the lodge had been vacant for some time prior to the arrival of Patrick and Mary. They had nine children. My Aunt Eliza, born in 1852, became a lady's maid to Annie Parker. My father, Patrick, born in 1864 was the seventh child. He was a year younger than Jack Parker of the Big House who died in Upper Burmah in 1896 far from 'the mother and sister he so dearly loved'.

As children, when visiting our aunt, uncle and cousins at Brookfield we loved to roam around the Lawn – two big, open fields at each side of the avenue – the Moor, the Horsepark and the Grove.

Between Dick Howard's farm in Mota down at the shore and quite close to the Belvedere quay is a stretch of swampy, rushy ground which in very wet weather is almost entirely covered with water. It was called the Móinín Ruadh (little red bog) by my Brookfield cousins. It contained an old mill (below) about which nothing is known.

Sources:
Primary Valuation Lists, Lower Ormond, 1852.
OHS, Gravestone Inscriptions, Kilbarron civil parish.
Eileen and the late Pat Carroll, Mrs Heather Bell (née Parker-Reeves), Dick Howard, George Stoney Diaries.

Photographs: p. 164, from glass plate loaned by Betty Williams; p. 166, taken by Paddy Carroll.

THE BRUCES OF LESSERRAGH

The Bruce family first came to Lesserragh circa 1870. Before that they lived in Williamstown – on the Co. Clare shore of Lough Derg behind the Twenty Islands. Major William Tyrell Bruce, the father of the Misses Bruce, built his house on the ruins of an older house called Mungo Park – it is named thus on the 1840 Ordnance Survey map. In fact it was not such an old house, having only been 'lately built' by Rev. Ralph Stoney according to John O'Donovan in his Ordnance Survey letters. It was destroyed by fire.

In 1840 'Mungo Park' was on the right of the road. This low-lying road was re-routed by William T. Bruce, as evidenced by a presentment for 'Special Works' placed before the Tipperary (NR) Grand Jury at the summer assizes of 1873.

> William T. Bruce, Esq., to make 96 p[erches] of a new line of road from the top of the hill of Gortmongo to the junction of the road leading down to Curraghmore so as to avoid the hill. £96.

Old people used say that the famous Scottish explorer, Mungo Park, who was lost in 1805 on an expedition to find the source and outlet of the River Niger, in Africa, was the inspiration for the name. This may well be so, but a more likely one is that it is a mis-translation from the Irish.

The townland adjoining O'Meara's Acres, on which 'Lesserragh' (below) stands, is called Gortmungo. P. W. Joyce's *Irish Names of Places* has the explanation. *Gort* means a garden while *mungo* can be seen as a derivation of *mong*: *long coarse grass/sedgy place*. An assumption that part of a Gaelic placename is a Christian name is not unusual. Another example in Co. Tipperary of this is in the parish of Drom-Inch, where *Gortannagh: marshy garden* has been translated as Annfield.

The road ran beside the old house, taking in the present avenue which, with its magnificent beech and sycamore trees, is such a feature of Lesserragh today.

Major Bruce planted those trees after the road was re-routed to its present higher position. The house was built by James Kennedy, civil engineer, Parsonstown (Birr), at a cost of £650.

The Bruce Line

Before settling at Williamstown the Bruce family lived in Athlone in Co. Westmeath. William T.'s father, John Bruce, owned property there and also in Nottingham in England. He held land in Westmeath from Viscount Castlemaine. John Bruce is described as 'gentleman and lieutenant in the Artillery Drivers'. William Tyrell Bruce was born in 1815, probably in Athlone. He joined the Royal Irish Regiment. In 1851 he was stationed at Calcutta, India, with the rank of captain.

He was a very accomplished flute-player and there is a letter dated 1851 from a famous firm of London flute-makers stating that they are sending him, by overland mail via Southampton, a Boehm flute which they had made for him. They wrote:

> ... as you expressed a great desire to have a Boehm flute as soon as we could send it to you, we put one in hand immediately spending our ultimate pains upon it and have forwarded it to you in this present mail. ... it is a magnificent instrument, far superior to the one you have been playing upon. ... and has been awarded The Grand Prize by the jurors at the Great Exhibition. We look forward with much pleasure to hear you play upon it when you return to England in a Trio with your band-master of whom you speak so highly and with whom we shall be happy to make an acquaintance. We have taken off £3 from the account being a friend.

The bill, including freight, was £26 7s 0d.

It would appear that Major Bruce married after leaving the army. His wife Sophia Susan was twenty years younger and they both died in 1896 – he aged eighty-one, she aged sixty-one. They had eight daughters and two sons. Frank went to South Africa. His family kept in touch with the Lesserragh Bruces, and in 1995 his great-grandson came to visit Mrs Rosamund Sterling, Castletown, and he was happy to be given a copy of an earlier edition of this chapter as an article which appeared in the Winter 1979 issue of *Cois Deirge*. He and his wife live in Plymouth, England.

The other son, Cecil, became a civil engineer and married Minnie Minchin and was the father of Dot and Gwen. The newly-weds emigrated to South America where he worked, but returned to this area and by 1906 Cecil and family were living in the old barracks at Coolbawn.

The Lesserragh family was large and they were probably not very well off. I have heard my aunt say that the plan was for Ellen Kate (Miss Ellie), the eldest, to be sent away to school to be educated and then come back and teach the others. The youngest, Sophia Mary, died aged eighteen. Two girls married Englishmen. Alice married Charles Pine and Louise (Tot) married Arthur Pike. They each had two sons. Ellie went to live at Thurlestone Hall, Cheltenham, perhaps as governess or as Lady Cheltenham's companion, and Janet trained to be a nurse.

Most of them played hockey when young – the local team was very good and won a lot of tournaments. Two of them, Eva and Alice Pine, were internationals.

The Bruce ladies, circa 1910.
Bertie is back right.

During World War I, Janet, Ethel, Eva and Bertie did war work. Janet was matron of a large hospital in the north of Ireland and received the decoration RRC (Royal Red Cross) for her services. The decoration is in marble over her grave in Kilbarron Church of Ireland cemetery. Eva was awarded the OBE for war work in Ireland, and Bertie the MBE for St. John's Ambulance welfare work in Birmingham. Ethel was in charge of the kitchen staff in a hospital at Bray.

A Full Life

They had inherited their father's musical talents and had their own orchestra when they all lived at home. It consisted of Major Bruce – flute; Louise – piano; Ethel – cello; Alice – violin; Bertha Marguerite (Bertie) – violin. Alice Pine's eldest son Tyrrell was a brilliant pianist and composer but died of TB in 1945/6. He had acted in the Gate Theatre, Dublin. Below is a programme of a concert they gave in Nenagh Town Hall in 1898.

Many local people will remember the open-air concerts Tyrell and Christopher

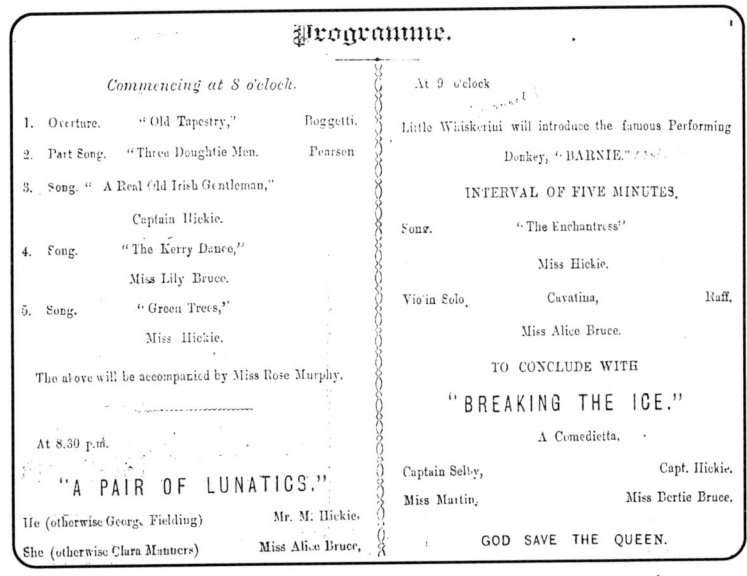

Casson (son of Dame Sybil Thorndike and Sir Lewis Casson), and the actress Meriel Moore, gave on the lake shore when they stayed during the war at Miss Grubb's 'Shack' which stood where the Bells' chalet now stands. Christopher Casson played the harp.

I myself remember the Lesserragh ladies when they were all in their fifties and sixties. Even Bertie, the youngest, must have been nearly fifty. They came back from their war work and resumed their busy, useful lives at home. Eva was the business woman and ran the estate. Ethel looked after the cooking, butter-making and bee-hives. Bertie drove the car and did the local first-aid work. Lily became stone deaf and was not able to do much. The two married sisters came every year with their husbands and sons for the 'dapping'/mayfly fishing. I can remember them all walking up to the church in Kilbiller.

There were other visitors also at Lesserragh – well-known people in the worlds of medicine and the St. John's Ambulance Brigade from Dublin and perhaps London.

The Bruce ladies loved to give pleasure to children. I still feel a shiver of delight when I think of the rather untidy and mysteriously lumpy brown paper parcels which would be delivered to our house, and to many other houses where there were childen, on Christmas Eve from the big black tourer. These parcels would contain toys – something quite rare to us in those days – and sometimes even books. Books were scarce and precious.

Colonel Dennis Pike, Louise's son, in a letter to me in 1979, wrote that:

Lesserragh was not a big house but it was a wonderful place, especially for children. Behind the house there was the 'marble hill' and on it was 'hazel hut' and the 'slide rock', the former built by my uncle for his little sister.

Every week there was a big wash and the big copper was on the boil in the outhouse and I was terrified lest Onnie Kennedy would put me into it! Also there was 'Peggy's Leg' and 'Surprise Packets' at Johanna Molamphy's shop at the Cross ...

My grandfather had a yacht, *The Meershaum*, kept in Anthony Fox's bay (beyond Curraghmore) but I do not remember it myself. In the old days (my childhood) Lesserragh got all its groceries in bulk, i.e. sugar by the half cwt. [4 stone] from Dublin and it all went into the storeroom.

Community Welfare

The Bruces played an exceptional role in the life of the community. Janet, the trained nurse, died in 1926 but the others' experience in the war was now used to help their neighbours. St. John's Ambulance Brigade, first-aid and home nursing classes were held at Lesserragh, 'Old' Dr Quigley, Dr Louis' father, being lecturer.

In about 1924 two members of the first-aid class, Mrs Jack Donoghue (Molly Tiernan) and Mary Moran went to Lourdes as nursing assistants with a national pilgrimage. These first-aid classes went on all during World War II.

Bertie Bruce and her sisters looked after the sick in their own homes, giving back-up help to Dr Quigley. At Lesserragh they dealt with a constant stream of minor casualties, cuts, sprains, boils, abscesses, sore fingers, and sore legs. One would have a bad abscess lanced by the doctor, as I had at age ten, and he would

Back (l to r): Gwen Bruce, Josie Spillane, Annie Armitage (Ryan), -, Christina Costelloe, Josie White, Nellie Moore (Molamphy), Liz Moore (Starr), Mary Darcy (Kelly), May Flannery, Jo Comerford (Carroll). **4th Row**: Mrs Michael O'Meara (Ballinagrass), Biddy Gleeson, Delia Carthy, Mary Brereton, Dr Luke Quigley (father of Drs Louis and Frank), Eva Bruce, Fr John Cleary, Bertie Bruce, Hazel Grady (Stanley), Nellie Kennedy (Stanley), May Graham, NT, Pauline Harkins (Hannigan). **3rd Row**: Maggie Lynch, Kitty Egan (Spillane), Annie Burke (Whelan), Mrs Jack Burke (Hogan), Maura Maguire (Byrnes), Monica Cahalan (Lynch), Nora Lynch, Ethel Bruce, Eileen Brereton, Nora Donoghue (Carty), Mrs Tommy Gray (Fortune), Mrs Jack Hogan (Treacy), Eithne Minogue (Concannon), Mrs Pat Donoghue, Bridget Grady (Treacy), Kitty Cormican (Sammon), Christina Molamphy, Nora O'Meara. **2nd Row**: Dot Bruce, Bridget Hogan (Treacy). **Front**: Jack Burke, Pat Donoghue, James Tiernan, Mick Needham, Jimmy Byrnes, Mick Hough, Danny Smith.

say, 'now go to Miss Bruce for the next week to have it dressed'. And one went as a matter of course. She came into the home and gave injections to ease the pain of the dying. It was her blessed needle which eased the agony of my father's last hours. She would tell those with gravely ill relatives to knock her up at any hour of the night by throwing gravel at her window. When one of my cousins was very badly burned as a child Ethel Bruce gave skin from the back of her neck to be grafted on to the burnt area.

These services were given freely, generously, without hope of reward or thanks. There was no condescension, no 'ladies of the manor' attitude. The sort of service which was given at Lesserragh can be compared with that given in the medieval monasteries or by the community care aspect of the health services nowadays. There was very little free medicine at the time and most people were poor to the extent that paying the doctor would be a hardship, particularly in a long illness.

Bertie Bruce lived to be very old, ninety-one, and was cared for lovingly in her own home until her death in 1964. The birds would fly in through the window and perch on her tray, unafraid.

Lesserragh is a handsome house, with much of the elegant simplicity of the nineteenth century. It is now owned by Peter and Mide Gerrard.

Sources:
Ordnance Survey Letters.
North Riding of Co. of Tipperary, *Presentments passed by the Grand Jury, Summer Assizes*, 1873.
P. W. Joyce, *Irish Names of Places*.
Civil Survey.
OS sheet 6.
Cois Deirge, 1979.
William Corbett, NT, Roskeen, Drombane, Thurles, for the 1898 Bruce concert programme which he found in a book bought at an auction in Co. Laois in 1997.

Photographs: p. 167 taken by Paddy Carroll; p. 169, glass plate loaned by Mrs Betty Williams; p. 171, Biddy Gleeson; p. 173, May O'Meara.

Red Cross with, perhaps, some LDF, *circa 1942*

Back *(l to r)*: Jack Gleeson, Kilcowran; Mick Donoghue (Red Lad), Bellevue; Mick Gleeson, Kilbarron; Tom Burke, Carrigagowan; Billy Ducie, Annagh; Michael Carroll, Coolbawn. **3rd Row**: Michael Hough, Lisquillibeen; Jack (Duke) Donoghue, Bellevue; Frank Flannery, Glenbower; Jimmy Grady, Curraghmore; Jack Hogan, The Curragh; Jack Ducie, Annagh; Pat Carroll, Brookfield; Michael Moran, Coolbawn. **2nd Row**: Paddy Loughnane, Springmount; Chris Dunne, Kylebeg; Tommy Treacy, Bellevue; Dr Luke Quigley, Borrisokane; Donie O'Meara, Gurteen; Jack Fleming, Kilbarron. **Front**: Frank Moran, Coolbawn; Jack Flannery, Bellevue.

THE BRERETONS OF OLDCOURT

Oldcourt House is situated on the road from Kilbarron to Borrisokane, on the left about a mile from Kilbarron village. There is a gate lodge which is in the process of reconstruction. About a quarter of a mile further on, on the right, there is a lane leading to a little clearing. This was the site of the old penal chapel in use until 1814.

The *Civil Survey* of 1654 states that the plowland (250 Irish acres) of Oldcourt was in the parish of Finnoe and that the proprietors in 1641 were Kennedys – amongst them Philip of Ballyfinboy, John of Graigillane, and Brian of Oldcourt. In the confiscation Graigillane was given to land speculator Nicholas White of Leixlip, Co. Kildare (an 'innocent' Catholic – i.e. he did not take part in the rebellion of 1641) in fee or freehold. Oldcourt was also given to him in fee. He soon sold the lands on.

In the *Civil Survey's* introduction to Kilbarron parish it states that the border between it and Finnoe parish 'contains the Gulfe of Corrlongy', which must be the Swallowhole at Cornaling on Brereton's land.

The Brereton family came to live at Oldcourt circa 1785. The main Brereton family then lived, as they still do, at Rathurles in the parish of Kilruane. They trace their line of descent back to a Thomas Brereton (d. 1776) who married Mary Carroll (1693-1783) of Ballycrenode in the early 1700s – they are both buried in Ardcroney graveyard. In 1785 a Richard Waller and his son Richard (we do not know which Wallers but not those of Prior Park who only came there in 1803) leased 165 acres of Oldcourt and 79 acres of Graigillane to John Brereton (1729-1813) of Rathurles, his heirs etc. (It seems to have been a very long lease!). The John Brereton (b. 1787) who subsequently inherited Oldcourt was son of the leaseholder and his wife, Margaret Watson, daughter of George of Garrykennedy.

According to the Tithe Applotment list of of 1826 this John occupied 225 acres in Oldcourt townland. He may have built Oldcourt House. We know he married Anne Hackett of Riverstown, but do not know if he had children or his date of death.

The House

From the Ordnance Survey Letters we know that circa 1840 Oldcourt House was already built, with the property, including the house, occupied by George Brereton (1766-1847), 'land steward' of John Brereton of Rathurles. Before taking up residence at Oldcourt House this George had lived in a house beside Cornaling Lake, the ruins of which were there until quite recently. It was always referred to as 'George's little house'. George, who was probably a son of John, married Mary McKenna. They were both Catholics although the original Rathurles family were not. George and Mary had, amongst others, a son Daniel (1816-1902). He bought out Oldcourt under the 1881 Land Act. He married Judith Cummins of Dunkerrin parish in 1842. They had seven children, George, John, Daniel (1857-1945), Denis, Patrick, Mary and Ellen (1854-1945), not necessarily in that order, but George was the oldest. He settled eventually in Liverpool. Denis for a time lived in Ballinderry and owned and worked the mill there. Mary married Matthew Slattery, Glenbower, who had bought the mill from Denis. She died, aged 26 years, leaving five children who were reared at Oldcourt by her brother and sister, John and Ellen.

Daniel Brereton, born in 1857, attended Kilbarron Boys N.S. where the teacher was Paddy Meagher, Coolbawn. He then went to Kyle Park school where he was taught by John Gallagher, and afterwards attended a school in Nenagh where he was taught by a Mr Brogan. From there he went to St. Flannan's College, Ennis and thence to Bell's Academy, Dublin. He obtained a position in a bank in Dublin. It was at this time that he purchased the instruments for Kilbarron-Terryglass Land League band. After four years he found he had only saved £20 so he decided to go to the USA where he had relatives.

Daniel (right) went first to Minnesota and, after a time, decided to go west. He travelled by prairie schooner – a covered horse-drawn wagon – to Montana, the home of  the Blackfoot Indians. While there he suffered frostbite and lost two of his toes. He mingled with the Blackfoot tribe, who were friendly, and smoked the pipe of peace with them.

Daniel's Homecoming

He returned to Ireland in 1898 after seventeen years, having made a goodly sum of money. He married Mary Matthews of Birr in 1903. They lived at Abbeyville, near Lorrha, where their first five children, Daniel (Danny), Mary, Eileen, Frances and Judith were born. In 1910 Daniel's brother John of Oldcourt died, leaving Daniel his half share of the property, with the other half going to their sister Ellen. In 1914 Daniel and his family moved from Abbeyville to Oldcourt where John (1915) and Breda (1920) were born. Daniel and Ellen farmed separately but in co-operation.

They were excellent employers. Six workmen were constantly employed and eight at busy times. In the holidays school children would get work. Unusually for such farms, the workmen all got dinner and tea. It was said, 'you got fed and ped (paid) at Breretons'. They would also have perks such as firewood, and when a beast was killed each man, as well as the neighbours, got his share.

Daniel (Danny), the oldest son, joined the Oblate Fathers at Piltown, Co. Kilkenny, as a late vocation. In 1941, the year before he was due to be ordained, he was killed in a tragic accident. While sitting reading his Office under a tree from which branches were being lopped, a heavy branch hit him and he only lived a day.

John, the second son, was not very interested in conventional farming but during World War II he successfully produced and marketed tobacco for a couple of years. The weather was not always suitable for growing this plant and the curing was a tedious and time-consuming process, so he did not continue with it. He built greenhouses and grew tomatoes on quite a large scale. He also grew mushrooms.

In 1952 he married Phyllis Clery from Hollymount, Co. Mayo. They had two children, Donal and Gertrude (Trudy). John died in 1990. The property was left between the two children. Gertrude sold her share a few years ago to Ronald Armitage of Uskane. Donal's share, which includes Oldcourt House, still remains in his possession.

His aunt Eileen Brereton lives near Thurles with her sister Mrs Mary Cleary. They are the two surviving children of Daniel Brereton and Mary Matthews. The Brereton burial place is Ardcroney cemetery.

Sources:
Eileen Brereton, Thurles.
OHS, Ardcroney Gravestone inscriptions.
TNFH research centre.
1901 Census.
Brereton Papers held by the late Tod Brereton, Rathurles.

Photograph on p. 175, loaned by Eileen Brereton.

THE HICKIES OF SLEVOIR

The rather extraordinary story of how the parish acquired a new and richly-furnished church in 1886 through the generosity of one family in the parish, the Hickies of Slevoir, has already been told. At that time the Hickies were comparative newcomers, having first taken up residence in the parish some fifteen years previously.

The family of Hickie or O'Hickie descends from Eochy Balderg, son of Cathan Fionn, son of Blod, son of Cas of the race of Cormac Cas, King of Munster. A branch of the family became chiefs of a district in the vicinity of Killaloe, in the barony of Tulla in Co. Clare. They had provided hereditary physicians to the kings of Thomond, the O'Briens and MacNamaras, and held their lands free from tribute.

The name Hickie in Irish signifies 'Descendant of the Healer' and some old manuscripts of their original prescriptions (or references to them) are to be found in the British Library.

At the time of the Cromwellian confiscations in the 1650s the estates of James Hickie in Co. Clare were granted to Philip Bigo and the confiscation was confirmed by the Act of Settlement in 1662.

At the Restoration of the monarchy under Charles II, James Hickie's son, William (1st), thereupon settled in Kilelton, Co. Kerry. His son, also William (2nd), married Pomel, daughter and co-heir of John Edmonds of Asdee, descendant and representative of Sir Anthony Edmonds by Margaret O'Connor of Carrigfoyle (O'Connors of Kerry) and became possessed of the lands of East and West Asdee which thereby escaped confiscation. The Edmonds had probably conformed to Protestantism.

The estate of West Asdee came into the hands of the second William who was succeeded by his son, also named William (3rd). This William married Phillis, daughter of James Trant, Dingle. This would have been in the early 1760s. Their eldest son, again named William, died and the younger son Michael inherited. Michael married Margaret Nagle and they had three sons. William (4th), the eldest, married Maria, daughter of James Murphy, Ringmahon Castle.

The Spanish Bride
One of their younger sons, James Francis, married Lucila, daughter of Don Pablo Larios y Herror de Tegada, a wealthy Spanish nobleman, and it was this couple who came to Terryglass in the 1870s.

Before the French Revolution in 1789 the younger sons of Irish Catholic gentry by tradition joined the armies of France, Spain or Austria, the only career open to them. When, towards the end of the eighteenth century, the penal law which forbade Catholics from holding commissions above the rank of lieutenant in the British army was repealed, it became usual for these young men to join the British armed services. For example Daniel O'Connell's younger brother, Maurice, joined the British navy.

James F. Hickie met and married his Spanish bride while serving in the army in Gibraltar. He soon left the army with the rank of Lieut.-Colonel, and the family came to live in London.

In 1871 he bought Slevoir House on the shores of Lough Derg from the representatives of Rev. Francis Synge who had been rector of Terryglass. The

Hickies had visited their cousins the Esmondes, who had lately bought Drominagh House, and fallen in love with the beautiful countryside around Terryglass and decided to settle somewhere nearby.

Slevoir and the Synges

Slevoir House (below), described in 1871 as a 'small Georgian house', was probably built by a Counsellor Monsell or Maunsell about 1800 or somewhat earlier. It is situated in the townland of the same name close to the Lough Derg shore. The Synges had bought it from his son, who was reputed to be profligate, in the 1840s.

A gravestone inscription in Terryglass old cemetery records the death of a Thomas Monsell in 1831, a Margaret Monsell in 1841, and a John D. Monsell in 1844. It may have been after the latter's death that Rev. Francis Synge acquired Slevoir.

Maunsell was a well-liked man and treated his tenants well to the extent of giving each one a lease, which was fairly unusual at the time as most small tenant farmers were mainly yearly tenants-at-will.

Synge wanted large fields, probably to let them out as grazing which was cheap to run, or possibly for tillage. He offered to buy the leases from the tenants and every family accepted except one, the family of Billy Hough. Billy Hough was the great-grandfather of Michael Parkinson and his siblings (a Parkinson from Muckloon having married into the Hough farm, there being no Hough sons).

Some tenants took the money and went, while others 'ate and drank their leases' and refused to go. Synge had them forcibly evicted, burning down or unroofing some of the houses when the occupants were absent. Some of these tenants are remembered in the names of fields – Fahey's, Grogan's, Blake's, Barry's. There is a tradition in the family of the O'Mearas of Islandmore that they were evicted from Slevoir but they were on the Island much earlier than this – circa 1812-15, going by the records.

The Murdered Steward

Rev. Synge soon acquired the name of being a bad landlord. It would appear that he had a very harsh steward named Liddle who was eventually murdered in April 1847. A native of Scotland, he had been steward to Synge for thirty years. The *Kerry Evening Post* carried an account of murder and described him as a 'respectable gentleman' and that he had been shot in 'his house in the village of Terryglass'. There is a tradition that he lived in Shannon Lane in the house later occupied by James Griffin, the carpenter, who worked on Terryglass new church.

Liddle had already received a warning the previous November as noted by the *Nenagh Guardian*.

Sarah Parkinson, daughter of Billy Hough. The first Parkinsons came from Dublin to Firmount as stewards.

Three armed men, undisguised, on the evening of Tuesday last, before it was quite dark, entered the house of the Rev. Francis Synge at Slevoir, and when passing through the hall they met one of the servants of whom they enquired if the steward was in the house. The servant stated he was in his bedroom. They then went up to his room and with pistols levelled at his head they swore him on a piece of paper to quit his place before the fair day (yesterday) or he would get the death of Waller. Neither Smith, the steward, nor the servant who met them knew the parties. This we have no doubt of, as the Terrys are generally brought from a distant part of the country to do duty.

The Waller reference here related to the murder of Thomas Waller, Finnoe House, in 1843 and is dealt with in a later chapter. The Terry Alts were an agrarian organisation committed to redressing what they perceived

Rev. F. Synge in front of the hall door of old Slevoir House, circa 1858, with his son Edward, daughter Sylvia and unnamed groom.

as injustices – usually land-related. Their actions extended to injuring and damaging persons and property.

Rev. Synge cannot have been unaware of the goings-on of his steward and it is strange that it was the steward only who was blamed. Blame must surely be attached to the landlord for unjust dealings between steward and tenants.

Enhanced Slevoir House

In 1871 the 'Mansion and Demesne of Slievyre', with adjacent townlands of Firmount, Lacken and Killeen, 'held in fee simple and partly under Lease for Ever', came on the market. Of the total 1,150 acres there was 700 held as demesne lands. The sale advertisement concluded: 'The lands are of good quality and the tenants are punctual in the payments of their rents.

When Lieut.-Col. James F. Hickie and his Spanish-born wife bought the property they proceeded to carry out extensive rebuilding and enlargement of the 'small Georgian house'. In fact, the old house is buried in the new one. The only visible sign of the Maunsell and Synge house is a curve in the wall which is on the side that faces the lake. While the alterations were in progress James F., Lucila and family rented Ballyeira House. This is on the road to Portumna, less than a mile past the turn-off for Lorrha. It is a biggish house on the left-hand side.

The alterations to Slevoir were finished about 1875. Manuel Hickie was born that year and was brought to Slevoir as an infant. He told this to his son James, Dublin, who furnished all this information.

When the house (below) was rebuilt it was the most modern Big House in the area. A piped water supply was installed in the house, yard and garden. Water was pumped from nearby Lough Derg by horse power into tanks in the tower. This method was used, as far as Michael Parkinson knows, up to the early 1920s when a petrol engine was installed. The house and coachyard were lit by gas made from coal. The gas plant and gasometer were where Lavelle's house is now situated. The carpenter's workshop, where James Griffin worked making seats and doors for the church, was also there. There was an ice-house down by the lake where meat was stored on ice collected from the lake during the winter. A barn belonging to the old farm at Slevoir is still there. It was known as the bell barn and has lately been renovated. It had a small belfry with a bell which was rung at 7 a.m. to start work, at 12 noon for dinner, and in the evening to finish.

One unusual feature of Slevoir is that the yard and stables are about one hundred yards from the house and are connected by a tunnel wide enough for a donkey and cart. All the maintenance of the house was done through the tunnel,

e.g. all the food and other necessities of daily life were thus brought from the yard and everything that was required to be carried out of the house was transported in the same way.

The Angelus
Manuel Hickie introduced the Angelus into the parish. As there was then no bell at the parish church the Angelus was rung on the bells at Slevoir and at Drominagh. Later on, when Manuel Hickie bought Old Court, it was rung on the workmen's bell there. When the belfry and bell were erected at Terryglass church the practice of using the farm bells ceased. It will be noted that the house has a tower. The architect who designed the Hickie renovations also designed the Sacred Heart Convent at Mount Anville, Dublin, which has an exactly similar tower.

William Parkinson, Michael's father, was steward at Slevoir from circa 1910 until 1923 when Major-General Sir William Hickie, a son of Col. James F. and Lucila, moved to Dublin. Sir William was succeeded by his brother Carlos and the farm was divided between him and his brother Manuel. On the death of Carlos he was succeeded at Slevoir by his son Brigadier-General Séamus Hickie, who had returned from World War II.

In 1965 Séamus Hickie, and his wife Pauline (below), sold Slevoir House and lands to a community of Salesian nuns. In 1983 the nuns sold it to a Mr Miworm. In 1987 he leased it to the present occupier, a German citizen, Dr Petersen. The Hickies built themselves a new one-storey house in the Georgian villa style in Slevoir woods and near the walled garden of the Big House.

Major-General Sir William B. Hickie

Major-General Sir William Bernard Hickie, KCB, was born on 21 May 1865, the eldest son of Lieut.-Colonel James F. and his wife Lucila. He was educated at Oscott College and the Royal Military College at Sandhurst.

His father had been an officer in the Royal Fusiliers and William followed him into that regiment in February 1885.

William served in the South African (Boer War) with great distinction, firstly as a major and then as a brevet Lieut.-Colonel. He had graduated from the Staff College at Comberly before going to South Africa.

He attained the permanent rank of Lieut.-Colonel in 1909 and was promoted to Colonel in 1912.

He was serving in the Curragh, Co. Kildare, at the time of the 'Curragh Incident' in March 1914. General Hubert Gough of an Inishlounaght, Clonmel, military family led approximately sixty officers (of the seventy stationed at the Curragh) who offered their resignations rather than obey potential orders to enforce Home Rule on itsUlster Unionist opponents. But Hickie was one of the few officers who were prepared to be loyal to their oaths and obey orders, and said so openly. The affair was settled by the War Office backing down in the face of the virtual mutiny.

At the outbreak of the Great War in 1914, he was holding a staff appointment in the 11th Corps of the British Expeditionary Force with the rank of Major-General. He took part in the retreat from Mons (Belgium) and the advance to the Aisne (France).

In April 1915 he was appointed to command the 53rd Brigade in England, and took it to France in July of that year.

In December 1915 he was appointed General Officer Commanding the Sixteenth Irish Division, being promoted to Major-General in January 1916. He led the Division during the battle of the Somme in 1916, at Guillemont and Guinchy, at Messines, and at the third battle of Ypres in 1917.

He relinquished command in February 1918. He was created a Companion of the Order of the Bath (CB) in 1914, and received the French Croix de Guerre. He was created Knight Commander of the Bath (KCB) in 1919. He retired from the Army in 1921 as a Major-General. He subsequently went on to found the southern division of the Royal British Legion, the organisation which looked after ex-servicemen and the widows and dependants of those killed in the war.

He was always a strong advocate of Home Rule which, true to his character, he did not disguise. During the War of Independence he was nicknamed the 'Republican General'.

In the election to Seanad Éireann in 1925 the Irish Free State was one constituency and there were seventy-six names on the ballot paper. Sir William B. Hickie (Independent) was fifth in first preference votes and was the first member elected. He continued to be an active member of the Seanad until its dissolution in 1936.

He lived for a while at Slevoir, but in the latter part of his life he was based in Dublin. He died a happy and peaceful death in 1950 and is buried in the Hickie plot in the new cemetery in Terryglass.

Michael Parkinson's personal Memoir of Sir William

When coming home on holiday he came by train to Cloughjordan where his carriage met him. A large crowd of locals would meet him at Starr's house in Roran, a couple of miles from the village. The horses would be unyoked and the men pulled the carriage as far as Heenan's hill where a huge bonfire was blazing. He would order a half-barrel of porter from the local pub and a great night was had by all.

After the war when he took up farming he gave constant work to five or six men and many more at harvest-time and seasonal field work. When he got into financial difficulties the workers offered to take a cut in wages to help him out; he refused this offer. It would not help.

General Hickie was a lovely man, a perfect gentleman and very charitable. Old soldiers called on him in droves and would each get a half-crown. He gathered up five or six unemployed men in the neighbourhood and employed them, finding little jobs they could do and enjoyed their company.

Sources:
OHS, Gravestone Inscriptions for Terryglass civil parish.
Nenagh Guardian, Nov. 1846.
James Hickie.
Brigadier Seámus Hickie.
Michael Parkinson.
William Corbett, NT.

Photographs: (all loaned), pp.178, 181, Wilsie Nolan; pp.179, 182, Michael Parkinson; pp. 179, 180, James Hickie.

7
Eugene Esmonde, VC, DSO

FAMILY AND CAREER

The Esmonde family had come to Ireland with the Normans in the twelfth century and settled in Wexford, where the main branch of the family remains to this day. The first Esmonde we hear of is Henry Esmonde, seneschal of Wexford in 1294. They have always remained Catholic, with one exception – Sir Lawrence Esmonde, the first baronet, who conformed to the Protestant religion in the reign of Elizabeth I. The 11th baronet, Thomas, succeeded at the age of nine years. His uncle James became his legal guardian and remained in the family home of Ballystranagh until Thomas came of age. James then married and bought Drominagh, a handsome early Georgian mansion with 600 acres, on the shores of the River Shannon on Lough Derg. It was adjacent to a fifteenth or sixteenth century O'Kennedy tower house known locally as Drominagh castle.

Drominagh Esmondes

James had three sons. Two died young and unmarried, but John Joseph (b. 1862) qualified as a medical doctor and married Rose McGuinness who bore him three sons and three daughters before dying prematurely. John Joseph re-married, his second wife being Eily O'Sullivan, of the O'Sullivan Beare family in Co. Kerry, by whom he had seven children – one daughter and six boys. They were Owen, Donal, John Witham, Eugene and James (twins), Carmel and Patrick.

On the death of his father, John Joseph gave up his medical career and went into Irish politics. He was a committed Nationalist and Home Ruler and was elected Member of Parliament for Tipperary North in 1910 as one of John Redmond's Home Rule party. At the outbreak of World War in 1914 he enlisted in the Royal Army Medical Corp (RAMC) as a captain and was appointed M.D. to the garrison barracks at Templemore. After a minor illness in 1915, he died of a heart attack at the age of 53.

His sudden death caused complications. Eily had seven children, the eldest Owen only nine years of age, but the Drominagh property was left in trust to all the children of the first marriage. Drominagh House and 300 acres were bought back by Eily whose family was wealthy. The money thus realised enabled the children of the first marriage to finish their education and get a start in the world.

Eily and her son Owen and his family continued to live at Drominagh until it was sold by Owen in 1946 to the Mosses, as recounted in chapter 6.

Early Life

The twins Eugene and James Esmonde had as their nurse Priscilla Stanley, sister of Dick Stanley, Ballinderry, who became the mother of Bill Donoghue. They called her Agnes rather than Priscilla and never failed to visit her when home on leave. The long summer vacations were spent at Drominagh when the boys learned the lake shore and the ways of birds and animals from Danny Donohue, steward and gardener at Drominagh, and his son Jack, a one-legged survivor of World War I.

Donal Esmonde had joined the Mill Hill Fathers, and Eugene and James were sent to the Jesuit college, Clongowes Wood. After a few months Eugene decided to follow in Donal's footsteps to become a foreign missionary. He spent three years in the Mill Hill seminary. Holidays were still spent at Drominagh where Owen had taken up farming.

About this time Eugene came reluctantly to the conclusion that the religious life was not for him. He returned to Drominagh very depressed. It is said that he had an unhappy love affair about this time. He looked around for some new career or profession. One day he saw an advertisement by the Air Ministry in London offering suitably qualified applicants a short-service commission in the Royal Air Force (RAF) for five years. He applied and was accepted on 28 December 1928.

Eugene as a boy in Drominagh woods.

He proved to be a 'natural' pilot and received his RAF wings on 13 December 1929. His first posting was to Catterick, Yorkshire. After a year there he was posted, in March 1930, to 43 Squadron at Tangmere, Sussex.

43 was a fighter unit and was regarded as an elite unit within the RAF. Here he learned to take part in 'formation aerobatics' in which he excelled. In May he was despatched to the RAF base at Gosport, Harts, and promoted to Flying Officer.

He now underwent a 16-week course of instruction in the handling of aircraft operating from aircraft carriers, as preliminary to joining the Fleet Air Arm of the Royal Navy for active duty. This included deck-landing techniques and, especially, torpedo-dropping tactics. On completion of the course he was posted in October 1931 to No. 463 Fleet Torpedo Bomber (FTB) of the Fleet Air Arm. He embarked on the aircraft carrier *Courageous*.

Esmonde saw his career as flying and, having failed to get into the RAF permanently, he decided to get into civil aviation. At the end of December 1933 he was officially transferred to the Class A Reserve. He remained in the RAF reserve for four years, being promoted to Flight-Lieut. with effect from 1 April 1936.

Civil Pilot
In 1934 he applied and was accepted by Imperial Airways as a First Officer. Skill, determination and courage were his hallmarks, as evidenced by the remarks made after his tragic death by David Humphreys, an engineer with Imperial Airways,

who had been based at Karachi during Esmonde's service there. 'I was a passenger on one of his flights between Karachi and Singapore and we were flying along the Burmese coast in tropical monsoon rain ... Esmonde [right, at Drominagh in 1939] was fighting the controls every inch of the way; the visibility was so bad that the only way he could see where he was going was by following the coast line at almost sea level. When we reached Akyab the aerodrome was almost a lake and our landing must have looked like a flying boat landing. It was a superb feat of airmanship. My admiration for him, both as a man and as a pilot was profound, and I was not surprised when I heard he had won the Victoria Cross.'

First Commission

In January 1939 Esmonde received a letter from the Admiralty offering him a commission in the Royal Navy's Fleet Air Arm – in a position of responsibility. He accepted the offer and on 14 April 1939 he was enlisted as a Lieut.-Commander. Esmonde's first ship was HMS *Victory*. His squadron flew Walrus amphibious and Fairey Seafox float planes.

Within five months Britain and France were at war with Germany. About this time he wrote to his mother – after the sinking of HMS *Courageous* within three weeks of the outbreak of the war, which he referred to 'as a straightforward act of war and I don't blame either party ... for Heaven's sake if *I* am ever missing I hope it won't upset anyone, because I can think of no greater honour nor a better way of passing into eternity than in the cause for which the Allies are fighting this war.'

On the same day as the massive evacuation of troops from Dunkirk was underway, 31 May 1940, Esmonde was appointed to the command of 825 Squadron, a position he was to hold until his death. It had been the first squadron to be fully equipped with Farrey Swordfish torpedo-bombers in 1936.

The 825 Squadron had a lucky escape inasmuch as they were disembarked from the *Glorious* and based on HMS *Kestrel* when the ship, with several air units on board, was sunk by gunfire from the German battleship *Scharnhorst* on 8 June with the loss of 1,515 lives.

THE HORROR OF WAR

About ten days before Esmonde was appointed to the post of commander the 825 Squadron had moved to the RAF base at Detling in Kent for operations under Coastal Command – mainly over the English channel and French coastline. The war situation was desperate. The Allied armies were being battered by the Luftwaffe (the German air force) as they made their way back to the Channel ports.

825 Swordfish were engaged in dangerous daylight bombing and lost eight

aircraft in May-June 1940. Accordingly, after six weeks of intense operational activities the squadron was withdrawn in early July 1940 for replenishment of its crew and aircraft.

By early September they were up to full fighting strength again and embarked aboard the carrier *Furious*. There were nine Swordfish planes in 825 Squadron. Their first operation, on 22 September, was a torpedo attack on enemy shipping in a Norwegian port. It was not a success, due to inclement weather conditions, inadequate maps and other factors. Three planes and crews failed to return to the carrier.

It was back to base again to recruit replacement crews and aircraft. The *Furious* returned for refurbishment. Squadron and ship were re-united in early October. This was to become the operational pattern of 825 Squadron – a torpedo-dropping mission with losses of crew and plane, followed by return to base of commander and survivors for replacements and intensive training sessions.

Special Targets

Between February and April 1941 they were engaged as an anti-submarine protection force to supplement the naval escort of destroyers for HMS *Furious* who was delivering an important cargo of fifty Hawker Hurricane fighters to the RAF depot on the Gold Coast, West Africa. The journey was uneventful.

In May 825 Squadron was ordered to join a new aircraft carrier, HMS *Victorious*, then anchored at Scapa Flow off the Orkney Islands and about to load up forty-eight crated Hurricane Fighters for transportation to Gibraltar.

However, as it was about to sail the Admiralty was forced to make radical changes to the plan. This was dictated by the German depredations on Allied merchant shipping by U-boats and surface ships, particularly in the Atlantic zones. Part of that success had been achieved by the two renowned battleships, *Scharnhorst* and *Gneisenau*, based at Brest, the principal German naval port on the west coast of France. They were known to the Allies as the 'Ugly Sisters'; between them they had sunk no less than twenty-two Allied vessels between January and March 1941.

The Admiralty now became aware that these two ships were to be joined by the heavily-armed 'pride of the German Navy', *Bismarck*, and the cruiser, *Prinz Eugen*, in an all-out attack on the Atlantic convoy routes. The plan was that *Bismarck*, *Prinz Eugen* and *Gneisenau* would rendezvous in the Atlantic in April for a co-ordinated offensive. *Scharnhorst* was to remain in Brest for repairs.

Before the movement of the ships began *Gneisenau* was attacked in that port on 6 April by a member of No. 22 squadron RAF. The pilot was killed in a fury of anti-aircraft fire and received a posthumous VC. But he had succeeded in putting the *Gneisenau* out of action for eight months. *Prinz Eugen* was also slightly damaged in another incident.

In spite of these setbacks Grand Admiral Erich Raeder decided not to postpone the rendezvous in the Atlantic of *Bismarck* and *Prinz Eugen*. This was named, 'Operation Rheinburg', and confirmed for 18 May 1941. Nine German supply ships and four weather ships took up their positions at the point of the rendezvous.

Bismarck and *Prinz Eugen* made their way northwards from Brest, under cover of dusk and keeping close to the coast, to a rendezvous in the Baltic with a minesweeper and two destroyers. They then took a zig-zag route northwards by the Norwegian coast. By 21 May they were south of the port of Bergen.

From intelligence reports coming in the Allies had been able to monitor the movements of the two ships. Two photo-reconnaissance men had photographed them and suspected what they might be. Admiral Sir John Tovey, Commander of the British Home Fleet, was shown the photos. Tovey acted immediately without awaiting further instructions from the Admiralty and signalled the captain of the *Victorious*, Capt. Bovell, who had not yet started for Gibraltar, asking him whether the Swordfish on board were able to undertake a torpedo strike against the German battleships.

Sea Engagement
Bovell summoned Eugene Esmonde and the aircraft carrier's Flight Operations Officer; all three agreed that such an operation might be possible.

Due to deteriorating weather Tovey was unable to ascertain if the German ships were still lurking in the Norwegian fjord where they had been seen, or whether they had already moved out into the open Atlantic. Notwithstanding the lack of precise information, he ordered HMS *Hood*, *Prince of Wales* and six destroyers to take up positions to cover the sea gaps, Iceland-Greenland and Iceland-Faroes.

But they were already too late as the German ships were off Greenland's southeastern coastline.

In the early hours of 24 May the *Hood*, at 25,000 yards range from the *Bismarck*, began to engage its guns. Within four minutes one of *Bismarck's* shells plunged into Hood's innards, exploded, detonating two magazines and tearing the huge ship in two. It slid into the ocean with the loss of the entire crew of 1,419 men except for two ratings and one midshipman.

Bismarck and *Prinz Eugen* now turned on the *Prince of Wales*, damaging her to such an extent that she had to return under smoke cover. She had managed to inflict three positive hits on the *Bismarck* and to rupture her oil tanks. With her 1,000 tons of oil flowing away, the *Bismarck* was forced to reduce speed.

The German ship now began altering her course towards the south and home, thus bringing her near *King George V* and *Victorious*, with Esmonde and his Swordfish aboard, and several others speeding towards her.

In the late afternoon of 24 May *Victorious* was ordered to proceed to within 100 miles of *Bismarck* to enable the launch of a strike by the Swordfish of 825. The expectation was that injury sufficient to slow down the vessel would be inflicted, thus enabling other Royal Navy vessels to sink her.

Air Attack
With darkness coming on, and the weather deteriorating, the order came at 10 p.m. for 825 Squadron to make the torpedo attack. Eugene Esmonde, with Colin Ennever as his Observer and Pilot Officer Parker as Torpedo Air Gunner led off the windswept deck in Swordfish 5A. The other eight followed. The question was: would the planes arrive back on *Victorious* before dark? Very few of the pilots had done deck landings at night, although Esmonde himself had.

There then occurred an incident which, indirectly, would appear to have contributed to the unsatisfactory outcome of the mission. Due to a breakdown of radio communication between the planes, HMS *Sheffield* was mistaken as the target and a descent made. Fortunately, she was recognised in time and no torpedoes dropped. This meant that they had to regroup and gain height.

The Swordfish, heavy with their torpedo cargo, gained altitude slowly, climbing only at a speed of 75 knots. At this point the *Bismarck* guns sighted them and opened fire. Luckily, the Germans did not believe that any aircraft would fly at less than 100 knots and so had set their fire control system on that basis. This meant that instead of hitting the plane the shells burst ahead of it.

Eventually Esmonde went into attack, followed by some of the others, and dropped their torpedoes. Few enough made direct hits and little damage was inflicted by any of the falling torpedoes.

The mission accomplished, albeit not highly successful, their problem now was to find the carrier and land in darkness. The carrier's captain radioed them his position, and led by Esmonde, they all landed safely though some were damaged from the skirmish. Esmonde's plane had a large hole in it and was immediately grounded for repairs.

The full horror of war is brought home when one reads that another force of Swordfish from the carrier *Ark Royal* finished off *Bismarck*, crippling her to such an extent that she could not get away. The Royal Navy closed in and she went down with 2,287 men. Only 107 were rescued from the sea.

Squadron 825's part in the destruction of the German ship was recognised in September 1941 when Esmonde was awarded the Distinguished Service Order (DSO), two of his colleagues received the Distinguished Service Cross (DSC), and two the Distinguished Service Medal (DSM).

Re-grouping

The carrier *Victorious* did not participate in the final stage of *Bismarck's* destruction on 27 May, having returned to port, loaded the Hurricanes and set sail for Gibraltar with Eugene Esmonde's 825 Squadron on board in their original role of an anti-submarine protection force.

Having witnessed the safe take-off of the Hurricanes for their Malta destination, Esmonde and his squadron returned to Gibraltar. There they were told to transfer from the *Victorious* to the *Ark Royal* carrier. The latter was a member of the Royal Navy's convoy protection force operating in the Mediterranean. Squadron 825 were one of three Swordfish squadrons on the carrier with a total of fifty aircraft. He was to remain on the *Ark Royal* for five months, participating in various escort, attack and reconnaissance operations, until it was torpedoed and ultimately sunk in mid-November 1941. Only one crewman lost his life. Esmonde was one of the skeleton crew who remained aboard with the Captain during the ship's final hours.

Esmonde's squadron returned to England on HMS *Nelson*. The unit, depleted in personnel and aircraft, re-assembled at Lee-on-Solent to commence rebuilding to operational strength under Esmonde's direction. By this time he had been in command of 825 Squadron for over eighteen months.

Home Leave

Eugene Esmonde came home to Drominagh for Christmas 1941. He spent it with his mother and his brother Owen's wife, Antonia, and her two small children. Owen was a pilot in the RAF and stationed in England.

Matt Fogarty, Drominagh Lodge, told me of his only meeting with Eugene which was during that leave. Eugene and Matt's father Denis were old friends. The Fogartys were near-neighbours and always threshed for them. Matt, then a small boy of seven or eight years, was walking along the road with his father when they met this man who was a stranger to Matt but obviously known to his father. The man was carrying a gun and a bag with, perhaps, one dead pheasant in it and was accompanied by two dogs. Denis Fogarty and the 'stranger' chatted about the war and one thing and another. At the crossroads the man shook hands with both before parting with them, saying, 'I don't suppose we'll meet again'. Young Matt was struck by the saying and never forgot it.

Years earlier, when Eugene was in the RAF, he borrowed a small biplane from his cousin Osmond Esmonde and took his brother Owen, Denis Fogarty and Danny Donoghue on a hair-raising flight over Lough Derg where he had 'looped the loop'.

After the holidays Eugene Esmonde returned to Lee-on-Solent to continue his rebuilding task. Two problems faced him: assembling crew members with operational experience and acquiring extra planes.

Operation Fuller

After the sinking of *Bismarck* in May 1941 the other two battleships, *Scharnhorst* and *Gneisenau,* and the cruiser *Prinz Eugen* took refuge in Brest harbour. Their presence there still presented a dreadful threat to Allied naval shipping on the Atlantic. Attacks by RAF bombers on the harbour had done no great damage to the ships other than to necessitate some repairs and so delay their return to action.

Meanwhile, the Admiralty had devised a highly confidential plan of action known as 'Operation Fuller' which extended to making all-out naval and air attacks on the ships in the English Channel should the Germans decide to move the ships into the Atlantic. The plan was to remain secret until the ships were on the move and in the Dover Straits.

Ironically, the decision to move the ships out was not based on a German plan to resume attacks on Allied shipping, but in response to the 'intuition' of the German Führer, Adolf Hitler. Hitler got the idea that any Allied invasion of Europe would be through Norway. Accordingly, he instructed Admiral Erich Raeder that all German battleships would be better employed guarding what he perceived would be the point of attack. Raeder managed to put him off the idea for a while but in December 1941 the Führer issued an ultimatum to his naval commanders that either they move all three ships from Brest or he would have them dismantled and their heavy guns sent to join the defences being built up in Norway.

Operation Cerebus

Immediately a plan to move the ship was devised and code-named 'Cerebus', though this was later changed. There was blanket security – only the ship's captains, Chief of Staff Reinicke, the navigator of the *Scharnhorst*, Helmut Gresler, and a handful of other senior naval officers were in the know. Admiral Otto Ciliax was in overall charge of the plan.

The aim was to sail from Brest in the early evening darkness of a moonless night – until the full moon on 15 February such a night in conditions of low cloud would provide twelve hours darkness from 7.30 p.m. to 7.30 a.m. The night of 11 February 1942 was decided on. Maximum air and sea cover would be given to the three ships as they progressed under cover of darkness up the French coast.

If all went according to plan such a sailing time should ensure that the ships and their escorts entered the narrow stretch of water between the English and French coast, known as the Dover Straits, at about mid-day on 12 February – at which time two-thirds of the voyage would be behind them.

The Allies expected a German break-out from Brest and kept a close watch on movements in the harbour. They were prepared for most alternatives. The general opinion among the Admiralty and RAF senior officers was that the prime attacking weapon should be torpedo bombers, including Eugene Esmonde's 825 Squadron.

The Admiralty planners believed that the German ships would pass through the Dover Straits in darkness, probably some two hours before dawn and could therefore be relatively safely attacked by the vintage Swordfish in the protective cloak of night and without need for a fighter escort.

Accordingly, an order went to Esmonde to transfer his squadron from Lee-on-Solent to the RAF airfield at Manston in Kent. Some days before this Esmonde had been present at a secret conference. It was made plain that the attack would be made at night and that as far as the Fleet Air Arm unit was concerned participation would be on a voluntary basis. In the light of these circumstances Esmonde volunteered his squadron. On 4 February 1942 he flew his six Swordfish into Manston – he was short three of his full complement. Nobody at Manston knew why they were there.

As with all other air squadrons earmarked to participate in 'Operation Fuller' Esmonde's preparations were geared towards a night attack. This extended to his squadron being in a state of full readiness at 4 a.m. each morning until ordered to stand down at dawn. In the event of a night attack, Hurricane planes from the Manston base would drop illuminating flares over the German ships, thus giving the Swordfish a clear sight of the targets. Esmonde planned his part in the intended attack in detail.

On 11 February he took the day off to go to London to attend an investiture ceremony at Buckingham Palace to receive his DSO for his part in the sinking of *Bismarck* in May 1941. As he returned by train to Manston in the late evening the operation which was to end his young life had already begun.

Break-out

On that 11 February the three German ships were slipping their mooring ropes preparatory to making their 'dash' when the air raid sirens sounded. The RAF was attacking Brest. The intensive bombing raid did considerable damage in the town but none hit any of the ships in the harbour.

The formidable head-on view of the battleship, *Scharnhorst*, on 12 Feb 1942, showing the many extra flak guns mounted in addition to the ship's main guns.

The forty-five minute raid was over by 8.30 p.m. but the 'all clear' did not sound until 9.14 p.m. Admiral Ciliax then gave orders to sail immediately – supposedly on night training manoeuvres and with *Scharnhorst* in the lead. Given good fortune, the ships could still make up the time lost and break through the English Channel at the precisely appointed time. By midnight they were sailing past Ushant, only seventy-two minutes behind schedule. Ciliax now informed the *Scharnhorst* crew that their task was to sail through the Channel eastwards into the German Bight. The escort for the three ships was formidable – destroyers, torpedo-boats and mine-sweepers, while overhead flew a minimum of sixteen fighter planes at any one time. The *Scharnhorst* had mounted additional guns supplementary to her usual contingent of armoury.

Blips
There now followed a sorry saga of missed opportunities and no small degree of inefficiency and disorganisation of the British defences. The British radar stations along the southern coast failed to identify the various German movements for what they were. As already stated, hardly anyone knew about the planned German operation to move the ships and of the intention to attack them. Other radar blips were ignored as they were not approaching England.

At 8 a.m. the leading German ships were nearing the coast off Barfleur which lies only 80-90 miles south of Portsmouth. The Germans could hardly believe their luck to have got so far unobserved.

The reason for this is partly explained by the fact that, though the ships seemed to be getting ready to move when photographed by a Reconnaissance Unit in Brest harbour at 4.15 p.m. on 11 February, they were still there according to film taken between 7.30 and 8.30 p.m. by the RAF engaged in the bombing raid on the harbour and town. Accordingly, no report based on the original pictures was sent to the Coastal Command headquarters, so no alarm was raised.

In a later inquiry which investigated the incident the explanation given as to how such an enormous convoy of ships could move undetected, practically within sight of the English coast, was that the regular air patrols suffered a series of radar and other technical faults resulting in their early returns to bases.

The explanation as to why the radar stations scattered all along the southern coast of England failed to identify the air and sea movements for what they were was attributed to jamming of the signals which had been going on for several weeks. The jamming had been interpreted by the operators as due to atmospheric interference. Blips were seen on the radar screens during the night but were mistakenly identified as 'normal' German shipping coastal movements, air-sea rescue patrols, or air testing of aircraft stationed on the French coast. A contributory factor of course was that neither the RAF fliers or the radar operators knew of 'Operation Fuller'.

Confusion
One of the first to question the radar signals being received was Wing-Commander Jarvis, senior controller of the radar filter room at Stanmore, the headquarters of the RAF fighter command. He came on duty shortly after 8 a.m. and at 9.30 a.m. he interested himself in a persistent plot of an aircraft circling near Le Havre which he interpreted as Luftwaffe aircraft escorting coastal shipping. He reported this to

No. 11 Group HQ at 10 a.m. and had it dismissed as 'probably aircraft exercising'.

At this stage of this dramatic and tragic story there occurred an incident which, unknowingly, linked Eugene Esmonde and another young man from Nenagh.

When Nenagh-born Squadron-Leader William A. K. (Bill) Igoe, came on duty at 8 a.m. in Biggin Hill airfield, where he was the controller, he noticed on the screen a series of circular radar plots moving from the Cherbourg area. Igoe, one of the few junior officers who knew of 'Operation Fuller', was immediately suspicious. It was too fast a speed for any normal convoy. Taking into account the aerial escort circling those large blips, Igoe concluded that they must be the *Scharnhorst* and the *Gneisenau*. He telephoned the same unit as Jarvis had – No. 11 Group H.Q. – and told them, 'I think it must be "Fuller"'. As the man at the other end of the phone had never heard of the break-out plan, Igoe, unable to explain due to the security blanket, then telephoned RAF Squadron-Leader R. W. Oxspring at Hawkinge and, still obliged to withhold information of the plan, asked him to 'go and look at some Hun fighters circling off the Somme Estuary and see what they're up to'. At 10.20 a.m. Oxspring and a colleague took off in two separate Spitfires.

Around the same time as this take-off the station commander, at Swingate airfield at Dover, Flight-Lieut. Gerald Kidd, began plotting three outsize blips on his radar screen which had aroused his suspicions due to their enormous size. He, concluded rightly, that the German ships were actually in the English Channel. He immediately set about alerting RAF headquarters in Dover but both the ordinary phone and scrambler line were out of order.

So far none of the three – Jarvis, Igoe and Kidd – had succeeded in convincing senior officers that a crisis existed.

Up the Line

Kidd eventually made phone contact with Dover HQ and duly reported his interpretation to Wing-Commander J. Constable-Roberts, the air liaison officer on Admiral Ramsay's staff. He immediately contacted No. 11 Group and got the same lack of interest accorded to Jarvis and Igoe. Undeterred, he then contacted the RAF coastal command unit at Thorney Island to suggest that a squadron of fighters [Bristol Beauforts] be sent to Manston immediately. Sensing the RAF's lack of response to his message he went straight to his naval boss, Admiral Ramsay, in the hope of getting action.

Ramsay, a realist, knew that within the time frame available he had only one air striking force immediately accessible to him – Eugene Esmonde's 825 Squadron at Manston. The idea of ordering such poorly-equipped and ancient craft to attack the formidable German naval force was repugnant to Ramsay. But, once acquainted of the crisis, he was obliged to follow a certain line of action. He immediately contacted the First Sea Lord (a naval member of the Board of Admiralty who administered the navy) in London and requested that he, Ramsay, *not* be ordered to send in the Swordfish. The reply he got was a Lord Nelson quotation: 'The Royal Navy will attack the enemy whenever and wherever he is to be found'.

In the meantime, Oxspring and his colleague, whom Igoe had asked to 'go and look ...' had indeed found the German fighters – a dozen Messerschmitts – and seen what they were up to. They discovered a large convoy of German shipping with three large German ships heading towards Dover. Breaking the silence rule for all pilots engaged on operations, Oxspring broadcast this message. Either the RAF did not receive his warning or ignored it, for nothing happened. But the message was picked up by the German listening service – information they used shrewdly and wisely. Oxspring and his colleague, unaware, remember, of 'Operation Fuller', landed at their airbase at 10.50 and reported that one of the large ships looked like the *Scharnhorst*.

Oxspring then spoke with Bill Igoe at Biggin Hill who, in view of his previous near-rebuff, suggested Oxspring ring 11 Group HQ direct and try to convince them of the battleships' presence in the Channel. Oxspring and Igoe were told that the Air Officer Commanding, Air Vice-Marshal Trafford Leigh-Mallory, was reviewing Belgian airmen at Northolt and ... was not to be disturbed.

By this time RAF Group Captain Victor Beamish, who knew of 'Operation Fuller', returned from a reconnaissance flight, having seen the battleships and their formidable escort. His persistence eventually brought Leigh-Mallory to the phone. After some persuasion the AOC agreed to execute the 'Fuller' plan. The time was now 11.35 a.m. – over three hours since Igoe first noticed the blobs on the radar screen and an hour since Oxspring's broadcast.

For those immediately involved in 'Fuller' things now began to move quickly. Information was conveyed to the various HQs and to coastal alert stations. Indeed one of these, at South Foreland, commenced firing shells at the German convoy now moving ten miles west of the French port of Calais. None found its mark.

Esmonde and a Wing-Commander Cleave at Manston had also been alerted. Esmonde was instructed by Dover HQ to prepare for take-off and to load 825 Squadron's Swordfish with their torpedoes. About this time Dover HQ also sent a request to Fighter Command and the RAF 11 Group to arrange a strong fighter escort for Esmonde's attack which was now going to take place in daylight.

'Operation Fuller', it will be remembered, was geared towards a night attack. Its plan included providing a simultaneous surface attack by destroyers on the German convoy in co-ordination with the Swordfish torpedo-dropping operation – a multiple attack from several quarters and so diffusing the full power of the convoy's gun power in any one direction. Employment of motor-torpedo boats was also part of the Admiralty's plan. The torpedo attack would be backed up by coastal gunfire and other naval vessels plus massive air bombardment. However, some of these were no longer in a state of preparedness and others, as in the case of the torpedo boats, had in fact being withdrawn and dispersed.

The Fateful Day

On the morning of 12 February Esmonde and his crew had, as usual, clocked in their two-hour's standby until dawn, followed by breakfast and training practices. Esmonde was, at this stage, still geared in his preparations to a night attack which, though dangerous in concept, seemed attainable. The morning was cold and a frozen dusty snow was being whirled around the air field. The airfield was a-buzz with various crews taking off on training exercises while off-duty crewmen went about their domestic and personal chores.

Meanwhile, down in Dover harbour, the atmosphere was similar to Manston until a telephone call from Admiral Ramsay's office – 'the German battleships are off Boulogne' – galvanised senior personnel. The order, 'man all boats – *Scharnhorst* and *Gneisenau* are in the Straits', rang through the operations room.

Around the same time as Dover was alerted Commander Constable-Roberts rang Manston to say that the German ships 'are out and approaching the Straits of Dover. Tell Esmonde'. Esmonde summoned his crews. However, being Royal Navy he had to wait for Admiralty confirmation. This came at 11.40 a.m. He then turned to his crews and in an unemotional tone told them to 'get ready'.

The battle plan for the break-out operation was in a locked safe but the Intelligence officer in charge had gone on twenty-four hour's leave, leaving the secret orders locked up with no one able to find the key.

There was a mad scramble to assemble the fighter escort. Bill Igoe at Biggin Hill was contacted to send five fighter planes to escort Esmonde's six Swordfish on their torpedo attack. A few other fighter units were cobbled together. Esmonde's biographer summed up all this as follows: 'The lack of a full briefing of these fighter pilots, combined with the last minute haste in mounting the escort, led to near complete confusion, total lack of co-ordination and ultimately pure tragedy'.

Squadron-Leader Brian Kingcombe, a veteran of the Battle of Britain, was in charge of the squadron of Spitfire fighters. He knew nothing of the plan to attack the escaping battleships and did not know the reason for the 'flap'. He was not given the full facts now – nor indeed were any of the other fighters who had been detailed to escort the Swordfish.

All the fighter escorts summoned were to rendezvous over Manston. Esmonde was relieved to hear this and replied, 'tell them to be here by 12.25 and for the love of God get them to us in time'.

Option

Esmonde was given a final opportunity to opt out of making the attack, which, given the circumstances, would have been understandable. This was conveyed to him by Constable-Roberts at Dover Castle who said, 'Admiral Ramsay wants to know how you feel about going in?'

Esmonde's reply was brief and to the point: 'Yes, the Squadron will go in, where is Jerry? What's the speed?' He was told and immediately studied his maps to work out the ships' likely position by the time he could reach them. Constable-Roberts came back on the phone again to enquire if he was satisfied with the fighter escort, concluding, 'if so, the Admiral says it's OK to go'. The RAF controller in the briefing hut where that conversation took place was later to recall his own feeling of shock as he looked at Esmonde's face who, he said, 'looked like a man torn apart'.

Esmonde then proceeded to instruct his crews, commencing with the direction that they forget all they'd learned about a night attack. He said the intention was to hit and slow down any of the big ships. He assured them they would have plenty of fighter cover so they need not worry 'too much' about enemy aircraft.

Having outlined their flight formation, height and so on, his final direction was that once they had cleared the escort surrounding the battleships each Swordfish was to attack independently. He last instruction was: 'now, get to your aircraft, warm up and stand by'. Each plane had a crew of three men, pilot, observer and a torpedo air gunner.

The telephone now rang to say the fighter escort might be a few minutes late. Esmonde replied, 'we're taking off at 12.25. I'll orbit the coast for a few minutes'. Wing-Commander Tom Gleave, at RAF Manston, met Eugene Esmonde as he

started to walk to his aircraft and wished him luck. He afterwards said, 'the look on his face shook me. It was the face of a man already dead. I'd known him as a vital man, alive and eager for anything. Now his eyes were dulled, his face grey, almost haggard, the sort of vacant lifeless face you read about but never expect to see. He barely recognised me, although his mouth twitched automatically into the semblance of a grin. And an arm lifted in a vague way. It shocked me as nothing had done before nor has done since'.

Esmonde got a last minute message from a runner who arrived panting, 'Dover says the enemy's speed is now estimated at 27 knots, sir'. Esmonde strapped himself into his plane and checked the sky for the expected fighter escort. In his mind he must have been recalculating the location of the target in the light of the last-minute revision estimate of the ships' speed. He had even less time to guarantee reaching the ships for any attack.

Take-off
The Swordfish (above) rumbled along the frozen grass runway and lifted shakily into a wintry sky. Eighteen young men (the oldest was aged 25) in six elderly biplanes off to challenge almost half the German navy as well as a part of the Luftwaffe of unknown strength. The time was 12.25 p.m., almost four and a half hours since Bill Igoe and others noted the ships on the move.

They set course for the town of Ramsgate on the east coat of Kent. They were there within four minutes and began to circuit the town searching the skies for those vital fighter escorts. Within three minutes only ten Spitfires had arrived – four squadrons in all were promised. Esmonde waited two more minutes and then decided to 'go in' – every minute lost meant that the quarry was speeding even further to safety. Esmonde's biographer, Chaz Bowyer, points out that he could easily and logically have abandoned the operation at that point as the situation was completely different to that which led him to originally volunteer Squadron 825 to participate in 'Operation Fuller'. However, he chose not to and set course for the target.

Near the half-way point they were viciously attacked by German Messerschmitts but were only slightly damaged. Brian Kingcombe, the leader of Esmonde's fighter escort who were flying ahead (the fighters had difficulty holding back their speed to match the old and heavily-laden Swordfish), attacked the Germans and drove them off. Then he saw a big ship. Because it was heading for Dover, he assumed it was a Royal Navy vessel. Suddenly the air was full of German planes

The black dots indicate, very roughly, the route of the German battleships and escorting convoy from Brest to point of attack. Ramsgate was where Esmonde was to rendezvous with his fighter escort.

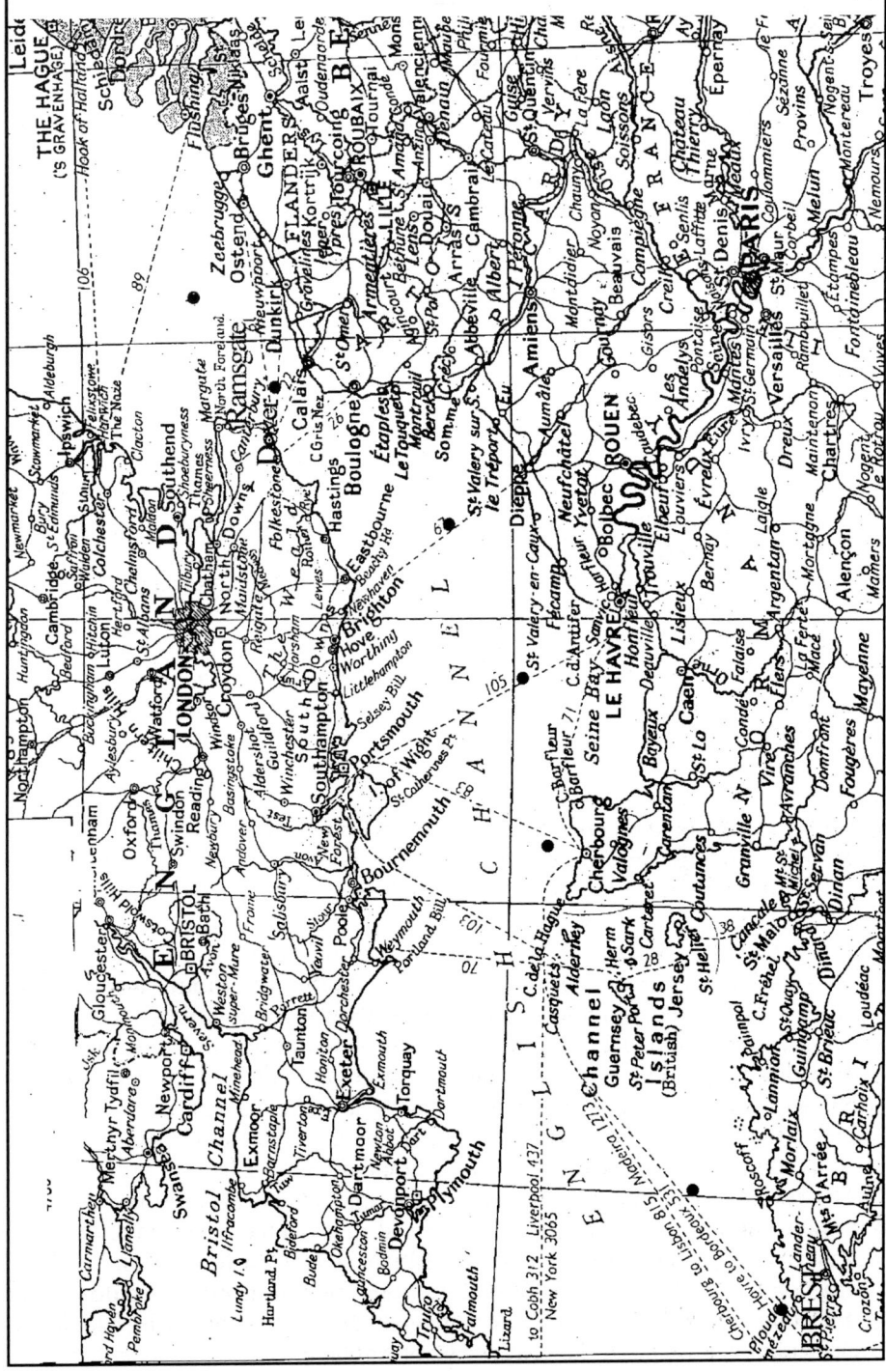

and to his horror he recognised the ship was the *Prinz Eugen*. He quickly brought his fighters back over the Swordfish.

Targeted

At 12.50 the Swordfish first saw their prime targets – huge battleships, destroyers, and E-boats which were putting out a dense smoke screen along the port flank of the main formation. Above the convoy, layered from 50 to 2,000 feet, was a host of German fighters – Messerschmitts, the elite units of the Luftwaffe. These now concentrated on the approaching Swordfish – a massacre was inevitable.

Esmonde's leading trio were less than two miles from their battleship targets when the German fighters bore in on them with cannon and machine-gun fire.

Esmonde flew on relentlessly. He got safely through the smoke screen, followed closely by two other Swordfish. They withstood a further machine-gun and cannon attack from the air and ongoing fire from below.

Then Esmonde's plane suffered a direct hit from the air which set fire to the tail, followed by a shell from *Prinz Eugen*'s gun which sliced away the lower portion of his port wing.

He continued to fly the severely damaged plane towards his target. Then their previous air assailant made one more pass, the gunfire killing the observer and air gunner and hitting Esmonde in the back and head.

The Swordfish nosed up slightly, then its torpedo fell away – apparently released on track for *Prinz Eugen* by the injured Esmonde. No damage was incurred to *Prinz Eugen* as she easily evaded the approaching torpedo.

Eugene Esmonde's aircraft nosed-dived into the sea and disintegrated.

The two Swordfish flying behind Esmonde were also wiped out with only one survivor of the total nine crewmen. The other three Swordfish suffered similar fates. Of the eighteen crew who had taken off at 12.25 p.m. on 12 February 1942 only five had survived.

Post-mortem

Esmonde's biographer records the following. In his report of the day's operations Wing-Commander Tom Cleave, RAF, Manston, concluded: 'I am of the opinion that Lieutenant Commander Esmonde is well worthy of the posthumous award of the Victoria Cross' – an RAF officer recommending a naval officer for the supreme award had no precedent in the history of the honour.

It is worth noting at this point the reaction of Admiral Bertram Ramsay who, it will be remembered, did not countenance sending in the Swordfish in the first instance, and gave the OK to Esmonde's decision to opt in only because he was assured that the fighter escort for the operation was all lined up. He told the Admiralty office that had he known the full facts he would have ordered Esmonde to stay on the ground. He described 825 Squadron's 'gallant sortie' as 'one of the finest exhibition of self-sacrifice and devotion that the war has yet witnessed'.

The reaction generally to the fiasco was one of outrage. Prime Minister Winston Churchill faced a storm of protest and anger in the House of Commons over an exercise which had seen six Swordfish, seventeen fighters and at least twenty bombers lost, a total of almost 100 airmen and sailors killed and dozens of others wounded, with no worthwhile damage to enemy warships who had dared to sail within gun range of the south coast of England.

The Victoria Cross
Lieutenant Commander Eugene Esmonde was awarded the V(ictoria) C(ross). posthumously at an investiture on 17 March 1945. His body had not yet been recovered. Four of the survivors received DSOs and the fifth a Conspicuous Gallantry Medal (CGM).

The prepared citation falls well short of the full truth:

> On the morning of Thursday February 12, Lieut.-Commander Esmonde, in command of a squadron of the Fleet Air Arm, was told that the German battle-cruisers *Scharnhorst* and *Gneisenau* and the cruiser *Prinz Eugen*, strongly escorted by some 30 surface craft, were entering the Straits of Dover and that his squadron must attack before they reached the sandbanks north-east of Calais. Knowing that his enterprise was desperate, Lieut.-Commander Esmonde and his squadron of six Swordfish set course for the enemy shortly after noon and after ten minutes of flying were attacked by a strong force of enemy fighters. The [RAF] fighter escort was lost and in the action which followed all the Swordfish were damaged, but he flew on against hopeless odds, and was met by intense fire from the battle-cruisers and their escort. The port wing of his Swordfish was damaged, but Lieut.-Commander Esmonde led his squadron straight through the fire from the ships in steady flight towards their target. Almost at once he was shot down but the squadron went on and launched a gallant attack in which at least one torpedo is believed to have struck the battle-cruisers and from which not one of the Swordfish returned.
>
> His high courage and splendid resolution will live in the traditions of the Royal Navy and remain for many generations a fine and stirring memory.

Mrs Eily Esmonde, who was confined to a wheelchair due to arthritis, made the journey from Drominagh with her sons Owen and Patrick, both active servicemen, to receive the posthumous VC from King George VI. As the day was St. Patrick's Day all wore shamrocks. Royal protocol was set aside to allow all three (instead of the regulatory two persons) into the investiture and again to allow all three to approach HM to receive the VC which was handed to Eily by the King. Eily held the tiny box in her lap as they returned to their seats, then each in turn kissed the cross, murmuring 'For Eugene'.

Burial
Five weeks later, on Sunday 26 April 1942, a body was found in the Thames estuary. It was identified as that of Eugene Esmonde by his uniform and a gold ring on his left little finger bearing the word, 'Jerusalem' This word appears on the Esmonde coat of arms.

He was buried with full naval honours in Gillingham new cemetery four days later. The religious ceremony was presided over by a Roman Catholic chaplain from the nearby naval barracks, who, incidentally, bore the name of Egan. His mother did not make the journey but Patrick, Owen, Carmel and her husband were in attendance.

Some years later a permanent monument to commemorate him was erected in St Michael's church, Lee-on-Solent. This was an inscribed brass plaque mounted on oak and a pair of brass candelabra.

Inquiry

Esmonde's biographer, in the course of his Epilogue, examines 'Operation Fuller' in some detail and highlights the circumstances and errors which turned it into such a disaster. The inflexible security ruling on the plan contributed in no small way to making it into the fiasco it became.

The Government was forced to set up an immediate official inquiry board to investigate and report on the debacle. The board, presided over by a judge, consisted of senior members of the Admiralty and of the RAF. They sat for fifteen days. However, it became nothing more than a 'whitewash' in the interests of restoring confidence in the Government and senior service chiefs. When, for example, Squadron-Leader Bill Igoe attended the board in Whitehall he was approached by an official and asked what evidence he proposed to give. In Igoe's words: 'I said, "the truth" and when I reached the stand I was asked if I had heard the previous officer's evidence, which was unconnected with mine, and if I disagreed with anything in it, I replied that I found it accurate – we were then both discharged without further consideration, without me being questioned at all, so that my evidence was never heard'.

The report was duly presented in Parliament but 'in the interest of national security' its contents was not made public. This same reason was given when fielding questions in the House. It was made public only in 1946.

The irony of this tragic story is that Germany's concentration of the battleships within the North seas suited the British Admiralty very well. It also meant that the RAF's protracted aerial campaign against them in Brest could now be directed at other important targets.

Sources:
Chaz Bowyer, *Eugene Esmonde, VC, DSO* (London, 1983).
OHS, Gravestone Inscriptions,Terryglass.
Burke's Landed Gentry.
TNFH research centre.
1901 Census.
Mrs Antonia Esmonde.
Personal memories of Bill Donoghue & Matt Fogarty.

Photographs: p. 185, copied from the Esmonde biography with the author's and Antonia Esmonde's permission; pp. 186, 191, 197, reproduced from the biography with the author's permission.

8
Other Houses and Lodges

ORMONDE COTTAGE

This is located in Finnoe. It shares an entrance with and is in close proximity to the deconsecrated Church of Ireland church. The first mention we get of it is in the *Topographical Dictionary* of 1837, when it was the residence of Samuel Waller. Samuel may have been a brother of the ill-fated Thomas of nearby Finnoe House who was murdered in 1843.

In Waller's time Ormonde Cottage was a two-storey house with three bedrooms, kitchen, dairy and wash house. We do not know who built it but Samuel Waller added to it extensively – his several additions being clearly idenifiable in the aerial photograph taken in 1962 (above). He built an upstairs sitting room in one extension which had very large windows through which he could look out over his fields and see his men at work.

Sometime before 1875 the property passed into the ownership of Robert Donald/Donald's son. The next occupants we know of are the Costelloe family. They may be the same as the Garryncurry family. Mrs Margaret Costelloe made a will in 1897 and died the following year. The will is in the possession of Mrs Nancy McCarthy, the present occupant of Ormonde Cottage. Margaret Costelloe's son, William, married Margaret McCarthy, Ballycapple, Cloughjordan. They had no children. After William's death Margaret married a Tuohy man from Toomevara. They had no children and after his death her brother, John McCarthy, who had a small farm at Crowle, but needed a bigger place, bought Ormonde Cottage and the large farm for £1,670 from his sister at an auction on 10 December 1910. He was married to Bridget Cahalan, Carneybrack. They had two children – Patrick and May. Patrick married Anne (Nancy) Cahalan, Borrisokane in 1952 and they had one son and four daughters. The son, Vincent, runs the farm with his mother Nancy.

Springfield House

Springfield house is located on the road running between Congor graveyard and Finnoe.

In 1826 it was occupied by John Falkiner, the head landlord being Thomas Sadleir. In 1852 Robert Walpole was the occupier 'in fee', so he must have purchased the lease from Sadleir.

James Cleary became the owner of Springfield after Walpole, having come from Kylebeg. He sold it in 1930 to the McCarthys, the present occupier being John McCarthy who is a brother of Mrs Margaret Cleary of Ballycolliton House.

Carrigagowan House

It is described by O'Donovan in 1840 as 'a respectable and commodious farmhouse in the occupation of Daniel Hogan Esq.' It was located on the road which runs parallel with the Puckane-Coolbawn road and links Cloghprior graveyard with Kilbarron village.

Daniel Hogan wrote to the Ordnance Surveyors asking that it be entered as 'Castle Carrig' on the map – and so it was.

It was a T-shaped house and seems to have been demolished around 1912 and a new house built on the site by John and Babs (née Casey) Bourke of Kylebeg and Lisquillibeen, respectively, shortly after they married.

Ballycolliton House

This house, which is probably about 200 years old, is situated on the main Nenagh-Portumna road about halfway between Puckane and Coolbawn and near the junction signposted 'Luska' going towards the lake. It is built beside Ballycolliton tower house and some of its out-offices are incorporated into that old 'castle'.

The settlers who acquired these tower houses, most of which are described in the *Civil Survey* as in a 'ruinous state', used to put up a lean-to against the tower house walls. There is a very good example of this at Ballycolliton. It is a strong, slated building and now houses tractors and other implements of the present owners, Cornelius (Con) Cleary and his wife Margaret. Margaret has found traces of decoration in the old lean-to, indicating that it was once a dwelling-house.

There is also a small, one-storey house attached to the back of their present house, now used as a kitchen and bathroom by the family. Margaret Cleary thinks it was built, perhaps, a hundred years before the main house.

The various changes of ownership which the Ballycolliton lands went through have already been recounted. The Cambie-Cleburne marriage of 1680 brought it into Cleburne occupation. A Richard Cleburne of 'Ballycoltaen' figures as a

witness in Minchin to Cambie and Sadleir to Cambie leases of 1723.

It is not known when the Cleburnes left but they are not there in the Tithe Applotment list of 1824 when the head landlord was a Joseph Palmer and the occupier Richard Gray. In 1840 a John Parker of the Lansdowne, Portroe, branch, was living there. In 1852 George Fawcett is living there 'in fee', i.e. having the freehold of 181 Irish plantation acres. This George Fawcett is one of the five people who, in 1878, granted a lease of Ballycolliton for 31 years to John O'Connell reproduced below.

John O'Connell married the 'girl next door', Winifred O'Brien of Kilbiller House. They had five daughters and one son, Michael John, who never married. Two of the sisters became nuns. Another, who married a Gleeson, was the mother of Mrs Maureen Buckley who inherited Michael John's bungalow at Luska.

In 1960 Michael J. O'Connell sold Ballycolliton House (above) and land to Cornelius Cleary of Ballylusky, Ardcroney, for £7,500 and in 1970 Con married Margaret McCarthy of Springfield House. They have two sons who farm the land with their father.

At the top of the old tower house, which I believe is at its original height, stands a belfry built of red brick. It contained a bell, probably put there by some previous occupier as a workmen's bell. The belfry was obviously not part of the original old building. Michael John gave the bell to Father Sheppard of Cloughjordan who was on the missions in Africa so the bell is probably now pealing out from some mission station on that continent. Michael John had a good idea for supplying water to the house. He had a concrete tank built at the top of the old tower house to which water from the nearby Ballycolliton river was pumped by a motor pump. The water then fell by force of gravity through pipes enabling the house to have a bathroom and flush lavatory.

Landlord and Tenant

The landlord-tenant system evolved in the 1700s and as the population grew sub-letting by tenants became the pattern. The landlord set his land to the tenant for a rent fixed by the landlord to be paid on 1 May and 1 November each year. The tenant held as 'a tenant at will' or 'year to year', or on a 'lease'. For the first two the agreement between landlord and tenant was subject to regular review and annually, respectively. The tenancy need not be renewed and there was no restriction on raising the rent each time

A lease spelt a degree of security for the tenant. Leases could take different forms and were for different lengths of time. The ones common to this area were for 21 years, 31 years, or three lives. A 'three lives' lease meant that a tenant or his heirs could not be disturbed if he paid the rent which in turn could not be raised until the three named persons had died.

Gradually, during the nineteenth century more tenants were given leases instead of being merely yearly or tenants-at-will. We have written evidence of this in the case of the Minchin and Cambie estates and anecdotal, but sound, evidence in the case of Slevoir when owned by Mr Maunsell who sold out to the Hickie's predecessor, Rev. Francis Synge, in the 1840s. Some were given leases for thirty-one years.

Many nineteenth-century leases are still in the possession of the families whose ancestors were parties to them. John O'Connell's lease is in the possession of Con and Margaret Cleary, Ballycolliton, who kindly allowed me to copy it. It is very elaborate but probably standard for the time.

Leases could be very restrictive. In this instance the lessor kept the rights to all fishing and shooting – even rabbits; all minerals or ores whether worked or not; all turbary (turf banks) rights, 'with the right to work all such minerals ...' Retained also were rights to loughs, watercourses, all trees, mills, mill sites, mill races, and so on.

The extent of the holding leased was 109 acres Irish plantation measure, and the yearly rent was £215 – nearly £2 per acre. However, apart from 25 acres which were allowed to be tilled, the lessee had to pay £10 for every acre more that he tilled, unless he had a licence to do otherwise. Also, he was restricted as to the type of crop he could sow.

John O'Connell was lucky because before his 31-year term was up the Land Act of 1903 enabled him to purchase the property – all the more fortunate because, if he had to vacate the property on its expiry, the terms of the lease debarred him from an important tenant entitlement under the 1870 Act - seeking any compensation for improvements made.

O'Connell came close to eviction within a few years of acquiring the lease. Obviously he supported the Land League's policy of seeking a reduction in the rent to Griffith's Valuation – in his case £134 as against the rent fixed in the lease, £215. An eviction writ was served on him by post and in court in May 1881 he had to pay up the full amount, plus costs.

The 1878 Ballycolliton Lease

October 11th 1878 between Archibald Robinson of 14 St. Stephen's Green, Dublin, Esq, lessor of 1st part, George William Fawcett of Madras, Presidency of India and Frederick Fawcett, Madras Presidency of India and J. Maude Crament, 12 Melbourne Grove, Gilston Road, West Brompton, London. Caroline Crament his wife herein afterwards called lessors of 2nd part <u>and John O'Connell, hereinafter called the Lessee of Ballycolliton in the County of Tipperary (farmer)</u>

herein called the Lessee do herewith demise the lands of Ballycolliton (otherwise Ballycollitane) contained one hundred and nine acres Irish plantation measure or thereabouts with the dwelling house and all offices standing therein together with labourers' cottages in as large and ample measure as same was lately held by J. W. Harvey Esq.

Except all mines, minerals, mineral ores, coals, quarries & beds of stone, limestone, marble and slate whether same has ever been opened or worked or not. All timber, plants and stumps of trees, underwoods, plantations, all turf and all bogs and turbary rights save as herein after giving pasture & commonage. All loughs, watercourses, mills, mill sites, mill races, mill dams and permission for lessors, their agents, heirs etc., to enter land & dig, bore, raise, saw, cut & manufacture & carry away the same, making reasonable compensation to Lessee for any damage done. And also except & reserving all birds defined as game by any Act of Parliament and all other birds or animals usually known as game or wildfowl & all rabbits and fish and to allow Lessors, their agents, heirs etc at any time to hunt, course, shoot, fish and to destroy any animal as aforementioned and carry away same.

To have and to hold such lands for a term of thirty-one years from 25th day of March 1878 paying a yearly sum of £215 (two hundred and fifteen pounds) half-yearly on 29th September & 25th March being Quit rent, Crown rent and landlord's proportion of Poor Rate, Grand Jury cess and Income and Property tax.

And further paying ten pounds for every acre Irish plantation measure in excess of the 25 such acres in any one year which shall be sown or planted with white or exhaustive crops without such licence as aforesaid, which rent to be paid from the commencement of the ploughing up of any such improper cultivation or mismanagement & to continue while such cultivation continues. If, after notice, the said rents, two hundred and fifteen pounds and additional rents, is not paid at the appointed time without having been demanded, the Lessor, his agent, heirs etc. has the right to distrain, distress, take away, lead, drive & carry away & dispose of according to law for satisfaction of said rents or any part thereof in arrears together with all such costs and charges as Lessor shall incur.

And if Lessee has fallen in arrears he will pay to the Lessor's agent George Waller McQuestion the half-yearly rent of £107 10s 0d one hundred and seven pounds, ten shillings in respect of the six months owing and all assessments, deductions and outgoings (except Quit Rent & Crown Rent & the Landlords proportion of the Grand Jury's Cess & Poor Rate & Income and Property tax).

And will throughout the same term and at his own expense sufficiently repair and keep in repair all Buildings for the time being on the demised premises & if any of said be destroyed or damaged by fire, lightning, tempest or in any other manner will, within six calendar months at his own expense repair all damages and will insure and keep insured all buildings etc against loss or damage by fire in such amounts as shall be not less than the full value & insurance be effected in such offices as shall be approved by the Lessor & will expend all such monies received in repairing, rebuilding and reinstating to the satisfaction of the Lessor.

And will not allow, without licence in writing from Lessor etc, any trees to be cropped, lopped, cut down, felled, injured or destroyed & preserve same to the best of his ability from damage by cattle etc. by putting fences around where necessary.

<u>And</u> during this period (31 years) will not allow more than twenty-five acres Irish plantation measure to be ploughed or broken up or set out or planted with flax or hemp crop or a succession of white crops or any other crops of a light kind or equally exhaustive nature and manage and cultivate the land in such a way as to leave it in good heart at the end of the demised period.

<u>And</u> to consume by cattle in an orderly & husbandlike manner all corn, grain, straw, chaff and all green crops (other than potatoes) & spread dung produced from such crops on the lands.

<u>And</u> not without licence bequeath, sub-let or sub-divide any of the demised lands & not cut turf or fuel save for the use of the dwelling.

<u>And</u> allow Archibald Robinson his agents and heirs to, at any time, come and inspect the demised premises.

<u>And</u> at the end of term deliver up demised premises in the state in which found.

<u>And</u> that the <u>Lessee</u> shall not at the end of the demised period make any claims for improvements under Landlord & Tenant (Ireland) Act of 1870 or under any subsequent Acts.

<u>And</u> the <u>Lessee</u> shall only bequeath the demised premises to one member of his family for the period remaining & this family member shall be bound by all these covenants as fully as if he been named in the original lease.

<u>And</u> if the rent is not paid after having been legally demanded or if the <u>Lessee</u>, his executors, administrators or any of them, shall be convicted of treason or become bankrupt or commit any other act of default or if this Indenture is offered as a security <u>Then</u> the <u>Lessor</u> his agents heirs etc, may repossess the demised premises.

<u>And</u> provided rents are paid and all covenants observed the said <u>Lessee</u> may peacefully & quietly hold use & enjoy the said premises for the thirty-one years without any interruption by the said <u>Archibald Robinson</u> etc and any of their agents, heirs etc.

George William Fawcett and Frederick Fawcett shall, except for the last six months of the lease, pay the <u>Lessee</u> interest on the said sum of one hundred and seven pounds ten shillings from the date of payment thereof at the rate of five pounds £5 (five pounds) per cent per annum.

Under power of attorney George Waller McQuestion has set his seal to & ascribed the names of George William Fawcett and Frederick Fawcett.

Signed sealed and delivered   Archibald Robinson
by the said John O'Connell   George William Fawcett

Various other persons and witnesses had also signed the document.

CASTLETOWN

Castletown, in the townland of the same name, is located a short distance from Coolbawn Cross on the road to Kilbarron/Skehanagh quay. It is surrounded by some of the fairest and richest land in Ireland which sweeps down to the lake shore. The chimney stacks and gables of the house can be seen from the Coolbawn-Ballinderry road and also from the road leading from the lake to Coolbawn. The first modern mention of it as a residence is the Taylor and Skinner road maps of 1778 where it is described as 'Castle Cambie', having come into the possession

of that family in 1714 by lease to Anne Cambie, widow, from Charles Sadleir, whose father had purchased it from the Briggs family in 1706.

Castletown (above) is the only one of the parish tower houses which, as far as we know, has been lived in since it was built by the O'Kennedys in the fifteenth or sixteenth century. It is also one of the very few in the county to enjoy this status still. As the photograph shows, the earlier tower has been extended to become a commodious residence with the addition of two extensions. The one on the right, dates from 1956 after G. M. (Jimmy) Sterling, who had inherited it from the Towers family, married Rosamund Barrow. The building work was carried out by Michael Egan of Puckane.

This extension is in character with the earlier addition directly on to the tower. It would appear that Charles Cambie, who sold it in 1856, was responsible for this wing which included a new timber stairs and spacious rooms at first and second floor level. The sale prospectus stated that Castletown was a family residence 'in excellent order, the owner having expended a large sum of money on its restoration'.

The house stands on an elevated position looking out over the islands and across at the Co. Clare hills. When I visited it on a sunny November day the Virginia creeper, which covers the walls, was russet and golden.

Henry J. Cambie, the young emigrant to Canada, wrote in his reminiscence that 'a courtyard in front of the house was enclosed with high walls and during part of my boyhood if any visitor came after dark he had to ring a bell outside the courtyard gate and give an account of himself'. The courtyard and lower portion of the wall are still there.

As stated elsewhere, work on Castletown estate was the only alternative to emigration for the younger sons of small farmers in Coolbawn and adjacent townlands.

There are some domestic records of the years 1924-9 which Mrs Rosamund Sterling has made available to me. There was the foreman, William Stanley, who had a free house and the grass of a cow – perhaps of two cows as he had a large family – and wages which varied from 30 weeks at £1 10s 0d (£1.50p) per week to 22 weeks at £1 5s 0d, making up to £72 12s 0d per annum for a typical year. Mike Kennedy, the herd, had 30 weeks at £1 1s 0d (£1.05p) and 22 weeks at 16s 0d (80p), making in all £49 2s 0d (£49.10p) less national insurance stamp @ 17s 4d.

He had a free house – the little house at Coolbawn Cross beside the pump – and free milk. The lower wages must have been for the less busy time of the year. Labourers, all local men, who varied in number from 2 to 4 in that period had 30 weeks at £1 and 22 weeks at 15s (75p). One worker who was married had a free house and the above wage. Two others, who lived at home and were unmarried, had 18s. for 30 weeks (£27) and 22 weeks at 13s (65p) making £45 for the year.

When we look back at the wages or salaries of teachers at that time – approximately £5 per week – the farm wages were not bad. In my first teaching post in 1938 in a convent school in England, with a university degree and higher diploma in education, I earned £60 per annum, living in.

Crops

The records of 1924-9 show how lands were used on 1 June in the years to which accounts relate – area under gardens, lawns, orchards etc was classified as pasture.

Meadow	70 acres
Oats	14 acres
Barley	4 acres
Wheat	Castletown 12, Coolbawn 24
Potatoes	1 acre
Turnip & mangolds	9
Flax	0
Other tillage	13
Waste	13
Pasture	421
TOTAL	545 + 36

There are detailed, but hardly decipherable, accounts of ingoings and outgoings and comparisons between Cameron, Coolbawn and Castletown. Only fragments of these accounts for those years were found by Mrs Rosamund Sterling but they attempt to give some idea of outlay and income. I believe the accounts were kept by Thomas Towers himself. He was becoming ill at this time and the writing becomes illegible. Agricultural wages for one year were £466 15s . Hire of grazing, £115, shoeing of horses, £14, repairs to farm implements £3. Long lists of produce, such as eggs, pigs, poultry, butter, potatoes, etc, have no prices. There was very little tillage, most of the land being under pasture and livestock the chief product. There is no indication of the price of livestock. I remember that those pre-AI days, Mr Towers, had the only bull in the neighbourhood and small farmers from round about took their cows to his bull for insemination.

It is not clear from the accounts if the farm was profitable or not. The big prices received during World War I were a thing of the past. What is clear from the

Towers documents is that the family had extensive investments both here and in Canada with each member of the family having his or her own portfolio.

House Servants
Two house servants were always kept in Castletown at this time – a cook and house parlour maid. This was 'good' service and the girls would probably be the daughters of small farmers from the parish or neighbouring parishes. In the afternoon the parlourmaid always wore the proper uniform of black dress, smart pleated white apron and matching cap. I know this because as children living at the post office we delivered telegrams. The parlour maid lived in and on their afternoon off on a Sunday would visit and have tea usually at Ryans, but sometime also at Morans or Gormans or our house. Their wages, living in, might be five to ten shillings a week.

The Towers Household
Mrs Lucy Wolfe Towers, mother of Thomas and the girls, was a widow for twelve years and until her death in 1893 seems to have kept her hands firmly on the reins. This is evident from various correspondence with solicitors and the local authority. For example she had a running battle, which she won, with the Co. Council not to have a labourer's cottage built on her land, saying that she already had five or six workmen's houses more than other neighbouring landlords, and that one was empty. These were the first rural local authority houses. There is an interesting notebook which unfortunately has not the year's date simply 'Sept. 1st Dress Account'. It is written in rather quaint, spiky old-fashioned script, obviously by Mrs Lucy Towers herself. An example of the content is given below.

Item	Cost		
	£	s	d
Children's cloaks	1	2	0
Shirt Ben*		11	0
Stays [corsets]		4	0
Hose [stockings]		1	4
Flannel for petticoats		10	2
Winter petticoats		6	0
Shawls, garters		5	4
Collars for Tom		1	6
Battledore & shuttlecock		–	–
Shawl for Nurse		3	6
Pelisse for Ann		4	10 1/2
and much of the same			

* This gives an idea of the date as Ben died in 1881.

Raided
A practice during the War of Independence was to raid a Big House for firearms. In Castletown's case this happened later on, during the Civil War. On 14 October 1922 five armed men entered the house, stole money and damaged a considerable quantity of valuable property. The list is five pages long and does not include any

firearms the acquisition of which was ostensibly the object of these raids. It is impossible to reproduce the list of items here because of its length, but includes damage to, and destruction of, various items of antique furniture, loss of much jewellery, valuable motoring coats (fur-lined), money, and so on. Each member of the Towers family compiled a separate claim. James O'Brien, Solicitor, Nenagh, dealt with the claims for the family. In a letter dated 4 August 1923 he wrote to Thomas Towers as follows: 'On 16 Oct last [i.e. 1922] I sent a claim to the Government for £340 14*s* 5*d*.' The solicitor goes on to say that 'it is now necessary to re-lodge the claim on the enclosed form which must be completed and sent to the Government by the 12th inst.' The list seems exorbitant but the final sum claimed quite small. There is nothing to show that the claim was met but it probably was. The Free State Government was usually quite meticulous about meeting such claims.

Curraghmore House

It was situated near Curraghmore Point close to Bellevue and Brookfield and reached by a lane (avenue) beginning at the entrance to Lesserragh.

It was inspected in 1840 by a Mr O'Callaghan, Hugh Costelloe and Daniel Hogan, in the presence of John O'Donovan, and is described as 'a commodious farm, the residence of Mr Alt'. The proprietor was Counsellor Grady. This is the Henry Brady (or Grady) who owned Islandmore until the Holmes family bought it in the mid-nineteenth century.

No traces of the house survive.

Garrane House

This house (below) is in the townland of the same name off the road between Kilbarron village and Ballinderry. In Lewis's *Topographical Dictionary* of 1837 it is given as the seat of Michael Legge Esq. Legge was one of the two people, the other being Rev. Ralph Stoney, who compiled the Tithe Applotment list for Kilbarron parish in the 1820s.

In 1840 it was leased by Joseph Falkiner of Rodeen House, who occupied it as a dairy and kept a caretaker there. In the Primary Valuation list of 1852 it seems to be be occupied by the 'constabulary'.

The house was also lived in at one time by the Fortune family. the house later came into the possession of the Sydneys, a Catholic family. In 1901 it was owned by Anastasia Sydney but not lived in by her. She was living at Gortmore with her brother, Colonel Sydney. He died before 1901 and she continued to live there.

The steward in Gortmore in the Colonel's time was Morgan Cahalan but the Colonel sacked him because Morgan would not fit in with what some people would call the Colonel's eccentric ideas. He refused to have the briars cut back and would not allow any rabbit to be killed. One can imagine the result. He also insisted on providing sticks for the crows to build their nests.

He took on as his new steward Jack Carty. I believe the Cartys came from Oughterard, Co Galway. He and his family may have lived in the big house. The Carty children, of whom people of my generation would know, were born there. Mick, Bill, John and Mary. I think Nora was the youngest. I went to school with her. She was a couple of years older and married Willie Donohue of Bellevue lodge. Their daughter Geraldine married Joe Ducie, Puckane.

Anastasia Sydney died in the mid-1900s. Many old properties, like Garrane, had mortgages on them and provided the sitting tenant, or steward paid them off, and fulfilled the conditions for buying out under the 1903 Land Act the Land Commission was satisfied. John Carty did this. When the last of the Carty family, Bill, died, the farm was inherited by a nephew and present owner, Oliver O'Meara. Garrane House, now uninhabited, is not in good repair.

GARRYNCURRA HOUSE

This house (below) is also off the road between Cloghprior and Kilbarron village.

In the Tithe Applotment list of 1824 Lord Ormonde is given as head landlord and Hugh Costelloe as occupier. O'Donovan in his O.S. letters of 1840 describes it as 'a comfortable farmhouse' occupied by Hugh Costelloe. O'Donovan adds that Costelloe told him that the proper name of the townland is 'Garrynacurragh', i.e. *garraí na currach: the garden of the marsh(es)*. Hugh Costelloe was one of those who gave local information to O'Donovan's team.

The Primary Valuation list gives the occupier as George Walpole. The Lynch family bought it from them and they in turn sold it to the present owners, the Clarkes, in 1956.

Luska House

A left turning, signposted Luska, on the main Nenagh-Portumna road about half way between Puckane and Coolbawn Cross, brings you to the shores of Lough Derg. Continuing straight on beside the lake one comes to Luska House, a Victorian villa standing on an elevated site on the left and approached by a short avenue.

This house (below) was built as a holiday home by George Arthur Waller, son of William Thomas Waller of Prior Park and grandson of George Waller who had purchased Prior Park in 1803. William T. had married Eliza Guinness, a grand daughter of Arthur Guinness, founder of the Dublin-based brewery.

The Wallers had four sons, the eldest and most interesting being George Arthur (1835-1923). After graduating in Science and Engineering at Trinity College, Dublin, he joined his cousin's firm of Arthur Guinness Ltd and quickly rose to be both chief engineer and chief brewer. He set up his brothers, Robert (1837-1915) and Francis (1846-92), as barley buyers and malsters at Nenagh and Banagher respectively. Both these ventures were very successful. Edmund (1839-94), the fourth brother, also joined the Guinness firm where he was in charge of the extensive horse transport department.

George Arthur married Sarah Atkinson from Cangort near Shinrone. They had six sons: Richard (Dick) (867-1942); Guy (1870-1950); Ned (1882-1970), George

(1872-1956), Harry (1873-1911), Robert (1879-1963), Jim (1884-1968), who all had successful careers, and Jocelyn (1877-1967) who came home to Prior Park when he was nineteen, his grandfather William Thomas being old and blind and his Aunt Selina unable to manage on her own. Jocelyn was born at Luska while his parents were on holiday there.

In middle age George Arthur decided that his religious principles would no longer permit him to take any further part in the production of alcoholic drink. He resigned from Guinness and started up a pottery factory in Co. Leitrim which did not succeed through no fault of his. He became bankrupt and was forced to sell Luska House. The family decided to emigrate to Tasmania. The journey took three months in the sailing ship and the baggage included a cow to provide fresh milk. Jocelyn had his fifth birthday the day they landed in Tasmania. George Arthur prospered, first as a farmer near Hobart and later as a successful businessman. Circa 1910 he returned to Ireland and re-purchased Luska House where he died in 1923, aged 88. He had originally sold it to a man named Peel whose wife was a Miss Headach of Johnstown House. At his death he left the house to his eldest son Dick, an engineer who was building railways in Spain, amongst other places.

The house was let to various people, both while Dick was working abroad and after he died. He came to live at Luska when he retired and died there in 1942. J. F. Tumpane & Co., Nenagh, had their goods carried by boat from Limerick to Luska quay where they had a storehouse. This traffic ceased when road haulage became easier and cheaper, and the storehouse was no longer needed. With his own hands Dick converted the old storehouse into a pleasant residence which he later sold to his cousin Bertie Waller of Bellisle. In the 1960s it became the home of the Hodson family. Sadly, Mrs Felicity Hodson was killed in a road accident in 1994. Her daughters sold the house to a Dublin business man in 1996.

Luska House had remained in the Waller family after the death of Dick Waller who had no family. In 1956 it was sold to a Mr and Mrs Frank Wylde. Mrs Wylde's niece, Amy Hamilton, came to live with her and some years ago married Myles Sterling of Castletown. The young couple made their home at Luska House.

Mota House

Mota House (below) is located down the road which leads to Mota quay. The quay is signposted on the main Coolbawn-Ballinderry road where there is a rather elegant little gate lodge in some disrepair. According to the Tithe records of 1824 Mota House, 'offices and land' were occupied by Theobald Pepper Roberts, the head landlord being Thomas Sadleir. It was described by John O'Donovan in 1840 as a 'good dwelling house', who also noted that there were 'two good dwelling houses' in the townland. Whether the second one is Rowdly House or Waterloo Lodge is not clear.

The present owner of Mota House, Richard Howard, when he was having the roof repaired in 1975 found on an old rafter the initials A.T. (probably that of a carpenter) and the date 1756. After T. P. Roberts the Tuthill family lived in the house. Very little is known of this family but a headstone in Kilbarron Church of Ireland graveyard has the following inscription:

Sacred to the memory of the beloved sons of Marcus and Emily Tuthill of Mota: Ernest died Feb 27th 1864, aged 15.

John Frederick died May 9th 1864, aged 14.
Francis died August 16th 1872, aged 18.
They sleep in Jesus.

It is said that they all died of tuberculosis. The sorrowing parents left for Australia in 1875 and no more was heard of them.

However, recently an interesting document was forwarded to Tipperary North Family History Research Centre in Nenagh. It relates to a Patt Cleary (born 1858), one of six children born to Rody Cleary and Judy Costelloe whose address in the registers is given alternately as Lisquillibeen and Gortmunga. It appears that after Roger and Judy died the Tuthills took in Patt and another brother – the older Cleary children, having emigrated. Around 1870 Patt emigrated to his brothers and sisters in Michigan, USA. He stayed with Needham cousins for a while. He taught himself to read and write while working at a lumber camp. With money saved he left work and went to school for two years, then took a teaching course followed by a business course. He then took to the road giving lessons in 'penmanship' and went on from that to found a very successful business school called 'Cleary College' in Ypsilanti, in the State of Michigan in t he mid-1880s. His descendants live in Virginia, USA.

Telfords

The property was leased to the Telford family who bought it out, probably under the 1903 Land Act. There is a tradition that the parents of William, Alfred, Henry and Elizabeth Telford were butler and housekeeper to a wealthy aristocrat who left them a legacy which enabled them to take out a lease on Mota as well as purchase some good furniture. This was auctioned on the death of Elizabeth, the last of the

Telfords. Some local people bought pieces at the auction; my brother Paddy bought a Queen Anne desk in need of restoration.

In July 1935 William, Alfred and Elizabeth Telford sold Mota House and 163 acres of land to Richard Howard's parents and took up residence in the old constabulary barracks at Coolbawn.

Henry Telford had married Emily Dagg – a very colourful and delightful lady – circa 1920 and after his mother's death in 1923 he went to live in her family home, the former Kilbarron Glebe House, where the Daggs had come to live from Kevanstown after the death of the last rector of Kilbarron, Rev. Samuels, in 1921. Henry and Emily had one son, Ian, who emigrated to America and died there rather young.

Alfred Telford had lived in Athy and I believe had been married and widowed with no children. He died in 1945. William Telford died in 1937, aged 86; Elizabeth died on 22 April 1941, aged 84; Henry died in Feb 1951, aged 88, and Emily his wife on 27 Feb 1960, aged 85. They are all buried in Kilbarron Church of Ireland graveyard.

Land Divided

There were two Telford farms, Mota and Balllyscanlon. William Telford sold his Mota holding to the Howard family; Henry Telford sold his to the Land Commission. Part of it was divided. Henry Telford had already given their house and some land to the Ryans of Ballyscanlon who had always worked for him. Hogans of Clonmackilladuff may have got a divide. Local man, Pat Meara, an ex-RIC man and first cousin of Paddy Tierney, who was living in England, bought some of the land – 5 or 6 acres – for a holiday home, but later had it taken from him by the Land Commission. He did in time build a house there.

Kilgarvan House, not far from Mota, has been dealt with in relation to the Cambies. The estate was never divided. It has been resold again since its 1976 purchase by a syndicate. The present owners are Dr David and Mrs Conlin.

ROWDLY HOUSE

Rowdly (below), in the townland of Mota, is not mentioned in either the

Topographical Dictionary of 1837 or the Ordnance Survey Letters of 1840. It was a shooting and fishing lodge belonging to the Vaughan family of Golden Grove, Roscrea. Felicia McIvor was the Vaughans' niece and inherited the house from them in 1936. Mrs Vaughan was one of the Lloyd family of Gloster near Roscrea.

Felicia McIvor died tragically in 1951 in an accident involving an electricity generator. The house was bought by Samuel (Uel) Biggs in December 1951. He had married Ruby Jupe of Dublin. They had no children. Uel Biggs died tragically in July 1974. His wife had predeceased him in 1968, also in tragic circumstances, having fallen down the stairs and fractured her skull. She died in Nenagh hospital.

The next owners of Rowdly were the Bishop brothers of Bruree, Co. Limerick, who bought it in 1975. They in turn sold it in 1986/7 to the present (1998) owner, Bruno Ospelt, a native of Liechtenstein.

Waterloo Lodge

This was built later than Mota House. It has a gate lodge situated on the right-hand side of what would have been at one time Mota avenue. This gate lodge is shared with Rowdly House built later, probably in the mid-nineteenth century. It was inherited from Mrs Ruby (née Jupe) Biggs in 1974 by her niece Angela Jupe, a Dublin architect. She had it renovated to a very high standard indeed and it is now owned by the Ospelt family who live in Rowdly House.

In 1824 Rev. Richard Vaughan was occupant of Waterloo Lodge, in the

townland of Mota and described as belonging to Thomas Sadleir. Richard was also a member of the Golden Grove family. He was still there in 1837, and in 1840 when it was described as 'a neat cottage'. The Vaughan family may have built it and the name Waterloo points to a date of circa 1815.

It is situated right on the lakeshore and has a deep harbour. It was inherited by

Capt. Robert McIvor, brother of Miss McIvor who had inherited Rowdly. Capt. McIvor died in 1943 and the property was leased to the Goodbodys of Clara from 1943 until 1951. In 1951 it was bought by the Huskinson family who came from Langer Hall in Nottinghamshire, England. In 1983 it was sold by them to Dr George and Mrs Hilary Henry of Dublin. They in turn sold it to Bruno Ospelt who had already bought Rowdly. The Henrys had upgraded the house, building on a fine conservatory and turning the coach house into living accommodation, a task which had been begun by the Huskinsons. There is a story, supposed to have been told by herself, that Mary Robinson, the former President of Ireland, spent holidays here some time during her childhood.

KILBILLER HOUSE

Kilbiller House, two storeys over a basement and now more or less in a ruinous state, is situated behind Rody O'Meara's new house which is approached by an avenue going uphill from the Puckane-Coolbawn road (i.e. section of the main Nenagh-Portumna road) on the right-hand side going towards Coolbawn. It faces Annagh Lodge, also in Kilbiller townland. Facing the avenue gate is a classical little lodge now in a state of disrepair.

Kilbiller House is associated with the Cambies. In 1714 Anne Minchin Cambie, widow of Solomon who had died a year earlier, had the lease from John Minchin, Castleinch, Co. Kilkenny, renewed on Kilbiller and other lands totalling 140 acres. In the lease Anne undertook to 'build a good farm house of line and stone on part of the premises and plant a hundred apple trees and some flax and hemp and plant and preserve the full number of trees as directed by Act of Parliament. Her son David, Bunnadober, was a witness to the lease. David (d. 1775), married to Anne, daughter of Edward Ledger of Ballinderry, lived in Kilbiller later. It is probable that the present ruin is the 'good farm house' of above.

Kilbiller and the Minchins

In 1824 we find John Minchin living in Kilbiller House. The property, like all Minchin property, was freehold. How or why the property reverted to Minchin ownership remains unexplained. We can only surmise that the lease was not renewed by the Cambies and as Annagh Castle was leased to a tenant Kilbiller was the Minchin home until Annagh Lodge as built.

The next inhabitants we know of are a family called O'Brien. They had made their money through taking contracts for the making or maintenance of stretches of road under the grand jury system of administration. Winifred O'Brien, Kilbiller House, married John O'Connell who had leased Ballycolliton. She inherited Kilbiller on the death of her father and the two properties were joined and farmed together.

In October 1911 Winifred O'Connell sold Kilbiller to Albert G. Waller (Bertie) of Shannon Grove, Banagher, Co. Offaly. In January 1920 Major Waller sold it for £5,520 to Martin Charles Maher of Roscrea, and on 19 June 1920 Maher sold it to Rody O'Meara of Ballythomas, Ardcroney for £6,625. The sale was registered by Rody O'Meara in October 1920.

In the O'Meara family there were four sons and daughters: Rody, Jack, Bill, Jim, Katie who became Mrs Kennedy of Bantis, Cloughjordan, and Nora who had died before they left Ballythomas. The boys were all great hurlers and I remember them all very well as young men when we were children. Jack became a priest and spent his pastoral life in North Dakato, USA. Rody died comparatively young. Only Bill married and on the death of James (Jim), the last of the brothers, Bill's son Rody inherited. He and his wife Margaret (née Dunne) live there now with their three children. They farm and breed horses. Jim O'Meara was the last to live in the old house. It had fallen into disrepair and Rody and Margaret built themselves a bungalow in front of the old house.

The O'Meara family taken in front of their Ballythomas home two years before they moved to Kilbiller in 1920.

GORTMORE HOUSE

Gortmore House is also treated of in chapter 6 in relation to the Biggs family. It is located off the old road to Terryglass. After Anastasia Sydney's death the house, left untenanted, became badly run down and it and the land were taken over by the Land Commission in 1925 and divided.

Nobody wanted the house so John Gleeson, the principal teacher in Terryglass N.S., bought it and ten acres around it sometime between 1925 and 1927. He would not be eligible for a divide. It took him two years to bring the house back to some sort of habitable state. He was gifted in many ways and one was carpentry. He married in 1928. As mentioned in chapter 6, it remains in his family.

The rest of Gortmore was divided. People got farms of about thirty acres and an effort was made to give them to descendants of those who had been evicted from Ashgrove estate during the years of the Great Famine. Only two or three of these took up the offer. Paddy Ryan, Coolbawn, got the biggest farm – over 30 acres.

Gortalougha House

This (below) is one of the best-known of the Big Houses in the parish because of the high profile it achieved as a 'Hidden Ireland' Country House when owned by Michael and Bessie Wilkinson up to 1997. The Wilkinsons were founder members of the 'Hidden Ireland' collection of houses which accepts paying guests. It is near Drominagh House, both by the lakeshore and by road, being located on the old road between Ballinderry and Terryglass where the entrances to both are almost side by side, with Gortalougha having no lodge. The two demesnes are divided by the Ballyfinboy river.

Gortalougha House was built more than 150 years later than Drominagh. The building is thought to have been begun by William D. Ferrar who, according to the Primary Valuation lists of 1852, owned hundreds of acres of land in the parish, particularly in the Ballinderry area. He died before the house was finished but his son John, who had been a captain in the Life Guards, finished the building. John went bankrupt before he managed to build the lodge, although the foundations were dug and were visible within the memory of people still living. He and his wife Violet, and at least one daughter. are buried in a vault in the woods. There is a story that the girl contracted some sort of fever from a polluted well. There is also a story in the neighbourhood that in a certain light the figure of a young girl can be discerned in the large glass window at the front of the house!

In early February 1998 I visited the vault with Wilsie Nolan. We had permission from the present house owners. The vault is a fine cut stone building, now almost entirely covered with ivy and other foliage. The front is elegantly shaped. The vault is reached by going down very steep steps and, on the day in question, the entrance to the vault was flooded after heavy rain. Inside it was very dark and we had forgotten to bring a torch. However, Wilsie had been in there before with a torch and knew the layout. When my eyes became accustomed to the dark I could make out on my left against the wall a large, rather rough-looking oak coffin. Facing the door was a similar but slightly smaller one, and on the right hand side a small coffin made of some pale metal, possibly lead. I could not tell although I scratched it with my fingernail. The metal had at one time been encased in oak as some wood was still clinging to the casket. In spite of the darkness Wilsie

remembered that there was a glass breastplate on the largest coffin which was not attached to the wood and could be picked up and taken outside to read. Something like a coat of arms was inscribed. The legend went:

    John Ferrer D.L.
    late Captain
    1st Life Guards
    12th Sept 1873
    Aged 57

I was surprised at how young Capt. Ferrer was when he died. There is no indication of when his wife and child died. The property must have been sold after his death as it is said he went bankrupt. He entertained lavishly, including all the titled people in the area. Some say that the daughter died while they were living abroad and was brought home in a lead coffin and the father must have built the mausoleum for her. His wife's name was said to be Violet but when she died is not known. Ater the Ferrars' deaths the property passed to a Sir William Austen who kept a pack of hounds there. After a while Sir William leased it to the Gleesons of Tinarana, in Co. Clare.

During World War I George Kent of 'Elmville', Terryglass, bought Gortalougha from Austen for his son Harold who had just got married. Earlier, George Kent had bought Belle Isle near Portumna bridge, which was Lord Avonmore's shooting lodge, for his son Ralph. George had leased it for thirty years from Avonmore who then offered to sell it to him. At one stage it had been lived in by Sir Henry Seagrave the famous motor racing driver who lost his life in one of his water speed record attempts on Lake Windemere. Indeed L. T. C. Rolt in his book *Silver & Green on Irish Waterways* states that Belle Isle was Seagrave's birth place.

Around 1948 Harold Kent sold Gortalougha to Captain Alan Hilgarth, R.N., and bought Killeen House, the former Terryglass glebe house. Hilgarth changed the name Gortalougha to 'Illannanagh' – *Oileán na n-each:island of the horses* – after a small island of that name not far offshore.

Alan Hilgarth had been the British Naval Attache in Madrid during World War II. After the war Duff Cooper wrote a thriller called *The Man That Never Was*, based on real facts. One of the chief characters was based on Alan Hilgarth. Coming up to the opening of the Second Front during the later years of the war the Germans were very anxious to find out where the invasion of Europe would take place. The Allies were equally anxious to put them off the scent so they got a corpse, dressed him in naval uniform, put documents in his pockets and dumped the body off the Spanish coast where it eventually came ashore and the Spaniards found it. The British legation found out – perhaps the Spanish authorities informed them. Alan Hilgarth. as Attaché, was given the task of demanding in no uncertain terms that the Spanish return the body and that on no account was any papers found on it to be read or to be allowed to fall into enemy hands. After much blustering the body – and papers – was returned to Hilgarth. However, as Spain's General Franco was pro-German, the Spaniards already had sent copies of the papers to Berlin. The information contained therein showed invasion was planned to take place in the Gibraltar area. The Germans believed this to be true and so left the eventual landing place, Normandy, less defended.

Captain Hilgarth, who was a widower at that time, had to go from Madrid to

Lisbon to send his secret messages to London. The Spaniards were not to be trusted but the Portuguese were honestly neutral. In Lisbon the cypher clerk with whom he dealt was an English girl named Jean. They fell in love, married and after the war came to live in Gortalougha. Sadly, Jean died at a relatively young age in 1975. He died in 1978. Both are buried in Terryglass new cemetery.

Alan Hilgarth received a CMG (Commander of the Order of St. Michael and St George), and an OBE (Order of the British Empire), replicas of which are carved on his gravestone in the new cemetery in Terryglass.

In the third volume of Winston Churchill's history of that war, *Their Finest Hour*, he thanks the people at the British Embassy in Madrid for the help they gave and mentions the 'British Naval Attaché, Captain Hilgarth, who had retired to Marjorca before the war but on its outbreak he returned to duty equipped with a profound knowledge of Spanish affairs'.

When Alan Hilgarth died in 1978 his sons sold Illannanagh/Gortalougha to the Farmer's Co-Operative which was not successful and they eventually sold it to the Wilkinsons who resold it in 1998.

ASHGROVE HOUSE

This house (below) is situated in the townland of Terryglass, on the left-hand side of the main road going from Ballinderry to Terryglass. It was first mentioned in 1824, the head landlord being Benjamin Talbot and the tenant Oliver Lodge Esq. It is next named in the *Topograpical Dictionary* of 1837, being described as the seat of B. Talbot, Esq. This Benjamin (1781-1839), was father of Rev. Benjamin B. Talbot, whose residence it was in 1840. John O'Donovan, in his Ordnance Survey Letters, described it as 'a commodious building'. Rev. Benjamin B. died in 1878, aged 67 years. He was married to Rev. Ralph Stoney's daughter Ruth (1818-1900).

One can reasonably presume that it was built by the Talbot family who had extensive lands and several residences in the area. It was called Ashgrove because of an adjacent ashgrove, recently cut away.

The Talbots & Heenans
A perusal of the Primary Valuation lists of 1852 shows that the Talbots were tenants themselves who sub-let on a large scale. For example, the immediate lessor for Ashgrove and 251 acres, occupied by Rev. Benjamin, was a Sir John Power.

There is a tradition that the Talbots were harsh landlords and did not hesitate to evict their tenants. The year is not clear but somewhere in the late 1840s or early 1850s twenty-eight families were evicted from Ashgrove and took shelter that night on a grass verge beside the road near Barry's Hill. Bill Donoghue's grandfather remembered as a small boy coming back from the well with his mother and finding the roof being taken off their house. The last of the Talbots to live at Ashgrove was Fanny Talbot (sister of Rev. Benjamin) who died in 1902, aged 72. She is buried in Terryglass old graveyard. Her steward, William Heenan, either inherited or purchased the property – as well as Shannon View, also a Talbot house.

William Heenan had several daughters. One married Michael Tierney of Macloon and they took up residence at Ashgrove. They had one daughter who died very young and then the mother died also. Michael Tierney married, secondly, Alice McCarthy of Ballycapple near Cloughjordan and the couple had six sons. Another daughter married Daniel Fogarty and they lived in Shannon View. Tierney and Fogarty families still live at Ashgrove and Shannon View, respectively.

During the War of Independence Ashgrove was looked on as a 'safe' house. I have heard that one of the girls was being courted by a Cronin of Lorrha, a member of a well-known Republican family who used visit there. Probably other activists would meet there, or men on the run might be hidden.

The true facts are all now lost in the mists of time but it is still said that one night the police got a tip-off that a crowd of the 'boys' was at Ashgrove. There was, in fact, a card school going on, one of the players being 'Kruger' Heenan. The story goes that two lorry loads of Black and Tans were sent to raid the house. Technically, it would be lorry-loads of police, as the Black and Tans were RIC reinforcements and an RIC Head Constable, or District Inspector, would have been in charge. It is, however, quite likely that the lorry loads had a heavy sprinkling of these 'heavies'. One lorry crashed at Pat Heenan's, near Crossanagh bridge. The other lorry came by Roran and took a wrong turning before Ashgrove and stopped at Neill's house to ask the way. Mrs Neill gave them the directions, then quickly sent her young son Jim out the back window to take a short cut up behind Nolan's house and get to Ashgrove before the raiding party thus giving the 'boys' time to escape. Another version of the story has only one lorry which crashed at Pat Heenan's. The police then marched towards Ashgrove and were delayed by Mrs Neill's tactics.

Shannon View

Shannon View, a neat south-facing Georgian dwelling, is situated on the old road to Terryglass from Ballinderry up a short avenue to the right. The site is elevated enough to provide a view of Lough Derg, hence the name.

In the Tithe Applotment List of 1824 there are two houses in the list called Shannon View (the word 'View' is not clear, being written in a somewhat illegible hand – indeed it might be Lodge). Benjamin Talbot, Snr., is both the head landlord and occupier of the Shannon View whose name is clearly legible, the other being occupied by John Hough in the townland of Terryglass.

In 1840 John O'Donovan described Shannon View (above) as 'a good dwelling house with extensive views of the lake and Shannon'.

OLD COURT, TERRYGLASS

James Hickie, son of Manuel, has no record of when this house (below) was built. When Manuel Hickie was a young man it was owned by an O'Flanagan, a retired

civil engineer. O'Flanagan sold the house to an Arthur Dawson from whom Manuel Hickie bought it with about 150 acres of land. He let the Dawsons stay on as tenants until he married James's mother, Mary McDermott of Killimor, Co. Galway, in September 1914. James Hickie says it was a very small house but Manuel Hickie added on and altered it slightly to make it very comfortable, all on one level. The word 'small' is relative – by some standards it is quite a big house. A 'for sale' advertisement in 1992 described it as a mid-nineteenth century extended fishing lodge with three reception rooms, five bedrooms, and two bathrooms in the main part. The ruins of Terryglass Norman castle are located on the lakeshore behind the house.

Old Court passed out of Hickie ownership when it was purchased by Alex Kent. A later owner was a Kevin Darley, followed by Jack Tiernan of Lesserragh, Coolbawn, whose father Patrick had been born on Illaunmore. He in turn sold it to its present owner, Mr. Murtagh.

When the present owner was doing some clearing near the house he found a headstone erected where a horse had been buried. The horse belonged to Manuel Hickie who had him during the Boer War and brought him back to Slevoir with him. It has the following inscription:

Confidence
He carried his master 6,700 miles in South Africa
during the 1900-1902 war and he died at Slevyre from
a disease contracted in that country.

TERYGLASS GLEBE/KILLEEN HOUSE

Miss Ellie Esmonde had lived at Drominagh until her brother Dr John Joseph Esmonde came home from England to take up residence there. She purchased Killeen House, formerly Terryglass Glebe. She kept seven servants – the last of

the gentry to have a full establishment. Mike (Bush) Hogan was her chauffeur (right) and drove the Austin Seven to Mass in Terryglass at about ten miles an hour at her request. When he and Georgina (George) Guest, who had also been on the staff, got married and wanted to build their own house she would not hear of them leaving and fitted up married quarters for them. Their two children, Ettie and Ben, were born there. Ellie brought Mary Clancy, her housekeeper/lady's maid with her from Drominagh. She was a sister of Joe Clancy. Mrs Nancy Horan (née Ryan, Ryehill) worked there from 1932 to 1938 when Ellie Esmonde died. Mrs Horan told me they were the happiest years of her life. It was a real 'upstairs, downstairs' situation. They were like one big happy family. Mike Hogan (right) hated wearing the uniform cap but Ellie insisted that he did.

Anne Darcy of the mill worked there, as did Nora Darcy of Kilfadda who was the cook. Jane Donoghue, afterwards Mrs Fox, also worked there and after her came Nancy Horan. At one time there was a staff of seven. Ellie Esmonde thought of them all as her children. After her death Killeen was bought by Maurice O'Connell who was taken prisoner of war in the Far East during World War II. He came back looking like a skeleton. He had married Lucila Deasy, whose mother was Dolores Hickie. Lucila had lived in Killeen during the war. After their deaths the house was purchased by Alex Kent. The Kents lived there until Elmville in Terryglass became vacant on the death of Olive Kent.

Ellie Esmonde is first on the left in this picture of cyclists ouside Drominagh House, *c.* 1910.

Gate Lodges

Gate lodges have always fascinated me, one reason being that my father was born in one and I was familiar with it from an early age. 'They were usually very pretty houses, being built beside beautiful entrance gates, gates hinged to cut-stone ports dignified as pillars in a temple, and gate lodges were designed with appropriate distinction.' So writes Molly Keane in her last book about the Anglo-Irish, *Loving and Giving*. She describes the West Gate Lodge.

> It was one-storeyed as usual. It had deep eaves and little stone eyebrows above each lead-paned window. An architrave, of the exact proportion to become this perfect doll's house, was over the door. The door was permitted to be of the cottage order, double, the bottom half, lower than that of a stable door, was designed to keep children in and chickens out – not that chickens were approved – their appearance was not conducive to the small dignity of the Gate Lodge. Children, too, were rather expected to play and to play quietly, behind the house – no balls or tin trumpets were ever to be left on the gravel sweep.

Kilbarron area abounded in gate lodges, now mainly in disrepair or demolished, although a couple are still inhabited. The first on the road from Puckane coming from Nenagh is *Ballycolliton Lodge*. Curiously, it is on the other side of the road from the entrance as the function of the lodge keeper was to open and close the gates for carriages to pass through. This is a little classical gem, completely plain, hipped and slated; it probably had leaded, diamond-paned windows. It is very small like all the gate lodges, probably two-roomed, and is in a bad state of repair which has been aggravated by the pipe-laying process for the regional water scheme at Skehanagh which almost wrecked it. Every time I passed by during the operation I dreaded seeing it a heap of rubble. The last family to live there were the Butlers.

Not far on from this, on the left, is one of Annagh Lodge's two gate lodges now incorporated in John Slattery's farmyard. It was very pretty in its day. It was last lived in by Robert Brien, the Annagh coachman, in the late 1920s and early 1930s. The second lodge at the entrance to the second avenue is in good repair, privately owned and inhabited. It has the look of a fairly modern bungalow

Small Dwelling

> In summer the little vacant house beside the pump at Coolbawn Cross is covered with fuschia. Houses of this size and design are fast disappearing from town and country. This one, built of rubble stone, was a two-roomed dwelling. Its chimney breast, with crude unplaned supporting beam, is intact as are the lintel over the door and windows.

Thus was described a few years ago the traditional home of the Castletown herdsman. In my childhood Jim Kennedy was the herd. The old age pension had come in but nobody knew how old Jim was. He had been baptised a Protestant but their parish records were destroyed in the Four Courts in 1922. I remember the hoo-ha when the time came for Jim to get his pension. I believe someone was found of approximately the same vintage who testified to his age. His son Mike succeeded him as herd. After Mike's death the cottage was left empty as the post of herd had become extinct. This 'housheen' was not a gate lodge but was of the same genre.

Not far from Coolbawn Cross on the road to Kilbarron/Skehanagh quay is *Castletown gate lodge* (below). Although in a bad state of repair it is a quaint and interesting structure, being made up of three distinct little houses joined at the gable ends. The middle one was the kitchen. Mick and Nellie Kennedy lived in it at least forty years ago and were its last inhabitants.

Next on the main road was *Lesserragh lodge* which stood on the opposite side of the road from the entrance gates. It was the home of the Tiernan family and again had the typical doll's house look. Inside these lodges, it was another story. They were very small and dark and mostly two-roomed. Nothwithstanding this, quite large families were reared in them. This gate lodge was demolished within the last few years.

About a mile from Lesserragh is the road off which is the avenue to Bellevue. A little way down the road to the left are the entrance gates and *Bellevue lodge*, on the left. It is a little gem, with leaded diamond-paned windows. It has fallen into disrepair since Willie Donoghue died.

Brookfield lodge, in which my father was born, has been dealt with in the chapter on the Parkers. The entrance to Brookfield had, until a few years ago, an old ruin facing down the avenue. It was known as 'Patt Wall's old house'. Walls were Godparents to some of my aunts and uncles.

Next on the main road is *Mota lodge*. It resembles Ballicolliton, only somewhat larger and somewhat less dilapidated. It is slated and hipped. The last person to live there was Jack Hough of Ballinderry who worked for Dick Howard. The present road down to Mota quay must have been at some time a private avenue leading to Mota House, which would account for the situation of the gate lodge.

Happily, *Kilgarvan gate lodge* is still lived in by Nancy Ryan, the last of her family who were all born and reared there. It also, like Ballycolliton, is on the opposite side of the road to the entrance gates. It more nearly resembles Molly Keane's gate lodge than the others and is very pretty indeed.

On the old road to Teryglass is *Drominagh lodge* (below) now lived in by the Boyle family. When Pamela Hinkson wrote *Irish Gold* it was inhabited by the Donoghue family. Bill, and probably all his siblings, were born there. Extended since then, it is a very pretty, well-kept house.

There was at one time a building by the entrance to Finnoe House. It was on the opposite side of the road inside the wall as you go from Kilbarron to Borrisokane. It was a beautiful cut-stone building and may have been an RIC barracks or a gate lodge, or may have served as both at different times. Unfortunately, it had to be pulled down as it obstructed the view of the road and was a traffic hazard. There are some piers still to be seen in the wall.

Slevoir gate lodge was a small thatched two-roomed house, probably going back to the time of Maunsell's small Georgian dwelling. During the few years when General Sir W. Hickie was running Slevoir, circa 1918-23, he had this gate lodge, as well as other houses on the estate, slated and renovated. He had the lodge itself extended and it is now a pleasant four-roomed one-storey house with a kitchen, sitting-room and two bedrooms. The Ryan family have lived there for at least two generations. The last member of the family, Dinny Ryan, died a few years ago and left it to his niece. It is at present uninhabited but in good repair.

Terryglass Glebe gate lodge is quite a little way, perhaps a 100 yards, from the present main entrance. It is an interesting, small slated dwelling. Anthony Fox the carpenter and his family were born there, including Bill, father of Rose and Helen. It has not been lived in for at least twelve years and has become somewhat overgrown and dilapidated. There is a story that it once served as a police barracks for a time. There is indeed a small stone extension at the road side which I am told might have been the cell where prisoners were kept.

Sources:
Tithe Applotment Books.
Primary Valuation.
Samuel Lewis, *A Topographical Dictionary of Ireland*.
Ordnance Survey Letters.
OS maps no.s 6, 7, 9, 10.
Registry of Deeds, Deed no. 127-558-88062.
Mrs Nancy McCarthy, Ormonde Cottage.
James Hickie.
Dick Howard.

Photographs: pp. 203, 207, 210, 211, 214, 219, 221, 223, 224, 227, 228 taken by Paddy Carroll. Others loaned as follows: p. 201, Nancy McCarthy; p. 212, Amy Sterling; p. 215, Laura Dwyer; p. 216, Hilary Henry; 218, Rody O'Meara; p.223, James Hickie; p. 225, Wilsie Nolan.

An aerial view of Islandmore, taken when it was put up for sale in 1987 (reproduced from the newspaper advertisement).

9
Islandmore

Islandmore/Illaunmore, the largest island in Lough Derg on the river Shannon, is one mile wide and 218 acres 12 roods and 15 perches in area. It lies one and a half miles from Whitegate in Co. Clare and one and a half miles from Skehanagh in Co. Tipperary.

It is officially in County Clare and in the parish of Whitegate since 1898. However, according to the 1841 and 1851 censuses, it was situated in the barony of Leitrim in Co. Galway and in Kilbarron parish.

After 1854 Islandmore belonged to the Holmes family of Peterfield and later of St. Davids, to whom the Buggawn Island and the Corrikeens also belonged. Until that time it was the property of a Hugh Brady (sometimes called Grady) who sold it in the Incumbered Estates Courts.

The timber on the island was planted by Bassett Holmes, grandfather of Mrs Rosaleen Goodbody (née Holmes), about 1856. The Holmes remained the ground landlords until 1903 when the land was taken over by the Land Commission and the O'Mearas and O'Gradys bought out their farms under the Wyndham Land Act.

Until 1990 the island belonged to Martin Winston, a descendant of the O'Meara family who went out there about 1816. That year he sold out to the Manke family of Germany who already lived in Killeen house, Terryglass. Martin Winston had bought the island in the early 1960s from his O'Meara uncle and cousins and from Willie and Michael Tiernan who had bought the O'Grady farm of 52 statute acres just before the World War II of 1939-45.

Island History
The history of the island prior to 1771 is obscure. Like almost all large lake islands it may have had a monastic settlement but probably not since the tenth or eleventh centuries. There are the ruins of an old church resembling the ruins of Kilbarron old parish church – see chapter 3. There are no traces of a graveyard. There are legends galore of monks fleeing before invading armies and dropping precious altar vessels into the lake en route to Iniscealtra/Holy Island. We know that great battles did take place on the lake at the time of the Viking invasions. The folk memories of fleeing monks probably go back to that time. Rev. John Gleeson in his *History of the Ely O'Carroll Territory* writes of Islandmore:

> On the S.E. side of the island about a mile from the land are shown the foundations of a church which was forty one feet long and twenty feet thick and built of lime and grit hammered stones, cemented with lime and sand mortar. In the time of O'Donovan (1840) the natives asserted that there was originally seven churches on this island but no trace of any other building was visible in the beginning of the last century (1800).

John O'Donovan, who surveyed the site in 1840, refers to it in his Letters as a 'Fransciscan Abbey'. However, this isn't tenable as any monks who ever lived on the island would be from the Early Christian times and before religious orders like the Franciscans came to Ireland in the thirteenth century.

About half-a-mile to the south-west of the side of the church, and thirty yards from the water, there is a remarkable standing stone [below], measuring eight feet ten inches in height, and three feet ten inches in width and one foot ten inches in thickness. [It goes four feet underground but O'Donovan does not say this]. It is a rough limestone said to have been put up by the Friars to commemorate their departure from Islandmore to Iniscealtra or Holy Island in the same lake.

A curious stone stands at Frank's Quay which Frank O'Meara, and later his son Jim, always kept whitewashed so that it acted as a warning for boats in the dark.

There is a field at the back of Tiernan's house called Gortnasillia (*gort na sailí: field of the sally/willow*) where human remains were uncovered when Frank O'Meara's workmen went to plough the field. The matter was reported to the parish priest at Whitegate who advised that the 'scrape' be put back, which was done. The field remains unploughed to this day. A tradition exists in the Kilbarron neighbourhood that during the Penal Days a friar lived on the island and ministered to the people on the mainland.

Ancient Stones

Fifty or so years ago the old church was much less ruined and worn away than it is now. Michael Tiernan remembers seeing what might have been pieces of an altar stone. Bertie Bruce of Lesserragh had some visitors who lived near Birr. One of them took away such a part of a possible altar stone and kept it in his house. The people in the house never had a moment's peace thereafter. There were constant noises and comings and goings in the night. The people of the house told Bertie this story which she disbelieved. They invited her to stay the night and she did this. After midnight the handle of her door turned. She put on the light, but there was nobody there. She then heard steps going back and knocking. This went on for the best part of the night. She never slept. Next day she went to see Canon Darcy, the parish priest at the time, and told him the story. He advised her to tell whoever had taken the objects from the ruin to put them back. They gave the stone to Pat Tiernan, Michael's brother, and he put them back. The Birr family had no further nocturnal manifestations.

In 1956 historian, Dermot F. Gleeson (formerly of Nenagh) visited the Island and later wrote in the *North Munster Antiquarian Journal* of two incised cross slabs seen there by himself and his companions. He also states that he was told locally that another one 'was taken away by some vandal'. The crosses were within the ruins of the island church and appeared to date to the seventh or eight century. From the photograph included with the article the stones look similar to those dug up in Latteragh graveyard in the early 1980s and now on display in the Heritage Centre, Nenagh.

Island Families

Circa 1814-16 the O'Mearas had been evicted from their holding near the present Long Lane Cross, close to Kilbarron village. Every small holding from Carrig to Carigagowan, Coolbawn, was cleared to make large fields for sheep grazing. The 'clearances' stopped at Coolbawn where Castletown estate began. The only house spared was Hogans of Coolbawn because they were 'good' with horses.

Michael O'Meara (1894-1982), Ballinagrass, when he was a young boy heard an old woman aged one hundred and five years, a member of the Hogan, Clonmakilladuff, family and mother of Eamonn Maher's grandmother (whom I remember), describe the day of the evictions. Thrown out of their home, the O'Meara family, father Patrick, mother, two small boys of about three and four named Michael and Patrick, and a little girl, Sarah, later Mrs Conlan of Eglish, walked to Skehanagh where they found an old flat-bottomed boat which they repaired and in it 'emigrated' to the island.

There were, at that time, about twenty families living there. They managed to put up some kind of dwelling and got a garden. They later acquired a small farm as evidenced by this Tithe Applotment list of 1824. The head landlord was Hugh Brady.

Name	*Acreage*			*Tithe*		
	a	r	p	£	s	d
Martin Flaherty	19	2	0	2	7s	2d
John & Darby Fahy	19	2	0	2	7s	9d
John Meara	21	0	0	2	10s	9d
Patt Meara	22	0	0	2	13s	9d
John Mulvihill	19	2	0	2	7s	2d
Ml Scales & partner	19	2	0	2	7s	2d

This makes roughly 120 acres out of a total acreage of 212 acres. The remainder of the island would have been held by people with less than one acre and so not liable for tithes. Obviously, the island was thickly populated. This is borne out in the later census figures.

	1841	1851	1861
Population	97	78	46
No. of houses	13	12	6

We get another list of the island occupants from the Poor Law Rate Books of 1843.

Name	Description	a	r	p
Martin & John Mulvihill	house and land	31	2	18
Pat Meara, Michael Tierney & Pat Hickey	house and land	69	2	38
Thomas Houlahan Jerry Minogue	house and land	15	3	6
Darby Fahey	house and land	24	11	5
Thos Hogan & Pat Fahey	house and land	7	1	5
William Collins	house and land	15	3	6
Charles Cambie	house and land	5	1	1*
Michael Hynes	house and land	15	3	6

* He may have had a fishing lodge on the island.

When the island was put up for sale in the Incumbered Estates court in 1854 the prospectus prepared for the sale shows that Patrick O'Meara now had 56 acres and that Michael had 45. One can only conjecture that the Patrick here is a son of the emigrant rather than the emigrant himself.

About this time Patrick Snr.'s son Michael (1812-96) built himself a 'good' house – the one in which Francis Tiernan now lives.

We can assume that some time earlier Patrick O'Meara, Jun., (c.1810 - ?) had built what became his son Frank's home. That Frank O'Meara (1860-1945) was Martin Winston's grandfather. He was also grandfather of the Flannerys of Glenbower and the Hollands of Nutgrove, Whitegate. Frank died in Raheen Hospital, Co. Clare, in 1945 and was buried in Clonrush, Co. Galway – as was Patrick, Jun.

This is the house which was lived in by the island gamekeeper, until he moved to the mainland in the mid-1980s because he had young school-going children. The house was originally thatched and had farm out-buildings, whereas Michael's was slated – unusual for the time – and had no out-buildings.

The timber for Michael's house was brought from Aughinish Wood near Tinarana on the Clare shore, the tree trunks lashed together and towed after the boats to the sawmills in Mountshannon. This Michael had a large family, all of whom except Joseph (1852-1914) left their island home and prospered. Joseph prospered on his Islandmore farm and, about 1890, married a Miss Minogue of Scarriff. She made it a condition of marrying him that he would buy a farm and build a house on the mainland. This he did, buying into Kevanstown for £650 and building the original thatched house there with his own hands.

In 1894 Joseph and his family moved out to Kevanstown, their son Michael of Ballinagrass (1894-1982) being then six months old. Joseph kept his land on the island. His father Michael was still alive and came with them to Kevanstown and on his death in 1896 was buried in Terryglass old churchyard.

The little boy Michael would go around with the old man, his grandfather, talking to him, and had one or two vivid memories of him, one being of their first sight together of a Buckie reaper and binder.

The move to Kevanstown left the house on the island empty. In 1881 three brothers named Tiernan had come down from their home on the largest island on Lough Ree to carry on their trade of eel fishing on Lough Derg. One of them, James

(1862-1945) lodged at Garrykennedy and married a Mary Ryan whose family had a public house there. They needed a home and Joseph O'Meara let them have his house in return for James's services as a herd. Another Tiernan brother, John, had a small holding at Skehanagh and was drowned in a boating accident in 1905 with John Cleary and his son. John Tiernan's son Jack lived all his life in Nenagh in a small house at the junction of Ormond Street and the Birr road. He and his wife Bridget died in 1994. Their daughter Mai is married to my nephew, Paddy Corbett. The third Tiernan brother, Patrick, also lived on the island as can be gleaned from the 1901 census.

In 1901 there were three households on Islandmore:
(i) Frank and Ellen O'Meara, farmers and their eight children, all born in Co. Galway; boarders Bridget Hogan, a teacher in the island school, born in Co. Tipperary; Nora Ganly, a ten-year-old scholar, born Co. Westmeath (the Tiernans' niece); Pat Phelan, farm worker, born Co. Tipperary. The O'Mearas had one more child after 1901, Margaret.

(ii) Patrick and Bridget Tiernan and one daughter, Kate, all born in Co. Westmeath. Also living with them was Bridget Ganly, Patrick's niece, aged 13 years. Like James, Patrick's occupation was that of fisherman but he also worked on the O'Grady farm on the island, as that family had moved to the mainland. Apparently, Patrick and his family later returned to live in Westmeath – possibly to their island in Lough Ree.

(iii) James and Mary (née Ryan, Garrykennedy) Tiernan had five children, and Sarah Ganly, a cousin – presumably from Westmeath, though this is not stated on the census return: James was born in Westmeath. Mary Ryan Tiernan was born in Chicago. James's occupation is given as fisherman. They had five more children after 1901.

Tiernan Family, Islandmore, *circa* 1911
(l to r): Pat, Tom, Mrs Mary Tiernan (née Ryan, Garrykennedy), her husband James, Kitty, John, Willie, Lizzie, Michael, James.

From time to time relatives of the O'Meara and Tiernan families came to live on the island in order keep up the numbers in the island school. This probably explains the presence of the Tiernan cousin and nieces.

The census shows that there were twenty-five people in all living on the island. Frank O'Meara owned his own house, Joseph O'Meara of Kevanstown owned James Tiernan's house, and James Grady of Ballyalla owned Patrick Tiernan's.

The Island School
Like his brother Michael, Paddy O'Meara, Islandmore, had a large family which dispersed and prospered, leaving only Frank. Frank married Ellen Hogan, Urra, and they had nine children. James and Mary Tiernan had ten. In 1900 the island got its own school. It was built on to the Tiernans' house by a man called Martin Mulvihill from the far shore. The first teacher was Bridget Hogan of Kildangan. She later married Constable Ryan, RIC – their son Michael lives in Newtown, Youghalarra parish.

The island's other school teachers during its lifetime were:

Unknown	1900-1910
Mary O'Halloran	1910-12
Margaret Maud Casey	1912
Mary K. Leonard	1913
S. O'Callaghan &	
Matilda Brogan	1914-17

The school closed for five days in 1911 to celebrate the coronation of King George V – I expect all schools did.

The last teacher, Matilda Brogan, became the teacher in Carney school, Monsea & Killodiernan parish. She married Michael Keane, Frolic. She is seen here with the pupils ouside the Island school in 1902.

As shown above, Tiernan cousins from Lough Ree and Westmeath would

come down from time to time, in order to maintain the pupil average and so keep the school going. Hogan and Ryan cousins from Urra and Garrykennedy would come in. But by 1917 all the O'Meara children had grown up and there were only three Tiernans left: Michael, born in 1905, his younger brother Willie, and sister Lizzie. So the school was closed, and after this the three Tiernan children rowed themselves to Skehanagh every day and walked the three miles to Kilbarron school where their teachers were Patrick Curtin and Hannah Nealon.

The O'Mearas and the non-resident O'Gradys were all farmers on the island. They burned their own lime and two old limekilns can still be seen. Peat for firing came from Coose on the Galway shore but there was plenty of timber on the island for firewood. In theory they still had to ask permission of the ground landlord to cut a tree. The land was remarkably fertile and I have been told that it was a 'lucky' place. Animals rarely fell sick – when you put sheep in you always brought out one more: a ewe would have a lamb when you would not expect it.

Island Field Names
All the fields on the island have names such as the *Fern Field, Hickey's*, the *Drill Field, Annie Rohan's Field, Jack's Field*, the *Stillhouse Field*, a reminder of the island's poitín-making days, *Tuohy's Acres, Gortnasillia, Jackson's, Riordan's, Uncle Pat's* etc. Those and others appear in the Ordnance Survey Letters of 1840. They recorded that Islandmore was about one mile from the shore of Kilbarron and that all was under cultivation. The report continued:

> ... contains along the east side a Franciscan Abbey [see above], a graveyard, sandy ridge, and Poolagher.
> In the south side there are Paddy Hickey's quay, Standing Stone, Paddy O'Meara's quay, and Ringrove on the south side of the island about 1 1/2 miles NE of Williamstown Quay. In the west are Big Quarry and Tinkers' Point. There are also several houses scattered around the verge of the island.

Poolagher/*pol a leathair*: *the Leather Hole* is the point on the island facing Kilbarron mainland where the float, used for transporting goods from the marina at Skehanagh, docks.

Tinkers' Point was so called because of being frequented by tinkers in the act of fishing. Only inhabitants are aware of its being so named.

Fishing
The Tiernans were eel fishers. Two lines, 12 foot apart with 500 hooks on each, backed with worms, would be set in the centre of the lake between Coose and Islandmore where the water was 150ft. deep. The lines would be weighted with stones to the bottom of the water and have a cork to show position. A mark/sighting would be taken on Portroe or Williamstown and one in the opposite direction. These lines would be put out about 4 p.m. and taken in at day-break.

Once a week a consignment would be taken to Dromineer and thence by horse and cart to Nenagh railway station and put on the 4 o'clock train to arrive at Billingsgate fish market, London, in the early morning. Fishing stopped in October when the first frost set in.

The largest eel James ever caught was a beautiful fourteen pounder. He often regretted not having had it stuffed but at the time the money was too badly needed. The family lived mainly on fish, Michael says. They might have fish three times a day but his mother could cook it in different ways. They had a vegetable garden and grew a little oats and wheat which would be taken to the mill at Ballinderry to be ground. In the late 1920s the E.S.B. took over the lake and the Tiernans were forbidden to fish and so lost their livelihood. They got no compensation because James could not produce the receipts for the fish he had sent to London.

James Tiernan (*c*.1861-1945), and Michael's father and mother Mary are buried on Holy Island, down lake in Scarriff Bay, as is their son John, the boatbuilder of Mount Shannon who is mentioned in Henry V. Morton's book, *In Search of Ireland*. James Tiernan used to say that he was born on an island, lived his life on an island, and so wished to be buried on an island.

Island Funerals and Mass-going

When James Tiernan died in June 1945 he was 'waked' in his home on Islandmore, the neighbours and relations from each shore coming in their rowing boats and leaving at first light. In the evening they congregated again to escort the coffin to Rynskaheen, the quay for Whitegate, where the priest met them. As the cortege of about twenty boats set off for the mainland James's little terrier, who had been hiding under the bed since his master's death, ran out and followed the boat along the shore until they rounded Meara's Point where it stood crying piteously until the boat landed at Rynskaheen. It then ran back to the house, hid under the bed again and refused food and drink until it died within a few days.

Frank Flannery, whose mother Julia was a daughter of Frank O'Meara of the island, was at this funeral and told me how he and Mick Whelan of Annagh, having got a lift in a boat to Whitegate, attended the Requiem Mass and then got another lift in a pony and trap from Jim Bolger of Kilcooley to Mountshannon.

The funeral procession of horses and traps and bicycles arrived at Mountshannon, the landing place for Holy Island, after about an hour. The neighbours there gave lifts in their boats to the mourners and the funeral procession crossed the silent channel to Holy Island. The priest and coffin were in the first boat. They disembarked and the relatives and neighbours carried the coffin on the rather long journey to the graveyard at the far side of the island.

On the way home the three 'boys' stopped at Shay Bulger's public house in Mountshannon for a drink. Mrs Mary Tiernan's funeral in November 1947 followed the same pattern.

The O'Meara and Tiernan families went to Mass in Whitegate in the old days, each family in its own boat. From the quay to the church it was two or three miles around by the road past the Ash Tree at the Crossroads, but sometimes they went over the fields by the 'Mass' path. In later years, after Frank O'Meara's daughter Nell had married a Holland from Whitegate, Frank kept a donkey and car there to help the older people on their way.

The most recent Tiernan family living on the island came to Mass in Kilbarron, James Tiernan (*c.*1900-1981) having married Brigid Quirke from near Kilbarron village. James and Brigid are now dead. Their daughter Sally Ann is now married and living in Coolbawn. Their son Francis comes out from the island every Sunday morning at 9.40 a.m. on the dot, for 10 o'clock Mass.

Our house is on the shore directly facing Tiernan's island house and every Sunday morning, when my son was small, the cry used to be, 'hurry up, we'll be late, they're coming out from the island'.

The lake often froze over. In old James Tiernan's time it once froze for seventeen weeks and a hurling match was played opposite Slattery's quay. It froze over for seven weeks in 1947 and Michael Tiernan and his brother James walked out to the mainland pulling a boat after them – the ice not being completely reliable – and wearing socks over their shoes to keep them from slipping. It froze for three weeks in 1963.

The Island Postman

Until 1920 the Island had its own postman who came twice a week – on Wednesdays and Fridays. His name was Michael Egan and he was caretaker of Williamstown House. On 16 November 1920 three young IRA men – Martin MacMahon, Alphonsus Rodgers and Martin Gildea – who were 'on the run' took refuge there. The military found them and took Michael Egan with them by steamer to Killaloe where all four were shot on the bridge. A memorial tablet, inscribed in Irish, was later placed on a wall of the bridge. It is not even certain that Michael Egan had anything to do with the Independence movement. The island did not get another postman.

Yellow Island

According to O'Donovan's OS letters, 'Yellow Island, close by the north-east end of Islandmore is a small island generally covered by floods in winter'. In fact, it has never been flooded in living memory. There is only a very narrow passageway between it and the main island, Joseph O'Meara's land being nearest to it. The smaller Green Island which adjoins it is merely a clump of trees. It too is never flooded.

From the mainland Yellow Island looks as if it is part of Islandmore. It is about 300m/823feet long and is covered with mature pine trees. Its name may well have originated in the yellow sandy shore which surrounded it until the lake water level was raised by some six feet when the hydro-electric scheme was built at Ardnacrusha in the early 1930s.

The present owner of the island is Anne Louise Gurney, daughter of Denis Pike whose mother was 'Tot' Bruce of Lesserragh. The Bruces acquired the island from Joe O'Meara, Kevanstown, for £100 about seventy or eighty years ago and built a holiday home on it. Denis Pike married a widow and his stepson, Piers Skidmore, wrote a comprehensive account of the birds and butterflies to be seen on the island, their habits and other details, in the 1983-4 issue of *Cois Deirge*.

Sources:
Tithe Applotment Lists, Kilbarron parish.
Nenagh Union, Poor Law Rate Book, ED Kilbarron, 1843, Co. Library, Thurles, for island occupants of 1843.
Incumbered Estates Sales, 1854.
1901 Census.
Rev Michael O'Flanagan, ed., Ordnance Survey Letters, Co. Tipperary.
Rev. John Gleeson, *History of the Ely O'Carroll Territory*.
Mrs Rosalie Holmes Goodbody.
The late Frank Flannery.
Michael Tiernan.
Tape recording made by late Michael O'Meara (1894-1982).

Photographs: p. 231, courtesy of Nenagh District Heritage Society; p. 234 loaned by Mrs Angeline Starr; p. 235 loaned by Holland family, Whitegate.

Shannon's Lough Derg Shore

In my mind's eye there's a memory of the young years and the pals,
  Where the hills and vales and inlets are galore,
  And the ancient game of hurling will never, ever die,
You will find it all by Shannon's Lough Derg shore.

Ramble down through Ballinderry or tidy Terryglass so clean,
Overlooked by green Kilbarron hills where the hazel grows supreme;
The view you'll see from Coolbawn hill will prompt you to once more
Walk in the evening sun along Shannon's Lough Derg shore.

Go to Dromineer on Sundays, or to Kilgarvan quay,
Up to Garry or to Luska as you please;
Row out to Islandmore, fishing trout along the way,
In your hair you'll feel the Shannon's Lough Derg breeze.

There'll be jigs and reels in Garry or a sing-song in Puckane,
Sure there's handball up in Youghal as in yore,
A game of cards in Newtown or a dance in high Portroe,
Looking down on lovely Shannon's Lough Derg shore.

From Duharra's hills to Woodford and Arra to Whitegate,
Sure Portumna to Mount Shannon is a dream;
The people you will find there: you can walk in any door –
There's a welcome there by Shannon's Lough Derg shore.

Now to all my friends and neighbours from Coolbawn to oul' Loughtea,
To the people around the lake I love so well,
If you're far away or lonely, close your eyes and dream some more,
And remember lovely Shannon's Lough Derg shore.

Michael Moran,
Coolbawn & Dublin

10
Villages

FOCUS ON COOLBAWN

Coolbawn, strictly speaking, does not merit the status of village – it is really a townland with a crossroads at which are situated the post office and shop combined and kept by the Molamphy family, a pump, a telephone exchange and a public telephone box. The Cross is roughly halfway between Nenagh and Portumna on the main Nenagh-Portumna road and is halfway between Puckane and Ballinderry. Today the townland contains eight households and there are the ruins of four other houses.

According to the *Civil Survey*, there were six cottages in 'Cuilebane'. The survey records that the townland was made up of an estimated 170 plantation acres, 150 arable and 20 rocky.

At that time the land was owned by John Hurly of Annagh, William Kennedy and Hugh Kennedy of Cuilebane/Coolbawn. These three men also owned property in several neighbouring townlands in the parish. The land, as was the case in many townlands, was not clearly divided between the owners. The comment that 'the land is totally waste and without improvement', which is made of some townlands – mainly in other parishes – is not made for here, so we can assume that the land was being profitably used.

There had been a period of comparative peace from the end of the Hugh O'Neill/earl of Tyrone's rebellion (known as the 'Nine Years War') in 1603 and up to 1640. People were able to get on with their lives and farm the land. Where the six cottages stood we do not know. The Coolbawn people would not have been isolated as there were eight cottages and the still inhabited tower house, with its bawn intact, at Castletown. There were also three cottages at Tullawn (Lisquillibeen) with the tower house there still inhabited by Arthur Geoghan, Gent, one of the jurors enlisted for the Survey. Another juror on the panel of twelve was Teige Hogan of Coolebane, Gent. Assuming that all these eight cottages in Coolbawn area were inhabited, and that each had at least six inhabitants in each, the population of Coolbawn area would be nearly 50 persons.

Tithe Applotment List
The next listing we get is the Tithe Applotment compiled by the rector of the parish in the mid-1820s. A person with an acre or more of tillage had to pay tithes to the (Established) Church of Ireland based on his or her overall acreage. The rectors had to make a return of the acreage and value of each person eligible. It is useful insofar as it lists the names of persons holding at least an acre of land. However, perhaps half the population are omitted as they held only gardens which were usually less than an acre each.

In Kilbarron parish names like Cambie, Biggs, Minchin, Sadleir and Sir Henry Carden were dominant as landlords, while the tenants' ones were Kennedy,

Brooder, Slattery, Costelloe, Cleary, Gleeson, Flannery, Cahalan, Leenane, Ryan, Meara, Carroll, Donohue, Loughnane, Boucher and Toohey.

The names of individuals liable for tithes in Coolbawn townland were: Mary Ryan, Patt Meara, Patrick Cantrell, Darby McGlenn, William Healy, Darby Meara, John Cormican, Patt Cormican. None of these families, except the Ryans, own land in Coolbawn today. John and James Carroll were not direct ancestors of Michael Carroll, though probably related. Mary Ryan's descendants, who live at Clonakenny near Roscrea, still own the land she held in 1824. The last of the family in Coolbawn was Mick who died at the home of brother Jack and nephews in Clonakenny.

Though the 1824 Tithe List does not give us any idea of the real population, we know from tradition that Coolbawn was a busy and populous place and 1824 was a period of relative prosperity. The building of the Church of Ireland church in 1822 and a parish school in its grounds in nearby Kilbiller would have given it a sort of village status, certainly in the eyes of the local gentry.

Primary Valuation
This document is often called 'Griffith's' after Richard Griffith who directed its compilation for tax purposes. It recorded the names of all occupiers of land, regardless of acreage, and/or of houses and offices from humblest cabins to mansions, and put a valuation on them. It also recorded each person's 'immediate lessor'. However, the lessor was not necessarily the owner of the land – in many instances he is a tenant who had sub-let part of his rented holding. Dated 1852, it is almost two centuries on from the *Civil Survey* and also incorporates the amalgamations brought about by the Great Famine.

In Kilbarron parish William D. Ferrar, associated with Gortalougha House, is there, in addition to the 1824 Cambie, Biggs, Carden, Dancer and Sadleir, with tenants bearing the names Cleary, Darcy, Donoghue, Tuohy, Hogan, Tierney, Meara, Moran, Costelloe, Tracy, Bruder, Burke, Ryan, Gleeson, Scurlock (Sherlock), Hobbins, Waldron, Mullamphy, Corboy, Walpole. There were six individual Kennedy occupiers with a John, Brockagh, on 17 acres and William, Gortmungo, on 19 acres.

The occupiers of Coolbawn townland were: John Gorman, Michael Ryan, Michael Ryan (cousins, probably first, and grandsons of above Mary of the Tithe list), Elizabeth Meara, Joseph Slattery, Richard O'Brien, Anne Meagher, Honoria Healey, John Lennon, Jane Feeney, Margaret Kelly, John Moran, Sgt. F. Griffin in the constabulary barracks (below) and Michael Moran (teacher) in the schoolhouse. The immediate lessor was Charles Cambie who held the townland on lease from Thomas Sadleir. Sarah Cambie, Charles's sister, had 34 acres in her own right, with no buildings.

Many of these surnames are preserved in field names – *Gormans' Garden, Kellys' Garden, Feeneys' Garden, Healys' Garden* (Ned Haley's). The ruins of Meagher's house are still there, as are those of one Ryan house, while the other Ryan house is inhabited by Michael Carroll. The border ('mearing' in the *Civil Survey*) between Coolbawn and Lisquillibeen is the wall between Michael Carroll's yard and Michael O'Halloran's (formerly Moran's) garden.

Censuses
In the Census of 1659, which did not include children under the age of fifteen years

in the count, the population of Coolbawn townland is given as 19, of which 5 were English and 14 Irish. Assuming each person had an average of two children, this would give a population of 52 – again in keeping with my 50 estimate for 1640. We have definite figures for the townland in the years 1841 to 1901.

Year	Pop	Year	Pop
1841	124	1881	53
1851	89	1891	50
1861	76	1901	49
1871	65	1998	38 (own count)

The first complete census for Ireland for which the household returns survive is that of 1901. Both Forms B and A for 1901 and 1911 can be consulted in the National Archives or on microfilm in the County Library, Thurles. Form B was filled out by the enumerator and lists the householders in the townland with details of the dwelling, such as type of roof, number of rooms, and number of windows in the front. Form A was filled out by the head of the household or, in many cases by the policeman-enumerator, and lists all occupants of the house on census night.

In 1901 there were nine households in Coolbawn townland. The names of their heads were James Kennedy, Johanna Molamphy, Patrick Smith, Denis Dwyer, Honoria Brien, Timothy Ryan, Michael Ryan, Edward Maher (or Meagher), John Needham. The total population came to 49. The constabulary were gone by this time and the barracks were empty. They left some time between 1889 and 1901.

Today (1998) there are nine households in Coolbawn. They are Michael Carroll, Noel Teefy, Michael Molamphy, Jun., Michael Molamphy, Sen., Patrick Corbett, Brendan Carroll, Tony Halifax, and Ernest Reed who lives in the former barracks (below). The total population is 33. If the O'Hallorans are included, and they are only technically in Lisquillibeen, it would be 38.

The 1920 Scenario

The three oldest Carroll children, Bridie, Paddy and May in 1923.

When my father, mother and their three small children (a fourth was born within two weeks) came to live in Coolbawn in April 1920 it had a shop, a separate post office, and a forge. Johanna Molamphy, who kept the shop at the Cross was also a dressmaker. The forge closed after a couple of years. It is described in a later chapter. The house we came to live in was a short distance back from the Cross on the Nenagh side. It had been occupied until 1916 by Mike Ryan and his wife Margaret, who kept a shop. His father Timothy had been a baker and was probably a son of the Mary Ryan of the 1824 list. Mike did not continue the bakery trade, but when we came to live there the brick oven was in place in the Bakehouse – now a little slated house, with a good fireplace, in my brother Michael Carroll's yard.

The great wooden trough in which the dough was kneaded was intact and served as our horse Charley's manger. The Ryan-baked bread when ready was taken to the Big Houses in the neighbourhood by a woman called Mary (Mane) Dominick in her donkey and cart. The donkey, whom she loved dearly, was named Wattie. She lived in Kilbiller in a little house beside the road nearly opposite Mary Cormack's.

One reason why Mike did not continue his father's trade may have been that he had a wooden leg. He lost the leg as a result of an accident when cutting timber in the fort on land in Coolbawn. His wound turned gangrenous and the leg had to be amputated. It is possible that he had served his time to the bakery trade before this misfortune.

Mike was quite a legend in the neighbourhood and was much quoted. He comes across as an intelligent and rather unusual type of man. Mike and Margaret spoke in a very precise and rather pedantic fashion. History does not relate whether he learned from her or she from him. One day a woman came in for a pound of bread soda. Margaret had none so she proceeded to explain how the weather was so bad Mike was afraid to go to town in the donkey and cart. This was how she said it: 'Michael went to prognostigate upon the atmosphere. The clouds were rolling and the air was low and he feared it would come to desolation in the afternoon, so therefore he had to postpone his journey to town – so we have no bread soda'.

Mike and Margaret had a fine orchard with all kinds of apples and delicious sugar plums which were still there in our time. There were colourful stories of his attempts to outwit the youngsters of the neighbourhood, the 'other' Ryans, Morans and Hogans, who plagued him by raiding his orchard. He declared that Michael Moran kept a 'retreating ground for robbers', meaning the apple stealers who could gain access by creeping up Moran's lane.

Mike's was a 'ramblers' house. There might be porridge (stirabout) in a black pot over the fire. He would say, 'stack the fire under the pudding, Margaret', to give the impression that they didn't only eat stirabout.

Mike and Margaret had no children. Two of his sisters kept a public house in Nenagh. One sister married Daniel Hough who had a public house and farm in Borrisokane. Madge Hough, their only daughter, married Michael Seymour of Monsea and they were the parents of Michael (Brud), Maureen (Mrs Heenan of Terryglass) and Ebie.

The 'other' Ryans, who were our next-door neighbours, were also descended from the Mary Ryan of the 1824 list. In 1920 their father Timothy was already old and had a long white beard. His wife Mary, who was a Tierney from the Rock, Terryglass, was also very old to our eyes. We understood that they had both lived through the Great Famine.

The Morans

Martin Moran was the youngest brother of Patrick, the hedge schoolmaster of the 1820s. Their father had been a carter and at the time of the building of the church in Kilbarron in 1814 had been engaged in carrying slates from the quarries above Portroe to Kilbarron for roofing the church. One day he was set upon by highwaymen and murdered – perhaps for his horse and cart and its load. His wife at the time was expecting Martin. She had several older children and was left destitute. According to the story, which was told me by her grand-daughter Mary Moran, my first cousin, the widow went to Father McCormack, the parish priest, for help but he was unable, or unwilling, to do anything for her. She then went to the Protestant rector. As this was before the erection of the new church in Kilbiller there was no resident cleric so he was probably Rev. Ralph Stoney, the rector in Terryglass. He helped her, and I have no idea what the deal, if any, there was, nor had my cousin Mary.

Anyhow, the story goes that she promised that when the child was born she would have him/her baptised and brought up in the Protestant faith, which she duly did and named him Martin. She and the other members of the family remained Catholic while he practised Protestantism diligently.

In the course of time he married his neighbour Judy Ryan, sister to Timothy and, of course, a Catholic. Tradition does not tell by whom the ceremony was conducted, but Judy brought up all her children, including Michael, my aunt's husband, as Catholics.

Every Sunday she and the children went to Mass in Kilbarron and Martin walked up the avenue to the Protestant church in Kilbiller quite near his home. He would be dressed in a Caroline hat, swallow-tailed coat and buckled shoes – a description brought forward for us by Tim Ryan. In due course he died and was buried, not in the graveyard by the Protestant church, but in the chancel of the old church in Kilbarron which happened to be the Morans' traditional burying ground. I do not know, nor did my cousin, if they tried to convert him on his deathbed but would hope not. So the Cleburne father and daughter of Ballycolliton are not alone among the papists!

When we arrived in Coolbawn in 1920 we were the only children in the immediate vicinity of the Cross. At each side of us we had our Moran cousins who, though young, were all grown up by comparison and busy with their own lives, except Pat who took us 'nutting' and generally out and about on Sunday with the dogs. He emigrated to the USA in 1926 and left a gap in our lives. We did not see him again for nearly forty years.

The Ryans
The Ryans were older and had more time for us. We followed them about. They were full of old stories about the past to which, unfortunately, we did not listen carefully enough. You could say they filled for us the gap that television fills for the children of today. They had a great fear of poverty and horror of ending up in the workhouse and felt that they could never sit down except on a Sunday. The Great Famine, or 'bad times' as they were called, were not spoken of but had touched them very closely.

There had been six boys and two girls – Ned, Dan, Mick, Tim, Paddy, Jack, Kate and Mary. Before our time four brothers had left home. Ned had married and gone to live in Carney and Dan had gone to Australia. Snaring rabbits had been one of his ways of making a little money and one night he gathered up all his snares and next morning set off for Australia, without telling anyone where he was going. He came back to France with the Australian Expeditionary Force and fought through World War I, but never came home on leave. When the war was over he returned to Australia with the army. Jack Ryan had gone to Ennis to be a coachman to Dr Michael Fogarty, Bishop of Killaloe. It is Jack's children who still own the land in Coolbawn. Paddy had also married and moved away. Kate, Mary, Tim and Mick remained.

Tim was the gardener at Castletown when we came. He was a good gardener and had worked as one in Tadcaster, Yorkshire, with a Colonel, and recounted stories of his time there. He was not really the marrying kind but did not get on all that well with his siblings and fancied the idea of a house of his own. It was the 1930s and cottages were being built by the County Council in rural areas. A couple of cottages were 'going up' on the Castletown estate and Tim decided he would put in for one. Alas, they were only for married men. Tim thought the cottage worth the risk of marriage and proposed to a neighbouring spinster who lived with her brother. He had probably indicated to the brother that with her gone he too could get married – which he did.

The lady in question accepted Tim and the wedding took place. They had two boiled geese and dumplings for the wedding breakfast at the bride's home. Joe Slattery was best man and Mary (Ciss) Hogan (Mrs. Lynch) was bridesmaid. It was, by all accounts, a tempestuous union. Tim's sisters, Mary and Kate, were very 'tasty', good housekeepers and good cooks. The new woman was neither. The crisis in the marriage came when she put some hyacinth bulbs, which Tim had been cherishing for Autumn planting, in a stew thinking they were onions! A veil has to be drawn over the ensuing scene and the wife returned to her brother's house.

Mary was the Ryan housekeeper and Kate worked 'outside' with Mick. Visiting Ryans at any time was a joy, but especially so on a Sunday evening. There would always be a big, blazing, cheerful fire and the kitchen sparkled. A huge carved dresser built into the wall was covered in dishes and jugs of all shapes and sizes. At each side of the wide hearth were forms (which we pronounced 'forrums') where we sat. Over the fire and hanging from the crane would be a black pot full of rice. This was no ordinary rice but thick with currants and spices. It was ladled out to us in generous helpings. Our mother just made plain, rather anaemic, rice with milk and a little sugar. I can still taste Mary Ryan's rice pudding.

Sadly, Mary, who was the youngest, was the first to die, relatively young, in her sixties. I was not at home during those years but have been told that Kate and Mick found it hard to manage on their own. Kate died before Mick and he was taken and looked after by his brother Jack's children in Clonakenny, as was Tim in his old age, bereft of wife.

The Shop
Molamphy's shop was, and is, an important landmark in the townland.

Johanna Molamphy's sister Ellen had come to live with her from Bellevue and married Martin Gorman of Bellevue who was a carpenter and came to live in the shop. Another sister, Margaret, married Martin's brother Johnny in the old home in Bellevue. Johnny was also a carpenter.

Ellen and Martin Gorman had no children, but Johnny and Margaret had a son and a daughter, Jack and Nellie. Nellie came to live with her aunts and uncle at the shop in Coolbawn and it was she who took me, my brother and my sister to school for our first few days, and 'minded' us until we got used to going. Although aged seven, six and four and one-half we all started school the same day, 26 May 1922.

Besides the jars of sweets and boxes of toffees, sugar sticks and Peggy's leg, Molamphys sold almost everything, including sacks of flour and paraffin oil. All the heavy goods came by barge to Kilgarvan Quay from Limerick and Martin Gorman brought them home on his horse and cart.

The Molamphy 'girls', i.e. Johanna and her sister Ellen Gorman, wore Edwardian dress – high-necked blouses with cameo brooches tucked into long skirts with narrow waists. To us they were the height of elegance.

After a long period of being called 'Gormans', the shop reverted to 'Molamphys', the present postmaster having inherited it from the grandfather of the same name, who was a brother of the Molamphy 'girls' – Nellie Gorman and her brother Jack having died unmarried.

There had been a shop there at least as far back as 1840, kept then by Joseph Slattery. There had been a tanyard earlier on the site, probably back in the eighteenth century or even earlier. The tanning of hides was done locally to supply leather for boots, horses' tackling etc. The process required a deep pit into which the layers of skins were placed with the necessary organic matter, often obnoxious, between them. This organic matter was required for the tanning process. There is evidence of the existence of such a deep pit at the back of Molamphys, now covered by foliage and woodwork. One side of the pit, built up with stones, was visible up to the 1930s.

Mahers and Needhams
The other two families in Coolbawn were the Mahers, or Meaghers, and the Needhams. The older Maher brothers, as well as the two sisters, had already married and gone to live elsewhere. Ned, the eldest, lived in Castletown lodge and worked on the Castletown estate. He seems to have been a sort of personality, as well as being the oldest of the young men and women in the townland, and was

often quoted and spoken of even after leaving the lodge. Their uncle Paddy had been the schoolmaster at the boys' national school until it closed in 1874 for a few years.

Needhams kept the post office a short distance from the Cross down the road to Kilbarron village. Again, some of the older members of that family had already gone away before we came. Two sisters had become nuns and the eldest son, Jim, who had been in the RIC, had emigrated to New Zealand. Mick worked at Castletown, Lizzie looked after the post office, and Jack and Pat worked on the farm. Bridgie was away doing hotel work. At that time there was a system called 'cooring', coming from the Irish words, *ag cabhair: helping*. At busy times neighbours came together to help one another, at haymaking, harvesting, getting in the potatoes, etc. We 'coored' with our neighbours. Meals would be taken at the house where the work was going on. We enjoyed having these neighbours in for meals and I remember we particularly liked having Jack Needham. He seemed to have a brightness about him.

These small farms of, perhaps, ten or twenty acres were hardly viable and certainly could only support one family. The families were big so the sons had to go to work on the Castletown estate or emigrate. Around 1910 Robert Waller's land in the Long Lane was divided and each farmer in Coolbawn and Lisquillibeen got a 'divide', possibly ten to fifteen acres each.

Jack Needham had a fund of stories about the old people, particularly about Mike Ryan. John Needham, his father, 'rambled' at Mike's and would take the young Jack with him. Mike, who was always formal, would put down the paper which he had been reading and say, 'good evening John, good evening Boy', on wet days sitting with an umbrella over his head, because of the drip. He and John Needham would then proceed to discuss the great and small events of the day. As they left he would say, 'goodnight John, goodnight Boy'. After we came to live

in Mike's house I got to know that drip very well and it was only cured when slates replaced the thatch. (House as it is in 1998 on previous page).

The Coming of the Garda Síochána

After the Irish Free State came into being in 1922 a new police force was set up. Late in 1923, or in early 1924, the Gardaí came to Coolbawn. They had to live in the forge house for a few months until the old constabulary barrack was made available to them. The first four Gardaí were Sgt. Danny O'Shea from Kerry, Patrick Carroll, John Cahill, a tall, fair young man who became grandfather to Shane McGowan of the musical group, The Pogues, and a man named Burns. They were all very young – in their early twenties – except Burns who may have been an ex-RIC man.

Regaining the Land

Many tenant farmers availed of the terms of the 1903 Land Act to buy out their farms, including the farm my father later acquired in Coolbawn in 1920. The purchase price, paid off in an annuity to the Land Commission, was paid annually until about six years ago when legislation was brought in to allow the payer to buy the remaining years outright. My brother Michael Carroll did this for £125 for about 30 acres.

Some holdings were uneconomic, often as small as four acres. A farm of forty or fifty acres was rare, eight to ten being the norm. The biggest landowners in Kilbarron, like Minchins, Towers, Biggs, Telfords, Reeves and Breretons, still held substantial acreages and, to a greater or lesser degree, were giving employment.

Once tenant-purchase was out of the way the political movement of the time, the United Irish League, applied themselves to getting the large estates divided among smallholders.

In 1910 the townland of Clonmackilladuff, circa 260 acres, was owned by Robert Waller, the malster, who lived in Nenagh. He did not farm his land but let it out for grazing to a neighbouring landowner. The smallholders of Lisquillibeen, Coolbawn and Clonmackilladuff felt that this was unfair and that the land should be bought by the Land Commission and parcelled out between them. Robert Waller did not agree. Accordingly, a number of men from these three townlands, mainly Lisquillibeen, devised a plan to force Waller to sell his to the Land Commission. They decided to drive the grazier's cattle off the land and to continue to do so until their object was achieved. This practice of 'driving' had a long tradition behind it. The group called themselves the 'Hazel Brigade' – perhaps they met in a hazel wood! – and then organised a big cattle drive from Clonmackilladuff in order to put pressure on Waller to divide. The cattle were not Waller's but nobody would take the grass if there was a danger of their cattle being 'driven'.

The group got ready in a house in Lisquillibeen, disguising themselves by blacking their faces. The drive was a great success, some cattle being driven as far as Borris wood (now gone). The cattle were all found eventually, unharmed. The spokesman for the group was the local schoolmaster who wrote to the *Nenagh Guardian* to justify the action, signing himself the 'Hazel Brigade'. Robert Waller succumbed to the pressure and agreed to sell his land to the Land Commission. Eventually every small farmer got some land, although it has been said that those who were most active in the 'driving' did less well than others. The average divide was about seven or eight Irish acres, except for Paddy Smith, the steward, who got a full farm and the house and farmyard where Robinson the overseer had lived. A full farm was about 30 acres.

Those who got land in Clonmackilladuff – it was also known as the Long Lane – were Mrs Ellen Hogan of Lisquillibeen, Mrs Peter Carroll of Lisquillibeen, Michael Moran, Timothy Ryan, Mrs Meagher, John Needham, Mr & Mrs John Hogan (Whittakers) all of Coolbawn, the Meaghers of Kevanstown, Smiths of the Bog, and (John) Hogan of Clonmackilladuff.

Coolbawn Today
Apart from the post office, and the thriving general shop attached to it, Coolbawn is a quiet place. The deconsecrated Church of Ireland church awaits a new life. under its owner, actor Patrick Bergin, who plans to make it into a poetry centre. Several new houses have been built; the pump is still there and the ruin of the little house beside it in which the Castletown herd traditionally lived. During the 1930s and 1940s a platform of timber dance boards flourished beside the pump, and the Cross was always a gathering place for young people. They got off their bicycles on their way home from the hurling matches and there was much talk and laughter.

As a child I thought America was at Coolbawn Cross. Now the cars fly by or pull up to do their business in the post office and shop and are off again. The post office is still a place where one meets the neighbours and has a chat and where the local news is passed on and discussed. Its going would leave a sad and empty void in the community.

Coolbawn is my own townland, the one I know best and is I believe, and has been, a microcosm of much of rural Ireland.

Sources:
Civil Survey, Tithe Applotment Lists, Primary Valuation, Census 1659-1996.
Paddy Carroll, Michael Carroll and author's personal memories.
Minchin Papers.

Photographs: p. 242 taken by Paddy Carroll; p. 243 sent by Genevieve Moran, USA; p. 247, loaned by Michael Carroll; p. 249, loaned by Julia Slevin.

The Costelloes and Mary Hogan of Lisquillibeen Lane, circa 1924
Back (l to r): John, Jack (father), Willie. **Front:** Mary Hogan, Mrs Mary Costelloe, Bridget Costelloe (later Mrs Fahy and mother of the late Julia Slevin).

Kilbarron (New Chapel)

This village is situated in the townlands of Upper and Lower Ballyquinlivan, four miles from Borrisokane and twelve miles from Nenagh. It was a greenfield site when the Catholic church was built there in 1814. It came to be known officially as New Chapel but the local people always called it Kilbarron, taking the name from the townland where the ruins of the pre-Reformation parish church was situated. A little village, hamlet really, grew up around the 1814 church. To further complicate terminology, as already pointed out in the chapter on churches, both Upper and Lower Ballyquinlivan are actually in the parish of Finnoe.

Up to and for some time after World War II, or the mid-1940s, the village consisted of the chapel, the boys' school and the girls' school, Donoghue's (now Hannigan's) public house, Treacy's public house, Quinlan's shop, Mark Bourke's house, an old unoccupied house called Ned Hogan's beside the girls' school and, a little way up the Coolbawn road, Pat and Mossy Meara's cottage, occupied until the last couple of years by the Gleeson family who now have a new house beside it. Meara's was one of the very first labourers' cottages to be built by the Board of Guardians.

Mossy Meara was the church sacristan until she became too old and was replaced by Mrs Quirke in the late 1920s. Her husband, Pat Meara, was an eccentric character who amused himself by making up parcels of stones wrapped in newspaper and leaving them along the roadside to intrigue passers-by. As schoolchildren we soon got used to them, just calling them 'Pat Meara's parcels' and ignoring them.

Mrs M. B. Fleming's cottage was built in the early 1930s and was first occupied by Bill Hyland, the blacksmith. In 1850, according to the Primary Valuation list, Thomas Hackett held all 103 acres of Ballyquinlivan Upper in fee and was the 'immediate lessor' of the boys' national school site and of the chapel and yard.

In the 1870s it became the property of the Wallers of Banagher. Major Bertie Waller inherited it and Firgrove in 1919 from his mother who had lived in Banagher.

The 1820s Roots

In the Tithe lists of 1824 the landlord with the most land in Finnoe parish was Thomas Waller who had bought in earlier in the century. Many of the tenants' names, like Meara, Treacy, Hogan, Gleeson, Corcoran. Hough, Ralph, Stanley, Darcy, Hodgins, Moran, Fox, Kennedy, Brooder, Cleary, Brereton, still occur in the parish today.

In that list Michael Clear had 22 acres, and John Clear 10 acres in Ballyquinlivan townland. Patrick Clear/Cleere who built the chapel in 1814 also built what is now Hannigan's public house in 1819. This date was found inscribed in plaster over its door when the first renovation to the building was undertaken by the late George Hannigan about fifteen years ago. The inscription was plastered over. It seems to have been built as a police barracks and is marked as such on the Ordnance Survey map of 1840 but sometime before 1850 a new barracks was built in Coolbawn on the Castletown estate and presumably the Clears applied for a public house licence for this house in the village.

Patrick Clear's daughter married Michael Donoghue of Carney. Their son John married Kathleen O'Rourke of Ferbane. They had no family and brought Mrs O'Donoghue's niece, Pauline Harkins, Athlone, to live with them. Pauline's mother had died and her father had remarried. In 1956 Pauline married George Hannigan, the local garda sergeant and a native of Donegal. Joseph is their only child.

Of the ten persons who figure as 'immediate lessors' in the Primary Valuation lists for Finnoe parish only three appear to be resident – John Brereton, Joseph and Richard Falkiner. Edward Waller (son of Thomas of 1824) lived outside the county. Non-resident William D. Ferrar was a newcomer-owner since 1824.

Again tenants with names of Gaelic origin are in every townland – Gleeson, Hogan, Cleary, Carroll, Dwyer, Burke, Meara, Darcy, Corboy, Phelan and Hough. The largest amount of land in the parish occupied by an O'Kennedy is in Kilcowran where William was a tenant of Ferrar's on 14 acres & 29 perches.

The Tithe record has a Widow Anne Cleary with one acre in Kilbarron village area. By 1850 the Primary Valuation list shows us that four Clearys, Jeremiah, Roderick, Timothy and James (Short), presumably her sons, had about 140 acres there. One of these sons, Jeremiah, built a house around 1913 or so. It became Quinlan's after his daughter Molly married Rody Quinlan. Molly Cleary Quinlan kept a general shop. She and Rody had three daughters, one, Pauline, my exact contemporary, died at the age of twenty-one of tuberculosis, and Margaret and Nancy died at a fairly young age, all unmarried. The site of the former Cleary-cum-Quinlan house is now part of the village car park.

James Cleary bought Springfield House and farm. His son, Michael, bought Rodeen House and farm (above) in Finnoe. Michael's son, James K., started a stationery, tearooms and confectionery business in Pearse Street, Nenagh, trading as J.K.C's. This flourishing business is continued by his son Michael, noted Eire Óg, Tipperary and All-Star hurler, and other family members. Michael Snr sold Rodeen to Michael Flynn, Borrisokane, in the 1930s and moved to Kildare. He later returned to Nenagh and had a vegetable shop in Pearse Street.

Either Timothy or Roderick Cleary acquired Rose Cottage, which is located nearly opposite the entrance to Finnoe church and graveyard. It is now owned by Michael O'Donoghue. As already seen, nearby Ormonde Cottage was originally the property of Samuel Waller (1785-1853).

Loughnanes, who occupied 30 acres in Kilbeg townland in 1824, probably built what was up to recently Mark Bourke's house (now demolished) about the same time as the Quinlan one was erected. Loughnanes were still in Kilbeg in 1852. The Bourkes came to live there in 1898. According to the *Nenagh Guardian* column, '100 Years Ago', of October 1998, Thomas Bourke bought the tenant interest in Kylebeg farm of 28 acres for £355 plus fees. The rent was £16 per annum. Mark Bourke became the owner of the old Loughnane house circa 1908-10 and married, circa 1914, Gretta Gleeson, a teacher at the girls' school. He kept a shop for a while. Gretta, who was from Bodyke in Co. Clare, was a cousin of John Gleeson, principal teacher in the national school in Terryglass, and of the parish priest, Canon John Darcy.

Pub and Parlour

Treacys' public house was owned by people named Grace. They came in 1889. They sold out to Martin Treacy of Bellevue and went to live in Dublin. Martin Treacy had come back from the States with Julia Tierney from Ballymassey, Borrisokane, to whom he was engaged. They married in 1904 and renovated what had been a small, thatched house. The public house business was carried on by their daughter Bridget and her husband Tommy Hogan of Clonmackilladuff until they gave up the licence but kept on a small shop until quite recently. Mrs Bridget Hogan died in 1995, aged 87, and Tommy in March 1997, aged 81.

A FÁS scheme to modernise the village has been going on for several years and has improved its appearance enormously. Fine walls have been built, trees planted and many other improvements carried out. In 1992 Joseph Hannigan practically rebuilt the public house to a very high standard and added a general shop. The old public house was lovely – square, with an eighteenth-century look about it and covered in Virginia creeper. The pub facilities were rather inadequate but upstairs there was an elegant parlour – a mixture of the Victorian and Edwardian eras. I was reminded of that parlour when watching the scene in the film, *Michael Collins*, where Collins, Harry Boland, Kitty Kiernan and her sisters are gathered in the Kiernan parlour in Granard and Kitty (Julia Roberts) sings (or mimes rather to Sineád O'Connor's singing) 'She Moved Through the Fair', and Michael declaims the first of the eighteen verses of 'Farewell to Skibbereen'.

The ceiling of Pauline Hannigan's parlour was an exact replica in miniature of the ceiling in Kilbarron chapel. Pauline had a beautiful singing voice and played the piano. She knew all the old songs and ballads and on our holidays during the war when life was grim in London, my sister May and two or three other friends had many happy evenings there listening to her play and sing. She had a wonderful repertoire of the sweet old Victorian and Edwardian songs, Irish ballads, and Moore's melodies. I can hear the lines from them and the tunes go through my head as I write.

Genevieve, Oh Genevieve I'd give the world
To live again the lovely past ...

Soft o'er the mountain wakes the day too soon ... (Juanita)

I dream of Jeannie with the light brown hair ...

How we loved 'Chérie' with its memories of a lost and darkened France.

Love's last word is spoken, Chérie;
Now my heart is broken, Chérie;
Faded the hours I spent with you,
Roaming the boulevards content with you ...

We wallowed happily in the rich escapist schmaltz. Then we would have a Moore's melody, another evocation of lost, tragic love.

She is far from the land where her young hero sleeps,
And lovers around her are sighing,
But coldly she turns from their gaze and weeps,
For her heart in his grave is lying ...

It seemed a million miles away from London and the war.

Muintir na Tíre

Muintir na Tíre: People of the Countryside was an organisation founded by Canon John Hayes of Bansha in 1931 for the betterment of the rural dwellers. The idea was that people should come together in the parishes and generally improve the quality of life. Improvement was badly needed. After we got Independence in 1922 there was the tragic Civil War and before the country had recovered from that catastrophe there followed the depressed late Twenties, and the hungry Thirties and its Economic War, 1932-8, with Great Britain. The British refused to buy our cattle in retaliation for de Valera's refusal to hand over only half the land annuities which had taken the place of the rents paid to landlords. No sooner had this been sorted out than there came the outbreak of World War II, known in Ireland as The Emergency, and its period of rationing. Many young, able-bodied Irishmen joined the British army, navy and air force and many others, men and women, went to work in the armaments and other factories across the water.

Muintir na Tíre was a godsend. It gave people an incentive to be up and doing and we are today enjoying the amenities which this organisation provided.

At first the whole parish combined in the great effort. Meetings were called and committees elected. Most of the people on these committees are now dead and we have to rely on the memories of those few left for the names and offices of the early members. Inevitably mistakes will be made and some will be left out or given the wrong office.

The first Chairman was Joe Slattery of Kilbiller; others on the committee were John Heenan of Clooniniha, Secretary; Paddy Fox, Mick Whelan of Annagh, Danny Smith, Pakie Hogan, Martin Horan, Wilsie Nolan, John Molloy, Dinny Starr, Ormond Allen, Jack Bourke, Marty O'Meara, Tommy Bourke, Carrigagown, Joe O'Meara, Kevanstown, Christy Carty, Jim Coen. At first the meetings were held mainly in Terryglass. Transport was a problem as few people had cars;

owners were rationed for petrol and most relied on bicycles. After about a year or so it was decided that, owing to the difficulty of transport and also because of the differing needs of the two communities, that they should have two separate branches of Muintir with one based in Terryglass and the other in Kilbarron.

Terryglass Branch, 1950-1
Paddy Fox was first chairman and John Heenan, Clooninihy, the Hon. Secretary. On the committee were aforesaid Pakie Hogan, Martin Horan, Wilsie Nolan, John Molloy, Dinny Starr, Ormond Allen, and Commander George Gaynor. The first task they undertook was to put a temporary wall around St. Augh's eye well in Shannon Lane. They then cleared away the old bank in front of the new church where people used to tie up their horses and vehicles while at Mass. Inter-parish hurling tournaments were held to raise funds. Tipperary (NR) County Council got involved in cleaning up the old quay. Muintir then put pressure on the Board of Health, a subsidiary committee of the County Council, to have the dispensary sited in Carrigahorig in Terryglass parish rather than in Lorrha. The Board argued that there was no suitable site there. Members of Muintir canvassed and came up with six suitable sites. The Board gave in and the dispensary was duly built on the Terryglass road, a short distance from Carrigahorig.

As already recorded in chapter 4, they worked hard with the parish priest to get a new national school sanctioned and built. Their efforts were rewarded and the school opened in 1954.

A feature of Muintir na Tíre were Rural Weeks for members. One in Mullingar was attended by Wilsie Nolan and John Heenan (Terryglass), Jack Ryan, Kilgarvan gate lodge, and Mick Whelan (Kilbarron).

Kilbarron Branch
After the break with Terryglass area in 1951-2 a Kilbarron-based committee was formed. Joe Slattery was the first Chairman and for a very short time Paddy Carroll was Hon. Secretary. He was soon replaced by, I believe, Mick Whelan. Other committee members were Danny Smith, Jack Bourke, Marty O'Meara, Joe O' Meara, Kevanstown, Christy Carty, Jim Coen, Boysie Moore and Mary Lynch, Oliver's sister. She was also Hon. Secretary for some time.

Projects Undertaken
The building of the parish hall was the biggest undertaking by the committee. This hall was badly needed and the idea was first mooted by Rev. Matthew Fogarty, Drominagh, who had returned from the New Zealand mission. Marty O'Meara saw an advertisement saying the Carnegie Trust was offering villages £2,000 towards such projects and it was decided to go after this grant.

A committee was formed within the branch to get this specific project off the ground – the date was 1957. Joe Slattery died in that year. Jack Bourke, Firgrove, was first chairman; Hon Secretary: Susan Slattery (now Mrs John Ryan, Summerhill, Nenagh); Trustees: Jack Gleeson (The Rally), John Ryan (The Professor); Joint Treasurers: Tom Bourke, Carrigagown, Donie O'Meara. Other committee members were Mark Bourke, Danny Smith, Marty O'Meara, Dinny Costelloe, Danny Corbett, Mick Gleeson, Joe O'Meara of Kevanstown, Tom Casey, Mick Whelan of Annagh, Joe O'Meara, Ballinagrass.

The contract for the building was given to Marty O'Meara. The original contract was £5,418 7s 6d, but Marty had to quote for extras after that. The architect was Dermot O'Toole, 2 Lr. Hatch St., Dublin. The first task was to find a site, and a suitable one was duly identified beside Ned Hogan's old house (beside the former girls' school, now a hall). It belonged to Bridget Treacy, later Mrs Tommy Hogan. Negotiations were entered into for the purchase of a quarter of an acre, but before these could be finalised in a satisfactory way Jack Bourke asked his uncle Mark if he would donate the site on the opposite side of the road which Mark agreed very generously to do.

However, it was not an ideal site as it was very low-lying and a great deal of expense and labour, particularly labour, were needed to fill it in and raise it to road level. This was all done by voluntary labour with most able-bodied people in the parish giving a hand. Some material was drawn from the walls which had surrounded the old Mass house in Carney Commons. Finally the site was level and Marty was ready to start building. Jack Hough was a tradesman on the job with an apprentice Pat Prout. As well as these there were Patsy Dunne, Ned Coen, Johnny Houlihan, Lorrha, and some Costelloes of Lisquillibeen. Some of the voluntary labour – mostly for the infilling of the site – was provided by Patsy and Billy Meara (Lisquillibeen Lane), Paddy Corbett, Michael Carroll, Mick Moloney, Jack (Duke) Donohue, Tim Cleary, P. J. Grady (working for Dinny Costelloe) – and probably other people whose names have not been remembered.

How the Funds Were Raised
Carnivals, with marquee dancing, were the key method. Donie Collins and his big band played for the first time in Tipperary at the opening dance in the marquee. The work went on fairly slowly but, fortuitously, in the summer of 1959 John O'Meara, Marty's brother and also a builder, came home from the States. The extra help made all the difference. Soon the building was roofed and all was completely finished by the end of December 1960. It was formally opened on New Year's Day, 1 January 1961, in a snowstorm.

The Grotto
Rev. John Cooney came as curate to the parish in 1959. He came from Monsea-Killodiernan parish where he had been instrumental in the erection of a grotto in Puckane village to mark the Marian Year. He now applied himself to the building of one in Kilbarron. There was a good site available where the old boys' school had stood. He designed the grotto himself and all of the work was done by voluntary labour. The actual construction of the grotto was carried out on a voluntary basis by Marty O'Meara. He made the shapes and moulds and did all the stonework and the tiling by hand. Special stone had to be brought from different parts of the country. The mica or shiny stone came from Blessington in Co. Wicklow, and the brownstone from the Hill of Howth. Stories are still told of the bringing of the brownstone. Marty O'Meara, Mick Gleeson, and Michael Carroll set off in Joe Kitson's lorry to bring it back. At Kildare on the way back Joe's lorry broke down and they had to spend two days in Kildare waiting for it to be repaired. Hilarious stories still abound about that journey. Finally, the grotto was finished and stands as a memorial to the vision of Fr Cooney and the skill and hard work of Marty O'Meara and other voluntary helpers.

New Cemetery

It was evident about this time that a new burial ground was needed in the parish. The old graveyard attached to the pre-Reformation Church in Kilbarron townland was overused. Graves in family plots were being re-opened to such an extent that they were becoming desecrated. Tipperary (NR) County Council responded to the demand and purchased a field from Jack Bourke adjoining Hannigan's (then Donoghue's) public house. Marty O'Meara built the surrounding walls. The first person to be buried there was Patrick Smith of the Bog, brother of Phil and Penny and known as Paddy Dagg as he had spent his life working for the Dagg family, first at Kevanstown and later at the Glebe, Kilbarron; he was really like one of that family. The cemetery was consecrated and officially opened in 1957.

Of all who worked on the building of the cemetery wall only two are alive – Marty O'Meara, Ballinderry, and Roger Corcoran, Co. Council engineer, aged 96, and living in Dublin, hale and hearty.

A few years ago Jamesy and Theresa Burke and family laid out a very pleasant pitch and putt and mini-golf course on their lovely, upland field facing Hannigan's shop. This is a good amenity for the expanding village.

Sources:
Tithe Applotment Lists, Kilbarron parish.
Primary Valuation, Kilbarron parish.
OS Letters.
Ordnance Survey Sheet no. 6.
Bassett's Book of Co. Tipperary, 1889.
Wilsie Nolan, Marty O'Meara, Michael Carroll, Donie O'Meara, Joe O'Meara, Ballingrass, Paddy Corbett.
Susan Ryan (née Slattery), Nenagh.

Photograph on p. 251 loaned by Mary (née Flynn) Egan.

Carney Commons

Carney Commons is situated about five miles north-east of the village of Kilbarron in the Finnoe end of the parish. This fifty-two acre site, a section of the townland's overall 280 acres, has come to the headlines in recent years following a botanical survey which was carried out on the area in 1996-7 by three students, Shirley Armitage, Denis Duggan and Marie Cormican of Borrisokane Community College.

Their survey revealed a diversity of plant life, surpassed only by places such as the Burren in Co. Clare. The students entered their findings in the Aer Lingus Young Scientist Exhibition in 1997. They came second in the Biological and Ecological Sciences section and won the overall National Heritage trophy. They also won the Young European Environment Research Award.

It was not always appreciated just how special this area is. It is historically renowned as an area of very infertile soil which is completely unsuited to agriculture. The 1840 Ordnance Survey Letters recorded:

> A large portion of it is inundated to a depth of thirty feet during the winter and spring seasons. In the month of May the water entirely dries up. During a great part of the summer season farmers are occupied drawing marl for manure out of this place, that which a few days previous was a great lake.

Tradition has it that the area was so worthless as agricultural land that Richard Chysers, the grantee in the Cromwellian era did not bother to even claim the land and returned to England instead. Ever since, the whole of Carney Commons has belonged to the adjoining farms as commonage.

Because Carney Commons was relatively undisturbed by agriculture down through the years, and because it has such a rare and unusual soil, very uncommon flora exists there.

Plants such as the Early Purple Orchid (*Orchis Mascula*), and the threatened species, Green Winged Orchid (*Orchis morio*), Pignut (*Conopodium majus*) and Perforate St. John's Wort (*Hypericum perforatum*) are among the spectacular ones which can be seen in abundance there through the year. In all over 160 plant species were identified and catalogued by the three Borrisokane Community College students. Right: St. John's Wort, which has yellow flowers and many traditional medicinal uses.

Incredibly, up to this time no comprehensive survey had been carried out, although it has always been widely acknowledged by locals that the flora here was something special. Thankfully, a firm record now exists for generations to come of the plants of Carney Commons.

(based on material supplied by one of the students, Marie Cormican)

BALLINDERRY

The village of Ballinderry grew up around the grist mill and distillery. The side of the village where the mill, barracks, and Mill House is located is in the townland of Newlawn, while the other side is in the townland of Stonepark.

In the *Civil Survey* we read that in the townland of Broccagh 'standeth a water corne-mill upon the river of Inihy[(Ballyfinboy] belonging to John Hurly'. Brocka was then quite large and contained parts of modern adjoining townlands. This John Hurly was proprietor in fee of one and a half of the four ploughlands of Broccagh.

John Hurly's is the earliest mention of a working mill which may well have been where the present mill is sited. There is a local tradition that the monks in Terryglass monastery had a mill somehow connected with this one. Many years ago a visiting archaeologist said that the wall which extends beyond the end of the Ballindery tailrace is much older than the mill and could be medieval, but this was not verified.

Interestingly, Ballinderry's was the last flour mill to be in use in the parish. It flourished under the ownership of the Hogan family from 1887 until 1962. The process of refining and making white flour was to come later. Indeed, a mill may well have functioned here continuously from the seventeenth century, or even earlier, until 1962 with alterations and/or additions.

These flour mills were in reality what is known as grist mills as they only ground wheat into wholemeal flour and oats into oaten meal.

1840s

In O'Donovan's Ordnance Survey Letters of 1840, the information having been obtained from a Mr O'Callaghan and the Catholic curate Rev. Mr Bugler, Ballinderry was described as 'a small collection of houses on the road from Puckane to Terryglass'. It had an extensive distillery and a good dwellinghouse owned by Dr James Dempster, Nenagh – presumably what is now known as Ballyfinboy House. We are not told who actually occupied the house but it may have been the man in charge of the grist mill which may have been distinct from the distillery. The distiller was named as Egan and lived in Newlawn House.

In 1846 William Egan, a Roscrea man, was carrying on a distillery, as well as a flour mill there. According to the Primary Valuation list of 1852, William Egan occupied 'a house, offices, flour mill, distillery and land'. A Timothy Hogan (no relation of later owners) was the 'immediate lessor', but this does not necessarily mean that he was the owner as he may well have been a tenant who had sub-let it to Egan. The land was 50 acres, 2 roods, 14 perches and was valued at £30 10s 0d, while the buildings were valued at £97 – a total of £127 10s 0d. Trush Darcy (Mrs Patricia Lyons, Ardagh, Co. Longford), a granddaughter of a later miller, Patrick Carroll, thinks the Egans were a branch of the Egans of Tullamore – P.H. Egan Ltd – who later merged with D. E. Williams Ltd.

Some time between 1852 and the early 1880s William Egan disposed of the property to Denis Brereton, Oldcourt, Finnoe. Brereton did not keep it for long and disposed of it to Matthew Slattery, Glenbower, who was married to his sister Mary. She had died at 26 years of age and left five young children who were reared by her family in Oldcourt.

While Slattery occupied the property the distillery went on fire and was destroyed. The flour mill remained intact. The concept of insuring against fire had just come in and when Slattery left and went to England or the USA, Brereton was left with the property on his hands. Brereton is reputed to have offered to sell the mill to Patrick Carroll the miller but Carroll could not come up with the necessary finance. Slattery had been living at the Mill House (now Ballyfinboy House) so this now became vacant.

Hogans Arrive

At this time a family named Hogan (the Bush Hogans) lived at Ryehill – where the Ryans live now, Mrs Ryan having been a Hogan. They had come to Ryehill early in the nineteenth century from near Carney – The Sheltery Bush – a well-known meeting place. At the time, circa 1887, when the mill and other property was put up for sale there were two Hogan brothers living in Ryehill – Patrick and Martin. Their sister Anne was married to the miller, Pat Carroll. Pat Hogan had a small bit of land at the top of Ciss Corboy's hill. He sold this to Will Leenane for £95 and, with this money and, I suppose, some borrowed finance, he bought the mill, the Mill House, the barracks, the then public house and 60 acres of land for £280. All the property was in Newlawn townland, except the thatched public house which was in Stonepark. This change of ownership was a contributory factor to the subsequent growth of the village.

Millers

The mill (below) continued to flourish as a grist mill. People brought their wheat to be ground into wholemeal and their oats into oaten meal for porridge. Patrick Carroll the miller was accidentally killed. After Pat Carroll came miller Kieran Dalton from Belmont, Co. Offaly, who married Julia Hough of Ballinderry, sister of Jim. She was the local midwife. After Dalton came Jimmy Madden from Finnoe. Jim Carroll, son of Patrick Carroll and father of Tom Carroll who still lives in Stonepark in the family home, was the miller in 1962 when it closed. Successive

millers and their families had lived in the house adjacent to the mill which is still there but has no permanent resident. Actually it was a double house, with Kieran Dalton living in one half and the Darcys in the other. It is now one house owned by Darcys.

The mill buildings and weighing scales also exist though in a rather ruined, ivy-covered, state. The current owner is Elsie Hogan who has a ledger with all the mill accounts going back probably to her grandmother Elizabeth's day. The last five entries are:

	£	s	d	
Mrs Geoffrey McNeill Moss	7	5	0	(248 stone Barley)
Michael Meara, Ryehill	5	18	3	
Pat Tierney, Macloon	1	17	0	
Mike Tierney	15	3	4	(Oats 44 stone)
Mike Flannery, Shanbally	25	3	3	

Ballinderry Distillery [Michael Parkinson memoir]

This distillery was rare in the country at the time of its operation. It carried out the complete process of turning barley into whiskey. The barley was purchased from farmers in the area. It was then kiln-dried and stored until needed. It was made into malt as required.

There was a special floor where the grain was steeped in water to make it grow. When it had good buds on it, it was dried again and the buds combed off. It was then malt and ready for use in the stills. The distillery was a great boost for the economy of the parish. As well as buying barley they provided a ready market for turf. They needed good brown or black turf for drying the corn. They used light turf or white turps [turpentine] for heating the stills. All the turf was bought by a measure known as a box. All the by-products of distilling – malt combings and grain – were bought back by the farmers for feeding to cattle.

Patrick Hogan, who bought the mill and other village property, married Elizabeth Cummins in 1879. He became involved in the Land League, this being a time of much agrarian agitation. As a result of attending late meetings, travelling long distances and getting wet, he fell into poor health and died at aged 44, leaving four children, the eldest Michael (Mike) being only nine years old.

Mrs Elizabeth Hogan must have been what in the west of Ireland they call a 'mighty woman'. She reared the family, kept the businesses going, renovated and slated

Michael Hogan's horse, Precept

the pub, and built on the extensions which are at right angles to the original house. And when her son Michael was old enough he added the loose boxes at the back – all the work was done by Will Fox. Very interested in racing, Michael kept several racehorses, the best-known being Precept. Mrs Hogan managed to send her son Tom and daughter Anne (Nan) to boarding school at Rockwell and Eccles Street respectively.

Michael Hogan married Nora Wells, a local girl. Elsie, Mrs Lucy Kennedy and the late Paddy are their children.

Dick Stanley

At the Stonepark or left-hand side looking down from The Tavern, approaching from the Terryglass end, there were two thatched houses, one at a right angle to the side of the street. They were the homes of the Foot and Tierney families. The latter was a public house – a sort of 'shebeen' (nothing to do with the present Tavern). The Foot and Tierney dwellings were demolished sometime around 1926 and replaced with Dick Stanley's house. When Dick died he left the house to his nephew Bill Donoghue. Bill and his wife Carmel now reside there.

Dick Stanley came from Woodford, across the lake in Co. Galway. He was one of twelve children of Charles and Helen (née Clancy) Stanley. Charles was a baker by trade. Dick went into that business, first of all with his father, and later with Duggans of Scarriff into whose family he married in 1934. Dick also worked for a period in Lawrencetown (between Portumna and Ballinasloe) before building the house in Ballinderry, where he opened a shop, and built a small bakery where for a time he made confectionery.

Dick was a sort of Renaissance man, of remarkable and diverse talents – athlete, hurler, musician and maker of beautiful violins. He was an fine hurler and won championship medals in 1913 and 1914 with the Woodford club. In 1914 he won a Clare county medal with Scarriff, thus getting medals in two counties in the one year. He won again in Clare in 1916-17.

During the War of Independence Dick was Commandant of the 4th battallion, East Clare Brigade. After the Treaty he took the Republican side and was captured in Galway. He was brought to Gormanstown Camp in Co. Westmeath, and was actually sentenced to death for his anti-Treaty activities in December 1922 but the sentence was commuted. The blessed candle, which was given to him after he was sentenced, as was the practice, is part of the Stanley collection of items carefully preserved in his former home by the Donoghues.

While in Gormanstown Dick furthered his education at the camp classes, and among the collection are certificates from the 'Gormanstown Education Board' – unique documents indeed. This educational board was set up by the prisoners themselves. On the 'Board' were such notables as Frank Gallagher (a youthful friend of Eamon de Valera's and later a journalist of repute and first editor of *The Irish Press*). Sean T. Ó Ceallaigh (a later FF Government minister and President of Ireland), and Matt Neill. A certificate which records that Richard Stanley passed the examination for the Fáinne on 26 June 1923 is signed by Oscar Traynor (a later FF Government minister) and Ó Ceallaigh.

Dick Stanley's own preferred musical instrument was the flute. But though he never played the violin, he could create instruments which could rank with the best. L. T. C. Rolt, an English travel writer, made a visit to Ballinderry in the early 1940s during a boat trip on the river Shannon, subsequently described in his book called *Green and Silver* (1949), and visited Dick Stanley.

> ... His art is entirely self-taught, he uses the crudest of tools and finds and seasons his own materials. He showed us one instrument which he had recently completed and another which was in the course of construction.

> Holt, expecting to find the end product a crude object, was most surprised when Dick placed the finished product in his hands.

> Had I not seen the same fine craftsmanship exhibited in the other instrument under construction, I doubt if I should have really believed that he made it. The soundboard was cut from a pinewood beam salvaged from a ruined mill nearby, the body was of sycamore, the pegs of holly wood, while the bridge and frets were of black bog oak dug from the neighbouring bog.

There are several violins made by Dick in the former Stanley home, all fine examples of his craftsmanship. Even the last one made when he was over 80 years – a little crude and rough, perhaps, as hands were growing old and stiff – bears witness to his skill and attention to detail. Dick died in 1975, aged 82.

The Village, 1887-1926

After the Foot house came the Costelloe-owned house in which Ger Buckley, ex-RIC, lived. It was later lived in by Dan and May (née O'Connor, Nenagh) Darcy. After they died their son Bernard sold it to Mrs Hilary Henry, Waterloo Lodge, near Mota Quay. The old house was demolished and replaced by a new building of similar design to house her very successful Lakeshore Foods, whose story is recounted in chapter 13.

Next was the home and forge of the Costelloe family beside Hogan's public house and extended residence. Thomas Costelloe was the occupier in 1850 of 77*a* 1*r* and 36*p* in Newlawn townland, the immediate lessor again being Dr James Dempster. Mary Anne Costelloe, Thomas's sister, perhaps, had 24 acres, and Joseph Clancy occupied 6*a* 3*r* 11*p*. Hugh Kennedy, father of Sylvester who had the post office, held 3*a* 3*r* 11*p*.

These two buildings were also demolished to make way for Lakeshore Foods.

The Costelloes kept six cows and supplied the village with milk. Thomas Costelloe's children were Martin, Tim and Maggie. Martin was the blacksmith from whom Jack O'Meara took over. Jack's son, Danny O'Meara, part-time postman and blacksmith, kept on the forge until the mid-1940s – see chapter 14, 'Forges'. Danny was married to May Bourke of Fort Nesbit and they later moved to Kildare.

At the outbreak of the Great War in 1914 Tim Costelloe joined the British Army. He was very good-looking and when he returned on leave in uniform a Miss Wallace of Shanbally, a Protestant and of the gentry class, fell in love with him and they were married. They had three children including a daughter named Maud. Mrs Costelloe, née Wallace, later became a poultry instructress – her husband had gone back to live with his brother and sister, Martin and Maggie, as the marriage was not a happy one.

At the bottom of Elsie Hogan's long garden is a little house on the left in which a family of Hogans (not related) had lived. The father Matt had been a member of the RIC, as had his two sons, Martin and Rody. Martin died young, rather tragically, and in the 1920s and early 1930s Rody and their sister Mary lived there. After their deaths it was the home of the Boyle family. While they were living there the river overflowed and flooded their home. They went to live at the gate lodge of Drominagh House and are still there.

Here I must go over the bridge and into Ballinderry townland.

Up to the 1940s there was a dispensary on the Nenagh road, opposite what is now John and Lucy Kennedy's house and beside their farmyard. When not used as a dispensary a Miss McDonagh came there to give lessons in housekeeping to young girls when Anne (Nan) Hogan and Mary Anne Hogan of Ryehill (later Mrs Danny O'Meara, Gurteen) were young in the early 1900s.

This house was later lived in by Anne (Nan) Hogan and her brother Tom, children of Elizabeth Cummins Hogan. Nan kept a shop and Molly Conway did the housekeeping and the yard work. The Hogans had lived in the barracks after the RIC left in 1922 and up until the Gardaí came circa 1930.

Mrs Elizabeth Cummins Hogan had bought Costelloe's farm over the bridge and her son Tom, who never married, built a handsome house on it in 1925. His niece, Lucy Kennedy, now resides there. After he moved to his new house the dispensary was occupied by Garda Pat Walsh and his family.

Returning now in the mind's eye over the bridge, the RIC barracks was located just a very short distance down the lane to the miller's house and the mill. Close by were two thatched houses, rather down in a hollow near the river. They were occupied by two Hough families. The one nearest the barracks was the home of Mrs Betty (née Fleming) Hough mother of Mrs Julia Dalton the midwife. When that was vacated before World War II it became the home of Harry and Maggie (née Conway) Donoghue of Ballyscanlon. The other house (below), known as 'Muddy' Hough's, was pulled down when the last of her family left or, perhaps, after she died.

Police and Distinguished Descendants

The RIC barracks (above) is a neat three-storey building. The date of its building is not known but it is not in the 1850 Primary Valuation list. It still functions as a barracks, though there is no resident Garda now.

Some RIC Sergeants who served in Ballinderry

Kilowran	1887
Nicholas Corish	1893
Devaney	1894-98
Thomas Commins	1900
Mulally	1902
Morrison	1905-08
Greene	1909-14
Waters	1914
Scanlon	1919

Constables in Ballinderry

Matthew Farrell	1897-1905
– Dea	1899-1908
David Storey	circa 1901
Leahy	1908
Ger Buckley	1910
Tom Ryan	circa 1916

Constable Matthew Farrell, a native of Kilkenny, lived in Ballinderry village in a house owned by Elizabeth Hogan. Constable Farrell was the enumerator for the 1901 census of that year for much of Kilbarron, including my grandfather's house at Brookfield. In 1903 his young wife Mary (née Neville) died of tuberculosis leaving him with seven children aged 6 to 13 years. The following year he married Mary Byrnes, daughter of James of Shanbally and a sister of Tom whose family now own the well-known restaurant, Brocka-on-the-Water. They had one child who died in infancy in 1907.

Matthew Farrell died in January 1908, aged 46 years. In October 1911 his widow, Mary Farrell, married Michael, son of Stephen Costello, Clooninihy, Terryglass. The seven orphaned Farrell childen, whom their step-mother Mary had reared before and after Matthew's death, were now aged 13 to 21 years. Mary and Mick Costello had three children of their own – Martin who died in 1996, Christine, and Una with whom I went to school.

All the Farrell children, who had attended Terryglass national school, emigrated to New Zealand. The first to go was Jack who went to work on his step-mother's uncle's farm. This was Peter Byrne who had emigrated years before. James Farrell became a Jesuit priest and later moved to Australia. Michael became a policeman in NZ. Margaret (Madge) Farrell married Peter Byrne's son. Matt Farrell, Jun., married a Nannie Cahalan in 1920. They emigrated immediately to New Zealand where they became very extensive farmers and parented ten children.

Paddy Farrell, who had qualified as a tailor in Nenagh, emigrated to his brothers in 1913 when he was 21 years old. He subsequently married Mai Sullivan of Tower Hill, Borrisokane, in New Zealand. The celebrant was a friend from Ballinderry, Rev. Matt Fogarty, Drominagh, who was a priest in Rangiora parish near Christchurch. Mai's parents and their seven children had returned to Ireland from New Zealand when she was about 4 years old. They settled in Borrisokane where they became well-known house painters. She and her sister Chris returned to NZ as young adults.

Paddy and Mai settled in the small mining town of Greymouth where he engaged in tailoring. They had two sons and daughter Mary. The eldest son, Tim, became a Dominican priest, Mary died when she was fourteen and the youngest son, Patrick, holder of a personal chair in history at the University of New South Wales in Sydney, is the doyen of Irish-Australian historians.

Professor O'Farrell (left) has written on aspects of the Irish in New Zealand and Australia and on Anglo-Irish relations. In his *Vanishing Kingdoms* (1990), sub-titled 'A Personal Excursion', he interlaces Farrell and Sullivan biographical material from Ireland and New Zealand with contextual accounts of social life, religion, politics, recreation and 'dreams of Ireland'. The book has marvellous family photographs as well as some of people and places in this area.

Another resident of the parish in 1901 was Wexford-born Sergeant Nicholas Corish, RIC, who was stationed at the barracks in Carrigahorig from 1898, having transferred there from Ballinderry. The Corish family of seven children lived in Garryclohy townland in Terryglass. He was grandfather of Brendan Corish, TD for Wexford, a former leader of the Labour Party, 1960-77, and Minister for Health and Social Welfare, 1973-7. Brendan Howlin, TD, who was successively Minister for Health and for the Environment, and is now deputy leader of the

Labour Party, is Sgt Corish's great-grandson.

Tom Ryan, RIC, married Julia, daughter of Martin Hogan, and went to live in the Hogan homestead in Ryehill after disbandment of the force. Another constable who remained on in Ballinderry, was Ger Buckley, a widower with one daughter, Geraldine, who went to work in Dublin and married a man named Harris. They had three sons, one of whom is the well-known millionaire businessman, Robert (Pino) Harris. Geraldine died only a couple of years ago, aged over ninety years – she is in one of the school group photographs in chapter 4.

Ger Buckley married as his second wife Mrs Kate Grady, a widow, of Curraghmore, Coolbawn. They went to live in Dublin and any of their former neighbours visiting the capital was always welcome in their home. I remember once visiting there as a hungry student and being regaled with a sumptious 'fry'.

Mill House

In front of the mill is the Mill House (above) with its own entrance off the main road and now known as Ballyfinboy House. It is referred to by O'Donovan in his OS Letters of 1840 as 'Ballinderry House', and described by him 'as a good house in a demesne with some trees contiguous'. It is a two-storey house with three windows at upper floor level and a fine doorway.

When the Mill House became vacant after Matthew Slattery, the mill-owner, emigrated, the new Hogan owners rented it to the parish priest, Rev. John Kennedy. His housekeeper was his niece, Nora Kennedy from Lorrha, who afterwards married local man, Joe Clancy, an RIC sergeant stationed elsewhere. The curate at that time, Rev. John Darcy, lived in Rodeen House, Finnoe, now the home of the Flynn family.

Father Kennedy died in 1900. Fr Darcy became PP. He and his curate, Fr Murray, lodged in Hogans. When Fr Toohey came as curate he went to live in Mill

House; thereafter it was known as the 'curate's house'. When Rev. Michael Flannery lived there his housekeeper was Nora Carroll from Newtown. During his ministry, and that of his successor Rev. Michael McNamara, a big renovation was carried out on the house. Danny Tierney of Terryglass was in charge of the work, assisted by Jim Meagher and Frank Hough, 'Muddy's' son, who died shortly afterwards with tuberculosis.

In 1964 Mill House-cum-curate's house was sold on behalf of the parish to Dr Vincent Ryan, who had been Medical Superintendent of a tuberculosis sanatorium in Knaresboro', a beautiful village about three miles from Harrogate, North Yorkshire, England. Dr Ryan was a native of Co. Limerick. They renamed it Ballyfinboy House. His widow Aileen and daughter Mary still live there.

When Patrick Carroll the miller was accidentally killed he left eight young children. The eldest, Margaret, was the mother and grandmother of the Darcys of Ballinderry, Terryglass, and Bellevue. Four of the family – two boys and two girls – emigrated to the United States and did very well there.

Golden Days
The Darcys all grew up in Ballinderry; Trush (née Darcy) Lyons, has happy and very vivid memories of her childhood and of the people in Ballinderry she knew as she grew up. Trush spent a lot of her childhood with Nora Carroll, Fr Flannery's housekeeper, and when the house was being renovated she loved to hear 'Muddy' Hough's son Frank, who was working there, singing 'I'll Remember You Love In My Prayers'.

The Tierneys lived over the road from Trush in what is now The Tavern. There was John Tierney and his wife and John's brother Willie. Trush spent much of her spare time with John and Mrs Tierney and they had great fun. Mrs Tierney would go up in the apple trees and pick the apples. Trush would have the basket and then the Angelus bell would ring in Terryglass. All work stopped and Mrs Tierney gave out the Angelus in the apple tree and genuflected up there! Mrs Tierney loved children and Trush says it was a shame that she had no family.

Julia Dalton, M. Kennedy, Joe Clancy, Mrs Clancy, Biddy Clancy, Margaret Darcy.

Margaret Darcy, Nan Hogan, Bess Meehan, Rose Meehan, Nora Hogan, Mary Ann McShane, Mike Hough, Elsie Hogan, Lucy Hogan, taken in 1932.

There was a tiny little room in Tierneys. It was on the way up to the shop on the left and Mrs Tierney used to have a fire there at Christmas and on special occasions. She would send Trush down to the kitchen for more turf and Willie Tierney would give her a dirty look. He was always saving the turf. Mrs Tierney would roll around the place when she came back with two sods! John Tierney always seemed to get the first news if someone died and he immediately put up the half shutters on the outside of the shop window facing the street. The Darcys had a full view across the lawn and Trush would be sent to find out who had died.

Trush spent a lot of time with Mrs Dick Stanley too and also with the Clancys and, of course, at the post office. Another acquaintance was Bill Donoghue's grandfather Danno and uncle Jack who had lost a leg in World War I and was a great character. He could travel very fast on crutches and used chase the Darcy children down their lane. He could also ride a bicycle – I myself saw him ride a bicycle in a race at a sports.

The Tavern was run by Gerry and Ina O'Meara until 1997 when it was sold on and the name changed to The Pickled Pig. It is now leased to Philomena (née McKenna) Quigley, Borrisokane, who has revived its original name.

The Tavern was inherited in 1963 by Gerry's mother, Bridie Whelan, from her aunt Bridie (née Whelan) Tierney, whose mother was a Slattery from Ballinwear and a niece of John Tierney's wife. Bridie Whelan married Marty O'Meara whose mother was Mary Anne Hogan, Ryehill. The fine caravan park adjacent to the public house, developed by Marty and Bridie O'Meara in 1968, is now run by their son Seán. It was the first caravan park in North Tipperary.

I have long wondered about the origin of this public house. Marty and Bridie O'Meara told me the story of it. According to oral tradition it was originally a police barracks, but a long time ago – first half of the nineteenth century, I imagine. When the O'Mearas were renovating it some years ago they discovered that the large tap room, now the lounge, was the main part of the barracks and separate from the rest of the house, and that the lock-up was the little room out the back called 'Willie Tierney's room'. Over the years additional bits were added on to the pub so that the original barracks is buried in the modern building.

Fine, new bungalows have also been built along the road to Terryglass. At Clancy's Cross, the house which once was Clancys is now owned by Tadhg Cahalan. This is opposite the garage, petrol pumps and car sales founded by Bill Donoghue. He was succeeded by his son Kevin who recently sold it to Joe Hannigan of Kilbarron village, who has changed the garage to a supermarket. Kevin now carries on his business near his home.

Kennedys and Storeys

Trush has lovely memories of the Kennedys of the post office, Katie, Mary Anne and Bridget (in that order, l to r in the snapshot below). Katie was Trush's godmother. Her godfather was Stephen Kelly who died in Bushy Park nursing home, Borrisokane, in October 1998, aged ninety-five years. After the last of the Kennedy sisters died Trush discovered they had left her £15 in their will. After the Kennedys the post office was taken over and is still kept by Gertie (née Tierney) and her husband Mick Quinlan.

The three Kennedy 'girls' are immortalised in Pamela Hinkson's novel, *Irish Gold*, the outcome of her long sojourn with the Esmondes in Drominagh House and published in 1939. Pamela Hinkson was a daughter of the writer Katherine Tynan. It was what one would call 'historical faction', inasmuch as it was based on a real place and peopled with real people. It deals with various aspects of Irish life and several chapters deal with the immediate surroundings of Ballinderry and its inhabitants, many of whom appear in the book. Even though she changed the surnames they are easily recognisable.

She called Drominagh 'Golden Wood'. When I first saw Drominagh House I could see why. It was evening time and the setting sun was lighting up the grey stone of the elegant eighteenth-century outline and turning it golden. It was April and the park bloomed with daffodils.

The Donoghue family, who lived in the gate lodge to Drominagh House where 'Old Michael' was head gardener, figure largely in *Irish Gold*.

She wrote almost a full chapter on the three Misses Kennedy of the post office – thinly disguised as the Misses Hogan. Even though the

writing was sympathetic and complimentary to them and to their father Sylvester, they disliked intensely being 'put in the book' and returned their presentation copy by registered post.

The sisters, children of Sylvester and Kate (née O'Meara), were in their early to mid-forties at that time. Their father was a first cousin of Catherine Kennedy, Clooninihy, the only member of her family to survive the journey to America in 1848, as recounted in Jim Minogue's moving play, *Flight to Grosse Ile*. Heenans now live on the site of their house; a field is still known as 'Kennedy's Field'.

Pamela – or Miss Pam as she expected to be addressed – seems to have been curiously ignorant about the Ireland of the pre-Cromwellian era, attributing the building of all the tower houses she encountered to the Normans. She seems never to have heard of the O'Kennedys, apart from the girls in the post office. She also displayed a complete ignorance of Irish literature before the emergence of the 'Anglo-Irish' writers.

Bridgie Kennedy prepared Trush Darcy for the journey into the great wide world in the late 1930s. She advised her to get work in a post office and gave her her first lessons in how to use the telephone and send a telegram. They then got her a job with the Misses McCormack who had the post office in Moneygall in 1938/9. A fee of £40 had to be found and to this day she does not know how her mother scraped that amount of money together. The Misses McCormack kept a very close eye on her and she was never allowed to go out alone. She was allowed out just one night to the carnival dance for about half an hour and one of them came with her and sat inside the door. Trush later got a post in Co. Longford where she met and married Mel Lyons and had five children. They live in beautiful Ardagh which, like Terryglass, is a winner of the overall Tidy Towns award.

Trush's grandmother Carroll had a sister Mary who was reputed to have been a very beautiful girl. She married a David Storey, a member of the RIC stationed in Ballinderry in 1901. He was a Protestant. They lived in Shanbally House, had no children, and were comfortably off. Trush's grandmother was not in very good circumstances, being a widow with eight children. The Storeys were very good to her and she visited them often. She always referred to him as 'Mr' Storey, and to his two sisters (above), who visited sometimes, as the 'Miss' Storeys. When David Storey died he was buried in the Carroll plot in Terryglass old cemetery. Mary Storey died some time later. Trush's grandmother Carroll and Biddy and Ann Clancy were first cousins. Joe Clancy and her mother Margaret Darcy were second cousins. The Fox family were related, as also was Dick Stanley.

The Pump
The pump was erected circa 1895 by the combined initiative of Rev John Kennedy, PP, and James 'Guardian' Cahalan of Clooninihy. James was a member of Borrisokane Board of Guardians and so the family got the name 'Guardian' Cahalans. His grandson Patrick, who is now over eighty, still rides his bicycle to Mass in Borrisokane. According to Patrick, the Bracket Stone on the hill at Clooninihy on the rise above Cappinesmear lime kiln was said to have been a Mass rock. There is a path on top of Clooninihy called the 'White Horses'. It is said to have been a path the monks used going from Terryglass to Cloghprior. The grass is always better on the site of the path and the difference in colour can be clearly seen.

The 'Guardian' Cahalans were the last people to thresh with a horse-drawn steam thresher. It belonged to Costellos of Shanbally and, as a boy, Wilsie Nolan played on it in Shanbally yard in the mid-1920s. They were the first family in Terryglass parish to own a combined reaper and binder and cut corn for many neighbouring farmers. The remains of the reaper and binder still exist, lying in a ditch near the Cahalan house. My uncle Bill Carroll of Comenthus also had a 'horse power thresher'.

James Cahalan, another grandson of the 'Guardian', has a son Paddy. They are skilled tradesmen, carpenters and cabinet makers.

Ballinderry Today
Ballinderry has always been a picturesque village but today, after the work done by the various FÁS schemes, as well as the efforts of the inhabitants to beautify their homes, it is even prettier. The unusual cement fretwork trimming which decorates Kennedys' handsome house by the bridge, which was built by Tom Hogan, was done by Garda Benn and his brother. They also did similar decoration on Dick Stanley's house when it was built in 1926.

The new Lakeshore Foods buildings are in harmony with their older neighbours. Elsie Hogan's fine premises and house are enhanced by a beautiful garden.

Sources:
Civil Survey, 1654.
Nenagh Guardian, July 1846 (re Egan miller).
Ordnance Survey Letters, 1840. Primary Valuation Lists, 1852. 1901 census.
Pamela Hinkson, *Irish Gold* (London, 1939).
Patrick O'Farrell, *Vanished Kingdoms – Irish in Australia & New Zealand. A Personal Excursion* (1990).
TNFH research centre.
Elsie Hogan, Bill Donoghue, Michael Parkinson, Marty O'Meara, Patricia (Trush) Lyons, Hilary Henry.

Photographs: pp.259, 260, 264 taken by Paddy Carroll; pp. 262 loaned by Elsie Hogan; p. 265, sent by Patrick O'Farrell; p. 266, loaned by Mary Ryan; pp. 267, 268, 269, 270 loaned by Patricia (Trush) Lyons.

Kilgarvan Angling Club

The importance of Kilgarvan quay as a local port is illustrated in the account of Kilbarron hurlers and supporters taking off for distant places aboard a hired steamer on a Sunday afternoon to play a match. The quay had a Grand Canal Company stores (later known as Wallers') and an important commercial function, as evidenced by Daniel Grace in his *Portrait of a Parish: Monsea and Killodiernan*: 'But Dromineer was being superseded by Kilgarvan quay further up the lake as the chief point of dispatch for grain. Most of the barley was grown in the Borrisokane-Terryglass district and Kilgarvan was closer for shipping'. In his statistics for grain shipped out of the two quays in the 1913-15 period, Kilgarvan topped Dromineer in each of the years, sending 1,110 tons out in 1915 as against the latter's 320.

When the government of the young Irish Free State championed the growing of beet in 1925 the farmers of the parish almost all welcomed the scheme. Prior to the erection of the sugar factory in Thurles in 1934 beet grown in the area was sent to the Carlow factory. Beet would be carried in horses and carts to Kilgarvan quay, weighed on its weighbridge, then loaded on 'Barrow boats' – long narrow boats designed to operate on the river Barrow – and taken by them to Carlow, via the Grand Canal to Lowtown near Edendery and then down the Barrow canal link to Athy and the rest of the way by river.

As getting beet out the ground at that time was primitive in comparison to today's methods, each root must have carried its own weight of muddy clay in mid-November or early December. Bill Donoghue's grandfather, a dedicated gardener, would look sadly at the muddy loads, shake his head, and say, 'all that lovely Tipperary clay going down to Carlow'. The first leg of the journey, to the bridge at Portumna, took about an hour and a half.

One of Bill's tasks as a youth working at Kylenoe orchard was to drive a large float to the quay, drawn by a yellow cob called Charley, laden with apples for the Dublin markets. The apple auctioneers were J. Lightfoot & Sons, and during the war years (1939-45) boxes of apples fetched 28*s* (£1.40) per box.

Transport of cargo by water gradually declined and the canal company was wound up in the late 1950s. The last four store managers were: Martin Flannery, Johnny Kelly, Brian Graham and Thomas Heenan.

Put to Good Use
After this, local initiative soon brought about a new life for the redundant stores. This began with the foundation of Kilgarvan Anglers which emerged from a public meeting in Ballinderry in September 1969, convened by Tom Heenan, Richard O'Donoghue and Oliver Kennedy. The first officers were: Patrick Tierney, MCC, President; Basil Leenane, Chairman; Patrick O'Meara, vice-Chairman; Bernard Darcy, Secretary; Martin O'Meara, Assistant Secretary; Tom Foote, Treasurer; Tom Fox, Assistant Treasurer. Committee: Matt Fogarty, John O'Meara, Christopher Boyle, Richard O'Donoghue and Thomas Heenan. Soon they had a membership of a 92 adults and 8 juniors.

Kilgarvan quay had not faded into oblivion with its decline as a port. It became famous for its annual regatta, with the former stores utilised for music and dancing, and as a tranquil spot for locals and visitors to spend a Sunday afternoon.

The infant angling club soon swung into action and voluntary labour saw a sheltered harbour created for fishing boats, the acquisition and development of the former grain store for clubhouse facilities, and the replacement of the decayed timber jetties with concrete ones. Over the years facilities have been upgraded with on-shore lighting, toilets, drinking water, a new slipway and winter storage for boats.

Understandably, the club places most emphasis on enhancing the fishing facilities and organising fishing competitions for members and visitors. The club celebrated its twenty-fifth birthday in style in November 1994 when it was able to report a membership of 120 people.

Sources:
Nenagh Guardian.
Daniel Grace, *Portrait of a Parish: Monsea & Killodiernan.*
21st & 25th Kilgarvan Anglers' anniversary programmes.
Bill Donoghue to author.

The lake was a dominant aspect of lakeshore dwellers' lives, using it as a means of transport, and familar with its hazards, as these two stories illustrate.

SHANNON STEAMERS

An inspection of the *Fairy Queen*, the first of the new Shannon steamers, by the Commisioners of Public Works, took place on Tuesday afternoon.

The *Fairy Queen* is a stell [fixed] screw steamer and has been built under a special Board of Trade survey for passenger service. Her promenade deck extends her entire length, and she boasts a dining saloon capable of accommodating sixty persons. The patent steam cooker with which her bar is fitted calls for some notice, as it is capable of supplying 200 persons with tea within thirty minutes. The first-class saloon, richly upholstered in ruby plush and furnished with marble tables, occupies the after end of the steamer, and the windows of both the first and second class saloons are of plate glass, fitted in solid frames, thus affording an excellent means of viewing the scenery. – *Midland Tribune*, 10 May 1897.

A follow-up letter in the newspaper to this Press Release had the following observations to make on the 'Fairy Queen'.

> ... She may do very well for the narrow river but I question very much her sea worthiness to cross the broad Lough Derg in all weathers, so to command the confidence of the travelling public. Steamers, to be successful in developing passenger traffic on the Shannon, should to my mind be sufficiently long enough to cover three waves on Lough Derg in a gale, and have beam in proportion to her length, meantime she could be of light draught, say 4 feet to 4 feet 6 inches, with a speed of 14 miles out on the lake.
>
> Her light draught would enable her to run full speed over the fords. Low paddle steamers offer least resistance to the wind, therefore would be more suitable than screw-propelled boats. Such, for instance, as the late Shannon passenger steamer, the *Duchess of Argyle,* which belonged to the Midland Railway and did the running

between Killaloe and Athlone some thirty-five years ago. A like steamer would cross Lough Derg in all weathers, as she did, and command the confidence of the most cowardly on board. ...

Signed: 'Shannon Wave', Banagher, 10 May 1897.

GALLANT RESCUE ON LOUGH DERG IN NOVEMBER 1914

By degrees we hear of the damage done by the severe storm of Friday night last. The Lower Ormond district of Tipperary suffered much by the falling of timber, but the most exciting scene of all was witnessed on Friday evening in Lough Derg. It appears that early that day Steamer No. 13, with two barges, No.s 14 M and 15 M, belonging to the Grand Canal Company, left Portumna on their way from Dublin to Limerick.

The boats were buffetted about Lough Derg all day, and the crew had a terrible time, and little headway was made. When off Goat's Reef, Curraghmore Point, on the Tipperary side, the captain decided to make for the shore. In the attempt the two barges became submerged and the cargoes were swept overboard. The crews took refuge on the steamer, which had also got badly damaged. The terrified men raised cries for help, which, fortunately, were heard by Martin Cleary of Curraghamore, whose house is quite near the shore.

Mr Cleary with his brothers, Rody and William, immediately set to work, manned their boat and set out in the teeth of the gale. They first rescued six and, having landed them safely ashore, again went to the assistance of the others, and succeeded in bringing six to land. On a roll-call being made it was found that one of the crew was missing.

The brothers Cleary set out again and brought off the thirteenth man who happened to be in the engine room of the steamer, the hatch of which was battened down. No sooner had the boat got clear of the steamer, than the latter sank, the thirteenth man being a lucky number this time. Shortly after the rescue the wrecked boat was smashed to pieces on the rocks.

The rescued men were entertained and made comfortable by the Messrs Cleary. Some of them were also housed by the Misses Bruce, Lesseragh, until such time as they could get home.

During the storms other boats on the lake had to take refuge in the harbours on both the Tipperary and Galway shores. The brothers Cleary deserve great credit for their courage in rescuing these men, and it is to be hoped that their pluck will be recognised by the proper authorities. As far as the family knows this did not happen.
– *Nenagh Guardian*, 11 June 1914.

TERRYGLASS

Until the new church was built in 1886, the parochial house in 1905 and the new school in 1954, the buildings which made up the village were clustered together on the east side of the river in the townland of Terryglass. This townland extends into Lough Derg and, accordingly, has an extensive shoreline.

In the Tithe lists of 1824 the landlords in Terryglass parish were Firman, Sir Amylard Dancer, Talbot, Going and Monsell. The tenants names were largely of Gaelic origin – Meara, Brooder, Griffin, Cleary, Cahalan, Kennedy, Fogarty, Ryan, Carroll, Hough, Sammon, Tierney, Gleeson, Tuohy, Heenan, Halloran and Darcy.

In 1852 Edward Biggs figures as the 'immediate lessor' for most of the land in Terryglass in parish. Additional to the 1824 landlord names are Dempster, Kent, Watson and Messrs Saurin. The tenants names are much the same as in 1824. The holding of William Kennedy in Lacken townland, at 58 acres, was the largest amount held by a tenant of that name in any of the three parishes.

1840

John O'Donovan's Ordnance Survey Letters of 1840 contain some information on the village area. O'Donovan relied on local people for information. Edward Biggs of Castle Biggs/Drominagh and Rev. Benjamin Talbot were his local informants for most of Terryglass. Most of the tower houses and Big Houses which O'Donovan commented on have been dealt with in earlier chapters.

O'Donovan cites Kylenoe Wood as the property of the Globe Insurance Co. In Shanakill Lower & Upper Edward Biggs gave the information that he had a record of grants given in the reign of King Charles I. The record included the plantation plan which was devised during the reign of Charles I by his minister and financial

The house at the corner of Shannon Lane

advisor, Thomas Wentworth, later earl of Strafford. Charles was always short of money and this was a plan to raise some cash.

O'Donovan recorded that Terryglass townland '… abounds with forts, gravel pits, quarries, rocks and some plantations'. He described the holy wells, and other ruins, a schoolhouse (this must have been the private hedge school on Ballinderry road), burial ground and bridge, and the grianán (or solarium in Latin/a sunny place) on the right of Shannon Lane going down towards the lake. It is said that in later years there was a foundry on the site.

Curiously enough, there is no mention of the Church of Ireland church which had just been renovated and a tower added by Rev. Ralph Stoney.

In the Primary Valuation list of 1852 Rev. Benjamin Talbot of Ashgrove was the immediate lessor of the Church of Ireland church and graveyard (part of). This is the old cemetery which was attached to the pre-Reformation church and which lies in two different townlands, one part in Cornamult and one in Terryglass – only a small corner lies in Cornamult. Sir John Power (Bart) was lessor of the RC chapel and yard.

Twentieth Century

From the 1901 census which, thankfully, has survived in total, we can recreate the village as it was then and who lived in which houses. Houses, with or without businesses attached, were categorised 1st, 2nd, 3rd or 4th. At this time there was a national school in the former chapel, a post office, three public houses and a forge. There were also some private houses, e.g. Elmville, the very picturesque house of the Kent family beside the bridge.

Public Houses

The pub now known as 'Paddy's Bar' was kept by 55-year-old Daniel Whelan and his wife Anne, aged 45. Daniel was also a blacksmith and the forge was attached to the house. It is interesting to note that in 1852 a Denis Phelan had kept a forge at Roran – they may have been related, even father and son, the names Whelan and Phelan being synonymous. The Whelans kept the local schoolmaster, thirty-three year-old Co. Clare native, John Scales, as a lodger. He knew Irish and may have been a native speaker.

Before the Whelans the public house had been kept by Pat Heenan After the Whelans Pat Sammon had it until 1959, John Moloney up to 1966, Paddy Murray up to 1970, Paddy Wilkinson to 1977 when it got the name Paddy's Bar, Madeleine Mitchell up to 1988, P. J. Galvin up to 1992. Successive owners since then have been Michael and Mary Comerford, and Valerie Cotter and Conor Hyland.

The Derg Inn

In 1901 this pub was kept by Anne McGovern and the landholder was George Kent. It is rated as a 'first class' house, Paddy's having been only a second-class one! After Miss McGovern the house was taken over by her nephew Jim Glynn, who sold it in 1977 to James Brunnock.

In 1980 it was sold to Don Drennan and in 1985 to Madeleine Mitchell. In 1988 she sold it to Jerry Brennan who leased it to John Maher and later to Tom Sheridan, the present occupant.

The third public house was kept by Ellen Kennedy and her husband, the landholder being George Kent. It was a second-class house.

The Post Office
In 1901 the post office was kept by Pat Hogan and was a second-class house occupied by two people. It was situated in a little row of houses which are still there, opposite the present Old Church craft shop & gallery. Ellen Kennedy's public house was beside it.

In all there were twenty-six households in the townland of Terryglass: two first-class ones, twelve second-class, ten third-class and one fourth-class. Of these nine were their own ground holders. J. J. O'Flanagan, who lived at Old Court House, was ground holder of the national school. James Griffin, the carpenter who had been in charge of all the timber work at the building of the new RC church, was aged 50 and lived with his wife Catherine in Shannon Lane (below) James could read but not write; Catherine could do both.

The chapel-cum-school continued to be used until the new school was built in 1954. It then became a parish hall and in 1988 was completely renovated by Morcome Builders Ltd. Much of the money for the reconstruction was raised by giant auctions organised by the late Rev. P. J. O'Connor, CSSP, who came to the parish as curate after a lifetime on the missions.

Shannon Lane leads down to what was, in O'Donovan's day, a small boat quay on the shore of Lough Derg. Before the Terryglass Improvements Association got to work in 1949 the quay might have one or two boats. Shannon Lane itself had Egan's house on the top corner, the holy wells, and a few small cottages on either side farther down. Driving down Shannon Lane in June 1998 one might have been in the south of France. Lovely houses have been built at each side and the quay itself is extensive and beautiful. Another new jetty had just been completed and boats of all shapes and sizes, and indeed nationalities, were moored in the quays. John A. Weaving (1911-87), the noted Shannon sailor, river barge dweller and naturalist, who contributed so much to the conservation and improvement of the waterway, is commemorated by a bronze head sculpture sited on the quay and facing towards Slevoir and Portumna. The bust was erected by the Inland

Waterways Association of Ireland and his many friends.

Weaving, a bank official, gave up that post to devote his time to the rivers and canals. He worked on the building of the new jetty at Terryglass which was funded by the Co. Council in 1973. He was helped in this work by Oliver Darcy.

In the old days local transport on the lake was provided by Griffins of Terryglass. They had a large barge for hire. Local farmers travelled to Banagher to buy callow hay and bring it down by barge to Terryglass. Griffins had a mooring of their own as there was no quay as such in Terryglass. A survey of the lake in 1839 shows just a mooring for a boat. The quay was not made until about thirty years later.

ORGANISATIONS IN TERRYGLASS
Irish Countrywomen's Association (ICA)
– Memoir by Biddy Gleeson (née Kennedy, Brocka), founder-member.

Terryglass Guild of the Irish Countrywomen's Association (ICA) was founded in October 1949 by the chief organiser, the late Phyllis O'Connell from Fethard in South Tipperary. It was the first guild of this national organisation to be formed in North Tipperary. The officers were:

President	Angela Gaynor, 'Ardeevin', Borrisokane, wife of Wing-Commander George Gaynor.
Vice-President	Mai Flynn, Carrigahorig.
Hon. Secretary	Maggie Fox, Killeen, Terryglass.
Hon Treasurer	Alice Tierney, Ashgrove, wife of Mick.

The meetings took place on the first Wednesday of the month in what was then the national school – formerly the old chapel and now known as the Community Centre.

Fiftieth Anniversary, 1989
Back (l to r): Nance Horan, Maggie Hayes, Maggie Fox. **Front**: Maura Lavelle, Biddy Gleeson, Brigid Leenane. M. Lavelle and Mrs Leenane are since deceased.

It was the only night out for a lot of the ladies at that time. There were always demonstrations – of rush-work, traymaking, patchwork and crochet, horticulture and poultry-keeping. Cookery demon-strations were given by Eileen Murray (now Scroope), then a domestic economy teacher in Borrisokane Vocational school. One of the members would bring along a gas cooker for the demonstration. Most of the ladies travelled to the meeting by bicycle or walked. All meetings ended with a 'social half-hour' and a cup of tea made from water boiled on the open fire in the big black cast-iron kettle. The members brought the turf and logs for the fire. Everyone made sure she had plenty of tea leaves left in her cup (no convenience tea bags then!) as one of the members was an accomplished reader of fortune in tea leaves and it was always a great laugh.

The annual outing of the guild was to Salthill by car. A few of the members had their family cars, and the local hackney car, owned by Joe Harris, would be hired. The cars left Terryglass early on the morning of the outing loaded with picnic baskets. It was a great treat – all dining out on the sandy beach at Salthill. As the years went by they progressed to hiring a bus and went further afield to such places as Tramore, Ballybunion, Lahinch, Kilkee, Fota Wild Life Park in Cork, Powerscourt gardens and many other interesting places.

The guild did the catering for all the social functions in the hall including socials to raise funds for the renovation of the hall. Tickets for the socials were sold beforehand at 2s 6d (12.5p) each to give an idea of how many had to be catered for.

In 1973 the guild had a 'Tree for Peace' planted in the green patch in the square in Terryglass by Pat Harrold, Horticultural Instructor. Twenty-four years later it is still flourishing.

On Tuesday 5 November 1985, to mark the seventy-fifth anniversary of the foundation of the parent ICA, the guild organised an Ecumenical Service in the Church of the Immaculate Conception, Terryglass. The ceremonies were conducted by Rev. John Hogan, PP, Rev. P. J. O'Connor, CC, and Rev. Canon Camier, Rector of Borrisokane. The Service was attended by past and present members. The choir and organist were all members of the guild. Prayers were read by the then President, Chrissie Corboy, and other members. Two founder members, Biddy Gleeson and Bridie Leenane, read prayers for the sick and deceased members of the guild. The ceremony was followed by a social in the hall.

In 1989 the guild celebrated the fortieth anniversary of its foundation with a dinner dance in Dooley's Hotel, Birr, in October. Members and former members had a great night's entertainment. Six founder members were presented with framed Honorary Life Membership certificates in recognition of their service to the guild. They were: Bridie Leenane, Maura Lavelle, Maggie Hayes, Biddy Gleeson, Maggie Fox and Nancy Horan.

Improvements and Tidy Towns
The first meeting of what was to become known as the Terryglass Improvements Association took place on 18 September 1970. The stated object was to encourage the development of the quay, the harbour area generally, and Shannon Lane. The first committee was:

Jim Guest	Chairman
Paddy Wilkinson	Hon Secretary
Eileen Donoghue	Joint Hon. Secretary
Kevin Darley	Hon Treasurer

Committee: Tom Downey, Jack Egan, Bill Fox, Paddy Fox, Brigadier Séamus Hickie, Martin Horan, Marty Nevin, Michael Parkinson, P. J. Starr, Pat Walsh.

The same committee carried on for three or four years. About 1974 a meeting was held in conjunction with the local guild of the ICA. The Tidy Towns competition had to be entered through an organisation; Mrs Mary Donoghue of Lacken (formerly of Bellevue) and her daughter Eileen, had, at the instigation of Brigadier Hickie, been entering Terryglass village for some years under the aegis of the ICA branch.

At the joint meeting, on the proposal of Wilsie Nolan who had joined the Improvements Association in 1974, it was decided to amalgamate this body and the Tidy Towns group of the ICA. A collection was taken up of about 2s 6d (12.5p) each and this yielded £5. Jack Molloy had a digger and was given the £5 to do as much clearing up as he could. He cleared up a lot of rubbish which had accumulated in the harbour area which had been used as a dump. He did a half day's work for nothing to get the job finished.

In the very early 1950s – about 1951 – Muintir na Tíre had done the improvements already mentioned in the account of that organisation in relation to Kilbarron. This extended to putting a concrete surround around St. Augh's well to keep the cattle from trampling in it. Amenity grants became available and these were applied for and secured from the County Council and Shannonside Tourism. The County Council started a group water scheme and most of the material dug up when laying the pipes was used as infilling in the harbour area and it was all levelled out. A dragline (a big digger), being used for dredging at Kilgarvan quay by Kilgarvan Angler's Association, was brought down and did £80's worth of work to clear the harbour.

Overall 'Tidiest Town', 1983 and 1997

Terryglass Improvements Scheme continued with various projects. Each year

Celebrating at Malahide Castle, 1983
Madeleine Mitchell, Bridie Darcy, Bobbie Mitchell, Oliver Darcy, Maura Lavelle, Biddy Gleeson, Mary Nevin, Monnie Hogan, Pake Lavelle, Maggie Hayes, Nora Hogan, Kitty Egan.

they kept entering for various awards and gradually higher marks were gained in the national Tidy Towns competition. In the meantime more people became involved. The area won individual awards. In 1981 Mrs Bridie Darcy won the award for best rural post office in the country, while Bobby and Madeleine Mitchell's Paddy's Bar won the Pub of the Year Award. In 1982 the Rent-an-Irish-Cottage scheme was finished. Terryglass was on the map of Ireland in a big way.

In 1983 came the final accolade – the overall award for 'tidiest town' in Ireland. This brought great rejoicing and Terryglass became very well known. New families came to live there and some quite luxurious homes were built, many in Shannon Lane. Overseas visitors were attracted and Terryglass is now quite a cosmopolitan village. The deconsecrated Church of Ireland church was purchased by Tom and Lucy (née Wilkinson) Sanders and converted into a residence, pottery and craft shop. The Sanders later sold it to Jeremy Castles and his wife, the well-known landscape artist Jenny Boelens. The Sanders then built a splendid modern guesthouse – 'Riverrun House'. The builder was Christy Cormican, Coolbawn. The design of the guesthouse fits in with the existing landscape and enhances the beauty of the surroundings.

Since 1983 the village has been a consistent prize winner at county, regional and national levels and in 1998 they emerged as the overall national winner once more.

Part of the prize for the 1983 win was an Arts Council commissioned sculpture. This can be seen on the grass verge of the main road opposite Kent's farmyard. It consists of granite blocks and a heron, by Gerard Cox.

Above: The Presentation of the Award in Terryglass in 1983. (l to r): Sean Browne, Shannonside Tourism, Rev. John Hogan, PP, Rev. Thomas Comerford, CC, John Leenane, NT, John McGinley, Co Manager, Tipperary (NR) Co. Council, John Ryan, TD, David Moloney, TD, Michael O'Kennedy, TD.

Sources:
Civil Survey, 1654; Primary Valuation; 1901 census.
Wilsie Nolan, Michael Pakinson, Biddy Gleeson.

Photographs: pp. 275, 277, 281, 282, loaned Wilsie Nolan; pp. 278, 280, loaned by Biddy Gleeson; p. 283 taken by Paddy Carroll.

The Arts Council's commissioned sculpture.

Wilsie Nolan, Chairman, receiving the first Lotto grant for communal projects (the hall), 1992-3, from Michael O'Kennedy, TD. **Back:** Michael Hough, MCC, Jim Guest, Sadie Tierney, Tony Fox, John Downey, Oliver Darcy, Pake Leenane, Cosi Zcenema, –, Basil Leenane, Raymond Molloy, Eileen Cahalan, P. J. Starr. **Front:** Tom Downey, Rev. P. J. O'Connor, CC, Senator Tony McKenna, Jim Casey, MCC, ex-Senator Liam Whyte.

Carrigahorig

This border village is located in the extreme north of the townland of Garryclohy where it meets Firmount and Ballyquirke. A few of its houses are in Kilbarron-Terryglass parish, but once across the Ballyfinboy river bridge one is in Lorrha parish.

At first the police barracks for the area was in what is now the Tuning Fork Restaurant and so in our parish. It was then moved to a building across the river and so in Lorrha parish. The building (below) is still there, though now an outhouse. I don't know the exact date of removal but the RIC were in the Lorrha building during the War of Independence, 1919-21. It was on an elevated site behind and between Hough's pub (now O'Meara's) and Sammons, now The Waterfall.

After the famous rescue of Seán Hogan at Knocklong railway station in during the War of Independence in 1919, members of the rescue party, Dan Breen, Seán Hogan, and possibly Seán Treacy, were on the run and stayed at Houghs for at least a week. The police were looking down into the yard and could see them out for a walk every morning but they kept silent about it in order to save their own lives. William Parkinson of Slevoir was ordered by the IRA to have his boat ready at the mouth of the river to take them across the lake to Woodford to safe houses if trouble arose, but everything passed off quietly.

Some RIC

Sergeant David Lavelle was married to Hannah O'Sullivan, a native of Co. Kerry, and they had twelve children, the youngest, Claire, born in 1894. A son married a Tierney of the Rock. They were the parents of Maura Lavelle and her brothers.

Sgt. Nicholas. Corish, 1898-1901 who transferred from Ballinderry.
Sgt. Owen Pathe, 1902-20.
Constable Connolly, 1900-1908.

Prior to serving in Carrigahorig Owen Pathe was stationed in Nenagh where eight of his nine children were born. All of the Pathe children and their mother, Mrs Anastasia Pathe (née Sullivan), emigrated to the USA. Three of the boys became priests. Some of the girls returned to Ireland; Eileen settled in Roscrea where her son now lives.

One of the children was Rev. Michael Pathe (1892-1971) who emigrated to America in 1910 to join the Redemptorist order of priests. He was ordained in Oconomowoc, Wisconsin, in 1916. He went on to become an eminent missionary, travelling for over forty years throughout the United States and in Canada and noted for his oratorial skills and singing voice. In 1929 Michael made his first, and only, return visit to Ireland in the company of his mother and priest-brother Timothy. The country and its people enraptured him so much that he recorded his impressions and experiences in a little book, entitled *A Summer In Ireland*, which was published in the USA in 1931.

> There is a little village with the big melodious name of Carrigahorig. I had spent much of my boyhood there. To the casual visitor there is nothing very attractive about this village. But to me it was the 'open sesame' to a thousand pleasant memories. Up that hill we trudged our daily way to the school in Terryglass, to meet the children from Kilbarron and Ballinderry, to see John Scales, the good old teacher, and 'read the day's disaster in his morning face'. ... The schoolhouse is there – the same as ever. Some of the old schoolmates of nearly thirty years ago were now the owners of property in and about the village. And their little children occupied the places where we drew our maps, or laboured through fractions. ...
>
> Back to Carrigahorig. In that river, at the foot of the hill, we played. It was our barefoot trail. We caught the speckled trout, we trapped the wild ducks here ... Against the side of Bridge House we fought our handball tournaments. From Flynns to Houghs we showed our prowess in cycling. In Donoghue's mill we tramped the drying corn. Under the bridge we probed for eels or hid from an angry parent. ... But the river is now smothering in grass – no children's busy feet to keep it down. The bridge is deserted and the waterfall sings a lonely song. Old friends were there to greet me. I fear they sometimes thought that America had changed me. Ah, they never knew how much I loved that village and its people. ...

Fr Pathe was closely associated with the nine-day Perpetual Help public novena in the 1920s. He re-introduced the concept in 1943. The response to it everywhere it was held was phenomenal. In the cathedral of Detroit it was conservatively estimated that up to 15,000 attended Mass daily.

As he grew older and his travelling had to be curtailed he specialised in week-end retreats, giving only occasional week-long missions. The last of these was in 1970. He died with the Holy Redeemer community in Detroit in September 1971.

Mills
In the *Civil Survey* we are told that 'upon the river of Inyhy [Ballyfinboy] standeth two decayed mills belonging to Bryan Kennedy'. These may well have evolved to become the two which appear on the Ordnance Survey map in the vicinity of Carrigahorig village – one in the townland of Garryclohy on the Terryglass side of the river and the other in Ballyquirke and Lorrha parish. Samuel Palmer is

returned as the occupier of the former in the Primary Valuation list, with the representatives of T. P. Firman the 'immediate lessor'. The entrance is beside the restaurant on the Kilbarron-Terryglass side of the river. The mill has recently been converted into a family residence by Tom Sheridan of the Derg Inn, Terryglass.

A flour mill with the exotic, and unexplained, name of Santa Cruise, sometimes spelt Santa Cruz, meaning Holy Cross, also appears on the Ordnance survey map and is also mentioned in Lewis's *Topographical Dictionary* of 1837 and in O'Donovan's Letters. It was fed by water diverted into a mill race below the bridge. Though the mill entrance is on the Portumna side of the bridge, it is in the townland of Firmount and, accordingly, in our parish. In 1850 Samuel Palmer was also the occupier and the representatives of Thomas P. Firman the landlords. The Firmans were the owners of the house at Firmount and were absentee landlords. The first Parkinson came from Dublin about 1800 as steward to Firman.

This one, also known as O'Donoghue's mill, was demolished a few years ago and the stone sold for wall building but the mill race is still intact. The mill house is lived in by Colm Keane.

Rickard Deasy

Rickard Deasy (right) put Carrigahorig on the map when, in 1966, as President of the National Farmers Association and leader of the Irish Farmers' Rights campaign, he was instrumental in bringing 30,000 farmers from all parts of Ireland to Dublin seeking to establish negotiating rights with the Department of Agriculture. They were successful in their aims and thereafter took an active role in the establishment of proper marketing structures for Irish agricultural produce.

Rickard Deasy was born in Dublin in 1916 to Hugh Peter (known as Peter) and Dolores (née Hickie, Slevoir) Deasy. Peter Deasy grew up in Carysfort House, Blackrock, Co. Dublin, which later became the teacher training college. His father died young and he was left in the charge of two tutors from the O'Connor Don family. These two were religious fanatics and to excape their clutches the young Peter joined the British army which was not at all a tradition in the Deasy family, unlike the Hickies. He was sent to India but did not like the peacetime army life there and after five years left and went exploring in the Himalayas, parts of which he mapped. He rejoined the army during World War I, but as he was then too old he was given tedious clerical jobs. In May 1916 he was working in Dublin Castle and in charge of the whole place at night.

By this time almost all of the insurrectionaries holding the rank of Commandant had been executed.

Among the others sentenced to death was Eamon de Valera. Attempts were being made to have him reprieved on the grounds that he was an American citizen, but the reprieve had not come through.

As Major Deasy made his rounds in the Castle he found a heap of signals beside the signalling machine which had been neglected. The first on the heap was a reprieve for de Valera. He took immediate steps to see that the document reached the relevant authority in time and de Valera lived to fight another day.

In 1930 Peter and Dolores Deasy and their family moved to Firmount/Cnoc na Faire, Carrigahorig, which until then had been part of the Hickie estate.

Their son Rickard was educated at Ampleforth College and Oxford University where he read PPE (politics, philosphy and economics). He joined the Irish Defence Forces in 1939 as a private and retired with the rank of Captain at the end of The Emergency in 1945. He then took over the family farm. His father, Peter Deasy, died in 1947.

Rickard Deasy is married to Sheila Marie O'Kelly of Gurtray, Portumna, and they have four children.

They have been called the 'Sixpenny' Deasys because of the following traditon. During the Cromwellian persecution the Deasys were wiped out but for one woman with her infant son, a few weeks old. In the words of Rickard's great-grandfather, 'one soldier still had a bit of humanity left in him, if only to be bribed'. She gave him her last sixpence and fled to West Cork (somewhere between Clonakilty and Timoleague) where she reared the child who was to be the ancestor of the Deasys.

Sources:
Civil Survey.
1901 Census.
OS Sheets 6 & 7.
Primary Valuation.
TNFH research centre.
Rev. Michael Pathe, *A Summer in Ireland.*
Eamon Horan, Roscrea, son of Eileen Pathe.
Michael Parkinson, Ricardo Deasy, Marie Deasy.

Photograph: p.283, taken by Bridget Adams, Tunbridge Wells.
p. 285, loaned by Marie Deasy.

The Landlord and Tenant Law (Amendment) (Ireland), 1860, was known as Deasy's Act, after the Rt. Hon. Richard Deasy, Irish Attorney-General, grandfather of Rickard Deasy.

Later a judge, his portrait hangs in the Four Courts, Dublin. The above photograph of it was made by Wilsie Nolan, Terryglass.

11
Parish Personalities

PADDY TIERNEY
SOLDIER, FARMER, SENATOR & TD

Paddy Tierney's roots were deep in the soil of Lower Ormond and in Ballyscanlon. In the Hearth Money Rolls for 1665 there is a 'Philip Terney de Kilbaran'. Paddy Tierney's is still the only Tierney family in Kilbarron although the name abounds in Terryglass. In 1850 John Tierney, Paddy's grandfather and a blacksmith, had a house, forge and 12 acres 39 perches of land in Ballyscanlon. In 1883 Mrs Bridget Tierney, Ballyscanlon, Paddy's grandmother, is named as one of the farmers in the postal district of Coolbawn. In 1901 an aunt, Mary Tierney, had a shop in Ballyscanlon. They were known as Tierneys of the Stream (pronounced locally 'strame'), because a stream ran by their house. Paddy's father was also a blacksmith and it is likely that the trade went farther back than the grandfather.

Paddy's father, also called Paddy, became involved in agrarian agitation during the Land War of the late 1870s or early 1880s. Looking across the lake from Ballyscanlon the uniforms of the soldiers could be seen glinting in the sun as they guarded the bailiffs who were evicting the earl of Clanrickarde's tenants on the Co. Galway shore. Paddy described to Patricia Feehily, in her excellent interview with him for the *Nenagh Guardian*, 23 October 1978, how his father went across the lake to help the Galway tenants. He came to the notice of the police and had to leave home, moving first to Portlaoise and then on to Newbridge, Co. Kildare. He married Anne Doyle, a native of Kilcullen, and followed his trade as blacksmith.

On 24 April 1904 Paddy was born. In 1916 at the age of 12 Paddy joined Fianna Éireann, the republican youth organisation. As the republican movement got going again after 1916 he acted as a dispatch rider. After the signing of the Treaty in December 1921 he was a member of the Free State Army (below) who took over Beggars Bush barracks from the British forces, having been issued with one of the very scarce green uniforms of the new State.

When the Free State troops attacked the Four Courts which the anti-Treatyites had taken over he decided to go with the latter but had to stay in the army uniform as he had nothing else to wear. After a week of bloody fighting between the two sides in which some of the finest buildings in Dublin were destroyed the Free State troops took over the city and the fighting moved out into the countryside. *The Civil War 1922-23* by Eoin Neeson, p. 134, recounts that 'the 6th Kildare Brigade (anti-Treaty) went to Ballymore Eustace, a small village in Kildare west of Blessington, commanding the Naas approach and the main road from Dublin … when Blessington was occupied the men of the Kildare Brigade held a line extending from Kilteel near Blessington to Coolcarrigan … cutting the main Curragh-Dublin road.'

Paddy Tierney was acting as a dispatch rider in this area. He was sent to Coolcarrigan with a dispatch and told to get there before dark so that he could be identified. He got delayed, arrived after dark and was shot by mistake. The bullet passed right through his body below the breast bone.

He was taken to Naas General Hospital (at this stage both sides in the war were still behaving in a civilised fashion) and placed under heavy guard. He had been carrying a gun. Eventually he escaped from the hospital with the help of Nan Sheehan, whose brother is still alive and verified this story a short while ago in a letter to May Tierney. He was put in the well of a pony and trap and brought to Tommy Harris's house (later Tom Harris, TD) in Caragh where he was hidden.

When news came that the Harris house was to be raided he was placed in a manhole until the raid was over. The following day he was to be sent to a hide-out at a place called Mooresbridge near the Curragh where five other men were also hiding out. His mother, on hearing of this arrangement, was not happy as his wound was not healed and still needed attention. She arranged for his brother-in-law Christy Kennedy, who drove an oil lorry, to drive Paddy to his Aunt Kate Tierney's house in Ballyscanlon. As it happened the other five men in the hideout were captured. I have been told they were later executed but am not sure about this because the summary executions came later in the Civil War.

When Paddy arrived at his Aunt Kate's he was still very weak and the wound had not healed. A Cumann na mBan nurse, Nonie McDonnell of Carrigatoher, who later married Jim Sullivan, Kickham St., Nenagh (now Rocky's), came down regularly to dress the wound until it was healed. The late Pat Carroll of Brookfield, the Tierneys' nearest neighbours, remembered Paddy when he first came. He was still wearing a tattered army uniform and could hardly walk. Pat must have been a very small boy then and when I commented on this fact to him, he said, 'I used hear them talking about it.' The good Shannon air, and his Aunt Kate's bacon and cabbage and homemade bread and butter, soon had him on his feet again.

From the beginning Paddy was a great favourite with all his neighbours and remained so until the day he died. He loved playing cards and every evening there would be a card school going at Kate Tierney's. At this time Paddy was still only eighteen years old. Kate had a workman, a Galwayman called Tom Kildea. When Paddy's mother wrote to Paddy from their Kilcullen home she addressed the letter to Tom Kildea. Paddy helped around the farm and he was very mechanically minded. Peter Carroll, his neighbour, had acquired a model T-Ford but had not the slightest idea how to drive or manage it. He treated it as if it were a pair of horses. Paddy drove Peter around and taught him to drive.

Into Politics
When eventually de Valera formed the Fianna Fáil party and led his followers into Dáil Éireann in 1927, Paddy took up politics again and organised a Fianna Fáil cumann in this parish. Church gate collections were the only way of collecting money at the time and Fianna Fáil was badly in need of money. The parish priest of the time, and nearly all the clergy, were very anti-Fianna Fáil. You might even say it was an obsession with this particular man. I suppose it was hard to blame him

after a bloody civil war. I myself remember vividly a sermon he gave before either the 1932 or 1933 election in which he thundered at us – the congregation – that 'we were to vote for our good government!'

One Sunday around 1928 the Fianna Fáil party decided to have a church gate collection in Kilbarron. Their table was placed outside what was then Quinlan's shop, now the carpark at the side of the church gate. It was manned by Paddy Tierney, Danny Gleeson of Lahesseragh, and Jack Whelan of the Hill, later of Gurteen. The parish priest got his driver to drive right up near the table – normally he would have driven into the chapel yard – then got out and aimed a vicious kick at the table. There was money on the table but the boys had seen the PP coming. Danny Gleeson had the presence of mind to lean with all his might on the table and it held firm. The money did not get scattered. Afterwards in the sacristy the PP grumbled to the altar boys that he had hurt his toe in the process. Paddy did not go to Mass for a long time afterwards.

It would appear that a similar incident had occurred at Terryglass the Sunday before when the 'boys' manning the table were not prepared and the money got scattered all over the footpath. To us in Kilbarron and Terryglass at that time Paddy Tierney was the face of republicanism, 'a soldier of the legion of the rearguard'. In 1930 he married May Grady, the only daughter of a neighbouring farmer. They had a long and happy, if sometimes hard, life together until his death in 1990, aged 86. They had fifteen healthy children and May, who was younger than Paddy, is still hale and hearty.

Into Labour

Paddy remained a Fianna Fáil supporter until 1939 but failed to get a Fianna Fáil nomination to contest the Tipperary (NR) County Council election. In any case he was becoming disillusioned with the party. His natural place was in the Labour Party and he had great admiration for Dan Morrissey, TD, Nenagh, who, he recalled in his interview with Patricia Feehily, 'was the first to take the labouring man in North Tipperary off his knees'. Paddy had been influenced also by his near neighbour Peter Carroll who had been for a short time a Labour member of the County Council. He too had worked all his life for the labouring man, having been a close associate of Dan Morrissey and having helped Ned O'Donoghue of Toomevara to get the workmen's insurance scheme underway.

During the 1922 general election Sinn Féin had endeavoured to prevent the Labour Party from putting up Dan Morrissey as a candidate for Tipperary. They then abducted Peter Carroll and several other of Dan's personating agents, taking them out of their beds at crack of dawn on the morning of the election, and shutting them up in Garrane House near Ballinderry village until the election was over.

Councillor

In 1939 Paddy won a Tipperary (NR) County Council seat for Labour, being easily elected for Borrisokane electoral district. He remained a member until 1974, having being at one stage in the chair for five successive years, 1950-5, as the only acceptable candidate to both Fine Gael and Fianna Fáil councillors.

Always active in council proceedings, he was particularly so during the long drawn out 'degrouping' debate which went on from July 1955 to January 1969. Tipperary had been divided into two halves, or ridings as they were called, in 1838.

They were virtually two normal-sized counties but with only one County Manager after the County Management Act had been passed in 1940. John P. Flynn who resided in Nenagh, was County Manager, while Pádraig de Buitléir, the Assistant County Manager resided in Clonmel. Some councillors were now advocating that each riding should have its own Manager. The whole saga has been told in some detail in Donal A. Murphy's *The Two Tipperarys*. Of Paddy Tierney he wrote:

> Paddy Tierney, Senator in 1956 and TD from 1957 to 1969, was trenchantly against degrouping initially. He mellowed to the extent of abstaining, though recording his dissent, in December 1964, simply abstaining in 1966, and rowing in with the unanimous opinion not to degroup in 1968.
> Nov. 1964 – As it was there were far too many County Managers in the country – he never agreed with the Managerial Act anyway.
> Dec. 1964 – He hoped that he was not hitting too hard but he believed it was the truth that they would finish up with two County Managers and two Assistant Managers for County Tipperary. If they thought that the Manager resided too far away, that Council and South Tipperary County Council could pass a resolution that he reside in Thurles and be accessible to both counties.
> Interpreting Tierney, one must recall that he was by nature agin-the-Establishment, whoever and wherever. He had been, in the Flynn era prior to those quoted opinions, the veteran of a hundred public rounds vis-a-vis that Manager. They were well-matched – assertive, combative, often abrasive; debate often livened and lightened with a mischievous wit and throwaway phrase; each informed and incisive – frequently on practical nuances which never reached print in local newspapers with a councillor-bites-manager news sense; each, out of the arena, capable of considerate human relations (remembered by many for the big heart and the good turn) with a mix of genuine charm and purposeful *plamás*.

This is a very good interpretation of Tierney the public man. He was one of the four Labour candidates to contest the 1943 Dáil Election when County Tipperary was one constituency with seven seats available. It was then one of the largest constituencies in the country and Paddy had to travel its roads entirely on a bicycle while canvassing. He told Patricia Feehily that he was the only one of the four Labour candidates with a bit of property and that his aunt had to sell three pigs to pay their solicitor. He was eliminated on the twelfth count. He did not contest the 1944 or 1948 elections and was again defeated in the new constituency of Tipperary North in its first election in 1951 and again in 1954. It was not until Dan Morrissey retired from politics in 1957 that he was finally elected to Dáil Éireann. Dan held the Labour vote even after his leaving that party and being successively on the Cumann na nGaedheal and Fine Gael tickets. This vote now went to Paddy.

Senator
Although unlucky in the Dáil election of 1954 he was elected to Seanad Éireann, gaining the final seat on the Labour panel. Seanad Éireann was a complete change of scene for Paddy as he entered it on 22 July. He made his first speech there on 25 November, supporting a motion that all British parliamentary elected members should be allowed an audience in the houses of the Oireachtas. He didn't debate much in the Seanad. However, when he did he wasn't one to 'sit on the fence'. He

enjoyed success in the House on 17 January 1957 when a motion of his was adopted by the Minister for Lands, Joe Blowick. Paddy's motion argued that future divisions of land under the Land Commission should take into consideration claims of cottage holders. He believed it to be unfair that in these divisions, 'smallholders were brought in from four or five miles away, while twelve or thirteen cottage holders living on these lands did not get as much as an acre'.

Teachta Dála

His election to Dáil Eireann in 1957 was to be the first of three consecutive successes. He entered the Dáil for the first time on 20 March. He was of the genre of 'ex-freedom fighters' who were present at the time in almost all parties across the political spectrum. Predominantly, it was the needs and issues of the people of Tipperary that Paddy took up, leaving the national issues to the more experienced members of the chamber. That is not to say that he didn't make such a contribution.

His first major speech in the Dáil was on 6 June 1957 on the Health and Mental Treatment Bill, in which he opposed the increase in hospital charges. He didn't let the occasion pass to put one over on his former party, Fianna Fáil, who were then in government.

> ... when the government gets into difficulties and wants to make a saving, it is at the expense of the poorer sections the saving is made ... while the Labour Party advocated that the poorer sections of our community should be helped.

Paddy paid particular attention to such areas as unemployment, emigration, housing, agriculture, and social welfare. Speaking on 30 April 1958, he made his best speech to the Dáil, when he appealed to the political parties to put aside their differences and unite in dealing with the unemployment problem.

> Is it not time to make a joint effort, and some sacrifice, to help to get us out of our present difficulties? Is it not a fact that all our parties seem to have lost their love of country and to harbour instead a love of party? I appeal to all parties here to co-operate to put this little country back on the map and make our economy one in which we shall not be like the old age pensioners and others, waiting for remittances to come from England from the emigrants who were forced to leave this country.

As one can see, emigration was another issue on which Paddy felt very strongly. On 16 December 1960 he made a very aggressive attack on the government's policy in this area and warned them:

> If the flight from our shores, of all our able-bodied young men and women, continues at its present rate, in a few years we will have a nation of very old people with very few young people. That is the rock upon which we will perish.

Having established himself in Dáil Éireann, Paddy held his seat in two more general elections, coming in third in 1961 behind John Fanning (FF), and in 1965 second behind Mary Bridget Ryan (Lacken) (FF). In early October 1966 Paddy wasn't slow to attack the Fianna Fáil government on their housing record in North

Tipperary. He went on to say in his satirical style:

> We were always led to believe that any government other than Fianna Fáil were short of money, but that the Fianna Fáil government had an abundance of money. We find in North Tipperary, in Thurles, Roscrea and Nenagh, and in rural areas a waiting list of up to at least 200 priority cases for housing.

During a debate on agricultural produce, Paddy rather surprised the Minister for Agriculture Patrick Smith with his knowledge of European affairs. He asked the Minister to respond to the comments of a Dr Sicco Mansholt at the EEC conference on Regional Economics, who was warning against the promotion of easy forms of agricultural produce and the subsequent subsidies which would be needed to sell them. Needless to say, the Minister's answer was unsatisfactory!

However, throughout his Dáil career, Paddy's 'pet' subject was pleading the case of the old IRA pensioners. Paddy congratulated one minister 'for recognising the group of people who made this house possible and without whose help none of us would be here. I refer to the old IRA'. Paddy was no doubt thinking of his own 'ex-comrades in arms' when speaking on this issue.

Defender of the Constitution

In one of his final speeches to the Dáil, Paddy pleaded the case against Fianna Fáil's wish to abolish the proportional representation electoral system by an amendment to the Constitutuion, *Bunreacht na hÉireann*. In his simple style, Paddy hit a note of realism when he introduced his thoughts on the debate:

> Knowing Fianna Fáil for a long number of years, when I heard that they wished to abolish P.R. again, I wondered what was behind the move. I know Fianna Fáil do not have the country in mind. Fianna Fáil come first and the country comes after.

Paddy went on to say that P.R. kept alive the healthy element of competition between TDs for the representative job they are paid for. However, if P.R. was abolished he argued that TDs (most probably Fianna Fáil TDs) would monopolise elections and leave people with no choice. He went on to claim rather ironically, what he would do if he was a TD under the proposed single vote system:

> I would make it my business to pick out the people with the widest connections and I would work for them. In that way I would build up a huge vote, possibly dishonestly.

He then went on to analyse why Fianna Fáil wished to abolish P.R.

> Over the past 30 years Fianna Fáil have got a huge grip on the older people in particular. Every job – rate collector, water-inspector or anything else – was in the giving of Fianna Fáil because they had the majority on most of the local authorities.
>
> The reason Proportional Representation is being abolished is that the younger people are not so easily influenced as people were in the past. They are better educated and more intelligent and they will not countenance graft or corruption.

As it turned out, Paddy was correct. The new generation kept proportional representation in the referendum which followed.

Life in Dáil Éireann

Paddy was very well liked by his fellow members for his witty style. He told a story against himself about his first encounter with James Dillon, ex-Minister for Agriculture, businessman, acknowledged as the last of the great Irish parliamentary orators, and an imposing patrician figure. It was Paddy's first day in Leinster House. In a corridor the new arrival, the small farmer from Lower Ormond, met the statesman and deferentially asked the way to the toilet. James Dillon looked over his glasses and said – according to Paddy, and perhaps he did – 'Go to the end of that corridor, turn left, and you will see a door marked "Gentlemen" - but don't let that deter you.'

It is from about that time too that the story comes of himself and County Manager Flynn both getting their tickets at Nenagh railway station. Flynn was in front and booked for the first-class carriage. He moved away and Paddy ordered 'third-class – do you know why I want third?' The booking clerk, sure he was on the scent of an anti-manager revelation, obligingly asked, 'Why?' The answer: 'Because there's no fourth class'.

Paddy had a friendly relationship with his North Tipperary colleague, Mary Bridget Ryan. There was a rivalry between the two but it was never bitter, possibly because both believed in helping anyone they could, regardless of political allegiance. The two often received one another's letters, asking for help, having been sent to the wrong address. They laughed over those. Paddy always maintained that the public were too much under the illusion that TDs 'got things done'. Usually, he argued, it was just a case of convincing people of what they were entitled to. People, however, liked the insurance of having a TD's backing.

Paddy enjoyed his time in Leinster House. He particularly enjoyed the visit of President John F. Kennedy in 1963. He was a member of inter-party delegations to visit Tel Aviv and Ottawa. His wife May says, however, that though he enjoyed his career, it was never easy. There was one small comfort in those years; the Tierneys were one of the few houses to have a telephone. May remembers well: their number was 6. He was always in Dublin from Tuesday to Thursday at least, and the allowances for expenses then were not generous. Towards the end of his career, his salary had still only reached £2,000. There were fifteen children to feed and clothe and the farm was small. It is no surprise that when asked by Patricia Feehily what his greatest moment in the Dáil was he replied 'my greatest moment was when I drew my first salary'.

That answer, self-mocking but with a grain of realism, was matched by his canvassing ploy for one of the later election campaigns: 'Missus, this time it's either Leinster House or the poorhouse'.

His political heroes were Dr John O'Connell, Dr Noel Browne, Tom Coyne and Dan Spring. The few Labour TDs shared one office. He was on good terms with Brendan Corish and was on very good terms with Steve Coughlan of Limerick and Dan Spring of Tralee. He and Dan shared the same republican background. When Dan's youthful son Dick was at Trinity he would come down to Leinster House in the lunch hour and he and Paddy got to know one another well. It was no surprise therefore that on the pouring wet day we buried Paddy, the tall, slightly stooped figure of An Tánaiste stood by the graveside and gave the funeral oration.

Retirement

Everyone expected Paddy to run as usual in the 1969 general election. He went to the constituency convention and was nominated. It is understood, however, that Paddy perceived pressure there to stand down and consequently he decided 'on the spot' not to let his name go forward. In the subsequent election, the party felt the loss of his large personal vote and saw their vote drop by 40 per cent on the 1965 figure – and the loss of the seat.

He continued as a member of Tipperary (NR) County Council until 1974. However, in July 1971, he left the Labour party and became an Independent Labour member. His reasoning was that the national leadership was not presenting the party in the way it should have been.

In retirement, the humour – often at his own expense – was still there. Pádraig Dolan in a Radio Éireann interview asked him how he then divided his time between his occupation as farmer and his favourite hobby of fishing. Paddy replied, 'When the Lord made the world, he made it ten per cent land and ninety per cent water – and I try to follow the Lord's example'.

After his eventful life, he had no regrets except possibly for not realising sooner that the Civil War was a 'no win' situation. He blamed the leaders on both sides for letting it happen. In an interview in the late 1970s, he said 'they should have been locked into a walled garden ... and let them shoot it out between them'. He remained a republican, however, until his death on 29 September 1990. He was aged 86.

Most of all, Paddy Tierney was a labourers' man, who did his best for the considerable 'working class' and underprivileged peoples of North Tipperary. He certainly deserved to spend his final years living beside and fishing on his beloved Lough Derg. Upon his death, his fellow North Tipperary councillors called him a 'tireless worker'. Perhaps the greatest tribute to Paddy Tierney came from the leader of the party he once represented in Dáil Eireann. Dick Spring, when delivering his funeral oration, described him as 'one of the hardest-working Labour representatives in the history of the State'. Entering the church Paddy's coffin was draped with the Plough and the Stars. Next day on the way to the cemetery for burial it was draped with the Tricolour.

Sources:
Mrs May Tierney.
Alan Kelly, M.Litt, UCC, who researched the Seanad and Dáil Debates and wrote up most of the contents of sections headed Senator, Teachta Dála, Defender of the Constitution, Life in Dáil Éireann, Retirement.
Donal A. Murphy, who supplied some information for those sections and allowed me to quote from his *The Two Tipperarys.*
Patricia Feehily in *The Guardian*, 1978.
Hearth Money Rolls, 1665-6-7; Primary Valuation, 1852; Bassett's Book of Co. Tipperary, 1889.
Author's personal knowledge.
Photograph on p. 286 loaned by Mrs May Tierney.

HAROLD CARDEN KENT, INVENTOR

Harold Kent was the son of George Francis Kent and Mia Hickie. He married Dorothea Jessica Balmain in Paris during World War I, his best man being Wing-Commandor George Gaynor, later a near neighbour whom he had first met at the Curragh. The Gaynors lived near Cornalack, Terryglass. Gaynor was a native of Co. Meath and moved, with his second wife Angela, to the area on account of their friendship with the Kents.

Harold's father was born in 1849, son of Thomas and Esther Kent. Either Thomas or his father, also named Thomas, built 'Elmville', the picturesque house (below) in Terryglass village which has the Terryglass river running through the grounds. George Kent's children, Harold, Ralph and three sisters, Eileen, Olive and Elizabeth, were all born at Elmville. George's wife, Mia Hickie, came from Scarriff, Co. Clare. She belonged to a branch of the Hickie family who had kept their lands in Co. Clare, having converted to the reformed religion – unlike the branch which later returned to Slevoir after a sojourn of nearly two centuries in Co. Kerry. It is recorded in the Subsidy Roll of Charles II, a seventeenth-century document, circa 1665, that 'William Hickie was still in possession of "Tomgreany in the Barony of Tulla" and was the largest taxpayer (£2 3s 6d.) in the district'.

Aviator

At the outbreak of World War I Harold Kent, aged 25 years and an excellent horseman, joined the South Irish Horse, then stationed at the Curragh. He later transferred to the Royal Flying Corps and came back to the Curragh for training as a pilot which would take just eight hours. On his marriage during the war his father bought Gorthalougha House for him and his English-born wife and they returned there after the war ended. Their children, Alex, Donald and Eileen, were born there.

While learning to fly at the Curragh Harold would come home sometimes with a companion to have lunch with his wife at Gortalougha, flying one of the flimsy aircraft of the day. It was not possible to land an aeroplane at Gortalougha which is heavily wooded so he would land at Killeen where the family owned a large open, level field, and then proceed to Gortalougha. On one occasion, I have been told by his son Alex, he arrived unexpectedly and thought he would let Dorothea know he was arriving for lunch. Alex produced for me a long piece of coloured linen at the end of which was a little pocket in which was written on a scrap of paper in pencil: 'Expect me to lunch after a flip to Gortalougha . Landing same field. Cold day. Harold'. Fortunately, the back door was wide open and it was a rather breezy day. He threw out his rolled-up length of linen and it blew in through the door and half-way up the stairs where his wife picked it up. Lunch would be ready!

Another story, this time of World War II vintage, involved Harold's son Donald who was in the RAF, and his next-door neighbour, James (Jimmy) Esmonde of Drominagh. Jimmy Esmonde was a mining engineer in what was then called the Gold Coast (now Sierra Leone) in West Africa whose capital is Freetown. Donald Kent's field of operations was in that vicinity, patrolling up and down the coast looking for survivors of torpedoed ships or anyone else in trouble. Both young men had just been home on leave about the same time. Each set out to return to work, Donald by air and Jimmy by ship. Somewhere in the vicinity of the West African coast Jimmy's ship was torpedoed. Donald's squadron happened to spot the survivors in the water and alerted the MTB – fast motor boats used for such rescues. Jimmy Esmonde, amongst others, was picked up. Neither man knew that the other was involved in the incident. A few days after they both happened to be in a pub called the 'Tipperary Bar' in Freetown and were exchanging news of their recent exploits. It was only then that Jimmy Esmonde learned that his next-door neighbour had been involved in his rescue.

Inventor

It is however as an inventor that Harold Kent (below) deserves to be remembered. Most of the inventions that he patented dealt with the cultivation of crops, the best-known being the Big Gapper and the Seed Dibbler. His automatic dry pig feeder was awarded a silver medal at the Royal Dublin Society (RDS) show in 1924.

Inflator: Patent No. 16739, accepted 21 May 1914. Improvements relating to the inflation of the Pneumatic Tyres of Bicycles and other like vehicles. This allows punctured tyres (or tubes) to be pumped while bicycle is still being ridden.

The Seed Dibbler: winner of the N.A.I.D.A silver gilt medal, patented 1939-45. This was a very important invention as it saved seed which was very scarce after the war years.

Gapper: Patent No. 18000, granted on 12 October 1946, for improvement in or relating to gapping machines for thinning turnips, mangolds, beet and other crops. This was a horse-drawn gapper.

Horse Gapper: Patent No. 477793 from the Belgian Government, an invention which seems to be the same machine as patent No. 18000 – written in French.

Mechanical Harrow lifter: Patent Specification 596928, accepted 14 January 1948. 'Agricultural harrows become choked when in use with grass, mosses or other accumulated matter, and in order to continue work effectively they require to be cleaned from time to time which is effected by lifting the harrow to free the material. In the case of flexible harrows such periodical lifting by hand for cleaning is a very difficult and tedious operation and it has been proposed to effect this mechanically and the object of the present invention is to provide improved means for this purpose whereby the harrow may be easily cleaned from time to time when in use, the action of raising the harrow for this purpose being effected from the drag action of the harrow over the ground.'

Thinning Machine: Patent No. 25707, 4 September 1954, for an improved machine for thinning and/or weeding root crops. 'In contra distinction to removing bunches of growing plants at a time, it is an object of the present invention to provide a thinning machine which will lift only one or two plants out of the ground at a time, whereby the operation of the machine may more nearly approach the usual hand operation of singling the plants, facilitating subsequent hand singling and leaving the plants remaining in the ground more regularly distributed. It will maintain an extremely accurate course in steering the tractor in order to keep the gapping disc aligned with the row of plants being thinned.'

Big Gapper: Patent No. 851612, 5 January 1959, for machines for improvements in or relating to tractor-towed root crop gapping machines. This was the one called the 'The Bentall-Kent Patent Gapper'.

> # KENT'S
> # SEED DIBBLER
> ### N.A.I.D.A. SILVER GILT MEDAL
>
> Kent's Seed Dibbler is an Irish invention, manufactured in Eire, and recently got the highest award at the Inventions Competition held by the N.A.I.D.A.
>
> The main object of this invention is the saving of seeds, plus the saving of labour.
>
> I think it can be safely claimed that it is the world's most economical seed sower.
>
> Seeds can be sown at any desired spacing or depth and any average number of seeds can be sown per bunch.
>
> Working this machine is just like going for a walk, as it has a walking-stick action and is not the least bit tiring to operate, in fact two Dibblers may be worked by one operator and in this way one can do double the acreage, which is roughly about two Irish acres per day.
>
> In a bad season when misses are likely to occur, the blanks can be re-sown with the Dibbler and so avoid waste ground.
>
> The approximate amount of seed used when dibbling is as follows:—
>
>   4 to 5 lbs. Mangold Seeds per Irish Acre
>   5 to 6 lbs. Beet   ,,   ,,   ,,   ,,
>   1 to 2 lbs. Turnip ,,   ,,   ,,   ,,
>
> This little machine is not only useful on the farm, but is ideal for the garden, as most vegetable seeds can be sown with it. Only a limited number of these machines will be available for this season, so please place your order now.
>
> PRICE, £3 17s. 6d.   (Carriage extra).   (Cash with order).
>
> Obtainable from:
>
> **H. C. KENT, Ballinderry, Borrisokane, Co. Tipp.**

Other Inventions

The following are more of his inventions, most of which were patented.

A windscreen wiper before World War I. This was sold for £500 to a company which went bankrupt and was never exploited. It was refused a patent as it was considered too much of a luxury.

A Sack Loader: for winding loaded sacks up to the loft.

A Grease Gun: used by loading it with grease and putting pressure on the trigger to put grease into machinery or cars.

A Swing for Children: patented. Sold to Perks Amusements, Youghal, Co. Cork. No more known about it.

A Gun for Scaring Birds off Crops: fuelled by carbide (a mixture of carbon and water which creates an ignitable gas). Though patented, the number and date is not known.

The foregoing are only some of the inventions, patented and unpatented, by Harold Carden Kent. Many medals, one gold and five silver, were won by him over the years for various inventions. His family have all the original patents and the medals. He had one of the first combine harvesters in the area which were imported into Ireland by a firm called McCulloghs of Dublin sometime in the 1950s. Harold Kent never made money from his inventions. He had a small annuity from

Bentalls, the firm which manufactured the Big Gapper.

He died in 1970, aged 81, and is buried in the cemetery beside Terryglass former Church of Ireland church.

Source:
Alex Kent
Photographs: p. 295, 298 loaned by Alex Kent; p. 296 loaned by Nenagh District Heritage Society.

The Medals awarded to Harold C. Kent

A patent granted to Harold Kent in 1959 for 'an invention for improvemensts in or relating to tractor-towed root gapping machines'.

MICHAEL CONWAY, POSTMAN

Michael (Mike) Conway was born in Turavoggaun, Terryglass, on 14 September 1895, the son of John Conway and Maria Hough. John had come across the lake from Douras near Gorteeny, Co. Galway; Maria was from Lorrha. They had five children of whom Mike was the fourth.

John Conway was a labourer and signed the baptismal certificate with his mark. Pamela Hinkson in her book, *Irish Gold,* describes him as standing at the post office window and looking with nostalgia out over the lake to Douras from whence he came. Mike attended school at Terryglass where he was taught by John Scales. He probably left school at twelve years of age and went to work for neighbouring farmers. There was always plenty of work in the bog and he was later in his life described as the best 'barrowman who ever worked in a bog'. The postman at the time was Sylvester (Syl) Kennedy whose family kept the post office in Ballinderry. When Syl got beyond doing the post in 1911 Mike Conway, then aged sixteen, got the part-time non-pensionable job which he was to perform on foot and by bicycle for the next fifty-four years – with the exception of the four years he spent away in World War I.

War

The war broke out in August 1914. According to his discharge papers he enlisted at Nenagh on 11 February 1915. He was discharged in consequence of 'Termination of his Period of Engagement', having served with the colours 'four years, one hundred and thirty-six days', and in Section B, Army Reserve, 'seven years, two hundred and twenty-nine days', His date of discharge was 10 February 1927. He is described as 5' 6" in height with a fresh complexion, grey eyes and auburn hair. His rank had been driver and his corps the Royal Artillery. His decorations were 14/15 Star, the British War Medal, the Victory Medal.

During Mike's tenure as driver with the Royal Artillery he drove the great horse-drawn carts called 'limbers' which were used to transport ammunition of all kinds, as well as the other necessities of life, right up to the front line. A 'limber' might require two or even three horses to draw. It was a most dangerous job. The driver had to go right up to the trenches, sometimes under shell fire, to control his often frightened horses. The terrain over which he drove was horrendous, pitted with huge shell holes. These were often so large that they had to be filled in somehow to take the wheels.

Young Michael recalls that although his father never spoke directly to his children about his experiences at the Front, he sometimes overheard his father's conversations with other neighbours who had been in the war. Michael once heard him say that sometimes he was so desperate to get the shell holes filled and get on his way that, unable to find enough debris he might have to gather up the dead bodies lying around and use them to fill up the hole, then level the ground and so let his horses and limber get by.

Mike did speak to Michael of one incident which haunted him. On 11 November 1918 at 11 a.m. the armistice was declared. News of this did not reach all the front lines at once, certainly not the German one. Mike was watching a soldier, probably a Royal Engineer, who was astride a tall pole disentangling some wires, and as he watched he saw the man fall to the ground, shot dead by a sniper's bullet from the German side.

In 1939 Mike joined the Local Defence Force and remained a member until 1945. Whenever he got a few hours free and after his retirement which lasted only five years, his greatest pleasure was fishing for trout in the Ballinderry river.

Family

While Mike was away at the war his job was carried on by a son of the late Matthew Farrell, police constable, Brocka. Mike returned in 1919 and resumed his postman's duties. In 1922 he married Brigid (Ciss) Hough of Ballinderry. He and Ciss had nine children in all, but three died in infancy. They included Brigid (Mrs Coen), Michael, Christopher, Nora (Non), Philomena and Teresa. I believe Teresa was one of those who died in infancy.

Mike and his wife worked hard while rearing their young family. He started his post round at 10 a.m. and finished at 3 p.m. After finishing he worked in the bog and for neighbouring farmers snagging turnips to augment his wages of £3 p.w. Ciss would go out with him to work in the fields.

When Brigid, the eldest child, was about seven or eight years old Ciss fell ill. Her sister Ellie, who was married and living in Finnoe, had contracted tuberculosis. Ciss went every other day to look after this sick sister, do her washing and mind the two children. She too contracted tuberculosis. This terrible disease was rife at the time and was very contagious. Ciss was sent to the sanatorium in Roscrea and died within a year on Christmas Eve 1932. She was only thirty-three years old and had been married ten years.

While Ciss was in the sanatorium in Roscrea Mike visited her every Sunday, cycling the twenty-two miles. Sometimes she had bad turns and the hospital staff would send for him, thinking she was on the point of death. Michael remembers times when his father would come in from doing his rounds and then get word to go to Roscrea. He would get up on his bicycle and cycle the twenty-two miles there and twenty-two more back. After Ciss's death tragedy struck again when his fourth child, a beautiful girl named Nora (Non), aged 18, died as a result of a back injury.

Mike was left to bring up his family as best he could. There was a small baby Teresa who was delicate. She was taken by Mike's sister Margaret (Maggie) Donoghue of Ballinderry. She did not survive. Mike's son, 'young' Michael, who gave me all this information remembers the little baby.

At this time Brigid, the eldest, was

about nine years old, Michael eight and the others like steps of stairs. Philomena, now the youngest, was subject to convulsions. It was Michael's task to deal with her when she got the fit by pouring cold water over the back of her neck while holding her over a barrel of water. This calmed her down at once. He learned the treatment from a neighbour, Dinny Corbett.

As A Rule
Mike was very strict about saying the Rosary. Every night about 10 o'clock everyone in the house, and that might include neighbours' children – young Corbetts or Houghs – had to kneel while he went through the five mysteries and all the 'trimmings'. Needless to say there would sometimes be a certain amount of surreptitious giggling going on.

In the carrying out of his duties as a postman Mike was very strict. Michael remembers that his father spent some time every morning polishing his buttons, buckle and cap badge until they shone. There was an old rule which said that a postman could not carry matches, presumably in case they set fire to His Majesty's mail. He kept strictly to this rule and had certain houses at which he would get a light for his pipe. Such a one was Cahalans of Brocka. He knew where the matches were kept on a high shelf and would go to the shelf, take down the box of matches and light his pipe. He might go into another house and take a lighted coal from the fire on the hearth for the same purpose. He must have loved his pipe because Michael remembers it was his task each morning before school to take the 1/2 quarter of tobacco, cut it up and rub it up firmly between the tops of his fingers and the palm of the other hand, fill the pipe, and put the remainder of the ground-up tobacco in the pouch.

There were two houses on his route where Mike always had tea. One was Ryans of Drominagh whose niece Mary Treacy of Bellevue was the housekeeper, the other was that of Kate and Matt Costelloe of Clooniniha.

Half a Million Miles
When Mike first started as a young postman he walked his route. Then he acquired a bike of his own and used that. Finally, he was supplied with the grand, official post office bike which can be seen in the photo. It was a hard route, especially in winter where places often got flooded.

A part-time postman did not become eligible for an established and pensionable appointment unless his duties engaged him for a specified minimum of working hours. Mike did not work the minimum hours – the authorities made sure of that – so was not eligible for a pension. He worked until he was 70 when he became eligible for the old-age pension. He had walked and cycled a total of almost half a million miles and was one of Ireland's longest-serving postmen.

Happily, however, his colleagues and the people to whom he had given a lifetime of conscientious, faithful, and a very civil service, showed more appreciation than his impersonal employers. When he rode in to surrender his bag at about 3 p.m. there to meet him were representatives of all the people on his daily round, embracing areas including Ballinderry, Drominagh, Kilgarvan and Cloniniha.

Rev. Thomas Comerford, CC, made him a presentation of a wallet of notes as a token of their thanks and their good wishes.

There also to show his appreciation was Paddy Tierney, TD , Coolbawn, who joined in the tributes and adverted, with regret, to the fact that after over fifty years as postman, Mike was leaving the job without a pension.

The *Nenagh Guardian*, which carried a report of the above function, also noted that:

> Capt. A. Hillgarth, Illannanagh, and Sergeant Kelly, G.S., also spoke; others present to express their good wishes included Tony Hogan, Clooniniha, Chairman of the presentation committee, and Mary Anne Kennedy, the sub-Postmistress, whose father, the late Sylvester Kennedy, was in charge of the local office when Mr Conway first entered the postal service in 1911.

Sources:
Michael Conway, Jun.
Nenagh Guardian, 1960.

Photographs loaned by Michael Conway, Jun.

l to r: Paddy Tierney, TD, Mary Anne Kennedy, Mike Conway, John Conway (grandson), Nancy Hogan, Rev, Thomas Comerford, CC.

John Francis Waller

John Francis Waller (1809-94) was a barrister, landowner, writer and literary editor. He was son of Thomas Maunsell and Margaret (née Vereker) Waller, Finnoe House, Borrisokane. He was born in his mother's home city, Limerick, on 21 July 1809. He was a sixth-generation descendant of Richard Waller, a Cromwellian soldier who was granted the lands of Cully, Newport, renamed Castlewaller. This was Mulryan or Ryan territory and the original Ryan tower house was incorporated into the later Waller mansion – now in a ruinous state.

Thomas and Margaret Waller and family moved to Finnoe in 1821, when John Francis was eleven to twelve years old. He had two older brothers, Edward and Thomas, and a sister, Anna Henrietta, who married Thomas George Stoney, JP, Kyle Park, in 1829 – he looms large in the story of Kyle Park school.

John Francis entered Trinity College at sixteen years of age and acquired a B.A. degree in 1829. He followed his brother Edward as a student of the King's Inns in 1829 and of Gray's Inn in London in 1831. He acquired his L.L.B. degree and was called to the Irish Bar in 1833. He practised on the Leinster circuit which was how he had a brief at the first assizes in Nenagh in 1839. He wrote a legal reference book and some reports of law cases.

He was a contributor to the *Dublin University Magazine* almost from its foundation in 1833 and later became its editor. He edited *The Imperial Dictionary of Universal Biography* and contributed several entries.

Waller used a pen-name, Jonathan Freke Slingsby, for his humorous writings. His favourite literary device was to have stories, verse and songs come from the lips of characters in his stories. A notable selection of these was published in a volume, *The Slingsby Papers* (1852); they include a party scene, 'St Patrick's Day in My Own Parlour', which incorporates Waller's outstanding rhythmic translation from Irish of 'St Patrick's Breastplate'.

Among the settings of his tales, 'Castle Slingsby' and 'Carrigbawn' appear to be Castlewaller and Rockvale, another Waller-owned house also near Newport.

Literary

John Francis Waller was a leading figure in the Dublin cultural establishment. In 1852 Trinity awarded its B.A. graduate the honorary degree of Doctor of Laws, in recognition of his 'eminent literary attainments'. His best-known composition is 'The Spinning Wheel', made famous firstly by singer Delia Murphy and later by Mary O'Hara and Nana Mouskouris. Indeed, for a long time it was assumed that Delia was also its composer. The song actually appeared towards the end of 1853 and was printed for local consumption in the *Nenagh Guardian* of 4 January 1854.

John Francis Waller was Hon. Secretary of the Royal Dublin Society for some years. He was a Council member of the Royal Irish Academy, representing 'polite literature', and in 1864 became one of its vice-presidents. In 1872 he became founder-president of a literary society, 'The Goldsmith Club'.

In 1867 he was appointed to the office of clerk in the Rolls Court, a post which enabled him to devote much of his time to the cultivation of letters.

On retiring from that sinecure he went to live in London and worked for some years with Cassell, the publishers. Their records were destroyed in World War II though they have traced Waller's name listed as an author in the 1879 edition of *Cassell's Family Magazine*.

Countryman

Much writing of a century or so ago is ponderous and unattractive to late twentieth-century taste. Less so in the case of Waller. This eulogy of country life, by the city-based barrister, is from the *Slingsby Papers*, p. 12:

> Preparing the earth to receive the seed within her bosom; then sowing in hope, watching in trustfulness the mysterious and beneficent operation by which Nature works in our behalf – seeing the clouds dropping their fatness and the winds drying our saturated soil; the sun warming and cherishing the young vegetable life; the dews refreshing the plants exhausted by the parching heat of summer.
>
> Then comes the glorious time when the earth yields her increase, when the kine luxuriate in the rich pastures, and the swinging mower is hidden to the knees in deep meadows; and after that comes the reaping of the yellow corn and the gathering of the apples in the orchard; when we turn to indoor work, and the muffled beat of the flail is heard in the barn, and the rattling of the winnowing machine, as its revolving fans drive the light chaff in a dusty shower upon the wind; and so on to ploughing again.

An Dúchas

The same feel for the atmosphere of his formative years and the family homes in North Tipperary, to which he obviously returned frequently, is present in 'Snap-Apple Night at Castle Slingsby'. The setting is a Halloween party with snap-apple and other games alternating with dancing, story-telling and songs. The device enables Waller to weave his own compositions into the tale. In this one, 'The Rake's Apology', stated to be to an old Irish air called 'Shaun Staal', follows a jig danced by a young couple.

> I aver that an Irish jig is the perfection of dancing, the poetry of motion, the drama of the feet; and if you can show me anything to compare with it, either in lordly saloons or on village greensward, then will I, Jonathan Freke Slingsby, burn my quill, break my lyre, and retire into a monastery of Trappists for the rest of my life.
>
> There now, the dance is over, and the young couple somewhat flurried, sit down to recover their breath. Hush! look at that dark-eyed fellow, with the brown hair and black silk kerchief tied loosely around his neck: mark how he clears his throat with a cough and stares with all his might at the ceiling, though there is not so much as a fly creeping on it. That's the surveyor, our 'primo tenore', he's going to give us a song – listen.

How Waller acquired enough Irish to translate 'Mary o' the Curls' or 'St

Patrick's Breastplate' is not known; perhaps, like James Clarence Mangan with John O'Daly's translations, he versified literal translations made for him by others. O'Daly, John O'Donovan and Eugene O'Curry, leading Irish scholars, were contemporaries.

All of us can identify with this scene that Waller painted.

> My eyes grow dim with tears, and my heart is stirred when I call to mind four children, with impatient wakefulness, awaiting the dawn of morning, that they might dress and hurry down – stealing on tiptoe to the door of the parents' chamber – then artlessly singing their Christmas hymn, and when it was ended springing into the room with gay clamour, claiming their Christmas boxes, and wishing a happy Christmas and receiving the kiss and blessing.
>
> And those parents – where are they now? And we, where are we? One, the loveliest and meekest of souls, sleeps in peace, wearied of the world before it was well entered on; and the others have gone, each his different way, and now we meet but rarely; for we have no father's house to reassemble us.

Tragic Parting

John Francis Waller's own home life in Finnoe House (below) was brought to an end by a horrific incident there in November 1843. The account in the *Nenagh Guardian* makes for gruesome reading. Briefly, two armed men entered the dining room in Finnoe House on a Sunday evening in November while Thomas and Mrs Waller and their grandson, Mrs Waller's sister Harriet Vereker, and Thomas's brother-in-law, Captain Bradell, were at dinner. The intended shooting of Thomas Waller was thwarted by the action of their butler, Michael Larkin. A general mêlée followed, with extra attackers coming in from outside. Weapons like iron bars, a garden hoe, and gun butts were used. The end result of the attack was that Harriet Vereker died some days later from a fractured skull and Thomas Waller, in his sixties, succumbed to his injuries within two weeks. The butler, Mrs Waller and Capt. Bradell were also severely injured. Though some arrests were made initially, no one was ever brought to trial for the crime. In the weeks that followed suspicions were expressed in the local newspaper, and to the police, that the 'faithful butler', actually admitted the would-be murderers to the house.

Thomas Waller and Miss Vereker were buried in Finnoe graveyard. It is curious that there is no inscribed gravestone to mark the spot. However, when Anna Henrietta Stoney, who had separated from her husband, died she chose, as the inscription on her stone shows, to be buried near her father.

> In loving memory of Anna H. Stoney wife of T. G. Stoney J.P. formerly of Arranhill and Kyle Park who died 25th May 1880 aged 75 and is interred by her desire with her father Thomas Waller, Finnoe House, and Aunt Miss Vereker. This stone is erected by her son Edward Waller Stoney CIE MICE Aug 1910.

Former merchant-businessman, Thomas Waller, would have run his holding as a business. Accordingly, improved farm methods and restrictions placed on old ways would not have endeared him to his tenants. The murder occurred at a time when evictions were frequent as landlords set about recovering small holdings in order to increase their own demesne lands for sheep and cattle grazing. Reports in the *Nenagh Guardian* at the time indicate that he was popular with his peers. Mrs Waller and Harriet Vereker were said to care for the sick and poor in the area.

Early in 1844 the eldest son, Edward, heir to the estate, sold all the furniture, farm implements and stock and presumably set the house. We find that he died, without issue, some thirty years later in County Tyrone of which his wife was a native. They had no children.

Sale to Tenants

John Francis became owner of the estate on the death of Edward. Fifteen years later, acting through his son, Thomas Francis, he sold the Finnoe lands to its tenants who bore names like Corcoran, Hayes, Starr, Burgess, Bond, Ryan, Cleary, Powell and Treacy. To mark the occasion the grandson and namesake of the man murdered forty-five years before gave a dinner for the tenants, served in the barn of Finnoe House 'under the management of Mrs George Burgess'. This Thomas Waller became Commodore of Sydney Harbour Trust, New South Wales.

In the course of his address to them, Thomas Francis Waller said: 'I shall not paint the landlord as the saint and the tenant as the sinner, nor endeavour to prove that landlords were all in the right and tenants all in the wrong. Far from it, for I honestly believe both were in the wrong; that there was a lack of sympathy between both and, in too many instances I fear, on the part of the landlord, an utter neglect of the moral responsibilities devolving on every landowner'.

A spokesman for the tenant-purchasers in the course of his address said that all the landlords of Finnoe had been fair and just men and that the present landlord, John Francis Waller, had always proved himself to be a just and considerate man.

George Burgess became owner of Finnoe house and attached land. After the death of his son John in 1915 it was sold to George Hayes, Ballintotty, Nenagh, for £3,300.

Forever Finnoe

John Francis and Anna (née Hopkins) Waller had two sons and six daughters, three of whom married clergymen and one a barrister. In 1892 John Francis went to reside in Bishop's Stortford, East Hertfordshire, with his daughter Anna upon the appointment of her husband, Rev. H. T. Lane, as vicar of St. Michael's parish. St. Michael's church dates from 1400 and is a magnificent building in flintstone.

On 19 January 1894 John Francis Waller died in Bishop's Stortfort after a prolonged illness. His wife Anna survived him by six weeks only. Their grave in the town's cemetery is marked by a Celtic Cross in blue Pennant stone.

In death as in life he spoke of the place he regarded as home. His name is accompanied in the inscription on the cross not by that of his native Limerick nor by that of Dublin where he lived most of his life nor by that of his daughter's home but, simply, by the words: 'of Finnoe, Tipperary'.

Sources:
Donal A. Murphy, 'John Francis Waller of Finnoe' ('From Script and Stone' in *The Guardian* 150th Anniversary Supplement, 24 Dec 1988).
Elaine Burke Houlihan, ed., *Tipperary: A Treasure Chest* (Relay Books, 1995).
OHS, Finnoe Gravestone Inscriptions.

'God is Love'
In Loving Memory of
John Francis Waller, LLD
of Finnoe, Tipperary, Ireland
Born 21 July 1809 died 18 Jan. 1894
and
Anna, his wife, born 2 Feb. 1815
died 5 March 1894

This cross is erected by their children

The Spinning Wheel

Mellow the moonlight to shine is beginning,
Close by the window young Eileen is spinning,
Bent o're the fire her blind grandmother, sitting,
Is croning and moaning, and drowsily knitting:

'Eileen, a chara, I hear some one tapping' –
''Tis the ivy, dear mother, against the glass flapping'.
'Eileen I surely hear somebody sighing' –
'Tis the sound, mother dear, of the summer wind dying'.

Merrily, cheerily, noisily whirring,
Swings the wheel, spins the reel, while the foot's stirring;
Sprightly, and lightly, and airily ringing
Thrills the sweet voice of the young maiden singing.

'What's that noise that I hear at the window, I wonder?' –
'Tis the little birds chirping the holly bush under'.
'What makes you be shoving and moving your stool on,
And singing all wrong the old song of the Coolun?'

There's a form at the casement – the form of her true love,
And he whispers, with face bent, 'I'm waiting for you love;
Get up on the stool, through the lattice step lightly,
We'll rove in the grove while the moon's shining brightly'.

Merrily, cheerily, noisily whirring,
Swings the wheel, spins the reel, while the foot's stirring;
Sprightly, and lightly, and airily ringing
Trills the sweet voice of the young maiden singing.

The maiden shakes her head, on her lips lays her fingers,
Steals up from the seat – longs to go, and yet lingers,
A frightened glance turns to her drowsy grandmother,
Puts one foot on the stool, spins the wheel with the other;

Lazily, easily, swings now the wheel round:
Slowly and lowly is heard now the reel's sound;
Noiseless and light to the lattice above her,
The maid steps – then leaps to the arms of her lover.

Slower – and slower – and slower the wheel swings;
Lower – and lower – and lower the reel rings;
Ere the reel and the wheel stopped their ringing and moving,
Through the grove the young lovers by moonlight are roving.

– *John Francis Waller*

HENRY GIVENS BURGESS

A later resident of Finnoe House was to have considerable success as an executive of a leading railway company and to become a member of the first Seanad of the Irish Free State.

Henry G. Burgess, was born in April 1859, the eldest son of George and Anne (née Givens) Burgess, Finnoe. The parents purchased Finnoe House from John Francis Waller in 1888. Another son, George, was to become the Canal Co. Agent at Dromineer. He later had the Pier Hotel there (now the Dromineer Bay).

In 1898 Henry G. was promoted from District Superintendent of the London & N.W. Railway Co., at Glasgow, to General Manager of the same company in Dublin. His successful career in railways began, it is said, with a chance meeting on the train from Nenagh to Dublin with the manager of the Dublin & S.E. Railway Co. They got talking and the young Henry G. enquired if he might have a job for him in his company. The Manager made a note of his name and address and promised to get in touch. However, the manager suffered a fatal seizure after he got off the train in Dublin. Later the piece of paper, with Burgess's name and address, was found in the dead man's effects, the company got in touch, and his career in railway management began. He reached the position of vice-Chairman before moving to the London & North West Railway Co.

During World War I, 1914-18, he acted as director of cross-channel tranport and Coal Controller for Ireland and rose to Director-General of transport in Ireland. His war-time job included regulating shipping to and from Ireland and he is credited with keeping the coal supplies regular and adequate.

In 1919 he was appointed Irish Controller of Ways and Commnunications under a new Transport Bill, which gave powers to deal with Irish ships, harbours and railways. He was also a Director of some railway companies. He progressed to being Principal Assistant to the General Manager of the L & NWR Co.

While Coal Controller he was instrumental in getting the government to construct new rail links between Castlecomer collierys and the Great Southern and Western line, and with having the line to the Arigina mine upgraded.

As Irish manager of the L. & NWR Co. he became well known to the various strands of business and was noted for his fair and conciliatory approach. He chaired a conference between the Irish railway companies and the workers in 1919 which saw improved working conditions, wages and working hours put in place.

He was an avid promoter of the development of the Irish rail system. In an interview given after his appointment in 1919 he stressed the need to switch from narrow gauge to broad gauge line. He advocated the refurbishment of the canal system of transport, the development of a 'trans-atlantic port on the east coast', and the 'development of electrical power by tideways, lakes and rivers'.

Henry G. was one of thirty members of the first Seanad Éireann nominated by William T. Cosgrave, President of the Executive Council of the Irish Free State, in December 1922 to serve for six years. He did not seek election in 1928. He was then sixty-nine years of age.

Henry H. married Agnes Balderston, Paisley, Renfrewshire, Scotland. They had two daughters. They lived in Dun Laoghaire. He died in April 1937 and is buried in Deans Grange cemetery, Dublin.

Sources: *Nenagh Guardian*, 1898, 1919, 1922. William Corbett, NT.

12
Across The Seas

JOHN CARROLL, LISQUILLIBEEN

John Carroll was born on 23 February 1829 at Lisquillibeen, eight miles north of Nenagh in the parish of Kilbarron. His father Jeremiah (Darby) Carroll, born in 1782, also in Lisquillibeen and probably in the same house (class 3), married Elizabeth Kennedy, born in Urra in 1786. Both are buried in the old cemetery at Kilbarron. In 1824 they held four acres of land from Falkiner Minchin of Annagh. There was no middleman. The Minchins always held their land in fee. The four-acre farm was valued at £2 and the house at 10 shillings. Tithes of 5s 9d were paid to the rector of the (Established) Church of Ireland.

John had three brothers living: Patrick (1822-1909), and Peter (1828-84), both buried in the old Kilbarron cemetery; James (1823-1913) buried in the Rock Cemetery, Cashel. As registers of births and marriages were not kept in Kilbarron-Terryglass parish before 1827, those dates were gleaned from headstones and family records. After the keeping of registers of baptisms and marriages commenced, two further children were born to Elizabeth and Jeremiah: Darby (Jeremiah), 1831, and Elizabeth, 1834. As no more is known of these two, it is assumed they died in infancy.

The house (below) built on the site of the house in which John Carroll was born is still there and used as an outhouse. The original, which was thatched, burned down in the 1880s and was rebuilt as a slated residence on the same spot with the help of the neighbours. John's brother Peter remained at home in Lisquillibeen and his great-grandson Timothy and his family – wife Veronica and four children – now live in a modern house adjacent to the old home.

Emigration

John left Ireland in 1849, the same year as the parents of President John F. Kennedy. We know none of the details of his journey except that he arrived in Westmoreland (then called Bartlett), New York, via the Hudson River and a town called Rome. Many people from this area at that period left from

Arthur's Quay, Limerick, and landed in Canada at Quebec, but the fact that John travelled via the Hudson River makes one think he may have landed at New York. There was no railway at Nenagh at that time so he may have got to Limerick on the Dublin-Limerick Royal Mail coach which passed through the town morning and evening. I suppose he walked to Nenagh, being a young single man with no goods. The families who emigrated took as many of their worldly possessions as well as enough food for the journey and as there would have been small children there must have been carts. We do not know if John travelled alone or with neighbours; probably the latter as there was a flood of emigration that year.

He arrived in Westmoreland, Oneida Co., New York, and took up farming work. Rome was, and is, the nearest fair-sized town. He acquired his own farm and continued farming until 1882 when he came to Rome and became proprietor of the old Conger Hotel, afterwards known as Floyd Avenue Hotel. In the meantime he had married Mary Anne Galvin, born in Co. Meath, daughter of Daniel Galvin, a school teacher of that county. They had seven children: Elizabeth, Mary Anne, William J., Sarah J., Jeremiah H., Theresa Margaret, and a child who died in infancy. John's wife, Mary Anne, died in 1870. In 1883 he married Jane Clinch. In 1896 he gave up hotel work and again took up farming in Westmoreland on a small property that he cultivated until his death.

The above draws on his obituary in the *Rome Sentinel* of 26 February 1905.

Jeremiah (1860-1905)
Of his six surviving children we only have space to follow the career of one, Jeremiah, although the others are well documented. He was born in Westmoreland, Oneida County, New York, on 19 January 1860. After attending Whitestone Seminary he occupied himself with farming and hotel-keeping in Rome. He became deeply interested in public affairs, held most public offices in the town at one time or another, and was the successful candidate in his district for State Senator in 1918 and although defeated, made a phenomenal run. He became Mayor of Rome in 1925. In later years he became interested in real estate and erected the Carroll Theatre and many other buildings. There is still a street in Rome called after him. He was a highly respected public figure for over three decades.

He married Alice Flanagan of New York City on 17 June 1881. She died in 1916. They had four children, Alice Viola, Howard Emmet, Ruth and Mabel. After Alice's death he married a second time, to Helen Sweeney; they had one daughter Geraldine.

Jeremiah's eldest child Alice Viola, known as Viola, entered the Mercy Order as Sister Consolata when aged twenty-one. She had taught for four years as a Home Economics teacher before becoming a nun. She was a truly remarkable person in many ways and I have always regretted not having met her on her only visit to Ireland in 1950. She was very pretty, full of joie de vivre, loved nice clothes and having a good time. In the Seventies when it became acceptable for sisters to wear attire appropriate for the occasion she arrived for the community picnic in a floral print organza dress with matching lavender accessories and a picture hat.

Her study was in the field of English Literature. She graduated from Fordham University with an M.A. degree and spent a summer at Broadleaf School of English in Vermont and attended the writers' conference there. She later loved

Carroll Family, USA
Top: Mary Anne (née Galvin) Carroll,
John Carroll.

Jeremiah Peter (Henry) (son).

Children: Ruth Carroll Dowd (top),
Front (l to r): Mabel Dorothy (Sr M. Ruth),
Alice Viola (Sr M. Consolata),
Howard Emmet.

telling her students of her Broadleaf days and the famous writers she met, particularly Robert Frost and a young Truman Capote. She did not hesitate to chide the latter for arriving late one afternoon for a lecture given by a prominent author. Whenever Robert Frost was scheduled to present a recitation of his works in her area she would encourage her students to attend and meet with him personally; he always made a point of seeing her students. She had clearly made a lasting impression on the renowned poet.

Alice Viola wrote two books. *I Hear in My Heart* chronicles her long struggle to give up the world she loved so dearly and enter the religious life. It gives a vivid and humorous picture of life in a prosperous Irish-American Catholic family at the turn of the century. It is autobiographical, only the surname being changed from Carroll to Farrell. It was selected by the Catholic Literary Foundation for June 1949, as was her other book, *Pray, Love, Remember*, in 1947. This was a series of stories based on her childhood experiences. The title is from Shakespeare's *Hamlet*, Act IV – 'there's rosemary, that's for rememberance: pray you, love, remember'. In 1950 she was Professor of English at Georgian Court College in Lakewood, New Jersey.

Howard Emmet served overseas in World War I and became a sergeant. He was called after Robert Emmet but his mother insisted on the Howard against the wishes of father and grandfather. They thought of Robert Emmet as a great orator and as Jeremiah had always fancied himself as a public speaker he wanted Emmet to follow in his footsteps. Emmet had other ideas and became a great baseball player and later a famous baseball coach under the nickname 'Judy' Carroll. He married but had no children and died young.

I imagine that when John Carroll was a young man growing up in Kilbarron people would be familiar with Emmet's speech from the dock, 'And let no man write my epitaph' etc. As a majority of them could neither read nor write they had probably learnt it by heart.

Jeremiah's daughter, Mabel, entered Mount St Mary's College of Plainfield New Jersey and graduated with a B.A. degree. She later entered the Sisters of Mercy.

His daughter, Ruth, became a teacher and later married Francis Erwin Dowd. They had three children: Francis Erwin II, who became a Labour Relations judge in Washington, Richard Carroll and Mary Alice (in religion Sr. Ruth Cecilia of the French Order of St. Joseph of Carnavalet) with whom I correspond and get information about the family. Judge F. Erwin II has a son and daughter Tom and Mary Ellen. Mary Ellen married in 1989, and Tom. who practises law, won the John F. Kennedy Labour Law prize when he graduated from Georgetown University, Washington, in 1984. Erwin II has grandchildren as has Richard Carroll.

Granddaughter Returns

John Carroll's granddaughter, Alice Viola Carroll/Sister Consolata, spent the summer of 1950 abroad, six weeks at Oxford University, enjoying a tutorial experience in the contemporary novel and poetry. She also travelled in Switzerland, France, England, Italy and Ireland. She came to Ireland by chance. The family in Rome seems to have lost touch with home, although they kept up contact at least until John's death in 1905 because they knew James and Patrick were still living.

Consolata knew that her grandfather had come from near Nenagh and quite by chance met a Miss Heffernan from Lahorna who was on the staff at the college. She told her story to Miss Heffernan who wrote to her mother in Lahorna asking if she could place Sr Consolata's relations.

Peter Carroll of Brookfield, a grandson of John Carroll's brother, Patrick, was well-known in GAA circles. Mrs Heffernan sent this information on to Oxford and as a result Consolata wrote to Peter Carroll. We do not have a copy of her letter to him but have a copy of his letter to her. He invited her to Ireland. She stayed at McAuley House, Baggot St in Dublin, the head house of the Sisters of Mercy and at the Convent of Mercy, Nenagh. She visited Lisquillibeen and the home from which her grandfather had emigrated, the home in Brookfield in which his brother Patrick had set up house when he married in 1850, and visited the graves of her ancestors in Kilbarron old cemetery. At that time the old cemetery was in a disgraceful condition, completely neglected and overgrown with weeds. I do not know what she must have thought of it. I regret she cannot see it now, neat and tidy and showing respect for the dead.

When she retired from teaching she served as Director of Alumnae Affairs and as College Historian. In April 1978 she left the college for reasons of health and moved to McAuley Hall, the Mother House. A sister in religion, Sr Mary Catherine, wrote on her death in 1988, aged ninety-five: 'Pray, Love, Remember – the symbol of literary laurels and a most appropriate epitaph for your life as a Sister of Mercy. Alice Viola – Sister Mary Consolata – dearest 'Cons' – your history is written not only on paper, but in the hearts of all of us who have known and loved you'.

John Carroll's Brothers

Peter, the youngest and first to die, married Margaret Darcy of the Comenthus, Bellevue. They had seven children. William (Bill) remained at home; the others emigrated or married elsewhere in Ireland. Bill also had seven children. Bill died in a tragic drowning accident in 1940. His wife Hannah died in 1982. His eldest child, Peter, married Mary Brooks of Borrisokane. They had two sons, Michael and Timothy. Michael lives in England and Timothy lives in Lisquillibeen. Peter died in 1997, aged eighty-four years.

Patrick, the eldest, was my grandfather. He went to work as herdsman for John Parker of Brookfield in 1850. He married Mary Fennell that year. They lived in the gate lodge. They had ten children. My father Patrick, born 1864, was the seventh child. He married in 1914 and had six children of whom I am the second, born in 1916. My son Anthony was born in 1958. My great-grandfather Jeremiah lived through the rebellion of 1798 as a boy of sixteen, the Act of Union, Emmet's rising in 1803, the Great Famine, the rising of 1848 and Fenian rising of 1867, and died in 1872. My father was eight years old when his grandfather, who had lived through these eventful years, died, aged ninety.

James joined the British Army, the 87th Royal Irish Fusiliers, in 1839. He was later with the 4th Royal Irish Regiment. He spent most of his soldiering days in India. I do not know when he left the army but was still in India in 1852. He may have served in the Crimean War but of that I am not certain. He attained the ranks of quartermaster and colour sergeant. On his return home he settled in Cashel. His headstone can be seen not far from the round tower on the Rock of Cashel. In the Heritage Centre in the town are his uniform, hat, red coat, boots, sword, a letter, and a sort of catechism and handbook presented to him by Captain C. J. Campbell, 87th Royal Irish Fusiliers, in India in September 1852. He had six daughters and one son, Patrick, who died unmarried. Several of his daughters emigrated to America and contact has been kept up with some of them and their descendants. The family name now in Cashel is Phillips.

MARY CARROLL, BROOKFIELD

Mary Carroll was born in Brookfield gate lodge on 4 September 1863, the sixth child of Patrick Carroll and Mary Fennell who had married in 1850, and a niece of above John Carroll who emigrated in 1849.

As already stated, Patrick (1822-1909) was the herd at Parkers of Brookfield. Mary Fennell was born in the Cloughjordan area in 1831 and died in 1889. Her family had been evicted from their home and she never saw her six brothers again. Their daughter, Mary Carroll, became a dressmaker and made the wedding gown for Miss Annie Parker when she married William Reeves (right). Mary was, by all accounts, a talented and beautiful girl.

In those days it was the custom for a dressmaker to spend several days, maybe a week or more, in the home of a member of the gentry or strong farmer class and get all the necessary sewing done. While sewing in the area of Carrigatoher, possibly at Carrolls of Lissenhall, who were Protestant gentry, or at Hogans of Rosemount, she met John Hogan of Rosemount who was born in 1855. They fell in love and planned to marry. His father would have none of it. She had no dowry, was the daughter of a landless man, and in his eyes was no better than a servant girl.

Their daughter Elizabeth (Lizzie), remembered her father repeating to her, when she finally returned and stood on the hill above Rosemount, what his father said to him when he announced that he was going to marry Mary Carroll. Banging his cane into the ground, he told his son, 'if you do not do as I say you will not receive this much [the size of the bottom of the cane] of Rosemount'.

John Hogan left home after his father's ultimatum and seems to have worked for a while in the Silvermines. He then went to Australia where he worked on an island off the coast in some position which required the wearing of a uniform – possibly Tasmania and in the prison service. After some time in Australia he set off to go to the USA, going first to South Africa, then to South America and, finally, arrived in San Francisco – probably in 1886 or 1887.

True Love

Mary Carroll had waited for him, and when he sent her the passage money she set out for San Francisco, taking her spinning wheel with her. She sometimes spoke to her daughter Lizzie of the terrors of the ocean journey, and the three days rail travel across the USA through deserts and mountains, and great stretches of red earth, huge forests, and over wide rivers and lakes. There is no record but she probably left from Queenstown and embarked in New York. The ocean trip was so terrible that she would never go home again.

She left Ireland probably in the autumn of 1887 and they were married in August 1888 at Mission San Gabriel, California. While in San Francisco she worked as a dressmaker. They never returned to Ireland but their daughter Lizzie came home to Tipperary in 1982 when she was about seventy years old. With her was her daughter-namesake Elizabeth, Betty Osborne.

Mary Carroll & John Hogan with their children, John and Agnes.

Rosemount, USA

In San Francisco John and Mary Hogan made a friend from Ireland, a Mr Donoghue who, from what I can gather from Betty (who has given me most of this information), was a member of the Donoghue family of Kilbarron village. They had the public house which is now Hannigans – John Donoghue's father, Michael of Carney, spent two periods in the USA (see 'Kennedy Lisquillibeen Letters' in this chapter).

This Mr Donoghue gave them a quit claim deed to 100 acres in the Mud Mt district of Washington state, where they homesteaded and then purchased another 100 acres by Mt Peak (part of the property was on the mountain). The little town was called Enumclaw. They built a two-storey clapboard house which they called 'Rosemount'.

A news item in a local newspaper of 30 Oct 1891 noted that 'John Hogan, living near Enumclaw, has been quite a traveller and is an exceedingly interesting talker. He has had many wonderful experiences in Africa, South America, Australia and other foreign countries.'

John and Mary Hogan prospered. They had four children: Agnes, 1892; John, 1897; Willie, 1898; and Elizabeth, 1899. All, except Agnes, were born at Enumclaw. She may have been born in Seattle where John had spent some time working as an under-sheriff.

Tragic Fire
In August 1908 a terrible tragedy overtook them as recorded in the local newspaper, the *Courier*:

John, Mary and the children outside 'Rosemount',

> On Monday afternoon John Hogan's home at Rosemount was entirely destroyed by fire and his ten-year-old son William was so badly burned that he died a few hours later. No one seems to know how the fire originated. The boy was seen going to the house for wood it is supposed to prepare for the evening meal while his parents were working in the barn. Soon afterwards the house was in flames and the boy was found nearby with his clothing burned almost entirely from his body. Henry Corrigan and Fred Gulickson were working on the road near there and were first to arrive at the scene. The boy was in a pitiable condition and was wrapped in a coat and carried to the barn. As soon as possible Drs Van Der Valge and Chas Newman arrived and everything possible was done to relieve the suffering of the little victim who died about nine o'clock.
>
> Many friends and neighbours rendered aid and comfort to the stricken and homeless family. On Wed the funeral services were performed in the Catholic Church by Rev. M. Puyallup and Rev. Fafard. Interment was made in Enumclaw cemetery.

Mary's treasured item from Brookfield, her spinning wheel, was burned with everything else. John Hogan lost no time in beginning to create a new home for his family. In the *Courier* of 6 September 1908 there is a report that 'John Hogan has commenced building a house on his farm to replace the one recently destroyed by fire.'

Two months later the same paper was to carry his obituary.

> John Hogan died at his home on Thursday morning from a perforated appendix. He had been unwell for some time but took to his bed only four days prior to his death. He was 52 years of age

'Rosemount' number two did get built (over, with Mary).It was one-storey and a much more humble abode. The Hogans' neighbours were mainly Lutheran and German settlers, with a sprinkling of Irish. They were good neighbours.

The Indomitable Mary

Mary Carroll Hogan obviously did not lose heart. There is an news item in the newspaper of 24 Dec 1909 which says: 'Mrs John Hogan gave a party last Sat evening in honour of her son Johnnie's fifteenth birthday. Music, dancing and card playing were the amusements of the evening. Refreshments were served at twelve o'clock'. There follows a list of those present, among them some Irish names.

The *Courier* of 17 Feb 1911 records that 'Mrs Mary Hogan has sold her 40 acres on section 32 to John Bozousek for $2,500'. On 18 Oct 1912, per the *Herald*, 'a "Potato Party" was the chief attraction at the home of Mrs Mary Hogan last Saturday. About 20 ladies were present. A big chicken dinner was served by Mrs Mary Hogan'. The *Courier* of 3 Oct. 1913 announced that 'Mrs Mary Hogan is making use of a fine spring of water recently discovered on her place, Rosemount Farm by having the water piped to the house. The spring has some 40 feet elevation above the house'.

In another extract we learn that 'she has made a presentation of a fine sample of honey recently selected from a large quantity made by their own bees. The quality is excellent. We judge from the flavour that it is most extracted from white clover'.

Agnes, John and Mary's oldest daughter, was sent as a boarder to the Holy Name Academy for girls in Seattle (it is still there). After graduation she went to San Francisco where she married. She did not come home to Rosemount, Enumclaw, very often.

The younger children, Lizzie and John, had to stay at home after eighth grade and work the farm. Mary needed them but they were very intelligent and would have liked to stay on in school. John was in the medical corps in World War I, 1914-18. His niece Betty recalled that when he came home after the war he wanted to marry but Gran [Mary Carroll] said, 'No – can't have two women running the house.'

Lizzie and her husband, a German named Schlosser, lived across the fields from her mother. Their children, Betty and Mary, each had her own cup there and almost every day cut across the three-quarters of a mile of fields to Gran's for tea – really a treat!

Mary Carroll Hogan was the town librarian. She picked up the books from the train depot and delivered them. She drove a horse and buggy and was always accompanied by her two Irish pug dogs. The buggy had a large front seat plus the back to hold things. She died of bronchitis in 1931, aged 68 years. Her obituary in her local paper was quite long and stated 'she was born in Nenagh, Co Tipperary, Ireland'.

Home

Mary and my father were brother and sister, only a year apart in age and very close to one another. They corresponded fairly regularly and always at Christmas. Sadly, none of her letters have survived. Photographs of new arrivals in each family were sent backwards and forwards. She was talked of a great deal. Her misfortunes must have been a great heartbreak to him as well as her death at 68. We always referred to her as 'Auntie Mary in America'. America seemed very close to us. We were not told when she died. I only found out by accident. Her daughter Lizzie died in 1987. They always referred to returning to Ireland as 'coming home'.

Frank Moran, whose grandmother was Mary Carroll's sister, has visited Enumclaw and has seen their graves.

The Good Neighbours

A footnote to this emigration story is of interest.

The neighbouring family who took in the homeless Hogans after the fire were from the parish of Youghalarra-Burgess. Daniel Quigley had emigrated some time before 1852 and settled in Auburn in the vicinity of Enumclaw in Washington State. His wife, Nancy (née O'Brien), Tullaheady, Nenagh, was to follow with Malachy and Bridget, thirteen-year-old twins, and eleven-year-old Thomas of Daniel's first marriage, plus their own two, Patrick and Margaret, aged five and two years respectively. The statutory passengers' contract ticket deemed the family 'equal to 3 1/2 statute adults'. On arrival in Auburn Daniel wrote to Nancy giving her instructions about emigration procedure. Sadly, Daniel died before she and the children arrived.

At the time of the Rosemount tragedy her sons, Patrick and John Quigley, would have been in their fifties. We do not know if Nancy was still alive.

A copy of Nancy Quigley's husband's letter is reproduced below as it give a flavour of emigration a generation before Mary Carroll took off to join John Hogan.

Nancy Quigley left from Limerick on Francis Spaight & Sons' *Jessy* on 12 Aug 1852 and the fare for the entire family was £9 3s 9d payable to Mr Robert Burton at Nenagh, not later than two days before sailing. The ticket shows the amount of food and water supplied to each passenger by the Master of the Ship.

> Daily: 3 Quarts of Water.
> Weekly: 2 1/2 lbs of Bread or Biscuit, not inferior in Quality to Navy Biscuit.
> 1lb of Wheaten Flour.
> 5lbs of Oatmeal.
> 2lbs of Rice
> 1/2lb of Sugar.
> 1/2 lb of Molasses.
> 2 oz. of Tea.

In 1991 Thomas E. Quigley of Washington, USA, sent the copies of the Quigley letter and passenger ticket to Nenagh District Heritage Society, who were kind enough to let them be reproduced here. Patrick Quigley, the five-year-old emigrant, was Thomas's grandfather.

Auburn, April the 13th, 1852

Dear Nancy with love and great pleasure to my [illegible]. I send you those lines hoping to find you in good health and with all the children as this leaves me and your children and Mother, brothers and sisters in at present. Thanks be to God for His mercy on us all dear Nancy I inform you that you have the best natured brothers and sisters in the world. The are sending you seventeen pounds British. It will be posted on this day for Nancy Quigley, Tullaheady.

Dear Nancy living is not so easy got in America as peeple thinks in Ireland. I don't by any close nor anything else but mearly what you can't do without you will want 2 or 3 pounds when you land in quebeck. Mony is better in your pocket when you land than any other value. Still don't stint yourself of anything that is necessary for you and so it will be but very littill you will want to by of provision as the ship allowance will be near enuff. The most you will use is patties, herrings, trifill of meat and butter and other meale and ye will use these when ye will not care to use anything else. A small sup whiskey. Get Paddy Magrath to make a large chest that you will put your labile into. If you can bring the little cubhert the will be use full as you can pack all your delfe into them and other thing as the will be of no cost to you. In packing your chests put some of your patties into them as the will be stole from you. Be very carefull. Your mother and sisters wishes that want to bring them some oaten meale as the have none heare bring them some caps. When you are taking shipping write and let us know all perticlers and the name of the ship and what monny you will have. Your mother and sisters would wish your sister Sally wants come with you wheather John O'Neale will come or not. Now Nancy rember when you will come to quebeck take all the children with you to the emmegration office persevere on them to emmegrate you to Kingston as the must send you there. If the refuse you persevere. They may only emegrate you to Montreal. Apploy there at the emegration office for Kingston. You have to pay to Aburn. Don't say at the emetion office that you have to go apast Kingston as it is in Canada. When you come there to the warf ask for Mary Carroll and your old nabour Patrick Ryan. He lived in french village. Your sister Mary and family stoped with them. The received her kindly if you should come short of mony write for it and it will be no delay.

Patrick Dwyer and family joins in sending their love and best respect to Brother Ned and James and Thomas Quinn and James and Mary Magra and family, William Dwyer and family, Mikel Hogan and family, John Hogan and family, Michel Kennedy and family, Mikel Quigley and family, Patt Magrath and family, John King and family, James Gleeson and family, John Bryan, Carragal and his sister Mary.

Let Mary Magrath know that her son John is in good health he lives with Pat Dwyer. No more at present from yours true and loving husband Daniel Quigley.

Leaving Bellevue

On a June day circa 1890 twelve young men and women left together to go to America from a stretch of road in Bellevue not much more than a quarter of a mile long. Some came home again; others did not. I was surprised at the number who in fact did come home for good, some after retirement.

Martin and Dennis Treacy were brothers. Martin met Julia Tierney from Ballymassy in Borrisokane parish in America and they became engaged, came home, got married and had a daughter Bridget who died in 1995. They bought Grace's pub in Newchapel village. Dennis Treacy never came home.

Pat and Jack Molamphy emigrated to their uncle Michael Joseph in Maryland. He had bought a farm with money he made selling beer to the railways. They never came home. However, their descendants have come and their relatives here, Nellie (née Molamphy) and Boysie Moore, have visited them. The US Molamphys still have the timber box Michael J. made in Bellevue for his effects and food.

Mike Flannery came home. He did not intend to come for good, but after seven or eight years away came for a holiday. An older brother had died and he found he was needed at home to look after the farm. He married Molly Molamphy, a sister of Pat and Jack, and they had one son Jack who is married to the former Joan Stanley. Mike learned to play the harp while in America and brought home a small harp which he played. I believe it is called a Columbian harp and in Austria a zither. Mrs Nellie Moore (née Molamphy) has told me that as children they were fascinated by the harp and particularly by the gadget to put over the thumb while playing. He allowed them to play with the harp.

Frank Smith came home when he retired – quite well off. He had never married. He could not bear to live in Bellevue: it was so quiet. So he bought a house in Borrisokane and took his brother Jack (Butticks) and sister Mrs Flannery to live with him.

Mike Kane came home after retirement. His sister was married to Jack Smith. There was some story that he had been done out of his savings in America. He was a very intelligent man. In 1937 copies of the new Constitution were issued to every post office so that people could read it and make up their minds how to vote in the coming referendum. My brother Paddy has told me that the only person in the postal district who came in to our parents' post office and read it was Mike Kane. He came in, asked for the document, sat down by the kitchen fire and carefully read it through. When he had finished he said, 'I like that, I'll vote for that'.

Mike Smith was a brother of Bridgie Smith and Mrs Margaret Joyce. I am told he and my father, who were near neighbours, were great friends. He came home and lived with Bridgie and Margaret. When Margaret was left a widow, having also emigrated, she came home with her two children, Margaret and Michael. I went to school with the daughter Margaret.

Will Flannery from Brocka was killed in America.

Nora Donoghue, sister of Jack, Will and Harry Donoghue, Ballyscanlon and Bellevue, and aunt of Nellie Hough, and of all the Donoghues. She never came home.

Sarah Hogan of the Curragh, who married Bill Hogan of Tower Hill, Borrisokane, came home and spent the rest of her life in Borrisokane.

The night before leaving they danced the short June night away in a dip in the road outside Mike Smith's house where Jim Donoghue now lives. They had a quarter barrel of porter and, I expect, tea for the ladies. When morning came they were driven in several sidecars by neighbours who possessed such conveyances to Cloughjordan station to take the train to Queenstown (now Cobh), Co. Cork. One of those who drove them on his father's side-car was Rode Cleary of Curraghmore. Rode often told the story to his nephews and nieces and it was told to me lately by his nephew Martin Cleary of Curraghmore. Martin was born in 1912.

Rode Cleary was quite a character. He was a great talker and knowledgeable on many subjects. When he was a lad he spent a lot of time with his cousins, the Clearys of Kevanstown. They had a neighbour Kitty Hackett who was getting on in years and Rode was very good to her. When she died she left her burying ground in Kilbarron old graveyard to Rode. He is buried at an angle of the old abbey and over him is an iron cross which stands up like the prow of a ship looking out over Lough Derg. The Clearys had come from Ballyclogheen near Birr and the rest of the family, including his brothers Martin and Will, were taken back there for burial.

A scraw had to be taken from Curraghmore to go over them. The late Pat Carroll of Brookfield told me that he remembered Paddy Treacy of Bellevue going down to Curraghmore with a pony and cart to cut a scraw to take it down to Ballyclogheen for old Martin Cleary's burial. I have never come across this custom before; it may be peculiar to the Ballyclogheen area or, indeed, even to the Cleary family.

FROM LISQUILLIBEEN TO AUSTRALIA
– THE KENNEDY LETTERS, 1910-12

The Kennedy family lived in Lisquillibeen Lane, not far from Casey's house. There were at least two brothers, Dan and Michael (Mick), and a sister Margaret, later Mrs Kane. They had a very small farm, a few acres, and had first cousins, also called Kennedy, who lived somewhere in the vicinity. Sometime circa 1850 one of these cousins named Patrick emigrated to Australia. From what I can gather from the letters reproduced below, there was no communication between the cousins until March 1910 when Patrick in Australia seems to have written to the parish priest, Father Darcy, to find out if his cousins Dan and Mick and Margaret were still alive. A correspondence ensued between the cousins but ceased when Dan died. Mick died in 1930.

Mick Kennedy, cousin of the emigrant, was the godfather of the late Johnny Casey, husband of the late Nora Casey, and left him his bit of land. I remember as a child Johnny Casey coming every Friday evening to Coolbawn post office, which was our home, for his mother's and Mick Kennedy's pensions.

Four or five years ago some young Australians, descendants of Patrick, came to the Heritage Centre in Nenagh looking for their Lisquillibeen roots. Nancy Murphy got in touch with those of us who knew Lisquillibeen and we were able to show them the spot where the Kennedy home had stood. They gave me the copies of the letters, originally copied by a priest in Australia.

The letters give a hint of the land struggle and tell us who got Robert Waller's land. The photo of Patrick's family must have created quite a stir amongst the Lisquillibeen folk. Martin Kane, whose mother Margaret was a sister of the Kennedys, Lisquillibeen, probably emigrated to Australia after he discovered he had relatives there.

Lisquillibeen
28 March 1910

There is no landlord today in Kilbarron – all are bought out about half the rent it was in 1881 but is only recovering after the long struggle.

    Mrs Donoghue's husband Michael Donoghue is a native of Carney - he went to America and brought home some money and married Anora [Cleere] – he sold nothing but drink and he did not think he was making money quick he went back to America and died there. My friend John Donoghue went to America soon after you leaving Ireland.

    Your letter to Fr Darcy very nearly failed. Father Darcy lives in Terryglass and his mother died about the time the letter came. Father Darcy and Father Murrey his curate are both Tipperary men. Fr Darcy was born in Barbaha, Parish of Youghal and is a cousin to the Miss Gleesons that was with Fr Tim. Fr Murrey is a native of near Templemore. Margaret Kane and Martin Kane and Michael (Mick) [Kennedy?] join me in wishing good health etc.

Your cousin Dan Kennedy

18th April 1910

Strange names now in Nenagh. There is not many now in Nenagh that was there 50 years ago. The same with the country. There was strong farmers in Kilbarron when you left it and there is not a trace of one of them there today.

Pat Cleeson (gough)	Curraghmore
Bill Cleary	Kevanstown
Burkes	Carrigagoun

and strangers in their places.

    Michael Toohey Annagh was thrown out on the road by the sheriff and he was a well to do man when you left here. He died with his daughter in a cabin at <u>Balafinboy</u> Castle near Borrisokane.

Dan. K.

Note: See more about the Toohey eviction in chapter 8. The Burkes now in Carrigoun are not the same as above family.

2nd July 1910

Mark Bourke at the Chaple. Mark lives in Jim Loughnane's house opposite Mrs Donoghue's public house and keeps a shop there and has Jim Loughnane's farm and what Jerry Cleary had there. He is a son of Tom Bourke that lives in the lower house in Kylebeg. He bought all Kylebeg.

    Mrs Donoghue (publican) Mrs O'Meara (nee Mary Scully) John Costelloe (son of Matt Costelloe near the Black Castle) Mrs Peter Carroll (nee Darcy) John Tracey Bryan Casey Ned Maher Coolbawn Pat Maher who was a schoolteacher at Kilbarron.

Lisquillibeen
18th July 1910

Dear Patrick,
I recevied the Photos and papers alright and the Photos are splendid as every one that saw them said and we are very glad of the fine large respectable Family of Sons and Daughters you have and you and Mistress so fresh and healthy yet. You are in my memory yet and when I saw you I could not say I ever saw you before. Mrs Donohoe, Publican would not know you. Mrs Meara (Mary Sculy) you must remember her would know you well your not the same she says as when you were leaving Ireland but still she would know you. John Costelloe (Matt's son near the black Castle) would not know you. Mrs Carroll, she is one of the Darcys of Cuminthus she married Peter Carroll (Darby's Son) near Sheehans. She thinks she would know you. John Treacy old Johnny's son that lived in the lane thinks he would know you. Bryan Casey would not know you. Ned Maher Coolbawn his brother Patt was school teacher Kilbarron would not know you and I suppose you would not know any of them. Dear Patrick all of them rejoice how well you have done out there and the large and respectable family of sons and daughters you have brought up which is a credit to you and the old land. Half of century brings a great change on. People it would be hard to know them. I am sending you a drawing of the old Castle Nenagh. You must remember it. Also the new convent school in the jail. Martin expects to sail in the Moravian July 30th from London. The weather is warm here now with heavy showers of rain & thunder & lightening and we hear of great damage being done through the country. We are very glad of the fine Family you have in a good country as the papers you sint shows. May God bless you all we all join in thanking you for your kindness to us and wish you and your family good health and happiness. I will write soon again.

Your sincere cousin
Dan Kennedy

Lisquillibeen
16th May 1911

We got none of Mr Robert Waller's land – we got part of Tom Houghs – and over to Daggs bounds. Ned Maher Coolbawn got two lots of Daggs. Patt Smith got Robert Waller's 31 statute acres and Robinson's house.

Note: Robinson was Robert Waller's overseer. Albie Bourke's son lives in the house now.

•••••••••

Michael Parkinson, Slevoir, has some interesting emigration lore worth recounting here.

> Emigration affected nearly every family in the parish. Most never returned. Now and again a man would return when he could afford the passage money. Sometimes if they were lucky they worked their way on boats coming from America. They

always took back a few sods of turf. When they got back they invited their Irish friends to sit around a turf fire and kindle their pipes from the coals like they used do at home in Ireland.

My grandmother's brother, Paddy Hough, went to Vancouver in Canada around the 1850s. He was handicapped as he had only one hand, having been burned badly as an infant. Before he went he travelled around the country from one schoolmaster to another to educate himself. He arrived in Dublin and met a group of Marist Brothers who were going to Canada to open a college. He got on well and had a large estate outside Vancouver. When he died he left all his property and money to build and endow a college near the city.

Two aunts of mine, Margaret and Ellen Parkinson, joined the Presentation nuns in America in 1908. Ellen lived only two years there; she died from T.B. Margaret became a nurse and worked among the Indians in the beginning. She later became administrator in different hospitals. For her work she was presented with a relic of the True Cross. After her death the relic was brought to my sister by a nun from the convent by order of the bishop.

PATRICK MORAN, BELLEVUE
by Justin Moran, Australia

Forty-six-year-old Justin Moran is a medical doctor in general practice in Melbourne, Australia. He is fifth-generation Irish on all sides, all his forebears having emigrated from Ireland. This account shows how he finally found the place of origin of his great-great-grandfather and how successive generations of that emigrant's offspring went on to become successful in business, politics, and the professions. In the light of earlier chapters in this book there is some irony in the knowledge that the emigrant fought in the colonial forces against the native Maoris in New Zealand and was repaid for his service with land.

Patrick's brother Martin was the great-grandfather of Frank Moran and his siblings.

My interest in family history started as a wide-eyed young boy, listening to the tales of my mother's mother who lived to be 93, of how her mother had camped on the banks of the Yarra river, in Melbourne, after arriving from Ireland, and how she had escaped death by seeking refuge in a dam with her grandson when a bush fire had scorched the Mallee black. My father had been told by a nun when he was a schoolboy that a 'Moran was the first king of Ireland'. Then there was always talk in the family as to where the dominant brown eyes had come from. It was often conjectured that they came from the Spanish Armada, but as with many of these tales it was hard to separate fact from fiction. After four generations in this country all my forebears had migrated from Ireland.

An uncle of mine, who had travelled to Ireland, and his cousin had done some research into the family history. The cousin had discovered some photographs, letters, memorial cards, and newspaper cuttings amongst his mother's papers after she had died. When my uncle died in 1991, some of this research was passed on to me. In one of these documents there was an extract of the shipping record of the *Kate,* which had arrived in Sydney in 1850, and included in the passenger list was a Patrick Moran, stated to have come from 'Balligerry?' and to have a brother Patrick in Sydney. How could Patrick have a brother Patrick? Patrick's death certificate stated he was from Nenagh, Co. Tipperary, and with this information in hand I explored records in the State Library in Melbourne and was directed to the microfiche of Griffith's Valuation of Ireland. After several hours trying to make sense out of this document I had found two possibilities but neither fitted either Nenagh or 'Balligerry' with the closest being Borrisokane. Rather frustrated, I left the library and pawed over the records again.

I tried in vain to obtain the microfilm of the Board of Immigration lists from the library. Although it was in the library it had not been catalogued, and I was told that it might not be available for several weeks! It was suggested that I go to the Genealogical Society of Victoria and look at the film there. It was here one afternoon that I slowly wound through the microfilm and came to the list of the *Kate* and my heart raced as there in clear script was Moran, Patrick from Co. Tipperary, Ireland, whose parents Patrick and Catherine were living at Bellevue, Co. Tipperary. This linked with the Griffith records I had previously noted, where Patrick Moran was leasing land at Bellevue in 1850. And so began the slow process of piecing together the family records from official documents. certificates and oral history.

Patrick the Emigrant
In 1850, with much of Ireland still destitute after the potato famine and the Australian colony now out of a prolonged depression and again offering assisted migration, Patrick Moran, the twenty-year-old-son of Patrick Moran and Catherine Kennedy, left Kilbarron for this southern land, travelling first to Plymouth, where he embarked as a £2 assisted migrant on the *Kate*, a 786 ton ship. As one of 302 passengers he set sail for Australia on 29 June 1850 and after a 106-day voyage, he arrived in Sydney in the British colony of New South Wales on 13 October 1850. In the Immigration Board records he was listed as a 'farm labourer' and could both read and write which is hardly surprising as his father, who was living at 'Bellevue', Co. Tipperary, had been a school teacher at Lorrha in 1824 and later at Coolbawn.

We know that Patrick, the emigrant, had at least two siblings: James born circa 1826, who later migrated to New Zealand, and Bridget, born 1829, who married John Hough in 1855 and stayed in Ireland. The Houghs parented Timothy (1857), Mary Anne (1859) Eugene (Owen) (1860), and Eliza (1861).

On board the *Kate,* Patrick travelled with sixty others from Co. Tipperary, including brothers Thomas, aged twenty-four, and Cornelius Egan, twenty-two, from 'Dura' (Dorrha). We can only speculate whether Patrick knew them before the voyage, from the time when his father taught at Lorrha. However, two years later he married their niece Mary Anne Egan on 25 May 1853, at St Francis's Church, Melbourne, Victoria.

Patrick and Mary Moran's first son James was born on 22 April 1854, at Collingwood, Victoria, but they later moved to the Forest Creek diggings, on the Mount Alexander goldfields, close to what is now Castlemaine. It is here that Patrick tried his luck as a miner. His second son, Martin, was born on 4 November 1855, at New Years Flat, Fryers Creek. He had two further sons, Patrick, born in 1857, and Michael Henry in 1859, as well as a daughter Sarah Ann in 1861.

Gold Miner

Gold was first discovered in Victoria in February 1851, near Ballarat. Soon after, strikes were reported in other areas of Victoria, including a large alluvial deposit at Mount Alexander in November of that year. The goldfields were far from the mythical romantic places as some now imagine, but were raucous noisy places, with large batteries crushing quartz round the clock. The general uproar caused by spruikers selling their wares, arguments and fights, was never ending. The air was foul with slaughter yards and butchers, unpenned livestock and raw sewage in open drains; so that the drinking water was polluted by both the mines and effluent. Disease and sickness were common and children died in large numbers with an horrendous mortality rate from typhoid, scarlet fever, diphtheria, whooping cough and measles. Most miners did not make their fortune with licences at £1 per month and average yearly earnings of £100.

In 1861, at Golden Point near Chewton, Patrick's beloved wife Mary died of encephalitis complicating erysipelas. Following this, Patrick tragically drowned at Golden Point, in a mine hole filled with water, when he went looking for his lost pet goat. James died of sepsis complicating phlebitis, and Michael Henry died of diphtheria. Mary and her three sons are buried at Chewton Cemetery (near Castlemaine) in Grave 31. The headstone inscription (right) shows the tragic extent of young lives extinguished.

> IHS
>
> SACRED
> to the memory of
> MARY MORAN
> the beloved wife of
> PATRICK MORAN
> who dep this life 11th JUNE 1861
> Aged 26 years
> Also their son
> PATRICK MORAN
> who died 26th September 1863
> AGED 6 YEARS
> ALSO
> JAMES MORAN
> WHO DIED 14th FEB 1866
> AGED 11 YEARS
> AND
> MICHAEL HENRY MORAN
> DIED 7th FEB. 1872
> AGED 13 YEARS
>
> Requiscant in pace

Soldier-Colonist

It is unlikely that Patrick had much luck as a miner, for he joined the 4th Waikato Regiment on 20 January 1864, bound for New Zealand, registered number 62. He was part of the Australian Colonial Forces, serving during the Maori wars towards the end of this campaign, with the promise of land for soldier settlers. His son Martin, who was aged ten at the time, related to his grandchildren how he had been carried on his father's back across New Zealand during the Maori wars and how the Maoris made shot from chewing Kikuyu grass into hard balls. Patrick served as a private, earning 2s 6d per day, and was entitled to one town allotment and a farm section of 50 acres as a soldier settler.

The story of New Zealand during the nineteenth century is one of almost continuous warfare between the Maoris and the British colonists. No fewer than thirteen major outbreaks requiring military action are recorded and the year 1864 saw a total build-up of some 22,000 Imperial and Colonial Troops in an effort to subjugate the Maori tribes south of Auckland.

Unlike the nomadic Australian Aborigines, the Maoris were fierce, capable fighters and military engineers. They were armed with rifles, shot guns, tewhatewhas (clubs) and tomahawks. They preferred to fight from their pas – hill fortifications consisting of an outer palisade fence enclosing a deep ditch with an inner parapet of earthworks surrounding a series of inner compounds, with rifle pits, connected by narrow trenches. They engaged in sorties from the pas and tried to engage the Colonial Forces under the cover of thick bushland. However, they were no match for the superior weapons, particularly artillery, and better supplies of the British forces.

Teacher

The next record of Patrick is on 12 June 1877 when he joined the Victorian public service, appointed as an instructor to Ballarat Boys reform school which looked after orphaned and abandoned children, instructing them in the 3 Rs and teaching farming skills. It was part of the Chief Secretary's Department; he completed his working life there. He died on 27 May 1901 at his son Martin's home, in White St. Malvern, Victoria, his occupation listed as a Civil Service pensioner, Chief Secretary's Department. He is buried at Boroondara Cemetery, Kew, with his son Martin, and Martin's wife Mary Ann.

The Second Generation in Australia

Martin Moran, his only surviving son, joined the Post Office on 10 May 1875 and was a registered mail guard when he married Mary Ann Millane at St. Francis's Church, Melbourne, on 2 August 1882. He rose to become an assistant supervisor Grade 4 with the Commonwealth Post Office by his retirement in 1917. He first worked at Sandhurst and later moved to Melbourne and lived in the suburb of East St. Kilda. He later moved to Malvern in White Street, but was living at Erica Street, Malvern, where he died in 1927, in a house built by his son Walter. Martin Place, Malvern, which is opposite the old family home, is most likely named after him. His last years were affected by progressive rheumatoid arthritis, and after he was run down by a team of runaway horses he was largely confined to a wheel chair.

Mary Ann Millane was also a first generation Australian whose parents had come from Kilseily in Co. Clare, and Limerick, Co. Limerick. Mary Ann and Martin (above) had six children, five living to adulthood: Walter James, Irene Constance, Aubrey Maree, Kathleen Frances and Brian Vincent.

The Third Generation in Australia
Walter James Moran (1886-1949), my grandfather, is listed as a commercial traveller in the 1908 electoral role, Westgarth Street, Malvern, when he was living with his parents Martin and Mary. He worked in many occupations including as a builder, property developer and real estate agent. He married Catherine Gardiner on 29 March 1910. The family moved to Adelaide, South Australia, and Walter worked as manager for the International Correspondence Schools from about 1918 to 1922, before moving to Sydney, New South Wales, where he was a director of Exide Battery Co. He returned to Melbourne and was involved in real estate and property development. Walter was a good athlete and a keen punter and even in his youth gambled on himself as a cyclist and had won £2,000 by the time he was eighteen years. He was heavily involved in horse racing in the 1920s, at one stage having twenty-seven horses in training. Walter was the complete salesman and made his fortune in property speculation only to lose everything in the Great Depression of the 1930s.

Irene Constance (1890-1931) was the goddaughter of her first cousin Mary Moran, the daughter of Patrick Moran's brother James who had migrated to New Zealand. Mary was a nun in Hamilton, New Zealand (Sr. M. Helena). So there is good evidence that the cousins were in close contact over this time. Irene followed in her cousin's footsteps in the convent, joining the Dominican Priory in Dunedin, N.Z. as Sr. Mary Winifred. After some time in New Zealand, she was forced, due to ill health, to return to Australia and died in 1931.

Aubrey Marie (1892-1940) married Terrence O'Brien whose family came from Limerick and Clare. He was a wealthy man and property speculator until financially humbled in the stock market crash of 1929, when a large investment in property in Perth, W.A., was greatly devalued. He died of a pulmonary embolus complicating gall bladder surgery in 1934, leaving Aubrey to raise their seven children alone, with much of his money tied up in trust for the children. She managed for a short time as a newsagent until she died in 1940, with her youngest child still only nine years old.

Kathleen Frances (1896-1964) married Harold Glowrey who became the Member for Ouyen in the Legislative Assembly of Victoria and later chairman and manager of the Grain Elevators Board of Victoria. They had two sons and five daughters.

Brian Vincent became a diesel mechanic for Carlton and United Breweries in Melbourne. He married Dorothy Murphy and had one son John.

The Fourth Generation in Australia
My grandfather, Walter James above, and Catherine née Gardiner (whose roots were from Armagh and Cork) had nine children, seven living to adulthood: Ronald, John, Gregory (my father) Winifred, Brendan, Leslie and Kathleen.

Ronald Martin (1910-91) was educated at the Jesuit school of Xavier, Melbourne, until the age of fifteen when he left to join the Redemptorists and went to St. Clements College, Galong, NSW, and obtained several state exhibitions in his final secondary year. He later attended the Redemptorist seminary at Ballarat but contracted rheumatic fever; at the age of 22 he was considered unable to continue and, much to his disappointment, was discharged from the seminary. He left Australia in 1949 to take up a position as Sales Manager for Millington's

Advertising Agency in Singapore where he spent the next seventeen years. He won second prize in a world-wide advertising competition for the Parker Pen Company. He had several trips to Europe and spent some time in Ireland trying to look up his roots. He returned to Australia in 1966 and retired. The heart that the Redemptorists were so worried about finally gave out in his 81st year!

John Walter (1913-81), educated at Xavier College and CBC, St. Kilda, became the Victorian manager of the Union Theatres in Melbourne. He married Lillian Madigan in 1947 and after her untimely death in 1952 married Shelagh Durack. He had no children from either marriage.

Gregory Thomas was born in 1914 in Melbourne. The family lived for a time in Adelaide and Sydney before settling back in Melbourne. He was educated at Burke Hall (Xavier College) and C.B.C., St. Kilda, before going to business college, with his dream of becoming an architect cut short by the failure of his father's business. He worked at Lincoln Mills textiles from 1934 to 1962 and worked in the spinning mill, becoming the yarn store manager. He worked for a short time as the general manager of a hardware store before he returned to the textile industry as General Manager of I & R Morley's until his retirement in 1979. He married Mary Agnes McLaughlin in 1946 and with the aid of subcontractors designed and, largely by his own labour, built his house before moving into it in 1956. He still resides there today.

Winifred Catherine (Mollie), born 1915, looked after both her parents in their last days but contracted miliary tuberculosis from her father who had been nursed at home. She spent many months in a sanatorium and was not expected to recover. She later worked in the very same sanatorium for many years. She never married.

Brendan Joseph (1918-86) trained as a cabinet maker, but following the outbreak of World War II, he joined the AIF in the 8th Division artillery. He served the war in North Queensland, Darwin, during the bombing and later New Guinea. When the war was over he went into business with his brothers John and Leslie in a joinery business, but later worked as a successful salesman before ill-health forced him into premature retirement. He had two children, Michael, now a radiologist, and Susan.

Leslie Michael, born 1920, was a successful printer running his own business for many years. He served in the AIF in WWII in the 8th Division artillery as a radio operator. He was seconded to the US Navy for 3 months and later fought in New Guinea against the Japanese in this most bitter and torrid campaign. He infiltrated behind enemy lines as part of the advance forces to assess enemy positions and direct artillery. Here he contracted malaria and scrub typhus; the aftermath of this was progressive blindness. He was forced to sell his business and moved to Queensland. He has nine children.

Kathleen Margaret, born 1923, educated at Star of the Sea, Gardenvale, married Peter Griffin an engineer, and they have five children.

The Fifth and Sixth Generations in Australia

My father, Gregory Thomas, and Mary Agnes (née McLaughlin) had two children: Damien born in 1947, and myself, born in 1952. I was educated at St. Bernard's C.B.C. and later at Melbourne University and St. Vincent's Hospital Medical School, graduating M.B.B.S. 1975. I married Suzanne Rothacker in 1976 and we have four children – Matthew 19, Daniel 17, Kathryn 14 and Luke 11. My eldest son Matthew is at present doing a Law-Science degree at Melbourne University.

Patrick Moran's descendants now number over 150 and the present generation includes many teachers, managers, engineers, lawyers, tradesmen, and doctors and are a testament to the great opportunities that Australia has presented them with after so difficult a beginning. It is unfortunate that over the years much of the family has lost contact with each other, but with the opening up of archival records and the great interest in genealogy worldwide it is often possible to trace back the important movements of our forebears and so replace much of our lost oral history.

Sources:
John Carroll: Tithe Applotment. TNFH research centre for genealogical data.
Author's personal knowledge.
Sr M. Ruth Cecilia Dowd.
Photographs: p. 10 taken by Noreen O'Meara, Tunbridge Wells; p. 212 loaned by Sr Ruth Cecilia.

Mary Carroll: Betty Osborne and Joe Schlosser, USA; Christy Carroll, Brookfield.
Photographs: p. 315 loaned by Heather (née Parker-Reeves) Bell; p. 316 copy made by Paddy Carroll; pp. 317, 318, Betty Osborne.

*Leaving Bellev*ue: Martin Cleary, Curraghmore.

Patrick Moran: Text and photograph Justin Moran, Australia. His sources included Primary Valuation, Lower Ormond, 1852. TNFH research centre for Kilbarron-Terryglass and Lorrha RC parish records.
Lloyd's Register of British and Foreign Shipping (1764-1913).
Australian Archives, Immigration Department *Assisted Immigrants Inwards to Sydney*, Reference Number 4/4918, Archives Office reel number 2461.
Death certificate, Victoria 18631/No. 5459.
Helen Doxford Harris, *Digging for Gold*, Nunawading, Victoria: H. D. Harris, 1988.
Leonard L. Barton *Australians in the Waikato Wars 1863-1864*, Sydney (1979).
Victorian Government Gazettes 1877 to 1885: Public Service Lists.
Boroondara Cemetery, Kew R.C. Compartment B, grave 1708.
Copy of letter from Sr. M. Helena (Mary Moran) to Mary Ann Moran (née Millane), 30 July 1931.

A Journey 1943

Yesterday at home
The September morning had been sweet,
Shimmering cobwebs on the hedgerows,
Wild woodbine blooming,
Children ambling safe to school,
Farmers with plenteous churns on carts,
The cob clopping along at his own pace,
Our brother happy at the reins –
The war seemed far away.

Storm-force winds on the Irish Sea,
Vertical decks slippery with vomit,
Stinking life-jackets proffered by angry sailors –
Frail, false protection against the hidden U-boat.
Grey-faced men in shabby suits,
Drab, latter-day wild geese
Returning to fight the strangers' war in factory or on battlefield.

Morning on London Bridge Station.
We await our train,
Two female exiles sick for home.
Beside us a British Railway worker, grey-haired, middle-aged stands.
He opens his mid-morning snack of corned beef sandwiches.
At his feet lies the enamelled billy can filled, no doubt, with tea.
With tea!
He looks at us,
He looks at his two large doorsteps:
He breaks one in half,
Gives us each a half
And a drink of tea from the enamelled lid.

Home is not so far from London Bridge Station:
This morning too has its sweetness.

– Bridie O'Brien

13
Trades and Occupations

FORGES

Forges and blacksmiths always played an important part in the life of the people. In England the trade description of farrier or shoer of horses was applied to the Ferrer or Ferriers family who shod the horses of William the Conqueror, in much the same way as the royal household trades of steward, marshal and butler became family names. George Barrow, the chronicler of the gypsies, wrote in *Lavengro*, 'It has always struck me that there is something highly poetic about a forge'. The poor farrier sweating at his furnace might not have agreed with him.

Long before any kind of sophisticated farm machinery came to be used horses had to be shod and armour had to be fashioned; gradually, as machinery came into use, the blacksmith was no longer a simple farrier. The horse had been all-important, as indeed had been the donkey, jennet and mule. All had to be taken to the forge to be shod so the forge was the great, classic talking shop for all classes of people from the humble donkey owner to the gentleman – or lady – on a hunter. Before the 1798 rebellion the United Irishman oath was often administered by the blacksmith, who made the pikes for the rebels, and there are many stories from that period of blacksmiths having been ill-treated, tortured, and even put to death.

During the late 1930s and early 1940s tractors and motor cars were beginning to replace the horse, but the blacksmiths were still able to cope with the simpler farm machinery. During World War II, with the scarcity of petrol, horses were used again as traps, gigs, cars and carts had to be relied upon as conveyances. Horses were also used to pull the plough and harrow. In the decade or so after the war the tractor and motor car finally took over from the horse, donkey and jennet, and gradually blacksmiths became redundant.

Terryglass – In the Hearth Money Rolls of 1666 for Terryglass parish there is a Dermot Shelderton, 'smith'. It is not known where his forge was situated. His is the only surname of possible English origin in the Rolls for that year but with his Irish first name Dermot (Diarmuid) his father must have 'married out'.

Roran – We know from the Primary Valuation list of *c.*1850 that Denis Phelan had a forge in Roran. In the 1901 census a Danny Whelan (one wonders about the likeness in the names) had one in the village of Terryglass, where he also kept a public house (now Paddy's Bar). The forge was behind the pub and part of what is now the 'Derg Inn'. It closed circa 1920. Wilsie Nolan has found old blacksmith's tools and implements there in later years.

Lacken – A forge at Lacken on the Carrigahorig road existed into the 1940s. The last blacksmith was Rody Kennedy who died in 1943. His father, William, who was also a smith, did all the wrought-iron work for Terryglass new church as well as items like door hinges and locks. His wife was Donoghue from Bellevue and her niece and nephew, Mary and Pat Donoghue who were first cousins and had married, came to live with her and inherited the house. Mrs Mary Donoghue was a founder member of Terryglass branch of the ICA. She died in July 1996. Her husband Pat had been dead for some years.

Another skill undertaken by the blacksmith was the shoeing of timber wheels for vehicles like cars, carts and traps. Having made the iron band to the wheel size, the wheel to be shod was placed on a stone bed on the ground and the band affixed, heat and water being the components used to ensure a tight fit. In summertime if bands became loose, due to the timber drying out, the solution was to take off the wheel and lie it in a stream or cover it with wet sacks. The water made the wheel timbers swell so that it soon fitted tight within the band again.

Rody Kennedy's wheel-shoeing stone (below) is now preserved at Hickie's new house in Slevoir woods. It was originally a mill wheel in Terryglass corn mill. After Rody's death most people took their horses and farm implements to Joe Maxwell's forge at Kyle in Borrisokane parish. His son Willie Joe carries on the trade and is reputed to be an expert with farm machinery.

Ballyscanlon – There had been a forge at Tierneys of Ballyscanlon at least since the early 1850s. Martin Tierney was the blacksmith there in the early years of the twentieth century. His father and grandfather had been blacksmiths – and possibly farther back – as was his brother Paddy, subject of the profile in chapter 12.

Coolbawn – Sometime before or during World War I Martin Tierney moved to Coolbawn, where the Dwyers had been smiths, and lived in what was known locally as the 'forge house'. The Dwyer family had died out and Thomas Towers of Castletown owned the forge and adjoining dwelling-house, situated where the new telephone exchange was erected some years ago – nearly opposite Coolbawn post office. Thomas Towers farmed in a big way and had plenty of work for a smith, as would the neighbouring farmers.

Martin Tierney remained in Coolbawn until circa 1922. His brother-in-law, Thomas Maloney from Borrisokane, worked with him for some of the time. Living with him was his wife and a seventeen-year-old nephew who was apprenticed to the trade. When Martin left Coolbawn he took up residence at Belle Isle near Portumna bridge and worked a forge in Lorrha to which he and his nephew walked every day. I believe he lived in a house on the estate of Major Bertie Waller.

Some time after their move to Bell Isle the nephew was tragically killed when crossing the bridge on his way into Portumna. I have heard it said that he was on his way to buy a tin whistle for Martin who was a very convivial character and liked wine and song. The young man somehow got caught when the bridge was closing. I do not know the details but remember the shock on hearing the sad news.

He remained at Lorrha until he became too old to ply his trade and then returned to Bellevue where he died. His deep involvement in the GAA is seen in chapter 15.

'The Flaming Forge'

My brother Paddy remembers Martin's nephew well as we lived near the Coolbawn Tierney forge and he was allowed to frequent it and enjoy its wonders. I never got beyond standing on the road and gazing into the dark cavern with its blazing furnace and roaring bellows, and watching the patient horses – shoeing required that the horse's foot was held backwards between the smith's knees as his skilled hands tapped the shoe in place and inserted the nails while cradling the hoof against his apron. I could not yet read but had heard my father quote Longfellow's 'The Village Blacksmith', one of the poems in the Fifth Reader which was studied by all the national school pupils in the nineteenth and early twentieth centuries. It is a truly remarkable book. In those days children were not in classes, they were in 'books'. My uncle would ask us, 'what book are you in?'

>His hair is crisp, and black, and long,
>His face is like the tan;
>His brow is wet with honest sweat,
>He earns whae'er he can,
>And looks the whole world in the face
>For he owes not any man.
>
>Week in, week out, from morn till night,
>You can hear his bellows blow;
>You can hear him swing his heavy sledge,
>With measured beat and slow,
>Like a sexton ringing the village bell
>When the evening sun is low.
>
>And children coming home from school
>Look in at the open door;
>They love to see the flaming forge,

> And hear the bellows roar,
> And catch the burning sparks that fly
> Like chaff from a threshing floor.

The forge and house in Coolbawn lay empty for a year or two until the Civic Guards arrived at the end of 1923 or the beginning of 1924. They lived in the 'forge house' for a few months until the old Constabulary barracks down the road to the lake was made available to them.

After the closing of the Coolbawn forge in 1922 people in the neighbourhood took the work to Kennedy's in Puckane. That forge is described with great panache and affection in Daniel Grace's *Portrait of a Parish: Monsea & Killodiernan*.

Kilbarron – In the mid-1930s a Cloughjordan man, Bill Hyland, built a forge on the outskirts of Kilbarron village on the Ballinderry road at the top of Armitage's Lane. He shod horses and wheels and did other smithy work. I have heard it said that he was an excellent farrier. His wife was an O'Brien from Lower Graigue and they were the first family to live in the cottage now occupied by Mrs M. B. Fleming. Mark Bourke had given the site voluntarily for the cottage. Bill Hyland moved back to his native Cloughjordan circa 1936.

Bellevue – In 1852 Patrick Meara had a forge in Bellevue. It is one of five or six houses and plots of land bracketed together in Griffith's Valuation list which were on the right-hand side of the road going from Coolbawn to Bellevue just after the turn-off to Bellevue House, i.e. 'the continent' referred to in chapter 1. That comprised just over 12 acres. The occupiers held the land in common in alternative strips – rather in the old medieval style. Patrick Meara the blacksmith also held an additional 5 acres of land elsewhere.

Lisquillibeen – In 1852 William Meagher had a forge in Lisquillibeen. Its whereabouts is not known; he had no house or land. However, a Patrick Meagher had a house and about 20 acres of land in the townland and may have been his brother or father. The forge was valued at five shillings (25p). My great-grandfather's father, whose first name I do not know, had a forge in Lisquillibeen before 1800. Great-grandfather Jeremiah Carroll does not seem to have carried on the trade as he worked as a farm labourer at Minchins before becoming a herd in Brookfield. Until a few years ago there were old pieces of forge material lying around at the back of the old family home in Lisquillibeen.

Griffith's Valuation list does not record a forge there in 1852, but Jeremiah's father would, in any case, have been too old to be carrying on the trade of smith as Jeremiah was born in 1782. The Carroll house is not far from Lisquillibeen/Tullawn castle and we have a fantasy in the family that they may have been armourers to the O'Kennedys. There are a great many artisans and very few farmers amongst my great-grandfather's numerous descendants.

Ballinderry – The Costelloe family had a forge at the back of the house where Lakeshore Foods now stands. Martin Costelloe was the last member of that family to carry on the trade. He gave up some time after World War I and was succeeded in turn by Jack O'Meara, who came from a forge in Clooninihy. Jack's son Danny in the late 1930s or early 1940s, and Paddy McKenna of Borrisokane during World War II. After a few years he returned to his own forge in Borrisokane and so he was the last smith to work in Ballinderry.

Springfield – In 1852 Michael Bond had a forge in Springfield Glebe townland in Finnoe parish. Additional to this he was occupier of 'a house, office and land', the latter being 41 acres 28 perches. The total valuation of all was £15 15s 0d. He was a tenant of Rev. Mr Martin, Rector of Finnoe.

Finnoe – At the Pound of Finnoe Mick Kennedy, who had come from Carney, kept a forge. He ceased to ply his trade through ill-health about 1920. Neither of his sons became blacksmiths; Mick joined the army and Paddy became a postman. The only girl, Mary, with whom I went to school, was beautiful and talented but died very young. The ruins of the house and forge are still there.

LIMEKILNS

Lime has always been a very useful commodity – as limestone abounds in the parish we have been fortunate in having access to this product in plenty. The limestone (a rock of calcium carbonate) was calcined or reduced to powder by being burned in kilns. The uses to which lime were put were many, but were chiefly for building, i.e. the making of mortar by mixing it with sand, for fertilising the land, and for whitewashing the insides and outsides of houses.

The following method of manuring land with lime appeared in *The Farmer's Assistant* of 1838.

> Make a circular platform of the sods to be burned, about a foot thick, and six feet in diameter; bring roach lime according as it is burned and lay it on this foot-thick of sods; on the sods lay another layer of lime, and on alternately until you have built up this heap like a bee-hive, as high as your hands can reach; then cover it round airtight with sods and put some clay over the sods to prevent the gases from evaporating. The quick-lime will convert the sods into vegetable mould, more efficiently for manure than if burned in the usual way; and I will venture to say that no bench of magistrates in the country will fine you for burning land in this manner. … If you burn land without immediately liming it in some manner you do it a great injury.

Over the years as new products became available and the way of life changed lime was no longer needed and the limekilns became disused and mostly disappeared. Modern fertilisers imported from abroad were used, cement was substituted for lime in the making of mortar and, as people became more prosperous and built dwellings with permanent finishes, whitewashing became a thing of the past.

Nineteen sites where limekilns existed in the parish of Terryglass have been identified to me by Wilsie Nolan. As far as we can tell few traces of these are left, having fallen victim to land reclamation, but I understand that the one in Kylenoe can still be seen. There were two in Macloon, three in Lacken, two in Firmount and one each in Ashgrove, Roran, Gortmore, Ballinderry, Kylenoe, Dromingh, Shanbally, Slevoir, Turravoggaun, Clooninihy, Shannon View and Cappinasmere,

Clonmackilladuf and Luska. It is possible that overgrown traces of some may still be there but only those who know the land well would be aware of them.

Limestone did not abound to the same extent in Kilbarron as in Terryglass so limekilns were not as plentiful. Possibly they existed and cannot be identified. There were two on Islandmore; the bigger one on Jim O'Meara's farm was lined with brick and was there up to a few years ago and may still be there.

In the parish of Kilbarron there was one at Garrane, traces of which still exist. There was also one at Luska. It was a fine, fairly intact, stone building about fifteen yards off the road opposite the old military barracks. It is now incorporated into a boathouse. Jack Barry tried to get it going during World War II but without much success. The kiln must not have been correctly constructed.

Limekiln at Hogans, Clonmackilladuff

Before World War II the use of homemade lime had almost died out. However, the war brought shortages of imported commodities, among them artificial fertilisers. Tillage, particularly of cereal crops such as wheat, was carried on intensively, making the use of fertiliser more essential than ever. The Government offered subsidies to farmers who would lime their land.

The Hogan family of Clonmackilladuff had the remains of a very old kiln on their land which had not been used for generations. There is still a large lime-stone hill or quarry behind their house. The three sons, Michael, Tom and John, got the idea that they might reactivate the limekiln. In Kyleomadaun, near Finnoe, Paddy Burgess had been burning lime for Tom Corcoran. The Hogans, acting on his advice, got Simon Tuohy to rebuild the limekiln. The Kyleomadaun kiln was worked up to relatively recently.

There was an art in building a kiln and Burgess supervised the work. It is built of stone, a round building about 10' in radius, 36' in diameter and 4' high. Inside it is oblong, narrowing towards the bottom. One side at the bottom is what is known as the kiln hole, the mouth from which the lime comes out after it has been calcined. This mouth is about 3' wide. Over the kiln hole on this ledge are three round holes, about 2' apart (still visible in above recent photograph of the kiln) which John Hogan said were used for props for a canopy, probably of galvanised iron, to protect the lime from rain as it poured out of the kiln hole.

The fuel used to burn the stone was culm, a mixture of coal dust, or anthracite. In order to get this fuel the Hogans had to go to Castlecomer in Co. Kilkenny. Jack Lynch of Garryncurra who was engaged to their sister Mary (and whom he later married) possessed one of the few lorries on the road at the time. He drew the culm from Castlecomer. The kiln was filled with alternate layers of culm and broken-up pieces of limestone and then set alight. There was a great art in lighting the fire and Paddy Burgess lit it for them for the first time and supervised the whole operation. It would be kept burning constantly for three months, then allowed to go out, all the accumulated debris cleared out, and a fresh lot of fuel and stone put in. Hogans' lime was of excellent quality. I have heard or read somewhere that long ago there were primitive limekilns in which turf was used for the burning.

How The Stone Was Obtained
This was the hardest part of the operation. The limestone hill behind Hogan's house had to be blasted open by gelignite in order to get at the stones. Permission for this had to be obtained from the Co. Council who then sent their engineer and an explosives expert – I believe it was Rody Nolan – to do the blasting. A hole would be bored into the hill and the gelignite inserted. The Hogans, Mary Lynch, Anne Vallette and Julia McDonnell and John remember very vividly the day the quarry was blasted. Anne and Julia were quite young children at the time. The Civic Guards – Sergeant Hannigan and probably a guard or two – had to stand at the Long Lane Cross to make sure nobody came along as it was a dangerous operation and stone could fly in all directions. The blasting operations produced enormous boulders. These boulders had to be somehow got on to the chassis of a cart pulled by two horses and carried to where they would be broken up. The kiln is quite a long way from the quarry – several hundred yards by road and then down quite a long lane. The huge boulders would be broken up into small manageable pieces by the three Hogan brothers wielding sledges. John and his sisters agreed that Tom was the best sledge man.

Sale of Lime
Four butter boxes of lime constituted a barrel and it was sold at four shillings a barrel. One shilling's worth would whitewash the outside of a house. Tommy Smith the postman, who was the Hogan's nearest neighbour, whitewashed the outside of his house once a year on Good Friday! People would come on bicycles for enough lime to whitewash their houses. Jack Lynch was kept busy delivering lorry loads of lime to farmers far and near and people came with their own transport. When the Hogans sold a quantity of lime to a farmer they had to furnish details to the Co. Council who then paid out the subsidy.

I was driven down the rough lane by Anne Hogan's son Freddie Vallette in his four-wheel drive on Sunday 24 January 1998. It was a sunny cold day. I was surprised at the elegance of the little building. We walked around the ledge at the top and gazed into the now cold and empty kiln. I found it quite a moving experience and am very grateful to the Hogan family and Freddie Valette for making the visit possible and for telling me the story. Sadly, Michael and Tommy are no longer with us, having died in 1997. Tom was my exact contemporary.

When lime was no longer used to make mortar, cement was substituted to make concrete. One of the first buildings in Kilbarron, and possibly Terryglass, to be built entirely of concrete was the store at Kilgarvan Quay. The first dwelling-house be built of this material was the house built circa 1912 by Patrick Curtin, the national teacher in Kilbarron. His brother-in-law, Will Hogan of Lisquillibeen, helped by his brothers, did the building. All the extensive and handsome woodwork was done by Martin and John Gorman of Bellevue. The slates came from Quinns of the slate quarries, Portroe. The house is still lived in by Patrick Curtin's daughter Eileen (Nell) and her husband Paddy Carroll, my brother.

SAWMILLS

In 1901 there was a sawmill at Kylenoe/Drominagh wood owned by Joseph Owens, Liverpool. Besides those already mentioned below, and in the photograph (below), there were several more Englishmen who worked in the saw mills. There were enough to make up a cricket team and they played against a Borrisokane side sometime before World War I. Amongst the workers were James Alfred Idle, James Hodgson, John Henry Jackson, and William Popplewell.

Soon after the photograph was taken, Mick Carroll left for America with three of his siblings and never returned. He was one of eight children of the Ballinderry miller, Pat Carroll died tragically, as related in chapter 10.

Paddy Fox, the carpenter, had a saw mill in Killeen in the 1930s. He later moved to Esmonde's estate at Drominagh where he operated a mill for a few years. Brian Williamson worked with him. They took on contracts for building cottages and built Terryglass school in 1952-4.

The Sawmill Workers circa 1903
Back row: Johnny Donoghue (he later joined the Dublin Metropolitan Police (DMP), Will Starr, Mike Starr (father of Willie Starr, hurler).
Front row: Standing slightly apart, is a man with a moustache named Jackson who was English, Will Corboy, another Englishman named Ronald Dilly, Michael Carroll (Jim's brother), Ballinderry, and Englishman named Billy Popplewell.

In Minchin's Wood

Dan Cash from Dolla, Nenagh, as a young man had a saw mill in Kilbiller beside Minchin's wood during and after World War I – where John Slattery's farmyard now stands. It was the biggest wood in Kilbarron parish. Many local men worked there including Will and Paddy Hogan of Lisquillibeen. Nenagh people also worked there – among them the father of Dan Morrissey, who drew timber with his horse and cart. Dan as a very young man worked at the saw bench in the mill. Paddy Hogan used to tell that years afterwards he was in the Hibernian Hotel in Nenagh having a pint after a visit to his doctor when Dan Morrissey, now a TD and Minister for Industry and Commerce, came in with some friends. He recognised Paddy, went over and shook his hand, and bought him a pint.

Dan Cash continued in the timber business up to the end of World War II, where the Nenagh cattle mart now stands.

Scotsmen

In 1905 a 'big wind' levelled much timber in Minchin's wood. A Scottish timber firm set up a saw mill there and cut up the trees. The workers lodged with the local people; some stayed at Hogans of Lisquillibeen, some at Mike Ryan's, the house in which Michael Carroll now lives, and others with Timothy Ryan, the house next door. One can imagine the stir they created in the little community and were remembered and talked about for many years afterwards. They were all Scotsmen. It was a high-risk occupation and it is recalled locally that one of the men who lodged with Tim Ryan had three fingers missing from one hand.

ORCHARDS

Kylenoe Wood, also known as Drominagh Wood, was the property of the Globe Insurance Company in 1850. It later became the property of the Evans family from Cloughjordan who planted the first orchards at Kylenoe. The next owner was Harry Williamson who improved the orchards. Lime was burned in the kiln on this land and spread around the apple trees.

In 1933 Archie Moeran took them over from Williamson. Jack Dwyer, Paddy Downey, Christy Hough, Will Corboy, Mick Creenane and Martin Dwyer had worked for Williamson. In 1961 Kenneth Moeran took over the orchards and planted many new varieties. He too used lime as a fertiliser. Apples from Kylenoe went to all parts of Ireland. A lot of workers were hired for the picking and grading of apples over the years.

When Kenneth Moeran died his wife Virginia (née Goodbody) took over the farm. Changes extended to removing most of the apple trees, leaving only the Bramleys. The reclaimed land is now farmed alongside a very successful farmhouse holiday business. Mrs Moeran also breeds horses.

CHARCOAL BURNING

In the mid-1940s during World War II petrol was becoming very scarce. Archibald (A. E.) Moeran of Kylenoe, a former agent to Lord Clanrickard, Portumna, got the idea of burning charcoal to produce a fuel to make gas to replace the petrol. Tone Fox and Tom Downey built the first kiln in Kylenoe Wood which was not a success. Mr Moeran gave it up as a bad job and went on a fishing expedition, telling the boys to forget about it.

Tom Downey and Mick Foot thought they would make another attempt. They got a steel drum and buried it in the ground for about three feet. They left an opening on the top for ventilation. It was then filled with small blocks of oak. Any wood would do but there was an abundance of oak in Kylenoe. They set the wood alight and left it. Next morning all they found in the drum was white ashes. They started again. This time they sealed up the top completely, having put in the wood. They bored three holes down the side of the drum and put 3-inch pipes coming out of the holes. They set the wood alight and sealed the whole lot up with earth – except, of course, the pipes. They could see no smoke coming out and next morning when the drum was opened they had perfect charcoal.

The charcoal was emptied into drums to cool and then put into bags. Tom Downey and Danno Donoghue built another kiln on the same principle and it was a great success. The kiln was lined with brick. I'm not sure if there was more than one kiln. The remains of an old brick-lined kiln can still be seen in the wood.

Other men who worked the charcoal burning were Jim Downey, Jim Nevin, and Mick Kirwan. Martin and Jack Dwyer cut down the timber which was sawn into blocks manually with a cross-cut saw. A little circular saw to cut it into small pieces was then used. Later on Wilsie Nolan and Seán Mackey (son of John), and possibly others from time to time, worked at the cutting of the timber. The charcoal was drawn up to Kilgarvan Quay by Danno Donoghue in a horse and cart and then taken by canal boat to Limerick and Banagher. In Limerick it was used by McMahons and MacAinishes. Some charcoal was also taken to Limerick by lorry, the haulier being Mike Hogan of Borrisokane. Charcoal taken to Banagher by boat was used by Wallers in their trucks. The chemical company, May and Roberts, sent down big vans for it from Dublin.

Tom Downey started working in Kylenoe in 1933 and retired in 1994. He received a medal of the R(oyal) D(ublin) S(ociety) for long service. He explained the charcoal-burning process to Wilsie Nolan in August 1997.

THE GROWING OF ARTICHOKES

Synthetic rubber can be made from artichokes, which is a thistle-like plant with a large, scaly head. For some years before the outbreak of World War I England had become nervous of the prospect of being cut off from its natural supplies of rubber in the Far East in the event of a war with Germany. Accordingly, the British Government got the idea of getting farmers to grow artichokes from which to produce a rubber substitute at home. Seed and fertiliser would be free. Matt Fogarty, as a child, had heard some vague story about the growing of this crop – as indeed I had in my childhood.

Going through old papers of his uncle, Rev. Matt Fogarty, he found a letter from his grandmother (Fr Matt's mother) to her son, dated 9 March 1914. Its highlight was the story of the artichokes.

> Dr Esmonde [Dr John Esmonde, MP, grandfather of Tony] signed all the agreeements yesterday in Terryglass [re the artichokes]. 'The County' is giving the field at the back of the barn and the glen. ['The County' was the nickname by which her husband, Denis Fogarty, was always known as he was a member of Tipperary (NR) Co. Council].

This amounted to fourteen acres. Many other farmers signed up and the artichokes were planted. This was March 1914. Before the crop could be harvested, World War I had broken out and the Government had lost interest in home-grown rubber. It was too late. The farmers were left with the artichokes. History does not tell us what became of them or if the farmers were compensated.

TOBACCO GROWING

In 1932 the Government had a scheme to get farmers to grow tobacco under licence. The seed was paid for by the Government and a contract was entered into with a big tobacco firm to supply the seed and anything else necessary – know-how I expect – and then to buy the finished product. I don't think too many people took it up. John Gleeson, the national school principal, then living at Gortmore on his ten acres, decided to devote a quarter acre to tobacco.

Apparently, the sowing and growing of the plant, and then the harvesting of it, did not present a big problem. It was the drying which was the nightmare. Firstly, you had to have a suitable room. Fortunately, the Gleeson house at Gortmore was well supplied with rooms and a big back kitchen was used. The tobacco had to be tied in bunches of ten stems and these bunches had to be hung on hazel rods on crooks on the ceiling as evenly apart as possible. Then little fires had to be lit all around the room – quite a lot of fires – in little pots or any suitable receptacle. Only timber could be used, not turf. I'm not sure if a special wood had to be used. These little fires had to be going evenly night and day for as long as it took for the leaves to reach the correct texture. The bunches had to be moved to ensure that each got a fair amount of the smoke.

I do not know how long the process took but by the end of it John Gleeson had decided he would stick to teaching and not become a tobacco grower. Only someone who was a perfectionist could be bothered to go through the process at all. His wife, I am sure, had to do a great deal of the looking after. Clunes, the tobbaco manufacturers, bought the product and gave a good price. Apart from all the finicky work involved, the growing of tobacco exhausted the land.

A few people managed to get hold of some seed without a licence and grew tobacco illegally. Some even smoked it but it must have been vile. Even the properly dried leaves when ground into tobacco were too strong and fiery: it probably needed various spices to sweeten it. Perhaps one day the government will have a scheme to grow cannabis. It can't do much more harm than tobacco does! Incidentally, Christy Gleeson, John's son, says that to this day he has not finally got rid of the smoke stains from that back kitchen!

DRESSMAKING

Up to a few decades ago it was unusual to buy ready-made clothes, particularly for children. As children, and indeed well into adulthood, we had all our clothes made by the local dressmakers, Mrs Jack Donoghue (née Mary Tully) and her daughter Mary, later Mrs Pat Donoghue, Lacken. My father always referred to them as 'mantie makers', a corruption of the phrase 'mantua (or mantle) makers'. Going to the dressmaker was quite an outing as we were always given tea and hot scones at Donoghues.

The only ready-made garments I remember were our Confirmation dresses, which were made of embroidered voile, and possibly also the First Communion dress. Two outfits had to be provided for the Confirmation – one for the catechism examination by the bishop, and the white voile one, with a veil, for the next day's Confirmation ceremony. My sister May and I were confirmed together and Mrs Donoghue made us identical examination day dresses. They were saxe blue with white bows. The voile dresses and other accessories – white shoes, stockings and gloves – were purchased at Miss Meagher's, Borrisokane.

The dress was sometimes worn afterwards, or it might be passed on to a cousin or neighbour for another child. Mothers whose daughters had straight hair spent considerable time and skill making ringlets by winding the hair around newspaper.

The dressmaker would go to the Big Houses and spend the day, or several days, sewing for the family. Mrs Margaret Darcy (née Carroll) would drive down to Killeen House in the donkey and trap to Ellie Esmonde and spend the day sewing. Julia Kelly (Mrs Finane), Brocka, would spend several days there. She features in Pamela Hinkson's *Irish Gold* as Julia Gleeson. Mary Donoghue would spend days at Bellevue House and Brookfield sewing for Zelie Biggs and Mrs Parker-Reeves.

Ciss Hogan (later Mrs Cahalan), Macloon, was the dressmaker who made clothes for us when we were grown up. I remember cycling to Macloon with Eileen (Nell) Curtin, now my sister-in-law, on a sunny evening in August 1939, to collect dresses a few days before my return to London. Nell sang as we cycled along, 'Sweet Little Angeline' and 'Little Apples', two hit songs of the day. Within a week World War II had broken out.

A generation earlier Johanna Molamphy worked as a dressmaker, first at her home in Bellevue and later in Coolbawn. My aunt, Mary Carroll, whose story is told in 'Beyond the Seas', worked likewise up to her emigration in 1887.

PLOUGHING IN KILBARRON

John Slattery supplied this account, and I have adapted it.

Ploughing and the Slatterys have long been synonymous in this parish. John Slattery of Kilbiller, born in 1933, and his sons have carried on the tradition. His late father Joe, had a great love of ploughing and was a good horse-ploughman. He ploughed in a competition in the 1930s in Lahorna.

John's first ploughing match was in Cloughjordan in 1956. He competed in his first All-Ireland junior ploughing contest in 1963 in Athenry. In 1974 at Watergrasshill, Cork, he won the junior All-Ireland with the late Rodge Callanan, Horse & Jockey, as a team. John has been one of the pair representing North Tipperary in the senior All-Irelands since 1974, coming fourth in 1979.

The North Tipperary ploughing championships started in Cloughjordan and were held in that area for some years. They were then held in the Rathcabbin area and have been held in Kilbarron in 1993 and 1996. His first North Tipperary senior win was in 1967. Since then he has won the North Tipperary title in 1969, 1972-3, 1976, 1978-80, 1982, 1984-6, 1988, 1990, 1991-8 – a total of 22 titles to date.

From January to March every year he competes in ploughing matches nearly every weekend. He has won many titles in counties Clare, Galway, Limerick, South Tipperary, Kilkenny, Laois, Carlow, Offaly, Westmeath and Longford.

John says he always had great encouragement from his brother Tom and his neighbour, the late Seán Costelloe. Seán was a great horse ploughman and later on with the tractor, but he did not plough in competitions.

John's sons, Joe and Ciarán, have also ploughed competitively and won the under-28 All-Ireland championships in 1988, 1989 and 1990. Both of them won several North Tipp titles in the under-21 and under-28 classes. Ciarán came second in the All-Ireland under-21 in Limerick in 1991. He was second in the under-28 in the All-Ireland championships held in Ballacolla, Co. Laois, 1995.

John's grandfather, John Slattery of Glenbower, known as 'The Brown', was also a great ploughman. In 1911 Robert Waller's land was divided up by the Land Commission, mainly between the small farmers and smallholders of Coolbawn and Lisquilabeen. Many of these smallholders would not have the necessary equipment, i.e. horses, ploughs and other implements to plough and till the land which they received and it was the custom for the neighbours to lend the equipment and give a hand generally to the new landholder.

Such a one was my father's first cousin, William (Bill) Carroll of Lisquilabeen. In 1911 he still held only the 4 acres which Jeremiah Carroll, his grandfather – my great-grandfather – is listed as holding in the Tithe Applotment list of 1824. As part of his 'divide' Bill had got the fine field at the Long Lane Cross, on the left going to Kilbarron village from Coolbawn. His son Peter later sold it to the present John Slattery's son, and young John and his wife Madeleine have built a house there.

This field must have been left fallow for a very long time because the *meitheal* (gathering of helpers) which had gathered to plough it up in 1911 found it impossible to shift the ground. Jack Whelan of the Hill, and afterwards of Gurteen, very young at the time, was there with a plough and pair of horses. He attempted to open up a furrow but found it impossible. Grandfather John Slattery came along with his team of horses and soon showed the young ploughman how to yoke up the team the right way in order to get a grip on the hard, fallow ground.

John Slattery in action

Carpentry

In 1927 the first new house that I saw being built in Kilbarron was for Burkes of Firgrove. O'Meara's of Borrisokane were the contractors and Jack Carroll of the Finnoe Rd, my first cousin, was one of the tradesmen. I believe O'Meara's house in Kevanstown was built about the same time by the same contractors. The first two new bungalows in this parish were Treacy's of Bellevue and Hough's of Lisquillibeen.

In Terryglass parish the Fox family were noted carpenters. Will Fox and his sons Paddy and Anthony did much of the local carpentry work. In an earlier generation Anthony Fox of Curraghmore was a boatbuilder and carpenter. He may have been a brother of Will. There is a sundial on the terrace at Castletown which had a brass plaque inscribed, 'repaired by Anthony Fox pupil of P. Moran', i.e. Pat Moran, the schoolmaster. During alterations to the roof of the castle some heavy stone fell on the sundial and smashed it and after it was again repaired the plaque was not replaced and is now mislaid.

James and Patrick ('Guardian') Cahalan were, and are, noted carpenters and cabinet makers. They made the dresser for Danny O'Donoghue now in Joe's home. Willie Ryan of Ryehill served his time to John Egan of Borrisokane but died before he could do much work.

The Gormans of Bellevue and Coolbawn were carpenters until after World War I. John Gorman and Jack ('Butticks') Smith of Bellvue were sent to Portroe to be apprenticed to a carpenter there. When John Gorman had learned his trade he passed it on to his brother Martin. I am told that Martin was the better carpenter of the two. I do not think that Jack Smith ever practised his trade. John Gorman's son Jack learned the trade from his father but never practised it to my knowledge.

A Tree Nursery

Matt Fogarty is a man who not only loves trees and talking about trees but also has a great knowledge of them. He now has at Drominagh one of the most successful, and indeed beautiful, tree nurseries in Ireland.

He traces his initial interest in trees to two factors. Sometime in the early 1950s he was going through an old bookcase and came on a tree catalogue posted in 1930 to his mother (who was Anne O'Meara of Kevanstown). The little trees were advertised at prices like 3, 4, and 6 old pence each. The other factor was that his O'Meara uncle, Bro. Paul, was head gardener at the Cistercian monastery near Roscrea. During the war his mother would hire a car and go to Roscrea to visit her brother and take Matt with her. There he would spend much time with his uncle going around and admiring the gardens and trees of which his uncle was immensely proud. It would seem that love of trees was in his genes. It was not only trees he had a great interest in, but all nature and wild life.

Matt lives at Drominagh Lodge near Ballinderry, which his grandfather, Patrick Fogarty, a native of Kilcolman in Youghalarra-Burgess parish, purchased circa 1880 with a fine farm of about one hundred acres. His father Denis had farmed this in a conventional way, with a dairy herd and some tillage mainly.

Matt continued in that tradition. In 1957 he planted his first few trees –

softwoods. In the early 1960s he got more softwoods but in the late 1960s his interest spread to hardwoods – beech, oak, lime, ash, walnut, Spanish chestnut. 'Spanish chestnut', he says, 'is a lovely tree'. He began to feel that the future was in hardwoods. His enthusiasm for them shines through as he speaks of all the different types of beech and oak. He has a particular love for beech and oak saying that you could have up to ten or twelve varieties of these, which indeed he has.

He went on planting hardwoods and by mid-1987 had built up quite a selection of trees of various types. Friends would come and he would give them a few little trees to take away. They would offer to buy instead of taking them as gifts. Finally, someone suggested to him that he should start a tree nursery.

Crann

In 1987 a lady named Jean Alexander came from Australia. She was interviewed on radio about wanting to plant hardwood trees in Ireland. Matt said to his wife Mary, 'I'm going to meet that girl'. They met and developed a great rapport. She gave him every encouragement to go ahead and came to Drominagh Lodge on a number of occasions. She started the movement Crann (Irish for 'tree'), a flourishing organisation engaged in the promotion of growing hardwood trees. Matt was one of the founder members.

In 1989 he decided to develop the hobby into a business. Farming friends frowned on good land being 'wasted' under trees. He knew that no hardwoods were being planted. Even then he felt that hardwoods were the thing of the future.

When in 1989 he decided this was the way he wanted to go he went to the local bank manager to borrow the money for the initial expenditure. The bank manager required an outline of what was proposed, and how long it would take before any returns could be expected – five years was the shortest time before the investment would yield a profit. The manager said he would let him know as soon as possible.

It was a type of investment very unfamiliar to him and he probably had to consult head office. In due course a letter arrived: 'Dear Mr Fogarty ...' saying that the bank could not see its way to lend the money for the purpose suggested.

Matt waited a fortnight and then visited the bank again with a request for roughly the same amount of money to buy cattle. He got the loan at once. He went home, bought a few head of cattle, and spent the rest on trees. When he was paying back the last of the loan a few years later the bank manager inquired, 'did you buy cattle?' 'No', Matt said, 'I bought trees'. No doubt in a small community the bank manager would have been well aware that Matt Fogarty had been planting trees with the money which should have been spent on cattle!

The Old-Age Pensioners

When Matt got going and Crann started, all the hardwoods in the country were very old, with most going back to the 1780s and 1790s when the British Government got worried about the shortage of timber for shipbuilding.

The government of the day, according to Matt, gave financial assistance to landowners to plant trees. The Royal Dublin Society claim they were involved in planting two million hardwood trees at that time. All around us in this parish many of these hardwood trees are growing in the big demesnes and many of them are over two hundred years old. 'If you go to a beech wood you do not see teenagers, only old-age pensioners.' By the time the government-sponsored trees had grown to maturity, the first iron-clad ships were being built so the hardwood trees were no longer used for ship-building and were left to grow on. Beech has a life-span of 200-250 years; oak much longer – 600-800 years.

In the will of Solomon L. Cambie of Castletown and Brookfield, written in 1792, the year he died, there is mention of 'a large quantity of timber now growing on the lands of Castletown and Clonmackilladuff which have hitherto been carefully reserved and which is well worth one thousand five hundred pounds'. Some of the trees are still on the Castletown estate but those at Clonmackilladuff must at some time have been sold off to help pay legacies to his numerous progeny.

Travels
Matt Fogarty has travelled widely in pursuit of his interest in trees. He has visited the USA about six times, particularly loves Northern California and thinks the Californian Redwoods are wonderful trees. He has many on his farm. He particularly enjoyed three national parks – Yosemite, in the Sierra Nevada mountains about two hundred miles from San Francisco which contains about 400 redwoods, Big Sur south of San Francisco, and Murir Woods, which are twenty miles north of San Francisco.

The latter is named after a Scotsman named Murir who, with the American president of the day, Theodore (Teddy) Roosevelt, was responsible for preserving the Californian redwoods. They were being cut down indiscriminately and would soon have all disappeared had Murir not got the President to co-operate with him in having the destruction halted. They are now totally preserved. Matt crossed through New England in the autumn to experience one of the most wondrous sights in the world, the flaming golds, yellows and russet reds of the woods of north-east America – Vermont, Maine and New Hampshire.

In Poland on the border with the Ukraine he visited a great beech and oak forest where charcoal is burned. It is very well managed and a tree is never cut down but another replaces it. This forest was preserved in the time of the Czars, so that the Czar of the day could go boar hunting. The forest has the largest oak tree in Europe, four or five hundred years old. The first branch is sixty feet off the ground.

Every year about October Matt Fogarty goes to England to visit Kew Gardens in London, Hilliers Arboretum at Romsey in Hampshire; he also visits the Scottish forests and has visited New Mexico. A point he makes very forcibly is how his interest in trees has enriched his life through the many and varied friends of all nationalities he has made through a common interest – both on his travels abroad and when people come to his nursery at Drominagh.

The Farm Today
Most of the farm's 95 acres is planted to commercial forestry with a smaller amount given to a nursery from which Matt and Mary sell a huge selection of young broadleaves. He has over 200 types of trees and increasing every year. He has a huge variety of broadleaves and the more unusual conifers. These include the Giant Redwood, Tulip trees, Walnuts, Spanish Chestnut and a wide variety of oaks. To date he has sold to twenty-five of the twenty-six counties of the Republic. The Fogartys have had a number of very successful open days with a crowd of 600 on one occasion.

Among the important factors in growing hardwoods, soil is number one. The

Fogartys are fortunate in that for the most part their land is fertile, deep and well-drained brown earth. This land gives excellent growth rates to most conifers and broadleaves. Any problems with rabbits and hares can be overcome.

Matt says old trees should be cut down. The timber becomes brittle and they are liable to crash down. If one has any interest in the environment, one shouldn't plant a lot of trees at once; rather, plant gradually.

Matt Fogarty's great interest extends to his splendid library, including Thomas Pakenham's acclaimed *Meetings With Remarkable Trees* (1996).

RDS Award
Matt's and Mary's years of hard work and courage for their major investment in the hobby-turned-business were rewarded when they were picked as the outright winner in the Farm Forestry category at the RDS in 1995. On Tuesday 12 December 1995 they were presented with the perpetual trophy and £1,000 by Ivan Yates, TD, the then Minister for Agriculture.

My Three Oak Trees

My three oak trees stand in a group together
    Like old friends waking mem'ries of the past,
Discussing this day's news, tomorrow's weather
    And if the price of cattle's set to last.

I wonder if, in twice a hundred years
    Though stars may fade and all I love may lie
Beyond the reach of laughter or of tears,
    They still will stand and watch the times go by.

Last year they lay, small acorns on the grass;
    Now safe and warm behind their sheltering wall
They reach with eager tendrils, reach and pass:
    My three oak trees, six splendid inches tall.

- May O'Meara, 1990

Lakeshore Foods

Since the grist mill closed in Ballinderry in 1962 there had been no industry in the village or its environs to give employment to local people, especially young girls, housewives and anyone without transport. Hilary Henry (right), who had spent the first six years of her life in Cloughjordan, and whose family was grown up, had been living in Waterloo Lodge for some years and recognised those needs. Hilary, a Trinity College graduate, had worked as a teacher until resigning to raise her family.

She had always experimented with wholegrain mustard for domestic use and knew that no mustard was manufactured in Ireland and that imported products were very expensive. At that time, 1984-5, Nuala Fennell, TD, Minister for Women's Affairs, was encouraging women to become entrepreneurs.

In order to become registered as a business it was necessary to start at the Food Technology Business Unit, jointly operated by AnCO (now FÁS) and Shannon Development in Raheen, Hilary's enterprise began as a very small single-handed operation. Her own first recipe was for Honey Mustard, and to that she added Guinness Mustard and Irish Whiskey Mustard to appeal to overseas visitors.

The products were made by soaking mustard seed, then liquidising them with natural flavours. No artificial colouring, additives or preservatives were added. Some of her first few samples were taken to Peter Ward, Country Choice, Nenagh, to test the market and get a reaction before taking a unit at Raheen. They sold well. After six months in business she got grant aid from Shannon Development to renovate a mews building behind her Waterloo Lodge home. This became her first local production unit of 300 sq. feet as of 1 January 1987.

Her object had always been to employ local labour. Mrs Henry was getting a telephone call put through one day when she asked Mary Fox, the operator, what she was going to do when the new automatic telephone exchange in Ballinderry came into operation. Mary had no idea. Hilary invited her to 'come and work for me'. Mary came, and stayed on after her marriage to Gerard Hogan and the birth of their children until 1995. The business soon employed four girls, three of them named Mary Hogan which complicated matters for the tax people and such like! The fourth girl was Rosie Fox. Cora Coen helped with the garden at Waterloo where horseradish, another ingredient, was grown.

Irish Materials

Hilary Henry was very keen to use only Irish materials in her products. She even hoped to grow mustard seed in Ireland but was advised by ACOT, now Teagasc, that the climate was not dry enough. So she relied on seed imported from England.

Her next problem was to source containers – a specific shape of jar, but the Irish Glass Bottle Co., would not produce the design in the small quantities required, so she had to import the hexagonal jars which became her trademark.

To Ballinderry

In 1990 Hilary Henry bought the shop and petrol pump in Ballinderry from Bernard Darcy which his late parents, Dan & May Darcy, had owned. The old forge, also Darcy property, was restored as cottage tearooms, keeping the old-fashioned character with half-door and roses around it. The other buildings were demolished and, with Shannon Development aid, a purpose-built 3,000 sq. feet factory was erected to the highest standards. The builder was Christy Cormican, Glenbower. Lakeshore Foods transferred there in May 1991.

As the business grew the staff complement rose to 10 or 12, mostly local girls and women. On its tenth birthday in 1997 over twenty products were being manufactured in Ballinderry. These included mustards, three different dressings, a mint sauce, rum butter, brandy butter and a ham glaze. They also manufactured diabetic mince meat for the UK chain store, Boots, sun-dried tomatoes marinated in oil for a company in Cork, and herbs and spices for a company in Dublin. Ballinderry-made products are now sold all over Ireland and in the UK, Europe and the USA.

In 1994 Lakeshore Foods employed Boyne Valley Foods, Drogheda, as their distributors with an option for them to buy out. This option was exercised in 1997 but it continues to trade as Lakeshore Foods. The new owners did not continue the tearooms as they required it as factory space.

Lakeshore Foods has put Ballinderry on the map, somewhat in the same way as the orchards put Kylenoe, though much farther afield. Its success is due to the steely determination of one woman not to be put off by the many obstacles encountered, as well as the helpful assistance of Shannon Development and, as she readily acknowledges, a splendid staff.

A family tradition says that Hilary Henry's grandfather, when going hunting, always took mustard sandwiches for his lunch, washed down, I have no doubt, with some brand of Irish whiskey!

Sources:
Forges to Ploughing: Civil Survey. Hearth Money Rolls. Primary Valuation. Daniel Grace, *Portrait of a Parish: Monsea & Killodiernan.* Wilsie Nolan, Paddy Carroll, John Gleeson, John Slattery. Author's personal knowledge.
Tree Nursery: Matt Fogarty.
Lakeshore Foods: *Irish Times*, 1986. *The Guardian*, 1996. *Mag-Net*, 1996. Hilary Henry.

Photographs: pp. 334, 338 taken by Paddy Carroll; p. 340 loaned by Wilsie Nolan; p. 345 loaned by John Slattery; p. 350 loaned by Hilary Henry

14
Some Parish Folkore

During the 1930s the Department of Irish Folklore was set up in University College, Dublin, under Professor Séamus Delargy. Around 1933-4 the Department sent out questionnaires to national schools throughout the country asking the teachers to get their older pupils to go around the parishes to gather as much folkore as still existed, especially from the older people. In Terryglass principal teacher John Gleeson took the project so seriously that his school received a prize for the best project in North Tipperary. Extracts from the folklore collected by the children in Terryglass in 1934 are given below. I have added additional information or comments in chain brackets [ ].

It is a noteworthy that three contributions come from members of the Parkinson family, especially as Michael Parkinson has contributed current memoirs to the chapters, Religion, Across the Seas and Hurling.

Local Industries That Have Disappeared

Mrs Sarah Parkinson, Slevoir, born in Slevoir and aged 92 years, a farmer, related the following information told to her about sixty years earlier [in the 1870s] at Slevoir by her father, William [Billy] Hough, aged 70 at the time. She married Michael Parkinson in 1868.

My aunts (Houghs) were spinners and weavers of flax which was grown by the farmers then for the making of linen clothes – shirts for men and 'shifts' for the women, also table-cloths and all household linen required for the homes.

All the work from the scutching to the making of the finished article was done at their home. Sometimes they engaged travelling women to do the carding of the flax.

The scutching pool is still on the land and near it is the field known as the spreading green.

Many people from the parish, or outside it, who were in need of linen clothes came with their orders to the house and they were never long delayed in waiting for what they wanted.

William Heenan of Crossanagh, Terryglass, aged about 60, a farmer, born at Crossanagh, related the following which he heard from his parents at Crossanagh.

Flax was grown in Ashgrove about seventy years ago [in the 1860s]. Spinning was carried on by Biddy Mason and Nance Reddan who lived in Terryglass. The only weaver at the time in the parish was Stephen Darcy, Crossanagh. He was the last weaver in the parish as both spinning and weaving ceased about fifty years ago in Terryglass.

The Ashgrove flax was sown under the instructions of a man named MacLynchy who came from the North of Ireland. The hackling of the flax was not done in the district; it was done in Kiloganny mill [the ruins of which are still to be seen in 1998 on the Borrisokane-Nenagh road in Mount Falcon townland.]

John Parkinson of Slevoir, a farmer, born at Slevoir and aged about 50, gave the following information which he got from his father Michael, aged about 35 at the time. [John Parkinson was born in 1875; his father married in 1868].

About fifty years ago turf-cutting was an important industry in the parish as very large quantities were cut for sale. In some districts, like Nenagh and Portroe, there were no bogs so that people who lived in places with a plentiful supply of bog were kept busy during the summer months cutting and saving turf.

Men at the time were great turf-cutters and the slanesmen vied with one another as to who could cut the greatest number of 'kish' in the day.

Work was begun at sunrise and continued until sunset while the turf-cutting season lasted and the money made on the turf was hard earned.

When the turf was fully saved it was drawn in kishes to Terryglass quay. Boats called there and carried away this fuel to Youghal[arra], Nenagh.

Above John Parkinson got the following information from his grandfather, aged about 75 at the time.

About seventy years ago there were manufactured in Carrigahorig, Birr, brogues or strong shoes. No other footwear of the kind was made for men at the time. If the *bróg* maker was speedy and skilful at his work he got ready call for his produce at home. The people of the parish kept the *bróg* maker busy the whole year, so that he had no occasion to go to look for outside markets.

Now and again he would carry a *cliabh* of brogues to the local fairs or markets.

Horse-racing
Brigid Parkinson, Slevoir, aged 64, a farmer, born in Slevoir, got the following information on the races and the Great Famine from her grandfather when he was aged about 50.

Kyleagoona (situated about 3 miles west of Borrisokane and beside the main road from Terryglass to the former town) [in Tombricane townland] was the traditional centre for horse-racing. It was a place of note in its heyday. Gentry in their carriages and on horseback travelled from Galway, Tipperary, and Offaly to attend the race meetings. The race fields used be thronged with carriages, caravans, tents and stalls. Food and drink were supplied in the tents.

A permanent stand was erected beside the course and from it a general view of the race was possible. Also, the race could be viewed from the public road.

The Great Famine
During Black '47 many people died of famine and fever. In one townland in the parish of Terryglass – Garrownaglogh – all the people were completely swept away. Eviction helped the terrible famine.

Before the famine there were forty houses in this townland, but not one remained afterwards. One house got the special name of 'Black Jane', so called after one of the emigrant ships (at the time) which was engaged in rushing the starving people from Ireland to America. Many of these unfortunate emigrants spread the fever among others on board, and the dead bodies of the victims were cast overboard as soon as death had set in. In this 'Black Jane' house the entire family died of hunger and disease.

The poorest of the inhabitants – the labourers depending on their day's wages for food – were the first to fall victims to the hunger. Farmers could not afford to pay wages, and even later on in the Famine period it was only the well-to-do farmers who had even a store of meal for stirabout.

One day a poor man named Connell came to the house of Billy Hough (grandfather to the narrator of this story). B. Hough and his family were having their meal of stirabout at the time. The kind-hearted man of the house invited the hungry man to join them. He did so, eating ravenously the share set before him. When leaving, he returned his thanks thus: 'God bless you Billy Hough, that is the only bit of food that went into my stomach within the last three days'.

A certain family living near B. Hough were suffering from the great hunger, but pride kept hidden their wants. They would not ask or beg – they would die sooner than beg.

The kind old farmer skilfully made a bargain with the starving family for some worthless pieces of old irons. When the bargain was completed the irons were brought in a bag to Hough's house by one of the hungry children. Looking at the pinched face of the child the good man was moved with compassion. 'Give some meal to the child as payment for those things', he said in a matter-of-fact tone of voice.

Billy Hough was asked if he ever felt the hunger of those days. He replied that he was forced once to go to his work without his breakfast.

Faction Fights

Mrs Darcy, Ballinderry, Borrisokane, then aged about 50, a dressmaker, born in Ballinderry, heard the following story from her mother named Margaret Carroll about 35 years ago. Her mother was about 50 at the time. Story told in Ballinderry.

About one hundred years ago [early in the nineteenth century] there were in the parish of Terryglass two great faction fighting families; one came from Shanavalla, Carrigahorig, the other from Ballinderry. There was a long standing dispute between the two parties. They finally decided to fight out the matter at the annual Kyleagoona races.

In those days Kyleagoona was a noted racecourse and people from Galway, Nenagh and other distant places were accustomed to come to the famous races. All the people from the locality flocked there, walking long distances as there were no cars to speak of or bicycles.

The Shanavalla man and his friends came in strong numbers to the races to enjoy the day and finish the fight. The Ballinderry man with his backers was there too.

When the challengers met the fight began. The men fought with blackthorn sticks and loaded butts. The Shanavalla man was far the better fighter and he gave a savage beating to the Ballinderry man leaving him half dead on the field. To celebrate the event the winner and his friends got drunk. They marched home across the bog to Shanavalla singing and shouting.

Author's note: The names of the faction fighters were given by Mrs Darcy but the IFC would not permit their publication.

Hurling

Above John Parkinson, Slevoir, got the following information from his grandfather at Slevoir, then aged about 75.

About 80 years ago men loved hurling on Sundays and the matches were played in certain selected parks for the start of the match. Shanavalla, Carrigahorig, was the usual hurling ground. Hurling home was the oldest form of game known. Two teams met at a selected spot. The ball was thrown in and such a ball was big and heavy. The hurleys, too, were not like those used at the present day. They were long, stout wattles somewhat like a spade handle. With these awkward wattles the men could readily raise the ball off the ground and puck it a long distance.

An active young man would then pursue the ball with the speed of a hound, and catching up upon it would drive it back or forth, according to the direction of his own parish from the sport. Indeed there was much hurling back and forth as there were speedy men on both sides watching for the flying ball.

There was no referee and few rules were observed. These determined matches ended in free fights, the spectators taking part in the fight. A broken shin accidentally received was usually the cause of a big row.

In those days men dressed in knee-breeches with brass buttons, long stockings, brogues of strong, stout leather, heavy frieze coats and Caroline hats. Before the hurling match started the men took off coats, brogues, stockings and hats wearing nothing but shirt and breeches.

While men were engaged in the hurling the girls and young women present took up a corner of the field playing such games as High-Gates.

Sources:
Irish Folklore Commission S 530: 451, 466, 467, 468, Irish Folklore Collection, UCD. This material is published with the permission of the Department of Irish Folklore, University College Dublin.

15
Hurling

THE EARLY YEARS – 1885-1934

The game of hurling is known to have been played in Ormond as far back as 1765. It was sponsored and supported by the local landlords. Games played were challenge matches between parish teams or between teams from the landlords' tenants. Carrigahorig was the main venue for matches.

The landlords and local gentry often attended matches and placed bets on their favourite teams. Rev. Francus Synge of Slevoir was at one such game and was so impressed by a team of light, hungry-looking men that he got the idea that if they were fed well they would beat all before them. He brought them to Slevoir and fixed up quarters for them over the stables. He fed them well: the baker's cart came twice a week and the butcher's cart once a week. They did light training for a couple of hours every day. He challenged another team to play in Carrigahorig and backed them heavily. They were badly beaten – they were fat instead of fit. He lost a lot of money and lost interest in the hurling as well.

The Gaelic Athletic Association was founded in Thurles on 1 November 1884. In 1885 thirty-five clubs were formed, of which Kilbarron was one. We do not know the composition of this first Kilbarron club. Canon Philip Fogarty's *Tipperary's GAA Story* names Jim Darcy and Jim Dwyer, Kilbarron, as being amongst those in 1886 who helped the Gaelic revival in their respective parishes and were not otherwise prominent.

In March 1886 a convention of clubs was held in Nenagh and a North Tipperary 'branch' of the Association was formed. T. Brooder and T. Costello were named as the delegates from 'North Kilbarron'.

Prior to that, in February 1886, North Tipperary played the first inter-county match under GAA rules in Dublin against South Galway and won. The team included James Brooder, Brocka, Kilbarron. Although it was advertised as 'the Great Hurling Match of the Championship of Ireland' it was actually a challenge promoted by Michael Cusack, founder and general secretary of the GAA. He refereed the match in the Phoenix Park. Canon Fogarty as Tipperary historian claimed that 'the Connaught men failed to keep pace with the unbridled youths from Tipp'. But the Galway historian, Pádraig Ó Laoi, quoted *The Freeman's Journal*: 'The better team did not win'.

James Brooder (right) of Brocka was born in 1869 and would have been only seventeen at the time. I was told by his grand-niece a short while ago that he emigrated to the USA and was never heard of again. John Carroll of Brookfield would recall as an old man that he had been picked to play for Tipperary when he was twenty but because of family circumstances did not go to Dublin for the match. He was born in 1866.

A completely different group of clubs in South Galway now challenged North Tipperary who again won at Limerick in early April.

By October 1886, the North Tipperary branch were able to run a tournament whose eighteen entrants included Kilbarron and Carrigahorig. The trophy was the silver cup won in Dublin; it now found a permanent home with the tournament winners, Silvermines. Two vice-Presidents of the GAA, J. K. Bracken, Templemore, and F. R. Maloney, Nenagh, were billed to attend Carrigahorig for a general meeting of its 'newly-established club' on Sunday 10 October.

By February 1887 difficulties seem to have arisen. North Tipperary played Carrigatoher, a few miles south-west of Nenagh, 'for the championship of the Co. Tipperary'! Carrigatoher included some who were 'formerly of the North Tipperary team'; North Tipp 'suffered visibly, being at the loss of several of their back men, notably the Brooders, and their ever-vigilant goal-keeper, either John or Peter Carroll'. One assumes they were Kilbarron men.

There were no Lower Ormond hurlers in what is regarded by the GAA as the first All-Ireland (in which just five counties participated) – the 1887 final played between Tipperary and Galway at Birr on Easter Sunday 1888. Tipperary. won, represented by a selection who included players from a wide catchment in the Thurles area.

Problems within the GAA central council in 1887 saw a decline in the spread of the organisation. During a period in the early 1890s football, rather than hurling, was played in various places including Toomevara and Kilbarron. The 1890-1 political split over the Parnell divorce issue had reverberations in the GAA and there were several barren years.

KILBARRON

The only detailed records of the Shannon Rovers hurling club, Kilbarron, which are available begin in 1898 and go on until 1906. During this period Peter Carroll of Brookfield was Treasurer and Honorary Secretary of the club and kept meticulous and detailed notes of club membership subscriptions, fixtures and expenditure. These notebooks are in the possession of his family at Brookfield.

The inaugural meeting of what eventually became officially known as the Shannon Rovers Hurling Club was held in March 1898. The following officers were elected: President, John Lynch; Vice-President, Martin Tierney; Captain, Stephen Starr; Treasurer and Hon. Secretary, Peter Carroll. Committee: James Kemple, Stephen Coffey, James Ryan, James Bouchier, Pat Starr, Matt Costelloe, Thomas Cahalan, Wm. Starr, Wm. Heffernan, John Starr, Patrick Smith, Thomas Smith, James Cormack, Tim Hoctor, Patrick Smith, John Bouchier, Denis Madden. At first the club was confined to the Kilbarron end of the parish but later on it covered the Terryglass end also – perhaps after the rule which restricted a player to his own and one other parish came into force in 1902.

The subscriptions amounted to £1 0s 6d. On 6 March a match was held at Kilbarron between Youghalarra and Kilbarron (Shannon Rovers). Score: Kilbarron 1-0, Youghalarra 0-0. The refreshments cost £1, leaving sixpence in the kitty.

The following Sunday, 13 March, subscriptions are recorded from, besides the aforementioned committee, Dan Ryan, Bryan Casey, John Costelloe, Pat Cahalan,

John Lynch, Carney Commons (top left), first Chairman of Shannon Rovers in 1898.
Peter Carroll, Brookfield (top right), first Hon. Secretary and whose Minute Book is drawn on for the club's early activities.
Stephen Starr (above) was first captain.

John Carroll (left), Brookfield, selected to play on the Tipperary selection to play a Galway selection in Dublin in 1886, but he did not travel. Tipperary won that game and also the rematch in Limerick. He was on the club team of 1900.

Joseph O'Meara, John Donohoe, Edward Lawlor, W. B. Ainsley, Jerry Hogan, James Ryan, James Carroll, Wm. Kane, Captain Minchin, F. J. Minchin, P. Brien. These yielded £2 0s 6d which was spent on a trip to Newtown for a return match with Youghalarra. Score: Kilbarron 1-2, Youghal 0-0. So the Rovers set off trailing clouds of glory! The breakdown of the cost of the outing to Newtown was: brake, £1 5s, car for five men 7s, car for three men 4s, ball 1s 6d, balance 3s, which was then spent on hurling balls.

The cars would have been horse-drawn side cars. In the earlier days, back in the 1880s, there were no brakes or cars. According to John Carroll they would set out on foot in the middle of the night with a bit of bread in their pockets and when they got to the venue would have a rest and eat their bread before the match. It is likely that the young James Brooder would have walked to Nenagh or Cloughjordan to catch the train to take him to Dublin for that first Tipperary inter-county encounter.

The club numbers increased and in November 1898 forty-nine men gave subscriptions ranging from 3s to 6d, amounting to £2 1s 0d. Each man's name and his subscription are recorded. On 12 February 1899 a match was played at Kilbarron between Kilbarron and Silvermines, score: Kilbarron 2-0, 'Mines 0-2. The following is an account of the match in the Minute Book:

> The hurling match between the Shannon Rovers and the 'Mines was played at Kilbarron on Sunday and proved a splendid exhibition of the national game and resulted in a win for the Rovers. When the ball was set rolling the Silvermines made a splended run and sent the ball to the Rovers' ground but without scoring. The Rovers soon drove it to the opposite territory, proving their superiority as runners and by a splended rush scored a goal. After this the play was of an even character, very good hurling at both sides until half-time was called. When the ball was again set in motion the Rovers scored again. Mr Tierney and Mr Gleeson acted as linesmen, and Mr Lynch as referee gave general satisfaction.

The refreshments for the team cost £1 10s, leaving a balance of 11s. A return match was played on 26 February at Silvermines, score: 'Mines 0-4, Kilbarron 0-1. A further collection of subscriptions amounted to £2 7s 6d which defrayed the cost of the match in Silvermines: brake: £1 12s 6d, car, 10s, entrance fee 2s 6d, postage 2s. This left 1d 6d in the kitty. A raffle was held, which brought in £1 8s 0d, leaving £1 9s 6d in hand. There do not seem to have been any gate receipts at this stage, but no affiliation fees or payments to the County Board either.

On 18 June 1899 Kilbarron played a team from Fortal (near Birr), at Birr, score: Fortal 0-5, Kilbarron nil. On 23 July 1899 at Roscrea, Kilbarron played Lorrha, score: Kilbarron 1-2, Lorrha 1-5. The following letter puts Kilbarron's objection which was not allowed.

> Dear Sir: I would be much obliged if you would be so kind as to explain to me how it was that the referee would not allow a goal to Kilbarron at Roscrea on Sunday, the facts being as follows: The ball passed between the point posts and was struck back by a Lorrha player when it was immediately struck between the goal posts by a Kilbarron player before the whistle sounded or the flag was raised, and the referee only allowed a point. If Kilbarron was allowed this goal the score

would be Kilbarron 2-2, Lorrha 1-5, which would be even and I maintain that the match should be played again.

In 1900 a match was played at Kilbarron between Kilbarron and Roscrea, score: Kilbarron 2-6, Roscrea nil. The entertainment was: half barrel of porter, 17s, doz. lemonade 2s, pint and naggin whiskey, 2s 11d, quarter barrel porter 7s, bread 5s. The affiliation and entrance fee was 14s 9d. This is the first record of affiliation fee and still no gate admission charges – until an account of a match between Roscrea and Kilbarron at Kilbarron on 25 April 1901, score: Kilbarron 2-6, Roscrea nil.

Dear Sir: We carried out the match today. The weather was very bad but we had a fair crowd – gate-money £4 19s 6d. We would have about three times that sum under favourable circumstances. There was a match in Nenagh between two unaffiliated teams and it took away a great many people and the rain also deterred many from coming.

Mr Spain appointed neutral linesmen and goal umpires who were very satisfactory. Roscrea won the toss and elected to play with a slight incline in their favour and at half-time Kilbarron had registered two goals and three points, Roscrea nil. At change of sides Kilbarron kept the ball in the opposite ground nearly all the time and the final score was Kilbarron 2-6, Roscrea nil. There were several stoppages on account of rain and a couple of men got slightly hurt.

I will enclose money in a day or two. The names of the winning team are: J. McCormack (goal), P. Starr, S. Starr. W. Starr, P. Carroll (captain), J. Carroll, J. Kelly, D. Kelly, N. Moloney, T. Moloney, P. Ryan, P. Heenan, T. Cahalan, J. Madden, W. Deegan, P. Smith, W. Heffernan.

The Kilbarron team which had played Roscrea in 1900 included Peter Carroll (Capt.), Pat and Stephen Starr, Din and Jim Kelly, Paddy Ryan, Neil Moloney, Pat Heenan, John Carroll, Tom Cahalan, Tom Bouchier, Wm. Heffernan, John Costelloe (right), John Donoghue.

In a semi-final in 1902 at Beechwood, between Kilbarron and Roscrea, Kilbarron scored 1-2 to Roscrea's 1-4. This must have been a bitter disappointment to the Rovers after their recent successes against Roscrea. In his history Canon Fogarty goes on to say: 'Peter Carroll declares that Roscrea brought hurlers from two counties to knock out Kilbarron. The outsiders were from Offaly. The final had to be repeated'. This was not much consolation to Kilbarron who had lost in the semi-final. Surprisingly, there is no mention of this episode in Peter Carroll's records.

The 1901 North Board

For some years prior to 1899 there was a certain amount of friction between North and South Tipperary in the one County Board. At the County Convention in 1899 a request was read from Peter Carroll, Kilbarron, asking that a Board be allowed in North Tipperary to run off matches there and then to have the winners meet the South for county honours and medals. Remember that there had been a North Tipperary 'branch' of the Association in existence 1885-7. The 1899 request was granted but it took two years before the new board began to function.

Canon Fogarty comments that 'Peter Carroll got "Home Rule" for the North' and records that 'at Nenagh Institute on 30 June 1901, he formed his government, which was: Ned Keeshan, Roscrea, President; John Spain, Roscrea, Secretary; Michael Kelly, Nenagh, Treasurer. Committee: Messrs Peter Carroll, Dan Tuohy, Kilbarron; Michael Torpey, Ballingarry; Stephen Coffey, Pat Burke, Carney; Tom Ryan, Pat Gleeson, Michael Gaynor, Lahorna; Pat O'Brien, Nenagh; Jim Looby, Pat Donoghue, Toomevara; Ned Ryan and Neil Moloney, Newport. On this occasion Michael Cusack wrote, "Glad to see Ormond become again a flowering spot on the breast of the Emerald Isle"'.

In 1902 a new bye-law was brought in which stated 'that teams be confined to their own, and one adjoining parish'.

The meticulous record of income, expenditure, success and failure is continued on through 1902 and 1903. We read in the list of subscriptions in 1901: 'A Lady Friend 1s 0d'. This is something new. One cannot help wondering who was this lady friend who dared invade a man's world with her shilling subscription. Whose wife did she become, whose mother, whose grandmother?

It is impossible to give more than extracts from the very detailed records but on 15 March 1903 at Beechwood, Kilbarron beat Borrisokane in a championship match 0-4 to 0-3. The expenses were: brake £1 5s 0d, whiskey, 2 bottles 6s 0d, postage 6d. The gate receipts were £10 10s 0d, the highest recorded so far.

On 16 March 1903 in a match at Ballina, Kilbarron lost to Ballina. They went by steamer to Killaloe – probably from Kilgarvan. The steamer fares were £3 0s 0d. On 22 June delegates' expenses to Thurles were 17s 0d.

On 23 August a match at Puckane cost 5s 2d for whiskey and 8d for lemonade, while on 6 September a match at Kilbarron between Lorrha and Ballina cost 5s for laying out field, 5s 0d for printing, 2s 0d for flags and rosettes, 3s 6d for ball, and 10s 0d for objection fee.

On 2 September, a match for the Nenagh Cup was played at Nenagh between Kilbarron and Killyon, Co. Offaly, score: Killyon 1-6, Kilbarron 0-1. Kilbarron

were awarded the match but the reason is not given. For the first time 17s 0d for hurling caps is recorded in the expenses. Pat Starr (left), Kilbarron, was amongst the De Wets selection which represented Tipperary in the Munster championships and was beaten by a Cork team.

The year 1904 was uneventful for Kilbarron, the only match recorded being against Silvermines which the 'Mines won. The championship finals were played at Kilbarron – Lahorna De Wets defeated Ballycommon. The gate receipts were £5 2s 3d.

In the 1905 championships, Kilbarron was drawn against Ballinahinch. They met at Ballycommon and Ballinahinch won. Kilbarron was the venue for the match between Terryglass and Ballycommon in the same championship, Terryglass winning 2-8 to 2-5. The gate was £8 12s 6d, leaving £4-18-4 in the kitty at the end of 1905.

In March 1905 there is a record of £1 0s 0d paid to the Tiernan fund. This recalls a boating tragedy on the Shannon.

In the 1906 championships Kilbarron got a walk-over from Ballina in the first round and from Terryglass in the second. Kilbarron played Lorrha in the semi-finals in Borrisokane, losing to Lorrha who lost to Lahorna De Wets in the final. There is a line up in the records at this point which one assumes is the Kilbarron team for the 1906 championships: J. Clancy, M. Molamphy, J. Slattery, J. Neill, P. Smith, M. Collins, W. Flannery, P. Neill, J. Costelloe, W. Wells, D. Ryan, Danny Meara, Gurteen (right), M. Flannery, W. Parkinson, M. Cormack, W. Grace, E. Egan. Reserves: M. Bouchier, P. Bouchier, J. Haugh, John Heenan, M. Hogan.

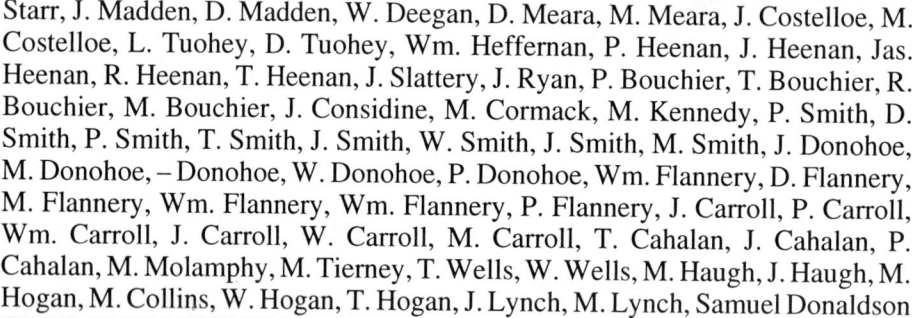

Roll of Members
The records for this period, 1898-1906, end with a list of Kilbarron (Shannon Rovers) club members in 1906: S. Starr, P. Starr, J. Starr, J. Starr, M. Starr, Wm. Starr, James Starr, J. Madden, D. Madden, W. Deegan, D. Meara, M. Meara, J. Costelloe, M. Costelloe, L. Tuohey, D. Tuohey, Wm. Heffernan, P. Heenan, J. Heenan, Jas. Heenan, R. Heenan, T. Heenan, J. Slattery, J. Ryan, P. Bouchier, T. Bouchier, R. Bouchier, M. Bouchier, J. Considine, M. Cormack, M. Kennedy, P. Smith, D. Smith, P. Smith, T. Smith, J. Smith, W. Smith, J. Smith, M. Smith, J. Donohoe, M. Donohoe, – Donohoe, W. Donohoe, P. Donohoe, Wm. Flannery, D. Flannery, M. Flannery, Wm. Flannery, Wm. Flannery, P. Flannery, J. Carroll, P. Carroll, Wm. Carroll, J. Carroll, W. Carroll, M. Carroll, T. Cahalan, J. Cahalan, P. Cahalan, M. Molamphy, M. Tierney, T. Wells, W. Wells, M. Haugh, J. Haugh, M. Hogan, M. Collins, W. Hogan, T. Hogan, J. Lynch, M. Lynch, Samuel Donaldson

& George. Donaldson (left), W. Parkinson, E. Egan, P. Neill, J. Neill, J. Griffin, P. Cleary, M. Gorman, P. Molamphy.

There is no record of Kilbarron taking part in the 1907 or 1908 championships. In 1911 the Lahorna De Wets are playing again after a two-year absence, but still no Kilbarron news. In 1913 Toomevara's star is shining brightly and our neighbours Borrisokane fight it out with them in the finals, Toom winning. Malachy McKenna was the Borris captain.

Blank Chapter and Revival
In 1914 there is the Great War and in 1916 the Easter Rising and still no Kilbarron news. In 1917 they are drawn against the De Wets and defeated. 'The Soldiers'

An early hurling scene in the Borrisokane area. This photograph, sent by Paddy Farrell, Ballinderry, to his brother in Australia, appears in *Vanished Kingdoms* by Professor Patrick Farrell and is reproduced here with his kind permission.

Song' is sung for the first time in the Sportsfield at Thurles. In the 1918 championships Glenahilty beat Kilbarron in the semi-final but were beaten in the final by Toom. The years 1919, 1920 and 1921 are overshadowed by 'The Troubles'. Many leading hurlers are in jail. On 23 October 1922 in the interdivisionals, junior and senior, Mid Tipperary beat North Tipperary. The North juniors included Martin Moran, Kilbarron.

This generation of Kilbarron hurlers I saw myself through a child's eyes. With my sisters and brother, sitting on our wall, we would gaze at them as they went on their bicycles along the white, dusty road carrying their hurls, calling out to one another and to us – young and strong and full of hope. We would watch them come home jubilant or downhearted. They would stop and gather around Moran's gate, stack their bikes and hurls under the sycamore tree across the road, and lie on the grass verge under my aunt's lilac tree. There they would play 'the match of the day' all over again and we would listen enthralled. The whole world seemed made up of hurling. We would be sent to Molamphys to buy packets of Players, 6d for 10, 1s for 20, and be rewarded with the cigarette cards.

At that time all the social life of the parish revolved around the hurling club. Dances, picnics, sports and raffles were held and at last the women and girls got some share in this bright, living, outgoing world of sport.

Canon Fogarty records that four teams participated in the senior hurling championship in 1923 – Nenagh, Lorrha, Kilbarron and Toomevara. In the semi-final Nenagh played Kilbarron. 'No mistake about it! Nenagh knocked the conceit of the Kilbarron men and put the "tin hat" on Mr Moran's hopes.' The score was Nenagh 7-5, Kilbarron 3-4. Toomevara beat Lorrha but in the final Toomevara beat Nenagh. Frank McGrath was the Nenagh captain. The Kilbarron team was: Martin Moran (Capt.), Dan Gleeson, Tom and Jim MacDonnell, Martin Hogan, Pat Fogarty, Matt Reddan, Willie, Mick, Jim and Rody O'Meara, Denis Cahalan, John Needham, John and Christy Mackey.

In the County semi-finals in March 1924, North Tipperary juniors included Jim O'Meara, Martin Hogan, Denis Cahalan (Kilbarron). Referees in 1924 included Pat Tierney and Dinny Costelloe, Kilbarron. In the 1925 senior championships Kilbarron was drawn against Nenagh and defeated in the first round. In 1927 in the interdivisionals North lost to Mid but only just. The North team included Jack Hoctor, Kildangan; Dinny Costelloe, John Needham, Kilbarron. In 1929 Kilbarron held its own in junior hurling which augured well for the future. North juniors included Maurice Corboy.

In 1930, when Tipperary annexed the 'Triple Crown', Kilbarron and Kildangan amalgamated successfully to become the North Intermediate champions. The team was: John Mackey (Terryglass), Martin Moran (Coolbawn), Pat Cahalan (Brocka), Joe Slattery (Kilbiller), Dinny Dwan (Carney), Jack O'Grady (Ballyalla), Jack Hoctor (Lisduff), Jack Kelly (Puckaun), Mick Hanrahan (Monsea), Mick Quirke (Kilbarron), Rody Gleeson (Peterfield), Dinny Costelloe (Kilbarron), Capt., Mick Foley (Knigh), Maurice Corboy (Parkboy), Bill O'Meara (Urra), Danny Gleeson (Kilbarron), Mickey Hogan (Macloon).

In 1932 Kilbarron-Kildangan won the North senior play-off against Borrisokane for runners-up medals. In 1933 Borrisokane beat them and went on to win the North. County juniors included Jack Hoctor, Kildangan, John Kelly, Kilbarron. In 1934 Kilbarron-Kildangan, having acquired Martin Kennedy (who transferred from Toom) won the North senior, beating Roscrea in the final. The team was Jack Hoctor (Lisduff), Capt., Jack Kelly (Puckaun), Danny and Rody Gleeson (Peterfield), Martin Kennedy (Castlesheela), Martin Moran (Coolbawn), Dinny Costelloe (Kilbarron), Jack Mackey (Terryglass), Jim Killeen (Monsea), Pat Cahalan (Brocka), Mickey Hogan (Macloon), Bill Hayes (Loughourna), Mick Hanrahan (Monsea), Mick Quirke (Kilbarron, later Frolic), Paddy Hogan (Urra), Jack O'Grady (Ballyalla), Jim and Joe Cleary (Kildangan), Dinny Dwan (Carney), Maurice Corboy (Parkboy).

The GAA catered for track and field athletics up to 1922. Matt Costelloe of Lisquillibeen was champion high jumper of Munster in 1899 and Peter Carroll of Brookfield the half-mile champion runner at about the same period. During the later Thirties and early Forties Michael Donohoe of Bellevue made his mark as a champion runner. Mick presented a cup, which he had won for rowing at Kilgarvan regatta, for cross-country competition. The Donohue Cup became the prize for an annual novice championship for North Tipperary clubs.

Matt Costelloe joined the Dublin Metropolitan Police (DMP) in 1900 and rose to the grade of Station Sergeant from which he retired in 1922. From 1902 onwards he belonged to the mounted section. In 1910 he competed in the International Horse Show, Olympia, London, winning the event (below). There were forty-two entries representing eleven police forces in various parts of the UK. The prizes were awarded for equipment and general neatness and training in the management

of large crowds. He lived out his life in Dublin and died in the late 1930s.

TERRYGLASS

I am indebted to Michael Parkinson for penning the following memoir.

A lot of tournaments were played to raise funds for the organisation and teams used to travel to venues in nearby parishes. Terryglass became an important venue for games. Training was in Terryglass every Sunday. Sometimes in the evenings a group of older men would arrive at the field and propose a match for a quarter barrel of porter. Porter was then 2*d* a pint and 8*s* 6*d* (42.5p) a barrel. Two 17-a-side teams formed; the losers had to pay 6*d* each but everyone drank the porter. The club cost very little to run as the carpenters on the team made the hurleys and my father, William Parkinson, made the hurling balls – a skill handed down from his father before him.

When going to play a match in Cloughjordan or places as far away the team travelled by brake hired from William Egan in Birr. If they had a game in Youghalarra or Ballina they hired a passenger steamer that plied the Shannon. When travelling by boat a large crowd from Terryglass and Kilbarron travelled also. It was a great day out for old and young with music and dancing on board. The local fife and drum band always travelled with them and used meet the Portroe band at the field. My father had great praise for Dan Nealon, or Dandy Nealon as he was known. He went to a lot of trouble to make sure everyone enjoyed a good day. On one occasion when coming home from Ballina the boat ran onto rocks coming into Kilgarvan Quay. Only for the skill of the captain it could have been a tragedy. All the Terryglass people got off at Kilgarvan and walked home.

Dan Tierney was club secretary and William Parkinson, chairman and captain for a number of years, and travelled to Nenagh to Board meetings on bikes.

There were some important matches played in the parish in the early years. On 2 April 1899 Lorrha played Terryglass in Carrigahorig. Terryglass won by 2 points. On 1 February 1905 the North Tipperary semi-final between Lorrha and De Wets was played in Terryglass. De Wets won by 5 goals 11 points to 3 points. In the 1914 senior semi-final, played at Terryglass, Lorrha beat Borrisokane 2-2 to 0-2. In the 1915 final for teams beaten in the championships Lorrha played Borrisokane. Borrisokane won by 1 point. In 1920 Lorrha versus Toomevara, first fixed for Terryglass, was played at Carrigahorig.

Teams from outside the county played in Terryglass, all challenge games. Killyon from Co. Offaly played often and Terryglass played return games in Killyon. Portumna played in Carrigahorig, as far as I know mostly football. Some time around 1890 Manuel Hickie presented a football to the club to move boys to play and get involved in sport. It never caught on.

SHANNON ROVERS, 1939-1990s

The club won the County Junior final in 1939 with a great win over Thurles Sarsfields, 7-4 to 3-5. They were the first team to bring the trophy to the northern division. The *Nenagh Guardian* report of the homecoming captured the heady atmosphere which prevailed in Ballinderry on the Sunday evening: 'They were met half a mile outside the village by a torchlight procession and the local band and their trainers and chairman, Michael O'Meara, was carried shoulder high through the village.'

The assembled throng was addressed by the chairman and David Fogarty, a local athlete, who mentioned especially the 'stone-wall back line of John Mackey and Paddy Cahalan'.

Following regrading, the club was senior for the 1940-3 inclusive, 1955-61 inclusive and for 1969. All their games at this level ended in first round defeats.

Win Celebrated in Song

After suffering defeat in the North Intermediate finals of 1963, '64 and '66, success came in 1967 and 1968. Up to 1985-6 Intermediate champions met the North Tipperary Junior champions in a play-off, with the winners going on to contest the County Junior title. The club regained the County Junior title in 1968 with a win over Lattin-Cullen, 6-3 to 2-5, Jim Egan scoring 3-1 for Rovers.

Shannon Rovers North and Co. Junior Chanpions 1939
Back (l tor): Denis Costelloe, Patrick Hogan, Patrick Starr, John Cahalan, Tom Ryan, Pat Cahalan, Bill Fox, Garda Michael McGowan, trainer. **Middle:** Chris Darcy, Michael Hogan (Top), William Starr, Michael O'Meara, Ryehill, trainer; Jack Costelloe, Paddy Hough, Danny Gleeson. **Front:** Jack Mackey, Jimmy Downey, Malachy Ryan, Tom Cahalan.

May O'Meara, Gurteen, wrote 'Salute to the Shannon Rovers' to the air, 'The Men of the West'. Marty O'Meara requested the song – his only stipulation being that every member of the team should be named.

> We honour Tipp's Sixty-eight Champions,
> The Rovers who came from the North
> And beat the brave South men at Thurles
> On November, the great Twenty-fourth.
> They came from Slevoyre and from Roran,
> Bellevue, Ballinderry, Coolbawn;
> The Burkes of Kylebeg and Jim Horan
> And the pride of the Cahalans, Seán.

Over the years the club had good successes in the various under-age groups, notching up victories in both hurling and football from u/12 to u/16. The above u/15 team won the North championship in 1946 – the club also won again in 1947, 1948 and 1952 in that age group.

Back (l to r): Pat Tierney (with cap), Seán Dunne, Billy Leenane, Paddy Tiernan, Billy Costello, Michael O'Meara (with bandage), Ailbe Burke, John (Rummy) Leenane.
Front: P. J. Starr, Paddy Gleeson, John Slattery, Jim Burke, Jack O'Meara, Frank Moran, Jimm Dunne, Matt Costello (partially obscured).

Shannon Rovers County Intermediate Hurling Champions, 1968
Back (l to r): Rev. Thomas Comerford, CC, Sean Cahalan, Raymond Guest, Albie Burke, Tom Ryan, selector; Jim Egan, Seamus Horan, Pat Prout, Matt Fogarty, Martin Horan, Tony Hogan, Tom Fox, Tony Darcy, Chris Boyle, P. J. Starr, John Cleary, Vincent McCarthy, Jack Meara, Martin O'Meara. **Front:** Michael Kennedy, selector; Timmie Tierney, Anselm Walsh, Martin Guest, Cyril Darcy, Michael Cahalan, Jim Burke, capt; W. J. Hogan, Tony Hogan, Tom Hourigan, Jimmy Sage, trainer.

They came from the farm and the cottage,
Magicians at scoring a goal,
From the carpenters' bench and the counter
And even from Garda Patrol.

The forwards were sturdy and fearless,
The backs they were eager and brave,
And many's the rally they halted,
Many goals did Sean Cahalan save.

The fleet-footed Guests and the Horans,
Brave brothers as everyone knew;
But the bravest of brothers at Thurles
Were Jim Burke and Albie so true.

For Jim was the Captain undaunted,
In years of defeat he fought well;
And so did Joe Hogan and Albie
With Matt Fogarty running pell-mell.

At centrefield Matt is a winner,
Anselm Walsh has the brains and the skill,
Mickie Cahalan too and Joe Hogan
Back them up with a heart and a will.

Jim Egan, a stout-hearted forward,
Timmy Tierney, a hurler of grace;
Tony Hogan is ever a danger,
They have stamina, courage and pace.

Cyril Darcy, the greatest of heroes
That day with the title at stake,
Forever and always his sallies
The South men's back line they did break.

So hail to the Sixty-eight Champions,
All hail to the deed they have done;
Their names will be always remembered
And the glorious victory they won.

Their names will live on in Kilbarron
Terryglass will remember them too.
And now I will finish my rhyming
And bid these great heroes adieu.

Won Some, Lost Some

The 1970s was marked with regrading back to Intermediate, a North final win in 1974 and 1975, and playing at senior rank 1976-79 and 1987-92, until regraded to Intermediate in 1993. In 1986 they won the County Intermediate championship by defeating Clonmore 0-9 to 0-8. This was followed by regrading to senior level. They reached the North semi-final the following year by beating Toomevara, followed by defeat by Roscrea. Having defeated Lorrha in a replay in 1989, Borrisoleigh beat them in the quarter-final.

They again got to the Intermediate North final in 1994, but were beaten by Silvermines. At that time they held the record of fourteen appearances in the North Intermediate final – as against Burgess's twelve.

Shannon Rovers won North Tipperary football titles at Intermediate level in 1990-1; at Junior level in 1988-9. The Minor team won in 1984 and their u/21 B team won in 1991.

Since 1934 Shannon Rovers have amalgamated at different times with neighbouring parishes – Kildangan and Borrisokane in four different grades of hurling, and with Lorrha, Borrisokane and Kildangan in senior football.

Board Officers

In keeping with the Peter Carroll tradition of the 1890s the parish has supplied officers to the North Tipperary GAA Board and County Bord na n-Óg. John Tierney, Ashgrove, was Chairman of the North Board, 1988 & 89. Liam Hogan, Killea, has been North Tipperary Board Youth Officer, chairman of the North's Bord na n-Óg, and County PRO for that body.

JIM AND ALBIE BURKE

In 1994, in the programme prepared for that North final Cyril Darcy penned a memoir of Jim and Albie Burke, Kylebeg, of which the following are extracts.

When I was asked to put pen to paper on my thoughts on the Burke brothers many wonderful memories came back to me for many reasons. The main reason was the influence the Burkes had on our parish, and especially on the game of hurling. Their influence has spanned from the 1940s to this very day in many different aspects of the game. The Burke brothers commenced

Shannon Rovers North & County Intermediate Hurling Champions, 1986
Back (l to r): John Tierney, selector; John Joe Costelloe, Joe Hannigan, Timmie Carroll, Noel Ducie, Michael Burke, Sean O'Meara, Timmy Tierney, Jim McLoughney, Ger Leenane, Liam Hogan, Tom Slattery, chairman. **Front**: Tomás Costelloe, Raymond Costelloe, Johnny Slattery, Seamus Sullivan, Gerard Darcy, Pat McLoughney, Tom Burke, capt, Gerry O'Meara, Sean Darcy, Pat Hogan.

hurling as juveniles for the Rovers in the late 1940s. They then played in various grades including a spell at senior 1955-'61 and continued on to the 1970s.

My very first memory of them was as a small boy and my father coming home from the Rovers' games and talking to the point of being obsessional about them. He would mention many others at that time in the 1950s, such as P. J. Starr, Pakie Hogan, but the two Burkes held pride of place.

When I started playing hurling myself we trained in Mick Leenane's field in Ballinderry. The juveniles and the senior team shared the field in training. That was when I first saw, and met, the Burkes. For us young fellows in the mid-1950s they were our idols. I remember going to the Rovers' games at that time, and a particular senior game: Rovers v Roscrea, with Billy Brussels and Martin Loughnane in their prime. On that occasion the Burkes excelled and the Rovers only lost by a few points.

As time passed by we grew from boys to men and it was a dream come true when some of us were picked to play on the same team as our local heroes. Of course before that we had many training sessions with them where they hardened us up, showed us really how to play hurling with spirit and commitment. These two men were full of passion, love for the game and there were no half measures.

Jim, who in the early years played outfield, often did so in his bare feet. He was a beautiful striker and had great control of the ball. He represented his club at county intermediate level and it was only fitting that he captained the team that won the county junior championship in 1968 to bridge a gap of 29 years. My greatest memory of that year was the many pep talks he gave us in the dressing room, and his powers of motivation. In that year he played beside his brother Albie and Seamus Horan on the full back line.

Albie played during the same period and shared many of Jim's honours with the club. He was also honoured by his selection on two Tipperary winning teams and subsequently got two All-Ireland medals at intermediate level. He played with many Tipperary greats such as Babs Keating, Mick Roche and Peter O'Sullivan. Albie was a real artist with a hurley, a marvellous striker of a ground ball and had great control of a ball and also of his opponent. He usually played on the inside back line and often wore a peaked cap on the field.

Outside hurling the Burkes were hard workers on their farms, great family and parish men – same dedication and commitment shown on the field of play also applied to their lives. They reared families that carried on the winning tradition and everything that was good in a rural parish. I am glad to say today that the Burke phenomena still continue on the field of play and on the sideline.

CAMOGIE

In the late Fifties and early Sixties the ladies of Kilbarron-Terryglass parish took up camogie. Their guide, mentor and trainer, was the late Paddy Grady of Curraghmore. They went on playing for eight to years, probably, until Paddy went to live in Dublin.

They played mainly in tournaments and at carnivals in places like Kilbarron and Dromineer. Amongst those that have been recalled for me as having played on the various teams were:

Bridie Whelan, Angeline Tiernan, Maria Burke, Sheila Slattery, Eileen Carroll.

Annette Leenane, Peg O'Meara, Phyllis Tiernan (capt), Julia Horan, Mary O'Grady, Bridie Cahalan, Anne Cahalan, the late Frances Costelloe, Pat(ricia) Nevin, Kathleen Corbett, Peggy Ryan, Mary Flynn, Betty Kennedy, Bridie Kelly, Teresa Kelly, Philomena Hogan, Moira Slevin, Bridie Tierney and Mary Coen.

Some of the team, including the captain Phyllis Tiernan, joined the Knockshegowna team when camogie was discontinued in the parish in the mid-1960s. The game was revived in 1985 but lasted only a year – but long enough for the juvenile ballad group to win a county Scór title in 1986.

Camogie was revived again after a five-year gap with a committee formed in 1991, consisting of Helen Fox, chairperson; Gráinne Stack, secretary; Bridie Brophy, treasurer. The trainers were Tadhg Cahalan and Annette Cahalan. The junior team got to the semi-final of a league in that first year and reached the county championship final. Catherine Burke got a place on the county minor team which defeated Kilkenny in the All-Ireland. The club also fostered and fielded under-age teams, and participated in coaching courses.

PAT McLOUGHNEY, CLUB, COUNTY AND ALL-STAR PLAYER

Pat McLoughney has been playing with Shannon Rovers since 1965 when he joined an u/15 team at wing forward and won a North Tipperary championship medal. He played with Borrisokane Vocational school and was in a centre-field position for their great win in 1969-70 of the Canon Fitzgerald Cup for all Co. Tipperary post-primary schools. Borrisokane was a very small school at the time. They played about five matches in all, defeating Thurles CBS in the final. Their coach and trainer was Denis Kelly, who retired from teaching this year, 1998. Pat is high in his praise for Denis's skills, dedication and patience.

In all Pat won four football and nine other hurling medals with the school.

Education completed, Pat became a full-time farmer on the home farm in Brocka, Ballinderry. His hurling genes come from both parents. His mother, Elizabeth Darcy, Bantis, Cloughjordan, played camogie with Kilruane in the 1940-50s. His father, Martin McLoughney from Soolmoy, Ardcroney, who died in November 1998, aged 84 years, also played hurling with Kilruane in the 1930-40s. The other members of the McLoughney family are Jim, Martin and Mary (Hogan).

Pat began as a wing forward with Shannon Rovers but soon became their valued goalie. He was on the team which won the North Intermediate championship in 1974 and 1975. He was selected to play in goal for the Tipperary u/21 team in 1976. They were beaten in the first round of the championship but Pat had a very good match, making some great saves.

The following year, 1977, he was selected as goalie on the senior county team – following in the footsteps of Seamus Shinnors, Newport, and Jimmy Duggan, Thurles. He was to be on the county panel from then until 1982. This was the 'famine' period of Tipperary hurling and Pat has no championship medal to show for his years of county net-minding. However, he won an All-Ireland National League medal in 1979 when Tipperary defeated Galway.

There then followed two prestigitious Bank of Ireland All-Star Awards – the best fifteen hurlers in Ireland as picked by the print, radio and television sports journalists. The All-Star team went on a two-week trip to the United States both years to play the winners of the All-Ireland championship – Galway in 1979 and Kilkenny in 1980. They also played matches in San Francisco, Chicago and Los Angeles. In 1980 Pat got the 'Player of the Tour' trophy put up by the American GAA Board.

Munster, with Pat in goal, won the Railway Cup in 1980. He was still on the senior county panel in 1981 but a serious injury (broken arm) sustained in club hurling put him out of the game for almost a year.

Looking back over his years as a county player, Pat pays special tribute to Séamus Hogan, Kildangan, and Seamus Shinnors, Newport. Both were experienced county players when he was first selected. They collected and took him to Thurles for training and were always available when support, advice – and sympathy – was needed.

During those years he was also a staunch club player. He won a North Junior football championship with Rovers in 1979 – a victory that was repeated in 1988 and 1989. His North Senior football successes were in 1982, '83, '84 and 1993.

Pat was still club goalie in 1986 when Shannon Rovers won the North Intermediate title but were beaten in the county semi-final by Moycarkey. He captained the Tipperary Junior team in 1987 and got to the Munster Final where they were defeated.

1994 was his last year in goal for Shannon Rovers. The club now had a good, young goalie coming up in Eoin Slattery and Pat was interested in returning to a position out the field – wing forward or centre forward.

He was now approaching his fortieth birthday and, apart from the year out with injury, had been playing club hurling for nigh on twenty-nine years. Once over the 40, the Masters beckoned.

The Masters, for players over forty years with no upper age limit, is directed from Croke Park and played only at inter-county level. To date he has played in four Masters All-Irelands, three as goalie and one as wing forward. However, he

Pat McLoughney (captain) and goalie, in action for Tipperary against Kilkenny's Kevin Fennelly in the 1998 Masters All-Ireland.

scored in all matches, coming out of the goal to take frees.

The Tipperary Masters have quite a spectacular record. They beat Kilkenny in the 1994 final, were runners up in 1995, and beat Clare in 1996. In 1998 Pat was goalie and captain when they were beaten by Kilkenny in the final. It seems Masters can go on almost for ever. When Tipperary recently played in London the opposing team's goalie was all of sixty-two years old.

Amongst Pat's trophies is the 'Guardian Player of the Year', 1979 and 1986 and the 'Tipperary Cidona Player of the Year', 1979.

Pat has also done his stint as club officer, serving as Shannon Rovers treasurer for eleven years, plus lending his expertise as selector, trainer and coach at differnt times. He is the club's current (1998) chairman. He also plays golf and racquet ball.

Pat lives in Kilgarvan with his wife Anne (née Collins) and their three children.

Upgrading the Grounds
The parish aquired a five-acre sportsfield on the road between Kilbarron village and Ballinderry in 1970. A pavilion was added by voluntary labour in 1974. It is not vested in th GAA but run by a parish-based committee.

In October 1992 months of intensive fund-raising and voluntary work saw the purchase of extra land and the opening of a sports complex in the sportsfield. The playing pitch already had dressing rooms and now a handball and racquetball court added a new dimension to the amenity. The extension was officially opened by the then parish priest, the late Rev. John Hogan.

The man credited with spearheading the work was the late Rev. P. J. O'Connor, chairman of the sportsfield committee. Ill-health had forced Fr O'Connor to return to Ireland from the mission field of Biafra, Africa. Due to the diminishing number of priests in the diocese the late Bishop Michael Harty had introduced the concept of retired missionaries serving as the second or third priest in a parish.

Sources:
The first two paragraphs were supplied by Michael Parkinson. The date 1765 come from Daniel Grace, *Portrait of a Parish: Monsea & Killodiernan.*
Tipperary Advocate, 20 March, 2 & 9 Oct 1886, Feb 1887.
Minute Book, Shannon Rovers Hurling Club, 1898-1906, kept by Peter Carroll.
Canon Philip Fogarty, *Tipperary's GAA Story*; Canon Edward Whyte, *Kilruane MacDonaghs and Lahorna De Wets*; Pádraig Ó Laoi, *Annals of the GAA in Galway*, vol. i.
Willie Gaynor, *Tipperary GAA Yearbook 1996.*
Nenagh Guardian, 1939,
Programmes prepared for the opening of the upgraded sportsfield in 1992 and for the North Intermediate Final, 1994.
Pat McLoughney, Liam Hogan, Frank Moran.

Photographs (all loaned): p. 358, Monica (née Lynch) Cahalan, Paddy Carroll, Jerry Moran; pp. 258, 361, Peg (née Starr) Donoghue; pp. 360, 365 Julia Slevin; p. 362, Donie O'Meara and Nancy Cohen; p. 367, 1994 programme; p. 368, Paddy Carroll, 1994 prog; p. 370, 1994 prog; p. 373, Pat McLoughney.

16
Wars at Home and Abroad

After the Treaty of Limerick the Jacobite soldiers, both officers and men, were given the option of going abroad to join the armies of France or staying behind and joining the Williamites. The majority of the officer class, including Patrick Sarsfield, opted for the former and many of their men followed them. These were the first of the Wild Geese and they fought in France, Spain, Austria and even further afield. All during the eighteenth century it was forbidden to Catholics to hold commissions in the British army but this law was relaxed towards the end of the century. As a result many of the sons of the remaining Catholic gentry joined the British army, e.g. the Hickies. As they had fought against the old enemy on the battlefields of Europe with bravery and distinction so now did they fight side by side with him in the same way.

During the latter part of the eighteenth century or during the nineteenth century there was a constant flow of Irishmen, both private soldiers and officers, joining the British army either for economic reasons, a love of adventure or as a career. It is said that in the fighting in the south-east of the country during the 1798 Rebellion there were more Irish speakers on the British side than on the Irish. The notorious North Cork militia who ravaged Co. Tipperary under High Sheriff Judkin Fitzgerald in a pre-emptive strike before the rebellion were mostly Irish-speaking.

No doubt many men from this parish went to the foreign wars but we only know the names of a few. There were Minchins, Hickies, Esmondes, Kents, who are all mentioned elsewhere in this book.

I cannot name for certain anyone from the parish who was in the Crimean War, 1853-6. My granduncle James Carroll may have been; there is a tradition in the family that he was. We know that Jack 'the Gunner' Donoghue, father of Rev. Tom Donoghue, was in the Boer War, 1898-1902. Daniel Maher of Clooninihy spent all his life in the British army, fought against the Boers in that war and was at the famous siege of Ladysmith. I have been told that Fr Arthur Hickie, an army chaplain and brother of Sir William, was also in Ladysmith during the siege.

Daniel Maher, whose mother was a Nolan, was a first cousin of Wilsie Nolan's father. When he died in England in the late Thirties or Forties, as Wilsie's father was next-of-kin the War Office sent him Maher's three medals with ribbons attached. After a few months another letter arrived with apologies saying that a will had been discovered in which Daniel had bequeathed his medals to the Matron of the Royal Chelsea Pensioners Hospital, a home for old soldiers founded by Nell Gwynn (favourite mistress of Charles II) in which he had spent his last days. Wilsie's father sent back the medals.

Captain Manuel Hickie served in the Boer War and brought his horse Confidence home with him. General Sir William and Brigadier-General Carlos Hickie served in the Boer War and World War I, as did Jimmy Smith, the fiddler, from Bellevue, Mike Conway, the postman, and several Houghs from Ballinderry.

Daniel Maher, who fought in the Boer War, is in the centre in his Chelsea Pensioners' uniform

The Houghs took part in bayonet charges, which they relived in their dreams to the horror of their parents.

Casualties in World War I
Michael (Mike) Hogan of Lisquillibeen had been in the Dublin Metropolitan police. He joined the Royal Navy and was a stoker in a mine sweeper in the North Sea, then the German Ocean. It was one of the most hazardous tasks a man could be given and the loss of life was high. His ship went down in 1917. He was aged forty-two. What his motives were for joining up one does not know. There was no military tradition in the family. He may have become disillusioned with the DMP who had got themselves a bad name in the 1913 lockout. He may have heeded Redmond's call. The War Office asked his mother if he had been helping her financially and she truthfully answered, 'No'. She got a pension of 4s 2d a week.

Thirty-year-old Garret Lavelle, son of Sgt. Owen Lavelle, RIC, and uncle of the late Maura and her brothers, was killed in France before he saw a single bit of action. He was going up to the trenches with his battalion to relieve the battalion coming down and amongst those being relieved he suddenly saw a neighbour from Ballinderry, Jack Somers. Naturally they stopped for a quick word. Just then a shell exploded beside them; it killed Lavelle but Jack survived. The last words Lavelle said were, 'Oh Lord, Jack, are you much hurt?' Jack Donoghue lost a leg but it did not prevent him from leading an active life on his bicycle.

Lieut. Geoffrey Esmonde was a son of John Joseph Esmonde, MP, by his first marriage to Rose McGuinness, half-brother to Eugene, and full brother to Dr Anthony, later Sir Anthony, father of Tony, who now lives in Lesserragh. Geoffrey was in the Northumberland Fusiliers and was killed in action in France, aged nineteen. When his mother died he was seven and his brother Anthony was five. They came to live at Drominagh with their grandmother Caroline, widow of James who had bought Drominagh.

World War II
Many Irishmen fought with great distinction in World War II. Brigadier Séamus Hickie, Slevoir, and Eugene Esmonde, VC, have been profiled in other chapters. Esmonde's was the only death. His brother Owen was a RAF pilot officer; brother

Patrick (Paddy), a doctor, was in the Royal Army Medical Corps,. as had been their father. Mick Bouchier of Annagh served all during the war in a submarine. 'Young' Jim Hough of Ballinderry, as distinct from his father 'Old' Jim who fought in World War I, was in the North African campaign under Montgomery and was wounded in the arm.

John Corbett was a son of Denis, a World War I veteran from Oola, who was given an ex-serviceman's cottage in Ballinderry. John, who had already left school at twelve before they came to Ballinderry and had been working for farmers in the Ballinderry area in the 1920s, joined the British army. He survived Dunkirk, where he narrowly escaped drowning, and was commissioned. Later he landed in France on D-Day and again narrowly escaped drowning. He fought his way to Berlin, rising in rank to Lieut.-Col., and was with the first group, mostly journalists including Richard Dimbleby, who entered Belsen concentration camp. It was only a brief call but enough to make him remember the horror for the rest of his life. He became Assistant Provost Marshal of Berlin and after leaving the army with an OBE studied law and became a barrister working for the British Board of Trade. After his wife's death he came back to live in Nenagh, but during one of his visits to England died suddenly of heart failure. He was aged eighty-three. His nephews, nieces, grandnephews and grandnieces still live in this area.

The War of Independence and Civil War
I must distinguish between the roles played in these wars between Kilbarron and Terryglass. Kilbarron had no rebel tradition. Parnell remained, in spite of his detractors, the un-crowned King. My aunts and uncles and their contemporaries who were in age two generations removed from me looked up to Parnell as my generation looked up to Pearse, MacDonagh and Connolly. When Parnell died his mantle fell on John Redmond and I would have no hesitation in saying that the majority of those in Kilbarron and Terryglass who took any interest in politics were staunch Redmondites. Another factor in the case of Kilbarron was the nature of the landowners. They were simple country gentlefolk and most of them had been there since the seventeenth century. There was friendship and respect between the classes and religions. There was no tradition of serious agrarian unrest or of evictions. Not a single Big House was burned in either Kilbarron or Terryglass during the 'Troubles'. Many families had members in the RIC.

However, in Terryglass there were folk memories of wholesale evictions. There were stewards who administered the estates for the landlords. However, the evictors, for instance the Synges and Talbots, were not always absentee landlords.

I only have scraps of information about the 1916-22 'Movement' in the parish. Terryglass and Lorrha adjoin and Lorrha was a hotbed of republicanism, due mainly to the Cronin family. One member, Felix, later reached a high rank in the Irish Free State army and, in 1927, married Kitty Kiernan, Michael Collins's fiancée at the time of his death.

In chapter 8 the Heenan's Ashgrove House has been identified as a meeting place for the Volunteers and the story is told of a raid, probably upon a tip-off.

Ballinderry Barracks
In 1920 an attempt was made to burn the barracks. Sgt. Scanlon, the last RIC sergeant in Ballinderry, had only arrived that day with a wife and three children.

Sometime during the night Mrs Betty Hough (née Fleming), mother of Julia Dalton the midwife, who lived beside the barracks, saw the flames and smoke. She raised the alarm and Mike and Tom Hogan who owned the barracks alerted the police occupants and helped put the fire out. I have been told that one little girl was standing at a window with smoke and flames behind her and a Hough man pulled her out. The sergeant's family went to Borrisokane for the remainder of the night.

Mrs Hough thought she saw a very big man with oil stains on his clothes at the scene. The police picked out three big men who might have been dealing with machinery. First they went for Denis Fogarty of Drominagh Lodge, Matt's father who had a threshing machine, and he was interviewed and taken to Limerick gaol for a few days where by all accounts he gave the authorities a great deal of impertinence to put it mildly. It is said that he hit a warder who told him off for smoking his pipe. Mick the 'Gunner' Donoghue was taken into the barracks for questioning but let go and Wilsie Nolan's father was questioned in his own house. None of the three had anything to do with it but there were mutterings that it was known who was responsible. By 1920 the Black and Tans had given the RIC a bad name and nobody was going to inform. The Black and Tans were a force of demobilised soldiers recruited by the British Government in 1920 to supplement the RIC. Due to shortage of the regular RIC uniform the new force was issued with khaki trousers and dark green tunic. This colour combination led to them being nicknamed after the famous Co. Limerick pack of hounds, the Scarteen Black and Tans.

The local IRA of the time drilled in Cooney's Grove in Clooninihy and Patrick 'Guardian' Cahalan remembers as a small boy seeing them come out from the grove and recognised some including a Nolan from Nenagh. Clooninihy would have been a safe place for the Lorrha and Nenagh contingents to meet for drilling as it had good look-out facilities.

Otherwise, no actual fighting took place in the parish. The role of the local Volunteers was mainly helping the active service units, e.g. carrying dispatches, carrying out raids for firearms, digging trenches in the road. Many were not even as active as this but merely had the name of being in the movement.

Some of the bitterness of the Civil War still lingers but is dying out and with my generation will have died. Although born in an RIC barracks in 1916 where my father was Head Constable, I have always been a staunch republican. My mother was a Galway woman and her family was republican and anti-Treaty. Politics were never discussed in the family and we were never influenced. The only political statement I every heard from my father was to call P. H. Pearse, 'the mad schoolmaster'. My father resigned from the RIC in 1920. We had been living in the barracks in Granard, Co. Longford. As well as being fearful for our safety he disliked having Black and Tans under his command. We came home to live on a small farm he had purchased in Coolbawn townland a short distance from the Cross. There was no animosity; he was amongst his own people. Michael (Kenneally) Hough from Ballinderry, son of Nora and Michael, a World War I veteran, was one of two members of the 'Flying Column' billeted in our house during the War of Independence.

I have no official list of names of those in the Independence movement although I am sure such exists. I have been given many names but whether these fought only in the War of Independence or in both wars, or whether others only joined after the Treaty, I do not know. For what it is worth, below are the names which were given to me, irrespective of whether they took the Treaty or anti-Treaty side. I got the names from several people, not just one.

John Gleeson, NT, was officer commanding; three Joyce brothers, Chris, Mick and Jack – Chris is the only one on the list still alive, now in Borrisokane; Tom Hough, Carrigahorig, known as 'the Manager'; Jack Whelan of Ballinderry, later Gurteen; Mick 'Gunner' Donoghue, John Neill, Paddy Nevin, Mick and Har Burchell, Tommy Mackey, Matt Reddan of the Lough, Jim Glynn, Bob and Bill Guest, Mick Tierney, Martin Horan, Jimmy Parkinson, Jim 'Duck' Hogan, Jim Tierney, Will Tierney, Slevoir, Jack Fox, Mick Kennedy of Brocka, Dan Elliott.

Cumann na mBan
This is the list of members of Cumann na mBan given to me by Mary Nevin (née Starr), aged eighty-eight and a pupil at Terryglass national school during the War of Independence and Civil War. She would have been about eleven at the time. Captain: Eileen Sammon (née Costelloe), from what is now Paddy's Bar, formerly of Clooninihy, assistant teacher to John Gleeson; Nan Doyle (née Cahalan), aged eighty-three, and the only one still living. She lives in England and is Wilsie Nolan's aunt, although he has his doubts about her involvement because of her age. Ellen Dervan and Delia Walsh, Portumna, both daughters of Stephen Mackey; Mary A. 'Gunner' Donoghue, Newlawn, later Mary Beavens, Shinrone; Kathleen Guest, later Mrs Phil Smith of Kilbarron (The Bog); Georgina ('George') Guest, later Mrs Mike (Bush) Hogan; Nora Darcy, Lorrha, cook at Killeen, Terryglass (Ellie Esmonde's place). She had brothers Jer and Joe; Mai and Sarah Flynn, Carrigahorig – Mai taught in Terryglass school, Sarah in Lorrha, neither married; Bridget Heenan of Ashgrove, later Mrs Mick Tierney; Bridget Flannery of Turravoggaun, later Mrs Billy Lawlor, Borrisokane. She and Georgina Guest were dispatch runners.

The group met in Terryglass school and mainly did knitting. I daresay the 'flying columns' would have got through a good many pairs of socks. When I asked if perhaps they made bandages or such I was told: they did knitting. There were certainly no bombs made! They also held dances to raise funds. Like their male counterparts, they were ancillary to the active service units.

I can verify none of this information. Names may have been mentioned who should not have been and vice versa. If so, I regret these inaccuracies.

One fact I do know to be true. During the Civil War, Bridie Whelan of Ballinderry, later Mrs Mick Leenane of Newlawn House, acted as a dispatch messenger and cycled as far as south Tipperary carrying dispatches.

Nan Cahalan with her brothers Tom and Steve.

Sources:
Thomas Pakenham, *The Year of Liberty*.
William J. Hayes, *Tipperary in the Year of Rebellion, 1798*.
Wilsie Nolan, Christy Gleeson, Mrs Mary Nevin (née Starr).
Author's own and family memories.

Photographs: pp. 371, 381 loaned by Wilsie Nolan.

V. E. Day 1945

Sister Maddalena walked under the lime trees
On her way to the kitchen garden,
Carrying her pail of hen food.
It was the month of May, sunny and windy.
That morning, Sister Superior had told them
That the war was over.
Superior did not speak of victory or defeat,
Only of peace –
She came from a neutral country.
'There will be celebrations', she said,
'At noon the bells will be rung.'
She looked at Maddalena.

Neat rows of vegetables
And upright raspberry canes –
There would be a good crop of raspberries,
As there had been last year when the buzzing bombs had come;
Red and ripe they had been as the thuds came nearer.
Scanlan had worked hard in the garden,
In spite of his sleepless nights as Air Raid Warden.
Once she had been able to help him;
Now she was stiff and old and could no longer stoop.
Maddalena looked away from the twisted mass of glass and metal
That had been the greenhouse.
She fingered her rosary.

Peace would come again to her home in the Ruhr;
Ludwig's sons were dead in Russia these two years gone;
Maria's grandson, little Magda's boy,
Would come home safely now.
Touching her rosary again, Maddalena fed her noisy flock,
Then made her way back to the chapel
Where she rang the bell
For the Victory celebrations.

– Bridie O'Brien

Census for Finnoe Civil Parish

Townland	Population 1659	Population 1841	1851	Inhabited Houses 1841	1851	Population 1861	1871	1881	Population 1891	1901	Population 1911	Population 1986	1991	Population 1996
Ballinderry		18	37	4	4	8	6	4	2	5	3			
Ballyfinboy	7	12	7	1	1	3	8	6	4	3	4			
Ballynamona		8		2		18	5	4	6	9	–			
Ballyquinlevan Lr		19	6	4	1	6	2	2	10	4	1			
Ballyquinlevan Upr		62	20	4	5	9	8	8	6	4	8			
Bellgrove		22	19	9	6	9	15	12	15	12	8			
Bellpark		21	5	4	1	11	10	8	7	5	5			
Boherleigh		69	20	12	3	54	28	38	34	26	24			
Commons of Carney		229	50	48	12	140	132	100	97	95	74			
Curraghmore		16	151	3	32	12	22	14	37	19	35			
Derries		34	9	4	2	–	8	4	4	–	–			
Gurteen		133	31	27	5	93	61	54	48	38	28			
Graigillane	2	64	101	12	17	25	29	40	30	12	6			
Green Lane		68	29	13	6	14	28	13	12	16	4			
Kilbeg		105	18	17	3	33	25	32	28	14	9			
Kilcowran	9	77	61	13	10	27	19	26	35	29	20			
Killea	6	109	18	22	4	74	49	52	44	27	25			
Kyleomadaun E&W		91	111	16	16	45	33	45	54	47	33			
Oldcourt		27	32	7	8	16	8	12	13	15	14			
Rodeen Lower		128	18	23	3	58	33	42	31	31	30			
Rodeen Upper	14	62	98	10	23	42	26	41	22	27	25			
Shesheraghscanlan		–	65	–	10	19	24	19	11	9	11			
Springfield		126	14	24	3	39	33	20	15	15	12			
Springfield Glebe		13	78	3	13	7	9	7	6	5	1			
Sragh		63	15	12	3	24	9	15	16	11	9			
Clyinkrokey	4		32		5									
Finmogh village	28													
TOTALS	**70**	**1,576**	**1,045**	**294**	**196**	**786**	**630**	**618**	**587**	**490**	**389**	**157**	**150**	**155**

NB Census figures for individual townlands are no longer published.

Census for Kilbarron Civil Parish

Townland	Population 1659	Population 1841	Population 1851	Inhabited Houses 1841	Inhabited Houses 1851	1861	Population 1871	Population 1881	Population 1891	Population 1901	Population 1911	Population 1986	Population 1991	Population 1996
Annagh	22	93	89	15	15	65	64	45	37	43	44			
Ballinagross	9	65	29	12	6	13	24	26	8	11	13			
Ballinderry	39	454	232	88	43	176	155	125	95	106	81			
Ballycolliton	32	40	28	8	5	34	30	32	27	29	12			
Ballyscanlan	7	123	45	23	9	29	20	22	15	19	16			
Bellevue		305	196	56	36	110	91	99	88	80	70			
Brockagh	12	275	194	44	36	159	145	94	72	64	54			
Brookfield		14	3	2	1	16	28	22	14	14	15			
Cameron Island		0	7	0		4	10	6						
Carrick	19	41	33	6	6	44	35	34	21	28	17			
Carrigagown Nth		30	12	4	2	9	6							
Carrigagown Sth		12	13	5		21	10	12	6		6			
Castletown	11	28	21	3	3	21	27	28	17	14	7			
Clonmakilladuff	33	166	97	33	20	39	21	22	29	20	17			
Coolbawn	19	124	89	24	17	76	65	53	50	45	42			
Curraghmore		122	78	19	11	38	39	29	22	16	14			
Firgrove						3								
Garrane		36	36	7	6	20	24	4	9	30	18			
Garryncurry		24	35	8	6	4	8	5		7	8			
Glenaviegh		32	14	6	3	10	11	12	8	6	6			
Glenbower		37	6	9	1	26	15	6	5	5	3			
Gortmunga		52	45	8	9	9	7	24	15	11	6			
Kevanstown Nth		44	23	7	4	27	17	14	16	20	7			
Kevanstown Sth		81	57	16	10	12	5	7	5	4	15			
Kilbarron	11	23	11	3	2	15	16	22	21	17	5			
Kilbiller	28	42	21	6	4	41	28	24	26	20	13			
Kilgarvan	10	58	51	12	14	14	7	7	6	10	13			
Lahesseragh		23	10	6	2	24	15	18	13	14	9			
Lisquillibeen	6	212	136	39	26	92	63	61	43	45	13			
Meelick		32	24	6	5						49			
Mota	11	12	5	2	1	3	6	6	5	3	13			
O'Meara's Acres	44	74	70	11	11	49	20	19	9	20	19			
Raheen		10	20	3	3		14	NR–						
Scarragh		16	14	4	3	19	8	9						
Scriboge	11	31	20	5	3	23	21	12	11	8	7			
Skehanagh		25	25	5	4	22	12	10	14	12	5			
Bounla Island			11		2									
Brieny's Island														
Goat Island														
Islandmore		97	78	13	12	46		27		25				
Thirty-five other islands														
TOTALS	324	2,853	1,878	518	344	1,313	1,064	936	707	750	600	541	530	530

The discrepancy between the figures for Kilbarron on this page and those on p. 6 is due to the insertion of figures here for Islandmore.

Census for Terryglass Civil Parish

Townland	Population 1659	Population 1841	Population 1851	Inhabited Houses 1841	Inhabited Houses 1851	Population 1861	Population 1871	Population 1881	Population 1891	Population 1901	Population 1911	Population 1986	Population 1991	Population 1996
Cappanasmear	10	164	120	23	16	64	52	63	44	NA	NA			
Carrownaglogh		164	65	30	9	28	22	22	20	20	22			
Clooninihy		241	206	38	33	131	88	83	82	74	50			
Cornamult		97	85	14	15	55	34	23	24	19	16			
Cornalack		28	16	3	4	3	6	5	4					
Crossanagh		45	42	7	6	32	38	47	46	33	33			
Drominagh		41	18	5	5	14	7	5	5	5	10			
DrominaghDemesne		11	12	1	2	13	20	13	17	20	30			
Drominagh Wood		8	10	1	1	6	—	3	1	15	7			
Firmount		182	111	32	22	150	104	121	95	90	69			
Garryard		168	121	29	24	42	38	34	31	NA	NA			
Garrycloghy	12	141	114	22	23	51	33	35	20	26	19			
Gortmore		50	26	8	4	19	20	3	3	4	5			
Killeen		68	28	11	6	5	13	16	18	13	8			
Lacken		293	55	11	6	37	31	15	21	17	17			
Muckloon		70	46	9	8	35	28	29	33	27	21			
Muckloonmodderee		119	105	15	15	88	69	72	68	56	51			
Newlawn		134	122	24	22	114	89	91	89	103	82			
Roegarraun		32	18	8	3	32	24	20	25	28	23			
Roran	24	191	143	32	24	101	76	66	71	67	56			
Shanakill Lower		130	21	17	3	29	24	24	19	24	17			
Shanakill Upper		31	26	5	5	21	9	2	8	8	22			
Shanvally		40	33	5	5	29	23	22	25	22	14			
Sheelruddera		32	28	3	4	14	12	10	6	14	12			
Slevoir	15	83	26	15	6	26	31	26	23	23	30			
Stonepark		114	99	15	15	81	42	34	43	42	32			
Terryglass		197	236	30	48	145	87	112	81	71	91			
Turavoggaun		79	54	12	9	43	40	36	33	37	27			
TOTALS	**61**	**2,953**	**1986**	**425**	**347**	**1,408**	**1,060**	**1,032**	**955**	**867**	**738**	**485**	**464**	**450**

NA = not available

This book is published with the support of Tipperary LEADER Group.

PUBLICATION COMMITTEE
Chairman: P. J. Starr, Terryglass; **Hon. Secretary:** Ann Carroll, Coolbawn; **Joint Treasurers:** Matt Fogarty, Drominagh, Ballinderry, and John Slattery, Kilbiller, Coolbawn.
Committee: William (Wilsie) Nolan, Terryglass, Joseph Hannigan, Ballinderry, Phylis Harnett, Terryglass, Michael Molamphy, Jun., Coolbawn, Loretta Tiernan, Bellevue, Bridie Hanafin, Coolbawn, Niall Heenan, Roran, Terryglass, Jimmy Cahalan, Clooninihy, Oliver Darcy, Terryglass, Liam Horan, Ballinderry.

SPONSORS
The publication of this parish history has been made possible by the generous financial support received from the sponsors who are listed here (list complete as of going to print).

Brigid Adam, Tunbridge Wells, Kent, England.
AIB, Main St, Borrisokane.
AIB, Pearse St, Nenagh.

Borrisokane Credit Union Ltd.
Noel Brennan, Auctioneer, Borrisokane.
Jamie & Daniel Burke, Clonmackilladuff.
John & Mairéad Burke, San Francisco.
Patrick & Brendan Burke, Kilbarron.
Teresa Burke, Kilbarron, Coolbawn.

Ann & Christina Carroll, Coolbawn.
Dermot Carroll, Dublin & Coolbawn.
Deirdre Carroll, Coolbawn.
Georgina Carroll, Kilbiller, Coolbawn.
Josephine & Jerry Carroll, Kilbiller, Coolbawn.
Michael & Ciss Carroll, Coolbawn.
Oliver & Marian Carroll, Caherdavin, Limerick.
Pat Carroll, Jersey, Channel Islands, & Coolbawn.
May & Willie Carty, Portumna.
Claffey Motors, Portumna.
Nancy Coen, Greenlane, Borrisokane.
Jo Comerford, Borrisokane.
Tony Conroy, Aglish, Roscrea.
T. F. Costello & Sons Ltd., Ciamaltha Rd., Nenagh.
Christina & Una Costelloe, Brocka, Ballinderry.
Donal Corbett, Middlesex, England, & Coolbawn.
Patrick Corbett, 'Corcool' Wood Products, Coolbawn.
Christy Cormican, Building Contractor, Coolbawn.
Crawfords Family Grocer, Borrisokane.

Cyril & Frances Darcy, Tramore.
Oliver & Sheila Darcy, Terryglass.
Michael Donoghue, Tiling Contractor, Lisquillibeen, Coolbawn.

Jim & Peter Egan, Building Contractors, Coolbawn & Puckane.
Seán Egan, Centra Foodstore, Borrisokane.
Europiping Manufacturing Ltd., Miltown Malbay.

F.B.D. Insurance, Kenyon St, Nenagh.
D. M. Fleming, London.
Matt & Mary Fogarty, Drominagh, Ballinderry.
Marie Fox, Fox's Book Shop, Mitchel St, Nenagh.

Tim Gleeson, Machinery Plant, Nenagh.

Tony & Agnes Hallifax, Coolbawn, Nenagh.
Joe & Jane Hannigan, Kilbarron, Coolbawn.
Robert Harris, J. Harris Assemblers Ltd. Dublin.
Al Hayes, Al Hayes Motors, Portumna.
Heaslip Insurances, Mitchel St, Nenagh.
Henderson & Bailey, Borrisokane.
Elsie Hogan, Ballinderry.
John Hogan, Clonmackilladuff, Coolbawn.
Joseph Hogan, Building Contractor, Terryglass.
Paddy Hogan, Kilrush & Bellevue.
Patrick Hogan, Cornalack, Terryglass.
Seán Hogan, Roran & Dublin.
Conor Hyland & Valerie Cotter, Paddy's Bar, Terryglass.

Irish Nationwide Building Society, Nenagh.
Irish Permanent Building Society, Nenagh.

Eileen & Donal Joyce, Gentian Hill Hse, Galway.

Pat Keller, Keller's One Stop Shop & Service Station, Nenagh.
Seán Kelly Tiles, Cork.
James Kennedy, Pub & Grocer, Puckane.
Kilbarron Festival Committee Fund.
Con Kinnane, Nenagh Plant Hire.

W. J. Lawlor, Borrisokane.
Rev. William Leenane, PP, Puckane.

Julia McDonnell, Ryehill, Ballinderry.
Michael & Angela McDonnell, Carrigatoher, Nenagh.
Sheila McDonnell, Portumna.
Lilian Madden, Dublin.
Margaret's Hair Affair, Carney & Horst Schlag Computers, Nenagh.
Virginia Moeran, Kylenoe, Ballinderry.
Mick & Mary Molamphy, Coolbawn.
Frank & Betty Moran, Coolbawn.
Michael Moran, Dublin & Coolbawn.
Morecome Builders Ltd., Coolbawn.

Nenagh Co-op Creamery, Nenagh.
Nenagh Co-op Mart, Nenagh.

Anthony O'Brien, London & Coolbawn.
Carmel O'Brien, The Chocolate Box, Kilcock, Co. Kildare.
W. J. O'Brien, Glenbower, Coolbawn.
O'Brien's Supermarket, Borrisokane.
John & Margaret O'Connor, O'Connor's Bakery, Nenagh.
O'Connor's Shopping Centre, Nenagh.
Jim O'Donoghue, Bellevue, Coolbawn.
Jim O'Grady, England & Mota, Coolbawn.
John O'Grady, Dublin & Mota, Coolbawn.
Michael O'Halloran, Forklifts, Coolbawn & Nenagh.
David O'Keeffe, Nenagh.
Michael O'Kennedy, TD, Nenagh.
Donie, May & Mary O'Meara, Gurteen, Borrisokane.
John O'Meara, Finnoe Rd., Borrisokane.
Marty & Bridie O'Meara, Ballinderry.
Mary & Joe O'Meara, Ballinagross, Coolbawn.
Michael & Teresa O'Meara, Kylebeg, Coolbawn.
Overhead Door Co., Ashley Park, Ardcroney.

Una Perrine, Arizona, & Tunbridge Wells, Kent.
Pfizer Corp Animal Feeds, Cork.

Phil Quigley, The Tavern, Ballinderry.

Bernie Reddan, The Tower Bar, Borrisokane.
Roscrea Oil.
John & Susan Ryan, Summerhill, Nenagh.
Patrick Ryan & Sons, Building Contractors, Coolbawn.

Brud & Ebie Seymour, Borrisokane.
Tom Sheridan, The Derg Inn, Terryglass.
John Slattery, Kilbiller, Coolbawn.
Michael Slattery, Slattery's Garage, Puckane.
Tommy Slattery, Lesserragh, Coolbawn.
Eamonn Slevin, Electrical Shop, Borrisokane.
Jimmy Slevin, Rodeen, Borrisokane.
P. J. Starr, Terryglass.

Texaco Oil (John McKenna), Roscrea.
Terryglass Improvements Committee.
Jack Tiernan, Surrey, England, & Bellevue.
William Tiernan, Video Shop, Cloughjordan.
Theo Tierney, Tippland Peat, Terryglass.

Ulster Bank, Kickham St, Nenagh.

Anne & Fred Valette, Yewston, Nenagh.
Valette-Kennedy Insurance, Kenyon St, Nenagh.

Index

Index does not include Ballinderry mill ledger entries, children in school pics, first-aid groups, foreign officers in Esmonde story, team and committee members.

Abbott, Marjorie 148
ACOT/Teagasc 350
Act of Settlement, 1662 16, 121, 145
Ainsley, W.B. 359
Aldworth, Richard 36
Alexander, Jean 343, 347
Alt family 41
Alt, Mr, Curraghmore 210
Amirath, Rev. Joseph 36, 39
Anderson, Elizabeth 135
Anglesea, earl of 17, 18
Annagh 1, 145; Castle 5, 146; eviction 323; Forty Acre Field 1; Lodge 147, 149, 154; Lough 5; tower house 25, 146
Armitage's Lane 336
Armitage's well 94
Artichokes 342
Ashgrove 222, 276, 352; evictions 222
Ashgrove House 221, 222; War of I incident 222
Atkinson, Sarah 212
Austen, Sir William 220

Baldwin, David 123, 128
Baldwin, Richard 124
Ballinagrass Lough 5
Ballinakill castle 145
Ballinderry 1, 37, 134, 258; acreage of 1; Clancy's Cross, 269; distillery 259, 260; forge 262; fort 8; in 1654 258; in 1998 271; mill 258, 259; mill – ledger entries 260; Mill House 66, 67, 259, 266; miller's house 263; post office 268, 269; pump 271; RIC barracks 259, 263, 264, 377; RIC names 264; river 4; Tavern 268; village 258; village houseowners 261, 262; village in 1840 258
Ballintrially 17
Ballycolliton 17; battle in 1598 26; Hearth Money Rolls 121; House 202, 203; lease 204; river 108; tower house 26, 203
Ballyfinboy House 180
Ballyfinboy 31; House 259; river 4; 'Sheela-na-Gig' 32; tower house 31
Ballyfinboy House 267
Ballyquinlivan 250; hedge school 76; Lough 5
Ballyquinlivan Upper 44
Ballyscanlan 134; school 74
Balmain, Dorothea Jessica 295
Bane, Aggie & Duncan, 'Murroughboro' 154
Barry, Jack 48, 153; John 37; Samuel 38
Bell, Heather & Alec 164
Bellevue 4, 5, 10, 321; emigration in 1890s 321; hedge & Kildare Place Society schools 82; House 142, 344; national school 82; new village 166
Bell's Academy, Dublin 175
Belvedere, the 165
Bergin, Patrick 50, 249
Biggs 134; Adelaide, Cornalack 137; 'Castle Biggs' 141; Cecil 139; Charlotte 135; division of land 143; Dr Edward 135, 138, 141, 143, 144; Dr Frederick 135; Dr William Ledger 135, 136, 137; Edward 8, 275; Elizabeth née Goodwin 139; George Washington 1st 82, 135, 139; Grace Robinson 139; Harriet (Babe), Cornalack 137; Helena, Bellevue 163; John, priest 136; Major George W. Bellevue 139; Mary, Cornalack 137; Mary Mason 134; Mrs Ruby née Jupe 216; Phidelia Matilda 135; Richard 37, 128, 134, 135; Richard, Terryglass 136; Robert 135; Samuel (Uel) 135, 139, 140, 143, 216; Samuel 2nd, Cornalack 137; Samuel, Cornalack 137; Samuel Dickson 135, 139; Samuel, Gortmore 137; Sarah née Hough, Cornalack 137; tenants 140; Thomas 135; threshing dances 140; Triphenia Anne Firman 135; Tudor-style house 141; vaults 134, 135, 139; William 2nd 135; William, Cloughjordan 134, 138; William Jun. 134; William, Newlawn 134, 142; Zelie 139, 142, 344
Black and Tan raid 378
Black Lough 5
Blowick, Joe 291
Boate, Godfrey, Dublin 134
Boelens, Jenny 72
Boer War, 1898-1902 375
Boland, Jane, teacher 87
Bond: Michael, smith 337
Book of Leinster 56
Book of Survey & Distribution 16
Bouchier 377; Jer 48, 153; Mick, Annagh 377; Patrick 150
Bounla Island 1
Bourke 84; James, Lisquillibeen 7; John & Babs, Carrigagowan 202; Mark 84, 94, 109, 250, 252, 323, 336; Rev. W. 68; Thomas 252
Bowles, Rev. Ambrose PP 53, 67, 76, 77; Rev. James 67
Boyle family, Ballinderry 263
Boyne Valley Foods 351
Brady, Hugh, Islandmore 230
Brannigan, Jimmy, Rodeen 117
Breen, Dan 283
Brereton, Breda 52, 175; burial place 176; Daniel 2nd 175; Daniel 3rd 175; Daniel 1st 174; Daniel 2nd 175; Denis 174, 258; Donal 176; Eileen 175, 176; Ellen 174, 175; Ellie 52; Frances 175; George 174; George 2nd 174; Gertrude (Trudy). 176; John 2nd, Oldcourt 174; John 3rd Oldcourt 175; John (4) 175; John (4) Oldcourt 175; John, Oldcourt 174; John, Rathurles 174; Judith 175; Mary 174, 176; Mary 2nd 175; Patrick 174; Thomas, Rathurles 174
Brien, Robert, coachman 148, 226
Brieny's Island 1
Briggs, George 124, 134; John 17, 18, 25, 27, 119, 120, 124, 134; John 2nd 134; Judith 134
Brock, Tony & Madeleine 138
Brockagh 134
Brooder, James, Brocka 356; T. 356
Brookfield 130, 163, 348; gate lodge 166; House 130, 165, 166, 344; Móinín Ruadh (little red bog) 166; old mill 166; private school 130
Browne, Emer, teacher 82
Bruce 140; Alice 168; Bertie 140, 170, 172, 231; Cecil 168; community welfare 170; Dot 168; Ellen Kate (Miss Ellie) 168; Ethel 172; Eva 168,

170; family line 168; Gwen 168; Janet 170; Janet, Ethel, Eva and Bertie 169; Louise (Tot) 168; Major William Tyrell 167, 168; orchestra & open-air concerts 169; Sophia Mary 168; Sophia Susan 168
Buckley, Ger, RIC 262, 266; Maureen 203; Mr, teacher 80, 82
Bugler, Rev. Fr 8
Burchell, Matt & Har 379
Burgess 309; Agnes née Balderston 309; Henry Givens: profile 309; Paddy 338, 339
Burk, Rev. Richard 35, 45
Burke, Annie née Whelan 108; James & Mrs 53; Jamesy & Theresa 256; Jim and Albie profile 370; Pat, Carney 361; Redmond 23; Rev. M. 67; Robert fitzDavid 21
Burns, Rody 48
Busherstown 145
Butler, James, 12th earl of Ormond 17, 18; James, Tullow 18; Rev. Piers 57; Rev. Piers 35, 36, 39; Richard, Ballyquirke 18
Byrne, Peter 265

Caddoo, Rev. D. G. 72
Cahalan Anne (Nancy) 202; Denis 364; James 271; James 'Guardian' 271, 346; Morgan, steward 211; Nannie 265; Patrick 'Guardian' 346, 378
Cahill, Garda John 248
Callanan, Rodge 344
Cambie 9, 11, 12; A. J., Vancouver 120; Alex 124; Alice née Craine 120; Alice née Craine 120, 121, 122; Anne 207; Anne née Ledger 124; Anne Minchin 217; Captain 120; Captain Solomon 1st 120, 121; Captain Solomon 1st 119, 145; Captain Solomon, Norwich 120; Castle Cambie 206; Catherine née Carlton 125; Catherine (Sabitier) 122; Catherine, Sedgemore 122; Charles 122, 123, 124, 207; Charlotte (Baldwin) 122; Colonel David 119, 120; David, Brookfield & Castletown 122, 123, 128; David, Bunnaduber 217; David, Kilbiller 122; David, Kilgarvan 125; David Solomon, Kilgarvan 125; Edward 2nd Kilgarvan 125; Edward 3rd 125; Edward, Mota & Kilgarvan 122, 123, 124, 125, 127, 129; Elizabeth 120; Elizabeth 2nd 122; Elizabeth (Lewis) 122; Elizabeth (Towers) 123; Elizabeth, Brookfield 122; Elizabeth née Watkins 125; estate, sale of 123; Esther Desbonnet 120; Fanny, Kilgarvan 125; George 122; Henry J. Vancouver 124; Henry J., Vancouver 131, 132; Jean 124; John 120, 121; John, Kilgarvan 125; Lieut. David 120; Lucy, Kilgarvan 125; Mary 122; MaryAnne 124; Mary, Brookfield 122; Mary née Walsh 123, 128; Miss, teacher 73; Rachel Harding 122; Richard, Kilgarvan 122; Richard William Camac 122; Sarah 122, 124; Solomon 1st 120; Solomon 2nd 120, 122; Solomon Baldwin 9, 125; Solomon Baldwin, Kilgarvan 125; Solomon, Captain 16, 17; Solomon Ledger 122, 126, 149, 348; Solomon Ledger, will of 123; Suzanne 120; Thomas 122; Thomas (Lalor) 122
Cambies of Norwich 120
Camier, Rev. James 72

Cappanasmear 18
Carlton, Catherine 125
Carney Commons, 257; cairn 7; Mass house 44; school 74
Carpentry 346
Carrick, crannóg 7
Carrigagowan: 'Castle Carrig' 202
Carrigagowan House 202
Carrigahorig 254, 355; mills 284, 285; RIC barracks 283; river 4; village 283; village – Pathe memoir 284
Carroll, Alice Viola, USA 311, 313; Anne, Brookfield 84; Bill 153, 271; Brendan 7; Brookfield 288; Eliza 166; Eliza, Brookfield 110; family 259; Garda Patrick 248; Geraldine, USA 311; Howard Emmet, USA 311; Jack, Finnoe Rd 346; James 310, 359; James, Brookfield 375; profile 314; Jeremiah (Darby) & Elizabeth née Kennedy 310; Jeremiah, herd 336, 345; Jeremiah, USA 311; Jerry 111; Jim 259; Joe (pedlar) 116; John 359; John (Golly), Borrisokane 66; John, Behagh 17, 27; John, Brookfield 358; John, Brookfield & USA 356; John, Lisquillibeen & USA 310, 311; Mabel, USA 311; Margaret née Darcy 314; Mary Anne née Galvin 311; Mary, Ballycrinode 174; Mary, Brookfield & USA 315, 344; May 252; Michael 8, 154; Mrs Peter 249; Nora 52; Nora, Newtown 267; Paddy, Coolbawn 340; Pat, Brookfield 322; Pat, Jersey 152; Patrick 310, 314; Patrick 2nd 166; Patrick, Brookfield: profile 314; Patrick, Lisquillibeen 166; Patrick, miller 259, 267, 340; Patrick, monitor 78; Peter 288, 289, 345, 357, 361; Peter (1) 310, 314; Peter, Brookfield 111, 314, 365; Ruth, USA 311; Sister Consolata 313; William (Bill), Bellevue 140, 345
Carty, Jack, Gortmore 211; Mick, Bill, John and Mary, Gortmore 211
Casey, Bryan 357; Jimmy 115; John 151
Cash, Dan 341
Casson, Christopher 170; Sir Lewis 170
Castles, Jeremy 72
Castletown 17, 134, 348; acreage 17; Buckle Park 147; Castle Camby 27; estate records 207, 208; estate, sale of 123; House 206, 207, 346; House, raid on 209; records 209; soup kitchen 124; tower house 17, 20, 27, 132, 207
Catholic Clergy: role of 14
Catholic clergy: registration of 42
Census, 1659 16
Charcoal burning 341
charcoal burning 342
Civil Survey 4, 16, 17, 19, 25
Civil War 379
Clancy 52; Joe RIC 52, 266; Mary 225; Mary Mrs 52
Clarke, Nurse 148; Rev. D 72
Clarke family: Garryncurry House 212
Clear, John 250; Michael 250; Patrick 50, 250
Clear's shop 250
Cleary 115; Anne widow 251; burial custom 322; College, USA 214; James 251; James K, Nenagh 251; James, Springfield House 202; Jeremiah 251; Jeremiah, Roderick, Timothy & James 251; John, Skehanagh 151; Margaret, Ballycolliton 203;

Michael 251; Michael, Nenagh 251; Patt 214; Rode, Curraghmore 322; Rody & Judy, Lisquillibeen 214; Roger 71; Thomas 58
Cleary, P. J. Annagh 146; Rode, Curraghmore 115
Cleary, Cornelius & Margaret: Ballycolliton 202
Cleburne, Eleanor 121; Elizabeth 48; family tree 121; graves 48; Richard 202; Richard, Bunnaduber 121; Robert, Kilbiller 151; Samuel 121; Samuel, Springmount 39; William 121; William, Ballycolliton 48, 121
Clery, Phyllis 176
Cloghprior 145
Clohedy, Rev. Daniel 68
Clonmakilladuff 134, 248, 348; cattle drive in 248; division of 248, 249; forts 7
Clooninihy 4
Coen, Cora 350; Julia 109
Coffey, Stephen, Carney 361
Collins, Jack, Claree 78; Séamus, teacher 82
Colmcille St. 55
Colum St. (Mac Cremthainn) 55
Comenthus 10, 112, 140
Comerford, Rev. Thos CC 8
Comerford, Rev. Thos CC 52, 66, 67, 301
Commissioners of Education Report 1826-7 74
Commissioners of Public Education, 2nd report 82
Concannon 84; Margaret, teacher 80, 84; Timothy, teacher 80, 82
Conlin, Dr David & Mrs, Kilgarvan 215
Conroy, Des 42
Conway 299; Brigid (Ciss) née Hough 300; Brigid, Michael, Christopher, Nora, Teresa 300; John & Maria née Hough 299; Margaret 300; Michael Jun. 300; Michael, postman 375; profile 299; Molly 263; Rev. John P. 67
Coolbawn 4, 114, 134; 1998 249; acreage in 1654 240; buildings at Cross 240; buying out the land 248; census 241, 242; Cross 9, 10, 208, 249, 378; division of land 247; field names 241; fort 7; gate lodges 148; Hurly, Kennedy owners 240; in the 1920s 243; landlords 240; Molamphy's shop 246; occupiers in 1852 241; platform 249; Primary Valuation 241; pump 9; school ruins 74; small dwelling 227; swans 5; tenants' names 240; Tithe Applotment 240, 241
Coolcarrigan 288
Coonan, Joe 153
Cooney, Rev. John CC 66, 255
Corbett: Lieut-Col. John 377; Paddy 234; Rev. George PP 61, 62, 68, 78; Rev. M. 67
Corboy, Ciss 259; Maurice 364; Will 341; William, Bellevue, lease 129
Corcoran, Tom 338
Corish, Brendan TD 265, 293; Sergt Nicholas 265
Cork & Orrery, earl of 18
Cormican, Christy, builder 53, 351; Mrs Kitty née Sammon 151; Mrs Thomas 53
Cornalack 136; House 138
Cornaling Lake 5, 109, 174
Cornamult 137
Costello, Anne, Kilbarron 84; Michael 265
Costelloe 109, 262; Dinny 364; family, Ballinderry 262; Hugh, Garryncurry 9, 212; John 357;

Margaret & William, Ormonde Cottage 201; Martin, Ballinderry 62; Martin, smith 336; Mary Anne 262; Matt, Lisquillibeen 365; Matthew 150; Seán 345; Tim 262; Vina 109
Cotter, Valerie 276
Craine, Alice 120
Crann 2, 347
Crossanagh bridge 222
Cubitt, Robin 154
Cuffe, Penelope, Kilkenny 146
Culberts coachbuilders 110
Cumann na mBan, list of members 379
Cummins, Judith, Dunkerrin 174
Curragh, Portroe 42
Curraghmore 41, 210; House 41
Curraghmore (Kilbarron: House 210
Curriculum for schools 91
Curtin 93; Eileen 93, 340, 344; Hugh, Co. Clare 93; Patrick, teacher 79, 80, 91, 340
Cusack, Joe 138

Dagg, family, Kevanstown 50
Dagg, Emily 215
Dalton, Kieran, miller 259
Daly, Rev. Wesley 71
Darcy, Anne, Ballinderry 225; Bernard 351; Dan & May 262, 351; Jim, Kilbarron 356; Margaret née Carroll 344; Mrs, Ballinderry 354; Nora, Kilfadda 225; Rev. John PP 13, 51, 52, 61, 63, 65, 68, 79, 91, 231, 252, 266; Stephen, weaver 352
Darcys: Ballindery 267
Darley, Kevin 224
Dawson, Arthur 224
Day, Rev. Dan 68
de Marisco, Geofrey 20
de Valera, Éamon 286
Deasy: Mrs Dolores 62; Peter 286; Richard, Attorney-General 286; Rickard, profile 285; Sheila Marie née O'Kelly 286
Dempster, Dr James 258
Dennison, Robert, teacher 85
Desbonnet, Esther 120
Disney, Jane 123
Doherty, Mr & Mrs Walter 53
Donald, Robert, Ormonde Cottage 201
Donaldson, Samuel & George 362
Donnelly, Michael, Borrisokane 67
Donoghue 137; Bill 137, 138, 143, 184, 222, 269; Cup 365; Danno 342; Danny 185, 190, 268; Frank 150; Harry and Maggie née Conway 263; Jack 268; Jack 'the Gunner' 143, 185, 375, 376; Jane 225; Kevin 269; Mary & Pat 334; Mary née Tully, dressmaker 343; Mary ICA 334; Michael 4; Michael (Mick), Bellevue 365; Michael, Carney 250; Michael, Knockballyea 152; Mick 'Big' 143; Mick 'Gunner' 378, 379; Nora 321; 'Old' Michael, gardener 269; Pat, Toomevara 361; Peg, Kilbiller 151; Willie, Bellevue lodge 211
Dowd, Francis Erwin & Ruth née Carroll 313; Sr. Ruth Cecilia 313
Downes, Rev. Michael CC 67
Downey, Jim 342; Paddy 341; Rev. Thomas CC 67;

Tom 341, 342
Doyle, Anne 287
Drominagh 4, 134, 141, 340; Dispensary Field 142; gate lodge 263, 269; House 4, 141, 181, 184, 269; Lodge 144, 346, 347; tower house 4, 22, 23, 141, 184; twenty cottages 141
Drominagh Demesne 22
Dublin Metropolitan Police 13, 365
Ducie, Billy 48; family 153; Joe, Puckane 211
Duggan, Jimmy 372
Dungan, Lord 17, 18
Dunne, Pat 42
Dwyer, Jack 67, 341; Jim. Kilbarron 356; John & Kathleen 5; Martin 341; Martin & Jack 342

Egan 346; Jack 63; Jim 109; John, Borrisokane 346; Michael 52, 238; Michael, builder 207; Rev. Connolly PP 43, 45; William 258
Elliot, Dan 379
employment 15
Esmonde 11; Carmel 184, 199; Donal 184, 185; Dr Anthony, Nenagh 138, 376; Dr John MP 342; Eily 199; Ellie 52, 62, 72, 224, 344; Eugene, VC, DSO 62,184-200; family history 184; James 142, 296; James, Drominagh 184; James2nd 184; John Joseph 184; John Witham 184; Lieut. Geoffrey 376; Osmond 190; Owen 142, 184, 185, 190, 199, 376; Patrick 184, 199; Tony 376
Evans family 341
Evanson. Rev. A.M. 50
Exshaw, John Jun. 151

faction fights 354
Falkiner, Benjamin 39; John, Prospect 39; John, Springfield House 202; Joseph 38
Farrell, Constable Matthew 264; Jack 265; James 265; Margaret (Madge) 265; Mary (nee Byrnes 265; Mary née Neville 264; Matt Jun.. 265; Michael 265; Paddy 265
Fawcett, Frederick 206; George William 203, 204
Fennell, Mary, Cloughjordan 166
Ferrar: John & Violet 219; vault 219; William D. 219
Field names 8, 108, 109, 112, 142, 153, 178, 270
Field names 6
field names, Islandmore 236
Finane: Julia née Kelly 344
Finnoe 34; acreage 2; census 16; church amalgamation 39; church new 38; church pews 38; church pre-Reformation 36, 37; church silver 40; Glebe (Curraghmore Hse) 41; graveyard 40; House 303, 305; lake in 5; landlords & tenants 250; Rectors 1612-1915 39; rectory of 35; school 85; Vestry Records 38
Firgrove 250
Firman 135
Firmans 135, 285
Firmount 180, 285
Fitzgerald, William 17, 18
fitzWalter, Theobald 19, 20
Flanagan, Rev. Michael 7

Flann, chief ollamh of Connacht 56
Flannery, Frank 237; Mike 321; Rev. Daniel 68; Rev. Michael 68, 267; Will 321
flax 352
Fleming, M. B. 250
flora 10, 70
Flynn, John P. 290, 293
Flynn, Michael 251
Fogarty, Anne née O'Meara 346; Daniel, Shannon View 222; David 367; Denis 189, 190, 342, 346; Dr Michael, bishop of Killaloe 60, 61, 69; Dr Michael, bishop of killaloe 63; Ger and Breda 150; Matt 189, 342, 346; Paddy, teacher 82; Patrick 96, 144, 346; Rev. Matt 265, 342
Fogarty's quarry 65
Foley, Rev. Michael 68
folkore 352
Foote:,Mick 67, 342
forestry 2; acreage of 2; Coillte 2
Forges 333
forts 7
Fortune family: Drominagh 144; Garrane 211
Fox, Anthony 228; Anthony, Curraghmore 346; Bill 228; Jack 379; Mary 350; Paddy 91; Paddy, carpenter 340; Rosie 350; Tone 341; Will 261; Will, Paddy & Anthony 346
Frend, Benjamin, Kings's Co. 134
fulacht fiadh 6

Gaelic Athletic Association 356; Carrigahorig club 357; North Board 1901 360; North Tipperary branch, 1886 356
Gallagher, John, teacher 78, 175
Garcin, Philip and Beulah 165
Garda Síochána 248
Garrane 210; House 210, 211, 289
Garryncurry 9
gate lodges 226-8
Gaynon, James 150
Gaynor, Jack, Nenagh 66; Michael, Lahorna 361; Wing-Commander George 295
Geoghegan 28; Arthur 29; James 17
George, Rev. Thomas 50
Gerrard, Peter & Mide, Lesserragh 172
Gildea, Martin 238
Gillespie: Rev. Henry 39, 42, 71
Gleeson, Christy 343; Christy & Biddy 143; Christy, Gortmore & Cornalack 138; Danny 289; Gretta 252; John, teacher 91, 93, 218, 343, 352, 379; Margaret teacher 84; Mick, Borrisokane 67; Pat, Lahorna 361; Rev. Cornelius 68; Rev. John 68; Rev. John PP 84; Rev. Michael 68; Rev. Tim 66; Rev. Timothy 68; Rev. Timothy PP 68
Glenbower 1, 10, 134; acreage 17; eviction 152; Hill 1
Globe Insurance Co 275
Gloster, Vivian St Claire (Edward) 154
Glynn: Jim 276, 379; John, Portumna 61, 65
Goat Island 1
Goodbody: Clara 217; Rosaleen 230
Gordon, Desmond, teacher 91
Gorman, Jack 346; John 346; Jon & Martin 346; Martin & Ellen 246; Martin & John, Bellevue 340

Gortalougha 4; House 219, 295
Gortmongo 167
Gortmore 134, 343; division of 218; House 143, 218, 343
Gould, Arbuthnot 147, 150; Rev. Pierce 39
Grace: Bernadette, teacher 82; John, Ballinvoyne 18
Grady, Kate widow 266; May 289; Paddy 371
Grady, Counsellor: Curraghmore, Kilbarron 210
Graham, May, teacher 82
Granard RIC barracks 378
Great Famine 353
Green, Catherine, Limerick 146
Greenshields 40; Rev. James 37, 39, 44; Rev. William 39
Griffin 87; Catherine & Jane 87; James 62, 87, 180, 278; James & Catherine 277
Griffiths, Elizabeth (Babs) 164
Guest 379; Bob & Bill 379; Georgina 225, 379; Martin 67
Gunning, Rev. Patrick 68
Gurney: Anne Louise 238
Gurteen 4

Hackett, Anne, Riverstown 174; Paddy 6; Thomas 250
Halifax, Tony 5, 7
Hall, Rev. John LLD 37, 39
Hally, Daniell 17
Hamilton, Amy 213
Hamilton, Captain Leslie 161
Hannigan, Joseph 251, 252, 269; Sergt George 250, 251, 339
Harding, Rachel 122
Harkins, Pauline 251, 252
Harris, Robert 266
Harris, Tom 288
Harty, Rev. William CC 66, 68
Harvest Thanksgiving 114
Hastings, Miss, teacher 85
Hayes, George, Ballintotty 306; Rev. Michael 68
Head, Rev. John C. 71
Hearth Money Rolls 134
Heenan, Bridget, Ashgrove 379; William, Ashgrove 222; Heenan, Pat 276
Heffernan, Mrs 153
Henry 262; George & Hilary, 217; Hilary 262, 350
Hickie 11, 177; Amelia Victoria 61, 62; Arthur Francis 63; Brigadier Séamus 59, 181; Brigadier-Gen. Carlos Joseph CMG 63; Brigadier-Gen. Carlos 375; Brigadier-Gen. Carlos Joseph CMG 62, 181; Dolores 225, 285; Fr Arthur 375; James 180, 223; James Francis 62, 63, 177; Lieut-Col. James Francis 59; Lieut-Col. James Francis 61, 180; Lucila Larios 177; Lucila Larios 59; Major-Gen. Sir William Bernard KCB 61, 63, 64, 181; Major-Gen. Sir William KCB 375; Manuel 61, 62, 63, 64, 65, 180, 181, 223, 366, 375; Mary 63; Mary Pauline 60; Mia 295; Pauline 181; William 3rd 177; William 1st & 2nd, Co. Kerry 177
Hilgarth, Capt Alan 220, 302; Jean 221
hill names 113
Hinkson, Pamela 112, 269, 270, 299, 344
Hipwell, Rev. W.E. 72

Hobbins, Patrick 151
Hoctor, Jack 364
Hodgins, George 109; George, teacher 87
Hodson, Felicity 213
Hogan 53; Bridget née Treacy 252; Ciss, dressmaker 344; Dan, Lacken 65; Daniel 71; David 9; Donogh 17; Elizabeth née Cummins 260; Elizabeth, USA 315; Ellen 249; Ettie and Ben 225; Gerard 350; Hugh 37; Jerry 359; Jim 'Duck' 379; John 17, 249; John & Mary née Carroll: 'Rosemount' USA 316-7; John and Elizabeth, Cregane 69; John, Ballintreally 17; John, Rosemount 315; Julia 266; Martin 364; Martin & Rody 263; Mary née Carroll USA 318; Matt RIC 263; Michael (Mike), Lisquillibeen 376; Michael, Tom & John, Clonmakilladuff 338-9; Mike 128; Mike (Bush) 225; Mr & Mrs John 249; Philip 18; Rev. John PP 10, 51, 67, 69; Rev. John PP. 53; Sarah 321; Séamus 373; Seán 283; Terry 150; Tom, Lisquillibeen 152; Tommy 252; Will & Paddy, Lisquillibeen 341; Will, Lisquillibeen 340; William, Lisquillibeen 150, 152; Willie Joe, Cornalack 138; Willie, Ryehill 138
Hogan (Bush) 259; Anne 263; Anne (Nan) 261; Elizabeth née Cummins) 263; Elsie 53, 260, 261; Lucy 261; Michael 261; Nora née Wells 261; Patrick 260; Patrick & Martin 259; Tom 261, 263
Hogan (Shelter), Michael, teacher 88
Holland, Anne, teacher 87; Robert 9
Holmes, Bassett 2, 230; Islandmore 230
holy wells 8
Horan, Martin 379; Nancy 225; Rev. P. 68
Horse-racing 353
Hough, Betty née Fleming 263, 378; Christy 341; Frank 267; Jack, Mota 227; John, Cornalack 137; John, Shannon View/Lodge 223; Julia midwife 259; Madge & Daniel 244; Michael (Kenneally) 378; Mrs Daniel 52; Muddy 267; Pat, teacher 78; Sarah 137; Tom, Carrigahorig 379; Tom, Lisquillibeen 115; William (Billy) 352, 354
Houghs, Ballinderry 375
Hough's well 4
Houlihan, Rev. Joseph 68
Howard, Dick, Mota 166, 213, 215, 227
Howlin, Brendan TD 265
Hurley, Edmundus, vicar 45; Rev. P. 68
Hurling 355-367; Terryglass v Lorrha 366
Hurly, John 17, 25, 26, 145, 258
Huskinson family 217
Hutchinson, Jim 116
Hyland, Bill 336; Conor 276

Igoe, Squadron-Leader William A. K. (Bill) 193, 194, 195, 200
Inihy river 4
Irish Countrywomen's Association 10
Islandmore 230-8; School & teachers 235

Jones, Rev. William, rector 71

Joy, Michael Jun. 42; Michael Snr 42
Joyce, Chris, Mick & Jack 379
Jupe, Angela 216; Ruby 143, 216

Kane, Mike 321; Wm 359
Keane 109; Michael 109
Kearney, Daniel, chalice of 53
Keeshan, Ned, Roscrea 361
Kelly, Denis, Borisokane 372; Elizabeth, teacher 89; Michael, Nenagh 361
Kennedy 52; Andrew, Kilgarvan 126; Brian, Oldcourt 174; Bridget 270; Catherine, emigrant 270; Christy 288; Dan, Lisquillibeen 323; Ellen, publican 276; Evelyn teacher 91; Honora Wall 126; James, engineer, Birr 168; James, teacher 87; Jim, Coolbawn 114, 115, 226; John and Lucy 263; John, Graigillane 174; John, Kilgarvan 126; Katie, Mary Anne and Bridget 269; Kitty 114; letters to Australia 322; Lucy née Hogan 261; Margaret, Kilgarvan 126; Mary Anne 302; Mary, Kilgarvan 126; Mary, teacher 84; Mick and Nellie 227; Mick, Brocka 379; Mick, smith 337; Mike, herd 208, 226; Oliver, Brocka 66; Onnie 114, 170; Paddy, postman 337; Patrick, Australia 324; Philip, Ballyfinboy 174; Philip, Castletown 17, 121; Philip, Kilgarvan 126; Rev. John 79; Rev. John PP 52, 68, 79, 88, 89, 116, 271; Rev. P. 67; Rev. Philip PP 82; Rody, smith 333; Sylvester 299, 302; Sylvester & Kate née O'Meara 270; Willie, Lacken 64. **See also O'Kennedy.**
Kent, Alex 224, 225; Alex, Donald & Eileen 295; George 220; George Francis 295; Harold Carden 72, 220, 295; Mrs Roland née Powell 39, 42; Olive, Elmville 225; Ralph 220; Ralph, Olive & Eileen 295; Thomas & Esther 295
Kerin, Rev. Josh 67, 76, 77
Kevanstown 134, 233
Kilbarron 2, 34; acreage 17; barracks 250; boys' school 250; boys' school re-opening 78; C of I church 41, 49, 50, 114, 115, 249; C of I school 85; carnivals, with marquees 255; census 6, 16; church donors 52; church, pre-Reformation 43, 45, 46; coming of electricity 116; curate's house 69; early schools 74; festival 10; first national school 76; girls' school 77, 84, 91, 93; Glebe House 50, 215; graveyard (old) 48; grotto 255; hedge school 82; hill names 111; Irish Baptist Society school 85; landlords & tenants in 241; Mass paths 108; new cemetery 256; new curate's house 66; new school 1842 76; new school 1942 80; old Abbey 9, 46; pitch and putt 10, 256; population of 74; Primary Valuation: landlords & tenants in 251; RC church 50, 53, 250, 252; rectors 1825-1921 50; rectory of 35; school attendance 77; school books 91, 97; school games 94; school reports 1880s 78; school reports 1890s 79; school reports 1900 79; schools 1920-30s 80; schools amalgamation 78, 80; second national school 82; stone church 35; well 9
Kilbarron-Kildangan, teams 364
Kilbarron-Terryglass, priests, list of 67
Kilbiller 145; forts 8; House 217, 218
Kilgarvan 129; Angling Club 10; House 129, 130;
quay 340, 342, 361, 366; regatta 365
Killea 5
Killeen 180
Killodiernan 145
Kiloganny mill 352
Kingsboro, E. 37
Kinnerk, Rev. Patk M. 68
Kirwan, Mick 342
Knockballyea 29; Thade's Castle 49; Thade's Castle 29
Kyle Park 78; Agricultural School 78; national school 78, 87, 175
Kyleagoona 353
Kylenoe Wood 275
Kyleomadaun 17

Lacken 64, 180
Ladies Club 10
Lahorna De Wets 362
Lakeshore Foods 262, 271, 350
Lakeview House 5
Lalor Cambie 120, 122; papers 120, 125
Lalor, Mary, Moyne 122
Lambert, Sir Oliver 25, 26, 30
land use 2
Larcom, Thomas A. 6
Lavelle, Garret 376; Maura 283; Sergt David 283
Lawless, Walter 18
Lawlor, Edward 359
Ledger 122; Anne 122, 217; Mary 128
Leenane 91; Bridie née Whelan 379; John, teacher 91; Mike 137; Will 259
Legge, Edward 37, 71; Edward, church warden 37; Michael, Garrane 210
Lesserragh 111, 167; first motor car 111; first-aid classes 170; House 167, 170
limekilns 337
limekilns, Islandmore 235
Lisquillibeen 28, 29; Black Castle 29, 48; forts 7; land agitation 248; tower house 28
Lisquillibeen Lane 152
Lloyd, Benjamin 37
'Lochiel' 154
Lonan, Ollamh (of Ireland) 55
Long Lane Cross 1, 112, 339, 345; evictions near 232
Looby, Jim, Toomevara 361
Lough Avon 5
Lough Derg 11
Loughawn 5
Loughawn, Trassey's 5
Loughnanes 252
Love, John, Annagh 146, 151
Lower Ormond: Hearth Money Rolls 18
'Loyall Answer' 1622 35, 42
Luscurry, M. 37
Luska 1, 4, 10; House 212, 213; J.F. Tumpane store 213
Lynch, Henry 150; Jack 339; Jack, Garryncurry 339; John, Carney Commons 117, 358; Mary 339; Michael, teacher 85; Paddy 48; Rev. M.J. 68
Lyon, Anne 49; Rev. Thomas 49, 50, 85
Lyons 267; Mel 270; Trush née Darcy 267, 270

MacCormac, Rev James 50
MacDermott, Mary 62
Mackey: Seán 342; Tommy 379
Mackeys: Gortmore 143
MacMahon, Martin 238
MacNeill Moss, Geoffrey 142; Gilbert & Fiona 142
Maggie Smith's Lake 5
Magrath, Marcus, Blean 17
Maguire, Dennis, teacher 76, 77
Maher 375; Daniel, Clooninihy 375; Martin Charles, Roscrea 217; Tom, Kevanstown 115
Mahnke, Klaus 72; Michael 72
Mailley, Rev. Patrick 67
Malone, Rev. Eugene PP 53, 67
Maloney, Mick 53; Pat Joe, Ballinagross 15; Thomas 335
Markison, Bob 52
marriage practices 11
Marrinan, Rev. Wm. 68
Marshal, John 20
Martin, Rev. James 39, 41, 337
Mason, Biddy 352
Mason, Mary 134
Mass paths 108, 109
Massey, Rev. Henry 39, 58, 71
Matthews, Mary 175
Maunsell, Counsellor 178
McCarthy, Alice, Ballycapple 222; John, Ormonde Cottage 202; John, Springfield House 202; Mrs Bridie 53; Nancy, Ormonde Cottage 201; Patrick & Vincent, Ormonde Cottage 202
McCormack, Misses, Moneygall 270
McDermott, Mary 224
McDonnell: Mrs Julia 8; Nonie, Nenagh 288; Rev. Peter 68; Tom 8
McGoldrick, William, teacher 77
McGovern, Anne 276
McGowan, Michael 138; Shane 248
McGuinness, Rose 184
McIvor, Capt Robert 217; Felicia 216
McKenna, Malachy 362; Mary 174; Paddy 337
McLoughney, Pat profile 372
McMahon, Rev. J. 67
McMerritt, Mr 37
McNamara, Jno 37; Rev. John 68; Rev. Michael 267
McQuestion, George Waller 205
Meagher 336; Jim 267; John 52, 137; Patrick, smith 336; Patrick, teacher 77, 78
Meaghers, Coolbawn 246
Meara, Pat 215; Patrick 336
Meehan, Rev. Thomas 68, 140
Menton, Rev. James 68
Meredith: Richard, teacher 78, 79, 110
Meredith's well 97, 110
Minchin, Alice, Busherstown 149; Anne 122; Brian 145, 149; Cambie to Minchin sale, 1668-9 145; Charles 37, 145, 146; Charles 2nd 146; Charles Rev. 41; Col. F.F.R. (Jack) 50, 148, 155-162; Commander F.H. (Harry) 145, 148, 153, 154; Dennis 148; Dick 148; division of estate 153; Falkiner 41, 147, 310; Falkiner John 147, 148, 150, 151, 359; Humphrey 145, 146; Humphrey, Busherstown 146; John, Annagh & Kilkenny 146, 149, 217; John, Kilbiller 147, 150; John, memorial 147; John, merchant 147; leases 147, 149; Lena 148; Major-Gen. Frederick 148, 149; Minchins 11; Minnie 168; Myles 149; papers 145; Paul, Ballinakill 146; Peggy 148, 149; Thomas, Annagh 146; Violet 148; William A. R. (Billy) 149
Mitchel, Madeleine 276
Miworm, Mr 181
Moeran, Archibald (A. E.) 341; Kenneth & Virginia née Goodbody 341
Mohilly, Dan, Nenagh 61, 65
Molamphy 84; Bernadette, teacher 91; family, Coolbawn 246; Johanna 170, 243, 344; Michael 84; Pat and Jack 321
Molloy, Jed 59
Moloney, Neil, Newport 361; Rev. James 67, 68; Rev. John CC 66; Rev. John H. 68; Rev. John PP 77
Monsell, Margaret 178; Thomas 178
Moran, Anne née Carroll 110; Frank 59, 319, 325; Honora, Courthill 124; James, teacher 77; Jerry 153; Justin, Australia 325; Martin 48, 151, 244; Mary 77, 170; Michael 249; Michael, Coolbawn 243; Patrick, Bellevue & Australia and descendants 325-331; Patrick, teacher 74, 77, 346
Morisy, Morrogh 17
Morrissey, Dan 289, 341
Mota 134; House 213, 214, 215
Mota & Ballyscanlan: division of 215
Mota House: auction at 214
Mr. Murtagh, Old Court 224
Muintir na Tíre 48, 253; first Chairman & Committee 253; first Chairman & Committee (Kilbarron) 254; first Chairman & Committee (Terryglass) 254; projects & participants 254
Mulvihill, Martin 235
Mungo Park 167
Murphy, Maria 177; Mr & Mrs Jerome 62
Murray, Rev. Michael 68
Murray Fr 266

Nagle, Margaret 177
Nealon, Dan 366; Hannah, teacher 84; Josephine, teacher 84
Needham, 246; Jack 153, 247; John 249, 364
Neill, John 379
Neville, Miss, teacher 82
Nevin, Jim 342; Paddy 379
Newlawn 65, 134; House 142, 258
Neylan, Rev. Francis PP 53, 67
Nolan, Rody, Nenagh 339; Wilsie 57, 137, 219, 271, 280, 337, 342, 375
Nolan's bog 6

O'Brien: John 51; John, teacher 82, 84; Pat, Nenagh 361; Rev. Wm D. 67; Sarah 84; Winifred, Kilbiller 203, 217
O'Bryen, Mortagh 17
O'Callaghan, Mr 8
O'Carroll, Colonel Anthony 145
O'Connell, John, Ballycolliton 217; Maurice & Lucila 72, 225; Michael John, Ballycolliton 203

O'Connell 52; Daniel, architect 60; John, Ballycolliton 130, 203, 206; Morgan Ross, Killarney 60

O'Connor, Margaret 177; Rev. P.J. CC 53, 67, 374

O'Curry, Eugene 7

O'Donoghue, Michael, Finnoe 252; Ned 289; Rev. Canon Daniel PP 52, 67, 69, 79, 91; Rev. Michael CC 67, 68

O'Donovan, John 7, 23

O'Driscoll, Rev. John PP 67, 70

O'Dwyer, Michael, teacher 82

O'Farrell, Professor Patrick 265

O'Keane, Rev. Francis 68

O'Kelly de Gallagh, Count Gerald 62

O'Kennedy: Anthony Rev. PP 43, 45; Brien 17; Bryan McMorrogh 17; David/Daniel 17; Dennis Rev. PP 43; Dermot 17; Dermot McDonnell 30; Diarmod na Brosny 28; Donagh, Lackeen 22; Donald McEdmond 30; Donatus Rev. 48; Donnogh Rev. PP 45; Donogh 17; Donogh Duff McBrian 25; Donough Rev. 45; Gilladuff 27; Hugh 17; James Óg, Ballyfinboy 30; Jeffrey McMorrogh 17; Joan 18; John, Ballingarry 18; John, Knigh 28; Keadagh 17; Lament For (poem) 33; M. J. 52; Morrogh 17; Morrogh McTeige McBrien 25; Owney, Drominagh 22; Owney McEdward, Ballycolliton 26; Philip 17, 27; Philip & Keadagh 31; Philip, Castletown 27; Richard McMorrough 17; Rickard 17; Rory 17; Rory & William, Brockagh 28; Rory, Criagh 26; Teige, Knockballyea 29; Teige McMorrough 17; Therlagh 17; William 17; William McDiarmada 26. See also Kennedy.

Old Age Pensions 115

Old Court 181, 223, 224, 277

Oldcourt 5, 174; House 174, 176; proprietors in 1641 174

O'Mahoney, William, Cloughjordan 67

O'Meara 50, 67, 234; Bro. Paul 346; Frank 231; Gerry and Ina 268; Jack & Danny, smiths 336; Jack, Bill, Jim, Katie 217; Jack, Lisquillibeen Lane 152; James 50; James, Islandmore 50; Jim 218, 364; Martin (Sandy) 152; Marty & Bridie née Whelan 268; Mary Anne née Hogan 263; Oliver 211; Pat & Mossy 250; Patrick 232; Rev. D 67; Rev. Daniel 68; Rody & Margaret 218; Rody, Ballythomas & Kilbiller 217

O'Meara family: Islandmore 234

O'Neill, Hugh, earl of Tyrone 23, 25

Onny Dunne's hill 111

Orchards, Kylenoe 341

Ordnance Survey Letters 7

O'Reilly, Miss, teacher 85

Ormond, Countess of 18

Ormond, countess of 17

Ormonde Cottage 201, 252

O'Rourke, Kathleen 251

O'Shea, Garda Sergt Danny 248

Ospelt, Bruno 216, 217

O'Sullivan, Eily 184

Over-60s Club 10

Owens: Joseph, Liverpool 340

Parker, Annie, Brookfield 164; Helena 164, 165; John (Jack), Brookfield 50, 164; John, Ballycolliton 9, 164, 203; John, Brookfield 123, 163, 164

Parker-Reeves 50; Annie 130, 164, 165, 315, 344; Eileen 164; Heather 164; Jack & Elizabeth 165; Robert William George (Laddie) 164

Parkinson 53; Brigid 353; Jimmy 379; John 353, 355; Margaret & Ellen 325; Michael 6, 57, 58, 64, 178, 180, 352, 366; Michael & Mary 53; Sarah 352; William 181, 283, 366

parochial house 65

Pathe, Rev. Michael 284; Sergt Owen & family 283

pedlars 116

Perdue, Rev. R.N. 71

Petersen, Dr, Slevoir 181

Petrie, George 6

Pheasant: Rev. Jasper 39

Phelan, Denis, smith 333; Dennis, Kilgarvan, lease to 130

Piggott, Leonard, teacher 74

Pike, Arthur 168; Col. Dennis 170

Pine, Charles 168; Tyrrell, composer 169

ploughing 344

Plunkett, Patrick, bishop of Meath 45

Popery, Report on, 1731 43

Powell, Abraham 42

Power, Sir John 276

Priest's Lough 5

Puckane 108

Quigley, Drs Luke & Louis 170

Quigley, Nancy: letter to 319

Quinlan, Mick & Gertie née Tierney 269; Molly cleary 251; Patrick, Supt of schools 76; Pauline 251

Quinlans, Kilbarron village 250

Quirke, Brigid 237; Mrs 250; Willie 48

Raheen 17, 134

Ramblin' 113

Reddan, Matt, The Lough 379; Nance 352

Reeves, Edward 130; William 130; William, Kilgarvan 164

Reformation 34

regional water scheme 10

Rider, John, bishop of Killaloe 35

Roan, Rev. John, bishop of Killaloe 37

Robbins, Sam 37

Roberts, Theobald Pepper 213

Rodeen 65; House 65, 251

Rodgers, Alphonsus 238

Roels, Paul 165

Rogers, Messrs 42

Roran 18

Rose Cottage 252

Rowdly House 143, 215, 216

Royal Dublin Society 347

Royal Irish Constabulary 13, 250, 259, 263, 264, 283, 377.

Ryan 45; Aileen & Mary 267; Dan 357; Denis, Borrisokane 67; Dr Vincent 67, 267; Elizabeth,

Ballymackeogh 122; family, Coolbawn 245; Jack, coachman 245; James 359; Judy 244; Mary Bridget TD 291, 293; Mick, Ballyscanlan 114; Mike & Mgt, Coolbawn 243, 247; Mike, Coolbawn 153; Mike, Lisquillibeen 341; Ned, Newport 361; Paddy, Ballyscanlan 15, 66; Paddy, Coolbawn 143, 218; Pat, Coolbawn 245; Rev. Laurence PP 45; Tim, Coolbawn 111, 244, 245, 246; Timothy 249; Timothy, baker 243; Timothy, Coolbawn 244; Tom, Lahorna 361; Tom, RIC 266; Willie, Ryehill 346
Ryder, Henry, bishop of Killaloe 36
Ryehill, fort 8

Sadleir, Charles 124, 207; Rev. Henry A. 71; Thomas 124, 134, 164, 213, 216
Sall, Rev. G.W. 71
Samsons, Rodeen 42
Samuels, Rev. F.S. 50
Saunders, Counsellor 38; Tom 72
Savile: Lady Anne 162
Sawmills 340; pic & names of workers 340
Scales, John teacher 89, 91, 284, 299
Scales, John, teacher 88, 276
Scanlan, Rev. Michael 67
Scarragh 5
Schlosser, Betty & Mary & Joe 318
Seagrave: Sir Henry 220
Seymour, Madge 52; Rev. Tom PP 66, 67, 70
Shanakill 134
Shannon Development 350
Shannon Lane 277
Shannon Rovers 356; 1901 team 360; 1906 team 362; 1923 team 364; 1930 team 364; 1939 team 366; 1946 u/15 team 368; 1968 team 367; 1986 team 369; Board Officers 370; camogie, cttee & teams 371; Co. Intermediate champions, 1968 368; first committee 357; football 370; members 1898-1906 362; North & Co. Intermediate Hurling champions, 1986 370; North and Co. Junior champions 1939 367; notebooks 1898-1906 357; subscriptions 357, 359; v Ballinahinch 1905 361; v Borrisokane 1903 361; v Fortal (near Birr) 359; v Glenahilty 1918 364; v Killyon, Co. Ofaly 361; v Lattin-Cullen 367; v Lorrha 1903 361; v Lorrha 1906 362; v Nenagh 1923 364; v Roscrea 1900 360; v Roscrea 1902 360; v Silvermines 1899 359; v Silvermines 1904 361
Shannon steamer 366
Shannon View 65, 222, 223
Sheehan, John 151
Shelderton, Dermot, smith 333
Sheridan, Noreen, teacher 91; Tom 285
Shinnors, Seamus 372, 373
shoemaking 353
Sinclair, Rev. Edward 49, 50
Sisters of Mercy 12
Skehanagh 10
Slattery 48; Eoin 373; Joe 153; Joe & Ciarán, Kilbiller 345; Joe, Kilbiller 48, 253; John & Madeleine 345; John (the Brown), Glenbower 345; John, Kilbarron 151; John, Kilbiller 148, 344, 345; Joseph 246, Joseph, Coolbawn 150; Joseph, Kilbiller 151; Mary née Brereton 258; Matthew 258, 266; Matthew, Glenbower 174; Tom, Kilbiller 345
Slevin, Eamonn, Borrisokane 52
Slevoir 10, 59, 295; evictions 178; House 177, 178, 180, 181; steward, murder of 179
Slyne, John, bishop of Cork 43
Smith, Bridgie, Nurse, Bellevue 164; Danny 153; Frank 321; Jack 346; Jimmy 375; Mike 321; Mr & Mrs P. J. 53; Tommy 153
Smythe, Edward Cecil 141; Frederick 141
Somers, Jack 376
Spain, John, Roscrea 361
Spellman's Well 9
'Spinning Wheel, The' 308
Sportsfield 10
sportsfield 374
Spring, Dan TD 293; Dick, An Tánaiste 293
Springfield 202; House 202, 251
St. Augh's Well 9, 55, 254
St. Barrfhionn 51
St. Colum 56
St. Colum's Well 9, 55
St. Flannan's College, Ennis 175
Stack, Rev. J. 67
Stanley, Dick 261; profile 261; Mrs Dick 268; Priscella, nurse 184
Starr, Alice 151; Pat 361; Stephen 358
Sterling, Andrew & Rachel 154; George Myles (Jimmy) 124, 207; Myles & Amy 213; Rosamund 124
Stonepark 1
Stoney, Anna Waller 40, 303, 305; Edward Waller 40; Edward Waller CIE MICE 305; George, Greyfort 163; Rev. Ralph 71, 77, 87, 167, 210, 244, 276; Thomas George 40, 71
Storey, David & Mary née Carroll 270
Sullivan, Mai, Borrisokane 265; May, teacher 82
Sweeny, Richard Thos 130
Sydney, Anastasia 211, 218; Colonel, Gortmore 211
Synge, Rev. Francis 177, 178, 356

Tabideau, Joseph M. 5, 147
Talbot, Benjamin 8, 221, 223; Edward 9; Fanny, Ashgrove 222; Rev. Benjamin B. 58, 71, 221, 222, 275; Ruth née Stoney 221; Thomas 37
Telford, Elizabeth 215; Emily née Dagg 215; Ian 215; William, Alfred, Henry & Elizabeth 214; William, Alfred, Henry and Elizabeth Telford 215
Terry Alts 179
Terryglass 9, 10, 34; 1983 award (pic) 281; 1983 win 280; abbots, list of 56; acreage 2; census 6; ancient stone 64; Arts Council's sculpture 281; bawn 21; C of I church 71, 72, 276; Calvary 64; castle 224; census 16, 276; Chapel of the Holy Cross 62; church pre-Reformation 56, 57, 58; 'Cobbler's Box' 21; craft shop & gallery 277; Dame School 87; Early Christian 55; Early Christian monastery 21, 34, 56; Elmville 225; first national school 59, 88, 277; first school 88; forge 62, 276; Glebe House 72, 220, 224; Guinchy

cross 63, 64; hedge school 88, 276; High Cross? 63; hurling in 366; ICA: first committee 278; Improvements Association 277; commitee and projects 279; Kildare Place Society school 85, 87; landlords & tenants in1824 275; limekiln sites 337; 'linear earthwork' 55; Mass house 44, 59; new C of I church 71; new C of I church tower 61; new cemetery 63; new RC church 59, 64, 333; new school 65, 341; Old Court castle 20, 21; old graveyard 58; old RC church 59; parish hall 277; post office 277; presentation of Lotto grant 282; public houses in 1901 276; rectors, list of 71; rectory of 35; school (in Roran) 88; school attendance 89; school curriculum 88; The Derg Inn: successive owners 276; Tidy Towns 280; townland in 1840 276; village 275

Thomas, 139; Fanny 109; Marish 120; Rev. Walter 39

Thompson, John 39

Thorndike, Dame Sybil 170

Thurles ring fort 7

Tiernan 153; Francis 233; Jack, Lesserragh 224; Michael 231; Molly 170; Pat 231; Pat, Bellevue 153; Willie and Michael 230

Tiernan family: Islandmore 233

Tierney, Bridget 287; Dan 366; Danny 52, 267; Jim 379; John 287; John, Willie & Mrs 267; Julia 252; Kate 288; Martin, smith 334, 335; Michael, Ashgrove 222; Mick 379; Paddy TD 302, 334; profile 287-294; Pat 364; Will, Slevoir 379

tobacco growing 343

Tobar Atáin/Aughan 9

Tobar Naomh Eoin 9

Toohey, Fr 266; Laurence 152; Laurence, Glenbower 152

Torpey, Michael, Ballingarry 361

Towers 124; Anthony Charles 124; Benjamin 124; Caroline 124; Elizabeth 124; Elizabeth Cambie 124; Frances Manning 124; household accounts 209; Johanna 124; Lucy 209; Lucy Ellen 124; Marjorie 124; Thomas 123, 124, 208, 210, 335

transport 110

Trant, Phillis 177

travellers 115

Treacy, Martin and Dennis 321; Martin, Bellevue 252; Paddy, Bellevue 48; Seán 283

Treacys, Finnoe 250

tree nursery 346

Trench, Rev. William 39, 40

Tuohy, Dan, 361; John, New York 53; Simon 338

Turavoggaun 6

turf-cutting 353

Tuthill family: memorial to 213

Vallette, Anne née Hogan 339; Freddie 339

Vaughan family: Roscrea 216

Vaughan, Rev. Richard, Golden Grove 216

Vereker, Miss 40

Victorian dress 115

'Village Blacksmith, The' 335

von Lowenstein-Wertheim: Princess Anne 162

Wall, Patrick 126

Waller, Albert G. (Bertie) 213, 217, 250, 335; Anna née Hopkins 307; Edmund 212; Edward, Finnoe 303; Francis 212; George Arthur 212; George Arthur & six sons 212; George, Prior Park 39; Jocelyn. Prior Park 213; John Francis 85, 308; estate sale to tenants 306; profile 303-8; Richard 174, 213; Richard, Cully 303; Robert 112, 212, 248; Samuel 39; Samuel, Ormonde Cottage 201; Sarah, Prior Park 148; Thomas 179; Thomas & Margaret née Vereker 303; Thomas, Finnoe 38, 40; Thomas, murder of 305; Thomas, New South Wales. 306; William 85; William Thomas, Prior Pk 212

Walpole, George 212; Robert, Springfield House 202

Walsh, Garda Pat 263; Mary 122, 123

War of Independence, the 377

Waterloo Lodge 216, 350

Watkins, Elizabeth 122, 125

Watson, Margaret, Garrykennedy 174

Weaving John A. 277

Westropp: Rev. John 39, 41, 42

Whelan. Daniel & Anne 276; Jack, Ballindery 379; Jack, of the Hill 345; John, Ballinderry 151; Mike, Borrisokane 52, 65

White, Charles, Leixlip 126

White, Sir Nicholas 17, 18, 26, 119, 174

Whittaker's field 4

Wilkinson, Michael & Bessie 219; Paddy 276

Williams, Betty, Bellevue 135

Williams family: Bellevue 143

Williamson 341; Brian 91, 340; Harry 341

Winston, Martin, 230

Wolf, Lucy Ellen 124

Woodward, Francis Sadleir 40; Jane 40; William 39

World Wars I & II, local participants 376

Wylde: Frank & Mrs 213

Yellow Island 238